John McCarthy was ~~born~~ ~~and brought~~ up in Hertfordshire. After graduating from the University of Hull, he had a number of jobs, finally settling in television news. He lives in London.

Jill Morrell was born and brought up in Yorkshire. She, too, graduated from the University of Hull and subsequently worked at UPITN. She lives in London.

SOME OTHER RAINBOW

John McCarthy
& Jill Morrell

CORGI BOOKS

SOME OTHER RAINBOW
A CORGI BOOK : 0 552 13953 X

Originally published in Great Britain by Bantam Press,
a division of Transworld Publishers Ltd

PRINTING HISTORY
Bantam Press edition published 1993
Corgi edition published 1994
Corgi edition reprinted 1994 (four times)
Corgi edition reprinted 1995
Corgi edition reprinted 1997

The line from 'Good Times' by
Burton/Briggs/Weider/Jenkins/McCulloch is used by kind permission
of Carlin Music Corporation, Iron Bridge House,
3 Bridge Approach, London NW1 8BD
and by Warner Chappell Music Ltd

'Wonderful Remark' by Van Morrison. Used by kind permission of
Warner Chappell Music Ltd, 129 Park Street, London W1Y 3FA

'Wait for me' by Konstantin Simonov, trans. Tom Botting, from *Let
the Living Remember: Soviet War Poetry*, compiled by L. Lazerev,
Progress Publishers, Moscow, 1976

John McCarthy and Jill Morrell would like to thank Apple
Computer UK for the donation of Apple Macintosh technology
and assistance to help write this book

The right of John McCarthy and Jill Morrell to be identified as
the authors of this work has been asserted in accordance with
sections 77 and 78 of the Copyright Designs and Patents Act 1988.

Set in 10pt Linotype Plantin by
Chippendale Type Ltd, Otley, West Yorkshire

Corgi Books are published by Transworld Publishers Ltd,
61–63 Uxbridge Road, London W5 5SA,
in Australia by Transworld Publishers (Australia) Pty Ltd,
15–25 Helles Avenue, Moorebank, NSW 2170,
and in New Zealand by Transworld Publishers (NZ) Ltd,
3 William Pickering Drive, Albany, Auckland.

Printed and bound in Great Britain by
Cox & Wyman Ltd, Reading, Berkshire.

This book is dedicated to
Sheila McCarthy

8 August 1923–8 July 1989

How can you stand the silence
That pervades when we all cry?
How can you watch the violence
That erupts before your eyes?
How can you tell us something
Just to keep us hangin' on?
Something that just don't mean nothing
When we see it you are gone
Clinging to some other rainbow
While we're standing, waiting in the cold
Telling us the same old story
Knowing time is growing old.

That was a wonderful remark
I had my eyes closed in the dark
I sighed a million sighs
I told a million lies – to myself – to myself

How can we listen to you
When we know your talk is cheap?
How can we ever question
Why we give more and you keep?
How can your empty laughter
Fill a room like ours with joy
When you're only playing with us
Like a child does with a toy?
How can we ever feel the freedom
Or the flame lit by the spark?
How can we ever come out even
When reality is stark?

VAN MORRISON, *'Wonderful Remark'*

Acknowledgements

We would like to express our thanks to the people who have helped us to tell our story. As novice writers we relied heavily on the professional advice of Mark Lucas, our agent, as well as on his personal support and friendship; our editor, Georgina Morley, patiently guided us through the writing process and coped with the mammoth task of giving our separate stories shape and structure; Broo Doherty rescued us from countless stylistic errors; everyone else at Bantam Press has worked hard to make this book possible; and Terence McCarthy was always a source of encouragement and practical advice.

We are both grateful to our family and friends for their support since August 1991; they were always ready to be there to help, but also, especially, allowed us the time and space to recover, and to get to know one another again.

We are indebted to Chris Pearson, Cathy Comerford and Karen Talbot whose practical assistance was invaluable and enabled us to maintain our privacy through the months immediately following John's release.

John: I would like to thank everyone at RAF Lyneham for their hospitality and for the sanctuary they allowed me in the first, strange days following my release. I am also grateful to Roby Burke and Lorrie Grabham-Morgan and other colleagues at WTN who did so much to ease the early pressures and ensure my privacy. A special thank you to Wing Commander Gordon Turnbull for his friendship and guidance since my release, and thanks to all his colleagues at RAF Wroughton. During my captivity the efforts of the Friends of John McCarthy were a vital

9

inspiration. Since my release I have gained a real sense of their efforts and achievements and I give my heartfelt thanks to all the Friends.

Jill: I would also like to thank Chris Pearson and Mary Delaney, whose encouragement, advice and memories I relied on, and Mary Lambe, for her painstaking and valuable research. I am grateful to my family and close friends whose loyalty and support sustained me through John's captivity. They were always there to listen and to offer advice and through them the true nature of love and friendship was, and is, constantly reaffirmed. They and other friends and colleagues formed the solid core of the Friends of John McCarthy and thousands of other people, many of whom I have never met, worked tremendously hard over the years to make the Friends a success. Their energy and commitment never flagged, and I will be for ever in their debt.

Contents

List of Illustrations

At UPITN, 1984.

At a WTN cricket match, 1985. This photograph was part of the display at the first anniversary vigil for John in St Bride's, Fleet Street, on 17 April 1987. *Courtesy of Moira Edmonds.*

With Pat and Terence.

With Sheila and Terence.

With Brian, 1961.

With Peggy and Brian, 1961.

Jim and Peggy Morrell, FOJM fifth anniversary rally, 13 April 1991.

Beirut. © *Sipa-Press/Rex Features.*

Nick Toksvig, Damascus, Christmas Day 1986.

With a beard. This is the other photograph Jill and Nick Toksvig took to Damascus with them.

First anniversary vigil, St Bride's, 16 April 1987. © *Times Newspapers.*

600 Days. Handing in a petition to 10 Downing Street, 7 December 1987. © *Times Newspapers.*

The launching of the Friends of John McCarthy, February 1988. © *Times Newspapers.*

With Alain Whyte, of *Sanctuary,* at 'An Evening without John McCarthy', Camden Palace, 17 April 1988. *Roy Cuckow.*

789 Days. With Jean-Paul and Joelle Kauffman on the FOJM Boat Trip, 15 June 1988. *Bob Gannon/Insight*.

With the FOJM dummy in its cage, Labour Party Conference, 4 October 1988. © *Yorkshire Post*.

900 Days. Releasing FOJM balloons from the top of Blackpool Tower, 3 October 1988. © *Times Newspapers*.

In the FOJM campaign bus at the Conservative Party Conference, 12 October 1988. *(L–R)* Joan Willows, Mary Delaney, Lawrence Harrison, Chris Pearson, Chris Jury, Gina Filose. *Johnny Haddock*.

FOJM display, Virgin Megastore, 14 January 1989. © *Times Newspapers*.

With Nasri, Yasser Arafat and Chris Pearson, June 1989.

1000 Days. With Peggy Morrell, Joan Ruddock and Chris Pearson, handing in a petition to 10 Downing Street. © *Press Association*.

With Pat McCarthy at the launching of the BBH poster, Finchley Road, 24 August 1989. © *Times Newspapers*.

Fourth anniversary vigil outside Iranian Embassy, 17 April 1990. *Jez Coulson/Insight*.

With Neal Davis, President of Hull University Students' Union, handing in a petition to 10 Downing Street to mark John's fourth birthday in captivity, 28 November 1990. *Jez Coulson/Insight*.

The FOJM Christmas card, 1990. Designed by Sue Brown and John Hewitt. *Courtesy of the designers*.

This photograph appeared with an article on the launching of the Friends of John McCarthy in *The Sunday Times*, 28 February 1988. *Anita Corbin/The Sunday Times*.

An Alphabet for John McCarthy, from the children of St John's C. of E. School, Heaton Mersey, Stockport. Their teacher, Ann Mettam, gave it to Jill at the fifth anniversary rally on 13 April 1991. In it are pictures, poems and letters from the children depicting all the things they thought John would be missing.

David Jacobsen, with his family, at Wiesbaden following his release, November 1986. *Piel/Frank Spooner*.

Frank Reed, with his wife and daughters, at Andrews Airforce Base following his release, May 1990. Robert Polhill, released only a few weeks before, is on the far right. Terry Anderson's sister, Peggy Say, is in the centre. *UPI/Bettmann*.

Brian Keenan with his sisters, Brenda and Elaine, on his return to Dublin, August 1990. *Syndication International*.

Jackie and Sunnie Mann with Group Captain Ian Corbett at RAF Lyneham, September 1991. *Syndication International*.

Tom Sutherland at Voice of America, shortly after his release, December 1991. *Reuters/Bettmann*.

Terry Waite with Lord Runcie at RAF Lyneham, November 1991. *Syndication International*.

Terry Anderson with his daughter Sulome arriving in New York following his release, December 1991. *Reuters/Bettmann*.

Arriving at RAF Lyneham, 8 August 1991. *Today/Rex Features*.

With Nick Toksvig and Chris Pearson, the Russell Hotel, 8 August 1991. *Sun/Rex Features*.

With the Friends, 8 August 1991. *(L–R)* Mary Delaney with Anna, Lawrence Harrison, Ronnie Wood, Sue Brown, Chris Pearson. © *Express Newspapers*.

At the Royal Scot Hotel, 9 August 1991. *Syndication International*.

With Perez de Cuellar, RAF Lyneham, 11 August 1991. © *Express Newspapers*.

Leaving Lyneham for Merrow Farm, August 1991. © *Press Association*.

New Year, 1993. © *David Secombe*.

Brian Keenan at the fifth anniversary rally, 13 April 1991. *Julius Domoney/Camera Press*.

2 August 1991, and still counting. © *Times Newspapers*.

Cathy Comerford, Brian Keenan and Pat McCarthy, NUJ Conference, April 1991. *Gladwin Photography*.

Camille Sontag's map of the Land of Grey and Pink.

Letter sent to the Foreign Office, received July 1990.

The only photograph of John in captivity, taken between February and May 1988, and issued by Islamic Jihad on his release. *Rex Features*.

St Bride's, 8 August 1991. © *Times Newspapers*.

Damascus, 8 August 1991. *Lionel Cironneau/Associated Press*.

Damascus, 8 August 1991. *Lionel Cironneau/Associated Press*.

With Karen Talbot and Chris Pearson at the FOJM Press Conference, the Russell Hotel, 8 August 1991. © *Times Newspapers*.

Still working, FOJM office, 8 August 1991. © *Times Newspapers*.

Cartoon by Heath which appeared in the *Independent*, 9 August 1991. © *Heath/Independent*.

With Pat and Terence in Damascus, 8 August 1991. *Lionel Cironneau/Associated Press*.

Cartoon by Tom Johnston, which appeared in the *Sun*, 12 August 1991. *Tom Johnston/Sun*.

With Terry Waite and Brian Keenan after receiving the CBE, 12 March 1992. *Rex Features*.

Wales, August 1991.

Note: All the above photographs, except where stated, are reproduced by permission of the authors.

Bequia, November 1991

We were sitting on a deserted beach. The white sand seemed to stretch for miles and it was a glorious day, the sky a brilliant blue. We had both caught the sun, and I was examining my many mosquito bites.

'Dab and spit,' John advised. 'Don't scratch, you'll just make it worse.' The mosquitoes had left him alone; during his years in captivity he must have become immune to them.

'Fancy a swim?'

'In a minute,' I replied, picking up the camera. I watched through the lens as John stood ankle deep in the waves, looking out to sea. It was his first swim in six years. It seemed such a perfect expression of freedom and I was happy to be sharing it with him. I watched as he continued to stare out towards the horizon. He looked exactly the same. The photograph I took, when it was developed, could be from any one of our holidays six, seven years before. But, after all that had happened since then, there was so much to learn about each other, so much to understand about that stolen time.

Later, we sheltered from a tropical downpour in the bar with three other couples. We were all chatting, laughing about the weather, when suddenly the conversation stopped. All eyes were on John. He tried not to notice, but became self-conscious all the same. He'd been talking to one of the men about the difficulties of buying a car; I had seen him lean forward, emphasizing a point with a familiar gesture. I knew he was totally engrossed in the conversation. 'When I was away,' he said, without thinking. Everyone, including me, had pricked up their ears, waiting for what was coming next.

I had to get to know him again, but how? Since he had come home everything had been so strange; coping with that had taken all our energy. For over five years we had been adrift on strange – and separate – seas, in the grip of powerful currents, buffeted by forces beyond our control. It was still difficult to know what lay ahead, but the most important thing was to find a way of putting those years in perspective. Only then could we look to the future.

Waiting on a Friend

I
Beirut, April 1986

We were late leaving for the airport. It had been a tense morning. A report, inaccurate as it turned out, that the body of a British journalist had been dumped somewhere on the outskirts of Beirut was followed by a rocket attack on the British Embassy Residence. Our West Beirut camera crew had raced to the scene and taken some good footage of the still smoking building. I was shocked by the damage; I had been there just a few days before to interview the British ambassador, John Gray.

I phoned my old friend Nick Toksvig, one of the duty editors in the London office of Worldwide Television News (WTN), with details of the coverage. We chatted briefly and agreed to go out when I got back that evening. Interrupting him, I told him I had to dash. My flight was due to leave imminently. 'Keep your head down,' he said. They were his last words to me.

We set off for the airport in two cars. I was in the first, a Cadillac driven by a long-term driver-cum-soundman for American Broadcasting Company (ABC), WTN's major American shareholder. Travelling with us was another ABC regular and Sami Zuneiddin, the WTN soundman for the Moslem areas. A cameraman was following behind with a friend who had good relations with Hezbollah, the fundamentalist Moslem militia.

Looking back, I was crazy to imagine that these men, who had close contacts with most of the political factions operating in Beirut, would be able to prevent armed men kidnapping me.

We left the city centre without mishap and seemed certain to make the flight. We were driving along dust tracks which cut across the barren wastelands between the southern edge of the city and the airport. It struck me that it was a different route from the one we'd taken when I arrived, which surprised me. I felt a bit tense, even though I knew we were nearly there.

A beaten-up old car was churning up the dust in front of us. We had to slow down behind it before making a right turn on to a narrower track between piled-up banks of earth. Seconds later, a Volvo raced past us and screeched to a halt in a shower of gravel. A tall, bearded man of around twenty-five jumped out and covered us with his Kalashnikov. We all sat rigidly in our seats, silently watching him.

The gunman started yelling at us. I couldn't understand a word. Sami got out of our car, shouting back. I assumed he was saying, 'Don't shoot, take it easy.' Seconds later, the gunman came round to my door, opened it and pulled me out by the scruff of my neck. He pushed me across the road and into the back of the Volvo, then down on to the floor. I noticed that the side window was smashed; perhaps it had been broken when the car was stolen. God knows why I gave it a second thought.

There was just one other man in the car, the driver, with greyish hair and a beard. The two men briefly exchanged words. I assumed they were waiting for the all-clear from a second car, into which I think they had put my luggage.

The gunman cleared his throat and spat. Then we were off. A blanket was draped over me as I crouched on all fours on the floor. I raised my head slightly. He gave it a sharp rap with his hand. A couple of minutes later he gave me a reassuring stroke, a curious gesture under the circumstances.

The kidnappers didn't say much. All I could think was 'This is just like a movie' – the car skidding to a stop, the gunman, the total silence in the Cadillac as we had sat frozen, as if in limbo.

It seemed so unreal; I wasn't frightened, in fact I felt close to laughing. The idea of being kidnapped was so

22

extraordinary that I felt more as if it were just my last image of the war zone – the final anecdote to tell the folks back home in the pub that evening.

After a brief stop where I was made to get into the boot of the Volvo, we arrived at the prison. Only then did I begin to know real fear. I was pulled out of the car and someone tied a rag over my eyes. Two men went through my pockets and took off my jacket and shoes at the same time. They sounded very excited when they found my wallet, which had several hundred dollars in it.

One of these men then led me down a number of flights of stairs. It felt as if we were leaving the world of light and hope. As we descended he kept asking me something. The main word sounded like *incatura* which meant nothing to me so I kept saying, 'Sorry, no Arabi.' It dawned on me, only as he relieved me of my wrist-watch, that he was saying, '*Inglaterra*'.

We stopped and he made me turn round and round, walk a few paces, then turn again, presumably to disorientate me. Then he sat me on a chair and I expected him to start beating me, not for any reason, but it just seemed inevitable. Instead, we set off again and I was pushed into a room. The metal door clanged shut behind me and I removed the blindfold and found myself in a tiny cell.

Almost immediately the door opened again. I covered my eyes, but sensed there were a number of men gathered outside. One, with a deep voice, older-sounding than the others, seemed to be in charge. He came in and went through my trouser pockets again. On finding a coin, it sounded as though he was berating the others for their laxity.

A heavily accented voice asked, 'Are you angry?'

'No,' I replied. 'Not angry, just scared.'

Another voice said, 'Don't be scared, this not your problem, this your country's problem.'

How reassuring.

They left me and I sat for a few minutes, unable to think clearly. Then the door opened and I was taken to another cell further up the corridor. Again I was asked if I was 'ahngry'. This time I realized it meant hungry. I said I was a little and was handed some bread with jam and an apple. The door closed again and they went away. Now I could inspect the cell. It was as small as the last, just high enough to stand by the door, just long enough to lie down in, maybe three feet wide. Thank heavens I wasn't tall. Some of my things were there: wash-bag, magazines and, weirdly, a light-weight jacket and tie. Even in a state of high anxiety this struck me as being comical – would I be expected to dress for dinner in this sub-basement club?

I sat down on the thin mattress, revolted by the foul blankets. I thought about Jill. Would she know yet? I tried to imagine how WTN in London would be responding to the news of my abduction. As my initial shock wore off I began to feel more confident. Surely with all their contacts, the Beirut office would be able to find out where I was and start working immediately for my release?

My first assumption was that I had been kidnapped by a Palestinian group. I thought about the two British teachers, Leigh Douglas and Philip Padfield, who were rumoured to have been kidnapped by Palestinians two or three weeks earlier. Perhaps I'd been taken in reprisal for the US bombing of Libya or maybe it was a pro-Iranian group. 'We consider all people from a country are responsible for their government's actions, so we can take anyone.' These words of a Hezbollah member who had been at the UPI Bureau Chief David Zenian's party a few days before rang in my mind.

I cursed myself for being so ignorant, for not being able to put this into some sort of informed perspective. It could have been any group taking me for any reason. If only I had prepared myself better for my first foreign assignment and made more use of the time in Beirut to trace the latest shifts in Lebanese politics. But then if I had been that well informed, perhaps I would not have been there in the first place.

* * *

In early February, 1986, John Connor, WTN's Managing Editor, told me that I would be going to Beirut for a month to stand in for the resident Bureau Chief, Ken Jobson. The previous summer I had hoped to go to Beirut or Damascus during the TWA hostage crisis. The prospect of visiting a war zone seemed to me not only potentially rather glamorous, but definitely an important step in my career.

Having been briefed by Connor, who had visited Beirut a number of times, and Roby Burke, WTN's Vice-President of News, I spent my last day in London with Jill buying shoulder bags and money belts. I also had taken a whole wad of passport photographs which I could use for press passes. I got quite a shock a year or so later when my captors gave me a newspaper cutting with messages from friends and family bearing that same picture.

Jill and I spent a quiet night at her flat in Baron's Court. Still a little bleary from the send-off party of the night before, I felt nervous, worried about how I would cope on my great adventure. Jill, as always, calmed me down. In the past few weeks, we had decided to get married and buy a flat together, so it was reassuring to look ahead rather than dwell on my chances of success or failure in Beirut.

We had booked an early cab to get us out to Heathrow in plenty of time to pick up some WTN camera gear from our shipping agents. The flight out was uneventful. I noticed with something of a shock that I was the only non-Arab on the plane; it was my first taste of a culture very different from my own. Looking back, it seems extraordinary that I was able to combine such enthusiasm for the Beirut assignment with such ignorance of the customs and manners of the Middle East.

It took a while to get through the airport. Eventually I was clear and greeted with much warmth by Ken and Sami, both of whom I'd already met in London. Mohammed Haidar, WTN's cameraman, and Ghassan Salem, our office manager, were also there.

After introductions we set off, Ken and the others in a Cadillac, Ghassan and I in his Renault. Ken later told me that he'd sent me with Ghassan as the Caddy had taxi licence-plates and therefore might be targeted as likely transport for visiting westerners. This remark came back to me when I was snatched from the same car barely a month later.

We drove through Beirut's southern suburbs, past the Palestinian refugee camps of Bourj-el Barajneh and Sabra-Chatila, past the former sports stadium. I had never imagined the extent of the damage: shell-marked buildings, areas laid waste. Yet what struck me more was the fact that, in the midst of this devastation, urban life seemed to be continuing at a great rate. There were roadside stalls selling everything from live chicks to army surplus – people everywhere and the craziest traffic conditions I had ever seen.

As we drove along Ghassan pointed things out to me. This first face-to-face chat (we'd often spoken on the phone) confirmed my liking and respect for him, feelings that only increased during my stay. When we arrived at the bureau I was shown around and met the ABC Bureau Manager, Shakib Humeidan. Shakib had a reputation for being a very effective 'fixer' – which I suppose meant he had good contacts and knew who to bribe. Privately I dubbed him 'Fatcat'. I called London to let them know I had arrived safely, spoke to Jill and called my father to give him my news and find out how my mother, who was about to have an operation for cancer of the stomach, was feeling.

I went across the road with Ken to my hotel. The Commodore was famous as a resting-place and watering-hole for foreign journalists. Connor had made sure that the bureau had booked me a suite on the top floor. It was the largest in the hotel, a huge bedroom and sitting room decorated in the foulest taste. It looked as though it hadn't been refurbished since the early 1970s, which would seem logical as there were no longer any tourists.

Ken and I had a beer at the bar and I was introduced to Coco the parrot who could whistle 'The Marseillaise' and do a very fair impression of an incoming shell. We nodded at various journalists from Associated Press who drifted in, then Ken went off home. I should have stayed in the bar and got to know the AP crowd, but felt a little tentative about doing so. I knew that there had been something of a rift between the AP bureau and the other western news operations in the city, and I wasn't sure if fraternizing with them might make me look like the new boy letting the side down. So I went up to my room.

Connor had stayed in the same suite on a previous visit and one of the cameramen, Raef Debaja, had scratched his name on the window. I'd got to know Raef well, since he had come to live in London the year before. Seeing his name made me feel a little less out of place.

The next day I woke early and went up to the roof terrace before heading for the office. The sun was already hot against my skin as I looked west over the roofs towards the sea, then northwards to the port area and the resort of Jounieh. Mountains rose steeply in the east and to the south a mass of high-rise apartments covered the low hills before the coastal plain. It looked, at first glance, a peaceful and beautiful city. But when I looked again I felt the presence of the invisible guns. They were all over those hills, trained on the Christian sector. There was another mass of guns pointing back from there to the hills and to the area in which I stood, the western Moslem sector. Somewhere between lay the Green Line which separated the two communities.

As if on cue a machine-gun rattled out over the din of the surrounding streets. Even in my ignorance I guessed that this was not fighting between Christian and Moslem factions, but between Palestinian refugees living in camps towards the south of the city and members of the Amal militia which controlled much of the area around the camps in the Shia Moslem-dominated southern suburbs.

I went downstairs and out across the road to our office, feeling totally conspicuous with my light brown hair and pale skin. Everyone seemed to be looking at me. A little boy tried to sell me some red carnations. A man was selling cartons of cigarettes from a barrow; a shop on the corner displayed carpets and Arabic coffee pots. The shell of a building under construction rose for several storeys on the opposite side of the street. There were no walls, doors or windows, yet I could see an old man sitting up there as if he were relaxing in his living room.

I went up to the office and asked about the gunfire.

'It was nothing,' I was told. 'Just part of the dawn chorus.'

There was occasional shelling of the camps by the Amal militia, but everything had been pretty quiet for a while.

I was given a more detailed tour of our offices and the tiny studios where visiting correspondents recorded the soundtracks for their reports. The windows and walls of the crew room and the edit suite were scarred with bullet holes – the result of another factional clash, this time between Amal and Druze militiamen. I remembered this incident clearly from Haidar's coverage of the fighting just before Christmas 1985. Terry Waite had been in Beirut on his first visit to seek the release of the American hostages held by Islamic Jihad. I was shown copies of Haidar's video and saw pictures of Waite visiting the neighbouring AP office which had been taken from my bedroom window. Somehow, even though I was standing at the scene of a recent battle, seeing it recreated on a television screen made it seem remote and unreal.

After the guided tour, we returned to the office Ken shared with Ghassan where an open window looked out over a building site. It was far warmer than I'd anticipated. Sitting in Ken's swivel chair, I turned from the white roofs and clear sky above Beirut to the rather dreary room, relieved only by a tired-looking cactus. I thought that the two big lights on the shelf were something to do with filming, but Ken soon put me right. They were for the inevitable power cuts. It felt good to be in charge, but then it dawned on me that I didn't really know where anything was – or even how the phones worked. Ghassan

28

explained everything, even showing me how to make the very strong, sweet, Arabic coffee that I came really to enjoy.

I read the wires to see what our colleagues in the print news services were making of Beirut so far that day. AP had described the fighting at the camps as a major battle. Reuters and UPI were far less dramatic, just noting minor exchanges of fire. My Beirut colleagues said that this was nothing new. I remembered Ken telling me that AP's habit of hyping stories often caused us major problems. The television news editors who we supplied around Europe would often request coverage after reading their reports and WTN London would panic, afraid that Visnews would beat us to a non-existent story.

I phoned London to let them know that so far nothing was expected for the day and told the WTN Eurovision (EVN) editor that should there be interest in the fighting in the camps he could advise our customers that it would be a waste of their money to have us cover the aftermath and then send the video to Damascus for transmission to Europe by satellite. I was beginning to feel a little more in touch with my new responsibilities.

I noticed that all the crew carried small radios so that they could keep abreast of any new developments as the local stations broadcast newsflashes as soon as an incident occurred. So I went with Ken to a shop across the road and bought a small short-wave radio. While we were there Ken spotted some baseball caps that had tiny radios fitted into a pouch above the peak. He bought three and I got the last one for Toksvig.

We went to have lunch in the Spaghetteria, a pleasant airy restaurant overlooking the coast road. It must have been a gold mine in the days when Beirut was a magnet for jet-setting tourists and expatriates, but now it was virtually deserted. Ken gave me some background on my colleagues which would help me work with them after he went back to England for his vacation. He volunteered a lot of good advice, but I realized after he had gone that there were many other questions that I should have asked him.

The days followed a similar pattern until Ken's departure. There was little action to cover. The boys decided that this was a very good omen and thought that I should stay longer in Beirut. They flattered me, suggesting that when Ken moved on to another bureau in the region I'd be the ideal replacement; if it stayed this quiet we could all relax and have a good time.

As most of the crew lived out in the southern suburbs controlled by Amal and Hezbollah, it wasn't safe for me to visit their homes and families. Instead I stayed close to the Commodore, where we managed to maintain something of a party atmosphere. Connor had suggested that I contact Sana Issa, who managed the *Newsweek* office. She became a good friend and introduced me to people from UPI and Reuters. I also got to know a British freelance camera team, working for NBC and later Con Coughlin of the *Daily Telegraph*. I was also very happy to meet Robert Fisk, whose reports for *The Times* had always impressed me.

Obtaining a press pass from the Ministry of Information and the Druze militia was a relatively simple process, but it was not quite so easy getting one from Amal. I was shuttled by Sami or Kasim, an ABC gofer, between Amal offices dotted all over the southern part of the city. The man we had to see, Ali Hamdan, was forever on the move. It appeared that all the offices had only just been occupied and that extensive and extremely noisy construction work was always in progress.

When we finally caught up with him, he gave me a glass of tea and explained that the situation in Beirut was not as lawless as the Western press made out. In the areas controlled by his organization there was no thieving, no street violence, no rape. I nodded, observing from my limited knowledge that such crimes were forbidden, *haram*, under Islamic law. Ali seemed pleased and Kasim later explained why. The Islamic code was used increasingly in Amal's statements as part of their efforts to reduce the appeal of the rapidly expanding fundamentalist Hezbollah movement.

I listened to this experienced PR man giving his organization's views on matters of local law and order, but I was far more struck by the little boy of about twelve who stood in full uniform by the gate of the Amal compound casually pointing his Kalashnikov at our car as we left. While there was no deliberate menace to us, the atmosphere of the place was of a vigilance stretched forever to breaking-point, dangerous and volatile.

Armed with my press passes I felt I was able to move round more freely. Connor and Burke had told me to take every advantage to expand my work experience, so I was looking for good television stories. If possible I wanted to write and edit some film reports myself, although the bureau chief's main function was to co-ordinate the activities of the camera crews and liaise with London on the details of their coverage and the best means of shipping the cassettes. This sometimes meant long periods of inactivity for all of us, but on the busier days everything became a frantic race to ensure that the crews were out, that a taxi had been laid on to take the coverage to Damascus and, above all, that London knew what was happening.

March 25th saw the first anniversary of the kidnap of the British journalist Alec Collett. Collett was believed to have been abducted by Abu Nidal, the Palestinian group who were reported to have an office or a spokesman at the Ain El Helweh refugee camp on the outskirts of Sidon, a city some twenty-five miles south of Beirut. I decided it might be worth a trip. It was also arranged that I would interview the Beirut Head of the United Nations Relief and Works Agency (UNRWA) for whom Collett had been working.

I set off early that day with Haidar and Sami. We drove down to Sidon and went into the camp. People were crammed into the narrow lanes and tiny breeze-block shanties. We kept asking for the '*majlis*', office, and were directed further and further in. Eventually we reached the office and Haidar explained why we were there. After more conversation in Arabic Haidar told me that no-one was available to make any comment whatsoever on Collett.

Throughout this exchange the office guard had been standing glowering at us, cradling his machine-gun and, as Haidar manoeuvred his car through a tight three-point turn to leave the office compound, the guard seemed to be staring straight at me with eyes full of hate. I stared back feeling increasingly nervous, wishing that Haidar would get us the hell out of there.

Once out of the camp Haidar made it plain that he had always thought this outing was a waste of time. Later, I realized that he and Sami were just as nervous as I had been and that I might have been exposing them to considerable danger. Now though, I was very much more preoccupied with the simple question of whether I would survive Haidar's driving. He was racing his Mercedes at a steady hundred miles an hour round blind corners on the wrong side of the road while trying to find an English word in his own, hand-written dictionary. I turned desperate eyes to Sami, who was sitting behind me, and asked him what Haidar wanted to say. Sami seemed blissfully unaware of the mortal danger we were in and had a lazy discussion with his friend about vocabulary. I can't remember what the word was, but eventually their calm rubbed off on me so that I began to enjoy the thrill of the ride and joined in their shouts of '*Yallah*', let's go, as we raced through Lebanese army checkpoints and overtook seemingly endless civilian convoys of trucks and beaten-up cars in the face of oncoming traffic.

Years afterwards I was to recall this trip when driving furiously round the narrow lanes of western Ireland with Brian Keenan. Perhaps taking oneself to the limits of safety is a way of burning up the adrenalin generated by looking down the barrel of someone else's gun.

Before visiting UNRWA we stopped at a major road junction at Khalde, near the airport, to film some general views of the spot where Collett was supposed to have been kidnapped. All the windows of the UNRWA building were

32

covered over with heavy metal shutters. I recorded a brief interview with the boss there, who was surprised that we had gone to see him. No other journalists had shown any interest in the anniversary.

Although Beirut was very quiet during most of my working stay, there were regular, if limited, exchanges of fire between the Christian and Moslem sectors. One morning we heard that a fighter from Amal and another from Hezbollah had died in some overnight shelling across the Green Line. The two men were to have a combined funeral. This was unusual in the light of the growing political rivalry between these two militias, so we decided to go and film it. Sami and Haidar agreed that we would set off early so that they could give me a close-up look at the Green Line.

We passed through densely populated areas of the southern suburbs, then turned off down a narrow street hemmed in with high-rise blocks which almost hid the sky. The road had disintegrated into a rutted track and I noticed that all the windows in the buildings had been blocked in and that the only openings were small, heavily protected, doorways. The lane twisted and turned once or twice, then we were at the front.

Leaving the car, we walked towards a tower block directly in front of us. Haidar and Sami exchanged greetings with the Amal fighters on duty; they explained who I was and that they wanted to show me the view. We were ushered into the building and stood beside a heavy machine-gun positioned on the first floor. Ahead of us lay a strip of wasteland with weed-covered hummocks where buildings had once been. Beyond that, seeming terribly close, were the concrete skeletons that marked the front line of the Christian Phalange militia.

The place was extremely spooky. A handful of militia-men kept company with rats, that scuttled about in the shells of what had once been a bustling community. The city had been divided by this line for years. The fighting consisted only of sniping at pedestrians if they showed

33

their faces or lobbing shells blindly into the night. It seemed incredible that nocturnal duels should be routine even when there was no threat of one side trying to advance across the no-man's land and no military gain was expected or sought.

I took some photographs of the fighters beside their weapons. While elsewhere Lebanese men carried on any conversation with much noise and gusto, here they spoke almost in whispers, perhaps in awe of the devastation they had already wreaked and that at any moment might start again.

We drove a short way to film the funeral procession. It was headed by an ambulance carrying one of the coffins and playing Moslem prayer chants over a Tannoy system. A string of jeeps and small trucks followed, carrying fully armed fighters and mounted machine-guns. All the men looked very young and many had Rambo hair-styles and head-bands. While Haidar and Sami were filming, I snapped away trying to feel like a professional, but realized that with my little instamatic camera I probably looked more like some misplaced tourist. Oddly I had no feeling that these hard and dangerous-looking men resented my presence. It was almost as if their staring eyes were merely a pose for our cameras, a stock display of strength to hide their real sense of loss and vulnerability.

We headed off again to film the procession arriving at the cemetery. Sami and Haidar took me in and it seemed as peaceful as any English country churchyard. A friend of Sami's arrived and explained in fluent English that he was the Amal officer in charge of the ceremonies. The image of a country churchyard rapidly dissolved as the sound of chanting began. We moved outside the gates and across the road to have a clear view of the procession, while maintaining a respectful distance. Some two hundred men, most waving guns, came down the road almost at a jog. In their midst the coffins bobbed along at shoulder height. As they saw the camera the mourners waved their guns more aggressively and raised the volume of their chants. Their eyes did now seem full of hate.

When the procession had moved into the cemetery, we walked back to our car; young faces filled every window of a building to our left, which was probably a school. They were shouting, whistling and laughing. I felt very conspicuous, convinced they were mocking me.

A trip across the Green Line to visit the Feghali brothers, Assad and Fadi, the WTN camera crew in East Beirut, gave me a very different view of Lebanon. Driving slowly across no-man's land with any number of snipers able to train their sights on us made me feel apprehensive. But once Haidar and I had turned a corner around the old museum building, and showed our press passes to the soldier at the checkpoint, we were relieved to see the Feghalis waiting for us.

Our destination was the ancient port of Byblos, some way to the north. After a few hundred yards we were clear of the potholes and shell-damaged buildings of West Beirut and cruising over a raised highway. The few checkpoints were manned by men turned out in smart uniforms and the streets were full of shops and cafés.

Leaving the main town of Byblos, we drove down a winding lane for lunch at a restaurant overlooking a picturesque little harbour. It felt as if we could be anywhere on the Mediterranean, yet we were but a few miles from scenes of total devastation and angry men waving guns and shouting as they buried comrades killed in battle.

Here, too, there were few, if any, men or women in traditional Arab costume. Beneath the terrace where we sat drinking Arak, groups of young people sauntered past, dressed in the latest designer gear from America and Europe. The furtive glances of the women of West Beirut were replaced here by level stares. Haidar and the Feghalis chuckled at me. Assad explained: 'The girls like foreign.' Ironically, I was being sized up as a potential passport out of all this.

Late that afternoon, when Haidar and I returned to the West, I was more acutely aware of the squalor and desolation of this part of the city, yet I also remembered a trip I had made to the seafront with Ken. He had taken me to a building whose exterior had looked quite derelict, while the interior might have been that of any exclusive boutique in Paris or London. I thought, too, of the vibrant street life where so much business seemed to be transacted. These people could do nothing to stop the shells coming down on them, but their spirit to make the best of things remained undaunted.

On one occasion, I thought the lull in fighting was over. The sound of countless guns letting off bursts of bullets drowned out any other sound. 'What's going on? Who's attacking who?' I asked. The men in the office laughed. It wasn't a battle, it was Amal fighters celebrating the re-election of Nabih Berri as their leader. 'Doesn't anyone get hurt?' I asked. 'Oh yes, maybe ten or so will die when the bullets land.'

Haidar and Sami went out to film some of the fighters as they drove through the streets, hanging out of cars and trucks, blazing away. They fired into the air, but, as the vehicles swerved round corners, the guns ended up pointing anywhere. I watched the cassette and saw one boy of about sixteen who held a pistol which he was waving right in front of the camera, loosing off shots willy-nilly. I heard Sami's voice on the tape. He told me he was shouting at the idiot to keep the gun pointing upwards. I said that the boy looked very wild and Sami said he was 'drunk'. When I showed surprise he explained that he meant drunk with excitement.

Two British teachers, Leigh Douglas and Philip Padfield, were kidnapped late on Good Friday night, 28 March. They had just left the Back Street night-club. We heard the news on 2 April. With a shock I realized that I had been there on the Saturday night with the NBC team.

I sent Haidar and Sami to take some film of the American University of Beirut (AUB) where Douglas worked, the International Language centre where Padfield had been director, and scenes outside the Back Street. As ever they returned with good coverage which we despatched to Damascus by taxi for EVN. I advised London of the developments and called the British Embassy in East Beirut to ask for an interview with the ambassador, John Gray. We arranged to meet at the Embassy Residence in West Beirut. It was very close to the Green Line, so was now only used for fleeting visits by embassy staff. As Sami, Haidar and I drove to meet Gray we passed high mounds of earth thrown up to protect the roads and buildings closest to the Line. At the Residence we were met by a number of Amal militiamen who controlled the area. Once inside the compound we were searched by the ambassador's two bodyguards, before being allowed into the elegant colonial-style mansion.

I wanted to know what moves were being made to bring about Collett's release. The interview was a dismal failure. When I'd talked to the head of UNRWA I had asked simple questions and received simple, usable responses. With Gray I thought I'd suddenly become a brilliant investigative reporter. I omitted the straightforward, obvious points in favour of a list of lengthy questions that I felt would draw out vital information on the Collett negotiations and the latest theories on the whereabouts of the two teachers.

I felt a complete fool when I reviewed the tape back at the office. Gray had answered the questions, but because they were long and vague so were his answers. I hadn't even asked the obvious one: 'What is your advice to British subjects still in Beirut?' Although it probably didn't matter to anyone else I never quite got over this failure. I'd learned another important lesson, but was never able to prove that to myself, or my colleagues.

Nobody claimed responsibility for the kidnap of Douglas and Padfield. Anti-Western feeling was growing in some quarters over President Reagan's display of power against Libya in the Gulf of Sirte, but it was rumoured that the teachers could have been taken for personal, rather than political, reasons. They had both been in Lebanon for some time and had many local contacts.

The British Embassy repeated its advice that all British subjects should leave the country if they possibly could. I felt that this didn't really apply to me; after all, I was a journalist and was meant to be here for just this sort of development. I had also been in Lebanon for such a short time and had moved about so little that none of the kidnappers would even be aware of my presence. I knew that a number of other British journalists were planning to leave, but they were off on vacations or to new postings, not escaping.

Thursday of the next week, 11 April, saw the rescue of French teacher Michel Brian who had been taken in West Beirut two days previously. Monsieur Brian had been sitting in a car with his kidnappers in the Beka'a Valley when a group of hunters, fortunately armed with machine-guns, came across them and opened fire. The kidnappers threw their hostage out of the car and raced off. He was handed over to the Syrians who took him to Damascus.

An Irishman named Brian Keenan had no such luck. He was picked up on the same day as he walked to work at the Hariri Institute where, for the last three months, he had been teaching English to students hoping for a place at the AUB. I went with Haidar and Sami to film Keenan's house and the street where he was thought to have been taken. We then went round to AUB to see if we could get a photograph of him. We did. Sami and I took one look at it and concluded that this hairy, wild-eyed fellow probably would be best avoided on a dark night or in a small room.

I called John Rowan, First Secretary at the Irish Embassy, and asked if he had had any news. He told me there was nothing so far, but that the embassy was going to place an advert in the local papers the next day to let the kidnappers know that Brian was an Irishman and therefore of little or no use to them.

Then there was silence.

Neither news nor demands about Keenan or the two Britons were issued. I began to have a nagging feeling that things were closing in around me. As more journalists left I felt increasingly conspicuous. I was woken very early on the morning of Tuesday 15 April by the WTN London overnight editor David Tucker to hear that the US, with the assistance of the British, had bombed Libya. David asked me if we could get the main Lebanese leaders to comment. I said that we would try.

'Which way do you think they will jump?' he went on.

I told him that I thought Gaddafi had few real friends in the Lebanese community and that relations between the various militias, their Arab backers and the West were too complex to allow *any* leader to 'jump' *any*where but away from *any*one holding a microphone at a time like this.

Reagan and Thatcher must have gone mad. Bombing Tripoli, even on the basis of allegedly solid intelligence that Libya was behind terrorist bombings in Europe, could only stir up greater distrust and dislike of the West and would do nothing to halt such attacks.

Despite everything, I was bitterly disappointed that Connor and Burke then decided to pull me out. I spoke to them both on Wednesday, the day after the raid, and agreed I would try to catch the first plane out – wherever it was going.

In fact the only flight that day, to Larnaca, was fully booked. There was a direct flight to London on Thursday, so, rather than go over to East Beirut that evening and see if I could get a ferry to Cyprus, I decided to wait for the plane. The WTN and ABC teams came and had a brief farewell drink with me at the Commodore and I gave them a quick outline of what I would be saying to the bosses about them when I got home.

I regretted leaving everybody so abruptly. Sami had volunteered to stay with me that night, so we went up early to my suite when the others went home.

I relaxed. I was disappointed at having to leave, but relieved that I was now safe.

It isn't much fun coming to terms with the fact that you have been a complete fool, realizing that it is now too late to make amends for past failings, being all too aware of present weaknesses. Through my own folly, I could not even reassure the people I loved that I was alive. My lack of foresight and a failure to address these, my real responsibilities, now found me in a tiny cell completely cut off from the world I knew. Frightened, I was underground, and, in more ways than one, in the dark.

I sat on the filthy mattress trying to make sense of my situation. Optimism fought with fear, but optimism had to win or there would be only despair and breakdown.

My mind switched back into acting Bureau Chief mode. I guessed it must now be one o'clock, so the taxi with the video of the attack on the Residence building should be in Damascus. The British news broadcasters, ITN (one of WTN's main shareholders) and the BBC, would want the pictures for their lunch-time bulletins. With any luck the Visnews coverage would be delayed and WTN, and therefore ITN, would have an exclusive. The item might well be the top story.

Then I thought: '*You* are probably the top story.' Somehow this gave me confidence. My plight would be well known and colleagues in London and Beirut would surely be able to sort it out. 'It will never happen to me', had now become 'It shouldn't have happened to me'. The kidnappers would soon realize that they had taken a Briton of no importance to his government, one who had been in Lebanon just thirty days and who was therefore too inexperienced to have developed any political connections. Posing no threat, having no value, it was certain that I would be out of this awful place in days, if not hours. Suddenly the foul conditions became more bearable. I could stand a week of them, confident that it was unlikely to take even that long.

So, the first thing I had to do was to make the cell as neat and tidy as possible, to impose my own order on the situation. I shook out the blankets and mattress, and plumped up the greasy pillow, creating a great cloud of dust. There was dust everywhere. I tried to sweep most of it into a corner with a copy of *Newsweek* that the guards had dug out of my luggage.

A china bowl, with a plate covering it, stood in the corner. My dinner service? It may have been once, but, as I lifted the plate, I saw that the previous occupant had defecated in the bowl. Good God, what kind of an animal would do that in his room, on his plate? Then came the awful realization that perhaps he had had no alternative; worse still, I might not have. How often would these people come round to feed me and let me go to the toilet? Was there a toilet? There was a plastic bottle that had been shoved under my nose with the words 'pee-pee', so maybe not.

This was unthinkable, intolerable. I lit a cigarette. The packet was almost full and a guard had given me some matches – a huge relief. Anyway I had had at least two full cartons in my suitcase. They would easily see me through till my release. I had two or three of my own books, magazines and some shorts, that would be handy if the power failed and the crude ventilation system that tempered the heat, stopped moving the air around. With these basic comforts I felt I should be able to hang on for a while.

The rest of Thursday passed without any more visits from the guards. No-one had shown me any deliberate ill-intent, nor indeed any great interest, although I felt sure that at some point I would be interrogated to find out who I was and what I was worth. I tried to work out some way of convincing these people that I was no use to them, but that as a television journalist, I could be, if released with some sort of statement. However, being completely ignorant of who was holding me and of what they might be holding me for, didn't exactly help.

The next morning when I heard the rattle of keys and the banging of cell doors I felt sure that now was my opportunity to make a humble, earnest, blindingly logical and convincing argument for my immediate release. If I could have just ten minutes with someone responsible who could speak English I'd be on my way home. The door opened and I had nothing over my eyes. Before me stood an elderly, round-shouldered man with wild grey hair and beard and very pale skin, wearing an old pair of pyjamas and battered straw shoes. He indicated that I should drape my jacket over my head, pointed at my water- and pee-bottles and beckoned for me to follow. He took me a little way along the corridor, guided me through a doorway and left me. A curtain had been pulled across the doorway so I removed my jacket and found I was in a very basic bathroom. Basic or not, it was there, one horror dimmed; but as I squatted, trying to make out whether the dark opening high on one of the walls might lead to freedom, I knew that there would be no immediate relief. Constipation had taken hold. I could only hope that when it passed someone would be around to bring me back to this grim chamber.

There were some slivers of soap lying about so I had a brief wash. The old man kept coming to the curtain and saying something in Arabic to which I could only reply, '*Moment*' in a sort of French accent which probably meant nothing to him. Having no towel, I dried myself with my shirt tails. I gathered up my bottles and wash-bag and tapped on the door-frame. The old man took me back to my cell and there I found some bread, cheese and jam on my mattress. I picked up the china bowl and gave it to him with a shrug. He took it and closed the door. I could hear him muttering to another man and then he went off to lead another prisoner to the bathroom.

Judging by his appearance the old man lived in the prison, perhaps had been a prisoner for so long that he had achieved 'trusty' status. So I nicknamed him Trusty. I sneaked a look through the grille on my door and saw him taking another man, head covered and bent almost double, along the corridor. I watched a younger man doling out bread and cheese for the other guests at a sort of bench. He was very tanned and had a pistol in his belt.

I sat down and contemplated the food. My appetite had almost disappeared, but I managed a few mouthfuls before I heard a young man screaming and the sound of blows. His cries were in Arabic, so, to my shame, I thought that perhaps he was not a hostage, but a prisoner who deserved punishment. Whatever the case, such brutality so close at hand killed any desire I had for food stone-dead. After half an hour the guard and Trusty left. The only sound now was the roar of the ventilation system.

That second night two men did come to see me. They spoke little English and probably wanted nothing more than to have a look at the new hostage. I asked them who they were and why I was there. They were the first of countless, unseen men who would say over the years, 'I don't know, not my business.' I begged some cigarettes. My large stock had disappeared and I was now given just six for the day.

I tried to lead them into conversation, talking about Palestine and Israel, hoping to pick up some clue about their reasons for holding me. Their response was that Israel was no good and that Britain had made it all possible. The tone wasn't excited so I was none the wiser. I had made one depressing discovery, however: I was frightened of them. Gone were the reasoned and irrefutable arguments for my release. Now I heard a timid voice agreeing that my country had done bad things. All I could say was: 'When will I go home?'

I was never to get over the habit of planning elaborate speeches, in English to start with, then later in poor French and, finally, in diabolical Arabic. But they rarely came off. The effect of my Churchillian eloquence was inhibited somewhat by the fact that I was speaking to someone I could not see, whose inevitable response was: 'It's not my business.'

After a few more minutes the two men said goodbye and left. I heard them go to a cell just up from mine, towards the bathroom, and I strained to hear what was said. I was certain they were speaking English again and decided that they must be talking to the two English teachers, Padfield and Douglas. I took great solace from this and spent a lot of time trying to work out how to make contact without simply shouting, which common sense told me would be foolish.

The next day, Saturday, passed much as the first with Trusty overseeing the bathroom jaunts and the guard dishing out the food and beating up the terrified young man. I couldn't imagine what he had done to deserve such automatic violence. That evening the narrow corridors in the basement seemed full of people. My cell widened a little by the door so I could look one way down the corridor, away from the bathroom, without my face appearing at the grille. I switched off my strip light and, in the gloom, moved into position.

I found out later that such inquisitiveness wasn't healthy, but now I couldn't resist the urge to see. At the end of the corridor where it turned off away from the line of cells, I saw a large door with a skull and crossbones crudely drawn on it. The door was open and two or three men were gathered around it, peering in. There were more inside. I sat down wondering what was going on when I heard a guard speaking in English.

Without success, I strained to hear what was being said. Then there was a shot. It was so close, and in such a confined space, that it seemed to explode inside my head. I heard the skull and crossbones door close and men file past me out of the cell block. As my ears stopped ringing from the shot I could hear the murmurs in English again.

Hysterically I jumped to the conclusion (quite erroneous as it turned out) that one of the two English teachers had been shot and that a guard was consoling his friend. I was devastated and terrified. After a while all the guards had gone. I remember stroking the wall between me and what I thought was the Englishmen's cell, mumbling words of condolence and encouragement. My mind was quite out of gear. I smoked my last cigarette, hoping to calm down, then decided to pee before trying to sleep. My aim was bad, urine splashed on my legs. Wanting to weep, but unable to let tears flow, I sank to my knees. How on earth was I going to cope?

2
London, April 1986

I was day-dreaming over breakfast, thoughts of Greece
flitting through my mind. It was going to be lovely,
stretching out on a beach in a few weeks' time with
John, especially after this month spent apart. I looked
at the clock. It was time to get on with the day and to
buy some food; there were only five hours until his plane
was due in at Heathrow. Already I felt a little nervous,
would he have changed? Would he find London a bit
of a let-down after Beirut? Pushing those worries away
I went to run a bath, but stopped in the doorway as the
telephone began to ring. It was probably John's friend,
Chris Pearson, ringing to see what time we would all be in
the pub for the welcome-home party. I sighed. I'd much
rather have John to myself this evening.

'Jill, it's Roby.' My heart sank. Roby Burke was a senior
manager at WTN and I could tell by his voice that there
had been some trouble at work. I hated being an NUJ
representative at times and today of all days . . . I made
myself sound business-like. 'Hallo, Roby. What's up?'
'Jill, I have some bad news. John's been kidnapped.' I
felt dizzy, a fog began to fill my head. Roby's words didn't
seem to make any sense. 'When?' was all I could think of to
say. 'He was on his way to the airport when some gunmen
stopped the car and ordered him out. We're doing our best
to discover what's happened . . .' Through the fog Roby's
grave tone frightened me. He had to be wrong. John was
already on the plane. It would have taken off by now. He
was on his way home. Roby's voice continued. 'What I
need from you is a photograph so that ITN can put it
on the lunch-time news. Can you find one and bring it in

46

to the office straightaway? Can you do that?' I raced into
the bedroom and searched frantically through packets of
photographs stuffed in a drawer. There was John pulling a
face; John adopting a dramatic pose; John wearing a great
big hat. My hands felt clumsy and I began to get angry.
Why couldn't he have one ordinary, decent photograph
of himself? I snatched up one from our holiday in Sicily,
back in October. John was wearing sunglasses and his
smile was slightly distracted because I'd made him look
up from the book he was reading. As I picked it up I
could hear him teasing me, saying, 'Jilly, you could have
found a better one than that.'

Two hours later, at WTN, the photograph flashed up
on the television as the newsreader reported the kidnapping in Beirut of John McCarthy, a twenty-nine-year-old
journalist working for Worldwide Television News. The
newsreader was explaining that his abduction was one of
several acts of retaliation against British interests following
the bombing of Libya. I stared at the screen in disbelief
and struggled to connect John with all this madness. Two
British teachers, Leigh Douglas and Philip Padfield, had
been found dead in Beirut that morning, their bodies
dumped on a roadside with that of an American, Peter
Kilburn, kidnapped months ago. A note attached to their
bodies said that they had been 'executed' in retaliation for
Britain's role in the bombing. I couldn't take it in. John's
photograph came up on the screen again. There he was,
peering out from behind sunglasses – perhaps being on
television would somehow keep him safe.

The WTN news room was still and quiet as the programme finished and colleagues reluctantly turned back
to work. Nick Toksvig, another close friend of John's, was
white-faced. I couldn't bear to look at him or at anyone
else. Everything seemed so unreal. On the way into work
I had looked through the cab window at the warm spring
morning outside, and people going about their business as
normal. I felt a long way away. I tried to keep calm saying
to myself, 'Don't cry. Don't cry.'

Roby called me into his office and gave me more details about what had happened. The gunmen had ordered John out of his car, pushed him into theirs and driven away with him. His colleagues had tried to give chase, but had lost him and returned to the office to alert London. 'We're doing everything we can,' Roby was saying. 'The British Embassy is pulling out all the stops and the Beirut office is keeping us informed. I'm sure there'll be news soon.' I still could not take it in. He must be on the plane, I thought. Only yesterday he'd rung to say he would be coming home a week early. Beirut had been quiet on the day of the bombing and there had still been no reaction to it the following day. We'd both thought that WTN was over-reacting by ordering him back and that he might as well wait another day for a direct flight to London. That conversation seemed from another time.

Roby asked me if I was all right and I nodded. I didn't want to leave WTN; I wanted to be there when news came in. When I called my dad to tell him what had happened, his shocked, 'Oh, love . . .' brought tears to my eyes and I had to hang up, telling him I would call as soon as there was any news.

For the rest of the day, I sat with three colleagues, Brad Mercer, Mike MacNish and Sean Ward in The Crown and Sceptre, the WTN local, waiting for news. In a daze, I drank the whisky they bought me, listening to them and others trying to work out what was going on. They were desperate to find reasons why John would survive, would not suffer the same fate as the two teachers, Padfield and Douglas. The very word 'executed' made the situation seem even more unreal. John was on the plane home. Soon he would walk through the door, embarrassed that he'd caused such a fuss when all the time he'd been drinking large G & Ts thousands of miles up in the air. Mike MacNish brought a weak smile to my face when he suddenly recited a scene from a Peter Sellers' film that John and I loved. Sellers as Inspector Clouseau is investigating a kidnapping. 'Now, what do we know,' he says in his exaggerated French accent. 'One! Prof Fassbinder has been kidnapp-ed! Two! Somebody has kidnapp-ed him!'

Within an hour or so, having heard the news, all our friends seemed to converge on the pub. Everyone looked stunned. The conversation revolved around what little we knew and speculation as to what might happen next. There were people everywhere. The noise was tremendous. The time that John should have landed at Heathrow passed. I realized he wasn't coming back. My closest friend, Mary Delaney, came through the door with tears rolling down her face; Nick Toksvig took a phone call from his sister, Sandi, who was distraught. Others, too, suddenly found themselves crying. I could stand the noise no longer; I had to get out of the pub. All I could think of was that three men had been shot. We had to keep John safe, but how?

That night, though, John seemed beyond my reach. I found it impossible to imagine what was happening to him; who he was with or what they were doing to him. There was just a void that my imagination refused to fill. I felt frightened and imagined how alone and terrified he must feel. I blamed myself for not realizing that he had been in so much danger and felt useless for not being able to help him now. I didn't really believe in God, but I prayed that John would survive. I concentrated on all the life he had in him, the spirit that, for me, turned the world into a magical place. I crossed my fingers, not wanting to leave anything to fate, battling against the dreadful feeling that if his unknown captors had coldly murdered three men already, why on earth would they spare John?

I awoke with a jolt the next morning to hear the phone ringing. Horrified that I'd gone to sleep, I ran to answer it, snatching up the receiver. At the sound of Roby's voice my stomach lurched. 'Jill, it's tragic news. There's been a call to a radio station in Beirut that John has been executed. I have to stress it's unconfirmed, but there's a report going out on the eight o'clock news and I wanted to warn you. I'll call you as soon as I hear anything, OK?'

I put the phone down and began to cry. Roby's phone call seemed to confirm the worst.

'He's dead, he's dead,' I sobbed. My flatmate, Geraldine Chmerling, came rushing out of her room, looking confused and alarmed. She and Barbara Mackie, a friend of John's who'd stayed the night, put their arms round me and led me back into the bedroom. I sat down on the bed, head in my hands. There was nothing to hang on to now, no hope left at all. Why hadn't I been able to help him? All the plans we had made disappeared in a moment, tossed away as if worthless. Barbara told me to get back into bed. 'We were going to get married . . .' I said. 'You will, you will; it's not confirmed yet. That's what Roby said, isn't it?'

The phone rang and Geraldine answered it; Roby again. I took the receiver, afraid of what was coming next. 'It looks as if that call was a hoax. There's been another call to say John's OK. The building where they said John's body would be has been searched and they haven't found anything . . .' I took a slow, deep breath. Roby's voice relaxed a little. 'We'll have to be careful or we'll all be getting emotional whiplash.'

Thank God. Somehow John had survived. He was alive. Roby told me that an anonymous caller had rung WTN in Beirut to tell them that the keys to a car stolen during John's abduction had been hidden in a certain place in the city. The caller had said that John was all right, but refused to give any more details. His authenticity was verified when the keys were found; while it wasn't cast-iron proof that John was alive, it was enough.

We waited desperately for more news. The West and the Arab world were still making sabre-rattling noises and I was terrified that the people who held John would kill him at any moment; every time a British politician spoke about the bombing of Libya, I worried that it would endanger his life. Helplessness made me angry. When the front page of the *Evening Standard* announced: 'Now London TV man is dead', I rang them up, shaking with trepidation. I told them that they were wrong, John wasn't dead, they should check their facts first.

'Who are you?' an impatient journalist asked.

'I'm his girlfriend,' I said, my voice trembling.

'Can I have your number?' the journalist said, eagerly. I put the phone down in despair. I'd just wanted them to acknowledge that they were wrong.

The day passed in an exhausting blur, as friends and colleagues converged on my flat to wait for news. About a dozen of us sat at the kitchen table, desperately trying to think of something useful we could do. We began telephoning people, anyone and everyone who might be able to help. As soon as the receiver was put down, someone else would snatch it up again with another idea; these became more and more desperate. We called Nick Toksvig's father, Claus, a Danish MEP. Perhaps the European parliament could help? Nick had completely lost his voice through shock, so was frantically passing us notes of questions to ask or of new people to contact. Mike MacNish suddenly shouted, 'Call the Pope!' and no-one thought it at all odd; anything was worth a try.

Normally I would not have had the courage to telephone a newspaper or an MP, but I was fooling myself that I could do something. Someone suggested I call Julie Flint, the *Guardian*'s correspondent in Beirut; all I got was a recorded message telling me to try later. I kept pressing the redial button like an automaton, waiting for the click which meant that the connection had been made. I had followed the same procedure when I'd talked to John late at night when the lines to Lebanon were less busy. Now, with the receiver to my ear, I could pretend that in a minute the phone would ring and I would hear his sleepy voice, saying, 'Darling! How lovely to hear you.' After countless attempts it was, of course, Julie Flint's voice I actually heard. I asked her what was going on. Did she know who had kidnapped John? What could we do to find him? She told me that she was doing all she could, but must have thought it better that someone told me now rather than let me carry on hoping in vain. 'Forget it, love,' she advised, 'they don't come back.' I put the phone down as a wave of hopelessness, and then anger, swept over me.

What did she mean? How could she say, 'forget it' like that?

I couldn't imagine life without John. We had met at WTN two and a half years earlier when I was a secretary and he had just started as a telex operator. Nick Toksvig had introduced us one day by the telex machine, after he'd discovered that we had all been at Hull University at the same time. John seemed quite shy but very charming. We didn't seem to have known any of the same people at Hull and I was unable to make any kind of conversation at all.

Not long afterwards, Nick and John were in the bar with Mike MacNish and invited me on an outing to the country the following day – in a chauffeur-driven Cadillac. I had already discovered that being with Nick and Mike was great fun; they made me laugh with their mad sense of humour and this sounded too good to miss. The next day I waited for them by the side of the road a little way from ITN House, clutching a bottle of champagne. I wondered for a moment whether their invitation had been serious. I was unused to Londoners and wasn't always sure how to take their apparently casual arrangements. In Yorkshire, people were more direct and you could take things at face value; you knew where you stood. But with Nick and Mike, with whom I felt quite comfortable, I should have had no doubts.

Later I looked back on that Friday as the most magical day of my life – everything had seemed perfect – but the best part of it by far was that I was beginning to fall in love with John.

Now, faced with what Julie Flint had said, I couldn't accept that John wouldn't come back. I picked up the phone again and called my local MP, Nick Raynsford, who did his best to be helpful. 'Why don't you call Terry Waite?' Waite was already on my list. I knew that he was trying to obtain the release of several Americans who'd been kidnapped in Lebanon the year before. He was the obvious person to turn to. When I actually spoke to him I was too busy thinking, 'I'm talking to Terry Waite!' to recall the conversation in any detail, but his reassuring manner and promise that he would help gave me confidence that something could be done. 'Thank God there are people like Terry Waite,' I thought. Whatever he could do would add to the efforts that Roby Burke told me were being made by WTN and the Foreign Office.

That evening I sat in a daze. The phone was ringing all the time and I kept jumping up to answer it. The flat was full of people, some of whom I didn't even know. Sometimes I wished everyone would go, but I didn't want to be alone.

On the second morning, Roby rang to say that the anonymous caller had been in contact again, repeating that John was alive and providing information about the stolen car. I was euphoric with relief. Everyone was confident that the return of some valuable camera equipment that had been in the car would be next, followed by John himself. Everyone gathered at my flat again to wait for that next call. It would soon be over. The war of words with Libya continued, but Roby said there was a feeling in Lebanon that enough had been done to avenge the bombing. We stopped telephoning people and I went out for a walk along the river with Mary while others stayed to man the phone. John would soon be home.

There was no third phone call offering information about John. Roby was in contact with people in Lebanon, and the FO, and over the next few days his bulletins were like a lifeline to which I clung for information. I was hesitant about contacting John's family. I didn't know them very well and I didn't want to call, imagining that they would be hoping, as I did, that each time the phone rang, it would be with news of John.

After a week, Roby rang to say that from now on he would only be calling when there was something definite to report. He suggested that I should get away, so I went home to my parents in Doncaster. Leaving London felt like abandoning the lifeline to Roby and through him to Beirut and John, and at home the silence of the telephone seemed even worse. I felt useless, unable to help John, and I tried to contact Julie Flint again. She rang back to say that she'd made all the enquiries she could, but had reached a dead end. How could he just disappear? What did that mean? I felt more confused and frightened than ever. My mum and dad, who are extremely practical and loyal people, were distressed to see me so upset. 'Are you sure there's nothing we can do, Jill? There must be something we can do, love,' said my dad. I told him that an international organization like WTN had to be able to find out who John's captors were, contact them and do whatever was necessary to get him home. Everything would stop for John. He had the weight of the Government behind him. If a British subject was kidnapped, the British government wouldn't rest until he or she was freed. It would merely be a matter of holding on for a few days more.

I sat up in my bedroom, feeling like I was being blown from one day to the next like a leaf in the wind. I looked out over the playing-fields of my old school. Nothing I'd learned there or since had taught me how to cope with a situation like this.

Life had been uneventful, with few surprises. The world I grew up in, the mining village of Woodlands on the outskirts of Doncaster, was very small and secure. It had developed above the coal seams of Brodsworth Colliery between 1906 and 1907 when the colliery created what it saw as an experimental community, the only one of its kind. Solidly constructed pit houses, built in a series of squares, slope down from the pithead to a parade of shops along the Great North Road. The houses have individual front gardens with low stone walls, but their backs look out on to communal greens reached by alleyways around the squares. It was all in keeping with the benevolent way that the mine operated up until a few years ago, playing a large part in most people's lives, providing employment, homes, youth clubs, miners' welfare clubs, a brass band and social activities like the annual galas and sports days which I loved as a child.

We lived in a council house on an estate built in the late 1940s for the families of young men returning from the war. It was an attractive estate running, like the older 'squares', from the pithead down to the Great North Road. By the time I was born in 1957 my dad was a draughtsman at International Harvester, a firm of agricultural engineers based five miles away in Doncaster. He had tried a variety of jobs including railway signalman, pit surveyor, even sailor during his national service and wanted to be a journalist, but had settled for learning a skill and having regular employment instead.

His family had come to Woodlands from Nottinghamshire in the early 1900s, when my great-grandfather had helped sink the mine. He worked down the pit all his life, as did my grandfather. As a child my favourite relative was my maternal grandmother, who lived nearby. She was a seamstress, widowed in her forties and had worked in a small room above a ladies' outfitters in town, supplementing her wage with money she earned making clothes for friends and neighbours. Her old sewing-machine was always out on the dining-table except on special occasions, such as Sunday tea. One of my pet hates as an impatient child was being draped in cloth and pricked with pins during endless fitting sessions for school clothes. As I grew older I began to realize how much she continued to be a source of support, understanding and constant practical help to all the family.

Our estate was full of families where the women had given up work, either after getting married or having children. My mum was bright and particularly good at maths, but, as the eldest of four, she had left school at sixteen to work as a clerk in an insurance company. After my brother Brian and I were born she stayed at

55

home, baking bread, cakes and pies, doing all the work around the house singlehanded.

I was very happy during the twelve years we lived there. The Miners' Welfare Association provided the adhesive which united most of the village in a way that was taken for granted and which provided quite a lot of entertainment for local children. I loved joining organizations such as the Church Girls' Brigade which had a special uniform and marched on Whit Sunday; and the local ballet and tap school which taught singing and dance. We even performed in concerts all around Doncaster. I was shy, but more than anything else I wanted to join in, mainly because I was anxious to miss nothing, especially at school. Apparently, when I was five I announced I wouldn't be coming home at dinner-time any more, but would be staying for a school meal instead. Nor did I want to be taken to and from school; I wanted to walk there and back with my friends. My mum cites this to show how determined I could be despite my shyness. Usually I was quite sure of what I wanted to do and fear ran a very close second to the idea of being left out of the fun. I always liked doing something, playing games, making things or sitting on my own, reading. In the evenings and at weekends I played with our neighbours' children in the street, but sometimes we went climbing trees on the land of a large house a mile beyond the pit. It always made me nervous. What put me off was a combination of being too far away from home and knowing we were trespassing.

A substantial respect for authority had been drummed into Brian and me quite early on. One of my dad's pet hates is rude and disobedient children, and we were wary of provoking him. Always the disciplinarian, stopping us short if we got too precocious or cheeky, he is really a softie at heart, too affectionate for his temper to last very long and he had endless patience when it came to teaching us things. Every week he took me swimming and walked me round the countryside beyond the pit while my mum was cooking Sunday dinner. He would point out interesting landmarks and places where he had played as a boy during the war: the bluebell wood and a well which Little John, one of Robin Hood's men, was said to have used. Through him I developed a liking for history and an appetite for reading and would lose myself in anything I could get my hands on. The one thing I wanted as a child that I didn't have was a garden shed like the one in which the Secret Seven used to meet. We just didn't have the space for it so I improvised with bits of wood; it was a recurring bone of contention between me and my dad for what seemed like years. We are quite alike, both hating to admit we are in the wrong, both unwilling to concede the last word.

My mum is quieter, less stubborn and hates arguments. When we were young, she would try to smooth things over, often distracting us with a plea for peace and quiet or more frequently with a joke. All her family have a great sense of humour and, because my dad shared it as well, there was mostly laughter and endless teasing at home. My mum and dad rarely rowed; the spot on the wall where my mum once threw an egg at my dad and missed was evidence of one of the rare occasions when she lost her temper. She likes music and would sing along to the radio, or my dad would accompany her on the piano in the sitting room. Her sense of fun spurred me on to take part in local concerts, enter fancy dress competitions, and compete in local sports days. I think that she was encouraging me to be as outgoing as possible, not wanting me to be held back by shyness or a lack of self-confidence, perhaps because that had stopped her from doing many of the things she would have liked to have done.

My brother Brian, three and a half years my junior, was more like her in temperament; he was quite sensitive as a small boy and liked to play quietly on his own or with one or two friends. We didn't get on that well when we were little – our interests were very different and I often made his life difficult by bossing him around. Occasionally he got his own back by climbing on to the piano stool after I had finished my daily practice and giving a perfect rendition of a piece of music I'd been labouring over for hours; it drove me mad. For years, I had taken piano lessons, but it was obvious very early on that Brian was gifted, that he had an extraordinary ear for music.

When I was about nine, I was told that I ought to look after Brian more and stick up for him if he were in trouble. Hostility was something I hadn't ever experienced and I had avoided it at all costs, but not long after that Brian was picked on while walking home from school. I suddenly realized I ought to do something. I found myself in my first 'scrap', spurred on by a mixture of anger, fear and an overwhelming desire to land a good punch.

When I was eleven, my twin ambitions were to teach and to be an athlete. I still enjoyed school and automatically thought about becoming a teacher whenever anyone asked that impossible question, 'What do you want to be when you grow up?' But my heroine was the runner, Lillian Board. I was doing well at sport and dreamed of representing Britain at the Olympics. The first news event I can remember vividly was the murder of the Israeli athletes at the Munich Olympics in 1972. I couldn't believe that people could behave like that towards one another.

When the embarrassments of adolescence struck, I became moody and uncommunicative. I found that moving to the other side of Doncaster when I was fourteen made things worse. It was such an upheaval and, although we were only twelve miles away, it seemed like a hundred. Gradually, I settled in and made new friends, but it took me a long time to get over the move. I lost confidence and began to worry a lot and I found that it helped to have plenty to do. I started a series of Saturday and holiday jobs, first as a waitress in a Wimpy bar where I learned to raise my voice shouting orders over the din, then at a 'superior' tea-room, which I hated, and finally as a sales assistant at Littlewoods. I also tried working as a pianist in a dance band on Saturday nights, mystifying the bandleader by pulling the curtain a little way across the stage in order to conceal myself. As the result of an attack of nerves, I missed the first four bars of 'The Last Waltz' and decided I was not cut out to be a performer. I seemed to lack ambition, doing whatever came along and with no idea about what I wanted to do in the future.

Of one thing I was certain; whatever the work, it must not be monotonous. I had reached this decision having spent a few summer holidays working at a canning factory in Goole where the workforce was directed by women who wore turbans coloured according to seniority and who yelled at everyone over the clatter of tin cans. They struck terror into the hearts of seasonal workers like me, who were often given a hard time for not catching on quickly enough or for not pulling our weight. I have never known time pass as slowly as it did when sorting through peas on a conveyor belt; strawberries were only marginally more interesting. Every minute seemed an age, and the five-minute break was the only time that talking was permitted. I preferred the harder physical work in the packing department; time shot by in comparison and I began to quite enjoy it. The comradeship of the women was tremendous, but the tedium of factory work was a killer.

Despite my uncertainty, I took it for granted that I would go to college. I had applied to some teacher training colleges in Yorkshire so that I could be near Steve, my boyfriend, and although I had been accepted at Bingley Teacher Training College, my mum and dad persuaded me to try to get into university, even though I had left it very late to apply. I wrote off quickly to universities in the Yorkshire area and was given a conditional place at Hull to read History. I realized that I had nearly blown my chances and I began to work again in earnest, sitting my A levels in the hot summer of 1976.

Not many of my friends from school went on to university, most were leaving to get jobs locally, and eventually to marry and settle down there. As my dad drove me the forty-five miles to Hull I felt about five years old again and spent most of the journey in silence. I remember him saying that I could always come back if I didn't like it, but I felt it was too late to have second thoughts.

The first few days were nerve-racking, particularly as I switched courses within a week, combining History with French. Luckily I didn't have a chance to be homesick as I had to get to know the eight other girls sharing our student house. I found they were all from the North and were easy to get on with, particularly my roommate and another girl, both called Elaine. We three became good friends and I began to enjoy the close relationships that university life makes possible and that I had missed in recent years at home. I was not very adventurous; I was still wary of people who were very different, like southerners, who seemed very confident and sophisticated – 'show-offs' they would have been called at home. So many people already seemed to have done a fair bit of travelling whilst I hadn't really left first base. Nevertheless, even though I wasn't very confident, I was still exhilarated by university life. My world was expanding, I was getting to know people from completely different backgrounds and life slipped into a comfortable routine of lectures, nights in the union bar and outrageous student parties.

At the end of the second year, in 1977, I began to travel. I went to Paris for six weeks to work at the French offices of International Harvester (IH). I had been spurred into going because I felt I should improve my spoken French, but the thought of the trip terrified me. When I found myself sitting on a suitcase in a siding of the Gare du Nord, wondering if I was destined for the white-slave trade, I was convinced I should have stayed at home. When help finally arrived in the shape of Laura, an Irish girl who was also going to work at IH, I stopped panicking and began to enjoy myself. The usual feelings of shyness and inexperience were kept at bay by the sheer excitement of being at large in Paris. I had to pinch myself every morning when I stopped off to buy a *pain au chocolat* for breakfast. I loved working and living in a totally foreign place; the unfamiliarity seemed attractive and stimulating instead of frightening and strange.

For the third year of my course, I went to work in a supermarket in La Plagne, a ski resort in the French Alps. Although he had initially been against the idea, Steve came with me and it made an enormous difference to me when he became enthusiastic about it. I doubt that I would have gone without him. The year away made me appreciate how pleasant it is to do nothing but study, and I regretted not having made more of my first two years at Hull. I returned there, in 1979, for my final year and was surprised by how interesting I now found the work. My results improved and I felt more receptive to learning than I had ever done.

As I began to explore and become more comfortable with different worlds, I felt dissatisfied with life in Doncaster. Most of the time I was at university I was going out with Steve. We had become engaged during my second year and I still saw my future in terms of the standard formula of marriage, a job and a house in or near Doncaster.

I graduated from Hull in 1980 with a 2.ii, with no specific idea about what I was going to do. Finally I decided to spend a further year there studying for a Secretarial Language Certificate at the College of Higher Education which seemed a way of widening my options. I was happy to stay in Hull; I still knew people there and had grown fond of the city, which in the late 1970s had the atmosphere of a place left abandoned while the world sped by.

After completing the course learning shorthand, typing and office management, I spent the summer of 1981 around Leeds, Sheffield, Nottingham and York in an unsuccessful search for work. It did not occur to me to look further afield. While I was tramping the streets of Nottingham my mum sent me a clipping from the job section of the *Daily Mail*. It was for a secretary to the General Manager of UPITN, which was, after a couple of years, to become WTN. The address given was ITN

House in London. I thought that my mum was mad, but applied for the job just to please her, only to find that I'd got an interview in London. Steve and my parents accompanied me, but on the journey down I was so nervous that I could hardly speak. London was the big, bad city; another planet. Steve and I walked down Tottenham Court Road and up Oxford Street feeling as if we were on an enormous Monopoly board where the prospect of working at ITN House seemed as remote as buying Mayfair or Park Lane. A little later I received a telephone call from UPITN and was able to tell my mum in a worried voice that they'd offered me the job.

The nerves I had prior to the interview were nothing to those I experienced on my first day at work. I felt sure that I couldn't possibly do a secretary's job, let alone in a place like this where the work surely must be above my head. I was saved from collapsing by another secretary, Anne Mellor, who took me to the canteen and to the ITN bar for a drink and generally saw me through the first few days, for which I will always be grateful. After a few weeks I relaxed and found that I was able to do the job after all. I discovered too that UPITN was a fascinating place to work. Despite ITN's substantial shares in the company, the two operations were separate and very different. They provided each other with news material, but principally UPITN gathered and distributed raw news footage abroad and had cameramen and clients all over the world. The small journalistic team in London decided what to cover, how to bring the footage in before our competitors, and what to distribute. The whole outfit intrigued me; the office in London was in touch with countries all over the world and the job of the journalists was to keep abreast of the interesting, important events that were taking place and provide film coverage of what was happening to TV stations all over the world.

My boss was the general manager, Eric Jessup. He had to keep our cameramen supplied with spare parts and small bits of equipment. Eventually I was put in charge of this side of things, but, although it made my job more interesting, it seemed to me that most of the excitement was going on in the news room next door. As I grew more confident, I tried to find out exactly what happened in there and how it all worked.

In those days the London operation was very small. Journalists, technical staff, administration, accountants, management and secretarial staff were all situated on one floor of ITN House, so it was easy to look in through a door and chat to people as they worked. I got to know film editors who explained what the various technical terms meant and what their job entailed, and became particularly friendly with an American girl, Taryn Gottlieb, who had just joined the news room. She saw I was curious about what went on in there and suggested that I came in one weekend and she would take me through her day. I had a stab at writing a script, a short twelve-to-fifteen-line factual account of a news event somewhere in South America. Trying to follow her instructions and give a decent résumé of what had happened by answering the who, what, where, when and how, took me several hours.

Although I had only a very basic idea of what was required I began to see, with Taryn's help, that the work wasn't quite as daunting as I had imagined and I told the news room manager that if they ever needed anyone to help at weekends, even if only for typing, I would like to be considered.

I had been very wary of people in the news room at first, scuttling in and out as fast as I could if I had a memo to deliver; but, as I got to know one or two people and then joined them for a drink in the seventh-floor bar after work, I realized that most of them were friendly and great fun. There were some very amusing people, great characters whose witty ripostes and famous victories and blunders were listed in the UPITN Hall of Fame and recounted for the benefit of newcomers like me. There were stories of drunken news editors directing operations from under their desks, still able to beat the opposition to a story; the experienced old hack who completely forgot to include the Royal Wedding in his news package on the day; the famous Clouseau impersonator who made every 'beumb' story a riot; the football cameraman who always seemed to be changing his film when the winning goal was scored; the seasoned journalist who stubbornly refused to extend a satellite booking by a few seconds so that viewers all around the world saw film of a world-record long jumper leaping into mid-air but never landing. They talked a lot about work, which I found interesting anyway, but I liked their enthusiasm and the way they worked as a team. Defeats were recounted with as much relish as victories and although the work was tremendously pressurized in its own way, nobody at UPITN actually appeared on television or was involved in the news presentation, so there were few of the monstrous egos that can be found elsewhere in the news business. They were friendly, workmanlike and didn't mind my endless requests for information.

Outside work life was also going well. Within a few weeks of arriving in London, I'd answered a flat-share advert and found myself living in a lovely house in Golders Green with two students, Mary Delaney and Jo Sheehan, who made me so welcome that I felt at home straightaway. I think they were a little bemused by my old-fashioned hair-style and northern accent, but we got on very well, staying together for three years, ending up in Holland Park.

Life in London was hardly dull or as lonely as I'd imagined it might be and I got the chance to do some travelling. In 1983, I went on a trip to Russia with a party of schoolchildren led by a friend from university; the dreariness of Moscow and the beauty of Leningrad gave me a glimpse, albeit a blinkered one, of life in the pursuit of communism. It was an impressive ideal, but practising it, I spent the week frustrated by how long it took to achieve the simplest thing; getting a soft drink outside mealtimes, visiting something not on the official tour; the incomprehensible system of queues –

one to choose your goods, a second to pay and a third queue to collect them. Nor did I like the claustrophobic presence of the State everywhere, nor the rows and rows of mean-looking tower blocks on the outskirts of Moscow. I thought how hard it must be for ordinary people to carry the burden of the Soviet ideal.

The following spring I joined Taryn and some of her friends on a tour of Scotland, and that summer went to Rome. It seemed to have all the qualities that I had loved about Paris only in greater abundance, and, remembering how nice it had been to live and work in France, I wondered if there was any way I could do it again, perhaps in Italy, this time on a more permanent basis.

Although I didn't acknowledge it at the time, the vague hopes I had for the future were taking me further away from home. During my first year in London, Steve and I saw each other most weekends. He had not gone into teaching as planned, but was working as a double-glazing salesman in Rotherham, at which he was extremely good. He liked the people with whom he worked, kept in touch with all his old friends and was still enjoying playing rugby for the local team and the social life that went with it. Sometimes I went home but most weekends he would drive down to London on Saturday after the match and leave again very early on Monday. Occasionally our separate worlds would overlap; Mary and Jo awoke one morning to find the entire rugby team from Doncaster crashed out in our flat, but in general it was difficult to bridge the two. We were going in different directions; Steve didn't want to leave Rotherham and I didn't want to go back up North. One weekend in Doncaster we decided to split up.

My mum and dad, now living back in Woodlands, comforted me as they had when Steve and I separated temporarily six years earlier. At the time it had seemed like the end of the world and my dad had been angry to see me so upset. This time, although the prospect of their daughter's marriage had evaporated, they realized that it was nobody's fault and my mum in particular was positive and encouraging as to what the future might hold.

Almost immediately life took off again. One Saturday the news room had a vacancy on the junior scriptwriting desk it couldn't fill so I was given the chance to try my hand. I spent virtually a sleepless night on Friday, listening to the World Service almost every hour. On the dreaded day, however, with the encouragement of colleagues like Brad Mercer and Mike MacNish, I managed to write some adequate scripts.

At the end of the day I joined the others in the bar for a drink and basked in the enormous pleasure of feeling part of the team, overcome by a sense of relief that I hadn't made any huge mistakes. I imagined that I might get another chance to do it in the future if another emergency arose and, in the meantime, decided to be better prepared. It happened much sooner than I expected. Out of the blue, the news editor, John Connor, called me into his office and said that he was going to offer me a job. Another junior scriptwriter was leaving unexpectedly and if I wanted to, I could take her place. It was such a huge stroke of luck. I was flabbergasted. Any immediate worries that I might not be able to do the job I kept firmly to myself. I was going to be able to call myself a journalist, even if I did feel it was a bit of a cheek.

I had other boyfriends, but the move into the news room brought more contact with John. We often made up part of the crowd in the ITN bar after work and I began to notice when he wasn't there. He was always very polite and unassuming, but his presence somehow made things sparkle. We began to see each other casually after a while and I soon had set my heart on him. John was unlike anyone I had ever met. He was open to anything, a free spirit who could seize the important moments in life and value them, whether during a drunken evening with friends, an intense conversation with Nick, or, as I hardly dared hope, during the time we spent together. We did ordinary things but they seemed quite magical to me. His enthusiasm for life was infectious and with him I felt more alive, more adventurous and a little wild myself. He was very charming, could make me feel the most interesting person around, and I loved his sense of humour. The first thing he said which made me really laugh was during the Cadillac trip when we arrived at the riverside in Bray and got out of the car. John sidled over to Nick and me, looked furtively over his shoulder at the chauffeur and whispered, 'What shall we do with him?'

As I got to know John better I found that he liked having quiet times, and that he was very sensitive and perceptive. He always listened carefully to what other people said, and was genuinely interested in their concerns, which gave him a remarkable ability to put himself in their shoes. For a long time, life seemed to revolve around WTN. After work we often went out to dinner or dancing with MacNish, Brad Mercer, Nick and others. We spent a lot of time laughing, just enjoying ourselves; sometimes, though, John seemed elusive, and I doubted if he was interested in anything too serious. We both experienced a certain amount of trepidation before our first holiday together and wondered if opting to spend twenty-four hours a day in each other's company was really a good idea, but actually we discovered that travelling together was great fun and that we made a good team. We both loved that feeling of being in a foreign country and not having a clue what's going on, so that everything becomes a series of educated guesses.

We went to Italy, having borrowed Chris Pearson's battered old VW Golf to transport us around Tuscany for three weeks. With considerable foresight, I practised the Italian for 'The clutch cable is broken,' all the way there and was to put the motoring section of the phrasebook to good use throughout the holiday as we suffered from various vital broken parts, were involved in a minor accident and were burgled. The predicaments in which we found ourselves became increasingly surreal and improved the holiday rather than ruined it.

We were forced by these calamities to hire motor bikes, but disaster struck again when John's was stolen. Up until then, I'd not seen John get really worked up about anything, and certainly hadn't seen him move as fast as he did when he saw his motor bike, complete with security chain, being dragged down the road by a nonchalant-looking Italian girl. He caught her up and press-ganged a passer-by to act as translator. He seemed more interested in chatting up the girl and we made no progress until, with a dramatic flourish, John produced the key to the security chain and proceeded to unlock the bike. The Italian girl then admitted that she had stolen the bike, adding that she felt entitled to keep it because someone had stolen hers. John had had enough; he leapt on the bike and roared off before he had to listen to any more nonsense.

I realized that what John had felt then had been straightforward fury. He was the last person to look for confrontation, but I remembered that I'd seen this side of him once before, at a party in the Holland Park flat. Mary had invited about a hundred people, the flat was absolutely heaving and there was simply no more room. My friend Angela came up to me, laughing, saying, 'Jill, I think you'd better see what John's up to.'

I squeezed my way through the throng to the front door. Standing at the top of the stairs was John, absolutely refusing to let in anyone else. He wouldn't budge, he was adamant that for them even to come up the stairs was absurd. I was astonished. I think it was then that I realized that, though John might be good-natured most of the time, there was a point at which he became totally immovable.

After the holiday, we were definitely much more of a partnership, and our relationship became more settled. I had fallen in love with John very quickly and it was nice being able to enjoy some less hectic time together. Things got better and better, but the first time he invited me home for the weekend I was very nervous. John came from such a different background and I had no idea what to expect. Needless to say, I had worried unnecessarily. They were all so charming and so much like John that I really enjoyed myself. Not long afterwards, John came up to Doncaster to meet my mum and dad. This time he was apprehensive, but my mum and dad loved him and Brian thought he was great. They talked about music for hours.

By the end of 1985 we were spending most of our time at the tiny flat I was sharing with Geraldine and we decided that it was time to find somewhere together. Through talking to other more widely travelled colleagues we'd formed a hazy plan of buying a flat, working abroad for a while, getting married and then having children. We had plenty of time to sort out the details. For the present, I was enjoying going around looking at flats; we'd seen one we really liked, but were pipped at the post. Before John left for Beirut he granted me Power of Attorney so I could secure it if it came back on the market while he was away.

The Beirut posting only became definite in February 1986. I was far more horrified at the prospect of his being away for a whole month than the fact that he would be in Lebanon, but I stifled any misgivings because John was so pleased that at last he had the chance, having proved himself on the desk in London, to go out into the field. I think I would have been more worried if he had been going to Columbia, or Peru, where the violence was hidden, unexpected and sinister. The fact that the civil war in Lebanon had begun in 1975 and that I had seen pictures of the fighting in the news room at WTN so often meant I'd become blasé. I knew John would make intelligent assessments of any risks connected with what he was doing, and wouldn't deliberately put himself in danger. In any case, there had been a lull in the fighting for some months. Although I knew that there had been a number of kidnappings, I was unsure why. As the men taken seemed mostly to be American or French, I had no fears that anything like that would happen to John.

When John and I left for the airport on 16 March 1986, he was very quiet. As we said goodbye, I became tearful. 'It's only a month, Jilly,' he said. Once he was out of sight, I felt silly for causing a fuss, but very lonely. The month stretched ahead, seemingly endless. I went up on to the roof of the terminal and took a photograph of his plane taking off which I thought I'd give him as a souvenir when he got back. Then I took the tube home to resume the search for our flat and begin planning our holiday.

Six weeks later I was in Crete after all, not knowing if John was dead or alive.

As I lay in a chalet trying to get to sleep I resolved that when John came back we would go on a much better holiday than this – the chalet Barbara Mackie and I were in and the nearby beach were nothing like those advertised in the brochure. If only I knew when he was coming home, I could book a wonderful trip; we'd be able to forget this nightmare as quickly as it had happened. I pulled the sheet up over my head to escape a lone mosquito careering around the room and tried to imagine what must be happening to John, but could visualize nothing beyond his actual abduction. I did not know where he was, who he was with, how they were treating him, in what circumstances he was being held. I knew nothing of Lebanon and wished I could picture the landscape, the weather, the people – even the food he was eating or clothes he was wearing – anything at all. Only now did I realize that Lebanon was such an alien country, a place where chaos was the order of the day and anything was possible. No normal rules of behaviour applied. All I knew was that we could see the same moon and might be trying to go to sleep at the same time. I tried to will him to hang on.

Most people saw John as an outgoing type, confident, relaxed and in control. Undoubtedly, most of the time, he was and I felt that he had the resilience and natural optimism to marshal his strengths for whatever he was having to face. But how could I predict that with any certainty when I didn't know what awful horrors he was being forced to confront?

And what, in the end, would his strength matter? When I closed my eyes I saw a photograph printed in *Newsweek* of the dead bodies of Padfield, Douglas and Kilburn. Images of John with a gun to his head haunted me.

Not Fade Away

3
Beirut, April–November 1986

It took me two or three days to realize that the screaming
had stopped altogether. The logical conclusion was that
the young Arab must have been shot on the Saturday
night, not someone from the cell next to mine, where at
least one English-speaker was held. On the one hand I
felt great relief that a Western hostage had not been killed
and the sense of being under constant threat of execution
largely lifted, but on the other, I suffered acute distress for
the actual victim. The young man had obviously spent his
last days in abject terror, the subject of routine abuse. His
cries and screams for mercy must have been addressed to
the guard, hoping to arouse some humanitarian response,
but must also have been a desperate effort to be heard by
someone or something else, perhaps to be forgiven, and
released from his torment. The stark reality was that there
was no-one to lend a sympathetic ear to the plight of these
captives. We were beyond all avenues of appeal, we had
no rights or sense of place, we could do nothing to end
this situation, only hope to survive it.

It took about a month for my appetite to pick up. I had
developed a routine to help pass the hours. After the daily
trip to the bathroom I would eat a little of the food the
guard had left on the mattress, read for what I thought
was an hour or so, do some exercises, have a cigarette, eat
a little more, then read and exercise again. Being so far
underground daylight didn't show even when the power
was off and the cell block in darkness, so I could only
guess at the time. Once or twice I was taken to a different
bathroom, next to the one I normally used. As it did not
flood, this made a very pleasant change. Trusty always

started with the prisoners furthest away from the bath-rooms and, since the plumbing was basic to say the least, the lavatory I usually visited – along with the floor – was soon awash. Fortunately, the guards had given me a pair of flip-flops from my luggage so, standing on a slightly raised piece of concrete, I could avoid having to stand directly in the other prisoners' filth. It all seemed wickedly designed to ensure that my bowels would remain firmly closed.

One day another guard appeared to oversee the food and bathroom round. I felt more of a fool than usual standing in the corridor with arms laden with wash-bag, pee-bottle and so forth, all topped off with a rather smart jacket draped over my head and shoulders. He tried to speak to me using his few words of English; he seemed an excitable sort, not aggressive exactly, but rather remi-niscent of a man joining lower management for the first time, anxious to show he could cope with a complex rou-tine. Anyway, he certainly threw Trusty's orderly progress out of the window (or would have done had there been a window), so, after a brief and mutually unrewarding conversation, I was ushered into the second bathroom with imprecations to 'Urry, urry'. I didn't hold much hope that the change in venue would bring any relief to my seized innards, but suddenly he fired his pistol right outside the door. I hurried myself.

Both bathrooms had a hole high in the wall. They looked out into a gloomy space that was presumably part of the foundations of the neighbouring building. If I craned my neck I could just see daylight shining through some sort of air vent. On days when the power was off I sometimes heard children playing in the street outside. I spent hours considering this as a possible route of escape, but the prob-lem was that I had so little time in there. Trusty and the guard were always in attendance and it was by no means certain that it would be possible to reach the air vent, let alone to get through it. I might also have been a little conspicuous emerging out of a hole in the ground, filthy, in a pair of shorts, emanating a ghastly subterranean pallor, into a street full of children. If this were to offer a way out then it had to be at night when the guards weren't around; that meant getting out of the cell in the first place.

The cell itself was tiny, the walls solid concrete and the door a sheet of steel with a grille at the top. The door was fastened by a padlock which was impossible to reach from the inside. On the door some former inmate had scratched an intricate cross – obviously a Christian. I knew that thousands of Lebanese had been kidnapped over the years of civil war so it seemed likely that some of the Christian victims had passed this way, indeed some of those currently held here might well be from the other side of the Beirut tracks. Somehow the possibility that there were prisoners who shared my Christian background and were very probably held with as little justification as I was didn't fill me with any kindred spirit – they were all part of an alien culture that had suddenly seized me and placed me in this underground limbo.

So it was with a distant, almost morbid, fascination that I followed one man's efforts to escape. He had managed to detach the ventilation duct where it turned in through the grille on his door. Every day after the guard had gone I could hear him prising off the duct. Then I would see a thick, hairy arm come through the grille and, with a piece of wire, he'd go fishing for the padlock. He never once made it in the ten weeks I was held there. I suppose I wanted him to succeed but really it gave me the creeps seeing him trying every day. There was something almost bestial about that hairy arm – an animal making its last, futile bid to escape the trap.

Although there seemed no real possibility of escape, fantasizing about it helped pass the time. These fantasies usually escalated from merely my getting out to me liberating the whole prison and solving all the problems of the Middle East. I would grow bored and embarrassed after an hour or so of this and then would try to imagine things that I might actually be able to achieve when I was released. My time in Beirut had reinforced my desire to become a successful journalist. I had been more and more frustrated by the need to find the television pictures without which WTN had nothing to offer its clients, and felt increasingly drawn to print journalism. This really covered a growing regret that I was so ignorant. I vowed that as soon as I was released I'd read volumes on politics, history, philosophy and art so that I would at least have a general idea of how the world – and I – had reached 1986 and, more importantly, have a clearer view of how I thought we should move on.

The reading matter I had with me didn't seem likely to help greatly in this project. One copy each of *Newsweek* and *Time*, a comic novel by David Lodge and a novel about a photographer's experiences in Vietnam and Beirut where he was killed, which, although well written, was hardly encouraging.

One book, though – *Beyond the Euphrates* by Freya Stark, which had been a Christmas present from my mother – stood apart from the others and gave me much encouragement and food for thought. The extraordinary courage and determination that Stark had shown as a woman travelling alone all over the Middle East in the 1930s was such an inspiration that I was very distressed when a guard took it away. Some time later I asked for it again and, when it was returned, I saw from some pencil notes that another prisoner had been reading it. I felt guilty at depriving him of the book, but enormously relieved that I could now finish it. Happily I had done so when a few days later it was taken again – clearly the other reader needed Stark's inspiration as much as I did. (I later found out that Brian Keenan was the other fan, and four years on that Terry Waite had somehow been given my copy and that he, too, had thought it marvellous.) I was particularly struck by one of her diary notes – 'Exercise, the attainment of knowledge, the practice of affection – the three best in mankind, and beyond these a gift of the spirit which is divine.' I was only now beginning to realize that that was my loose philosophy, too, although I had never had the time to develop and practise it.

I asked the guard to find me some other books and was given a blockbuster by Arthur Hailey about banking; the terrific detail on high finance was not matched by the characterization, which was a bitter disappointment as it was company I sought, even that of fictional people.

I desperately missed conversation. In the past I'd talked a lot of nonsense, playing with words, using humour to get to know people. It may have been frivolous, but it was contact, an intimate bond with others. Whether with a close friend or just an acquaintance, for me conversation had been the spice of life. But perhaps I had relied too much on superficial talk, choosing not to dig too deep.

Now, in prison, as ideas struck me, I would turn to tell this or that person, only to come up hard against the blank wall of solitude. I tried to commit things to memory – good one-liners that flitted across my mind, jokey songs about friends and colleagues. But although this brought some companionship into my bleak cell, the horror was that faces were already beginning to fade. I might be able to imagine what a friend's response would be, but that was all. It was increasingly difficult to hold anyone's image in focus. They might spring to life for a few moments, a remembered stance or look, then they'd drift away again, leaving me aching at the renewed loss, wanting only to hear a familiar voice even if I couldn't touch a face or hand.

Sometimes it was just too painful to think of home and other days. Exercise and the few books I had offered only a temporary diversion, so I'd sit there on the mattress trying to occupy myself with ideas that wouldn't remind me too much of what I was missing. I decided to write a novel in my head, but even that brought me slap up against the reality of captivity. Any research I needed to do had to come from memory – there could be no visits to half-remembered places, no-one whose advice I could ask, only the solitude of the cell.

As the summer heat grew more intense I realized that yet more weeks, maybe even months, might elapse before I was freed. I'd lie there wanting to escape into sleep, but was always too conscious of the noise of the ventilator, of the dust it spewed over me, and of the possibility of a visit from the guards.

I would spend ages looking out through the grille in the door, although there was little to see. The wall opposite was just two feet away. Down the corridor to my left were other cells, sensed rather than actually seen, and at the end, some twenty feet away, the door with the skull and crossbones on it, then another passage leading off from there. To my right the passage led to the bathrooms and beyond to the steps leading up from the cells. I couldn't see much here either, but in the foreground was a long concrete shelf where the guards stacked the supplies. I would look hungrily at the piles of Arabic bread in its plastic bags, at the tins of hummus and the long tubes holding beef sausage from Scandinavia, and, above all, at the cartons of cigarettes.

My own boxes of Marlboros had never materialized, but I still lusted after the ghastly Lebanese Cedars which had now become my regular brand. It seemed ridiculous that when cigarettes were so cheap we should be rationed to just five or six a day. I could appreciate that our Moslem captors would never give us alcohol, that was forbidden, but the craving for more cigarettes, or perhaps a wish for the rationing to be more logical, became something of a neurosis and I stared and stared at those wretched cartons.

Little light relief, then, was offered by the view from the cell. It only emphasized that whatever I would normally just reach out for, from the joy of company to the simple pleasures of food and cigarettes, was all too literally out of my reach. And during the many power cuts, frustration levels shot up. The ventilation system and all the lights would cut out, plunging the cell into fetid darkness. I had a candle and matches so could shelter from the even deeper solitude of the dark, but as the heat increased it became impossible to relax. Then the mosquitoes would descend. The candle attracted them even more, let alone raising the temperature. They made a phenomenal row, determined and aggressive, attacking me where my skin stretched tightly over my bones, on my ankles and wrists. The pain was excruciating and I soon learned that it was fatal to scratch the bites. Instead, I would ineffectually dab them with water or spit in an attempt to take the heat out of the stings. Sometimes it got so bad that I had to get under the filthy blankets to hide from the hordes. But in the dripping heat, that, too, was unbearable, so I would compromise and put on the pair of jeans I'd been wearing when kidnapped to cover my legs, socks for my all-too-vulnerable feet and a short-sleeved shirt to hide my torso. Then I'd sit, protected, in the dark. But the noise was as trying as the bites and my resolve soon snapped. I'd light the candle and go on the warpath. I'm sure that the only time it's gratifying to see your own blood spilled is when you've squashed one of those little buggers on the wall.

On good days, I felt really pleased with myself, believing that I could handle this prison existence. I tried to watch what little might be going on; I thought about food incessantly, developing unwonted cravings for school puddings like apricot crumble and custard; and I'd had the old lag's obsession with 'snout' since the first day. I'd even scratched the number of days on the wall. I was lonely and terribly bored, but I could cope. I remembered that when, in *Decline and Fall*, Paul Pennyfeather was sent to prison for some madly unjust reason, it was observed that 'anyone who has been to an English public school will always feel comparatively at home in prison'.

I was less certain that the supposed advantage of being used to having one's movements restricted by the boarding-school regime – being locked in at night, living with a whole gamut of petty rules and arcane lore – might not in fact be a handicap. I had often felt that having my choices so limited at school had hindered my ability to stand up to authority; not to challenge merely for the sake of it, but to be prepared to question a rule that was unnecessary or threatened one's dignity.

Now, although there wasn't any obvious way of fighting this new, absolute and malign form of imprisonment, in which I could test my nerve only by risking my life, I feared that all those years of accepting school rules might have compromised my freedom to think for myself.

I had, I think, always been unsure of myself. I was born on 27 November 1956 in Barnet and came home with my mother to Wood End, our house at Northaw in Hertfordshire. My earliest memories are of a funny little dame-school called Guildhouse which was run by two elderly sisters. No alterations had been made when the house became a school so we all queued up to wash our hands in the bath; I hated having lunch there and usually went home. We wore blue corduroy shorts and white shirts, but I have a clearer memory of my blue cap and heavy gaberdine raincoat. My mother always remembered the day I came home, sat down at the dining-room table, still in cap and coat, and furtively produced a tiny map of the world.

'See that?' I said, pointing to a little patch of colour.

'Yes, darling.'

'That's Japan.' The map disappeared back into the gaberdine folds. I think she was amused because I had just the air of a minor pornographer offering filthy 'snaps' in a Soho backstreet.

My mother was brilliant, a genuine eccentric. As a girl she had loved acting and dancing; her teachers thought she had the potential to make a career of it. But the war came and her subsequent marriage to my father and starting a family led her in another direction. I don't think she minded – she was very much in love with him and adored looking after her sons – but I think that she may later have regretted not having had a much wider experience of life. In part she remedied that when Terence and I were away at school by taking a degree in English. She had always loved literature and inspired that same appreciation in us. Despite a sheltered childhood my mother had seen quite a bit of the world and her experiences during the war in the Royal Corps of Signals had been a sort of education. She met people from different backgrounds and with a different outlook on life; she learned a good deal about human nature and this, with an innate common sense, she applied to her understanding and interpretation of literature.

The war also affected my father's education. Instead of going up to university he became an officer in the Royal Engineers, later becoming part of the airborne army serving in Norway and Palestine. He loved army life, particularly mixing with such a wide range of people. A wonderfully gregarious man he is always the life and soul of the party, with astonishing stamina for one who, in his own words, 'was a boy before the Second German War'. After that war he joined a firm in the City of which he later became a partner.

Both he and my mother were very attractive and, although she had many admirers, she always had her heart set on Pat McCarthy. He and his brother John were at school with her brother, Peter, and in the holidays they would all see a good deal of each other. In later years, my mother would say that the McCarthy brothers were quite different from other boys – they treated her with respect. Needless to say, she was still relegated to hauling a line of boys along on their little push-carts!

Between them my parents ensured that Terence and I had a safe and happy childhood. The garden at Wood End was large and wild; it was a perfect place to play. In school holidays Terence and I would build little huts under a huge rambling blackberry bush or make expeditions to the Great Wood opposite. The garden dropped steeply away at the back and offered a brilliant panoramic view towards Northaw and London beyond.

Also in the garden was a 'gypsy caravan' – actually an old baker's hand-cart that my father had converted for us; Terence and I used to love playing in it. I once decided to spend a night there on my own, but at the first owl hoot I shot inside to the safety of my parents' arms. The caravan still exists, in my father's garden, although it is now sadly rather derelict.

Living out in the country, there were few local boys and girls to play with, but there were still children's parties. I dreaded party games and got very nervous. At home, things were very different. Parties there were fun; I felt safe and my mother was always so relaxed and happy to join in. One of my schoolmates was an Irish boy called Gallagher. He was big for his age and made my mother laugh so much when he steamed through the dining-room to get back to the action, shouting, 'Out of the way, you English pig!' that it became one of our many stock phrases. Ever after, my mother liked to imagine that Mr Gallagher senior used to bellow this at all and sundry as he drove his car.

Terence and I both inherited, or learned, our sense of the absurd from our mother. We were always getting the giggles. In fact, when we were teenagers it finally reached the point when my mother and I had to sit separately at school concerts so as not to disgrace ourselves. Keen to make mischief, Terence either managed to control himself or would make a great to-do of exploding into his handkerchief – which always sent me into fits.

As a small child I was pretty happy-go-lucky, but when I was at prep school I went through a time of great nervousness. I suppose I was about nine or ten and, although I can't clearly remember what triggered it off, it became so bad that I was terrified of going to school. I'd will myself to be ill so that I could stay at home with my mother. Not surprisingly, my schoolwork suffered, even though I was quite bright. Terence was a good friend to me then. It was just before he left the school to go to Haileybury and whenever I was unhappy and worried, he used to tell me bedtime stories all about the adventures of an imaginary boy called Johnny Marks. Perhaps that was why, when I was first captured, I tried to find solace in thinking up a novel. Even after he went to boarding school, Terence would write me long letters with more Johnny Marks stories, until, eventually, my worries faded and I started to enjoy life again. But I've never forgotten the love and support Terence showed, when he, too, was very young.

In time, I went to Haileybury as well. It was a beautiful place, fine old buildings set in magnificent grounds. I was in the same House as Terence, which was a great blessing. In the two years he'd been there he'd made many friends and they all greeted me warmly, nicknaming me 'mini-T', and I immediately felt at home.

Like most public schools, Haileybury had its rather quirky traditions. New boys, called New Guv'nors, had to learn these as well as the House and School rules. At the end of the first term we all had to pass the New Guvs' test and then sing a song in front of the whole House. At the time, I didn't mind singing 'The Yorkshire Grenadiers' in front of fifty older boys, but by the time I left none of us could really see the point of what was often a daunting task. It wasn't so much the singing as the fact that pillows – and anything else that came to hand – were hurled at the singers to put them off. Nor did I mind sharing a dormitory with fifty other boys, nor being a fag for one of the House prefects.

It did no harm, and there was very little bullying, but I noticed early on that some boys took their little promotions very seriously. In my final year I was shocked when a school prefect shopped a boy, with whom we had both grown up, for smoking. It was quite unnecessary as no-one else had been there and so the prefect was not obliged to make an example of him to the younger boys. What bothered me was the ease and readiness with which some people appeared to accept the *status quo* and blindly adopt all its petty regulations and inflict them on their contemporaries. The idea, of course, was to inspire leadership, but the philosophy behind much of the school's structure seemed out of date. Most of it was handed down verbatim without any reference to changes in society outside. I felt that some of the masters were uncomfortable with the antiquated outlook and were often less than convincing.

My school record was scarcely spotless. My two greatest friends, Paul Marsh and Joph Gregson, had been at prep school with me and we were often in trouble. I tried to get away with as little work as possible, rather than getting on with anything. I definitely lacked a sense of purpose, and schoolwork seemed to lead to nothing but more schoolwork.

This lack of purpose was only heightened by the arrival of girls at the school in my last year – not because they were a distraction, but because the school's attitude' towards them was so hopeless. The idea of boys and girls being kept apart throughout adolescence seemed to me ridiculous, as it still does. Unfortunately, no-one at Haileybury had really thought through the potential problems and any developing relationships were regarded with deep mistrust.

When I started going out (or, more realistically, staying in) with one of the girls there was serious trouble. Zita and I really fell for one another. Once, we were sitting studying in the Library together when the headmaster came in. He made me sit at the other end of the room and later, through my housemaster, told me that I wasn't to see Miss Chen in any private way again. Neither of us ever understood what the precise reasons actually were. It was absurd. The school seemed completely incapable of offering any constructive advice, opting instead for the simple, negative, attitude of saying 'No' to everything. The aim appeared to be more for control than growth, the fear of scandal outweighing the responsibility of truly acting *in loco parentis*.

All this had repercussions at home. I was very distressed when my father once decided that my friends must be a bad influence and should be avoided just because the housemaster wrote a few lines to that effect in an end-of-term report. I became wary of talking with my parents about my friends for fear that they would disapprove. I was still very happy at home, enjoying the quiet sanctuary of Wood End and family holidays, but somehow life had split into two quite distinct worlds. There was one world of home and family and another of friends at school, with occasional visits to see Paul and others in London during the holidays.

Although my father was a good, kind and loving man, Terence and I had never built up quite the same easy familiarity with him that we had with my mother. When we were young, his working in the City meant that he was normally home after we had gone to bed, and he was often abroad. Terence and I missed his company and going away to school emphasized this. Even as an adult I didn't feel we had ever really got to know one another – at least, not to the point where we might feel comfortable talking openly about anything, however problematic.

As I sat in my cell in Beirut, reliving much of my life, I felt certain that had I been at a day school, this slight but significant distance would not have come about. We were a very united and happy family and, had we been able to spend more time together, I'm sure our relationships would have been that much stronger, and our dealings with one another less formal.

With the leisure that captivity gave me to review my life, I was able to see that this should and easily could be put right. I also realized that, although I could, with some legitimacy, blame the inadequacies of my schooling for my lack of a properly mature relationship with my parents, I was now twenty-nine and I hadn't done much to change things so far. If only I could go home, I vowed to be more attentive and supportive to everyone I loved.

Thoughts of home filled my mind all the time. In my dreams I always seemed to be back at Wood End. Very often I was still a hostage, and although my family were allowed to come and go as they pleased, they had to keep quiet about the presence of Arab terrorists in this quiet corner of the Home Counties. I resented their liberty and it took years for my subconscious to understand and accept that my family and friends were just as much hostages as I was. In waking hours I would think of my parents' present home in Essex. It's a mellow, red-brick house behind the church and I'd day-dream about sitting round the dining-room table for Sunday lunch, with my parents, Terence and Jill. There is a nice walk through the fields down to a little wood and as I did my exercises I'd lie on my back doing bicycle movements, close my eyes and pretend I was jogging to the dell and back.

Having no alternative but to face up to myself was at once terrifying and enlightening. There seemed to be no point in hiding from the truth, or what I imagined to be the truth about myself. I had to accept that the few minor successes I had effected were largely based on potential, rather than actual, achievement. I would sit on the mattress hating myself, the refrain 'if only, if only' constantly ringing in my ears. I felt so small, so insignificant, that even the tiny cell seemed to dwarf me.

It appeared that I had never had any ambitions. School followed school and then university and then a job. In those first weeks of captivity I often woke from dreams in which I was having to finish an essay or resit A levels; it took months for my subconscious to catch up with reality so that, while sleeping, I could say: 'Hang on, I've been to university, I've got a degree. I will never have to do any of that again unless I want to.'

Such dreams had been all too real in the summer of 1974 when I was sitting my A levels. I'd been typically idle and my A level results were poor as I knew they would be, although probably they were even better than I deserved. My parents wanted me to try for Oxford, so I stayed on at Haileybury for the Christmas term. This suited me. Zita, Paul and many other friends were still there. Needless to say I didn't get a place at Oxford, but was interviewed and was encouraged to try again the following year after retaking my English and History A levels.

At great expense my parents sent me to a crammer in London. Although initially I was very nervous about it, I came to enjoy travelling up to town and being able to wear ordinary clothes rather than uniform. My grades improved, although they were still not brilliant, and I resat Oxbridge, this time under the guidance of a tutor from Hatfield Polytechnic. Despite beginning to feel more confident, I still didn't get in and was left trying to think of what to do next.

University still seemed the only proper route to take but, in the meantime, I found myself a job working as a kitchen porter at Barnet Gas Works. Although the work was menial I really enjoyed my time there and, once my colleagues had got over my accent, I was made to feel very at home. I enjoyed working and earning a living and was sorry to leave in the early summer to do some last-minute revision to take my History A level for the third time, only to get the same low grade again. This wasn't surprising as I spent most of the time reading novels rather than studying. Evelyn Waugh seemed so much more rewarding than the Napoleonic Wars.

The prospect of actually being offered a place at university seemed remote, but thanks to my mother's keen research we found out that Hull University had an American Studies course which sounded interesting. I applied through the clearing system and was amazed to get a place.

Looking back from my cell, I regretted the fact that I had not travelled and worked abroad, perhaps using some of my father's many contacts. I wish my parents and I had taken the time to sit back and work out what I really wanted to do and how best to achieve it.

Nonetheless, I set off for Hull with much excitement. I don't know quite what I was expecting, but it was a relief that the hiatus of the past couple of years was over; I now knew what I was doing and was keen to get on with it. For my first couple of terms I shared a room in a hall of residence with another freshman, Steve, who proved remarkably tolerant of my late hours and tendency to be the worse for wear. In the summer term – probably to Steve's relief – I managed to find myself a single room in a neighbouring hall.

Being completely in charge of my life for the first time gave me a curious sense of freedom, but it didn't bode well for my studies. Lectures and tutorials soon seemed a bit of a chore; my social life was going far too well. In the first few weeks I made some good friends, most of whom were on the American Studies course and nearly all of them, like me, came from the south. It was at about this time I was introduced to Nick Toksvig, who also turned out to be on the same course. Nick's father, Claus, was Danish and they had lived for many years in New York where he was working as a journalist. Although Nick had spent two years at a boarding school in Brighton, he still had a discernible American accent. Our first meeting, typically, was in a college bar. As we queued for yet another pint, Nick suddenly turned to me and said, 'I really like you.' I beamed back. 'I really like you, too.' It was the start of a great friendship. We both shared the same absurd sense of humour which bound us together and tied us firmly to our other new friends, among them the two Chrises, Martin and Pearson.

Chris Martin arrived late for that first term. He'd run out of money on holiday in Greece and been delayed with a little problem over selling his blood, and police bureaucracy over an insurance claim. He soon made up for lost time. Needless to say, our first encounter was again in the bar. A group of us were having a drink and I offered Chris a cigarette, a Camel. When, later, I offered him a more modest Number 6, he declined, saying, with the trace of a smile, 'I only smoke Camels.' We were friends from that moment on.

It was through Chris Pearson that I kept in touch with the wider activities of the student body. Watching him going round Union meetings, pad in hand, pinning the politicos to the wall one could only think, 'This is a newshound.' His ability was obvious from the start. He joined the student paper, *Hullfire*, in his first week, and soon became its editor. It was no surprise when he won the *Guardian*'s student journalism award and later a place on the BBC's training programme.

Reliving student days as a hostage was at once a great source of succour and a bitter reminder of my loss. Those friendships were so positive; the only downside was the feeling of guilt that I had not given enough to them. But the happy joyful memories were a comfort. I couldn't find any solace in thinking about all my lost opportunities to study, to understand and to enjoy the world more. As I waded through Arthur Hailey again or struggled through some awful French novelette about twin sisters, one a nun, the other a call-girl, I kept kicking myself thinking of all the books I could have read in my life, of all the books I had read but had failed to take to heart.

I remembered how quickly I'd let my work slide while at Hull. I would get irate memos from tutors demanding my attendance or the presentation of essays. Often when I did the work and showed up the tutors would be kind enough to say that I was doing very well; my literature tutor John Mowat was particularly encouraging. As usual I abused their support by assuming it meant that I could get away with doing very little. It always seemed that work could easily be put off and I'd head for the Union Bar with Toksvig instead.

But I muddled along for the rest of my time at Hull, making no progress academically, although enjoying myself greatly. At the start of my second year, I fell in love with one of the drama students, Ronnie Wood. At the same time Chris Martin started going out with Barbara Mackie, another American Studies student, who was also a friend of Ronnie's. Chris and I were over the moon – until exams loomed in our final year.

Miraculously I got a degree and vowed never to sit an exam again. But having left Hull in the summer of 1979, I was then confronted with the problem of finding a job.

Initially I worked in a local iron foundry as a general assistant. I was, of course, furiously over qualified, at least on paper, for that sort of work, but – like most students – I had built up a large overdraft in my final year and wanted to pay it off myself.

After the foundry I spent a couple of years unsuccessfully trying to make the grade as a salesman. I hated the loneliness of being in the car all day, felt awkward 'cold-calling' on clients and never really grasped the knack of it. By October 1981 I had had enough – and so had my boss.

I was living in Clapham with Ronnie, Nick and Chris Pearson, when he wasn't away on his latest posting with the BBC. Nick had been working for some time as a journalist with UPITN. I had been in for a morning to see how things worked there and had tried my hand at writing a script for their general news service. A very kind woman showed me what to do. This entailed such basics as putting paper in the typewriter. The final script and the typing were abysmal. I went off not feeling terribly encouraged. It was the day Sadat was shot, but I left before the news broke and so missed an opportunity to see the news room going into overdrive as it covered a major breaking story.

I practised my typing at home and hoped that through Nick's good auspices I would be able to get some freelance work there. In the mean time, I signed on the dole and filled in time working the switchboard for the Scandinavian Broadcasting offices, coincidentally also based in ITN House. Nick's father was the Danish radio and television correspondent in London, so the Toksvig connection was a vital link for me at the time. Claus helped out by using me as a subject of a film he was making about young unemployed people in the UK. Just before Christmas I even worked for a few days at the Piccadilly Hotel as a wine waiter at some of the big office parties which were held there.

Just after Christmas Nick convinced the UPITN office manager, Derek Langsdon, that I was competent enough to stand in for the regular office telex operator while she took some leave. This entailed sending off all the news-room scripts and many of the messages on the wire machines and telex. It was one of those jobs that wasn't difficult in itself but, because of the heavy traffic throughout the day, one had to keep well on top of everything otherwise colleagues in London and clients around the world started getting irritable. Yet, despite the constant pressure of their workloads and deadlines, everyone in the news room was remarkably tolerant and always ready to lend a hand when I got behind. The only gentle nudge came from Derek who sent me a memo saying, 'Thanks for your efforts, but please try to use fewer thumbs when typing!'

In those days the UPITN news room was a rather wild place. It was full of eccentric characters with unusual pasts. Many of the team enjoyed long chats in the bar and it was part of the UPITN ethic that if you had imbibed too much liquor, it was too bad, you still had to finish your shift and leave everything in order. As I liked this slightly cowboy approach to working, I had to develop not only a better tolerance to alcohol, but, more importantly, try to grasp the activities of the various staff members as soon as possible. This meant keeping abreast of the main news stories of the day and keeping half an ear open to follow the experienced journalists plotting their day, anticipating disasters and trying to avert them.

Thanks to Nick's friendships with many of the staff and the high regard in which he was held, he managed to get John Connor, then one of the executive editors, to give me a shot at writing the 'dope' sheets that were sent to the daily satellite transmission customers. Again my typing held me back, but everyone rallied round so that I didn't get too behind or miss last orders at the bar. It seemed the perfect place to work. Not only was my best friend already there, but the rest of the people were fun and the work was exciting and seemed to have a real purpose. I felt at last that here was the way to earn a living.

In the spring of 1982 Nick was posted to an expanded UPITN bureau in Washington, DC. Pearson was away either in Belfast or in Newcastle, so Ronnie and I decided to take up Barbara Mackie's offer to move into the flat she shared with Chris Martin near King's Cross.

I was working many more shifts at UPITN and was even allowed to take on the then heady tasks of putting together satellite transmissions and running the Eurovision desk. This was the real cut-and-thrust side of news-room operations. I talked to our bureaux all over the world, made rapid decisions on how and when to move our film and video coverage of world events, and tried to convince our clients in Europe that our material was better than that of our competitors at Visnews. I was often 'skating' through these tasks. My understanding of the news business remained limited and I just managed to keep hold of the new details I learned each day. But I was always ready to take on a new 'desk' and would come in to work at the drop of a hat if a colleague fell sick. I think this readiness coupled with some journalistic ability and a general popularity with my peers helped me get a staff post at the beginning of August.

My first month on staff – although I had been taken on at the most junior level – was spent running the Eurovision desk. I had a successful month, beating Visnews and everyone breathed a sigh of relief that I had made the grade. I was very pleased when one of the old hands said that I had become a 'hack', and could handle problems.

On a personal level, life with Ronnie was not going well. Perhaps the new direction on the professional front emphasized that we had been growing apart for some time. At the end of the year we decided to live separately for a while.

From my cell in Beirut, I could see that I had been so carried away with the excitement of the new job that I had treated Ronnie very badly. I spent far too much time socializing with my new friends so that I saw her only briefly most days, often late at night. I was also finding it hard to keep in touch with my other friends – there didn't seem to be enough time for everyone. This wasn't strictly true; I simply wasn't organized enough. I kept thinking of the Animals' song with the refrain: 'When I think of all the good time that's been wasted having good times'.

There were no good times now; yet one day I was happily reminded of one of the best. A guard came into my cell. I covered my head with my jacket as usual, but he took it off and I saw that he was wearing a clown mask. He clearly wanted a chat, but, as he spoke no English and I no Arabic, the banter soon dried up. I had spotted some of my belongings on the food shelf outside the cell and thought that some photographs might still be there. Somehow I made myself understood and he went off to get them. We went through them all. He was most interested in some pictures I had taken with Sami and Haidar of the Green Line; I was more interested in some photographs that dated back to the previous year – they were of Jill on a holiday we had in Sicily. Better still were some pictures that Nick Toksvig had taken on the day that Jill and I had first got to know each other in 1983.

In early spring that year, Toksvig had come up with the crazy idea that we, together with Mike MacNish, a good friend and colleague, should hire a Fleetwood Cadillac limousine to drive down to Bray and have lunch on the Thames. Mike and I agreed and Nick arranged everything for the next day.

I arrived at ITN House at eleven o'clock as Nick had instructed to be confronted by the car. I was intimidated by the machine's size and presence. It was a mile long and completely black. As there was no sign of the boys, I thought I'd better go and check with Jim, the driver. He let me into the vast expanse of the passenger compartment; when Nick and Mike appeared we set off.

Nick said that we had to pick up Jill Morrell round the corner. I hadn't realized that Jill was coming. I had only met her very briefly in the ITN bar and exchanged a few pleasantries about the fact that both of us had been to Hull University. She had struck me as being very shy – and pretty.

We arrived at Bray without mishap and went to a very famous restaurant, took one look at the menu and realized that eating there would bankrupt us. So we went down to the river's edge to reconsider. I felt again the huge presence looming behind us, with the attendant Jim in full livery.

'What are we going to do with him?' I asked.

'How about some champagne?' asked Jill.

I was very impressed; it seemed an excellent solution. She produced a bottle, we toasted Jim and arranged to meet him again in a couple of hours.

We wandered around the village and Nick took snaps of us investigating a churchyard. We found a pub and thought it best to have a swift one before deciding on where to go for lunch. Jill went off to get some film for her camera. I was beginning to feel relaxed with her. Despite her shyness, she got on very well with Mike and Nick, renowned for their wild sense of humour and determination to have fun. I felt certain there was much more to learn about her. When she returned from the shop, she said in a soft voice, 'Was our car black? I've just seen a large black car driving out of the village.'

The car was nothing but black, monstrously black, yet she stood there, as Mike said, like a startled fawn, eager with her bit of information, but wary of coming out with it too directly. From this point I began to focus more on Jill and realized that as well as being pretty she was great fun.

We had an excellent lunch and, later, after tea, headed back on the motorway for London. Suddenly the electric window between the front and back seats rolled down and Jim said: 'Do you people like rock 'n' roll?'

To the cheers of Mike and Nick, Jill and I then began to dance to the strains of Chuck Berry. It had to be performed while squatting down on our haunches so freedom of expression was limited, but the real thrill was to see that Jill was sharing the absurdity of dancing in the back of a moving car and that for all her shyness she wasn't going to miss out. The day had been perfect – an eccentric plan made and carried out with two very funny and dear men, then given its full romantic potential by the presence of this lovely secret ingredient. It was, as they say, 'the beginning of a beautiful friendship'.

Having the photographs of this wonderful outing was a terrific comfort to me in the prison. It brought Jill so much closer. I could look at her and think of the plans we'd been making just before I left for Lebanon to buy a flat together and get married. In the drabness of the cell the colour photographs of her smiling face were a constant source of joy. One day they seemed to transcend being mere paper and reflect the vital part that Jill had come to play in my life.

I was peeking at the guard as he prepared our food. This was dangerous, but as he was facing the other way, I wasn't worried, nor was I particularly interested in him; but any form of entertainment was irresistible. What I hadn't realized was that the guard had a friend with him, who had gone down past my cell and on his way back saw me looking out. He gave the metal door a sharp rap. I sank back to the mattress cold with fear. 'This is it, they'll shoot me for sure.' I mumbled a quick farewell and apology to family and friends and waited for the inevitable. The guard put his hand through the grille and switched on my light. I covered my eyes. He came in.

'What is this?'

'I was looking at the food – I am very hungry.' I could think of nothing else to say.

'What is this?' He seemed interested in something in the cell. Suddenly he came right in to the room and was crouching down beside me. I tensed, expecting a blow, but none came. Instead he held Jill's picture under the towel over my face.

'What is this? You lovely?'

'Yes, yes, my lovely.'

'It is very good.'

'Yes it, she is.' My mind was spinning. I think the guy's about to blow my head off and he wants to admire my girlfriend. Suddenly his mate popped his head round the door and said, 'Naughty, naughty.' The Jill-fancier muttered something and 'Naughty' backed out again. The

97

photograph was carefully replaced and he started telling me in his very broken English that I had done wrong to peek. I said that I was sorry. The other fellow popped his head in for another quick, 'Naughty, naughty', and then they both left. I took a few deep breaths and thought that from now on I must remember Nick's last words – *Keep your head down*. I was just beginning to relax a little when the door opened again. The terror returned; this time it must be the end. But no, a light thump and there on the blanket was more bread and a heap of sausage and hummus. The door closed; I hugged and kissed the photograph of my guardian angel – 'It is good, oh yes indeed!'

I was to be in this solitary cell for less than three months, but after the first two or three weeks it felt as if I had slipped into a different time-scale. Days passed without any variation. The food-and-bathroom run and then nothing. I read and re-read everything available. I relived much of my life and made endless plans for the future. But after two months with not the slightest hint that I might be released I got more frightened. So many of my reflections had left me feeling inadequate that I really began to doubt that I could cope alone.

One morning these fears became unbearable. I stood in the cell sinking into despair. I felt that I was literally sinking, being sucked down into a whirlpool. I was on my knees, gasping for air, drowning in hopelessness and helplessness. I thought that I was passing out. I could only think of one thing to say – 'Help me please, oh God, help me.' The next instant I was standing up, surrounded by a warm bright light. I was dancing, full of joy. In the space of a minute, despair had vanished, replaced by boundless optimism.

What had happened? I had never had any great faith, despite a Church of England upbringing. But I felt that I had to give thanks. But to what? Unsure of the nature of the experience, I felt most comfortable acknowledging the Good Spirit which seemed to have rescued me.

It gave me great strength to carry on and, more importantly, a huge renewal of hope – I was going to survive. Throughout my captivity, I would take comfort from this experience, drawing on it whenever optimism and determination flagged. In the euphoria of the next few days I felt completely confident. But soon I found myself wondering how, even with the support of a Good Spirit, I was going to manage alone.

Sometimes when the power went off and the heat was intense, the other prisoners would start banging on the doors and shouting. I had no idea what they were saying, but presumably they were cursing the guards and demanding, 'Get some air down here! Give us some light!' I always found these occasions very spooky. At any other time there was silence along the passageway and when the banging and shouting started it was as if some spirit of madness, until then held in abeyance by the thin threads of neon light and moving air, snapped through in every cell. The demons could no longer be held in check; fear was out. It felt as though I were in bedlam, hoping that these wild creatures couldn't get at me. Then, one day, there was a lull in the eerie rantings and the fear, heat, boredom and loneliness vanished as a light, hoarse voice with an unmistakable Belfast accent called out, 'How much longer?'

But it was to be weeks before I could respond to that voice.

In those first terrible weeks of solitary confinement the date and the number of days of my captivity was the only information I had. Counting the days became an obsession. By keeping track of the date I felt I still had a link with the real world – a world which carried on beyond the influence of my captors. Each morning after going to the bathroom I'd make another mark on the wall.

Desperate to maintain my optimism I would play with the numbers, days and date, to try to see a pattern, some magical combination that would enable me to predict the day of my release. The idea was so fanciful that if these 'special' days passed without incident, I wasn't too depressed. It was, in any case, something to do; I would simply look more closely at my numbers and make a new calculation. The best results were those which set the next magic moment for a week or a month hence, so that I could sit back and say, 'OK, I'll be here for another week; I can handle that.'

One day my calculations pin-pointed 25 June, which would mark sixty-nine days in captivity. The roundness of the number, the neatness of ten weeks, all seemed right. So it was no surprise when on the 25th a guard came into my cell and told me to put on my '*pantalons*' and shirt and gather my belongings together. Taking my things didn't suggest immediate release but at least something was happening. The guard returned a few minutes later and led me, blindfolded of course, up the winding staircase that I'd come down two and a half months ago. Then I'd been terrified, now I was highly nervous but from anticipation rather than fear.

After sitting for some minutes on the stairs I was led by another man across what I sensed was an underground car-park to a van. I clambered in and was told to sit and make no noise. I was soon joined by two or maybe three other men. Then the guards got in with us. We set off and drove for about twenty minutes. All the while one of the other captives was hyperventilating, moaning and praying softly. When the volume of these murmurings reached a certain pitch, a guard would give him a thump and hiss at him. It was impossible to tell who the frightened man was or where he came from. I found it all very unnerving.

We stopped and sat, waiting; in these circumstances five minutes felt like an eternity. All manner of ideas would flit through my mind: unwanted images of a prison more dire than the last; hopes that it was just part of some delicate release procedure; the black hole of execution. In fact I was simply bundled out of the van and led, quick march, into a building, then a room and told to sit down and stay put. I waited, still blindfolded, and tried to sense the size of the room.

There was a commotion a little later as another man was dragged into the room and thrown on to something that creaked and groaned, perhaps a bed. Nothing was said. Two guards came in and gave us some sandwiches and bottles of Pepsi. We ate silently and then the guards left the room, locking the door behind them.

I raised my blindfold and looked at the other man. 'Fuck me!' I said, 'it's Ben Gunn.' I saw a mass of hair and beard that left only two bright, sparkling eyes visible. I'd seen those eyes blazing at me from a photograph months ago; I'd heard the soft Belfast voice in the past few weeks.

'You're Brian Keenan. I'm John McCarthy. How do you do?'

'All right, thanks. How are you?'

We stared at each other for a few moments. It was the first real, open, human contact for each of us in a long time. I raised my bottle of Pepsi, said it was a shame that it wasn't champagne and drank his health. We laughed and shared my last cigarette.

The room was large with a high ceiling. There were no windows and just one door. The floor was of rough concrete, very, very dusty with some thin plastic mats laid over part of it. In one corner was an old filing cabinet; in another, a tall cupboard stood, made of the same green metal; there was a dilapidated folding bed and a small straight-backed chair. Light came from one very bright bulb hanging from the centre of the ceiling. It looked as though we were in the backroom of some kind of business premises. Certainly it wasn't a prison.

Underneath his mop of dark brown hair Brian was wearing a yellow shirt and brown slacks. I'd seen them often enough as I peeked through the curtain in the bathroom doorway and watched Trusty take him, head covered, to the bathroom next door. Now he sat on the bed smiling but still a little tense. I was on a mattress on the floor feeling shy, yet somehow confident, even happy. I filled Brian in on all that I knew about the aftermath of his kidnap. It gave me a sense of immediate intimacy to be able to say that I'd been filming reports about him and had spoken daily to John Rowan at the Irish Embassy for any news on his disappearance. I sketched the outline of my brief time in Beirut and my kidnap. Brian told me about the three months he'd been living and working in Lebanon.

We talked about the last prison. He told me that he'd gone on hunger strike a week or so after having been taken and had become very weak. As an Irishman he felt sure he was of no value to the captors and, more importantly, had to demonstrate at once that he wasn't prepared to be used by them. He was clearly depressed that he hadn't 'gone the distance' with the strike.

A senior guard had come to talk to him about it and said that he understood Brian's point of view, but asked him to appreciate that they wouldn't consider releasing him even if he became really sick and further, that they wouldn't send his body back. It was this that cracked his determination – the thought of making the ultimate declaration of personal dignity, only to be dumped in the sewers.

I was shocked that he had taken such a dramatic stance so early. Yet again, I felt uneasy about my own reaction to captivity. If I'd thought of suicide it was to end my ordeal, not to make a statement to the guards. To me that seemed pointless. It was a theme that we would return to continuously over the next four years, developing through argument and debate, almost an amalgam of our different views. With this understanding we were able to think as one, offering each other appropriate comfort and support.

After some time the lights went off. There were no candles. If we spoke loudly a guard would hiss under the door. So we sat, Brian on the end of his bed, me on the mattress below or on the chair, our heads a few inches apart, talking nineteen to the dozen in hoarse whispers. Initially, with his soft voice and Belfast accent, I kept missing Brian's words, and would interrupt to ask him to repeat the last sentence. He likewise had trouble with the way I slurred my speech, soon dubbing me 'marley-mouth' because he said that I sounded as if I had a mouth full of marbles.

But in sharing experiences, feelings and the expression of them, we were following each other very closely indeed. As one of us spoke of the terrors in solitary cells, of what he had felt when the man was shot, of the awfulness of the heat and dark, of the concerns for those back home and of the shock and sorrow of all those things we'd done and not done in our lives, the other would butt in to say, 'Yeah, that's it exactly, and didn't you feel this . . . ?' The frustrations, anger and fear had been felt and were now expressed in the same way although our reactions had been different – Brian's hunger strike, my determined optimism strengthened by my numbers game.

Brian was from a working-class family, had been to a state school, leaving at sixteen to learn a trade and then deciding to go on to further education. I was a middle-class public schoolboy. Despite these differences, we soon found that our views on life and our interests were very similar. But Brian's experiences were far wider than mine. I assumed, wrongly, that, coming from Belfast but travelling on an Irish passport, he must be a Roman Catholic. He patiently explained that he had been able to see both sides of the conflict in the north of Ireland when he'd been a community worker and how he had come to realize that the problems were not based on religion, which he saw as too easy and narrow a definition. The real debate and struggle between the Irish and British was over power and national sovereignty.

Working closely in both communities had brought him into contact with the victims of the civil war, their families, many of the political leaders and sometimes the families of the 'hard men' on either side who carried out the 'military' operations. His accounts both of the suffering and of the huge community spirit that alleviated it were a revelation and an inspiration for me. It gave me an insight not just into Belfast, but also into the Lebanese situation which had so many parallel themes. Moreover his intelligent and sensitive observations on the psychological make-up of the 'boyos' gave me some help in understanding the mentality of our guards.

Our discussions on the problems of Ireland and Britain, although often heated, revealed very close similarities in political and social outlooks. But they also allowed us to explore and enjoy each other's sense of humour and reflected a growing bond. My McCarthy ancestors had moved from County Kerry in the early nineteenth century. Terence had traced them back to an Irish chieftain living in the 1300s, so I would argue that my claims to being Irish were stronger than Brian's, who'd grown up in the Protestant community of Belfast, which saw itself as being British. His response was typically brusque. My ancestors had obviously 'taken the King's shilling' by turning Protestant rather than adhering to the 'True Faith' and that by association I was a 'dirty shilling-taking Brit bastard'. Naturally, I then felt justified in calling him, often, an 'unspeakable Irish swine'.

Almost immediately I began to realize that not only was Brian's presence a great boon simply for his company, but also in the way we could deal with the guards as a pair, rather than individually. In the previous prison we had become accustomed to the fact that normally the guard would only turn up once a day to give out food and take the prisoners to the bathroom.

Here – at least at first – there seemed to be two men on duty. The senior, or at least more confident, one called himself Jack. His partner said that his name was Joker. Neither of them appeared nervous of us so we guessed that they were only expecting to be guarding us for a short while. I took this to indicate that we would soon be released. Brian, as ever more realistic, or perhaps sensing the danger of raising hopes only to have them dashed, argued that this was more likely to be an interim holding-place.

Jack took us to the bathroom once or twice, rather disconcertingly cooing, 'I love you' in our ears. He spoke little more English but did try to tell us about the World Cup. We said that we'd heard people playing soccer outside the building and he told us, with some help from Joker, that he played there himself and that he was a terrific goal scorer. He told us that he loved Lineker. To my shame I thought Lineker was the Arabic word for goal, which caused us all some confusion when I tried to further the conversation.

We felt that it was worth encouraging the guards to chat in the hope that they might let slip some information about our situation. In this we were unsuccessful; probably they knew very little themselves, but by building just a basic relationship we gave them the confidence to respond sympathetically to our pleas to have some of our things from the last prison. They gave us our books, some French magazines, my toothbrush and comb and the two pairs of shorts that I had had with me. Luckily one pair fitted Brian so we both felt far more comfortable in the stifling heat.

Soon, Jack and Joker began to spend less and less time in the building. There was one occasion when they did not appear at all for over two days, days in which we had no food and had to defecate in a small plastic bag which had been left in our room. Brian and I took advantage of these long absences to peer through the gap under the door in order to get a better idea of the layout of the place. For some reason, a finished surface had not been laid over the rough concrete so there was a gap of about six inches between the floor and the bottom of the door. Looking into the two rooms opposite we could see that one was set up as an office.

By climbing on the filing cabinet I was able to remove a small air vent, which gave a different view of the corridor; in the second room, where the guards usually sat and talked, I could see a Kalashnikov. We could also see the door leading to the street. It was so close and, being wooden like the door to our room, we felt that we must be able to find a way to break out. We looked all around the door-frame to see if we could attack the hinges or dismantle the lock. The prospects weren't encouraging.

Jack eventually turned up, said that conditions would get better, left, and then dropped out of the picture altogether. After that Joker would turn up once or twice a day on his push-bike to take us to the bathroom and feed us. All we were given was a small amount of bread with a meagre portion of processed cheese and apricot jam.

It was hard to take Joker seriously as a 'terrorist' when he arrived on his bike every day. Despite the poor food and the peculiar circumstances, he seemed to look on us as his guests. He was dismayed when we told him that the food was awful and a day or so later he came into the room in a state of barely controlled excitement, crying, 'What is this? What is this?' As our heads were covered we told him we had no idea. He stuck something under Brian's towel prompting the blunt statement, 'It's a fucking chicken!'

Joker liked to come and chat and wanted us to teach him English. He was unusually sensitive to the discomfort caused to us by having to talk with our heads covered, so, if he wanted to chat, he would wrap a scarf around his face and stick a pistol in his belt.

We had now been held for over three months and in that time, neither of us had had a haircut. Brian looked every inch the wildman and he assured me that I looked awful, too. We asked Joker to bring us some scissors and, if possible, a mirror. To our surprise he did so the following day. The mirror obviously had been taken from a bicycle. He insisted on playing the barber and wrapped his scarf round his face so that he'd have access to our heads without being seen. Brian went under the knife first. In a matter of minutes I witnessed Ben Gunn transform into Papillon. Before he'd looked wild, now he looked insane. We all became completely hysterical, me looking at Brian, Brian watching me turn into an almost bald twelve-year-old, and Joker laughing through nervous excitement – he thought the haircuts were fine.

After Joker had sat with us a few times, wrapped in his scarf, Brian decided it would be very easy to jump him, tie him up and escape. I could see the logic of this but was very wary. While we might get away, I argued to myself that if we had to hurt or even kill Joker, others might suffer as a consequence. I thought, too, of my WTN colleagues. While I'd been working in Beirut a leading figure in one of the Moslem militias had called the office with a warning that they knew where the camera crews lived, what family they had and how vulnerable they were.

The truth was that I was just plain scared of committing violence myself – I had never been in a fight in my life – and of being brutally beaten if we didn't get away with it. Memories of the merciless attacks on the young man in the last prison fed my imagination. However, after watching Joker sit with us again, I realized that Brian was probably right. I insisted that we rehearsed jumping Joker, that we had lengths of electric cable (stolen from redundant light fixtures) ready in our pockets to truss him up and that we had a gag on hand to keep him quiet. We decided that the best time to strike was when he gave us our cigarettes after eating. As we weren't allowed candles, the guards had decided that we shouldn't have cigarettes or matches in the room with us. So Joker would lean over the bed (which we took turns to sleep on) to give one of us a smoke and then light it for us. Our scheme was to grab the hand proffering the match and pull him over the bed. The man on the bed would straddle Joker and pull his arms behind him as the other gagged him. This plan, which I dubbed 'Operation Yallah', could be carried out even with towels half covering our faces. We practised often and with much gusto – no-one could have any doubts about Brian's determination. I was finally confident that we were ready. Then disaster struck.

Joker arrived as usual one evening to give us our food. He came in again a little later but left without giving us our cigarettes. When he'd gone we noticed two fags and a box of matches lying on the end of the bed. Why the change in practice? Suddenly the passageway outside our room was bustling with activity as at least three people started moving things around. The odd bits of furniture and boxes that had been left out there were being taken outside. Were we in for another move? Were we going home? It didn't feel like it.

Three men came in. Two spoke good English, but the other seemed to be in charge. We asked them what was happening? Why we were there? When would we be going home? Of course, there were no answers, only hollow promises that we'd be released soon. The two English speakers told us that they would be looking after us from now on and that they would bring a cooker and a fridge so that we could have decent food. One of them said his name was Abed, the other, rather oddly, called himself John.

After they had gone we sat back in horror. It was almost as if the room was bugged and they had known of our escape plan. Although we couldn't be sure, we feared that now we'd be guarded around the clock, which would be a far harder nut to crack than jumping little Joker.

The following day back they came. Abed seemed very relaxed and eager to talk about himself and his girlfriend Nancy who, he said, lived most of the time in the US. He did indeed bring better food and allowed us as much time in the bathroom as we wanted. It was wonderful to luxuriate in a shower morning and evening if we felt like it. His partner, John, was shy but spoke very good English and was extremely polite, so much so that I thought he'd make a perfect butler and we christened him Jeeves.

We knew that there was at least one other man being held in the building. We saw his shoes shuffling past as a guard led him to the bathroom. We suspected that there might be another prisoner too, but if so, he was in a different part of the premises and didn't pass our door. But now, Abed and Jeeves could often be heard talking to the man near us. They seemed to find him very funny. All we could hear from him were the words '*Merci, K'tir*', a phrase meaning 'Thanks very much', that Brian had often heard used in East Beirut. However, it didn't help identify him as the mix of French and Arabic could as easily be used by a foreigner as by a Lebanese, although he did sound like an old man.

Abed and Jeeves spent quite a bit of time talking to us; they even brought us a home-made version of the Arabic game *dama*, a more complicated type of draughts. They showed us how it worked – although we never really mastered it. Abed had made the pieces out of gold- and silver-foil cheese wrappers. Jeeves, ever the one to be exact, pointed this out to Brian: 'This is gold, this is silver.' I felt Brian tense and he muttered to me, 'He's winding me up.' I failed to see the problem. Certainly the fellow was stating the obvious, but I figured he couldn't think of anything else to add to the conversation.

After the guards had left us we talked about the incident. Brian had impressed and sometimes alarmed me by his determination not to be put upon by our captors or to hide his anger. He would tell them outright that the food was lousy, that what they were doing was wrong and inhuman. I was nervous of doing the same, fearing that they would only make our conditions worse, that the better avenue was to try and cajole them into improving their ways. This time he agreed that perhaps he had over-reacted. In general, though, I felt his attitude was quite correct.

As we got to know, love and respect each other, we would each modify our normal reactions to help the other. Sometimes Brian might be furious but would hold down his anger if he sensed that I didn't have the energy for a conflict. For my part I would reject my usual conciliatory tone when I knew Brian was much distressed and needed my support. We learned to use our different styles to make forceful, yet restrained, points to the guards while denying them their usual angry response to criticism. As I spoke better French than Brian, had a few more words of Arabic and spoke English with an accent that the guards found easier to follow, I would act as translator after Brian had exploded. This diverted the guards from his anger, which usually got them raging as well, and they would listen to my quieter explanations of the problem.

Abed and Jeeves would be on duty for two or three days at a stretch, then another pair would take over. These two spoke virtually no English and were far more nervous of us. When one came to take us to the bathroom, he summoned me first, and, as I walked to the doorway, head, as usual, covered by a towel, I suddenly felt the business end of a machine-gun pressed firmly against my chest. I moved very carefully so as not to startle him into pulling the trigger. I was alarmed that he should be so frightened of me and I wanted to reassure him by being as calm as possible myself. After he had locked the door on Brian, we moved very slowly to the bathroom. When I came back I whispered, 'This guy is very nervous and he has a gun.' But Brian already knew. He'd been watching through a little hole worn in his towel. These two were immediately dubbed The Brothers Kalashnikov.

Nerves apart, the Kalashnikovs weren't great providers. Abed realized that we needed better food than mouldy cheese and jam sandwiches and the odd glass of Arabic tea. When the shifts changed, he would bounce in, announcing, 'Abed's Hotel open in the morning.' Being a smoker, he was also more generous with the cigarettes. We spoke to him about the Kalashnikovs and he promised to have a word. It seemed to work. The food may not have improved, but they did relax a little and the guns were certainly less evident.

They even tried to talk to us, although conversation wasn't entirely straightforward. One spoke a little English but was reticent to use it. The other, the original Kalashnikov, had no English but wanted to chat. He could manage a few simple phrases of French which, while we could understand them, seemed to have a meaning unique to him. Once he sat asking us, '*Tu as famille en France?*' '*Non*,' we replied. He then went round much of Europe, the States and other places with the same question about family. Eventually I guessed that he wanted to know if we had travelled to those places – that for him *famille* meant *vacances*. Having made this link it was soon possible to build something of a conversation.

It was very important to be able to feel that I could communicate with these men in case we really needed something from them. Although I couldn't forget that, merely by holding us they were abusing us, it helped, when possible, to bring out their more human side so that we knew it existed, in theory at least, in times of crisis.

Despite the conversations with the guards, most of our days were spent with only each other as company. We talked incessantly about our families, our experiences at school, our hopes and ambitions and how, after only a few months of captivity, these had already changed. We also found that we had similar reactions to the few books which provided our only other intellectual stimulus.

Joker had given us an English copy of the Koran. It was a translation by an English convert to Islam, who had tried to capture the poetry of the original and give a flavour of the language that he had witnessed take devotees to heights of ecstasy. It was undoubtedly powerful writing, but without any guidance as to which might be the most important and relevant passages, much of it seemed repetitive.

Brian read out those passages he found particularly moving, including one that warned of the hell that awaited those who did not follow God's word. This was a place of great sorrow and suffering from which backsliders could never escape, from which they would never be reborn – an 'evil cradling'. Brian felt this phrase summed up our situation and decided that should he ever write a book about this time he would use it as the title, as indeed he has. Brian meant in no way to criticize the guards' faith. Rather he wanted to ask them that if this were God's ultimate punishment, could they be certain that, by punishing us – whom they knew to be good men – for the crimes of our governments, they weren't in danger of incurring God's wrath against themselves?

We still had Freya Stark's book and also a text book that Brian had used in his teaching. Fortunately this was a book for advanced students and included a beautiful essay by an American woman on autumn in New England. It was easy to lose oneself in their words, one's mind travelling and sharing the writer's experience. But the magic would always fade as I realized again that we might not see such things for a long time to come.

That sense of loss was sharply brought home to us as we heard the sounds of other people living near by. It gave us hope just to hear the children playing football or families clattering up the stairs to the apartments above. Hearing mothers chattering with their children, or couples coming in late at night, gave us a strange sense of community. Although they might not have cared and probably could not have helped us, it was comforting to think that the majority of the Lebanese would disapprove of our captivity. Our 'neighbours' were a link to the friends we'd made while at liberty in Lebanon.

We'd been there about a month when, one day, the key was left in the door. It struck me that we might be able to knock the key out of the lock, grab it and then open the door from the inside. That wouldn't necessarily get us out of the building, but we would be able to grab a gun from the guards' room and wait for the first man to turn up, 'arrest' him, then make off at our leisure. I managed to get hold of a shortish stick I had spotted just outside the door and by lying flat on the ground, with my arms out in the corridor, using Joker's mirror to help my aim, I could just reach the key. Brian looked through the lock and was able to tell me which way to tap it to get it straight. It took a while but success came just before my grazed elbows told me that enough was enough.

I remembered Terence performing a similar trick years before, copying the idea from a book he'd read. He had put a sheet of paper under the door so that when the key fell from the lock, it could be pulled through. Although we could easily put a whole arm under the door, I thought a magazine there might stop the key bouncing away out of reach. So I placed one of our precious magazines under the door and Brian poked the key through. It dropped on to the magazine. We'd done it. We hugged each other in triumph and then tried it. It wouldn't work. It had to be the right key but clearly it only worked from one side. We couldn't accept that, so we tried again and again – to no avail.

Eventually we gave up. I climbed up on to the filing cabinet, removed the vent and dropped the key on to the table. It was most unlikely that the guard would remember that he'd left the key in the lock. We drew a little comfort through lassoing a packet of cigarettes from the table's edge with a bit of wire and so had an extra smoke. I dropped the packet back through the vent and had just clambered down off the cabinet when a guard arrived. We had failed to escape, but knowing that somehow we could reach beyond the confines of that little room gave us a huge boost.

Yet, thanks to a strange guard who appeared once or twice, it was hard to forget the truly oppressive nature of the situation. He would simply come and throw our sandwiches under the door on to the filthy cement. One evening I lay on the mattress on the floor and, albeit from a distance of some fifteen feet, naturally looked over as the sandwiches were chucked in. The man peered under the door and, seeing me looking back, snarled. I was shocked. We were being fed like dogs in a cage, yet it was the 'keeper' who made the animal noises. On this occasion Brian was more amused than angered by the absurdity of our position.

At the beginning of August, a large number of people arrived. Almost immediately three of them came into our room. None of them spoke English. One of them reeked of garlic and, I could see from under my towel, was wearing a caftan. He took our shirts and trousers out of the filing cabinet where we kept them and gave them to me indicating that we should put them on. We did so and, without further comment, he led us separately outside. He'd tied the towel tightly across my eyes before we left the building. I felt panic rising but the feel of the fresh evening breeze diverted me as I concentrated on walking next to him, slipping slightly in a stretch of sand. He guided me into a truck where I sat and waited.

Soon Brian followed and then the old man we'd heard talking with the guards, but I felt sure that there was another captive there as well. We drove for a short while and then stopped inside a building, which I imagined was a garage. Here there were more guards. They took the old man out first, then Brian. I could hear a guard wandering around the van. The man sitting next to me started touching my shoe. I thought he said something but I ignored him. I was afraid they'd shoot me if I spoke.

After a few minutes I, too, was taken from the van, led a little way, then guided through a trap door, and down a ladder into an area that seemed to blaze with lights. Negotiating a hole and climbing down a ladder blindfolded is not easy. There were two men at the bottom, arms outstretched to catch me if I fell. They led me along a passage, down a few steps and into a cell. The door closed and there was Brian. I hugged him in relief; I had dreaded being alone again.

The cell was tiny. The two foam mattresses fitted, but one had to be lifted up to allow the door to open. The room was tiled completely in white. There was no light, but some sort of spotlight shone through the grille at the top of the metal door. At the base of the door there was an electric fan.

After a while a man came in. He spoke good English and said his name was Mahmoud. He gave us some cigarettes and a cup of tea. He was very relaxed and friendly, which heartened us a little. He said that they hoped to give us very good food now and more books. He added that he would tell his chief what we needed. He came back after a while, hissed through the grille and I looked up to see a mop of very curly hair. I stood up to take the sandwiches which he held in his hand, but, as I took them, he leant back so that I couldn't catch a glimpse of his face.

A number of cell doors were opening and banging shut, although we had no idea how many other prisoners were held here beyond the two who had travelled with us. After a while things quietened down. We took a couple of furtive looks through the grille and saw that there was another line of cells opposite ours, perhaps fifteen feet away, with a very low wall in between. We could see no-one else though. Clearly, this was a purpose-built prison and it suggested a long stay. We tried to cheer ourselves up thinking that if we had to be here a while, judging from Mahmoud, at least conditions might improve.

There was a lot of activity over the next few days as the guards continued to make small improvements to the prison. Two or three of them seemed to be on duty at all times. By looking up our line of cells late at night when the guards had quietened down, we could see that they lived in a room at the end of the cell block that was shut off from us by another heavy metal door with a grille in it. They had a television up there which would have on incredibly loud. We could easily hear the programmes and sometimes got a hint of the news when the local broadcaster was using a story from an American or British company. One of the guards, Mohammed, spoke fluent English and had a good sense of humour. I'd come across him once in the first prison and he'd given me extra food and plenty of cigarettes. Once or twice as we heard familiar theme music he'd bellow, 'It's Benny Hill', down the corridor, and later shout, 'Good night', to the block in general.

On 8 August, five days after the move and my mother's birthday, we were moved two cells further down from the guards' room. It was even smaller than the last, the mattresses taking up all the room. We had been given shorts, underpants and vests by two other regular guards, who called themselves Ali and Ayeesa, but our books and, most importantly for me, my photographs of Jill, which were taken in the move, never reappeared. In this new cell we found that Ali and Ayeesa had carefully made up the beds with heavy sheets that looked more like table-cloths.

There was a plastic jug each and cups, and even a bottle of eau de toilette. We'd just had a shower – there were two bathrooms and we were taken twice a day – and been given new clothes. It felt very odd. These two men, who of course we couldn't see, had obviously made an effort to make this tiny hole homey for us. We thanked them, Brian admitting, 'It's like the fucking Ritz.' They were very pleased. After a while they returned with ice cream and gave Brian a watch. A little later they came back and gave me one. They weren't our own. We couldn't make out what on earth was going on.

We kept asking for books, anything to help pass the time. Eventually they brought us a set of dominoes and a slim volume entitled *Into the Light*. After the first couple of pages it became clear that the story was about a small child in California who was kidnapped by a lunatic. It was terrible – the only thing we had to stimulate our minds was a novel about someone else being held hostage. I managed to derive some entertainment from it when Brian read it by misleading him about all the characters' motives so that he had no chance of guessing who the bad guy was. When he finished the book he stared at me and said accusingly, 'There wasn't any Roman Catholic priest.'

'What do you mean?'

'You said I had to keep an eye out for the priest, that he was central to the plot.'

'Did I?'

'Yes, you did, you lying bastard.'

'Didn't it add a little spice to the otherwise dismal mystery?'

'OK, OK.'

Our situation, like that in the book, was so miserable and beyond anything in our experience that we tried to get away from it as best we could. We played endless games of dominoes, telling each other more of our life histories or talking about books and ideas we'd found interesting. We sang each other very muted versions of our favourite songs and acted out scenes from movies we'd liked. I'd often take off on a flight of fancy, setting a scene, then playing all the parts.

For a while we escaped, as Brian tried to follow an argument between an Australian and a Glaswegian in a pub or a Hooray Henry from Sloane Square trying to negotiate with an Arab terrorist for his regular cup of Horlicks. Our own peculiarities and quirks were soon built into these routines and the often confused English of the guards gave huge scope for scenes of utter confusion and crossed wires. Laughter, especially when shared with such a patient audience as Brian, really helped me overcome the daily bouts of nerves and depression.

At night, especially if the power was off and the fans no longer roared, a guard would hang a small radio in the middle of the block and tune it away from any station so that it made an appalling hiss. This drove us nearly insane. Brian developed bad earaches and worried that he might be developing abscesses. He started demanding to see a doctor. The guards said they'd ask the *chef*, but nothing happened. Eventually he got so worried and frustrated that he found a piece of old razor blade in the bathroom, made a small cut between his toes, dabbed a piece of tissue in the blood and then put the tissue in his ears. He looked very comical with little pieces of paper sticking out on either side of his face, but they had the desired effect. A guard asked him what the paper was for and was shown the bloodstains. I was moved to a cell on the other side of the block right next to the guards' room, hoping Brian would be given the help he needed.

We'd never seen anyone in the cells across from us, but once or twice we'd heard American voices complaining about the conditions. We'd heard a clip on the television that I'd interpreted to mean that Vice-President Bush was going to visit Lebanon. It wasn't true, of course, but that's what we thought. When we heard these Americans talking, we figured that they must be a news team who had been sent to cover the visit and been kidnapped instead. We pitied them their innocence; Brian and I knew what bad conditions really were – the current situation was pretty good in comparison.

As soon as I settled into my new cell I realized that there were people next to me. I strained to hear what was said when the guards opened the door to take the men to the bathroom or to deliver food. Eventually I heard a distinct American accent, but nothing told me who they were. I tapped any tune I could think of on the wall, from 'Yankee Doodle Dandy' to 'The Star-Spangled Banner'. To identify myself I tapped out 'God Save the Queen'. Later I found out that they thought I was French and tapping 'The Marseillaise'. It didn't say much for my musical abilities.

I had found that by lying down and putting my face up close to the fan in the door, I could, as it turned, see through it without being spotted by anyone on the outside who was more than a foot or two away. I could look into the guards' room, when their door was open. Usually very little happened. Having to wear a blindfold whenever a guard was about meant that we came to identify them by their voices, even by the way they cleared their throats. Now I could catch an occasional glimpse of a guard and if he spoke, I would be able to put a name to him. But the sightings were so brief and at such an odd angle that I could have no idea what the men would look like in normal circumstances. Any brief image formed would rapidly fade.

I also looked at the passing feet as my fellow captives were taken to the bathroom. I counted five people as they were led past. The guard always walked a little behind, sometimes clad in jeans, sometimes in army fatigues, sometimes in pyjamas. I never quite got used to the sight of a vicious-looking machine-pistol dangling in the hand of a man wearing floral-print night-wear.

About four days later one of the men next door was taken away for some time, after the normal bathroom run. When he came back he bumped his head on a light outside my cell and an American voice said to the guard, 'I'll have to shrink if I'm going to be here for long.' When the guard left I heard him speaking to his cellmates, saying that he'd been taken to a room some floors up, where he could easily hear planes flying over from the airport. Then his voice dropped and I heard no more until, some time later, Mahmoud went in to speak to them. This time the voices were loud and I could hear them asking why they'd been asked to write a letter, and what was it that Jihad Islami wanted?

I sat back in cold shock. Islamic Jihad, the shadowy group who had kidnapped the first French and Americans more than a year earlier. These must be the same Americans, Terry Anderson from Associated Press and the others whose names I couldn't now remember. Our worst fear, one that Brian and I had tried to ignore, had come true. We'd smugly thought that they were new boys, but these men had been locked up for over a year. Now we had to face the same prospect.

That evening I saw Brian's trousers and shoes go past my cell. I hoped he was on his way to see a doctor and that he'd be released on humanitarian grounds. Yet an awful voice in the back of my mind prayed that I wouldn't be denied his strong, warm comradeship. I really couldn't see myself coping alone again with the new spectre that it might be a year before I went home. Later that night, when Mahmoud brought me some food, I asked how Brian was. 'He is fine, you will be with your friend again tomorrow.' Massive relief, along with guilt at feeling it, swept through me.

Sure enough, the following day I was back in the cramped little room with Brian. He was clearly angry and depressed that the doctor hadn't done the decent thing and recommended his release. Although he quickly overcame this, for my benefit, his depression returned when I filled him in on the terrible news about our captors.

We vaguely recalled that Islamic Jihad had demanded the release of some of their fellows from gaol in Kuwait in exchange for the French and American hostages. We also knew that generally Iran was considered to have

119

much influence, if not actual control, over the group. But neither of us could remember the exact state of relations between Britain and Iran. There had been arguments about embassies and minor wrangles over debts following the fall of the Shah, but nothing that seemed important enough to warrant holding us hostage. Nor could we see any value to the Lebanese in holding us. France and the US still played a large role in Lebanese politics as they did in other parts of the Middle East, but Britain tended to keep a lower profile.

Any snippet of news overheard on the guards' radio or television seemed directly relevant to us. Suddenly, any activity in the Middle East was motivated, to a large extent at least, by our own plight. When we heard that Britain had moved a resolution at the United Nations calling for an immediate Israeli withdrawal from southern Lebanon, and that the Americans had not vetoed it, we decided that this British action was made to meet a demand from the kidnappers and that we would soon be on our way home. I called it the Keenan–McCarthy resolution. We were sure that this was the best they could hope to get for an unknown journalist and an equally unknown teacher.

A couple of days after my return to Brian we noticed a towel hanging through the grille on a door opposite. We'd never seen this door open so wondered if there was some crazy man in there. That night the power went off and, as the guards came round in darkness with the food, I saw, from peeking through the fan, that as they shone a torch in the Yanks' cell it lit up the grille where the towel was hanging. It was obviously a double cell. My first reaction was, 'Hell, if they've got a double cell, what are they complaining about? They should try living like us.' Both Brian and I began to think that the Yanks received better treatment than us and felt quite resentful.

The power came back on but the cell-block lights and fans were immediately switched off. A bright light shone from the guards' room. Suddenly a loud voice spoke: 'My name is David Jacobsen, I am an American. When

I wrote my letter I was in a very depressed state of mind, and didn't make myself clear.'

It was very eerie and I came out in a cold sweat. Jacobsen was clearly reading a prepared script, probably for a video as they were using a spotlight. He went on to say that he and his fellow hostages were in good health but living in poor conditions and that they believed that the US government should meet the demands of the kidnappers. When the lights and fans went back on Brian and I went over every detail. From what I'd heard in the other cell we could guess that it had been Jacobsen who'd been taken upstairs a few days before and that he'd written a letter to the US government. This video recording seemed to have been made for clarification. We wondered if it was good or bad news in terms of our prospects for release. On the whole it seemed bad.

We'd long anticipated this situation, that our captors would want to back up their demands, whatever they were, with a photograph or something to show that we were alive. The only explanations for their not having done so already was that they still weren't sure if they needed us and so might let us go at any time – a theory I clung to – or, as Brian suggested, maybe they were just holding us in reserve and would use us when they wanted something from Britain.

Now, we discussed the likelihood of our having to send messages. The idea was not a comfortable one. Brian was quick to point out that to follow a script prepared by our captors, which might well say things we didn't agree with, would be collaborating. I argued that even so it would be a huge relief for our families to see us and know we were alive. We also hoped that discussing a message with the guards would give us a clearer idea of why they were holding us. We agreed that if we were to do something we should insist on knowing what their demands were before saying they must be met.

Although we now knew that we were being held by Islamic Jihad, not knowing why was the greatest strain.

However bad the conditions, they were finite, graspable. We could look around the cell, see the blankets on the mattress, a toothbrush and pee-bottle, could even take a look across the cell block. Brian and I had each other to talk to, to back each other up, but we had no indication of what it would take to get us out. We couldn't answer the only real question: when?

I started thinking about what I would say if I were able to add a personal message on to a video and, if not, how I would convey that we were in good spirits. Jill, Nick and I, together with a number of our friends, were great fans of Peter Sellers' Inspector Clouseau movies and often used some of his stranger expressions. It struck me that I could easily slip in a Clouseau-esque phrase. Although I wouldn't be able to use Sellers' crazy French accent, I knew that people in London would immediately pick it up and be reassured and, in turn, reassure my family that I could still crack the odd joke.

Often we talked about our worries over how our people were coping back home. Brian was very concerned about his mother, an elderly woman who wasn't in the best of health and who had lost her husband only a couple of years earlier. Brian regretted that he hadn't spent more time with his parents and realized that his community work, moving among both Catholics and Protestants in Belfast, had distressed them because of the potential dangers involved in that kind of job. His decision to leave Belfast eased that fear but moving to Beirut had hardly offered great grounds for reassurance.

Likewise I was terribly worried about my mother. She would still be recuperating from her operation. I felt aching guilt when I realized that my coming to Lebanon and then disappearing would have put her under an incredible additional strain. I thought of her darling voice on the phone when I'd called, triumphant, with the news that I was to go to Beirut. Her immediate response had been, 'Why must it be you?' I'd blithely replied that it would be good for my career, that things were quiet in Beirut, that I'd be safe. Now I couldn't get away from the realization that I hadn't thought through the consequences of my trip for friends and family at all. I'd wanted to do it and that had been that.

At night, the power cut, tossing and turning on the thin foam mattress, sweating, often wanting a pee (sometimes we weren't allowed bottles – according to the guards, 'This not good for health'), it was impossible to sleep. Thoughts of past failures and my responsibility for the current situation, but, more importantly, for that of family and friends, came back again and again. Every day I went through the same mill. The heat, the cramped conditions, Brian barely more than a foot away from me, usually snoring furiously, and, above all, the hiss from the mistuned radio outside, all seemed to act as goads, emphasizing the mental torment.

For the umpteenth time I made resolutions to be more attentive to my family's needs. I vowed to take more interest in all my friends rather than concentrating so much on those with whom I worked. I'd be more sober. I wanted to be a good son, friend and husband.

As the night wore on I would remake plans for my future with Jill. We had just started looking for a flat to buy together and I would spend hours planning what sort of place we would have, the number of rooms, the location, even bits of furniture. I imagined a holiday home in Tuscany where we had had our first, very happy, holiday alone together. I looked forward to having our friends to stay there, cruising around the ancient hill-top villages, looking at villas and views before finding a good place for a meal. I wanted to be with Nick, Chris Martin and Chris Pearson booming out over the Tuscan hills on powerful motor bikes. As these images came into sharper focus and I could hear friends talking and laughing and feel the wind in my hair, I would find my resolve again. Once more I had the determination to carry on for another day. Finally around three in the morning I would drop off to sleep after smoking one of the cigarettes that I should really have saved to share with Brian the following day.

The morning after Jacobsen made his recording we made contact with Tom Sutherland and Terry Anderson. They were living in the double cell opposite us. It was too dangerous to speak so, from behind our grilles, we exchanged names and nationalities using our hands to shape crude letters. Although pale and a little shaggy around the head and chin, they appeared well and uncowed even after such a long time. The fear that we, too, might be held for a year was dissipated by seeing that survival, in good spirits, was possible. With a lot of mime they told us that Jacobsen had been made to write the letter and then to make the video because the American press had said that the letter clearly hadn't been written by a native English speaker.

Jacobsen was now in another cell, on the same side as us but further towards the guards' room. Neither we nor the Yanks could see him as there was a wall between the two rows of cells at that point. Anderson wanted to know if we had a pen. Fortunately Brian had borrowed one from Mahmoud to make a board game for us. We agreed to find a hiding-place in the bathroom where we could leave the pen with a note so that they could reply by the same route. It took us a few days to find and describe a safe place, but eventually they got our first message.

Perhaps ironically, Brian had got his job at AUB through Tom's wife, Jean, who was still living and working in Beirut. Before his kidnap, Brian had got to know her well and so could pass on much of her news. I could tell Terry of the latest situation with his colleagues at the AP bureau and that I had met his great friend Robert Fisk. For their part they filled us in on what had happened to them over the past year. Their most exciting news was that Father Lawrence Jenco had been released a day or so before we arrived at the prison and that the guards had assured them they'd be going home as soon as the US had made 'the next step'.

As far as Terry and Tom knew, the demand for the release of the men held in Kuwait was still of prime importance, at least to the kidnap group in Lebanon. They also assumed that the Iranians were seeking other benefits for 'helping' the process. Although Jenco had just gone home, Ben Weir had been released a year before, and Jacobsen's separation from the rest of us might indicate that he, too, was on his way. Tom and Terry had grave doubts that the Kuwaitis would ever release the seventeen, no matter what else might be negotiated.

For the next few days we sent messages back and forth, but then Mahmoud took the pen back. Brian came up with the brilliant idea that we could scratch messages on a piece of cigarette foil, which the Yanks could then rub 'clean' and use again. I was so jealous of Brian's ingenuity that, having formally praised his idea, I couldn't resist adding, 'Of course, having a criminal mentality must be a great help to you. I hadn't really appreciated how much this situation, so outrageous for someone as wonderful and fine as I, is the perfect and rightful environment for you, you filthy, thieving Irish swine.' Brian lapped it up, cocky as all hell with his scheme. In Anderson's next message he told us that he would teach us the deaf-and-dumb sign-language. He'd learned it from a schoolfriend and after a couple of days, we were 'talking' fluently.

By this time we were all used to listening for the approach of the guards. While they were not going round the cells they would normally lock the gates into their room at the top of each line of cells. As long as we kept our hands within the grilles on the doors we were certain they could not see us. Whenever the gates rattled open, or at any unexpected noise, we would dive back down on to our beds.

The Yanks reaffirmed that our captors were very paranoid about being seen and that to be caught peeking was a major offence. The guards had told them that they knew the CIA had put a price of ten thousand dollars on their heads. Obviously they'd be furious if they caught us talking to each other. As far as the guards were concerned neither Brian nor I knew that the Americans were there, or that we were being held by Islamic Jihad.

Terry and Tom told us more about their former conditions and the personalities of the guards. This initially caused some confusion as they knew some of the guards by different names from the ones we used. Some of their former guards had treated them badly, abusing them physically and giving them awful food. Some had even spat mouthfuls of water at them, which, although really only an irritation, was very demoralizing. They had had plenty of books in the previous place. Sayeed, the senior guard, whom we'd yet to talk to, had agreed to bring these and arrange for better food. However nothing ever seemed to come of his promises and Anderson said he had a 'magic slate' mind – all information received could be wiped out as soon as he concentrated on something else. The Yanks felt Sayeed was basically reasonable and would eventually sort out our problems, but when Brian and I got to know him we disagreed, deciding that the man was a vicious, lazy psychopath.

As we talked across the cell block we realized that we were being treated in slightly different ways. The guards had got to know the Yanks well over the past year, but, because of the constant propaganda against America, 'The Great Satan', they'd never relaxed enough to discount their original belief that Tom, Terry and the others were all members of the CIA.

They seemed to view Brian and me quite differently. We'd had our problems, but basically the guards appeared to trust us. Perhaps they felt they could believe us when we said that we sympathized with the plight of the Lebanese, Arabs and Moslems in general, because their political and spiritual leaders in Beirut hadn't made such a big deal about Britain. As Brian was Irish and from Belfast, which, like Beirut, was a divided city, that helped further. They wanted to feel that we were part of their struggle and that we understood that their actions were necessary.

For some time we'd been aware that there was another captive in a little cell directly opposite us. We'd heard him speaking in a loud voice to the guards. He spoke English, but with a strange accent that we could not place. One day Ali and Ayeesa came round asking us all for our full names and fathers' names. The fact that it had taken them nearly six months to check exactly who we were was infuriating. Perhaps our theory that we'd been taken by a kidnap gang and only handed over to Jihad Islami when we got to this place was right. Whatever their reasons, it meant that we found out who our neighbour was. When Ali and Ayeesa went to the cell opposite and dropped their usual muted tones to bellow questions at the inmate, who was obviously partially deaf, we heard him say his name was Camille Sontag and that he came from Alsace, which perhaps explained his odd accent. Soon after this we actually saw Camille and tried to tell him who we were and where we were from. He was delighted to see us and we all raised clenched fists in gestures of support and solidarity.

Brian and I grew very fond of him. He seemed quite unconcerned by the antics of the guards who treated him as something of a joke. We were sure that he played up his apparent barminess to keep these delinquents at bay and reckoned that he simply didn't give a damn what they did to him. Sometimes we'd see him with a book held out through the grille under the flickering spotlight outside his door. Often, which amused us, he'd hit this with irritation, but when he called out, 'This book is Rousseau, very, very good!' we were seriously alarmed. We put our fingers to our lips to indicate that he should be quiet for fear of the guards, but he'd merely start blowing kisses at us. We liked to think that he would be released because of his age and pretended weakness of mind only to head straight back to Paris, get kitted out at one of the great couture houses and then go out on the town ordering jeroboams of the best champagne surrounded by a bevy of adoring women. He was an inspiration and when, some weeks later, he was freed, we hoped he did just that.

We'd not had a haircut or a shave since the manic butchery performed by Joker, so it was a relief, particularly as the late summer heat often made the cell unbearably hot and humid, when Ali came to take me for a trim. After he'd finished, leaving me with a little goatee beard, I was taken to the bathroom for a shower and given a clean set of clothes. Usually, the guards banged continually on the door to hurry us up so I showered quickly. Curiously, I had to wait for ages before being taken back to the cell. Brian wasn't there, and I assumed he, too, was sitting in the barber's chair. Half-formed jokes about Ali Barber and the forty thieves passed through my mind.

When Brian returned eventually, I was startled to see that his beard had gone. Only the moustache remained. He was obviously very distressed. He explained that when Ali had come for him he'd stated emphatically that Ali was not to cut off his beard, which provoked a bizarre response. Ali had said that it was better for Brian's health not to have a beard. Brian had responded angrily that he'd had a beard since he was sixteen and that to force him to shave it would take away his dignity. This argument was way beyond Ali's very limited English and so all he could hear was Brian's anger. This he took as a threat to his authority and went off to get his chief, Sayeed. At least three men returned with him. When Sayeed told Brian that he must do as he was told, he refused, saying he wouldn't allow them to humiliate him. Their response was inevitable. While his sidekicks pinned Brian down, Sayeed took what Brian described as 'a few digs' at him.

Brian had made his stand and further resistance was pointless. He suffered the haircut and lost his beard. His main concern while his hair was butchered had been that a small tear, born from the rage of frustration and humiliation, might run down his cheek and allow Sayeed and his cronies to think, however wrongly, that he was frightened of them.

I was amazed at Brian's courage. I was ashamed that I went along with the activities of the guards without offering any resistance, always being polite, acknowledging their jokes, being over-grateful when they met even the most basic needs. Yet I wasn't convinced that Brian's confrontational approach was going to be very effective, although I could see it gave him a huge boost to stand up to them regardless of the consequences. While I marvelled at his ruthless determination to maintain his dignity, I feared adopting the same stance.

Despite the crude banter that had become a focus of our growing friendship, we listened in silence to each other's stories, ideas and fears. Brian made me work my mind as I had never done before. He wants to understand everything, he always needs to know where he stands, where he's going and how best to get there. His mind is constantly racing and sometimes, pushed by his temper, goes up avenues that are often hard to follow. He has a great ability to explain abstract philosophical or political ideas through personal anecdotes. His language is brilliantly coloured with imagery and humour.

In our cell I'd listen, understanding the words, but, in the flow, felt uncertain about how to respond. The lack of confidence which had dogged me all my life, still held me back from arguing as each point arose. It didn't matter though, I was thinking and learning. I would mull things over so that when a conversation led us back to similar ground I could express my views more clearly.

Sometimes Brian's tales would be long and rambling. I'd quickly grasp the point, but I'd listen on, frustrated until he got to another point which would recapture my interest, anger me or make me laugh. The laughter I always allowed to come immediately; I had no doubts about shared humour. I might make a critical point by teasing him, but I knew he'd both accept it and enjoy it.

As time went on I'd show my anger and found that while our hushed arguments might become furious, it was an intense communication that, being based on certain friendship, was not damaging. We could let off so much steam hating each other for five minutes and then dissolving into body-wracking laughter as one of us took the fury way beyond hate.

Talking with Brian took me on mental voyages that happily compensated for those physical journeys we were denied by circumstance. One of us would tell a tale, the other would respond and take the trip further, the ideas spreading out, forming a progression, often drawing a circle and coming back, through stages of anger, laughter and sadness, to the point of departure. Yet we returned refreshed. We couldn't actually move, we were cramped, but we could grow.

Brian's fierceness was a challenge, demanding a counter-challenge that would stimulate us both. I came to relish it. I developed, not by answering any of life's great questions, but by finding my own emotional and intellectual base from which to look at them. I realized that it wasn't possible, wasn't even necessary, to understand everything in one go. No one book or statement could fix the world, there were too many variables. But I had a duty to try to understand and to challenge things if only on the basis of gut-reactions, a duty to myself that came through realizing that Brian wanted and needed me to knock him down so that he, too, could grow.

He was a forceful man but not arrogant. He would often pontificate but was always ready to laugh at himself, to accept my laughter at him. He told me a story about going to a riding stables with a girlfriend. The friend always used the same horse and, while it was being prepared for her, the owner of the stables looked at Brian, small and a bit nervous.

'Do you ride, Mr Keenan?'

'Oh aye, course I can ride.'

He had no doubts that he could bring anything, especially his fear, under the control of his will. The owner looked long at him. He stared back. She shrugged and turned to an assistant.

'Bring out Billy.'

She knew. She'd called his bluff. Billy was a giant black stallion. Brian had to try in order not to lose face. If he'd only had a step ladder he'd have been on that big bastard and away. But he hadn't had a ladder and sure as hell no-one was going to give him one. He tried but he couldn't climb the mountain. It was a funny story, but that wasn't the only reason he told it. He shared not only the joke with me, but also his sense of growth through failure.

In early October the guards took it into their heads to redecorate the cell block. First they tiled the floor, carting down the cement in a small bucket. Having come down the rickety ladder through the trap door it struck me that they'd have made the job easier by bringing the bags of sand and cement down and mixing them up *in situ*. When we went to the bathroom we were guided very carefully to avoid spoiling the alignment of the new tiles.

Then they painted the walls. The lower half was painted grey, the top half bright pink; the line between the two went up and down all over the place. It was very curious watching the guards as they went about this task. They splashed the paint on with such gusto that they ended up covered in a pinky-grey sludge, and so our prison became the Land of Grey and Pink.

Not long after all this frantic domesticity, the rains came. Tom's and Terry's cell was flooded. Tiles fell off the wall and the mattresses and blankets were soaked. The Yanks complained to Mahmoud (known by all of us as the Big M) and after some consideration he decided to move them to the cell next to the guards' room. Having watched Tom and Terry traipsing after the Big M, blindfolded of course, over the mini-wall with their mattresses and other worldly goods, we were surprised to see them doing the return trip half an hour later. Brian and I were anxious to know what was going on. Terry signalled to me what had happened. He was wearing dark glasses and waving his crucifix at me. It turned out that the new room had been filthy and, being right next to the guards' room, very noisy.

Terry angrily told Mahmoud that this was unacceptable. 'If this is how you expect me to live, then shoot me now. Won't God love you for killing a Christian?' Although the situation was undoubtedly serious and I could see how upset Terry was, I just couldn't stop laughing. Terry, being excited, was hand-talking at great speed, so that even when I could stand up straight and look at him through my tears, I couldn't always 'read' what he was saying. I had to keep asking him to repeat himself. Brian was sitting down laughing along with me, but was concerned to know how things worked out. We were both terribly upset for Tom and Terry, yet all we could do was laugh. The situation was so outrageous and Terry and Tom looked so pathetic as they moved back and forth; I could easily picture Brian and myself in the same predicament and felt it safer to laugh than cry.

A couple of weeks later Mahmoud came to us and told us that we would be moving to a larger cell and that, the following day, we were to clean our present one before the move. After he'd left Brian argued that we must refuse to do such menial prison work; we were not convicts but hostages, political prisoners. I quickly got caught up in this and the next day we refused to co-operate when Mahmoud came with water and cleaning gear. He wasn't happy but, although he was by far the biggest man in the group – when I walked beside him the top of my head barely reached his shoulders – he didn't get excited or threaten us. He just went away.

The following day Ali and Ayeesa took us across to the double cell where the Yanks had been and told us to clean it up. This time, Brian went ahead with much gusto. I was surprised that he suddenly felt able to do 'prison work'. After we'd finished and Ali and Ayeesa, again bizarrely, had made everything pretty with tins of talcum powder, bottles of scent and bags of paper tissues, Brian explained his change of heart: now we weren't jeopardizing our principles as we were cleaning our own room, not merely working for our captors. That made sense to me.

Through Brian, I was gaining important insights into how to maintain my dignity, although I sometimes felt that his ideas were based too much on principle, too little on pragmatism. Before we moved across to the larger cell he'd had a savage row with Ayeesa about being kept in a sweaty, stinking hole. Ayeesa had become alarmed, but his English was so poor that he couldn't follow Brian's argument. Brian was taken to the bathroom and while he was there Ayeesa brought Mahmoud down to talk to me. He began by telling me that Brian mustn't get angry and I quickly realized that if I acted as a go-between I could both divert the guards' attention from Brian and quietly demand better conditions. I was able to explain Brian's anger very calmly and at the same time make the point that if they wanted us to 'be good' then they must allow us the conditions to do that. Eventually – and perhaps surprisingly – they apologized and said that they'd get us new sheets, books and so forth.

Brian often tried explaining to the guards that he could understand their aims, but that they were completely wrong in trying to achieve them by taking innocent men hostage. They never knew what to say. I loved the way Brian would sit there wagging his finger at these guys and was delighted once when the guard he'd been lecturing just got up and walked away from the open cell door. He was still wagging and talking when I said, 'Bri, he's gone.' 'Oh God.' This became a standing joke and helped give me the confidence, when he later said that he'd tell the boss 'some political home truths', to observe, 'Yes Bri, but we aren't at home.' It was very difficult to find our feet in a situation where we were political prisoners, but where our politics were completely irrelevant.

Initially living in the larger cell was a great boon. We could actually walk around it and exercise without bumping into each other all the time. But having seen the cell block tarted up it was impossible not to feel that the kidnappers expected us to be here for a long time. We pressed ever more urgently for books and we were given *Madame Bovary* in French. I struggled through it outlining the story for Brian, but realized that had I not seen a TV dramatization a couple of years earlier I wouldn't have been able to make much sense of it either. The lack of any reference books added to the general frustration. If only we had a dictionary we could have had a thoroughly engrossing read and taught ourselves French. We needed to feel that all this time wasn't going to be completely wasted.

We were also given the last book in James Jones's *From Here to Eternity* trilogy, in which all the main protagonists ended up going bonkers and/or committing suicide. The Islamic Jihad library service seemed truly intent on forcing us into ever-deeper depression.

At the same time as our move, Tom and Terry had been separated which was a real blow for them. Terry was in the cell between us and the guards' room so could see nothing and was cut off from any direct communication. Tom was now in our old cell and we spent many hours hand-talking. After the move and separation from Terry, and with it the fear that Terry would be released leaving him alone, Tom had become so depressed that he told us that he'd tried to commit suicide by putting a plastic bag over his head. It was awful; I felt so hopeless and incompetent, and wanted to give him all the encouragement I could, to rebuild his optimism and determination to survive and beat these people at their own game.

But how could I reach out to him when all we were to one another was a face seen through a grille? I couldn't put my arms around him, but I could talk with my hands. 'What about your wife and daughters, Tom? They're keeping going for you, you can't let them down.' It was emotional blackmail and I felt that I sounded as bland as teachers at school who would, over almost any transgression, start in with, 'You're a disgrace to the house, to the school, to your parents and, most of all, to yourself.' It seemed to work and eventually Tom cheered up enough to carry on.

Now that Terry Anderson was unable to 'talk' to us, Brian and I started trading messages via the bathroom with him. We always passed on the latest news we had from the guards. Sayeed often spoke at length to Terry and, although it was probably just hot air, would always be very encouraging about an early release. We took these statements with a pinch of salt, yet we all clung to them. One day Terry wrote expressing confusion that Brian had signed off his last note, 'Obo and the Snake'. I wrote back explaining that as my 'shilling-taking' family had left Ireland Brian had decided that I fell into the pool of those thrown out by Saint Patrick and that, therefore, I was a snake. 'Obo', according to Brian, was the brand name of the world's strongest masonry nail and, as he was a hard Belfast boyo and 'tough as nails', he adopted the name for himself. From his next letter we got the clear impression that Anderson thought we were stir crazy.

Tom felt that the guards were too suspicious of him to feel safe sending messages via the bathroom so I'd pass on Terry's letters by hand-talking. Once as I did this the man next to Tom, whom we'd all believed to be Lebanese, appeared at his grille. He used basic hand-signals to tell me that he was Frank Reed, and American. I passed this on to Tom. Frank had already guessed who Tom and Terry were and I introduced Brian and myself.

After that whenever I was talking to Tom, who really needed the contact, Frank would interject with odd bits of information about himself. He told me he was a Moslem, by marriage; that he had been on the verge of introducing his 'Mastery of Learning' techniques into the whole of Lebanon's secondary school system; that he was born one of three triplets and that the other two babies were Siamese twins who had not survived. Then he would start telling me that because of his connections with the Lebanese establishment and his Moslem beliefs he was certain to be released soon. In fact he often reported guards' over-heard conversations that indicated 'I go tonight'. He later admitted that he spoke almost no Arabic so I couldn't understand how he knew what the guards were talking about.

He was clearly in a state of shock. Since he had been taken in early September, he'd had no chance to talk to anyone else. When, later, Jacobsen and then Sontag were released he asked me with obvious amazement why they'd been released before him. It hadn't occurred to him that it might be because they'd been held for longer than him. It seemed to me that he felt he was of greater importance inside and outside the prison than any other hostage. Although his attitude was infuriating, I suppose it was just his way of maintaining his self-esteem in such humiliating circumstances.

All contact with our fellows ceased when the power went off for a whole week. The guards would use a candle when they brought us food, then leave us in the dark all day. Despite the fact that Brian and I still had each other's company, the prolonged darkness and stillness, in which the sounds of cockroaches and mice scratching about became horribly amplified, wore heavy on my nerves.

As the weeks passed, our cell seemed to attract more and more visitors. Cockroaches and mice, presumably sheltering from the colder weather outside, appeared at all times. During the night I'd lie there huddled under a blanket trying to ignore the scratchings and scuttlings. Living in a hole in the ground with vermin and filth, the last remnants of civilized life seemed to have gone. I couldn't keep up the pretence that, when the door was closed, we were in our own place – not with these creatures invading it, potentially bearing some awful disease.

Brian would be asleep, snoring. The noise of the beasts would start me squirming, itching, slapping at imagined things running over me. I'd leap up, and start swotting the roaches with a plastic sandal. Embarrassed at my skittishness when Brian turned over with, 'What the fuck are you doing?', I'd reply, 'Ridding the world of pests like you.' He'd wearily get up to help me corner a mouse under a mattress, stamp on it, then go back to bed cursing me for a fool.

The noise of the fans as they became loose in their fittings on the doors were Brian's great bugbear. Now, in the double cell, we had two of them and the hum and drumming of the rackety machinery would become louder and louder until it felt as if we were lying right beside the engine in the depths of some huge and ancient steamship. We'd screw up pieces of paper and jam them around the fans. The rattling would stop for a day or so, then come back with a vengeance.

As the winter wore on, dealing with the creatures and the pounding fans was a nightly event. I'd sit up, shake Brian's foot and announce, 'Time for the Pest and Noise Abatement Society to meet.' At a time when my nerves were stretched by the gloomy environment and the tension of sending secret messages and hand-talking across the cell block, the pest invasions seemed to be just too much. But at least I could deal with them, so, while my reactions were probably over the top, it was a huge relief to drive them out periodically. I knew Brian thought I was an idiot for taking so much notice of these minor irritations. I also knew that, wanting me to be as calm as possible, he'd help me.

The guards, too, were involved in pest control. Sometimes they'd bring a cat down and leave it locked with us in the main cell block for a few hours. I don't think the poor creature ever caught anything; it was too busy crying, wanting to be let out of that awful place with the curious large animals in their cages.

Once, when Bri was in the bathroom, Ali came in. Beneath my blindfold I could see he was holding a red-glass flower vase. He was laughing, with his hand over the top of the vase. He clearly wanted me to look closer, so I did and saw a mouse moving about in the cramped space. Ali kept pushing the vase at me and suggesting that he would let the mouse jump out at me. I moved back quickly, my blindfold fell down and I looked straight into Ali's eyes. He didn't change his expression which was one of pure warmth, of a friend whose eyes are shining at a shared joke. For an instant we looked at each other as people do. Then reality took over again. I retied the blindfold, no longer friends but victim and persecutor. We let the joke run for a few seconds longer, but whatever fun there might have been was gone for me. I couldn't understand how a man, whom I'd actually seen giving genuine human warmth, could tolerate his role which demanded that I put on the blindfold, and sit quietly as he locked me in the cell and went off, probably still happy, to the real world outside. What made these people tick? How could they treat us so badly when it was clear they didn't really want to, when, at times, they truly wanted to be friends?

Another poignant moment came when Ali was taking me to the bathroom a few days later. On the way back he stopped me in the guards' room and took me over to one of the beds. I looked down beneath my blindfold and saw a baby wriggling about. I knelt down in awe. I put a hand out to touch a little foot – more wriggling and a gurgle. I pointed at myself, said, 'John', at Ali, said his name, then pointed at the baby. 'He Ali, Ayeesa Papa.' I congratulated the father: '*Mabrouk*, Ayeesa.' 'Thank you, thank you.'

Here, in this place of fractured, tortured minds and morals, was a living image of innocence, ignorant of the purpose of the place and of what his father did to other men in the name of God. I cherished those few seconds. It was a new beginning in one life and allowed me to believe that I, too, would be able to begin again.

Yet the thought that clung to me was that the men who held us could bring a child there. They simply couldn't appreciate that it was a bad place. Later Mahmoud and some other guards arrived and they all posed for photographs with the baby and proud father, using the same camera with which they had taken photographs of pale and frightened men. What caption would they put in the family album? 'Little Ali with Daddy and colleagues when they used to bury innocent men in holes in the ground.'

My heart went out to Anderson when I heard him say, as he, too, was shown the child, 'When am I going to see my baby? When will you let me see my baby?' They knew what he was saying even if their English was minimal.

They couldn't answer. The only right answer would have been to take the man out on to the street and given him his taxi fare home. No chance, no answer, back to your cell.

On 1 November we were given a Bible. That night I flicked through it looking for comforting, hopeful passages. Suddenly the block was full of guards. They kept opening and closing doors making as much noise as they could. Ali came in and took back the steel watch he'd given Bri in August. A little while later he came and took the gold one he'd given me. Brian and I realized that all the noise was a lunatic attempt to disguise the fact that somebody was being moved. Then I chanced upon the prophet Zechariah. Chapter 11, Verse 1 read '*Open thy doors, O Lebanon.*' It was the first day of the eleventh month. The words of the prophet must have been heard and I was sure Lebanon's doors were actually opening for someone. That night David Jacobsen was released.

4
London, April 1986–March 1987

I came back from Crete uncertain as to what to do next. There was still no news. The flat was empty, Geraldine was at work, all around me life was ticking over as normal, which seemed impossible: John was still kidnapped. I began to wonder if the kidnappers felt they couldn't lose face, and had decided to make the most of their mistake by trying to get something in return for John. Any day now Roby said WTN would receive proof that John was alive, a photograph of him holding a recent newspaper perhaps and then a list of demands. Until this happened I felt it would be a terrible betrayal to do anything normal, but I had to occupy my mind somehow. I decided to go back to work.

Roby warned me to expect that my colleagues would be getting on with their jobs, but I wasn't prepared for the shock that hit me when I returned to the news room. There was Moira, Audrey, Nick, James, all the familiar faces just getting on with their jobs, life turning over as if nothing had happened. I thought there would at least be the kind of 'war desk' that was usually set up to cope with a huge breaking story. I wanted to rush up to everyone and shout, 'Don't you realize John's been kidnapped?' As I sat down at my desk several people came up to ask if there was any news and I appreciated that I'd misinterpreted the air of normality.

Everyone in the news room felt a deep affection for John. He worked hard at his relationships with people, developing an intimacy with them, often through humour. He could tease someone out of being too self-important or too temperamental because he made them feel it mattered to him that they got on well. Roby had spotted this quality and singled John out for the Beirut posting. After John had disappeared I sometimes raged at Roby's decision, but John had done his job very well and proved that Roby's confidence in him was justified. No-one could have foreseen that the Americans, with Britain's help, would bomb Libya.

The news room felt strange without him. We had been working together for two years and it was nice to be able to look across the room and see someone you loved. The only real problem had been the danger of spending too much time at WTN; quite a few of our colleagues were good friends, so our social life could be a bit claustrophobic. Now I was glad of the closeness, glad to be among friends at work. The colleagues of whom we were particularly fond missed John a great deal and I sensed the concern they had for him was being deflected on to me. They organized little things, like ensuring I never dealt with Middle East stories, or taking me out for lunch, or, like Rachel Stabb, leaving notes in my pigeon-hole to cheer me up. With their support, WTN was not a bad place to be, especially as it was where news of John would first arrive.

Each morning I woke with the expectation that John's kidnappers would make contact. It was really only a question of going through the motions and somehow passing the time until they did. Sometimes I felt as if John had simply had to stay a little longer in Beirut, but would be back soon. I would keep up this pretence until someone asked me, 'Is there any news?' or until reports came through of more violence in Beirut. Then reality would hit me again.

I had only been back at work a few days when I walked into the news room to be buttonholed in the nicest possible way by Sean Ward, who didn't seem to want to chat about anything particular, but obviously was intent on edging me away from the photocopier towards the fire exit. I glanced over his shoulder and saw that he'd been trying to block my view of the many televisions fixed to the news-room walls and desks. They were all tuned to an incoming satellite showing grainy pictures of a body hanging from a scaffold. This was the video issued by the kidnappers of another Briton, Alec Collett, whose 'execution' had been announced after the Libyan raid. It was a terrible shock to see that the body was wearing a red shirt and blue jeans, clothes just like John's. For a second I thought it was him. I dashed out on to the fire escape in tears. Sean wrapped me in a big hug and said that he'd tell Roby's office that I'd been taken ill and had to go home.

I went back to work the following day, but would often get upset. The energy I was putting into getting through my shift would evaporate and one of my colleagues would have to take me home. I would wake the next morning exhausted, in a grey cloud of depression that I couldn't shake off. Not knowing what was happening to John was frightening and confusing; it left an awful blank that my imagination still could not fill. I couldn't absorb the fact that John had been kidnapped. I knew it had happened, but still felt it could not be. The fear that I dared not confront was that the calls to the WTN office saying John was OK were hoaxes. They were the only proof we had that John was alive, but after the shock of the first few weeks wore off it began to strike me as very odd that a group of Lebanese kidnappers should bother to return a stolen car. It didn't add up, which seemed to question the authenticity of the phone calls. I worried that the anonymous caller had not actually known that John was OK, which led me back to the awful first reports that he had been killed. I hoped that there would soon be proof of what I felt inside; that John was indeed alive. At night I prayed that some good spirit would keep him safe.

I went to see Dr Rettie, the ITN doctor, in the hope that he could help with the depression. He told me that what I was feeling was something akin to jealousy, a negative emotion that did no-one any good. He said that I had to accept that I couldn't help John and until he came back I should find an interest outside work to keep myself occupied. I could see the sense of his suggestion, but somehow it didn't seem to be the answer.

A month passed and with the kidnappers still silent, I tried to pay lip-service to Dr Rettie's advice. I tried learning Spanish, attempted to get regular exercise, saw friends for lunch and went to Brighton for the day. I tried to fill the hole that John's disappearance had left in my life by keeping busy. Life without him was dull and empty and I missed the quiet times we spent together at my flat. Until he came back I chose to spend as little time alone in it as possible and stayed out late so that I went to bed exhausted. Friends made a point of calling regularly and inviting me out, and all their concern touched me, as did the letters which arrived from my family in Yorkshire and from school and university friends with whom I'd lost contact.

I rediscovered the female friendships that I had neglected in recent years. My flatmate, Geraldine, shared the strain I was under, and I particularly relied on Mary's support. She made a point of calling often, and if I felt down, she would come round and make endless cups of tea. She was quick to understand how I was feeling and it was such a relief to pour it all out to her. I'd find my spirits lifting, and then by the time I'd become engrossed in entertaining reports of her latest news they would usually have recovered enough to make the next day seem not such a bad prospect after all.

Chris Pearson and his girlfriend Sue Barnard invited me out or came round to see me; Barbara Mackie and her boyfriend Tony Steyger did the same, as well as telephoning every few days for a chat. It was impossible not to respond to Barbara's irrepressible nature and as time went on we began to confide in one another and develop a close friendship from the foundations we'd laid in Crete. We all avoided the subject of what might be happening to John: it was too painful. Instead a kind of mania set in as the summer began. It was as if we had to find something to laugh about at all costs until we heard specific news from

Beirut. It eased my feelings of loss to sit with people who loved John and who shared his mad sense of humour.

But it seemed as if everyone else had someone special they could turn to for comfort and help. Trying to cope with not having a partner was made easier by Nick Toksvig's loyal friendship. Nick had lost his best friend, I had lost my boyfriend and I was grateful for his support. Often when I got upset at work he would be there and would take me home, or come round after his shift finished to see how I was. His sense of humour was so in tune with John's that he could have me chuckling when I thought laughter had deserted me for good. We shared an equal frustration at being unable to do anything to help John. Nick had had some experience of the Middle East and I turned to him when I wanted to discuss what various bits of wire copy might mean, what the significance of this or that development might be. Roby said that we were winding each other up but I felt this wasn't fair. Nick had a very calming influence and was a rock of support, always reassuring and optimistic about what the next day would bring.

Several weeks passed, and still the kidnappers did not make contact. I staved off fear and confusion by learning as much as I could about hostage-taking in Lebanon. I was desperate to find an explanation for what had happened to John and I tried to build up a picture of how the kidnappers might behave. It was another way of filling in the time and feeling useful. Nick and I went to meet journalists with knowledge of the Middle East and Lebanese people living in London. Everyone was willing to talk about the situation, but nothing ever seemed relevant to John's case. Concentrating on the facts and coming to terms with them was another way of keeping my emotions at bay and of feeling that I was doing something positive. I read Jonathan Randal's *Tragedy of Lebanon* and *Israel's Lebanon War* by Ze'ev Schiff and Ehud Ya'ari and photocopied articles from ITN's news information library. I bought a map of Lebanon and stared at the spot from where John had been abducted, hoping somehow it would reveal where he had been taken next. It looked quite a small country, and the urge to just go there and scour the streets was very strong.

Instead, all I could do was gather and file information. Thousands of Lebanese, both Moslems and Christians, had disappeared since the civil war began. Some were kidnapped for money, some for political reasons, and some were simply murdered, their families left to wonder what had become of them and to hope that one day they would return. The outside world paid little attention to them, in contrast to the few Westerners who'd been kidnapped. They were seen to be more valuable than the Lebanese hostages.

The groups hitherto involved in kidnapping Westerners had been Islamic Jihad, Abu Nidal and, more recently, The Revolutionary Justice Organization. Little was known about these groups and they were all described as 'shadowy' and 'mysterious' by the press. Islamic Jihad had ties with Hezbollah, a radical Moslem organization which followed Islamic law, virtually ran its own Islamic state, and aligned itself with Iran. As I went further back in the cuttings I discovered that this group had started kidnapping Westerners in earnest in 1984 and 1985 when they abducted two Britons. I noted with relief that both had only been held for a few weeks, until their nationality had been ascertained. Islamic Jihad seemed to be concentrating mainly on Americans and Frenchmen, some of whom had been held for more than a year.

The cuttings on Abu Nidal and the groups thought to be linked to it, such as the organization who had murdered Collett, went back further to the 1970s. They had committed many terrorist offences, most recently the murder of Israeli citizens queuing at El Al desks in the airports at Rome and Vienna. As far as I could make out, this was the only group with any grievance against Britain; one of its members was imprisoned here for the attempted murder of an Israeli ambassador. John's kidnap initially had been claimed by The Children of Gaddafi and his reported murder by the Revolutionary Commando Cells. Neither group had been heard of before.

But as John's kidnap was linked to the bombing of Libya, and Abu Nidal was thought to have links with Libya, it seemed possible that the group might be holding him. Other people we had spoken to also suspected Libyan or Syrian involvement. Now that I had a possible culprit for John's abduction I felt better. It gave some kind of shape to the confusion. I knew my theories meant nothing, but I pretended that they represented some progress.

It soon seemed even more likely that Abu Nidal was responsible. I read in the papers that in the weeks prior to the bombing, when Libya and the US had been threatening one another, 'freelance' gangs of kidnappers had been looking for Westerners to take hostage, knowing that they could be sold to the Libyans. That's what had happened to Padfield and Douglas; Gaddafi was rumoured to have paid one million dollars for each of them. British politicians later admitted that they had known the men were in Libyan hands. John had probably been taken by one of these gangs as well, but somehow, mercifully, had escaped the same fate.

Nick and I tried to follow what had happened to each of the Western hostages; how long it had taken for their photographs to be released by the kidnappers and for a list of demands to be issued. Terry Waite was trying to help the Americans kidnapped by Islamic Jihad in 1984 and 1985. They had all been seen in photographs and on videos since their abduction. Islamic Jihad wanted freedom for members of their organization who were in gaol in Kuwait for carrying out bombing attacks; they wanted America to put pressure on Kuwait to release them. But Islamic Jihad had also kidnapped a number of Frenchmen in 1985, again issuing photographs and videos of each one to prove it. No-one seemed to know exactly why they were being held, but some journalists were suggesting that the kidnappers were trying to persuade France to stop supplying arms to Iraq, currently fighting against Iran in a war which had been going on for the last six years. All this told us nothing about why John was being held. It was all too confusing, too labyrinthine, to follow.

Three months had now passed without word of John; no authentic claim for his abduction had been made by any group and no demands issued for his release. It was cruel, pointlessly so; why kidnap John, hold him captive, deprive him of his family and friends, and, in turn, deprive them of the peace of mind of knowing, at least, that he was alive? Why remain silent? I wanted to shout at the kidnappers, make them listen, shatter their complacency. I wanted them to stop hurting John and us, end these haunting fears about whether he had not, in fact, survived. I was sure John was alive; I just wanted to know it. I imagined his captors as volatile men, desperate, full of hate. I pitied them in a way, but I hated them too.

I was powerless. We'd begged them to let us know John was OK, appealed to them for news and none came. Under the circumstances, it was reassuring to know that another man was in the same position as John, in that there had been no news of him either since his kidnap in April. His name was Brian Keenan. He was from Belfast and had dual British/Irish nationality. He was young, too, a teacher. I picked up his photograph in the newspaper cutting and eyed it warily. He looked pop-eyed and his face had a startled expression. 'He looks a bit strange,' I thought. 'I wonder where he fits in.' Two British men, both kidnapped at the same time, both unclaimed. The silence was still incomprehensible, but it was now not so unusual, and I seized on this as proof that John was alive.

No-one seemed to be able to make sense of the situation. Lebanon was in such a mess; its people were suffering and the Government virtually powerless to stop the factional fighting, let alone deal with the release of the kidnap victims. I thought back to the previous year when two employees from WTN Beirut had come over to London for a few weeks. They were recuperating from having been briefly kidnapped and beaten up by members of one of the factions.

I remembered sitting with John in The Crown and Sceptre, asking one of them, Raef, to shed some light on a particularly bad car-bomb attack that had occurred in Beirut. 'Why do you think this has happened?' I asked, hoping for some local insight. He had looked at me and smiled. 'It's just games,' he said. 'It doesn't mean anything, it's just games.' I had nodded wisely in response but hadn't the faintest idea what he meant. Now that events in Lebanon had a direct bearing on my life, I realized how impossible it would be to offer, for example, to pay a ransom. There would be no way of finding a middle man to handle the transaction. How could anyone cross all the sectarian barriers and work through the various 'games' that were being played to negotiate with murderers?

As we waited through June and July for the kidnappers to get in touch or for the WTN and Foreign Office efforts to produce something, Nick had a brilliant idea. The World Cup was in progress and he had read that the fighting stopped in Beirut when Arabic soccer matches were being played. Perhaps John's kidnappers might be watching or better still, perhaps John was. Nick called Sean, who was in Mexico producing WTN's World Cup operation, and asked him if it would be possible to display a banner carrying a message to John during one of the Arabic matches. There was a long silence as Sean pondered this and then wrote down the message, which was wonderfully obscure. He said that he would see what he could do. Over the next few weeks we sat through several football matches, scanning every shot of the crowd in vain as we waited for the banner to appear. Then one evening, dutifully watching Morocco play someone or other, we both leapt to our feet. There, displayed near the scoreboard was a huge banner, with three-foot-high red letters bearing the message: 'John McCarthy Beirut: Tinker Taylor says TTRA.' This was a reference to John's and Nick's American Studies tutor at Hull, exhorting them that it was Time To Roll Another roll-up, a message that was bound to have John smiling were he to see it. It was a one in a million chance but the lift it gave us carried us smiling through the next few days. I felt as if John had been there in the room with us, sharing the joke.

'They don't come back,' Julie Flint had said, but in early summer two French hostages and then an American were released within weeks of each other. Philippe Rochot and Georges Hansen had been held for only three months; their kidnappers, the Revolutionary Justice Organization, said they were freed because of changes in French Middle East policy but the newspapers went into no detail. Both men looked thin and pale, but claimed they had been well-treated. Although I didn't think this was relevant to John's case it was good news generally; perhaps this was the start of a succession of releases that would free all the hostages. Father Lawrence Jenco, who was released in July, had been held for eighteen months. Islamic Jihad said they had released him on humanitarian grounds which newspapers attributed to Terry Waite.

When Fr Jenco spoke of the chains, the solitary confinement and desperation of his captivity I felt cold inside. Islamic Jihad were ruthless religious fanatics who were taking on the United States. I had seen coverage of their activities in the press and on television: in my mind they were a separate matter and they had no bearing on John's situation. I distanced Fr Jenco's experiences from what might be happening to John. I resented the fact that British newspapers had been full of Jenco's release and of Waite's role, but had made no mention of British hostages. If only Waite would hurry up and start work on John's behalf.

By August, four months after John's kidnap, there had still been no communication from the kidnappers, no claim, no demands, and I realized I knew very little about what WTN and the FO were actually doing. Roby was in charge, the only person at WTN who knew the score. He would call me into his office every week or so for a chat. His news seemed to be pretty general. I didn't know any of the details of what was happening with regard to John, so it was impossible to form a clear picture of what those activities were. When I asked for more precise information, I was told it was confidential; I realized that, as I wasn't John's wife, I had no automatic right to know or to be consulted on decisions that were being taken about him. Although I felt extremely frustrated, I had to trust that everything possible was being done for John, that WTN and the FO were still pulling out all the stops, talking to anyone and everyone in Beirut, making it clear that he was important. I wished I knew more about what was actually going on.

I could have told them that just before John left for Beirut we had decided to buy a flat together, had talked of getting married and starting a family; but the decision was so recent that I had told only my mum and dad. In the circumstances, it seemed both pointless and too personal to try to explain the state of our relationship to strangers. In any case, all our plans were now on hold and the future offered only the hope of news the next day. I believed in the idea of our future together for all I was worth, but nagging doubts were starting to surface in my mind. I have always been a worrier, and now I rose to the occasion. Had John really wanted to live with me? Had we really decided we were going to get married and have a family? When I discovered from Pat McCarthy that he had no recollection of John telling them of our plans, what turned out to be a simple mixup took on enormous proportions in my mind and I wondered if I was going mad.

While I was waiting for news of John, all around me things were changing fast. Already WTN was no longer the relaxed, pleasant place that John had known. Roby hadn't been there all that long and now was sweeping through the place with a new broom. Most of the managers whom John would remember had resigned and news-room colleagues were also starting to leave. Each time an old face left, the realization that the world John knew was changing provoked feelings of panic. He was missing so much. I wanted time to stand still until John was back so that nothing would have been lost, but it was like trying to hold on to a handful of sand and watching the grains trickle out, no matter how tight your grip.

With distrust and apprehension clouding the atmosphere at WTN, it wasn't surprising that there was a general feeling in the news room that the company wasn't doing enough for John. His colleagues were not being kept informed about what was happening and as I was being told little myself, it wasn't possible for me to reassure people with any conviction. I would come out of Roby's office after another update and as I returned to my desk would see questioning looks in the eyes of my colleagues as if they were saying, 'Well?'

Walking round the corridors between the news room and the editing suites or waiting at the coffee machine, people would ask, 'What's the latest?' or, 'Is there any news?' My reply was always a lame, 'No, not really.' Then I would feel sorry for the person asking who would be uncertain what to say next. I would try to think of something positive to cheer them up. It was exhausting.

The McCarthys were also finding other people's kind enquiries a strain. John's mother, Sheila, had virtually stopped going into the local village because she couldn't bear the sympathy in people's eyes. Nor did she want to stay too long away from the telephone in case it brought some news.

It had been obvious to me when John and I had visited them that they were a very close family, John and his mother, in particular, shared a sense of humour; she, too, always seemed to look for the fun in life and you only had to be with her for a few minutes to see that John must have inherited his wonderful warm spirit from her. Since May, Sheila and I had been writing to each other as she found this a less distressing form of communication than the telephone. Reading her letters brought home to me that there is no love comparable to a mother's for her son:

Each morning when I wake up I don't know how I'm going to get through the day, so what it must be like for dear John doesn't bear thinking about. I feel his loneliness and uncertainty must be terrible for him. To think that this should have happened to such a dear boy who loved being with his friends and family is so difficult to understand.

Sheila made several television appeals for John's release in the months following his abduction; pleading with the kidnappers, talking to them as people who had suffered great injustices and whose hopes for lives of honour and dignity she shared and understood. It had been an ordeal, but she had been eager to do it. 'Anything that's going to help John, I would go in, you know, head first. I didn't mind doing that at all. I thought if that's the way and if that's going to get the captors to say what they want and who they are, well, that's splendid, that's fine,' she said. She was so good, Pat and Terence dubbed her, 'One take McCarthy'. We heard that ordinary people watching those broadcasts on Lebanese TV found them terribly moving, despite their own suffering; but from the kidnappers they bought no response whatsoever. True to character, Sheila remained optimistic, determined to make a full recovery from the operation she'd had while John was away. In one of her letters, she wrote: 'Within minutes of each other, the song "When Johnnie comes marching home again", came to Pat and me, so it must be a good omen.'

The McCarthys were guided by the Foreign Office and by Roby, whom Pat had come to respect a great deal since April. 'He gave the most astounding performance at the FO,' Pat had told me over the telephone. 'He spoke for about an hour, without notes, about John's kidnap and everything that has happened since, recalling even the smallest detail. I could tell they were jolly impressed.' In the brief conversations I had with Pat during the summer there was no question in his mind that his son wasn't getting the best possible help.

The US and Libya were continuing to trade insults, just as they had before the bombing in April, and in August it began to look ominously like a re-run of the same disaster. I was terrified that if Britain became involved again John would not survive. Nick and I devised a plan to contact everyone who knew John and ask them to write to their MPs and MEPs expressing their concern about John's vulnerability and requesting that Britain would not become involved in any attack. Everyone lobbied MPs furiously and my Auntie Shirley's postman began to think she was running for parliament. The responses were passed over to Nick and me and we were inundated with official letters, some from the Foreign Secretary and Mrs Thatcher. The replies were virtually identical and stated that the Government was doing all it could for the hostages short of giving in to terrorism and could not say what would happen with regard to Libya. One aspect was encouraging, though, and that was how many MPs took the view that the bombing of Libya had been a bad idea in the first place and would oppose it happening again.

No sooner was that crisis over than another one started. A Syrian, Nezar Hindawi, was sentenced in London to forty-five years in prison for his role in the attempted bombing of an El Al jet at Heathrow on the same day that John had been kidnapped. There were allegations that he had acted on behalf of the Syrian government and Mrs Thatcher's response to the verdict was promptly to break off diplomatic relations with Syria. We held our breath and prayed that John would be safe, that the response from the Arab world would not be retaliation against British citizens held hostage there. Friends gathered again at my flat as we waited for some reaction from Lebanon.

There was none at all, which in itself took on sinister connotations. Doubts about John's survival surfaced yet again. Roby called me into his office and after a while talked about Hindawi.

'Jill, we have to ask why the kidnappers have not taken this opportunity to show that they have John, to use him to their advantage. It's been six months now and there's been nothing, absolutely nothing.'

'I know, but . . .' But what? He had voiced my own fears and I wanted him to be frank with me, but we shouldn't assume the worst until there was proof.

'But what about Brian Keenan? He's in the same position as John – no claim, no demands – John's not the only one that no-one has heard anything about. What about him?'

Roby sighed and looked doubtful. 'Jill, we have to seriously consider the possibility that John may be dead. We have to. It doesn't look good.'

I knew he was just trying to be realistic, but I didn't want to hear it and the conversation upset me.

As summer turned to autumn the intense activity of the kidnapping groups in Lebanon made the silence about John's fate even more puzzling and worrying. One faction had kidnapped two Frenchmen, one of whom was eighty-one years old, and two Americans, Frank Reed and Joseph Cicippio. Islamic Jihad released videos of French and American hostages criticizing their respective governments for doing nothing to help them. The videos were harrowing to watch, each man looking grey-faced and weary, their voices monotonous with despair and their eyes dulled through lack of light and hope. Despite that I thought how wonderful it would be to see John even in this way, to hear his voice again, and to know he was alive.

I needed to see him; it was becoming very difficult to summon up his face at will and to imagine what he would have said and done. I read and re-read the two letters he'd sent from Beirut, wanting more, marvelling at a line that had made me laugh at the time and now seemed to belong to a bygone age, carefree and innocent. 'If I ever get kidnapped,' he had written, 'I'll tell them they'd be better off with the parrot from the Commodore Hotel. It can whistle "The Marseillaise" and live in a much smaller cage.'

On 2 November, an American called David Jacobsen was set free by Islamic Jihad and thrust into the light. He managed to run a few steps across the tarmac at Wiesbaden airbase where, his voice shaking with emotion, he thanked Terry Waite for giving him hope in his darkest hour.

A few days later, I celebrated my twenty-ninth birthday in fine style, thanks to Nick, Barbara and Geraldine. I harboured secret hopes that John would be allowed to get a message through to me, but the newspapers were full of reports saying that Jacobsen, and Jenco before him, had apparently not been released on humanitarian grounds after all. Revelations of Irangate began slowly to emerge and what at first seemed preposterous gradually became accepted as fact.

I couldn't bear to read the details; the only thing that seemed important was that the Americans had lied. Lofty statements about leading the world's fight against terrorism – the very arguments that had been used to justify the raid on Libya – were nothing but a cover for dirty work that had achieved the release of a few hostages, but left those still in captivity more vulnerable and isolated than ever. The Americans had encouraged the kidnappers to think that taking hostages was a good idea, had raised the stakes by paying for them with arms, and had handled it all so badly that it was obvious that they had not considered the consequences at all. This was the Government whose fight against terrorism Britain had so enthusiastically joined and whose statements about not doing deals with terrorists it so faithfully repeated. Even the French now were thought to be involved in a huge deal to get their people out, but at least they hadn't lectured anyone else about ethics. I felt sorry for the families of the remaining American hostages who had been led so blindly up the garden path and I began to see things in a much more cynical light. Raef was right; these were games, moves on a gigantic chess board with pieces that could literally be sacrificed.

The newspapers and TV were full of the revelations and implications of Irangate, but again they largely ignored John and Brian Keenan and the fact that Terry Waite was helping them as well. On the Sunday after the story broke,

I was sitting at home listening to Radio 4's *The World This Weekend* as it, too, was reporting on the Irangate story. As the report ended, my ears pricked up at the news reader's words: '. . . well, even though Mr Jacobsen is free, there are still seven Americans missing in Lebanon, plus eight French hostages, a South Korean, an Irishman and an Italian. Although there are hints that other releases may be in progress . . .' My heart was pounding. What about John? They had failed to mention John. I stared out of the window. The report seemed to confirm my worst fears about John slipping through the net, about being presumed dead, about being forgotten. I wondered if I had misheard, but Chris, Nick and Pat had been listening to the broadcast and were all angry and upset. Chris called the programme editor to explain that there was a British hostage as well and at least he got a sympathetic and apologetic response; but I had no faith that John would be remembered the next time, or that the assumption that John was dead wasn't shared by the rest of the media.

Up until now I had thought that it was wrong to seek publicity for John's case, despite an urge to shout from the roof-tops that something ought to have been discovered about his whereabouts by now. I still thought it was wrong. The arguments put forward by Roby, Pat and the FO made sense. If we kept a low profile then the kidnappers would see that John wasn't an important pawn and might release him. If we didn't, then the kidnappers might think he was someone important and would set impossible conditions for his release. But six months now had passed and everything was collapsing around our ears – the lack of news, the break in relations with Syria, Irangate – I didn't know what to believe any more.

The moving television pictures of David Jacobsen being reunited with his family underlined the need to do something. Several colleagues at WTN felt that the company was now simply waiting for the kidnappers to make contact and when one of them mentioned this to me, I had been shocked; I'd assumed the idea was to do everything within our power to establish contact with them and that the attempts to do this would be as determined as I thought they had been in the days following John's abduction.

Nick and I felt that we had to act; to go out to the Middle East and see what was happening for ourselves, to talk to people. I just wanted to be closer physically to where John was. The McCarthys were enthusiastic about the idea and we devoted most of our time to planning a trip to Cyprus, Syria and possibly Lebanon, although Roby had told us we'd be fired if we set foot in Beirut. We were unclear quite what we were going to do but the journalists with whom we had made contact over the months, like Robert Fisk on *The Times* and Jim Muir at the BBC, all thought it was an excellent idea and helped us with names and telephone numbers of people to see. Fisk had been sympathetic from the start. He had met John in Beirut and he knew what it was like when someone you loved was kidnapped. Terry Anderson, one of the American hostages, was his best friend. Since he'd been taken hostage, Anderson's brother and father had both died and his girlfriend had given birth to their daughter. Anderson had been held for eighteen months – an inconceivable length of time. I wondered how on earth his family were coping. At least John was neither American, nor held by Islamic Jihad.

Nick and I were pleased when his father, Claus, an MEP, used his contacts to get us a meeting with Sir David Myers, the Permanent Under-Secretary of State at the Foreign Office. As we drove down Whitehall towards Downing Street and King Charles Street, where the Foreign Office is situated, I felt a sense of awe that we were about to enter a place where people ran our country's foreign affairs, where diplomatic deals had been negotiated for centuries and where decisions that affected all our lives were taken every day. Surely, with such influence, it wouldn't be too difficult to find a way of releasing John? In the huge reception area other visitors were reading *The Economist* and *Newsweek*, and watching them I realized that business here didn't revolve around what was happening in Lebanon; there were more important problems to think about. A guide came to show us to the right room and we silently followed her down long corridors, into tiny lifts and past magnificent ante-rooms. It seemed to take ages to get there. As we climbed up a grand, curving staircase past portrait after portrait of former sovereigns and ambassadors, I felt as if I was getting smaller and smaller like Alice in Wonderland and John's situation less and less important. So many things were going on in the world that needed attention. How much did one person matter to people here?

We sat around a table in a fairly bare, nondescript meeting room. Sir David seemed to act as if I wasn't there; I realized that every time I asked a question or made a point he would appear to address his reply to Nick. That disturbing habit aside, he talked a lot of sense and was very encouraging, telling us that individuals were sometimes capable of succeeding where governments had not. We left his office feeling that the corridors weren't quite so intimidating nor so remote, and that we had been given an enormous boost.

One of the biggest problems for the Foreign Office, as I was beginning to understand, was that Britain was seriously under-represented in the capitals of all the countries with which it needed contact if it were to make progress in locating John in Lebanon. We had diplomatic relations at the lowest level with Iran, a country which the Irangate revelations had showed as having a mysterious but productive role in the release of the American hostages and with which France was reported to be doing a deal over theirs. To make things worse, Mrs Thatcher, in the crude black-and-white way she approached foreign policy, had left Britain in the position of having no diplomatic representation in Libya or Syria, the two countries believed most likely to be able to help find John. Roby had been out to Damascus several times for discussions – we didn't know with whom – but Nick and I felt that there was no harm in a different approach from people who loved John and could speak from the heart. We decided to go to Cyprus, to talk to all the journalists who for safety had moved there from Lebanon, and to Damascus to talk to anyone at all.

All our friends, and especially our colleagues at WTN, were enthusiastic and eager to help. When the management told Nick and me that we couldn't, as we had planned, go over Christmas and New Year because of staffing problems, colleagues switched their holidays around to make the trip possible. When we realized we would need to organize a small fund-raising evening to pay our way we found ourselves bombarded with help from all sides. It was as if John's friends had been waiting a long, long time to be able to help in some way, to feel that they were at last doing something and to focus their attention on John in a positive way. Nick's sister Sandi persuaded the Comedy Store, where she was performing, to let us have the place for an evening and rounded up some acts for the show. We arranged the 'Party for John' on 24 November, the nearest available date to his birthday. My brother Brian said he would do a cocktail spot on the piano; Gina said she would cook all the food and supervise the catering; other friends designed the tickets and got them printed; a colleague, Nigel Parsons, fixed us up with bouncers; The Crown and Sceptre donated bottles of wine and beer; other friends devised a roster for the cloakroom and the ticket office; everyone else set about finding prizes for the raffle and ITN graphics ran up a poster for us to distribute in news rooms around London.

I was astonished when cheques and messages of support began arriving from those news rooms, from journalists at ITN, the BBC, TV-AM, Visnews and TVS. I'd been so disappointed by the lack of coverage of John's plight I'd assumed that fellow journalists just weren't interested; it was a marvellous boost to discover that they were. We had issued about three hundred tickets, but they sold out fast and people even made donations if they couldn't attend on the night. Our first donation came from an Australian colleague called Kerry Brewster who was leaving London before the event. She had a farewell party and at about two o'clock in the morning, when I was about to leave, she kissed me goodbye outside in the pouring rain and silently pressed two wet twenty-pound notes into my hand as she turned away. In the taxi home I marvelled again at two things: the spontaneous generosity of people; and the way John had made such an impact on so many of the people he had met. Even those who had only had a drink with him a couple of times, like Kerry, remembered him with enormous affection.

The big day began with a bouquet of flowers and a good luck card from the McCarthys and passed in a blur of frantic activity; the evening itself couldn't have been better. Nick made a moving speech, the comedy acts were brilliant and the auction was a great success. The generosity was staggering. Everyone seemed to be bidding money like there was no tomorrow – Mike MacNish looked only slightly perturbed when he realized he owed a hundred pounds for some Estee Lauder make-up, but a little more so when he discovered he was one of the prizes – Mary Lambe had won a night out to dinner with him. There was a real sense of love, commitment and fun in the room; optimism was in the air; people were elated to be doing something at last.

That sense of optimism and purpose lifted me through the depression of John's birthday on 27 November, when Mike MacNish, Nick and I went out for lunch and raised our glasses to John. We had just been watching a report that ITN had broadcast on the fact that he was still missing. Their interest had been roused by the party, and Nick and I had agreed that there could be little harm in being interviewed on the understanding that no mention was made of our plans to visit the Middle East. We were worried that the Syrians would deny us entry if they knew why we were going.

It was the first television interview I had done, and I was surprised when the reporter asked me two brief questions and then said that was the end; I thought I'd hardly said anything at all. Nick and I watched the report to see how we had done, then listened in horror to what the news reader was saying. 'Today is the birthday of John McCarthy, the journalist kidnapped in Beirut last April following the bombing of Libya. There has been no news of Mr McCarthy ever since then and now his girlfriend says she is going to Beirut to look for him.' I was appalled. They meant me. How could they do that after all we'd said about not mentioning the trip? It might mean that we couldn't now go if the Syrians heard about it; it might harm John in some way. Mike, Nick and I discussed it over lunch and I calmed down, but I had learned that in future, I would have to be on my guard.

Our leave approached with no sign of our visas to Syria. Since Britain had just accused the Syrians of running a terrorist state, why should they help us get into their country? After raising the money for the trip, it would be a terrible blow if the project had to be cancelled. Luckily, however, Nick and I had another card up our sleeves.

Earlier in the year I had made contact with the families of some of the other hostages and had spoken to Peggy Say, Terry Anderson's sister. She told me that the wife of the Greek Prime Minister, Mme Papandreou, had been very helpful; she had been sympathetic to the plight of the hostages and was in a good position to be of assistance because of the excellent relationship between Greece and Syria. By coincidence she happened to be in London with an EC delegation, so I wrote to her at her hotel explaining our predicament. Two days later the telephone rang early in the morning.

'Hallo?'

'May I speak with Miss Jill Morrell, please? This is the secretary of Mrs Papandreou. I have Mrs Papandreou on the line,' said a foreign-sounding voice.

'Er . . . speaking,' I stammered into the phone, trying to think how on earth I should address the wife of a Head of State.

'Miss Morrell, I have just received your letter,' said a smooth American voice. 'Would you like to meet at my hotel later today? Would that be convenient?'

Overcome with embarrassment and excitement as I put the phone down, I picked it up again straightaway to call Nick and tell him the news. 'Brilliant Jill, that's brilliant!' he said as I blurted out what had just happened. 'I'll come and pick you up at one and we'll go together.' That afternoon we were in Park Lane having tea with Mrs Papandreou, an elegant, attractive American woman who seemed completely *au fait* with events in the Middle East and especially the hostage crisis.

We explained John's situation, our plans to visit Syria, and the difficulty we were having acquiring visas; she said she would see what she could do to help. Downstairs in the foyer, Nick and I sensed that she would keep her word and we had a cream tea to celebrate finding such a good ally at last.

Our leave was ticking by, so we decided to fly out to Cyprus and take things from there. Before we left, on Sunday, 14 December, Mary came round and gave me a late birthday present, a tiny, silver photograph frame. We hunted through all the pictures I had of John and chose one from our holiday in Gomera in the Canary Islands. I remembered that we had walked up a deserted, dusty hillside, above the line of the trees, to the summit where we had found, of all things, an abandoned dumper truck. John had climbed on it and given a victory salute as if we'd conquered Everest. I cut out this tiny figure raising his arms in triumph and put it into the frame to take with me, wondering if this John, the one I had known then, was still hanging on. He looked robust and strong, but also small and vulnerable – as most people do when you stop to consider the physical horrors life can suddenly throw at them. I was sure he was alive, but was he still strong and optimistic or had he given up, letting go of all thoughts of home because they were too painful, shutting off his mind and abandoning himself to his fate?

When Nick and I set off for Heathrow on Sunday morning, it was as if those intervening months hadn't happened. I felt as if I were on my way to meet John at the airport as I should have done on 17 April, and would see him there as planned. Instead, here we were, sitting around a table in a café at Heathrow in bleak December, being waved off by the entire Toksvig family, Chris and Sue, and Barbara. I thought I detected a certain apprehension as we said goodbye and they wished us luck, as if we, too, might disappear into a void. If the unthinkable could happen once, why not again? Chris urged us to telephone him every day; he would co-ordinate anything we needed from London. I was nervous of what lay ahead but, with Nick's support, I was also eager to get on with it, to be closer to John, nursing a secret hope that, by accident, we might knock on the right door and find him waiting behind it.

On our first morning in Cyprus we both felt despondent; I had had a sleepless night mulling over the idea of travelling to Beirut by ferry. Now that we were so close, the current ferocious fighting and the dangers seemed that much more real, but what were we to do if, as seemed likely, we couldn't get to Syria? Nick came into my room as the telephone rang.

'Miss Morrell? This is the Greek Embassy. I am ringing to inform you that your visas for Syria are waiting to be picked up at the Syrian Embassy.' I beamed at a puzzled-looking Nick as I put the phone down. 'She's done it!' I said. 'They're here, our visas, they're here!'

We were the only Westerners waiting for the flight to Syria. It was a bleak reminder that we were leaving a world that we knew for one which I, at least, knew nothing of. We would soon be within a hair's breadth of the world which had trapped John and still held him in its grasp, a world where the irrational seemed to have taken charge. It made me very, very glad to be with Nick, who always managed to look calm and collected even if he didn't feel it.

No matter how much I had wanted to come to Syria, I wouldn't have done it without Nick's support and encouragement. I simply wasn't up to doing this kind of thing alone. His confidence and optimism had bolstered my flagging spirits time after time over the past months. In Cyprus when we met Robert Fisk and other journalists like David Hirst of the *Guardian* and Peter George of the Australian Broadcasting Company, I had been nervous of wasting their time, of being too much an amateur. But Nick had broken the ice and I relaxed when I saw that they were genuinely interested, wanted to help, and didn't mind talking everything through. None of them had any idea which group held John, but they had all been helpful and suggested who we might see in Damascus.

Once in Damascus, armed with copies of photographs of John with and without a beard, letters from the McCarthys and our address books, Nick and I began to contact the ambassadors of the countries most likely to be able to help. I had been given sound instructions by Audrey Purdie, a colleague who had visited Lebanon, on how to present myself, particularly with regard to Moslems. She advised me to respect the Moslem customs by wearing modest clothing and not shaking any man's hand or even looking a strict Moslem in the eye. With the Iranians, where I could have put this advice into practice, we had had no luck, but we could tell Mrs Papandreou had helped out again when an invitation arrived from the Greek ambassador.

Mr Constantin was a serious, plump little man with a kind face, who stared at John's photograph and seemed genuinely taken aback and saddened by how young he was. The photograph of John with a beard had been taken a couple of years before, when he was about twenty-six, on a holiday in Denmark with Nick and MacNish in the depths of winter. We'd stayed in the Toksvig's farmhouse, miles from anywhere, and John hadn't bothered to shave. He probably had a beard again now, so the photograph would be useful for identification purposes, but it was strange handing it over to strangers, however sympathetic, as if we were surrendering our lives to them as well. Mr Constantin said that he would try to arrange a meeting with the Syrian Foreign Ministry for us and, giving me a kiss, he wished us luck. His kindness brought tears to my eyes and I left the room, but a commotion in the room behind me made me turn back. Poor Nick had mistimed his departure and had tried to walk through the door at the same time as our portly host, and I was just in time to see him hurtling across the room. Nick was torn between acute embarrassment and a desire to laugh and, as he apologized profusely for shoulder-butting the Greek ambassador to Syria, we beat a hasty retreat.

It was an inauspicious beginning but it got us started and we found ourselves with no shortage of people willing to see us. The French Embassy official we saw wasn't very forthcoming, but the Danish ambassador to Syria and Lebanon took us to lunch in a battered, white embassy car with a little Danish flag flying proudly from it and told us he would ask about John when he was next in Beirut in a few days' time. He'd heard from a journalist that the British knew that John was with Abu Nidal, but didn't want to say so for political reasons. Incredible as it seemed, Abu Nidal had an office in Damascus as if they were a firm of solicitors. Tony Touma, the WTN representative in the city, promised to arrange a meeting with them and other Palestinian factions based in the capital.

The fighting in Beirut meant that most of the leaders of the various Lebanese militias were also in Damascus. An Associated Press reporter, Marwan Souka, offered to help us meet them and, over the next week, he would materialize out of thin air, announce that he had a meeting arranged for us that very minute and tell us that we had to go now, please. He took us to see Mustapha Saad, the leader of the Palestinian Liberation Army, and reminded us in the hotel lift that he had been blinded and badly scarred in a bomb attack several years before.

I remembered that Saad was regarded by most journalists as a decent man and an honest broker; at the time of the Libyan raid, he had been trying to negotiate Alec Collett's release. We were invited to sit on either side of Saad, an elegantly dressed man, and tell him about John. We handed over the photographs to the nearest bodyguard, explained the brief facts we knew about his kidnapping and then sat like lemons as he and his bodyguards chatted among themselves in Arabic and read bits of the newspaper out to one another as if we weren't there. Nick and I shifted uncomfortably in our leather seats for a while then Saad turned to us again and told us he would do what he could. We thanked him and left.

The meeting had been a good introduction to how such business was conducted in the Middle East, but I didn't feel in the least prepared for what was coming next. Mr Walid, the Abu Nidal representative in Lebanon and Damascus, didn't look like a terrorist, but his organization was seen as one of the most dangerous terrorist groups in the world. I kept telling myself that this man, sitting in his shabby black suit and black pullover, with black curly hair, might be responsible for John's abduction and here we were drinking tea with him. He told us in the most charming and sincere manner that his people did not practise kidnapping, nor were they responsible for the murders of women and children at Rome and Vienna. It was just that they had been blamed. My head began to spin as he said that he regarded children as little flowers that should not be cut down under any circumstances.

To be honest, I would have agreed with anything he said as long as there was a possibility that his group might have John. He listened politely as I showed him John's photograph and said that I realized John's case was a small problem compared to those of his people, but that we were desperate. He told us he would pass John's picture on to his comrades in Lebanon and through their contacts they would try to find out something concrete.

He asked for our addresses in London and feeling slightly apprehensive we wrote them down.

'Have you ever been to London?' I asked, rather nervously.

'Oh yes, I have been there many times.'

'Oh,' I said, a bit nonplussed, and then felt a complete fool as he smiled and said, 'I have many friends there, some of them are in prison. Well,' he continued, 'we are friends now. I will be in touch.'

Early one morning we took our second trip down to the Lebanese border to meet up with Ghassan Salem and Kasim Dirgam, who had been in the car with John when he was kidnapped. We drove along the main Beirut-Damascus highway, a wide road carved out of the mountainside, designed for the huge army trucks that thundered by, almost too close for comfort. The scenery became increasingly spectacular and as the sun shone through the rain, beautiful rainbows formed above us. The border area wasn't far, but by the time we reached it the rain was pouring down and the roads were swimming with mud. We pulled up near some makeshift offices next to a bridge and a kind of tunnel through which I could just about see Lebanon. My first glimpse of it was the nondescript stretch of earth that made up the no-man's land of the border area. I stared through the tunnel, overwhelmed by a feeling that John was within reach, that he couldn't be more than a few miles away at the most. I felt as if he was so close I could almost touch him. Then I looked again and saw the land stretching away into the distance, further than the eye could see and thought of the thousands of streets and houses and grim-faced people with guns like those who had stopped our car so many times on our first journey here a couple of nights ago. They had thrust their heads through the windows, making me want to cower in the back. It seemed easy enough to disappear here in Syria, let alone out there in Lebanon. A sudden burst of rain hit me in the face and the idea that John was within reach evaporated like a mirage.

Nick and I met Kasim and Ghassan in no-man's land, in a miserable hut furnished with a couple of tables and a few posters of President Assad. They were a funny pair, Kasim with his deeply lined face and grasp of the English vernacular and Ghassan so young and sweet. They told us they had no information for us, but that they were sure John would be released soon. They were all working hard on it and never forgot him. They told us what had happened on the day of the kidnap and I learned that John had been driven off in the kidnappers' car. I thought that the kidnappers had driven off with John still in the driver's car. It wasn't important, of course, but we had so few precious facts about what had happened and not even that part of the story was clear. It was hopeless, just hopeless, to think we could ever get to the real truth in this chaotic place.

Things brightened a little when Mr Constantin, the Greek ambassador, called the following morning. True to his word he had fixed up a meeting with the Syrian Minister for West European Affairs. Mr Suleiman Haddad, however, was not very encouraging. He told us that the Syrians were willing to help and had already had three soldiers killed in their attempts to find the French hostages, but they had not been approached by anyone from the British side. I offered him the photographs of John but he refused them, saying he knew all the facts: I was John's sister, wasn't I, Nick, his brother, and hadn't our mother made an appeal on TV?

We trudged back to the hotel to be met by Marwan who was beside himself with impatience. 'Where were you? We have meeting in five minutes with Mr Berri.' We were off again. Nabih Berri, the leader of the Amal militia, was an important figure in Lebanon, and we were suitably apologetic to Marwan as he drove us to Berri's plush house in the suburbs. He was an aristocratic-looking man dressed in a silk suit and, as before, we were invited to sit beside him and his bodyguards and tell him our story. He said that he would look into it, and that if we wanted to go to Lebanon we had better ask him for an escort as we might get kidnapped. Everybody in the room roared with laughter at this huge joke and then the telephone rang: a call for Berri from Senegal. The connection must have been bad because everybody in the room collapsed with laughter once again as he yelled into the phone with such gusto that I thought the furniture would shake. I was beginning to get the hang of these meetings. You were expected to sit around and chat for a while about this and that, then discuss your business almost as an afterthought. The only problem seemed to be getting the timing right and avoiding offending anyone.

One man we wanted to see was General Jalloud, Gaddafi's Number Two, who was staying at the hotel. If a Libyan-backed group did have John, surely Jalloud would know about it. We discovered he was in residence on our floor, which explained the number of bodyguards always silently watching us go by. We hadn't yet seen him, but one morning, as the doors of the lift I was in were just closing, some bodyguards jumped in with a small, foxy-looking man in their midst. He had the meanest eyes I had ever seen and I was sure it was Jalloud; but I lost my nerve and was unable to speak. Before I knew it, they were out of the lift and down the corridor. Later, with Tony providing moral support, I went to see the bodyguards and handed them a letter for Jalloud requesting a meeting. They went away for a few minutes, then came back to say, 'In one hour', a deadline that kept being extended throughout the evening as Nick and I sat nervously in my room, finally realizing at about two o'clock that the hour was never going to arrive; nor did it during our entire stay. I was so ashamed that I had missed the opportunity to confront him while we were in the lift.

After the fiasco with the Libyans I approached our meetings with two Palestinian groups the following evening with more than a little cynicism. The first was with the Democratic Front for the Liberation of Palestine, an organization housed on the first floor of a dingy apartment building. Their offices were cramped and basic, a million miles away from Berri's silk suits and exquisite furniture. Their representative, Jameel Hilal, looked like a gentle, kind man and he started by telling us that his organization was against kidnapping. Many of their people were in the hands of Amal, whom the Palestinians were currently fighting. He said that he would take John's photograph, of course, and distribute it in Lebanon, but there were difficulties. The refugee camp at Chatila was almost completely destroyed and his people were living underground. He said all this in a simple, matter-of-fact way, but Nick and I were on the verge of tears by the time we left and went straight to the headquarters of the Patriotic Front for the Liberation of Palestine without speaking. Children of about twelve showed us to their offices where young men were working on alterations and hammering at pieces of wood. Hani Habib and Abu Saber stressed that they didn't want to help with just words, they would photocopy John's picture and distribute it among their fighters and friends in other militias and let us know if anything came of it. Habib said we should keep pressing everyone for help, particularly Jalloud, and insisted that John's case was important. 'One innocent life lost,' he said, 'betrays the whole point of what we are fighting for.' It had been worth coming all this way just to hear that.

By Christmas Eve we had been in Damascus a week and I awoke to find the Sheraton buzzing with the news that a French hostage was going to be released as a goodwill Christmas gesture. Downstairs in the lobby the names McCarthy and Collett kept appearing on the AP newswire, but it was garbled and neither Nick nor I could make out what was happening. Eventually it transpired that the British chargé d'affaires in Beirut had made a Christmas appeal for information about the hostages. I felt a rush of anger at Britain's helplessness; all we could do was issue unanswered appeals while the French were getting their hostages out one by one. Auriel Cornea was released in Beirut that day, leaving Jean-Louis Normandin as the only French hostage held by the Revolutionary Justice Organization and the other four with Islamic Jihad.

We decided that now was a good time to leave. We had seen everyone we were going to see. I was glad to be there for Christmas, though. It meant I could still pretend that normal life was suspended, that time wasn't really passing. On Christmas Day we shopped for presents in the souk, took some photographs and raised a glass to John. As we left the hotel for the airport Marwan appeared from nowhere again and introduced us to a stocky, tough-looking man of about thirty-two, wearing an expensive leather jacket. Tony Touma was there, too, and he explained what we were doing in Damascus. We gave the man some photographs of John, but I couldn't think where I'd heard his name before. As we drove away Nick reminded me. Elie Hobeika was the leader of the Phalange militia reported to have carried out the massacres of hundreds of Palestinians in the refugee camps of Sabra and Chatila.

We flew back from Cyprus on New Year's Day. The journalists there told us that we had not done badly as innocents abroad, but I despaired when I thought of how many times all those people would need reminding that they had said they would help. We had handed out photographs of John to everybody we met, and reminded them of his situation. It still didn't seem nearly enough. Compared with the all-out effort I thought the Government was making, our visit was just a drop in the ocean. What worried me more, though, was that no-one we met had indicated that they had been asked about John before, let alone been shown his photograph. The Australian ambassador, who had represented Britain's interests in Syria since the break in relations, wanted to help, but said he had been told by London that he could not interfere. The Englishman who ran the British Interests Section at the Australian Embassy also said he wanted to be of assistance, but had little information and very few contacts. I had a nagging suspicion that the British government lacked the will to do anything for the hostages. The Australians had been told to do nothing, the Syrians hadn't been approached. What was going on? As we neared London I suddenly realized that all our meetings had been conducted on the assumption that John was alive. No-one had said that he was dead nor had they been in the least surprised that we hadn't yet heard from the kidnappers. John was a Westerner, a valuable pawn in someone's hands. If he had been killed, they would have known about it. I held on to that news. We might not have found John, but we had found another reason to believe he was alive.

Arriving in London I knew we had returned to the waiting. The past year had been a series of disjointed events; there had never been any feeling of momentum, never any sign that John might soon be released. Our only real hope now was Terry Waite who was due to return to Lebanon any day to continue his negotiations. In mid-January, a few days after he arrived, Nick called me to say that the journalists in Lebanon had heard John was about to be released. I sat by the phone and the TV all day, watching Waite as he announced that John's family shouldn't be dismayed, and in the evening Mary, Nick, Brian and I waited for some news.

The following day, at work, a reporter turned up at WTN saying he had some news for me. He'd heard that John was with Abu Nidal and what did I think about it? I asked him where he'd got his information from and he replied, 'Our man in Beirut.' Nick, who was standing there glowering at the man, asked who that was. 'Well, an Arab man,' said the hapless reporter, 'and if you give us an interview we could pay for a nice holiday for you and John when he gets back.' That was too much for Nick, he advanced on the man and sent him packing, furious at such insensitivity. The incident did nothing to calm us down. The teletext service Oracle was reporting that Waite had met John's kidnappers and knew where he was; Roby slapped Nick on the back and said he'd confirmed the story from another anonymous source. I had been sceptical at first, but now I started to believe it was true and felt like celebrating. Even if John wasn't released immediately, he was as good as home now that Waite knew where he was. I went out and bought John some new socks and underwear to add to the case of clothes I'd packed for him the day before.

A few days later, with our expectations at fever pitch, Terry Waite dropped out of sight to continue his negotiations. I was at work when news came through from the BBC that he was coming out with two Americans and one Briton; they were in the American Embassy in East Beirut. Roby called me over and said, 'Those who know are expecting Waite to come out with two Americans and John, but until they cross the Green Line no-one will know.' My mind was in absolute turmoil, but there was still nothing concrete to go on. Over the road in the pub that evening, I waited for news with Chris Pearson, Brad, MacNish – just as I had nine months earlier. The atmosphere, tense and expectant, was exactly the same.

Then, on 30 January, just as I had finished watching the 9 o'Clock News through to the end and learned nothing more, the newsreader said, 'News just in. Terry Waite has been kidnapped. A senior Moslem official who refused to be identified says that Waite has joined the list of hostages and was kidnapped ten days ago.' I stared at the screen, barely taking in the next few lines about how the phone call he received was a hoax and the rumours that he had taken two million dollars to free Jacobsen on his last trip to Lebanon.

I couldn't believe Waite had been kidnapped. Surely it was another false rumour, just like all the others we'd heard over the past week. But somehow it had the ring of truth about it. And when another few days went by, then a week, I began to realize what it meant. Waite had been the one person who offered any hope and now he was gone. No-one knew what he had managed to find out about John's kidnappers, and Roby now doubted that he had discovered anything at all. More hostages, Americans and French, had been kidnapped while we'd been hoping for John's release, and several of them had been threatened with execution, their kidnappers releasing photographs of one with guns pointing at his head. The Americans were threatening to bomb Lebanon if the hostages were harmed, and Ali Akbar Hashemi Rafsanjani, the Speaker of the Iranian Parliament, had revealed yet more details about the arms deal. What was going on? No-one seemed to be able to explain or to offer any hope.

What on earth would happen now?

At first I told myself that Waite's abduction had to change things. He was a national hero; the Government would have to get him out.

It didn't take me long to realize that I was completely wrong. Waite's kidnappers said nothing, giving the press nothing to report and the public no reminders that he, too, was in such a terrible position. When the Foreign Office put out a statement saying that it had warned Waite not to go to Beirut and it was discovered that he'd left instructions for no ransoms to be paid for his release, I had the awful feeling that there was going to be no public outcry after all, at least not a sustained one. I worried that Waite now looked like a fool and willing martyr and that the Government would prefer to distance itself from him rather than become embroiled in Irangate. After the initial shock of his abduction, the only headlines that consistently appeared were sensationalist: 'Waite shot whilst trying to escape' or, 'Waite faces death sentence'. It wasn't the reasoned analysis of government policy that I'd expected.

That policy had been spelled out to me by Roby shortly after John's kidnap. He had been in complete agreement with it and even though it had filled me with despair I had found it impossible to argue against. 'The Government's position is that it can't do a deal with terrorists to secure the release of British citizens held hostage,' Roby had said. 'The thinking is that if the Government did negotiate the release of a Brit, it would mean that more people would be taken hostage, and I have to say I agree, they just can't allow that to happen.' 'No, I realize that,' I had said, my heart sinking. Personally, I would have done just about anything to get John home, but I wouldn't have wished his experience on anyone else in a million years.

The policy's supposed pay-off was that the kidnappers would be made to see that abducting British people didn't pay and when they understood that John was of no value to them, they would then release him. It had sounded reasonable enough at the time, but I worried that the kidnappers were not the kind of people who would accept moral lessons from the British, and that even if they did decide that kidnapping Britons wasn't worth their while, they would not release John but kill him.

I couldn't understand why, after all this time, the behind-the-scenes diplomacy hadn't produced anything. I began to telephone the FO for news myself and I got on fairly well with Tim Gurney, a junior member of the Security Co-ordination team handling John's case. He was a pleasant man and our conversations were always amicable, but they never failed to leave me feeling discouraged and more depressed. 'Nothing much to report, I'm afraid,' Tim would say, apologetically, when I rang. I began to go in to see him occasionally and he would outline what else was happening in Lebanon, a summary which told me nothing more, and probably less, than I already knew from reading Robert Fisk in *The Times*.

Nor did the FO want publicity. Their argument, endorsed by Roby, was that it would increase the price on John's head. I wasn't at all sure they were right. I wondered if it were time to speak out and at night arguments for and against publicity would march relentlessly back and forth in my head. What must John be thinking of us, letting him stay wherever he was for so long, to endure unimaginable horrors? Would we make life worse for him by making his case public? Was it better to make him more valuable to the kidnappers, or worse?

I talked it through with Nick, but we always came back to the same thing: we simply didn't know. There were no guidelines, no rule book to follow.

Of one thing I was certain, in ten months nobody had yet discovered anything concrete about John. All the behind-the-scenes diplomacy had produced nothing. Nobody had any idea who held him and nobody could even tell me whether he was alive or dead. I was tired of people saying, 'Don't worry, he must be released soon,' or, 'I'm sure there'll be news soon.' 'Why?' I would think, 'why "must" it be over soon? What is there to make anyone think that he'll be released soon?' More and more I wondered if my colleagues were right – the main thrust of the policy being pursued by WTN and the FO was to wait: for the kidnappers to get in touch; for the other side to make the first move. But during all that waiting, winter was turning into spring.

Chris, Nick and I decided to make a few attempts at publicity. It was a huge step, but if we kept it fairly low-key and uncritical of the Government, I didn't see that it could encourage the kidnappers to think they had someone important. We just wanted people to be aware of John's situation. Besides, the main hope was that John might hear of it and be encouraged by it.

In February I read on the AP wires that it was Terry Anderson's six hundredth day in captivity and realized that the media liked round figures. It was as if they had a special significance that 438 or 599 days might lack. I counted up the number of days that John had been missing and worked out that in a few days' time it would be 300. It was an ideal opportunity to interest the press in the fact that John was still a hostage and to make an appeal to the kidnappers.

I telephoned Pat McCarthy to ask his opinion. Pat had complete trust in the FO and I didn't think he would agree to the idea of any publicity, however low-key, but, to my surprise and relief, he did. 'Good idea, Jill,' he said. 'I don't think there's any harm in that at all.'

On 10 February Chris Pearson and Nick met me in the Russell Hotel outside the room that they had booked for the press conference from where we were to broadcast our appeal. I peered in through the door. It was the first press conference I had attended and I marvelled at how professional it all looked. It could almost be real. At the far end of the room was a table and two chairs for Chris and myself. A jug of water and two glasses were waiting for us. Facing us were rows and rows of plastic chairs, where waiting journalists chatted to one another and photographers unpacked their equipment.

As a result of Waite's recent abduction, hostages were newsworthy again, and we had attracted a fair crowd. I was sure that I was going to be rendered speechless with fear as we took our seats. Chris read out our appeal to John's kidnappers to make contact. When he had finished he added, 'OK, now we'll answer any questions you have for Jill and myself.'

No-one spoke.

We waited, and still no-one spoke. I felt my fear giving way to panic: they were not interested in what we had to say, they were all going to get up and walk out and that would be that. In fact the journalists were keeping quiet because they all wanted to do their own individual interviews, and for the next hour and a half I answered the same questions over and over again about the circumstances of John's abduction, how the Government was doing all it could but perhaps needed a bit of help, and, in addition, something I hadn't really been prepared for, the details of my relationship with John. How long had we been going out together? Were we engaged? How had I felt over the past ten months? How did I know he was alive? I answered as best I could but went back to work feeling drained. It was as if I'd given away something precious and vital.

As I watched our press conference appear on the television news, I felt quite numb. The feeling stayed with me as I read about it in the papers the following morning. 'Let my love go, girl begs kidnappers' said one headline. It was strange, as if they weren't talking about John and me, but about characters in a story. At least, though, people reading the papers would now remember that Britain had hostages as well. I felt sure that if only they knew about them they would care, and that if John remained alive in people's memories it would somehow help him to survive – wherever he was and whoever he was with.

Months before, in Belfast, Brian Keenan's sisters had also decided to talk to the press. They now rang me to say that they were coming to London to appear on *Day to Day*, a BBC programme hosted by Robert Kilroy-Silk; its subject was the British hostages and they thought I, too, should appear. Apart from anything else, it would be a good chance to meet up for the first time.

We had made contact after I read an article about Brian and his family in *City Limits* and it had been such a relief to talk, even only on the telephone, to people who were going through the same experience and feeling the same frustrations. We discovered that we were all following the same tiring route, trying to find out as much as we could about Lebanon from books and newspapers and attempting to prise information from the various authorities with a marked lack of success. As representatives of Brian's family, Brenda and Elaine were talking directly to the Irish FO, and while I envied their status, I thought my difficulties paled in comparison with the extra anxiety and tensions of living in Belfast. The Keenans were Protestants, but Brian had chosen to travel on an Irish passport, which some Loyalists would regard as treachery. In publicizing his plight, Brenda and Elaine were potentially making themselves political targets.

When we met in the BBC studio for the *Day to Day* recording, there wasn't much time to chat and I was terribly nervous. We were seated on the front row of the studio panel, on either side of two former representatives of the British government, Lord Chalfont, an ex-foreign office minister, and Sir David Roberts, an ex-ambassador to Lebanon. Also taking part were people with various experiences of the Middle East, along with members of the public. As the discussion warmed up I almost forgot that the cameras were there.

What struck me most about that programme was how much ignorance and hostility there was to overcome. 'They should never have been out there in the first place,' said one chap. 'It's easy to deal with these terrorists,' said another, 'you just blow them out of the sky and sacrifice the hostages for the world to come.'

I could understand why people felt like that, but I was astonished when Lord Chalfont adopted much the same position. 'There aren't going to be any deals, ever,' he lectured the panel, wagging his finger at the rest of the guests, 'and I also want to make it clear to the terrorists that they are not as secure as they may think – sooner or later somebody will find a way of dealing with them and dealing with them in a tough, draconian and military way. When we find that that can be done effectively and successfully, it will be done.'

I was shaking with anger. Here was someone who had been in government, had considerable political influence and he was advocating bombing the kidnappers. What about the hostages, I thought, are they to have no rights in all this?

The experience had made me more determined to aim for regular, low-key publicity, but I realized that Lord Chalfont had dealt quite cleverly with the sympathetic reaction Brian's sisters and I would, as friends and relatives of the victims, naturally provoke on television. He'd said that although he felt moved by our position he still believed that there should be a tough response to the kidnappers otherwise we would have 'more emotionally disturbed people like these' around. Elaine's arguments had not been put emotionally at all. She had just pointed out that there was a difference between trading and negotiating: 'one's selling arms, the other's sitting down and working things out.' I had tried to express my alarm at hearing Chalfont talk of military measures when what was needed was communication, not bombs, but had felt myself getting too angry to think. We were being patted on the head, the emotional relatives. However angry I might have been, I knew that we had to remain calm and rational in order to be taken seriously. The Government insisted that its policy was a straightforward 'no deals with terrorists' and I could see that that sounded good, appealed to people, and had its merits. But I had learned more over the past ten months and was more confident that my own opinions were valid. No-one was asking the Government to do a deal. All we wanted to ensure was that it also looked for alternative ways of finding a solution that would bring the hostages home. They were British citizens and their rights as such should not be ignored.

Sometimes it seemed as if the friends and relatives of the hostages were the only people who cared and it was a relief for me to appreciate that Brenda and Elaine felt the same way. When I talked to them I stopped feeling like a freak; they knew what it was like to live without knowing whether someone you loved was dead or alive. They recognized the highs and lows; the feeling of constant tension; the way we functioned on two different levels, our minds on events in Lebanon, but still leading everyday lives.

We were living in limbo. Time had both stopped and started the previous April. Everything important since then seemed to refer to John's kidnap in some way. Each day since had only been marking time. There had been no death to mourn or rage against, no painful process of slowly consigning someone to memory; but neither had there been a way of picking up the pieces and moving on.

It was this limbo that I recognized in Brenda and Elaine even though I couldn't have articulated it at the time. Fate had thrown us together and I grew to like them. They were honest, direct and determined, and always ready for a laugh, even when their strong Belfast accents sometimes left me unsure as to what the joke was. They were certainly more confrontational in their dealings with the Irish Foreign Office than I would have dreamed of being when dealing with the mandarins at King Charles Street. Elaine, in particular, seemed quite tough, learning fast and seldom betraying her feelings about Brian. I wondered more and more what kind of person he was, and if John and he were together, whether they got on. I couldn't gain much of an impression of his personality from his sisters. Gina Filose once asked them with all the experienced, sympathetic air of the social worker that she is, what Brian was like. 'He likes a drink,' said Elaine. 'But what's he really like?' Gina persisted. 'He's a dirty pig!' said Brenda, and the two sisters killed themselves laughing, leaving our imaginations to fill in the rest.

For Brenda and Elaine, there had been a strong indication that Brian was alive the previous November, when the eighty-one-year-old French hostage, Camille Sontag, was released after four months in captivity. As television cameras were thrust in his face in Damascus, Sontag had told the world that a fellow hostage had handed him a note on which was written: 'I am Irish. Please tell my family.' There was only one hostage whom it could be. The news was a huge breakthrough for Brian's family and I drew immense comfort from it as well. If, despite the kidnapper's silence, Brian was alive, then it strengthened my hope that John might be too. When it was discovered that Sontag did not actually have the note, and had been without his glasses and hearing-aid, I heard via Roby that the general belief in London was that Sontag was confused and unreliable witness. It was so frustrating. The FO seemed quick to pour scorn on any indication that the hostages were alive. The First Secretary at the Irish Embassy, John Rowan, had spoken to the French FO and believed from what Sontag had said that Brian was alive. Why couldn't the British believe it as well?

I learned about Sontag's imprisonment from Brenda and Elaine. When representatives of the Irish FO and a friend of Brian's went to see Sontag, Brenda and Elaine had sent me copies of their notes and from them I had learned much more about the Frenchman's experience. He had been held by the Revolutionary Justice Organization. Although his gaol was underground, it had been something of a model prison, with good physical conditions. The cells were very small, but clean, and there was a shower; the food wasn't good, but there was enough to eat. It was reassuring to learn that Sontag hadn't been transported around in the horrific way that Jacobsen and Jenco had spoken of only recently on television. Perhaps not all the hostages were being treated in the way they described: being taped up like dummies and slid under lorries in containers that were little more than coffins. The thought of John going through that was unbearable. I found it impossible even to begin to imagine how Jacobsen and Jenco had coped with it physically, let alone mentally, but I held on to the fact that they were alive; they had survived the torture and they had been released. Again I felt relief that their captors, Islamic Jihad, were not holding John.

Brenda's and Elaine's notes told me that Sontag had managed to communicate with the person in the opposite cell by hand-signals; conversation between the prisoners had been forbidden, but the man had indicated that he had been held for five months. Sontag had seen him in September 1986, which meant he had been kidnapped in April which was when Keenan disappeared. When the man realized that Sontag was deaf and had bad eyesight, he had held up a note indicating that he was Irish. This Irishman had an outgoing personality and a good relationship with the guards, some of whom would lie outside his door while he taught them a few words of English. His health and spirits were good, he had demonstrated a 'certain kind of humour' and he had done his best to communicate with other prisoners when he could. The slit in the cell doors had only allowed Sontag to see the Irishman's lower forehead, eyes and upper nose, but when the man was taken out of his cell to go to the bathroom, he had managed to get a better look at him even though the blindfolds which the prisoners were forced to wear had obscured his view.

Sontag's descriptions of this man had convinced the Irish government that he was Keenan. The Frenchman hadn't identified him from any photographs which he was subsequently shown, but the Irish diplomat who had spoken to him said that his account of his captivity was consistent and coherent and that neither his age nor his ordeal had made his testimony unreliable. The Irish FO's assessment to Brenda and Elaine was that Brian was alive, and possibly being held by the same group, the Revolutionary Justice Organization, which had held Sontag. The notes said that the Irish had been in contact with groups close to the RJO as well as the Iranian and Syrian governments. Their positive attitude made me despair once again at the prevailing feeling at the FO and WTN that Sontag's evidence was unreliable and told us nothing. Why did they have to be so negative? What if John had been in one of those cells, too, for nearly a year now?

When Brenda and Elaine rang in early March to suggest that I join them on a trip to Paris to see Sontag and find out more, I jumped at the chance. We were to be looked after by Joelle Kauffman, the wife of one of the French hostages, whom I had seen on TV and admired for her fighting stance. Once in Paris I felt a surge of happiness at being there, but it wasn't simply the fact that the city looked beautiful bathed in winter sunshine. After being in France for a short time, I realized that it was the relief of visiting a country where the hostages were a big issue. The group campaigning for their release had a boat moored on the Seine on which a painted slogan acted as a daily reminder to people not to forget them. I was amazed that no-one needed to explain to the French to which hostages the slogan referred; everyone already knew. Every night the main TV news bulletin was preceded by their photographs as the newsreader read out the number of days each hostage had been held. I realized that here it was normal to believe it was the Government's duty to get them released; normal for the subject to be discussed at great length in the newspapers; normal for everyone to believe that the Government should be exploring all the possibilities available to them to get the hostages home.

Joelle was an elegant, competent woman whom I liked straightaway. Jean-Paul had been held captive for two years by then and she had become convinced that the Government wouldn't do anything unless pressured into it by the French people. Again, I experienced relief at meeting someone else in the same situation. I had expected Joelle to be terrifying but I felt at ease with her almost immediately. I admired her and was encouraged by her fighting stance, as well as by her concern for Brenda, Elaine and me. I had never been so glad that I had studied French and could talk to her and other people she arranged for us all to meet, one of whom was the former hostage, Philippe Rochot, who'd also been held by the Revolutionary Justice Organization.

Rochot had been released in June 1986 having been held for just a few months and was now back at work at Antenne 2, one of the French television networks. Now, nine months after his release, nothing about his physical appearance or bearing indicated what he had been through. He was anxious to help and told us that the conditions had been bearable and that he had not been harmed in any way. I seized on the fact that Rochot's captivity had lasted such a short time; it made the prospect of Brian and John soon being released seem that much more likely.

Rochot had been held in apartments for most of his captivity and his experience seemed to have differed enormously from that of Sontag and of the Americans, Fr Jenco and David Jacobsen. I'd managed to speak to Jacobsen in London and he had spoken of the same underground cell block that Sontag had described. He thought that several of the American hostages and possibly the French were there too. It struck me as strange that, although these men were being held by different groups, they were all living in the same place. But he hadn't seen or heard of any Englishmen, so it still shed no further light on what had happened to John. Jacobsen had seemed very angry, agitated and intent on persuading the State Department to rescue the hostages by military means; I learned more about which areas of the prison were vulnerable to attack from the outside than of the actual conditions. He didn't seem to take into account the fact that the hostages would almost certainly be killed in any rescue attempt. Listening to him I hoped that the State Department didn't take any notice of his ideas.

In Paris, Brenda, Elaine and I had hoped to meet Sontag to find out more about the prison and what exactly he had seen, but to our disappointment we found, on arriving in Paris, that he had just left for his home in the South of France. It was hundreds of miles away and we didn't have time to follow him. I telephoned him but his deafness made communication impossible. I shouted down the line to Antibes that I would write to him instead. Months later, Sontag wrote back and threw everything into confusion yet again.

I had sent him photographs of John as well as some of Brian, and after looking at them Sontag wrote that John corresponded exactly to the man he had seen in the opposite cell. He had never identified Brian from any of the photographs which had been shown to him and now he was saying it was John he had seen! The 'Irishman', he wrote, didn't have fluffy hair like Brian's, but thin, smooth, neat dark brown hair combed from right to left like John's; he didn't have a broad face like Brian's, but an oval, slightly elongated face like John's; he didn't have powerful shoulders like Brian's, but was of a smaller build, like John. Nevertheless, Sontag said, this was the man who had held up the sign saying: I am Irish.

Was he an unreliable witness as the FO had thought? He could have gone slightly mad after what he had gone through, but from his letter it didn't seem likely; he sounded as if he was trying to be scrupulously honest about what he had seen and was as confused as I was to find out that the man he had seen wasn't Irish. He had even taken the time to draw a precise little plan of the layout of the prison, marking his own cell, Number 4, and that of the Irishman, Number 7. After a while, the man had been moved, when the block was being painted, and Sontag had never seen him again. He wrote:

Eight days later, believing that I was going to stay forever in the place, I was freed. I admit that I was the most surprised of anybody. I end this account knowing that you must have found it a little long and that you may find it wasn't exactly what you were expecting, but I hope to have been some use.

I put down the letter, moved by his kindness in replying in such detail, but baffled. It just didn't make sense. Why on earth would John hold up a sign saying: 'I am Irish'?

On our return from Paris, Chris was waiting at the airport, eager to hear the news. I was touched that he had come to meet us; it postponed the sinking feeling I experienced on landing in Britain, where, if they weren't American or French, hostages just weren't news. I showed Chris an article I'd read in a French current affairs magazine, called: 'Who to negotiate with, and how'. It attempted to trace the links between the kidnappers of the French hostages via various possible intermediaries to Iran. It was informative and sensibly argued, rather than sensational or moralistic. I had never read anything like it in the British press.

In France I had also learned that rumours about John were circulating in Beirut. A French journalist who still travelled in and out of Lebanon had told me that he had heard that John was alive. A doctor had apparently been taken in to see him, and the group holding John was thought to be Ahmed Jibril, a radical Palestinian group with links to Syria and Libya. I had been amazed. I had learned more over a cheese roll in a pavement café than I had from WTN and the FO over the past eleven months. I had phoned Pat, Nick and Chris from Paris to pass on the information, but when I passed on the news to Roby he said the information was old and had apparently already been rejected. It made me realize how little I was being told about what was going on and frustrated me even more. The rumour may have been just tittle-tattle, but it was precious all the same; even rubbish has currency when you have nothing to go on.

The only people in whom I could confide and trust were my friends and those of John's that I now knew that much better. Mary was still my mainstay. Before the trip to Paris I had had a severe attack of nerves and was on the point of backing out when Mary dropped all her plans for the weekend and came with me. She was conscious of my fears and frustrations about what was being done for John and understood how difficult I found it to decide how best to proceed. Nearly a year of behind-the-scenes activity had produced nothing. I was becoming more and more doubtful about the effectiveness of government policy, of the efforts that were being made to find John and the advice that publicity would be harmful. I remembered how much happiness John had given me and how much I owed him. I felt the need to do something, anything, rather than just continue to wait for news. If I were kidnapped, I'd be frightened and would be hoping against hope that someone back home was doing something to get me out. If the FO and WTN were just waiting for news, it wasn't good enough; John needed – deserved – more.

5
Lebanon, November 1986–April 1988

A week after David Jacobsen's release Tom Sutherland signalled that he'd seen Camille Sontag and that the old fellow had shown him a broken set of false teeth. A few days after this we anticipated that something was about to happen as the place was busy with guards. We were conscious that Sontag had been taken out, dressed. He didn't return. After two days Brian and I toasted the old man, hoping that he would be fulfilling our fantasy of him downing brimming bowls of champagne and charming the ladies. We wondered if he'd broken his teeth on purpose; we liked to think so.

In the last few weeks before his release he'd started talking to himself quite loudly. Sometimes he'd just keep repeating, 'Yeah, yeah, yeah,' as if listening to a friend speaking or, more likely, looking back over his life and remembering things with the clarity and resolution that solitary confinement allows. The guards would tell him to stop the noise, but it seemed to amuse them and we'd hear them imitating him. A few days after his departure Mahmoud and Ali were playing dominoes with us, when another guard appeared doing the 'Yeah, yeah, yeah' routine. I picked it up. The guards fell silent. 'What happened to that man, Mahmoud?' I asked.

'He has gone home.'

'Was he sick?'

'No, but I think he loses his mind. He is very old man, more than eighty years.'

'He must have been a very bad man, Mahmoud, for you to keep him here when he is so old.'

'No, I think he is good man.'

I said no more, Brian remained silent. As Mahmoud thought over what we'd said we could sense his guilt, his uneasy awareness of what he was doing to innocent people. But my tone hadn't been angry, my words not deliberately critical, so he had nothing to vent his confusion on. After a few moments he left with his friends, unable to cope with the living, blindfolded evidence of his actions. He wanted to pull down the blindfold on his conscience. Within minutes the television was blaring in the guards' room and we could hear the shouts and thumps as they practised their karate and avoided thinking.

Over the years we found that this was the standard response to our condemnations of their work. Often they'd say, 'We same as you, we stay here all day and night.'

'Yes, we know that, but after a few days you will go home to your families, you will see the sky, walk down a street and meet your friends.' They would become uncomfortable and we could feel their need to escape us, their conscience. They didn't want to think. When we pushed them a little more: 'Why are we here? Why do you do this to us?' they'd say, 'I'm sorry, it is not my business, I do not like but I have orders.'

'But you choose to accept those orders, you can walk out of here now and go home and do another job, no-one is forcing you to stay here.'

For them, that was the real rub. They wanted to believe that they were doing God's work, wanted to believe that their leaders were right and so be free themselves of any responsibility. We were forcing them to accept it. They couldn't face it. Sometimes they became angry through their frustration and fear of thinking. More often they'd just get up and leave quietly, maybe returning later with a cup of coffee and biscuits to make amends.

For me these exchanges were a reflection of my own development. As I realized freedom means making choices, I also realized that like Brian, I, too, had to demand an explanation of the guards' use and abuse of freedom.

We could understand the difficulties that they had in dealing with our arguments. They'd spent all their adult lives dominated by the trauma of civil war, in an atmosphere of fear and mistrust, with their war lords claiming not only military and political might, but also the power of God's direct support. It was easier for our captors not to think. They had little education, never read a book, read only the party newspapers and the Koran which they interpreted as instructed by their radical clerics. The hints we gave them frightened them. We told them that they had to make their own decisions. They hadn't thought for themselves for so long and were now so vulnerable to their masters that they couldn't break out of their sad mould.

Terry Anderson had now been moved to the other side of our cell, where Sontag had been. Frank Reed was moved into Terry's place next to the guards' room. Terry could now talk freely with his hands to Tom, and through Tom to us. One day after the guards had been in our cell playing dominoes, Terry joked, 'Haven't you heard the old maxim that a man is known by the company he keeps?' Through Tom, I replied, 'Don't you mean a man is known by the company that keeps him?' We could have ignored the guards' efforts at friendship, and often did, but it was too difficult to be against them all the time.

On 27 November, my birthday, Sayeed took me across to a small cell, where he asked me many questions. Who did I know in Lebanon? Who had I met? I gave him some names, those people I worked with whose names his organization would already have. He was particularly keen on hearing the names of other Britons. I was careful to give only one or two who had left Beirut for good before my kidnap. 'Who else, who else?' I told him about John Gray, the ambassador. 'Yes, yes, we know him. Who else, who else?' I made up a couple of good English names and pointed out that I'd only been in the country a month before I had been kidnapped.

Then he wanted to know where I'd worked, what I'd done, all the countries I'd visited. I quickly rattled off the

European countries where I'd been on holiday, telling him that Lebanon was the only place in which I'd worked apart from England and that no, I'd never been to the US. I tried to give him information that could be easily confirmed at home should it be used to back up any demands for my release, but not to give him the names of anyone who might still be vulnerable in Beirut or details that might arouse suspicions against me. It certainly wasn't a heavy interrogation, nor indeed a very competent one, and, although I had felt very wary throughout, I was relieved that something seemed to be happening.

Brian went through the same rigmarole and we exchanged notes with Tom and Terry. Frank tried to talk to us by tapping out words on the wall between us. The only letters I got were CIA and KILL. Clearly Sayeed's cack-handed questioning had shocked him badly. For some time before his move into Terry's old cell, Frank had been signalling to me that he was about to go home or that the guards were talking about him or that when he'd heard them praying outside his cell it meant they were going to kill him. I'd tried to calm him down, saying that the guards were there because they were decorating their room which was filthy. He couldn't take it in.

We all took fright at odd things and developed scenarios that would explain them. But we could share those ideas, argue about them and then put them in proper perspective. Frank had had no chance to have his ideas, born of stress, tested among friends as the rest of us had. His imaginings became facts, the consequence of unavoidable neurosis.

Now we heard him speaking to friends in the world outside. We heard him calling on God, using some of the Arabic words of Moslem prayer, then asking, 'God, don't these people know that I am one of the greatest educators in the world?' Our hearts went out to him, but he frightened us. The likely wrath of the guards paled beside the appalling idea that we might lose our minds.

Against the background of Frank's apparent crack-up Brian and I remained on good terms with the guards. The day after the interrogation, Ali came in and gave me a pair of pyjamas. I put them on, then he sprinkled perfume over me and led me out with Bri to the guards' room. He sat us down on the floor with Ayeesa, Sayeed and the others. He raised my blindfold a little to show me the spread of cakes, fruit and sweets. 'This is Happy Birthday for you.'

I was flabbergasted. I'd hoped yet dreaded that they wanted me to make a video. Why else would they be dressing me up? We knew that Anderson had been photographed with a birthday cake and shown a video of his little daughter Sulome, born since his kidnap. But this was just a party. The guards made a dreadful racket, singing 'Happy Birthday' with Brian. It was extraordinary that they enforced quietness at all times so that the hostages in their cells shouldn't hear one another yet now they were bellowing an English song with an Irish baritone flowing free over the top of them. Then Brian explained that it was a tradition in Ireland for the birthday guest to make a speech. Sayeed therefore called on me to make one.

'Well, I'd like to thank you all for having a party for me. I wish I could thank you face to face. I have only ever seen your feet, but they look like good feet and I hope you are good men and that this will be the only birthday where we have to sit like this unable to look at each other properly.'

Sayeed translated rapidly for his friends and they applauded. He then said that they were all very sorry for keeping us in this place but that we would be going home soon and that they hoped we wouldn't think badly of them. I didn't know what to think. It was just so odd.

Back in the cell I asked Brian what he had made of it all. He thought that it was a mixture of guilt and genuine affection. They wanted us to like them. The next day, Anderson sent a tiny, elegantly wrapped package via the bathroom. A Panadol: *'To help you get over the hangover from your party.'*

Not long after my birthday, very, very early one morning we heard Frank banging on his door. No guards came; they must have been sleeping upstairs somewhere. After an eternity we realized that Frank had got out of his cell. He was walking around calling out, 'Don't you guys worry, I'm going home today, but you'll be out very soon.' I was terrified. He came close to our door: 'You guys awake in there? Don't worry, it'll be over soon, I'll tell Thatcher to get you out.'

Brian and I lay quite still, fearing that any movement would encourage him to talk more, to try to get in with us. He started banging on the iron door to the guards' room. We heard the sounds of metal on metal and guessed that he must be trying to prise the door open. I listened with horrified fascination, reminded of the man in the first prison. But that man had worked quietly, carefully, not shouting out loud. The door refused to move. Frank then started yelling at the guards, 'Hurry up, hurry up, yesterday you said tomorrow, now it's today. Hurry up, bring me my clothes.' He carried on for a while, then went back into his cell.

A little later Mustafa and Safi came down to give us breakfast. All proceeded quietly. They seemed to miss the fact that Frank's door couldn't have been properly locked. Then, suddenly, the place was full of guards. Our door burst open, someone grabbed me and dragged me out and down to a bright light at the end of the block. They looked at my hands, then hauled me straight back and threw me on the floor. Brian was pulled out and back again. We heard the occupants of the other cells being subjected to the same thing. Then we heard Frank in the guards' room. A man was shouting at him, 'Who you talk to?'

'No-one, no-one!' Then came the appalling thud of a heavy blow.

'Who you talk to – who?'

'No-one, I promise you.' More blows and Frank was dragged past us into one of the tiny cells at the end of the block.

We knew we would be interrogated. We knew that they knew we must have heard what had happened. Brian and I quickly agreed to say that we had heard what we thought was a madman raving in his room. We'd heard someone banging on his door and shouting but couldn't understand much. That way we felt we would seem honest and that they might treat Frank more gently if we convinced them he had lost his mind.

After an hour or two of intense nervous anticipation I was taken to the small cell off the guards' room. It was full of men. I was told to sit on a small stool. A man sat right in front of me. Sayeed told me this was a big chief and that I must tell the truth or there would be big trouble. They said they knew I was a good man and that if I helped them they would help me. I was breathing heavily, trying to keep calm. They asked what was wrong. I said I was very scared.

'Why you scared?'

'I'm scared of everything in this place, it is a bad place.'

'Don't be scared. Did you hear banging?'

'Yes, it sounded like a man banging on his door for help.'

'He was shouting. What did he say to you?'

'He didn't speak to us. It was hard to understand. I think he was praying and shouting for you.'

'Talking to us, why?'

I told them what he had said. The details about 'Yesterday you said, now it's tomorrow' took a while to translate, but in the end seemed to satisfy them that I was co-operating. When they asked again if he had talked to us or the others or if he had attacked the door with a crowbar I could lie confidently that it had never happened. They seemed to believe me and I said that it was very sad that a man had gone crazy in this place, that I was worried I, too, would lose my mind. I asked them when I would be going home. I knew that now of all times they wouldn't talk to me, but wanted to convince them that the situation was as simple and sorry as I'd explained it, that it was both nothing and finished. They seemed satisfied.

Then it was Brian's turn. He told the same tale as me and was clever enough to act his usual cocky self. When the boss told him that the man who tried to get out was dead, Brian said, 'I don't think so, there was no shot.'

'There are other ways to kill a man,' the chief answered as he put his hands round Brian's throat.

Then Terry and Tom were taken in. Terry had heard most of the commotion but Frank hadn't gone up to his cell, so he could truthfully say he'd heard some banging and voices but couldn't really hear anything because of the noise from the fans. Tom said the same, having in fact heard very little from his side of the block.

Things were quiet until late afternoon when we heard Franky shouting again. 'Hurry up, hurry up.' We sat rigid. No sound of blows. We couldn't tell if he were demanding his release or for the guards to get his execution over with. He probably didn't know either. We heard the guards rushing into his room and shouting, 'What, what?' Then we heard the sound of tape pulling. Were they tying him up? He must have been in an awful state – terrified enough to try escaping from that place, then taken right down into the darkest valley of fear in beaten failure.

Frank's breakdown and the brutal treatment he received made the prison into a complete hell. But this hell was freezing, the cold draining energies already sapped by fear. I shivered under my horse-blankets trying to decide if it wouldn't be better to let go, throw reason away and sit, foetal, untouched by anything.

Two days later Frank tried again. Ali opened his door to take him to the bathroom. Frank zoomed out. He only got as far as the stairs and was brought back by Ali and another man. We heard one or two blows then silence after they put him into the cell next to their room. He stayed there for a few days, then returned to the cell next to us. He didn't make any further escape attempts; indeed from what we could tell he was now refusing to go to the bathroom.

After that, things calmed down. In the month leading up to Christmas, Terry and Frank were moved around again, for no apparent reason. Then one day Sayeed came in with a newspaper. He told me it said that Jill and Nick Toksvig were going to Damascus. He quoted Jill saying, 'I just want to be as near John as possible for Christmas.' I was overjoyed. This was the first news we'd had of any friends or family. I was very proud that Jill should be taking such a trip for me and I couldn't help feeling that she must know something, that she wanted to be in Syria to meet me when I was released. We pestered Sayeed for more news. Would we be going home for Christmas? But all he would say was, 'You must pray very hard.'

After he'd gone I signalled the news to Tom saying, 'I think my relationship with Jill is about to become public property. The media will love having us running into each other's arms.' It felt very strange. We were both shy people and at work had kept our relationship low-key. I desperately wanted to think we'd be reunited soon but the atmosphere didn't bode well. I couldn't even come up with a 'magic day' by playing my silly numbers game.

The sense of unreality that the news of Jill brought was heightened between Christmas and New Year when Sayeed took us up to the guards' room. We sat down on a blanket facing a wall and were given tea and some nuts by Mustafa. When Sayeed told us to raise our blindfolds a little we saw a television. He played us a tape of the local news. My mother was making an appeal for my release. I heard only a few of her words before the Lebanese presenter blotted out her voice with an Arabic translation. Immediately it was over they put a war film in the video player for us. I could not tie all these things together. There we were sitting with armed guards behind us, watching a violent film, while the image and voice of my mother filled my mind as if from a dream.

As soon as the film ended Bri was taken back to the cell. When I turned to ask Sayeed to show me the news tape again he pushed his machine-pistol into my chest and fired it. Of course, the gun was unloaded although the jolt was heavy. I ignored it and continued to make my request, which was granted. Then Mustafa, one of the most considerate of all the guards, led me back to the cell with his arm round me.

Bri and I sat quietly. It was a huge relief for me to know that my mother was well. Her speech seemed a little slurred which worried me, but I thought perhaps she had taken a tranquilizer to bolster her for the ordeal of TV cameras. What really upset me was the fact that she, too, was blighted by this awful place. We had spoken often about our concerns for our mothers, realizing the horror they must be going through, but somehow we had hoped that they were untouched by the grim reality of the prison and that other distractions would help them. Seeing her there destroyed those hopes.

Brian gently brought me out of my depression. He teased me that he couldn't believe such a lovely woman could have a son like me.

'I always thought your mam was a lady from what you told me, but how could I trust anything you'd be saying?'

He sat, his face composed but his eyes burning, willing warmth back into me. 'Didn't you tell me, Johnny, that you all used to live in some Elizabethan manor? Was that where we saw her just now?'

'No, Bri, she was at the place they moved to after Broxted.'

'Oh aye, the Vicarage. Well, that's not too bad, a vicarage! And now that I've seen her myself I know she is a great lady, I'll call her the Dowager Duchess.'

He went on, saying he was looking forward to meeting the 'Duchess' and telling her the truth about her foul-mouthed offspring, how despite my innocent appearance she must realize that I was truly a 'wrong 'un' and that a spot of prison might be the making of me. He kept on until I could join in the light banter and detail fully the litany of faults I could draw to Mrs Keenan's attention.

By this time we'd talked so much about our families and friends that it was almost as if we could go out for an imaginary drink in London or Belfast and feel quite at home with the company, joining in the old jokes and discussing the latest career or social moves of people we had never actually met.

We might spend a morning with Buzz Logan and Jim McKilvenny in Belfast's Crown Bar with its preserved Victorian interior after having a huge fry-up breakfast with Brian's mother. We might go up to my parents' house for Sunday lunch after a late and drunken evening with my friends at The Crown and Sceptre pub near WTN's offices. We already loved each other so much that we couldn't wait to introduce one another to our friends in the flesh.

Having spoken so much and so intimately about our home circles we could include these people in our conversations so that if Brian was telling me a story I would say, 'No, I don't believe that, Elliot wouldn't say that.' Of course I'd never met Elliot, but he was a real person for me. Likewise, Brian loved my mother before he'd even seen her and delighted in the intimacy of being able to give her a nickname of his own.

When I told him that I had given Jill power of attorney before coming to Lebanon, so that she could buy a flat in a hurry if the right one turned up, he laughed and said, 'Well, boy, by now she'll have spent all your money on a Porsche and she'll be dripping diamonds.' From then to now he refers to Jill as 'Your woman, Dripping'.

I was happy that he teased me about Jill. He had seen pictures of her, but perhaps knew more from my talk of her. He would smile and nod when I spoke of our plans, sensing that whatever had happened to us, however long we might be separated, I had no doubts that she was the person with whom I would find the greatest possible joy.

During our captivity the guards might ask, 'You want us bring you girlfriend?' This was always posed as a naughty joke, but the idea of Jill having to be tainted by those foul dungeons was horrible. I didn't want her to see me like this. The thought of women being held in such conditions made me shudder with revulsion. I couldn't really imagine it, not so much because they wouldn't be able to handle it, rather that they simply wouldn't tolerate it. I have no idea how women would react in such situations but, because I felt awful accepting them, I wanted to think that they would have strengths we men appeared to lack.

There was more news in the New Year. Sayeed brought another newspaper and told us and the Yanks that Terry Waite was back in Beirut. He felt things were looking very good, especially for the Yanks. There was a report that the British ambassador was 'optimistic' and anyway Bri and I felt that if they let the Yanks go there would be no point in keeping us.

On 15 January the block was bustling. Tom, Frank and Terry were all taken into the guards' room for haircuts. Terry returned joyfully drumming on the wall between our cells. They were going home. The guards were getting shoes and clothes for them. This was it. That night they left.

Brian and I sat huddled together, straining to hear anything on the radio or TV. The guards had started nagging obsessively about the smallest noise, even the clack of dominoes. We assumed this was because there was now a new prisoner in the cell next to us. So when the power was off and all was silent we would barely mouth words straight into each other's ears.

One afternoon there was a sudden growl from the guards' room. Sayeed had woken up from his siesta. We heard him making a lot of noise as he loaded his Kalashnikov, then he came down into the block, stopping first with the man next door, then moving on to us. He didn't speak, just breathed very heavily. The atmosphere thickened. I felt the butt of his gun pressing down on my neck. Then he started clubbing my shoulders and arms. I was stunned by the attack, but more shocked that it didn't seem to hurt all that much. My initial fear diminished and I started wondering why he was beating me and what would happen next.

After what seemed like a hundred blows I thought to myself, 'OK, OK, you've made the point. Now if I've done wrong so has Brian, so why don't you go and give him a few, I'm done.' He did. He still hadn't spoken and when he stopped hitting Bri, he just stood there doing his breathing routine. He left, and we pulled up our blindfolds each asking, 'Are you OK?' We were both fine, but stunned and bruised. We could only guess that Sayeed had woken, heard whispering and, assuming we were talking to the man next door, had decided to punish us.

Almost immediately, Mustafa arrived with tea and sandwiches. I got the feeling that he wasn't happy with the beatings, but Sayeed was his boss, so there was nothing he could do, if in fact he did care. He took us both to the bathroom as normal. When we returned and the guards had gone, Brian raised his blindfold, smiled and said, 'It's a mighty powerful laxative, that beating.' 'You too!' I replied, laughing. But I was furious and still shocked. I'd started to ache, but the experience had been instructive. I'd always known that I might be beaten at any time, for no reason, but I hadn't realized that being battered with a rifle butt wasn't as horrific, of itself, as I had always thought it must be. Dimly my mind registered that a threatened beating was no reason not to stand one's ground.

The next day, the radio, as usual, was left hissing in the corridor. Suddenly, it tuned itself to an English-language station: 'There is still no news about Terry Waite, he has disappeared since he went to meet the kidnappers.' It was 25 January. Coming after Sayeed's attack it felt like the end. We tried to cheer ourselves up with theories that maybe this was all part of the release process, that he'd be coming round to see we were all right. But by now even my optimism had dried up. These people beat us up for no reason and now had snatched the only man whom we'd heard of who was trying to negotiate with them.

I wanted to believe that the beating had been a mistake, that they had some excuse for their behaviour, but

I couldn't come to terms with the way they thought. There had been small kindnesses – the birthday party, other moments – but now I couldn't escape the realization, long held but never so forcefully presented, that the guards could do anything they liked. There was no higher power, no avenue of appeal. They were free to abuse us at the slightest whim.

The day we heard the news about Waite, Abed Abdullah was back on duty. He had joined the team of guards in late November and spoke very good French, saying that his father taught it in school. He told us that his name meant he was the servant of God. He was a little creepy but eager to talk, bragging about being a regular member of one of the groups which made raids into the Israeli-occupied sector in the south. We took this with a pinch of salt. He was all piety and it sat uneasily with us. But, after the Yanks left, he spent more and more time with us, getting me to teach him English.

Although he hadn't been present on the day of the beating, he soon heard the news. He came in and inspected the bruises all over our arms. I was still so angry I kept asking in French, 'Why did this happen? Why? We have done no wrong. This a very bad thing for your friend to have done.' He said that he'd find out. I had no illusions on that score. I knew that despite his tales of bravado in the south he wasn't really a fighter, but a fraud, yet he was the only man (apart from Sayeed who was, unsurprisingly, staying away from us) to whom I could talk.

Any slight hope that Abed was at all sympathetic soon faded. He took Sayeed's action as *carte blanche* to follow suit. He allowed himself an *alter ego*. This creature spoke no French nor English, had a harsh voice and was brutal and stupid. Day after day, he would come into the cell, stand on our legs and put a gun to our heads. When he was bored with that he'd go and thump the other captives. It was an impossible situation. If we'd charged him directly with our certain knowledge that this 'new' man was he, he simply would have claimed that we'd been looking at him and have a high old time beating the hell out of us. He was a sick youth with too much power.

All optimism was dead. We were being persecuted by Abed; Waite had disappeared, probably for good; and the Yanks had gone somewhere that wasn't home. The strain was enormous. I'd lie there with the worry beads Abed had given me on one of his good days, not using them for prayer as a Moslem would, but more to help me concentrate on a sort of mantra. I'd click them through my fingers, repeating, 'My hope, my faith'. I was still uncertain what the 'ecstatic' experience I'd had in that first lonely cell had meant, but it had brought me back from the brink of total breakdown. I think I was now talking as much to my inner reserves, to Jill, to my family and friends, as to any God figure, trying to calm myself and rebuild my strength. Desperate to impose some control on my situation I reverted to the numbers game. Up came Monday, 16 February.

On Valentine's Day Mahmoud reappeared and came for a long chat. He told us it was his birthday. We congratulated him and explained that this was a special day back home for lovers. He liked the idea. He told us that he was now married and had twin boys. His reasonable attitude to criticism and open manner was always a breath of fresh air. It brought some sanity to the proceedings. Of course, he couldn't give us any news. 'I'm sorry I haven't got the order' was his standard reply, but he did at least sympathize with us and didn't revel in his power over us.

On the Sunday Mustafa gave us a haircut. While shaving my beard he nicked my chin – I gasped and couldn't help opening my eyes. He was smiling, saying he was sorry and I closed my eyes again; another second's glimpse of a normal man in a normal situation. Abed came around and took all our belongings, even the pyjamas and rough jerseys and blankets. He left one mattress.

We waited and waited, freezing, anxious about the move that was certain to come. There were still two other prisoners there. One we thought to be the Korean, the other we reckoned to be French or Belgian. Eventually Sayeed came. He gave us jerseys and shoes, then led us out of the cell block and into the back of a van. The other two prisoners didn't join us. Sayeed drove, while Abed and Mustafa travelled in the back with Bri and me. It was the first time we'd been above ground in six and a half months.

We drove for some fifteen minutes before stopping. There was some small arms fire near by and I guessed the delay was to ensure that we wouldn't get caught up in a situation where the van might be searched. It was so cold that my body ached and started going numb. Any movement prompted Abed to press a gun to my head, whispering, '*Doucement*'. Hours seemed to pass before Mahmoud slid open the door and handed in some of the inevitable cheese and jam sandwiches.

Eventually we moved again, driving down a road, then turning and pulling up. A guard walked beside me into a building. He had one arm wrapped tightly around me so that both my arms were pinned to my body. It was terrifying walking blindly, not knowing if I was about to fall down a staircase or drop through a trap door. I slipped a little in the shoes Sayeed had given me before leaving the prison. They were too big. Our blindfolds had been secured tightly, but mine had now eased a little so I could just see the ground around my feet.

We were in a lift. Abed was there gaily prodding us with his machine-pistol. Eventually we went up; how many floors I couldn't tell, but it took a while. Then we were bundled out, pushed up some stairs and into an apartment. Ayeesa and Mahmoud welcomed us like long lost friends. It was a huge relief to find them there; they had never hurt us. I begged a couple of cigarettes, then they left us.

As our eyes adjusted to the dark we realized that we were in a large room, with a carpet, on which all our stuff was neatly laid out. The windows were covered by metal sheets, but there were gaps around the sides and through them we could see the lights of Beirut. We were up in the land of the living; we could feel fresh, free air blowing on our cheeks; we could see signs of the real Lebanon and our hopes rose.

It was pure joy to feel safe from the psychotic Abed, to be in an apartment block, full of families doing normal things. I couldn't help grabbing at the most optimistic interpretations of the move. Having been brought to a much better place after the dreadful hiatus following the Yanks' move might mean that they were preparing us to go home. It had been a month since Terry Waite had gone missing, but we'd heard no more on the radio and hoped he might be free again and waiting for us.

The next day we realized that the Yanks were all in the room across the hall from us. Peeking through the keyhole as the guards took them food we counted three men. As I recognized Tom and Terry despite their blindfolds, the other had to be Frank. We couldn't see any way of communicating with them. To have left a message hidden in the bathroom would have been pointless without first warning them.

We walked for hours round the expanse of carpet, and I looked longingly through the cracks around the windows. I could see the apartment block across the road and peering down could see a woman in her yashmak, with a baby in her arms. In the early morning, after the dawn call for prayers, I'd often see a man on the building's roof throwing corn to the chickens he kept up there.

In the wall by my mattress I found a small hole drilled through to the outside. I couldn't imagine why it was there, but it gave me a view across a wide space to yet more blocks of flats and beyond them to the mountains. Judging by the movements of the sun we knew we were looking across Beirut to the Christian sector. Brian, who knew the city far better than I, felt sure we weren't in the southern suburbs, the stronghold of the Hezbollah and other extreme Shia groups, but in the heart of the city, close to the famous shopping street of Hamra. This, too, encouraged me to think we'd be off home soon, as did finding a small stash of dollars under the carpet.

I needed to take whatever good, hopeful impulses I could from any source. The sight of a person outside our situation, the sound of children's voices, light from the moon and sun coming in around the metal black-out – simple wonders – all encouraged me to hang on. Even the sound of battle helped – it made me realize yet again that there were people worse off than me. As I listened to the fighting I imagined families hugging together as they sheltered in the basement praying to escape for another night, determined to pick up their lives as soon as the shelling ceased. Sadly Sayeed decided to seal up the gaps round the window. We argued that we needed the fresh air. He just laughed. As normal the job was slightly botched so we got a little light through to remind us that the sun still shone and my little spyhole remained intact.

Day after day the guards would practise their karate, whacking away at each other and shouting. Some of them obviously needed to cultivate a macho image to bolster them up as they stood, gun in hand, beside us, blindfolded at their feet. Abed – sickeningly, back to being the sweet, considerate boy – was particularly fanatical. We could hear him thumping the walls or screeching, having been knocked down again by the far larger and more expert Mahmoud.

Sometimes, as he stood in the doorway while Brian was in the bathroom, he'd tell me to come over and stand with one hand in the air. Then he'd try to reach it with a karate kick. When he did so, I'd obligingly say, '*Bravo, encore.*' When he kicked again I'd catch his foot and stand there, saying, '*C'est très bon le karate, tu es très fort.*' He couldn't do a thing, I wasn't threatening him, just holding his foot in a game he started. It was strange realizing how frightened he was. I savoured the situation for a few more moments, then let the foot go and walked back across the room, triumphant.

Brian always revelled in such horseplay, often to the point of provoking the guards. I couldn't see the point of being knocked about, however gently, to amuse a bored guard. But I came to see the value in showing that, even blindfolded, I was ready to fight, and that I could still fight and hurt them. I learned that as long as it was done sparingly and calmly, keeping the guards a little edgy was a valuable asset, if only to maintain our own confidence.

We'd been in the apartment for about a week when Safi came in with Ayeesa and gave us some trousers and then took photographs of us. We were really fired up – this must be a good sign. Photographs proved that they had us and trousers indicated that we'd soon be wearing them home. I was distressed that they fitted so badly, I wanted to look smart when I came out of this. We kept asking if we were going home, but Mahmoud would only say, with a chuckle in his throat, 'Hope so'. It was hard to tell what he meant. He, too, seemed excited and happy, and I needed to think that it was because he had been given good news about us. I knew I was clutching at straws.

For days, we waited. Then, one morning I woke to an announcement from Brian: 'They've gone.'

'What? Who has?'

'The Yanks. They went early this morning.'

I didn't believe him. I knew that Brian always slept like a log and that I barely ever even dozed. He insisted he never slept despite snoring furiously. This time I couldn't deny the evidence. Looking through the keyhole I saw that the room opposite was empty, no Yanks, no mattresses, nothing. What did it mean? Would we, too, be moving soon? Had they been released? We debated the possibilities, but could be certain of nothing, although I took comfort from Brian's bald statement: 'Well, at least there wasn't any malarkey when they went.'

Frantically, I returned to my numbers game. I worked out that 3 or 11 March would signal our next journey. I tried to convince myself it would be the journey home, but couldn't ignore the great doubts in my mind. We strained our ears every time the guards had the radio or television on, but never heard anything about the Yanks. They'd gone with all their gear so it looked as though they'd just been shunted around again. I couldn't accept the obvious and doubted that I'd be able to stave off total depression if we were just going on to another prison.

We were on tenterhooks the entire time now, only diverted by a game Brian invented. It was a sort of darts-cum-skittles, played with dominoes and olive pits. The faithful dominoes were set up in rows and we took turns to aim the olive pits at the pieces with the most dots.

Days went by with no sign, but then one evening Ayeesa came and took everything but the clothes we were wearing. We were left like that for two days, lying shivering on the carpet, trying to sleep at night. Although spring was imminent the nights were still very cold. Mahmoud took pity on us and gave us a little electric fire. Every time he came in we asked him what was happening, where were we going, would we be released? He wasn't sure but he thought the heavy rains of the past two days had delayed the plans. I tried to hope that rains were delaying our journey to Damascus and freedom.

Early on the morning of 10 March we heard men arriving and strange voices. Sayeed was present, but seemed to be deferring to others, who sounded older. I was told to stand up and put on the ill-fitting shoes. I was led to the door of the apartment. A man linked an arm tightly through one of mine. He took my blindfold off and we walked down the stairs. There must have been ten flights. At each turn I looked out through the broken windows to the outline of the city showing vaguely in the dawn's earliest light. As we descended, the horizon came closer and closer until I could make out nothing in the murk. I was unnerved to be back in the darkness. Surely they would have said if we were going home.

The man walked me across the road into the back of a VW van. I clambered in and sat down on a cushion. He spoke to the driver, then told me to put my blindfold back on. They wouldn't want me to be able to identify them or the location even if we were going home, so that didn't mean we weren't. It felt close, so close. After all the ups and downs, the false hopes, the cruel treatment, the boredom, we were off, we'd done it. 'Fuck 'em all, fuck 'em all, the long and the short and the tall, for we'll not be mastered by no Jihad bastard, so cheer up my lads, fuck 'em all.'

Brian soon followed me into the van. We set off and drove for a little while. We stopped. It was getting quite light. Sayeed had joined the men guarding us. He said that we would be released soon. Then his friends wrapped wide strips of plastic tape around our bodies to keep our arms tight against our sides, and taped our legs together. 'Are we going home?' 'Yes.' They put tape around our blindfolds and then taped pieces of cloth over our mouths. Trussed, we were then carried a short distance from the van and pushed into what seemed to be a small metal cabinet. Panic was rising fast within me. But I still clung desperately to the hope that they were tying us up here so that we wouldn't wander away from the designated exchange point.

Suddenly an engine started up. I had no sense of being in a truck. Now I was terrified, imagining we were in a refuse crusher, that they were getting rid of any evidence of us. I started shaking uncontrollably, my body aching against the tight bands of tape. The engine stopped. Sayeed spoke through the metal walls of the truck. 'We are going for a drive, maybe twenty minutes, make no sound.'

Once we were moving I had to get more comfortable or risk permanent damage. I wriggled about, managing to loosen the tape around my body. Lying on my back I could now lift my hands and feel the metal sheets that formed the roof of the box. It could only have been eighteen inches high. I worked myself on to my side fearing that in bouncing over rough roads I might smash my face on the panels above. By curling up as far as possible I was able to reach my face, pull down the gag and push up the blindfold.

Feeling a draught on my eyes and being able to gulp in breaths of air eased the panic a little. I'd been terrified that the fumes from the engine would make me vomit and that

I'd then choke on it and suffocate. That fear began to fade. I started thinking about the time and the number of bolts it had taken to close up the back of the box encasing us. If there were an accident and we drove into a ditch full of water, or the engine caught fire, we wouldn't stand a chance, even if the guards bothered to try to get us out.

I knew I mustn't dwell on imagined horrors. The reality was bad enough. I tried singing, but could hear nothing over the roar of the engine. I felt Brian's hand in mine and sensed that he was trying to spell out a message with his finger. I couldn't concentrate on it, lost patience with him. How could he play games at a time like this? We crashed and bounced along. It was impossible to stay on my side. I rolled again on to my back and felt my coccyx being battered by every dent in the road. I tried to think of something that would stop me hyperventilating and relax the spasms that were still racking my body.

The ache was becoming unbearable. I told my body, 'Stop shaking,' but it wouldn't listen. For some reason I tried to work out how many more people a factory could employ if it put some of its workers on job-share schemes. 'If there are two hundred workers and half of them are on job-share that means that there are so many more man-hours to fill; that means; that means; the factory needs this many more full-time workers; that means; that means; oh God, how much longer? How much longer? Where are we going? What's going on?'

We seemed to have been travelling for at least half an hour, on the flat and at a good speed for most of the journey. That must mean that we hadn't gone east towards the Beka'a as the mountains start on the outskirts of Beirut. Obviously we wouldn't have gone north, that would have taken us into the Christian sector. We must be going south.

We came to a stop. At last we'd be able to move. But, after an age, the truck started up again, following a track off the main road. We were sliding from side to side as the truck skated on the wet, muddy surface. Despairingly, I thought we must be going over the mountains after all, but by the back roads. We'd be sure to skid off into a ravine. A few minutes later the truck stopped on the flat. All was peaceful. We heard chickens clucking, then the sound of four or five men's voices. After another age they started loosening the bolts on the box. I wriggled about to pull the blindfold down into place and tried to get the tape back low across my chest so that if we were to continue they wouldn't decide more tape was needed.

The back of the box came off. Under my blindfold I could see some faces peering in. I was pulled out, carried into a building over the shoulder of one of the guards and put on the ground. I couldn't move, all my muscles had seized up. The tape was torn off. We were taken into a room and lay down on mattresses. Sayeed told us to sleep and that he'd bring some food later. We whispered to each other, speculating on the reason for this latest move.

After a while Sayeed came and spoke to us. 'It was bad in the box?'

'Too fucking right, pal,' I replied. He liked the phrase and repeated it. We asked if we'd be released from here? He hoped so. The usual bullshit. I had a go at him about the beating we'd received. 'This was a mistake, the man who did this thing has been punished.' It was meaningless drivel, but it felt good to have made him admit, albeit indirectly, that it had been a bad error.

He brought us some food on a tray, which was obviously a meal prepared by someone living in the house, or nearby. We were taken to the bathroom. Through a crack around the frosted window-pane I could see a view of a small plateau, dotted with little houses and ringed with low hills. It was a tranquil scene which countered the menace of the man waiting outside the bathroom with a gun. As if reading my thoughts and wanting to break the fragile security my glimpse of countryside had given me, Sayeed tapped me on the shoulders with the butt of his gun as we walked back to the room. Evil little bastard, he couldn't resist jangling our nerves a bit more.

That night we moved again. This time it was just in the back of a VW van with no taping or gags. We only went a little way downhill. We were taken out, into a house and sat down in a room. There was an awful din as they ripped a door off its hinges. We were then taken into a room and found two mattresses side by side. Maybe our new home? At least there were blankets. Mustafa greeted us and we tried to sleep.

We had to keep our blindfolds on all the time as the guards were sleeping just outside the now permanently open doorway. In the light of early dawn I sneaked a look around the little room we were in. It was a kitchen. There was a sink right beside me, then a draining board and on the end wall a wooden dresser stacked with china. Various pairs of shoes, women's and children's, were stacked in one corner. It was definitely a home and had been until very recently. In a sense, it was reassuring to be in a proper home with normal family things lying about. But this family was working with our captors which rather demolished any feelings of sanctuary; the demons even reached into the home, to places where children played.

The next morning we were given breakfast by Sayeed and Mustafa and taken to the bathroom. Daylight flooded in, cheering our spirits. Then came the rattle of chains. They brought them into the room with them. They fixed a bolt to the wall, then the chains to the bolt. I couldn't believe it. I knew that the Yanks had been chained up before, but it was such an awful thought that I'd tried to blot out any notion that it could happen to me. Yet here it was. My immediate reaction was to laugh, 'You cannot be serious.' They were. No humour could break this impermeable human ice. They were set.

Brian was furious. He could easily believe they'd do it.

'I am a human being, not an animal. You are destroying my dignity as a human being.'

'We are sorry, this for your security.'

'For our security! That's crazy, you're destroying our security completely!'

'No, this is good for your security, if you chained then you won't try escape and we won't have to shoot you, so you safer with chains.'

With this surreal logic, they chained us up.

I was a man, and in my mind I knew it, but what was happening to my body told me otherwise. The guards lifted and pulled our legs around as if they weren't attached to a person. They experimented with the length and tightness of the chains as if it were a normal exercise, part of a regular working day, two men working on repairing a bit of office equipment, deciding the best spot for a new piece of furniture. It was bitterly demoralizing that men could do this so naturally, that it was possible for them to ignore our humanity so casually. It also boded ill for any ideas of release.

We'd had our blindfolds on for more than thirty hours. That meant that the guards were permanently around. Any move was tense, but this time we had moved continuously, and the blindfolds had been taped tight over our eyes. Physically this was very uncomfortable, but the torment of going, sightless, to an unknown fate was unbearable. Whenever we were like this I had to loosen the binding so that I could feel, even in the darkness of a metal box or the boot of a car, that I was going out with my eyes wide open.

There was also the difficulty of walking blindfolded. In the prisons we learned the route to the bathroom and anyway would be able to look down our noses and see a small area around our feet. Most of the guards were quite happy with this, even pulling up our blindfolds a little if we stumbled, so that we could move more easily. However, other guards, the nervous or sadistic ones, insisted we had them on tight. The sadists enjoyed pushing us around in our blind confusion.

You never, ever, get used to being blindfolded. It was always a cold shock when talking to a guard, especially if it was a friendly conversation, to realize, 'He's talking to me in this pleasant, intimate way, yet he can't see me, and won't let me see him.' Any warmth was rendered meaningless. It was so sad to think this was the only level on which these guys could operate. If they felt shame, their fear of us and their bosses overrode it – that's assuming they ever did consider what they were doing. Every time we took them to task for their treatment of us, we got nowhere. The incessant commands for silence, the chains, the blindfolds, all reflected their own insecurity, their lack of real power.

After the first couple of days, life settled back into the usual routine of food deliveries and bathroom runs. The pressure was slightly eased when they put a curtain across our door so that at least we could raise our blindfolds more often. But we still had to keep almost silent, speaking in only the lowest of whispers.

In the mornings, after the guards had finished their dawn prayers, they would usually go back to bed for a while. As the light strengthened outside I often peeked through a crack around the cardboard that had been taped over the window. Just outside I could see greenery, what looked like a privet hedge in the foreground and beyond that a tall tree. The glimpse of trees, the sounds of street life and the thin band of daylight moving across the ceiling and down the walls as another day passed never failed to lift my spirits.

We had no books now, nor even our faithful set of dominoes. We talked as much as ever despite the closeness of the guards – more so perhaps, for we were both highly nervous. The uncertainty of what might come next, Sayeed's insane praying and, above all, the new and terrifying shock of being chained up kept us constantly on edge. Even the homey nature of our cell was a vicious tease emphasizing, through its incongruity, that we might be displaced again at any moment. Our nervousness came not so much from fear, as from the impossibility of calming down, of 'settling' in this place. The slightest thing would set us off into uncontrollable fits of giggles.

Our nerves were so stretched that even pet jokes became

unnecessary. Merely saying each other's name or just sighing was enough to render us hysterical. This madness became more acute at night, perhaps as subconsciously we prepared ourselves for the eerie ordeal of listening to Sayeed's prayers. Faith, or psychosis, prompted him to pray all night, alternating the praying with readings from the Koran. These would almost immediately reduce him to tears, raving over the words. I know this can happen to fervent devotees, but in Sayeed it didn't seem genuine. He'd switch back to normal in a second if he got up for a drink or to give an order. He made a deafening racket and it was often so alarming that I couldn't sleep through it. Brian was less affected by it and once Sayeed broke off his wailing to pull back the curtain and tell me to make Bri stop snoring. It was crazy.

In the first week of April our guards were joined by a new man who spoke very good English. On his arrival he came and asked us how we were. He seemed more sophisticated than the others and was obviously more powerful. Brian made it clear that we were not happy and that while some of the guards were all right, others were evil men who had beaten us for no reason. He apologized, explaining that some of the 'brothers' were poorly educated and couldn't understand that hostages should be treated differently from enemies or criminals. He promised to speak to them and remarked that just as we were being tested by our experience, so, too, was God testing the 'brothers' in the way they treated us. Fine sounding phrases, but as meaningless as the claims that the guards were as much prisoners as we were.

The next day Brian was unchained and moved out of the kitchen. I was afraid that we would be separated or that we were in for yet another move. In fact Bri was only moved to the far side of the room next to the kitchen, where the guards initially had based themselves. I heard the English speaker talking to him. He seemed to be asking questions. He then came to me and gave me some sheets of paper with questions written out on them. I had to fill in the answers.

The questions struck me as being rather mundane, but their curious use of English made me smile. 'What is a news?' 'How you make a news for TV?' I could answer those fairly easily, concerned only that the answers might be too technical or boring. As with Sayeed's interrogation back in November there were questions about my life, family, work and all the places I'd ever visited. After a couple of hours I had worked my way through them. The man returned, thanked me and gave me another great wodge of papers to go through.

I was quite enjoying the limited mental exercise of planning the answers and putting them down coherently on paper, the only such opportunity, apart from the necessarily brief messages we'd exchanged in the Land of Grey and Pink, that I'd had in almost a year. But now the questions were getting more detailed. 'Give names for all your organization's offices in the world.' I listed as many as I could remember. They wanted to know how the company budgets were organized. This was something I'd never been involved with so said as much, but privately regretted that it took oddly phrased questions from my kidnappers for me to realize how little effort I'd made to understand the workings of my company.

I had a chuckle when they asked, 'List all details of corruption in your organization.' Apart from the odd lunch on somebody's company credit card, posing as an executive from another TV station, I really didn't know of anything. When the man came back again, I explained that I couldn't answer some of the questions but he seemed unperturbed. He said that he would give me more questions the next day.

I couldn't follow what was going on at all. There had been no threats, no force, indeed the man had been very polite. Nonetheless, I couldn't get one of Tom Sutherland's jokes out of my mind. Hand-talking one day about the difficulties of sleeping, he'd said, 'It reminds me of the joke about the guy who says to his wife, "Be sure and get a good night's rest, honey, there's something very important

I want to tell you in the morning." ' Like the woman in the story I didn't sleep a wink.

The following morning, after breakfast and the bathroom run, the man came to me again. My imagination had been working overtime all night, convincing me that things would soon get very unpleasant, that I would be 'interrogated' in a more direct and painful way. But no, I was just presented with another batch of written questions.

This time, however, they were more to the point. 'List all your contacts with secret services (any country)', 'Give the names of all secret people who have spoken to you in Lebanon.' This struck me as being quite barmy. If I had been a spy surely I would have known how to dodge the obvious questions? They repeated some of the earlier ones about news so I reckoned that there might be some method in their madness and decided that simple, honest answers would still be best. I wrote that I'd had no contact with any secret service people from anywhere and that if any spies had made contact with me they hadn't told me about their private business. Knowing that I wasn't a spy made it all seem rather pointless, even though it was mildly amusing. What did bother me was that they might find out that WTN was largely owned by ABC, the company who had managed to get an exclusive on the TWA hijack/hostages story in Beirut in 1985. This was widely seen as having been made possible through throwing bundles of money at powerful Shia leaders and having powerful friends in high places in and around Washington, DC. If they knew I was linked to ABC, I feared they would become suspicious, or feel that I was more valuable and hang on to me even longer.

When the fellow came back, I told him I'd answered his questions as well as I could, but that the replies seemed very dull. He didn't seem worried and asked if I would like anything. I said that I wanted to write a letter to my family and my girlfriend. It had been a year since I'd seen or spoken to them. Surprisingly, he agreed and gave me a sheet of paper. How could I convey in such a small space what had happened to me, my fears and my concerns for those I loved? I wrote first to my parents and brother. I wanted them to know that I was all right and that I was in good spirits. I hoped that their fears for me would be eased if my letter sounded optimistic. I said that I was fine and that conditions weren't too bad. I told them how much I loved them and how thinking of things in the past often had me laughing out loud. I said I was sure I would be home soon. I asked them to tell Jill that I loved her very much and that she mustn't worry about the time we'd lost, that we were both young and that we had the whole of our lives to live and enjoy together. The man took the letter away but returned after a while, saying he had read it and thought that my 'spirit' was very good. He said his friends felt the same.

I was pleased but felt rather uncertain. It seemed to imply that the guards thought I was co-operative. Brian and I had worked so hard to keep each other's spirits up and work together to maintain our dignity in the face of constant humiliation that it was a mixed blessing to have our success endorsed by the people who were holding us down.

The man also added that he was going to take my answers to some other 'brothers'. I just hoped they would be as satisfied as he seemed to be. I wanted to believe that all the questions were aimed at proving to the British government that my kidnappers did hold me, although I had to admit to myself that it was a very long-winded way of doing it. With this hope in mind, I asked the man what the 'brothers' purpose was in asking all these questions. 'We want to be sure you are what you say.'

'But I've been here a year, haven't you done that already?'

'No, now we will be sure and hope for negotiations.'

'You mean there haven't been any yet?'

'No, but now we hope for a quick solution to your problem.'

That quick solution was more than four years away.

It was a great relief when Brian was moved back into the kitchen with me. Our visitor had left, all his questions answered, and we tried to put some positive meaning into the little information we'd gleaned from him. It wasn't easy. In fact, he'd only confirmed our worst fears, that no-one had been negotiating on our behalf and we both had the clear impression that they hadn't made any demands for us. Like me, Brian had been allowed to write a letter. We could only hope that these would be sent so that at least they'd know back home that we were all right.

Mahmoud came in and told us he was very happy that we'd said good things about him. We tried to take advantage of his good mood to get a clearer idea of where things stood.

'Your friend told me that negotiations would now start. What do you want and how long will it take?'

'I am sorry I do not have the order, but I hope you go home very soon.' The same old story.

The next day was the first anniversary of Brian's kidnap, 11 April. That night Sayeed came and said we were moving to a better place. He unchained me, told me to pick up my clothes and led me to the front door of the house. Standing on the doorstep he put a gun to my back and said I must walk straight across the road to his friend. The night was very quiet. Underneath my blindfold I could see the rutted track in the moonlight. I sensed the village sleeping around me. Should I make a run for it? Would it be possible in these floppy plastic sandals? How far would I get barefoot with at least two men after me? What would Bri do if I made it without him? Sayeed pushed the pistol in my back. I stumbled across the road.

I knew that there were two guns pointing at me but at least I was walking freely, with no tape or chains binding me. It felt good.

On the other side of the road Mahmoud led me up a flight of stairs and told me to sit in the corner of a room. Brian joined me a few minutes later. Our mattresses were brought in and we were told to go to sleep – hard to do with the guards staying in the same room. We slept fitfully and at dawn they were up praying.

The next day they fitted bolts to the wall and chained us to them. Then they stretched some wires across our corner and hung curtains from them so that we found ourselves in a sort of tent. This gave us a little privacy and we could raise our blindfolds, but our guards were living in the same room and we never had a moment to forget them. A new man, Abu Salim, joined Mahmoud and Sayeed. The three of them were incredibly noisy. They would have the radio and television going full blast at the same time. At prayer times they would often have a tape machine playing 'Nadbars', Moslem chants, so that we found it impossible either to think or to relax. Their mattresses came right up to the curtain so that now I had one or two extra heads snoring within arm's reach.

Abu Salim soon demonstrated that he was one of the would-be holy-macho brethren and would compete with Sayeed as to who could pray the loudest, hissing and clicking his fingers at us if we whispered or even just sighed. He liked clicking his fingers. He'd click at us to indicate that we should leave the bathroom. It irritated me so much that he couldn't even bother to say '*dah*', come, that I would stand in the bathroom doorway clicking my fingers back at him until he either said something or came and grabbed me. One morning I was desperately tired and so furious at the row from the radio that I started clicking my fingers over the top of the curtain. He came over hissing like a goose. I kept on clicking until he put his head through the curtains and then, pointing to my ears, I whispered, 'Radio, radio', and made a lowering motion with my hands. He clicked and hissed, but did go and turn the thing down. It was a minor achievement, but it made me feel a hell of a lot better.

We soon realized that there were other hostages in the room next to us, but, because of the guards' heavy insistence on silence, we couldn't make out who they were. They had to go through our room to the bathroom so we'd been able to count three men and in bright daylight could see their silhouettes. It could have been the Yanks but, judging by their stature, and the way they moved, that seemed unlikely; one of them was very small and moved very fast, another moved slowly like an old man.

We discovered that they were French when Sayeed went in one day and asked them something in Arabic, but including the phrase, '*Qu'est que c'est que ça?*' One of them replied, '*Chou haidar mim saidar?*' Sayeed spoke a little more with them and we heard whispered French and someone translating it into Arabic. We guessed that these three must be Kauffman, Carton and Fontaine who had been taken about the same time as Terry and Tom and claimed by Islamic Jihad. We had learned from the Yanks back in the prison that they all had been held in the same Beirut apartment about a year before.

Although we had every reason to despise Sayeed after the beating he had given us, I was truly grateful when, a couple of days after the anniversary of my kidnap, he came and read me an item from a Beirut newspaper. He said that my friends had held a service for me at the journalists' church in London. There had been prayers and Jill had appealed for news of me and for my release. There was nothing more, or at least nothing more that Sayeed would tell. He would only say that he thought we'd be going home soon. As he was leaving he asked, 'You want picture?'

'What picture?'

'Of Jee, Jih.'

'Jill? There's a picture of Jill, please, yes please, give it to me.'

'OK, one minute.'

He went off. I sat there thinking this could only be a vicious trick. But after a few minutes he returned with a tiny photograph. He'd even sellotaped it to a piece of card so that it wouldn't fall apart. There was Jill looking as fresh, pretty and vulnerable as I remembered her. She was holding a picture of me. I remembered my mother

220

telling me of the time my father had gone on a business trip to Czechoslovakia when Terence and I were very little. The day after he left for Prague she received a letter from the insurance company saying that he wasn't covered in case of arrest, detention or disappearance. In a state of shock she'd imagined herself, head and face shrouded in a large scarf, going round Czechoslovakia showing anyone who'd stop a photograph of Pat, asking, 'Have you seen this man?' I wondered if this was how Jill felt now.

In the photograph I was unshaven, holding a beer can and smoking a cigarette. It had been taken at a cricket match two summers previously. It had been a good day; whatever the WTN team had lacked in skill had been made up for by our focusing on the contest's social side. Now I looked into Jill's eyes, noticing the slightly startled expression I loved so much, wanting to reassure her that I was fine, that I would be coming home.

That night I prayed that Jill, my family and friends would see that same strange light and feel its peace as I had done almost a year ago in solitary confinement. 'Please, Good Spirit, let them see your light.'

Looking at Jill and knowing that people were thinking of me was a tremendous boost. Playing my numbers game I felt sure that something would happen at the end of April, especially as it would be the start of the Moslem holy month of Ramadan. Perhaps it would be a good opportunity for them to release us on humanitarian grounds. Yet deep down I couldn't see it happening.

I wanted to believe Sayeed when he said that we'd be going home soon, but couldn't forget that the man with the questions had said, 'Now we start negotiate.' It might be a long time yet. In my mind I spoke to Jill, hoping that somehow my thoughts would reach her. 'I'm fine, but I may be here for a long time. Don't waste your time waiting for me, you mustn't put your life on hold just because mine has been.' I tried hard to believe that I meant it.

We found, we had to find, the energy to adjust to the new environment, even when any whispered conversation we started would be interrupted by Abu Salim. We were extremely bored as we only had a couple of English language text books to flick through. I yearned for the sort of boredom that Dunbar in *Catch 22* had revelled in, where every tedious moment was an extension of his life. But for us the boredom was so acute that we could feel all our energies burning up, sense ourselves wasting away as we went nowhere, achieving nothing, losing time.

To use up some of the excess adrenalin we tried to get back into an exercise routine, running on the spot and doing push-ups and sit-ups. We'd keep count and always try to do more the following day. We wanted to walk free upright, not hobbling like broken men. Exercise wasn't simply a way to burn off adrenalin or to pass the time, it was also a great tonic, taking our minds off other worries and making us feel fresh and positive.

Yet over the years we found that we couldn't keep up our enthusiasm for long periods. Sometimes the conditions – the length and tightness of our chains, the smallness of the room, the guards' paranoia about us making any noise – made exercising either impossible or simply too uncomfortable. Often it just seemed a waste of time. Towards the end of our captivity that changed, and we did more and more.

The English text books we'd been given encouraged Mahmoud to have some English lessons with Brian. We found that the guards could normally take twenty minutes of study before losing interest. Then we'd have a chat and Mahmoud sometimes made us a cup of coffee and gave us extra cigarettes – he smoked like a chimney. One day, as he was leaving, we thanked him for the coffee and the smokes. He said, 'It is nothing, for what we do, words cannot say how I do not like this.' He meant it, but his genuine regret changed nothing.

One advantage of the guards having the television on at full volume was that we could easily hear anything in English. There was a piece of plastic tape stuck to one of the curtains and Brian managed to make a little pinhole in it. By putting an eye up to it we could look over the guards' heads to the screen. In this way we learned about Irangate and that the American hostages so far released had been part of a secret arms deal between Iran and the US. We gathered from a CBS *60 Minutes* programme that the deal, contrary to all public policy claims, had been sanctioned by President Reagan, but that now, because of the public furore, it wouldn't happen again.

We were furious. The Americans' actions could only have convinced Islamic Jihad and anyone else with a grudge against the West that, if they held hostages long enough, they would ultimately get what they wanted. We hoped that by improving diplomatic relations our governments could ensure our release without handing over cash or arms. Although we could not pretend that we would not welcome release on any terms, we did not believe in striking deals that left some hostages in captivity and put other people at risk of being kidnapped.

Although we'd heard nothing about British government policy, we had no doubts that Mrs Thatcher would use the hostage crisis to her own political advantage and boost her tough image by refusing to negotiate on any level whatsoever. Having achieved that, she would then wipe her hands of the whole irritating issue.

With April coming to an end the weather was much finer. The window was usually open and we could smell the fresh air and see the sunlight above the sides of our curtained tent. One morning, when all the guards had gone out of the front door, presumably to take the air, Brian raised the edge of the curtain a little and looked along our captors' beds. He kicked me and hissed, 'Look, there's a gun.' I stared at it, an evil machine-pistol, just two feet away. If we took it perhaps we could turn the tables on the guards and escape.

Sayeed and Abu Salim chained to the wall, blindfolded, bound and gagged, was a brilliant image. Let them feel the gun at their heads. Let them know what it was like to expect a shot the next moment, and the next, until the panic

223

eased off to the point where you could breathe again and could, dared, move a muscle. But as soon as they saw the gun they might run out of the door. Could we shoot them? We could see more guns across the room. They might have others with them. If they refused to unlock our chains, could we risk a shot that might bring half the village running? What would the French think? Did we have the right to force such a desperate decision on them?

We did nothing. The guards returned, laughing, to prepare lunch. Brian and I looked at each other thinking, 'Next time, next time.'

There wasn't going to be a next time in the tent. On the night of 29 April we moved again. It was a short journey along winding roads. We weren't bound or gagged; Brian went in the car boot while I travelled in style crunched down in the back seat with a guard lying across me.

When we stopped we were taken upstairs and chained to a tap fitting in a tiny room. The guards were making tea on a cooker just outside the doorway at my side. As the walls were tiled I assumed we were in a scullery. Below my blindfold I could see the bottom of a sliding door which I tried to close so we could remove our blindfolds. Mustafa, who hadn't been with us since before we went to the tent, came over and stopped me. I mimed taking the blindfolds off. He said, 'OK,' and taped a sheet across the doorway. When he'd gone and we could inspect our new home we understood why he didn't want the door closed. In one of the walls there was a small window. It wasn't bolted. One of us might just be able to get through it with a lot of wriggling – if we hadn't been chained to the tap.

The next day someone came and fixed separate bolts beside each of us. When they finished they chained us with no more than eighteen inches of movement. There wasn't far to go. The two mattresses just fitted leaving a foot's space at the bottom for our water jugs and pee-bottles. During the day Mustafa's sheet kept falling down. He stuck it up again a few times, but then it stayed down. We were right next to the kitchen with guards moving in and out at all hours so had to keep our blindfolds on twenty-four hours a day. We were to be there for seven months.

Things soon settled into the familiar routine: breakfast of sandwiches and black tea followed an hour or so later by a visit to the bathroom; lunch, normally of rice with tinned vegetables and sometimes meat, followed by a long afternoon before more black tea and another sandwich. Depending on the mood of the guards we might be allowed to go to the bathroom again in the evening.

It seemed that the apartment had never been lived in before. Indeed some of the interior doors had yet to be fitted. It was a pleasant change from makeshift hide-outs or the greater horrors of actual prisons. But despite chains, blindfolds and guns, the guards were always nervous that we might see something through a window or be heard by anyone passing by.

They developed a new habit of leaving the door open when we were in the bathroom. With guards like Safi, Mustafa and a new man, Bilal, this was a nuisance, but not an obvious humiliation. We knew they had no interest in either looking at us or wishing us to feel embarrassed. They were merely following the house rules. However, with Abed and another new man, Mazzin, who replaced Mustafa, we felt very uncomfortable. They would leave the door wide open so that we had to sit on the toilet, blindfolded, knowing that they were looking in.

As the summer wore on, water got scarce and we were lucky if we had a decent wash, not quite a shower, once a week. Sometimes two or three weeks would go by with little more than a daily splashing of hands and face. The joy of taking a shower would be completely eroded knowing that Abed and Mazzin were leering through the doorway at us. It was obvious that they did so because if one of us turned round in the bathroom, even if the door was only slightly ajar, they would say, 'Why you look at me?'

Mazzin also irritated me and revealed his own fear when he tried to appear tough by putting a machine-gun to my head whenever he thought there were strangers in the road outside.

Despite being blindfolded all day there were benefits to 'scullery living'. We lay with our heads pointing away from the window. I lay beside the kitchen doorway, Brian next to me by the inside wall. A few feet from me, there was a frosted-glass door leading to a balcony. This was often left ajar and beneath my blindfold I could catch a glimpse of the valleys and hills, in the distance, dotted with small stands of trees. At night I could see the faint glimmer of lights from distant farmhouses.

The kitchen and our scullery would start filling with light just as I was getting off to sleep in the very early morning. But it was always a pleasure to hear the birds singing near by, smell the grass as the sun started to lift the dew and see my little strip of countryside come into focus. Each morning we could hear a helicopter flying some way off. We assumed that this was a United Nations aircraft. No-one else was likely to risk making such regular flights. Whenever I heard it my hopes that we had been brought to the south in order to be handed over to the UN in exchange for Lebanese prisoners from Israel were rekindled.

Once or twice Mustafa opened our little window, which still had no lock but was held shut with tape. Lying back we could half raise our blindfolds and look out at the wide sky. High white clouds contrasting with the pure light blue of the sky were a beautiful sight, which never failed to lift my spirits. Once, a dove fluttered just outside the window. The vision of the bird, its wings spread, framed in the square opening stayed with me as a powerful image of freedom.

It only took us a few days to realize that the Yanks were living down the hall from us, next door to the bathroom. We wondered if they'd heard the awful news about Irangate. We could think of no way of communicating with them, but it was good to hear them speaking to the guards occasionally and know that they were still holding on.

We were now allowed to watch television. Initially we

had to share a television with the Yanks – they'd have it one day, we the next. As usual Bri and I thought that Terry, Tom and Frank were getting special treatment. They always seemed to have it on Wednesday nights which had the best programmes, but Brian managed to shift the schedule so that we were able to see them, too.

News was forbidden. '*Mafi akbar* (no news), OK, John? OK?' 'Yes, yes, we know, *mafi akbar*,' and each guard made up his own mind as to whether we could change channels. Needless to say Abed enjoyed 'policing' our viewing more than anyone. Nevertheless the television was a great diversion, even though the volume always had to be turned right down. We'd put it at the end of the mattresses under the window and sit with our blindfolds slightly raised, our faces a foot or so from the screen. One day when Mustafa was on duty we flicked through the channels and found an Israeli station showing the film *Local Hero*. Jill and I had seen it together and loved its gentle humour. It must have driven Bri mad but I couldn't resist saying, 'You're going to love the next bit,' about twenty times. I felt so close to Jill that she might have been sitting beside me.

Mostly we were restricted to watching CBN, an evangelical network based in the States, but broadcasting from northern Israel. In the evenings CBN had some reasonable American comedy and drama series, although during the day it was aimed more at spiritual and physical improvement. We enjoyed the soaps and came to regard many of the characters as friends, looking forward to catching up with them each week. Brian got very carried away with Nancy Larsen, a keep-fit personality from Chicago. I never failed to find his desperate attempts to follow her routines on the end of a few inches of chain hysterically funny. Abed thought the show was 'no good' because Nancy wore normal Western exercise clothes. After a while – and for no apparent reason – we were forbidden to stand up so had to sit down all day and try to exercise as best we could from there.

Neither of us were committed Christians, but we found great solace in CBN's 700 Club. The programme was filled with people witnessing miracles and answered prayers. The hosts even had 'visions' live on the show. They would say, 'I see a little girl in a blue coat, I sense danger for her, pray God protect her.' A later edition would then report that a child had been knocked down by a car as she went to school wearing a blue coat, but by a miracle she had not been injured. Praise the Lord. We were both sceptical of these things, fearing that such fervent evangelism caused hysteria in people rather than bringing them to a deeper faith. Our fundamentalist captors seemed to bear that out. Having said that, however, we wanted to feel that some of it was true and when Pastor Ben said that he could see some pale men sitting close together in a room, we felt sure he was tuned in to us and we held hands and prayed, our free hands resting on the television.

It may seem contrived but, having watched it day after day, when Brian became very sick with dysentery, I did pray to Christ to help him and even tried the 'laying on of hands'.

For a week we'd been aware that one of the Yanks was very sick. We thought, correctly, that it was Tom. We could hear him throwing up and asking the guards to take him to the bathroom at all hours. We heard Terry telling the guards that his friend needed medicine urgently. Just as Tom recovered Brian became ill. It was pitiful to see him suffering so badly, still on an eighteen-inch metal leash, while his body writhed with cramps, spilling out filth at both ends. He tried to call the guards but the attacks were so violent and sudden that he couldn't wait for them even to come to the door, let alone unchain him and take him the thirty feet to the bathroom.

The guards, especially Abed, insisted that Brian should wait. For the first time I couldn't hold back my anger and snarled at Abed, 'If you want him to wait, get a doctor. This is your problem, you made it.' He didn't respond. Whenever a guard was near by I asked for medicine. Two or three days passed. No doctor, no medicine. They tried to get him to eat a bowl of yoghurt. He tried, only to spew it out again when he found it was horribly laced with garlic.

Brian was getting so weak that he could barely walk as far as the bathroom, even when he was allowed to. As his clothes and bedding got soiled I washed them for him, wishing I could make those bastards understand that he was seriously ill. Their only concern was the impropriety of shitting in a scullery. It didn't matter that the stench from their toilet wafted over us. To them, he was a dirty heathen, behaving like an animal. They had let that happen, yet they blamed Brian.

After several days of this Safi and Abed were sitting on the floor in the kitchen. Abed was murmuring in an undertone, stirring something up. Sure enough within a few minutes Safi told Brian to be careful with his blindfold. Brian wanted to rage at him but could only whisper, 'John, tell him I'm too near the edge for this nonsense.' Abed translated for me as I tried to explain that if something wasn't done for Brian soon, it wouldn't matter if he'd taken bloody photographs of them all because he would be dead. I appealed to Safi's better nature, forcing him to think about Brian's condition and realize that all he wanted to do was stay alive, not look at anyone. I think Abed translated my speech honestly because after a while Safi said, 'OK, no problem, Brian good.'

That night I prayed and put both hands on Bri's stomach. 'Cure my friend, make him well!' Bri leapt up for the plastic bag again and I gave up on that idea. But a day or so later I knew Brian was on the mend when one of the guards sidled over with a little cake for me. 'What are you eating?' a faint voice asked. He tried a bite and it stayed down.

I think our captors were impressed with Brian's stamina. Even Abed stayed friendly for an unusually long time. He abandoned the television one day and came over to me, saying, 'Your girl, Jill?'

'Yes, what?'

'She loves you very much?'

'I hope so.'

'She does much for you.'

'You've seen her? On the television?'

'Yes.'

'What did she say? What was she doing?'

'She is very belle.'

'Yes, but what did she say? . . . Abed, what did she say? . . . Abed?'

He'd gone. I don't think he was trying to distress me this time. Part of him wanted to be kind, but he was scared of telling me something without permission from his boss. He went through phases of being terribly sweet, then would abruptly turn dangerous, looking for trouble. It seemed to occur every month. Maybe his moods were dictated by the moon.

One night he came, opened the window and told us to stand and look at the night sky. It was a beautiful sight. But his kindness, risking the anger of his leaders, was unnerving. We knew him to be unbalanced and likely to twist things to cause us trouble. On another occasion he brought us extra cigarettes and some Arabic coffee at dawn. He even left us alone to enjoy them. For a moment I regained that happy, excited feeling I remembered from childhood. It had always come to me when getting up early to go on holiday.

We had accepted that the guards, even the best of them, ignored our humanity at times. They had no compunction about taping us up or gagging us. They liked to think the chains and blindfolds were for our benefit, so that we wouldn't escape or see them and have to be done away with. Whenever we moved to a new place they'd say, 'No noise, we are ready to do everything.' It never dawned upon them that we had fully appreciated that fact from the moment they had dragged us away at gunpoint. Even so their behaviour sometimes went beyond even our limits of credulity.

Bilal was a large young man with a powerful build

running to fat. He was always relaxed, although clearly followed the lead of whoever was on duty with him. He spoke good English and some French. He squatted down beside me one afternoon and asked, 'You teach me to dance?'

I sat up slowly. 'What did you say, Bilal?'

'You teach me to dance disco?'

Was I hearing things? I felt Brian beginning to shake beside me.

'Um, isn't dancing *haram*, forbidden, Bilal?'

'Not for me.'

'Um, do you have any music?'

'Yes, next time I bring Richard Clayderman tape.'

For someone whose dancing skills were limited to pale and essentially drunken imitations of Mick Jagger this didn't sound like a winning proposition. But it might be fun. Besides, what a story to tell back home. 'Did I ever tell you about the time when a member of one of the world's most notorious terror gangs asked me to teach him to dance?', 'I beg your pardon?', 'I said did I ever . . . ?'

An important question crossed my mind. 'Will you unchain me for your dance lessons, Bilal?'

'No.'

'Well, I can only move my left foot eighteen inches so I think it will be a little difficult.'

'No problem, we move the mattress.'

'Listen, Bilal, bring your tape and we'll talk about it then.'

It was completely barmy, but somehow endearing. How could these young men be so far out of touch with what they were really doing? As I thought it over it occurred to me that with a longer chain I could probably have managed a fairly snappy Tango, taking one, two, three steps and then whirling round as the chain tightened and bit into my skin.

The guards still spent a lot of their time practising their karate and fighting each other. They loved watching kung fu movies and any type of war film. They were surprised when we wouldn't watch yet another such offering. For them, they were the ultimate entertainment. It was hard not to see them as a bunch of children sitting around the living room with their cowboy hats on, holding pistols. Yet their make-believe was horribly close to reality. When they watched another low-budget re-run of the Vietnam War, with the Americans always winning, they had real weapons at their sides. We were very conscious that such movies often showed vicious treatment of prisoners and that these men had their very own captives to abuse. If there ever was an example for the need to control violence on television this must have been it.

Film violence may have influenced the guards treatment of us, but it clearly set them going among themselves. It was evident that the more immature men like Abed found this more fun than others, but they all seemed to enjoy it once the 'fight' was underway. Like us they were bored and wrestling passed the time as well as anything. Indeed I would often attack Brian to annoy him, and amuse myself, by throwing myself upon the mound in the blankets made by his feet, turning to him and saying, 'It's OK, I've got them, they can't get away,' and then start pounding the 'creatures' into submission. Brian, reasonably, responded by whacking me. As soon as he, being stronger, got the upper hand, I would immediately plead, 'I'm sick, you can't hit a sick man!' Then we'd dissolve into laughter and that would be that.

The guards, Abed particularly, liked to prolong their bouts for hours at a time. We were pretty sure that their need for such physical contact came from sexual confusion and repression. It tied in with their obsessive talking about sex. How many girlfriends had we had? Some of them wanted to learn English slang words with sexual connotations. They condemned the West for its sexual freedoms, while lusting after the unreal beauties seen on American television programmes. They seemed to have a fear of women which they tried to deny with macho talk of wife-beating and demands for slavish loyalty. The excessive praying, which did not appear to bring them peace of mind, and the obsessive way some of them cleared their throats (part of the ritual ablutions for prayer) seemed to go beyond religious fervour into some sort of physical blotting out of 'bad' thoughts.

Brian and I were confident and comfortable with our own sexuality – for us the wrestling was a consciously silly form of entertainment and sometimes also a controlled part of our exercise. Equally, we didn't apply these theories to all the guards. Some manifested few, if any, such 'symptoms', or managed to accept their sexuality as normal and showed a kindly appreciation of our situation. Safi, aware of our views about Mrs Thatcher, would often tease Brian that secretly he was in love with her. Using the hybrid language we were still developing with him, he would come to the door and say, 'John, Brian Tatcher amour, no?'

'I'm afraid you're right there, Safi. Brian veut Thatcher cul iyom (every day – all the time).' Then Safi would turn his attention to quizzing Bri on the subject. 'Brian, you veut Tatcher?'

'No!'

'But Tatcher fort. Brian fort, no?'

'Aye, I'm Rocky, me Rambo.'

'Yes, Brian Rambo, Rambo veut Tatcher, so Brian veut Tatcher.' These little exchanges normally ended with Safi turning back to me, 'John veut Tatcher?'

'No, Thatcher no good.'

'OK, Tatcher no good, so Brian no good!'

'Absolutely, Brian very no good, Safi.'

'Brian, John dit you no good.'

'Safi, you know English no good, Irish very good, John very bad man.'

And so it went on over the years.

Some of the guards, like Safi, picked up on the banter between us and liked to join in. They understood the basic problems between Britain and Ireland, although they, too, believed that the problems in Belfast were just down to religious sects, which fitted their view of their own country's problems. They were fascinated that we were clearly such good friends, yet would happily denounce one another as scoundrels.

As our relationship with Safi developed it was clear that he genuinely did like us. He enjoyed having a joke and, after the first year or so, would calm down his friends when they got annoyed with us or we with them. He'd make some coffee and come and say, 'Sorry, my friend fatiguee, OK?'

One day he came and sat with us to watch World Class Championship Wrestling on CBN. Having watched it for a while we were bored, but the guards loved it. As we sat there some ancient wrestling luminary came on and started an interminable spiel to camera. After a couple of minutes Safi said, 'OK, thank you, *hallas*, finish.' The luminary bored on. 'OK, OK, tomorrow,' said Safi. More luminary. 'OK, one dollar, *hallas*.' No chance. 'OK, OK, twenty dollar.' We laughed; Safi's timing and expressions had been perfect.

Most of the time the guards sat watching television or playing games. At last we had a reasonable supply of books. Nearly all of them had been printed twenty years previously and often fell apart, a process speeded up by Abed's deliberately prudish habit of tearing off any cover with a woman on it. Although many of the books were run-of-the-mill detective yarns, there were some serious novels that gave us a chance for a bit of intellectual exercise. We often went on to rewrite the books or to plan how to make them into films.

We even had a copy of *The Wooden Horse*, the Second World War escape story, although it was, sadly, a simplified edition for English language students. Despite this, we read with envy of the POWs' ingenuity in their bids for freedom. They could build things, dig tunnels and study maps. We were in a concrete block, chained to the wall armed only with plastic spoons. Yet we still thought incessantly of ways to escape.

In the summer's heat the guards often left the balcony door open at night. It would have been easy to climb over the low wall outside and drop to the ground. Often a pair of guards' shoes were lying about so we felt that if we heard two lots of snoring from the guards' room, across the hall from the kitchen, we could get away if we didn't make too much noise. Of course all this depended on getting the chains off. Here we were lucky.

The guards had taken to letting us fix our own chains, probably because the room was so small. We found that they didn't look too closely so we could hook the padlocks through one link, wrap the chain round our leg and then fasten the padlock around the chain like a slip-knot. It looked as though it was fitted tight but in fact was free to run and could easily be slipped off. Brian tore up bits of cardboard to fit inside a thick pair of socks in case there weren't any shoes handy. I had a pair of flip-flops. We'd been able to tell from the sun's movements that we were facing south so knew that we had to take the opposite direction to reach Beirut, although, of course, we had no real sense of our exact location.

The tape around our little window had been loosened when the guards had opened the window. Early one morning I decided to risk opening it to get a better idea of our surroundings. Easing it open millimetre by millimetre took ten minutes, but I managed it with very little noise and looked out. Before me, a narrow, deep valley stretched away to the south. It was peaceful and beautiful in the early morning light. Below me I could just make out the far edge of a dirt track. Beyond that was a small house with a tree in front of it. Further away, around the edge of the valley, was a wide, unfinished road leading off into the distance. I closed the window very carefully and settled down on my mattress once more. A few minutes later Mustafa was in the kitchen making some tea.

If I'd been caught things would doubtless have been very unpleasant. But I wasn't. Instead I had a vivid image of the outside world to hold on to and to picture again and again. The quiet landscape had looked so welcoming.

We whispered alternative plans at each other, plotting

the best way to lower ourselves off the balcony, arguing whether we could seriously go very far without proper shoes. It was possible that we would be picked up by another group or, indeed, anyone who felt we might be worth something. I still had the twenty dollars which I'd found in the Beirut apartment so we might be able to get someone to drive us back to Beirut.

One night everything was in our favour: the chains were OK, Abed was on his own and snoring loudly, the balcony door was closed and the key was in it. I think there was even some moonlight. But I had a bout of diarrhoea. I sat up and banged on the door for Abed. No response, no break in the snores. Brian asked anxiously, 'Can you travel?' I wasn't that sick, but it was a pretty big decision to make in a split second when most of my attention was on my stomach. My mind spun with potential problems that we hadn't yet resolved.

We might have been able to slip out on our own without waking Abed, but we needed to be sure that we could get away cleanly without him raising the alarm while we were still clambering off the balcony. That meant creeping into his room and grabbing both him and a gun. Then we'd have to tie him up. All this in silence so as not to alert the occupants of the flat below, who were probably also involved – or at least aware of what the apartment was used for. Where would that leave the Yanks? If we were to take the gun we had to be prepared to use it. It wasn't a question of right or wrong, more a simple desire not to. But with a gun we might be able to hijack a car. There were so many questions and they all had to be decided immediately.

My bowels matched the turmoil in my brain. 'Sorry, Bri, I've got to go to the bathroom.' I banged on the door again, more loudly, and Abed woke and came in. He took me to the bathroom without any bother.

Back in the room I realized that Abed wasn't going back to sleep. As my stomach-ache eased so did my mind, but I knew I had failed Brian. I hadn't had the nerve to go through with it. He was sympathetic saying that it was hard to make a gut decision when your guts were working to their own agenda and we agreed to try again as soon as I was well and another opportunity arose.

The following morning Sayeed turned up. We hadn't seen him since we'd arrived two or three months before. He was in a strange mood and spent hours killing flies at the balcony door with a length of elastic, just like a small child. It was a bad omen. He spoke to us, trying to wind Brian up, but Brian ignored him. Then, that night when other guards arrived for their shift, they fixed the chains themselves. It was nightmarish. Just like the year before, in the business premises, it felt as if they had somehow known of our plans and were now acting to thwart any new thoughts of escape.

But at least this time we had notebooks and pens. They'd been given to us at the same time as the books. The pages were divided into squares. After I'd kept a diary for a few days and Bri had written some poetry, we realized that we would never be allowed to take the books home with us, so decided to work on a few projects. We designed the interiors of little boats and 'motor-homes'. We wanted to make them as small as possible, just big enough for one person to live and travel in.

We spent many hours with these drawings. Our designs were influenced by the smallness of our room. I'd wasted a lot of time imagining my ideal prison where we could make the best of captivity without the appalling pressure of constant attention from the guards. Our boats and vans were an extension of this, a way of making the scullery, at least theoretically, a home.

We still had the dominoes and while we no longer found any entertainment in the game itself we used them as makeshift playing cards. We worked out the rules for *chemin de fer* from a James Bond novel and in about an hour we had both lost and won a fortune. By the end of the evening's session Brian estimated that I owed him a ten-year-old Mercedes sports car with cowhide seats. I have no idea how much money this was supposed to represent, but to this day, despite countless other gambling sessions in which I am sure he lost tens of thousands of pounds to me, Brian still insists that I should get him that car.

One night I dreamed I was lying in a room with him. In my dream I was angry with him for some undefined crime. I started kicking him as he lay beside me. When I realized that the fuzzy edges of the scene were filled with guards' faces, laughing to see me putting the boot in, I thought I must stop. Suddenly I was being shaken, my head cleared and I heard Brian hissing irately in my ear, 'What do you think you're doing? Why are you kicking me?' My first reaction was to turn round and look under the blindfold to see if any guards really were in the vicinity. Thank God they weren't. 'You were snoring so much I couldn't sleep, you bastard.'

'No, I wasn't. How can I sleep with you flailing away at my legs? *You* were asleep, it took me five minutes to wake you.'

'I'm sorry, I've not been well lately. I keep having these hallucinations that I'm chained to a wall, in bed with a little hairy monster.'

With pen and notebook I was able to give my numbers game rather more of a scientific flavour. I still took a ridiculous interest in trying to read meaning into the most bizarre 'signs'. If something optimistic occurred in the plot of a book I was reading I would take note of the page number and try to decide if it meant that we would be released in that many days' time. If that didn't feel right I might consider the chapter number and see if, by putting them together, I might get a day and month for our release. The Bible was great for this purpose, having books, chapters, verses, lines and page numbers that went over a thousand. It never occurred to me then that I would be incarcerated for more days than there were pages in the Good Book. Reading the many hopeful and uplifting passages provided great solace, but now, too, it gave this additional, albeit eccentric, stimulus for the numbers game.

I noted down the days and dates on which we had been moved. I played around with the duration of the stay in each place. Out of nowhere came the realization that every time there had been a Friday 13th in a month we had moved. The move from the first prison, the move from the second, then the move south and the next into the tent, had all occurred in such a month. This proved a real guide. Perhaps the old superstition about Friday 13th wasn't so barmy, perhaps it might somehow be a good day for us rather than the traditionally unlucky one. The next Friday 13th was in November. Perhaps I would be home for my birthday on the 27th or better still home for Jill's on the 6th.

Such idle, if encouraging, notions were blotted out in late October when Abed started getting troublesome again. We'd heard him going on at the Yanks about something. He'd been yelling and was claiming that they had bent a metal door. We heard Anderson saying, 'I did not bend the door. If you want to beat me then beat me, but I did not bend the door.' Then Abed came to talk to us, his tone cold with the menace of restrained hysteria. He criticized the West, Christianity, whatever. Brian quietly asked him how Moslems, with their belief in a good God, could take innocent men hostage. Did they use the phrase, *Bismillah, irahman, iraheem* (In the name of God, the compassionate, the merciful) when they killed or beat someone? 'Yes,' was his bleak reply. He left, clearly wanting a fight.

The following day he came and told Brian to open the window. Brian did so. Just as he sat down, Abed said, 'Close the window.' Brian got up and slammed it shut. Abed, triumphant, leapt into the room and threw Brian back against the wall. Brian retaliated, grabbing him round the neck. Bilal jumped in between them, holding Brian and pushing him down on to the mattress, but he didn't hit him.

Abed made us both lie on our fronts and tied our hands behind our backs. He tied a towel over Brian's face, then started hitting him with a stick. After a few blows I

239

asked him to stop, it was enough. He beat me a couple of times and went back to work on Brian, raining blows on him, chanting, 'Bismillah, irahman, iraheem.' Brian's hoarse screams escaped through the towel. It seemed that it would never end. I lay there praying for him to stop, for God's voice to fill the room and strike Abed down in fear. What should I do? What could I do beyond call out?

Abed seemed to be going for different parts of Brian's body. He'd started with his back and arms, then his legs. When Brian's screams went up in pitch I thought he must be hitting the soles of his feet – perhaps a trick he'd learned from one of those bloody war films.

Bilal came to the door, stood a moment, then said, 'Hallas – hallas!' Abed stopped. He was breathing hard, not from the exertion but from intense excitement. He stomped out telling us not to speak.

I asked Brian if he was OK. Stupid question. He tried to answer but was still so shaken and his murmured answer so muffled by the gag that it was incomprehensible.

After a while Abed returned, removed Brian's gag and untied my hands. Brian said that he needed to pee so would Abed unchain his hands? 'No.' But when he saw me trying to help Brian his screwed-up morals wouldn't let him force us into a position where I would have to hold Bri's penis. He released his hands.

After a while, huddled in a blanket, Brian's body stopped shaking quite so badly, although he continued to tremble from the physical shock for another day. He was bruised and cut all over, his feet already swelling. But he was remarkably calm, saying, 'You know, you feel very close to a man when you're fighting him.' I was stunned.

That evening Abed came in and they talked. He apologized but said that Brian had forced him to beat him. I was amazed that Brian then took the time to lecture Abed on the dangers of power. I sat there in a state of shock. The two of them seemed to have achieved a sort of calm that couldn't touch me. I was still distressed,

At UPITN, 1984.

At a WTN cricket match, 1985. This photograph was part of the display at the first anniversary vigil for John in St Bride's, Fleet Street, on 17 April 1987.
Courtesy of Moira Edmonds.

With Pat and Terence.

With Brian, 1961.

With Peggy and Brian, 1961.

With Sheila and Terence.

Jim and Peggy Morrell, FOJM fifth
anniversary rally, 13 April 1991.

Beirut. © *Sipa-Press/Rex Features.*

Nick Toksvig, Damascus,
Christmas Day 1986.

With a beard. This is the other photograph Jill and Nick Toksvig
took to Damascus with them.

First anniversary vigil, St Bride's, 16 April 1987. © *Times Newspapers*.

600 Days. Handing in a petition to 10 Downing Street, 7 December 1987. © *Times Newspapers*.

The launching of the Friends of John McCarthy, February 1988. © *Times Newspapers*.

With Alain Whyte, of *Sanctuary*, at 'An Evening without John McCarthy', Camden Palace, 17 April 1988. *Roy Cuckow*.

789 Days. With Jean-Paul and Joelle Kauffman on the FOJM Boat Trip, 15 June 1988. *Bob Gannon/Insight.*

With the FOJM dummy in its cage, Labour Party Conference, 4 October 1988. © *Yorkshire Post.*

900 Days. Releasing FOJM balloons from the top of Blackpool Tower, 3 October 1988. © *Times Newspapers.*

In the FOJM campaign bus at the Conservative Party Conference, 12 October 1988. (*L-r*) Joan Willows, Mary Delaney, Lawrence Harrison, Chris Pearson, Chris Jury, Gina Filose. *Johnny Haddock.*

FOJM display, Virgin Megastore, 14 January 1989. © *Times Newspapers.*

With Nasri, Yasser Arafat and Chris Pearson, June 1989.

1000 Days. With Peggy Morrell, Joan Ruddock and Chris Pearson, handing in a petition to 10 Downing Street. © *Press Association.*

789 Days. With Jean-Paul and
Joelle Kauffman on the FOJM Boat
Trip, 15 June 1988.
Bob Gannon/Insight.

With the FOJM dummy in its cage,
Labour Party Conference,
4 October 1988. © *Yorkshire Post.*

900 Days. Releasing FOJM balloons from the top of Blackpool
Tower, 3 October 1988. © *Times Newspapers.*

In the FOJM
campaign bus at the
Conservative Party
Conference, 12
October 1988.
(*L-r*) Joan Willows,
Mary Delaney,
Lawrence Harrison,
Chris Pearson, Chris
Jury, Gina Filose.
Johnny Haddock.

FOJM display,
Virgin Megastore,
14 January 1989.
© *Times Newspapers.*

With Nasri, Yasser Arafat and
Chris Pearson, June 1989.

1000 Days. With Peggy Morrell,
Joan Ruddock and Chris Pearson,
handing in a petition to 10
Downing Street. © *Press Association.*

With Pat McCarthy at the launching of the BBH poster, Finchley Road, 24 August 1989. © *Times Newspapers.*

Fourth anniversary vigil outside Iranian Embassy, 17 April 1990. *Jez Coulson/Insight.*

With Neal Davis, President of Hull University Students' Union, handing in a petition to 10 Downing Street to mark John's fourth birthday in captivity, 28 November 1990. *Jez Coulson/Insight.*

On the twelfth day of Christmas,
John McCarthy will have been a hostage for...

1715 days 1716 days 1717 days

1718 days 1719 days 1720 days

1721 days 1722 days 1723 days

1724 days 1725 days 1726 days

The FOJM Christmas card, 1990. Designed by Sue Brown and
John Hewitt. *Courtesy of the designers.*

ashamed that I'd done nothing to stop the horror. I simply couldn't follow what was going on.

It took me a while to realize that the two men had indeed been calm after the beating. Brian had made his stand and, although he'd been unable to resist, he didn't feel demeaned. Abed had burnt off whatever frustrations were tormenting him, and now justified his fury as fulfilling his duties. I was beginning to see what Brian had meant about 'feeling close'. One saw the basic, abandoned side of someone in a fight. But that side was so cruel and I felt so impotent that I just wished that we didn't have to study it here and now.

Brian's body was a mass of bruises and he had difficulty walking to the bathroom for a few days. A week or so after the beating Amin turned up to talk to us. We'd seen him several times and he seemed to have taken over Sayeed's role as the guards' immediate boss. He gave the impression of being one of the calmer types and was always optimistic, saying, 'You will go home soon and very soon, believe me.'

When he arrived I urged Brian to tell him the exact circumstances of the beating, knowing full well that Abed would naturally have rendered an account that covered himself in glory and Brian in wickedness. Brian didn't agree – the battle had been with Abed and was over. So be it; it wasn't my business. Certainly Amin gave Brian only a minor rebuke for causing trouble and then amazed us by producing a letter that Brian's family and friends had placed in one of the Beirut newspapers. This was a great moment for both of us. It was the first time we'd heard anything from Brian's family and he was delighted to know that his mother was well and that his sisters, Brenda and Elaine, were working with his many friends to get something done for him.

Amin left telling me that he would bring me a card from my friends, but would say no more about it. The idea that there were letters for both of us was very encouraging. Brian felt sure that, by reading between the lines, his folks were telling him that his letter of last April had indeed been sent home. It turned out that it hadn't, but at the time it was good to think that people on the outside knew we were alive.

With the immediate horror of the beating now fading, the mental stress along with the physical bruises, Brian's letter and the promise of one for me gave us a renewed optimism. I recalled my belief that November would be a special month because the 13th fell on a Friday and I decided that something had to happen. We got the impression that one of the three Yanks had been moved. We thought that we heard a mention of Sutherland when the guards were watching the news and hoped he'd gone home.

The week after Friday the 13th Amin turned up again and told me to get ready to move. He wouldn't say anything beyond, 'Do not worry, but remember we are ready to do everything, so don't make anything.' My hands were chained behind my back and, as usual, there then followed a long wait. I knelt down again beside Brian and asked him to light a cigarette and hold it for me while I took a few puffs. We wished each other good luck, Brian giving me last-minute messages in case I was going home.

Then we were off. I had my hands behind my back and was blindfolded, of course, but I don't remember whether I was gagged or taped up. I rode in the boot of a car. It wasn't a long journey and I was taken into a ground-floor room. It was very small with rough, newly concreted walls. The door was ten inches above the floor. I was chained up by the foot again. The door was left open so I couldn't risk looking around. It was very damp and cold and, despite the lateness of the season, was still swarming with mosquitoes.

Amin stayed with one or two other guards and I had to keep knocking to ask them to take me to the bathroom as they wouldn't give me a pee-bottle. The next morning before they were up I cautiously lifted my blindfold and looked about. There was a large bathroom directly opposite my door with a barred, but open, window on the far wall. This was not the bathroom to which I'd been. That was tiny with only a small air vent. Surprisingly it had a European-style toilet, but sadly lacked a sink. There was just a tap in the wall, which, together with a complete lack of hot water, made washing plates, cups and plastic cutlery difficult.

I could see that the corridor between me and the bathrooms went off in two directions, but couldn't tell which way the guards' room was. Although my ears were now highly attuned to picking up the smallest noise, the voices echoing down the corridor were unplaceable.

Amin had left some of his things in my room so I had a look through them. I found a bundle wrapped in a piece of chamois leather. In it was a photograph of a pretty little blond girl – so European-looking it seemed hard to imagine that she was a daughter or a sister – and a great wad of dollars. I still had my twenty dollars but reckoned getting someone to drive me to safety would be easy if I could get away with this stash. But of course, within a few hours, Amin came and took away his belongings.

Two or three days went by. I feared that I'd lost Brian for good, but Amin told me he would be coming soon. He did and it was a great relief. The door was now closed and we saw that there was a huge pipe just below the ceiling which led across to the guards' bathroom. My initial reaction on seeing the glimmer at the other end was to say, 'Look Bri, the light at the end of the tunnel.' Brian wasn't so impressed. The place had clearly just been prepared for us which didn't suggest that anything good was about to happen. Moreover, the 'tunnel' provided little light, but acted as a breeding ground for the mosquitoes and brought the stench from the guards' toilet right into the room. It was foul and we christened it the Pigsty.

A few days after Brian's arrival another captive was brought in. He was put in a room further down the corridor. Several days later we realized it was Frank. Neither Terry nor Tom showed up but we couldn't really believe that they'd gone home. Now we could take off our blindfolds for most of the day, but the Pigsty was still very depressing. The lack of daylight and a pitiful battery-powered lighting system left us in the dark much of the time. To keep the mosquitoes at bay we found ourselves wrapping towels around our heads, wearing the blindfolds and staying under the blankets regardless of the temperature.

True to his word Amin did turn up with a postcard. It was from a friend at WTN, Tom Browne. He'd sent it nine months earlier while on holiday in Switzerland. He said Jill and Nick were working tirelessly for me. It was terrific news. But the truly wonderful thing was seeing a friend's handwriting. I read and re-read the short message and felt home come closer. It amused us that it was addressed to *John McCarthy, British Hostage, c/o xxxxx, Beirut, Lebanon*. The word after c/o had been scratched out. It seemed daft that they didn't want us to know how it had reached us, when we'd be able to check immediately after our release, but we presumed it was through Hezbollah. Their fear of us knowing anything was usually infuriating, but on this occasion it afforded us a little light relief.

On 27 November, my birthday, Safi and a new guard, who called himself George, brought us some cakes and stayed for a chat. Suddenly they went round to Frank's room. We heard Safi saying, 'What, what? No good, no good,' followed by a series of blows. Frank said, 'Sorry, nothing. I do nothing.' Brian and I had a muttered discussion, the cake turning to ashes in our mouths as poor Frank was beaten. We later found out from him that he'd got into the habit of cupping his ear with his hand so as to be sure to hear the guards approaching. George and Safi believed he was doing this to overhear their conversation with us. We decided that it would only make matters worse if we protested or gave the cakes back. We didn't want trouble, and felt certain that the last thing Frank needed was more anxiety.

Abed turned up the next day and went straight into one of his psychotic moods. We heard him go into Frank and start hitting him, until Frank said, 'Please stop, I am hurting a lot, I don't need any more.' How Frank managed to keep his voice level I will never know. It was the second time that we'd heard him suffering vicious abuse, yet this time he sounded much stronger.

Elated by his violence Abed looked to see how he could torment Brian and me. An afternoon came when we both desperately needed to use the toilet. We knocked on the door and he came. We could hear the delight in his voice as he said, 'No.' We had little alternative but to use the plastic rubbish bag in turn – a pointless, depressing humiliation.

A day or so later, as if in compensation, Amin arrived with a newspaper cutting of birthday greetings from my parents, Jill and WTN colleagues. It was printed in Arabic so Amin translated it for me. He left the cutting which featured a photograph of me in which, Brian assured me, I looked awful.

I was reluctantly agreeing with him, when I suddenly remembered when it had been taken. I told Brian the story. I had been suffering from a rather vicious hangover the day before I left London a year and a half ago. Jill and I had been out the night before with Nick Toksvig and other friends for too many farewell drinks. We'd gone to the pub, then on for a very late meal at the Trattoria. After that we may have detoured to Nick's before heading back to Jill's flat in Baron's Court.

For a few seconds we were in The Crown and Sceptre, drinks in hand, plotting the night ahead and laughing. It was one of those perfect moments when Brian and I shared a vivid flight of fancy and left gloomy reality behind us. I was a little surprised to realize that it was the photograph and through it, the memory of that distant evening with my friends, rather than their birthday messages, that triggered our brief escape.

*   *   *

245

We had been in the Pigsty a couple of weeks when Brian suddenly blurted out, 'You've shrunk.' We were exercising at the time, touching our toes. I stopped dead. I looked at him beadily. 'If I've shrunk, you've shrunk a fuck sight more than me.' Aghast, we looked at one another. Surely we weren't shrinking because of the dietary deficiencies or lack of exercise? After all we'd been through, holding on to our sanity and keeping our spirits up, we were going to go home like a couple of garden gnomes. We started laughing, confused at this strange development. We examined each other more closely, standing against the wall and marking our height. I was still a little taller than Bri, so at least we were shrinking in proportion.

We both felt that we'd lost at least six inches. But was it really possible? Then it dawned on us that as the door was ten inches above floor level, it gave the little room a curious sense of proportion, so we tried to find something that we could use as a measure. All we had were pee-bottles, plastic spoons and a couple of paperbacks. We couldn't be sure how tall a paperback was but guessed. Using it as a ruler we worked out that we probably hadn't actually shrunk and stopped panicking.

Just before Christmas Abed came in and said that we were going to a bigger, better room. We hoped so. In fact they merely swapped us with Frank. The room was indeed bigger, but they made our chains so short that we couldn't move more than a couple of inches and so tight that I lost a lot of sensation in my left leg for months afterwards.

The weather now was wet and freezing cold. We huddled all day under our blankets, playing 'cards' with the dominoes, quickly putting our hands back into the warmth after each play. We hadn't had a good wash for months, nor changed our clothes and we both developed burning rashes around the crotch. Eventually Bilal turned up with a giant plastic bowl and a jug of hot water so that we could at least have a 'birdy bath'.

Safi developed a bad cold and cough so virtually banned our smoking, which was a bitter blow. It was unlike him but it showed that despite his general air of *bonhomie*, at heart he'd sacrifice any pleasures we had to suit himself.

Although cigarettes were out, we did get to see a few videos. One of them, *Trespasses*, had as its theme music Willy Nelson's version of 'Amazing Grace'. I'd never much cared for the song before, finding it too blatantly sentimental, but his reedy voice made it so much more sensitive and the words – 'I once was lost, but now I'm found, was blind, but now can see' – had a special resonance for us.

As the weeks wore on, our spirits slid further and further downhill. We still cracked the old jokes, but didn't have the energy to come up with anything new. Each day was a bitter, gruelling, stubborn wait for night and the next day. We had no news, and the severe decline in conditions, the presence of Abed and Safi's change in mood offered us no reason to think that we were any nearer going home. I could find little comfort in the numbers game, just blankly hoped that whatever happened we'd be moved somewhere else soon.

It was only after our next move, some time in February, that I realized I should have been able to predict it – another Friday 13th. But I was at such a low ebb that I couldn't even be bothered to keep track of the date.

We were moved in sacks in the boot of a car. It was a short trip and then two or three days spent chained together. We got the impression another man was also held there; presumably it was Frank. Abed gave us some volumes of an American encyclopedia to use as pillows, but we started to read them instead. 'No, you must not read. This is my book.'

'Abed, I taught you to speak English, now you tell me I cannot read your books. That's bad, Abed.'

A little later he gave in. 'OK, read if you like.'

'No thanks.'

One afternoon there were more guards than usual and we heard the dreadful sound of tape being pulled. I went into cold shock. Not the truck again. Not the endless jarring and the terror of suffocation. But, of course, it was, and with a vengeance. They taped us from head to foot, legs tight together, arms pinned to our sides. It was impossible to move even a fraction. We were mummified with just a small slit below the nose. Brian was carried out first. Abed held me teetering upright. 'You want pee-pee?' he asked, his voice full of mock concern. Like a fool I breathed, 'No.' More tape around my mouth, the bastard. Then I was taken and slid into the ghastly metal chamber of horrors.

'Calm, calm down, breathe easily, you won't suffocate, you've done this before. It'll only be half an hour, hold on, hold on.' For a few seconds I relaxed as I imagined that Brian and I must look like a pair of skinny Michelin men.

We set off after a long delay during which we listened to a sheep bleating very close at hand. We were in some kind of garage or barn adjoining the house as we could hear rain beating down, but not directly on to the truck.

We'd only been going five minutes when we pulled off the road. 'What now?' The driver tried to start the engine again and again. I couldn't believe it. However much they ignored our plight, it seemed insane that they hadn't got the truck in good shape to avoid any trouble for themselves. Maybe they'd just forgotten to fill up the fuel tank. It was a long delay with the freezing air biting through the plastic outer skin and our thin clothes. The roads must have been awash, we had heard the tyres swishing along, water finding its way even through the tiny hole round my nose.

Eventually we were off again, arriving back in Beirut in – as far as I could guess – the early afternoon. We were dragged, limp, from the truck and the tape cut away from us. Then we were bundled into the back of a VW van, given a blanket and told to keep quiet and still. We tried to sleep but the cold was too deep in our bones. My shivering was exacerbated by the muscular spasms from attempts to brace myself against the van's bouncing on the journey.

Abed and Safi were with us. After a while we heard them walking away from the van, talking. I peeked through a crack in the screen between us and the driving compartment. I could see that we were in a huge building. There were piles of sand lying about and I guessed that it was still under construction. It was so large I couldn't see the roof and wondered if it was a mosque, if, up there in the dark, was a dome that would soon be covered with beautiful gilded scriptures. If it really was to be a mosque, then this was a pretty sad use for it.

We were cold, dirty and very tired. The bare metal floor of a filthy van wasn't the place to recuperate from the frightful journey. It was a relief when Amin turned up and we were loaded into sacks with our hands tied behind our backs. We went a short distance in the boot of a car. They took me out first and when my head got caught on the top inside lip of the boot, they just yanked on the rest of me as if I were an awkward object. Fearing that my neck would break I couldn't help shouting, 'No.' They got the message and handled me more gently until they could lift me clear. I was carried into a building and left with a guard in what I imagined was a lift. Somebody kicked me lightly, presumably in irritation at my crying out. I assumed that there would be more of this to follow. It must have made them nervous that I had called out in English on a quiet street.

Brian arrived; the lift went up and we were taken out and into an apartment. We found bedding and the rest of our stuff all ready for us. Amin asked me why I'd called out. Bluntly, I told him.

'I am sorry, but don't do it again.'

'OK, I hope not.'

That was that. I was relieved. I didn't have the strength to cope with any nastiness.

We found ourselves in a big room with a well-tiled floor. There was a large window, covered as usual, but this time by metal shutters, so, with a bit of luck, they might be opened. We were both chained to the same bracket in one corner and the mattresses were side by side. But it was clean, there was space, proper electric light and, as we discovered the next day, a decent bathroom.

Other conditions improved as well. Ali was back with us and he made an effort with the food which came on plastic trays with little partitions, just like on an aeroplane. We started getting fruit and fresh salads and much more meat than we'd ever had. We had a few books and a television, although, of course, we were still forbidden to watch any news. We were even given great thick duvets with pretty covers. Showers and a change of underwear and pyjamas were a weekly treat.

After a couple of days we realized that Frank was next door. A week later we got the impression that there was another man with him, presumably Terry or Tom. Then, one morning when the guard was bringing breakfast, we heard a voice say clearly, with a strong French accent, 'Am I disturbing you?' This surprised us. Why were they mixing Frenchmen and Americans. Had the other Yanks and Frenchmen gone home? Were we the last ones left? The move back to Beirut and the dramatic improvement in treatment could mean that they were 'feeding' us up before release. I did some calculations and realized that there wasn't a Friday 13th until May, all of three months away. Perhaps the Friday 13th business was just hocus-pocus and I tried to find a 'magic' date early the following week. Nothing really fitted, but it didn't matter – things were definitely looking up.

Needless to say little Abed had to try to spoil life. I slept on the mattress nearest the wall with Brian beside me. One day Abed noticed some mess from a candle on the floor on the far side of Brian. He told me to clean it up. 'No problem, Abed, I'll do it next time I'm off the chain.'

'No, do it now.'

'OK, but undo the chain. I can't reach it from here, the chain is too short.' I was damned if I was going to lie flat out, blindfolded, and try to clean up a little mark just to make that boy feel powerful.

'You must do it now.'

'If you unchain me, I will do it.'

'No, you must do it like that.'

'Shan't,' said Toad with great spirit, but I think the *Wind in the Willows* reference was lost on him.

'This will be bad for you.'

'It already is, Abed.'

He stormed out. Brian was quite impressed. Abed returned and told me to stand up. Then he punched me and kicked me. It didn't hurt, but I sank down on my haunches with my back to the wall saying, as more blows landed, 'Abed, this really isn't right. Why don't you go and ask your *chef* what he thinks you should do?' He cleared off again. I felt a vague sense of victory.

A few days later a strange man turned up. As was often the case for visiting dignitaries, the guards, on this occasion Safi and Abed, would make a great to-do about being on the alert, guns would be dusted off, and while one of them made coffee for the guest, the other would nip round the hostages whispering in determined tones, 'Make everything good, all comfortable.'

'You want us to tidy up?'

'Yes, make nice.'

So we'd shift a tissue here and a matchbox there until everything was adequately shipshape, then consider the more pressing matter. 'Who the hell is the VIP? Why's he here? What do we want to say if we get the chance?'

In twenty-two months of captivity we'd spent just three weeks living in a normal room in a normal home. It had been good the last time, almost exactly a year before, now – after the long months in the Scullery and the Pigsty – it was even better. Abed's spiteful bit of malarkey had seriously blotted the Jihad's otherwise improved copy-book. We agreed that I must explain this to the visitor.

He came in, alone, and squatted down between us at the head of the mattresses. Nothing happened. 'Who is he?' He didn't exude the dangerous confidence of some of the senior types. I wondered if he was just an idiot chum of the boys who wanted to look at the freaks. It must have been a disappointment to those characters who came to peer at us over the years. All they saw was little groups of huddled, motionless men.

The man was working up an English expression. 'You OK?'

'Yes thanks, how are you?'

'Thank you, I am good.' He obviously considered his words carefully as two minutes passed before he said, 'My friends, you, good?'

'Well,' I said.

'Go on, John, tell him,' urged Brian quietly. It crossed my mind that months before when he was recovering from Abed's torture he'd refused to say anything about it to Amin. As I'd wanted him to speak up then, I couldn't really back down now. I spoke very slowly.

'We have a problem with one of your friends. The other men are good, but this man makes problems.'

'Who friend?'

'Tell him, John.'

'His name is Abed.'

'OK, what problem?'

I explained as simply as I could what had happened. He listened with great patience and made me go over it again and again as we gradually sifted all the details into English phrases that he could follow. His attention and sympathetic manner encouraged us to try and convey that, while we could almost understand them holding us hostage, we could not accept stupid ill-treatment. Again he made sure he followed everything, before he said, 'OK, this finish, now, today, everything good.' Then he left.

We could hear him talking to Safi and Abed for a while. Then Abed came in and asked us if we wanted anything. When we said, 'No thanks,' he bizarrely offered to bring us some clean pillowcases the next day, sounding desperate to please. We thanked him. He left.

Safi followed a little later and closed the door. Usually he'd speak to us, but now he just padded silently round the room. We could hear the man talking on and on in very subdued tones. It was still cold so Brian offered Safi a corner of his duvet under which to warm his feet. 'No, thank you, Brian, me chauffage,' Safi chuckled. They had an electric fire in their room. I tried to start a conversation, '*Fi akbar*, any news, Safi, *chou*, what about, Thatcher?'

'*Mafi akbar*.' We got the point. He wanted to eavesdrop on the conversation across the hall.

Abed went home the next day. He returned a few weeks later for a couple of days, then never appeared again. It was a triumph. We'd got rid of a major problem, a serious drain on our failing reserves of energy and optimism. I was pleased that Abed had been removed without any drama on our part. By keeping my temper when he had attacked me I had left them with no opportunity to blame me for the situation, yet I had maintained my dignity and taken back a degree of control from them. It was also a great relief to know that there was someone in the organization who understood our needs and was prepared to take our side against his own. Some of them could be rational. Over the remaining years this knowledge was to give us greater confidence.

At the time, though, we didn't know how successful our lobbying of the mysterious *chef* had been, so when Abed turned up for what was to be his last shift we treated him with the usual cautious politeness, anticipating that he might seek revenge for my complaints. He didn't.

It must have been early April – coming up to our second anniversary – when we had our photographs taken for the second time. Safi was on duty and came in to give us a haircut. I'd got fed up with my beard as it only seemed to itch all the time. We weren't able to trim our beards and mine got in the way when eating and drinking and, as it got thicker under the chin, I was always conscious of the ruff of hair there.

I fantasized about being able to trim and shape my beard properly as it grew. It became a bit of a neurosis, I suppose, in the same way that not being able to cut and file my fingernails used to get on my nerves. When I could I would spend ages trimming and filing my nails so that they wouldn't catch on clothing or blankets. I'm pretty sure that the time I spent doing this used to irritate my various companions. The guards would often say, 'Five minutes with clips, OK?' If they came back in less than twenty minutes I was always still manicuring away.

Safi hacked off most of my beard, then asked me, 'John, *cheveux*, zero or one?'

'What, Safi?'

'Zero or one?' he repeated, taking my hand and running it over his own head. It felt bald, or more like a moleskin. 'This zero.'

'OK, me three, *claytee*, please, Safi!'

'OK, tree, *trois*,' he said, laughing. He'd just begun the shearing when another guard arrived. Safi told me 'Now photo.' I knew I looked pretty rough although it wasn't until the day of my release that I discovered the true horror of the captured image when I saw that it had been put out by my captors before my arrival in Damascus.

Soon afterwards, we were watching the television when the programme suddenly went off the air and rather murky pictures of an airliner on the tarmac appeared. There was a caption, 'CNN live from Algiers' and an American voice saying, 'The hijacked Kuwaiti plane has been on the tarmac here now for some hours. It is still not clear what the hijackers want, although it is believed a member of the Kuwaiti Royal Family is among the passengers. PLO leader Yasser Arafat is believed to be helping with negotiations to get the passengers off the plane.' Our immediate hope was that the demand might be for the release of the seventeen in Kuwait and, given there was royalty on board, that they might have it met. Mazzin shot into the room and switched off the set. *'Qu'est-ce que tu regardes?'*

'Un avion sur la terre.'

'Alors tu comprends toutes choses.'

254

Not really, but he told us to keep the machine off until further notice.

Generally we didn't really bother to try and see the news. The odds of catching something about us were too slim and if we were caught we'd certainly lose the TV and maybe even be mucked about a bit for good measure. Yet for no apparent reason Brian flicked on the late news, some time around ten in the evening, on Friday 15 April. The first image we saw was a banner reading: 'An Evening without John McCarthy'. We both sat rigid in shock. Brian then leant over by the side of the television and put his ear right up to the little loudspeaker, his hand on the off switch in case a guard should bound in. I sat with my eyes riveted to the screen. I was so excited, so aware that at any moment the guard might appear, that I could hardly concentrate on the pictures.

After the banner, two young men appeared, dancing a little, obviously singing. Then a stream of images. Jill talking, Sir Geoffrey Howe, a few shots of my parents, more of the singers. As soon as it finished Bri switched off the TV and we exchanged notes. 'There was some singing, something like, "we want you home", or, "John, you're not alone", then a young woman's voice . . .'

'That was Jill, that was Jill. What was she saying?'

'That the Government wasn't doing enough, that she wanted to draw more attention to you and get the Government to find out what's happened to you.'

'Right, right, then there was Howe, the Foreign Secretary.'

'Aye, posh man saying they were doing all they could, but no-one had claimed you and they had no information yet.'

We talked over the remaining shots trying to tie the words to the pictures. The fact that that story should be on the news the one night we'd risked a look, was amazing. It had to mean something, had to be a good omen. Yet the hard fact was that nobody knew what had happened to us. We were excited that Jill was getting something going and taking the Thatcher government to task. But we couldn't understand why Islamic Jihad hadn't claimed us yet. It had been two years and it seemed as much a waste of their time as of ours. But we weren't forgotten. Friends and strangers remembered us, people were even singing songs for us. Brian couldn't resist singing his own. A whining version of the one he'd heard. 'Oh, John, we want you home, oh, darling John, you're not alone . . . too bloody right, I'm lumbered with you, you shilling-taker!'

6
London, April 1987–April 1988

It hardly seemed any time at all before the days started to get warmer and spring was here again. I love the fresh smell in the air when everything seems to be coming to life again and I felt a natural surge of joy, as if in a few weeks' time John would be coming home from his first trip away just as he should have done the previous April. The feeling almost wiped out that terrible year as if it hadn't happened at all.

It had been impossible to think of the future since John's abduction, but 17 April was only weeks away and I had been discussing with Chris and Nick how we might mark it in some way. As I tried to think about what we should do, the day began to represent something we could work towards and almost look forward to, at a time when Waite's kidnap had left us nothing to hope for. I knew now that I might have been foolish to have expected so much from Waite, but he had been the only person who'd been willing to treat both kidnappers and hostages as human beings and to attempt some kind of understanding about how the situation could be resolved. Now he was gone.

In the pub on the night of John's kidnap people had tried to reassure me that if he wasn't freed soon then there would be nationwide protests demanding his release. The reality was that he seemed to have been forgotten and nothing was going to serve as a reminder unless the kidnappers broke their silence. Our recent low-key attempts at publicity, the *Day to Day* programme, the press conference to mark the three hundredth day and a few other interviews – had been fairly successful and hadn't offended or worried Pat or Sheila, although Roby had been against them.

I had been taken aback by the extent of his feelings. 'How many times are you going to want to do this, Jill?' he had said. 'Who do you want to convince, the man in the pub?'

I was upset, but when I'd calmed down, I wondered if Roby was right. Did I want to seek publicity just to make myself feel better? It satisfied a need to do something, I could see that, but I didn't think it was my only motivation. My real aims were to get through to John and to keep him alive in people's minds so that he couldn't be forgotten. When Pat told me that he'd been pleased with what I'd said on *Day to Day* I felt better; I couldn't have coped with his disapproval as well.

The main problem was how to interest the media. I wrote to the editors of all the major newspapers and television channels asking them to cover the anniversary. Hardly any of them replied and Chris, Nick and I decided to follow up the letters with phone calls. As soon as I heard a journalist say, 'John McCartney? Who's he when he's at home?', any doubts I had about badgering them disappeared. However, a few newspapers were interested and I found myself giving about a dozen interviews. It was draining, but I was grateful to any journalists prepared to listen, even if it was obvious that some papers only felt it was a good story because of the 'love interest'.

After a while, the numbness I'd experienced after the press conference set in, and I felt again as if I were talking not about John and me, but about two different people. I repeated the story constantly. It was hard to keep any freshness in my replies, and it was difficult to examine and display my feelings.

But it was encouraging that some journalists were genuinely interested in trying to help and did feel that what had happened to John could have easily happened to them. One such person was John Curran, a producer at ITN, who had already demonstrated his kindness by giving me an answering machine so that I could screen any calls from the press. John was keen to help in a practical way and it was he who came up with an idea for marking John's year in captivity.

'What you need is a permanent display somewhere in London; perhaps John's photograph and the number of days he's been held. You need something that can be changed every day as the number grows, somewhere people can see it every day. That way the press will have something to photograph to accompany their stories. You've got to feed them, make it easy for them, give them something visual.' I could see that he was absolutely right, but where could we do that? How would we change the numbers? Would it need to be waterproof? Suddenly, I thought of St Bride's, the journalists' church in Fleet Street. 'We could try there,' I said, tentatively. 'I found out a few weeks ago that the canon there says prayers for John every day.'

Nick and I went to see Canon Oates and we knew after only a few minutes in his company that he wanted to help very much. His interest and concern calmed me and sitting in his study at the back of the church I felt more at peace than I had in a long time. Despite the phone ringing insistently in the background, I felt as if I could have sat there for ever. 'I'd be privileged to help,' he said, when we asked him about the display. 'Why don't we have a prayer vigil here the night before the anniversary?' Brushing aside our thanks he asked when the anniversary was. 'It's 17 April,' I said and then wondered if the church was booked because the canon suddenly looked preoccupied – he seemed to be somewhere else entirely for a minute. 'That's Good Friday,' he said in a hushed voice. Good Friday, the day Jesus died, to rise again three days later. I hadn't realized the significance of the date until now. 'Yes,' he said, shaking himself, 'we'll have the vigil here the night before and put up a permanent display inside the church.' We thanked him and as we were leaving he added that we could leave all the press arrangements to him. 'We have to nudge the politicians in the right direction. Sometimes I think God needs a little help at times like this!'

On 16 April, the day of the vigil, I put on my smart suit for the last of the interviews and went into work to look through the papers. In Beirut the siege of the Palestinian refugee camps by the Amal militia had just ended and the starving inmates were finally being allowed to leave. A British doctor, Pauline Cutting, had returned home to a heroine's welcome and was featured on several front pages. 'I wish that I had her guts,' I thought. I wanted to be in Beirut for the anniversary, to be near John, but the trip seemed too daunting, too frightening. Instead, I had sent an open letter to John that I hoped to get printed in the Lebanese press. It was just possible that the kidnappers might show it to him. It had been difficult to know what to say. I was terrified of saying anything that the kidnappers would view as a coded message or as offensive in any way, in case John should suffer for it, but how was I to put a year's worth of thoughts and feelings into a few lines? Nothing that I thought of seemed adequate, but in the end I decided to keep it simple. I typed on to the telex: 'Darling John, It seems unbelievable that you have been away from us for so long. More than anything I wish I could be with you. I am fine and your family is in good health and send their love. All your friends miss you and think of you all the time. We won't let you down. Don't give up hope, my darling. All my love Jill.'

I leafed through the newspapers, glad that I had done those interviews. There were articles about John in several, including a two-page spread in the *Daily News* by Duncan Campbell, a former colleague of John's, and Martin Jackson, the editor of *Broadcast*, had even written an editorial urging fellow journalists and broadcasters not to let the anniversary pass unrecorded. 'John McCarthy is one of our own,' he had written. 'Let it not be another year.'

Pat and Sheila had been busy, too. Sheila had made another video appeal and they had sent letters, via WTN, to Sheikh Fadlallah and Sheikh Moussawi, both prominent members of the Shi'ite community in Beirut and leaders of

Hezbollah, asking for them to help secure John's release.

It was a hectic day. Friends rang round to remind each other of the vigil and colleagues rallied as many people as they could to come to St Bride's. Chris and I delivered the display, which the ITN graphics department had made up as we waited. Next to a photograph of John were a few words of text which Chris had just written off the top of his head:

> John McCarthy was working as a journalist in Beirut when he was seized on his way to the airport to leave. He is a colleague of yours; you may have worked with him; you may have met him; please, pray for him.

'It'll do,' he said, with his customary offhand modesty, as we stood admiring it in the church. By the time everyone began to arrive the church looked wonderful. An altar to the side had been decorated with flowers and large candles now lit up John's photograph. A few TV companies came and went; it seemed very dark when their harsh lights had gone, but gradually my eyes got used to the gloom and I knew if I looked round I would see comforting, familiar faces, as people took their seats in the rows of chairs in front of the altar. Pat, Sheila and John's brother, Terence, arrived, having driven up from Essex. As they walked towards the altar, Sheila stopped to say hallo. 'I was so excited all the way up here in the car,' she whispered. 'I felt as if I was going to see John.' They didn't stay very long. The experience seemed to exhaust Sheila. It was much too painful for her and Pat decided that they should leave. After they'd gone, I sat near the front next to Nick and looked round. I felt very tired.

Suddenly, a complete stranger jumped up and said an impromptu prayer for John, and then another. It was a bit unnerving; they didn't even know John. I stared at his photograph. It had been taken by a colleague at a WTN cricket match and had captured his lovely face and warm smile. He had a slightly shy look in his eyes. It was odd; I found it difficult to focus on the time that had passed since he'd been kidnapped; sometimes it seemed like moments, at others like years. I wanted to feel warmed by the love and laughter in those eyes, to have all my worries reduced to nothing again just by seeing him. It was so difficult to conjure him up at will now, to truly remember what he was like and bring him to life again. I had to keep reminding myself that the plans we'd had weren't just a dream and that he had loved me. I stared at the photograph again, concentrating hard. After a while it worked. John's face seemed to come alive and his spirit escaped the prison of the photograph releasing brief images of happy times; John dancing along the pavement, John tilting his head back to exhale smoke from a cigarette, John talking to a cuddly toy in a supermarket and making me laugh. How could this be happening to him?

Sometimes I imagined that he'd sneaked back into the country and was leading another life. Mad. But how could life have changed so much that this was happening? What was the use of this endless silence? What was the point? How could his kidnappers be so cruel and not explain their reasons why? I felt a stab of hatred for his captors. As I understood more about Lebanon I had felt sympathy for them, seen them as victims who had themselves experienced terrible deprivation. Now I felt like bombing them, hurting them, kidnapping one of their own families and torturing them with their own tactics.

But what if they weren't tactics at all? What if John was dead, as some people seemed to think? What if I was fooling myself? It was unthinkable that John could be dead, but it had been unthinkable that he would be held for this long and it had happened. I wanted it to be over, to return to the innocence and freedom of life before the kidnap, for John to be safe, for us all to know some kind of certainty instead of this constant doubt and anxiety, to be able to think of the future again. I felt Nick's arm take mine as he saw my tears; I was grateful, but felt little comfort. It was finally sinking in that if a year could go by, then so could two, or even three. This silence could continue and we might never find out what had happened to him, never get any answers, never know for sure.

A friend's drunken voice from the back of the church interrupted this miserable train of thought. 'It's a load of bullshit!' the culprit shouted before being strong-armed out of the door. I had to smile; the outburst was outrageous, but it was the type of thing that John would have laughed about. For a moment it seemed to have broken the spell and punctured the mournful air of the church. The vigil was very moving but some elements of it were a bit odd. A few people got terribly carried away, leaping up to voice their guilt at John being kidnapped and saying that it should have been them. Other people looked on in amazement. I wondered what on earth John would think if he saw all this; his friends in church, many for the first time in years, strangers saying prayers for him, me weeping over his photograph. Perhaps it would have been better to have organized an evening in the pub.

Nick and I got up and went outside, where groups of friends were gathered. Some of them could not believe that they had found themselves in a church, and were only stopping off *en route* to a nearby pub. For some people prayers were the obvious answer. For most of us they weren't, but everyone had felt that they had to mark the day, and what else could we do? We shared a laugh at the strange goings on inside, finding it hard to understand why life had taken such a bizarre turn for John and us all. It was difficult to connect this with the vibrant person we all missed so much.

I found myself standing next to Ronnie Wood, John's ex-girlfriend. We had met at parties previously, but had carefully avoided one another after exchanging polite hallos. Ronnie had written to me a few months before, saying that she had hesitated to get in touch but wanted me to know how concerned she was about John. Her kindness broke the ice and as we began to chat I discovered that instead of feeling awkward I was eager to talk to her. Our thoughts and concerns about John ran along similar lines. Ronnie had loved John too, and knew his vulnerabilities. It was such a relief to share my secret worries with her. The calm, thoughtful way she acknowledged them and talked them through with me made me feel that we had taken the first step towards friendship.

I thought back to something Barbara had said not long before, that John had been the glue that bonded all his friends together, the magnet which drew everyone closer. John might be absent, but he provided the focus of the evening; he was the reason everyone was at St Bride's, sharing this strange experience – and even if it was strange, it had also been very moving.

If only John was here; I longed to talk to him, to laugh about the funny, surreal side of all this with him. In Damascus he would have loved baiting Marwan, the AP reporter, with Nick; at the Comedy Store he would have laughed at the idea of the song someone had written for him – 'The Hills are Alive with the Sound of Bullets'; and my début at live interviews would have provided another entry for his file of great lines.

I had met Chris and Nick at Bush House to be interviewed about the anniversary for the World Service; it was important because of the possibility that John or his kidnappers might be listening and I was very nervous, even more so when I arrived late to discover that the interview was live. 'Live?' I wailed to Chris and Nick as a BBC producer bundled me up the stairs 'I've never done a live interview before . . .' Seeing my stricken face the producer tried to offer some comfort and advice as he propelled me through the studio door. Still hurrying along at a hundred miles an hour he leaned over towards me and lowered his voice. 'Now,' he whispered confidentially, 'the thing to remember is that the Greek Orthodox priest is the one on the left with the beard,' and with that flung me determinedly into my seat. John would have loved it.

Life was marching up such a strange road that it was sometimes hard to take it all in. I'd even had a call from the Archbishop of Canterbury, Robert Runcie, who had been kind enough to phone to say that he had been greatly moved by the vigil and had wanted to let me know that the situation wasn't hopeless. He told me that Lambeth Palace was pursuing its own contacts in an attempt to locate Terry Waite. It was a heartening conversation and I was grateful to him for contacting me. I was thrilled that someone as important as the Archbishop of Canterbury had taken the time to call me, although I couldn't help but think it odd that an Archbishop was now leaving messages on the same answering machine as my mum.

Building up to the anniversary had been the focus of my life for several months; now it was over I felt depressed and despairing again. The way people had responded to it had been very encouraging, with news bulletins showing Sheila's appeal and a photograph of the vigil even appearing on the front page of the *Daily Telegraph*. Despite the huge amount of work that had gone into making the vigil a success, though, I was sure that the whole thing would be forgotten again – just as John's actual kidnap had been the year before.

I received a few letters from strangers which made me realize that people did care. One lady had sent me a poem called 'Wait for Me' by a Russian poet, Konstantin Simonov. It was obviously written as encouragement to the soldiers and families separated during the long years of the Second World War, but it seemed to express the yearning that so many young men must have felt when they were far from their families, desolate and frightened:

> Wait for me, and I'll return
> Only wait very hard
> Wait when you are filled with sorrow
> As you watch the yellow rain
> Wait when the winds sweep the snowdrifts
> Wait in the weltering heat
> Wait when others have stopped waiting,
> Forgetting their yesterdays.

Wait even when from afar no letters come to you
Wait even when others are tired of waiting
And friends sit around the fire,
Drinking to my memory,
Wait, and do not hurry to drink to my memory too.
Wait. For I'll return, defying every death.
And let those who do not wait say that I was lucky.
They will never understand that in the midst of death,
You with your waiting saved me.
Only you and I know how I survived.
It's because you waited as no-one else did.

Because I felt that John would be relying on the people he loved not to forget him, I kept it. It was a moving tribute to the power of the human spirit to overcome an experience which threatened to crush it. I hoped that John would 'defy every death' as the poet said, secure in the knowledge that people loved him.

I felt drained and weary after the vigil. Before the anniversary I had intended to try to mark every hundred days of John's captivity in some way, but the prospect of battling through another summer of silence seemed impossible.

Throughout May and June nothing was heard from the kidnap groups at all. As far as anyone could make out none of the hostages whose lives had been threatened earlier in the year had actually been harmed, but the stream of communiqués from the groups had dried up. The newspapers said that this was due to the fact that the Syrian army was tightening its ring around the southern suburbs of Beirut where the French and American hostages were thought to be. There was still no news of Waite, but I read that Archbishop Runcie's offer to help Iran locate four of its diplomats still missing in Beirut had received official welcome. In return Iran was going to help Runcie find Waite. More and more, ever since Irangate, Iran seemed to have a crucial role to play in the release of American and French hostages. Not that that was much help; it still looked more likely that John was with a group backed by Syria and Libya. We still had no idea why he had been kidnapped.

Chris, Nick and I continued with little bursts of publicity, setting up an organization called the Friends of John McCarthy. Roby and Pat were behind us and we also had support from Nick Raynsford, Martin Jackson, David Nicholas, the editor of ITN, Harry Conroy, the General Secretary of the NUJ and several members of the House of Lords. Our aim was to co-ordinate the various efforts being made and bring them under one umbrella. We didn't really do anything with it and certainly didn't get much coverage. The hostage issue only hit the headlines again when Charles Glass, a British-based American journalist, was kidnapped in mid-June.

Within a few weeks of Glass's abduction, a group calling itself the Organization of Good against Evil released video pictures of him allegedly confessing to being a spy. The group had followed the usual procedure of a claim followed by proof of abduction. There had still been nothing of that kind from John's kidnappers and for the first time I began to have serious doubts about whether he was alive; I began to feel less sure of it deep inside, where it mattered.

I decided to throw myself into buying a flat, and avoid thinking about Lebanon as much as I could. I had planned to buy a flat with Geraldine but realized that if – no, when – John came back I would rather have a home all set up for him. I bought something very quickly in the area where we had planned to buy before, and moved in in a matter of weeks, decorating the place with the help of my mum and dad and furnishing it with the family's cast-offs and a sofa-bed which Nick gave me. Brian had decided to move in with me and help pay the mortgage. He was a professional musician now, still sensitive and happy doing something he loved. As he regaled me with his adventures on the road, I began to feel more normal. I was really touched when all the McCarthys drove up with a few bits and pieces. We went out for dinner that evening and I asked Sheila why she'd brought an egg poacher. 'John's always liked poached eggs,' she told me.

Since John's abduction I had kept a diary, hoping somehow that I could capture the time John was missing, to keep things from fading so that I could share them with him when he came back. I had even tried to record all his favourite television programmes. Now I stopped. Nor did I cut every article on Lebanon out of the paper. I had decided that I had to face up to the fact that John might not come back or he might be gone for a long time and that when he did come back we might not love one another. Even if he still felt the same it was no good if I was going to drive myself mad by becoming obsessive. I had neglected my friends, family, job, social life, virtually everything to do with living a normal life. I wanted it so much. I was tired of trying to hold back time; it just swept ahead regardless. Friends' lives were changing as they split up with old partners, found new ones, bought flats, changed jobs. Colleagues, too, were moving on, leaving WTN, being posted abroad, getting married. Everyone was adapting to the shifting landscape around them. Even Britain seemed to have transformed itself. The Thatcher revolution had got into its stride and in June 1987 had been given the right to power ahead in a landslide victory. Any hope of the Government modifying its aggressive response to terrorism went out of the window.

Following the video from Charles Glass, there was much talk of the Syrians doing their utmost to release him. His abduction had been a blow to their attempts to show that they were bringing Lebanon to order. High-level American diplomats went to Syria to discuss the kidnapping, but one morning Glass appeared at a Beirut hotel looking tired and dishevelled, saying that he had escaped. When Mary phoned to tell me he was free I was elated – he might have news of John.

He didn't, but experts on TV and in the papers set off flurries of speculation that negotiations were finally under way to release all the hostages. Suddenly, everyone was talking about Syria and Iran – which country had more power over the hostage-takers, which was leaning more to the West. All in all, excitement reached fever pitch and it was confidently expected that there would be releases within the next few weeks. I felt my spirits lifting even more; things were on the move at last.

Chris, Nick and I carried on working under the umbrella of the Friends of John McCarthy. Canon Oates held another vigil to mark John's five hundredth day in August. Sometime during the summer the media remembered that there was a British angle to the hostage story and contacted me more frequently for interviews. Colleagues covered for me when I slipped out of work to do them. I was still trying hard not to rock the boat, not to upset either the FO or WTN, and was desperate to find a way of making uncontroversial remarks sound interesting. I had sleepless nights before every television interview – not just from nerves, but from the effort of working out what I was going to say. A few minutes of television time was so precious. I spent hours trying to come up with a brilliant argument that would demolish the 'no deals' policy in seconds and solve everything. But all I could do was remind people of John's situation. Perhaps, then, they would ask themselves and others if enough was being done to get him out.

Despite the amount of time I spent worrying about them, the questions themselves were usually the same: what happened to John? How do you know he's alive? What do you think should be done? When asked, 'How do you know he's alive?' I would talk about the call to the WTN office in Beirut saying that John was OK, and tell them that Sontag's sighting of Brian showed that silence from the kidnappers didn't necessarily mean that a hostage was dead. I could see interviewers thinking that, frankly, this evidence didn't add up to much. Most of them, though, were sympathetic and some, like Jeremy Paxman on *Breakfast Time*, made the whole thing that much less of an ordeal. 'You again,' he would say, 'what should I ask you this time?'

By the time the summer was over, the predictions that Syria was about to release all the hostages had come to nothing and the issue was dead again. There'd been a repeat of the sensational reports about Waite – he'd died of a heart attack in an Iranian prison camp and his body returned to Beirut, or the island of Cyprus was on alert for his imminent release – and a three-day series on all the hostages in the *Independent*, but there was still no questioning of government policy nor a proper analysis of what was really happening. I was disillusioned with all the experts who'd been predicting one thing or another; they obviously didn't know any more than anybody else. The only fact that now seemed beyond doubt was that Syria and Iran were obviously the two countries who were crucial to getting all the hostages released, whoever was actually holding them. What was also becoming more evident was something that one of the experts had pointed out.

Amir Taheri, an Iranian author, said on television that all the governments with hostages in Lebanon – America, France, Germany, Britain, South Korea – were treating it as a bona-fide political problem – apart from Britain. All these governments, despite what they were saying or had said previously in public, considered the abduction of their citizens as a political act and were negotiating over it. According to Taheri, Britain regarded the hostage-takers as criminals and saw the problem largely in terms of policing, rather than negotiating, which was why British hostages were a low priority and would be bottom of the list when it came to any subsequent releases.

His words had the ring of truth about them. The British government didn't seem to have a coherent policy for dealing with the hostage situation, they just wanted to teach the kidnappers a lesson. I despaired when I heard Sir Geoffrey Howe, who was Foreign Secretary at the time, speak at the Tory Party Conference in October and heard him repeat the same old stock phrase: Britain will never make a deal over its hostages in Lebanon.

As if to mock us, Howe's remarks preceded the release of the South Korean hostage Do Chae Sung by just a few weeks and the liberation of two French hostages by just over a month. Ironically, the two French hostages were released on John's birthday, 27 November. We had decided to print birthday messages to him in the Beirut press and once again our love and thoughts went over the telex and into a vacuum. My colleagues at work sent a message, saying: 'Dearest John, on your second birthday in captivity your good friends at WTN send their love. Their thoughts are with you.' I wrote: 'Darling John, I can hardly believe that your birthday is here again and you're still not home. I wish I could tell you myself how much I love you and miss you. We are all fine and Chris and Nick send their love. Keep strong and remember that I'm with you every minute.' John's mother wrote: 'My Darling John, today is your second birthday away from home and our thoughts are with you every second.'

We had no way of knowing it, but those messages were to bring us the first concrete news of John for eighteen months.

The release of the Frenchmen, Jean-Louis Normandin and Roger Auque, by the Revolutionary Justice Organization on John's birthday took place against a backdrop of bombings and embassy sieges in Paris and Tehran. There were allegations of a huge cash deal and changes in France's Middle East policy to accommodate Iran. There had also been rumours that Germany had paid a ransom to get two of their hostages out a few months earlier, and what with Germany breaking ranks, Irangate and now this suspected deal for the French hostages, British newspapers were of full moral outrage at the weakness of other countries and their capitulation in the fight against terrorism.

It was the final straw for me as well. When I watched the TV news and saw Auque and Normandin waving to the crowd on their release, something snapped. How many more hostages were we going to see walk free while our Government still couldn't tell us if John was alive?

Three days after the French were released Joelle Kauffman arranged for me to see Normandin and I flew to Paris, with Mary, to see him. It was unlikely, but just possible that he might have news of John. Normandin was a precious link to that other world that held John and I was more excited than nervous as we walked to his apartment near the Champs-Elysées. But when Joelle introduced us I realized that I hadn't really been prepared for the meeting at all.

In those days, it seemed to me that released hostages had come out of deepest, darkest Africa. I knew so little about who had held them and how they had got out, it seemed as if they had come from a different world, a different time. It was a shock to see the bare evidence of what that kind of captivity could do to a man, and feel the sense of despair at what he had lost. He had a bad cold and was shivering inside his dressing gown. I felt foolish that I hadn't been prepared for the fact that his skin would be so bad or his teeth so deteriorated. I stammered in French that I was very happy to see him and very grateful that he had made time to see me. He had no news of John, but once we had overcome an initial awkwardness, he tried to tell us about his experience.

He spoke without much prompting and I was encouraged by his composure. He had never been kept in a cell, unlike Sontag and Jacobsen, but in various different apartments where the conditions were always similar: a comfortable mattress on the floor, books to read, and occasionally, a television to watch. He had been held with two other French hostages who had also now been released, and two Americans, Edward Tracey and Joe Cicippio. The three men had established a routine of playing cards between breakfast and lunch, draughts between lunch and dinner and chess between dinner and lights out. He said that he hadn't been treated 'badly', but had, like Jenco and Jacobsen, been chained by one or both ankles for most of the time. He recounted all this without any anger or bitterness, but as he got up from his chair to go to the kitchen I had to turn away rather than watch him move around his flat as though he were still hampered by chains.

I asked him how he had coped emotionally with his captivity. 'My spirits varied between depression, acceptance, and hope,' he said, 'although I found it easier not to think of my son, Antoine.' There was a silence and then he added something that stayed in my mind more than the chains, more, in fact, than anything else he had said. 'I didn't lose hope of being released eventually because I knew other French hostages had been freed and that the French government would be working hard to free me.' I asked, 'How much did it mean to you to know that people at home were working for your release?' He looked at me as if the answer was obvious. 'It saved my life.'

I was drained after meeting Normandin and when Mary and I got to Roger Auque's hotel, it was almost a relief to find that he was out. Mary and I flew back to London, but did leave some photographs of John for Auque, just in case. That evening he rang me. On the last morning of his captivity, on 27 November, his guards had shown him a newspaper and in particular a photograph on one of the pages. There was only one photograph it could have been – the picture of John that accompanied our messages. 'The guards, they showed the paper to me and they pointed at the photograph and said: "He is with us".' 'What?' I said, trying to stop my voice from rising several octaves. 'And it was John, are you sure it was John?' 'Yes, I am sure.'

I put the phone down and slumped in a chair. John was alive. It had taken a year and a half to find out, but now – at last – I was sure.

A few months later I was sitting at a table opposite three Foreign Office officials.

'Roger Auque is an unreliable witness,' said one. 'He thinks he saw all sorts of things, including Terry Waite. We can't take his testimony seriously.'

'But why should he lie?'

'Anyone coming out of a situation like that is very confused, their recollections change. His story has many inconsistencies. There are things that don't add up.'

'But are you going to follow it up? The same group must have John. We could at least find out. At least we know who to talk to and can ascertain why they've got him.'

'We are not putting out any signals which might make the kidnappers think we are going to do a deal. The moment we ask any questions they'll think the British government is going to do just that, and it's not. They have to get the message that the British government isn't going to pay.

'John has a better chance of being released if the kidnappers realize there is nothing to be gained by hanging on to him. The moment they think he is valuable, the price on his head goes up, and it makes it that much harder to release him.'

'Don't you think they'll have got the message by now? It's nearly two years since he was kidnapped.'

'As soon as we start asking questions the message goes out that the British government is prepared to deal and that's not going to happen. It's better that they understand that than make demands that aren't going to be met.'

'But this could go on for years.'

'We really believe that this is the best way. As long as he's unimportant, the kidnappers might release him.'

I looked across at Ivor Roberts, the Department Head, his manner was, as ever, supercilious. He had an uncanny way of making me feel simple. In the early days, I had tried to make a few suggestions about what the FO could be doing. I knew that they had been on the point of shipping dialysis machines to Lebanon in an attempt to free Alec Collett just before the bombing of Libya. I had wondered if we might not try something similar. Coldly, he had dismissed the idea. He seemed to have no interest in doing anything.

I left the FO feeling bruised and battered; they had really given me the works. Why were they so negative?

Why did they want to dismiss positive news, potential proof that John was alive, and do absolutely nothing about it? The Government insisted its policy was a straightforward 'no deals with terrorists', but the idea that 'no deals' could be accepted as a comprehensive response appalled me. It was at best inadequate and, at worse, an excuse for doing nothing. I could see the attraction for the Government; a positive response was more difficult to formulate and meant more work. But I could not believe that the policy went unchallenged when there still was scope for negotiation and diplomatic intervention; yet the Government seemed unwilling to try either. It occupied the moral high ground and refused to budge.

It was spring 1988. In Doncaster over Christmas, I had been thinking constantly about criticizing the Government. Whenever I went home, my mum and dad had asked me what was being done for John and why there had been no news of him. I was touched when my dad told me that every night he stood on the back doorstep and said good night to John. I knew John's predicament worried my family, too, and that they were solidly behind him. I had told them what others were saying to me: people were working hard behind the scenes and publicity could be dangerous. They accepted what I said, but weren't happy. At home people rallied round automatically; it was taken for granted that if someone was in trouble then it was everyone else's business to help. I, too, was beginning to wonder why I wasn't speaking out. Keeping quiet had not done any good. I was haunted by Normandin's remark that knowing people were doing something had kept him alive. John had no such reassurance. I'd stuck to the rules and nothing had happened. The FO and the Government weren't doing anything effective and, worse, they seemed proud of it. I'd pretty much made up my mind that they had to be forced into action, but it was such a difficult decision. Was it right? Did I really think I knew better than the FO, full of clever people who were experts on British foreign policy? I had been left in no doubt that any other way of handling John's case might endanger his life. Then there were Pat and Roby.

When Auque and Normandin were released the previous November, Pat and Sheila had spoken out about their frustration on television. 'Jaw, jaw is better than war, war,' Sheila had said. I had been heartened by their performance, but Pat really thought that, in its basic approach, the Government was right. I knew him well enough by now to know that he would never presume to tell me what to do. He would just gently let me know his opinion. 'You see, Jill, I see John as a sort of prisoner of war. The British can't change their policy and negotiate with these terrorists, can they? I mean what else can they do, dear?'

I like and respect Pat. He fought in the last war and is a very intelligent and basically optimistic person, like John. He always looks for the best in people or in any given situation. He seemed to be much better equipped to accept political realities than I was. He was encouraged that, under the circumstances, everything possible was being done for John. The FO telephoned him once a week, to keep in touch. He spoke to Roby every day. From them, Pat felt he had all the available information and that kept him going. In addition, he used any contacts he had in the services, or the Government, in case they could be of help.

In the end, I was left with two voices in my ear, Normandin saying, 'It saved my life' and the Government saying that making a fuss could have severe consequences. Who was right? All we wanted was proof that John was alive and to know why he was being held, but government policy was so rigid that there could be no contact, no discussions. What must John be thinking after all this time? Nine hostages had been set free since John was taken. In Britain people seemed to think that asking the Government to establish the most basic facts about the fate of our hostages was equal to asking them to ship arms to Iran. The suffering of the hostages didn't seem to come into it. In effect, the message being sent to John and the other hostages was that they had to keep a stiff upper lip and hope that, one day, the kidnappers might let them go. It wasn't enough; it hadn't been enough for a long time.

I thought about the options open to us. I had to consider seriously the potential risk to John, but if the hostages could be made an issue at home, at the very least the Government wouldn't be able to ignore their plight and might, consequently, be influenced in their dealings abroad. The *status quo* was unbearable and the Government's lack of interest might also endanger John. What was to stop anyone just shooting him if they thought he was worthless to them? Pursuing this *laissez-faire* policy may have been in the national interest, but it didn't seem to be in John's or that of the other hostages. I didn't know what I was going to do, but I had to do something.

If only more people were questioning the Government. But it was difficult to see why they would, given that everyone seemed to agree with the current policy. As if to underline how huge the task of changing public opinion would be, and of making people see that the hostages mattered, it had been spelled out in a television programme I had taken part in the previous November when Mary and I had been in Paris.

The passionate concern for their fellow countrymen shown by the French contrasted sharply with the stiff upper lip of the British. Amid the furore over the French deal for Normandin and Auque, Joelle Kauffman and I had both taken part via satellite in *The Time, The Place*, which discussed whether the British government was right to say 'No deals'. That the programme was taking place at all was an amazing thing in itself, but when I heard people in the studio audience talking of the need to sacrifice the hostages now for the sake of others in the future, just as they had in *Day to Day* nine months previously, I wondered why so few people seemed to share my view that we were being duped into believing that teaching the terrorists a lesson was the sole issue. If the hostages were to die it would be because their government had failed, whether through lack of expertise or lack of interest, to find a solution. It was a difficult case to argue, though, without sounding as if I were asking the Government to give in. I talked about the conditions that Normandin had described and kept repeating that it wasn't a question of doing a deal, but of looking at other ways to get the hostages out. I was given a sympathetic hearing, but it seemed as if the only people who really agreed with me were the relatives of the hostages. Even then, we were not united in our approach.

David Waite, Terry Waite's brother, was in the studio audience in London, together with Brian Keenan's sisters. I had never met David Waite and didn't know what he thought. My heart sank when I heard him say he was in full support of the government's policy. 'I want to send out a very strong message today,' he had said, 'one thing I learned when I was young is that you don't give in to the village bully. The kidnappers have to realize that the British hostages aren't like bottles of pop,' he went on. 'You don't get money back on the returns.'

Sitting in Paris, listening to this through my earpiece, I thought, 'It's hopeless. No-one is ever going to listen to us and our appeal to the Government to start talking.' Then Amir Taheri, the Iranian author, spoke, answering David Waite's point perfectly. 'The British government doesn't want to talk about it,' he said, 'but every other country has broken the united policy. Britain should either unite its allies or talk – it cannot leave its hostages undefended by standing alone.' 'There *are* people out there who think the policy wrong,' I thought, 'we've just got to keep repeating ourselves until enough people change their minds.'

After the broadcast finished Mary and I thanked Joelle for coming on the programme and being a target for all the anti-French feeling flying around at the time. As we said goodbye, her companion, Michel Cantal du Val, the president of *Les Amis de Jean-Paul Kauffman*, gave us some startling advice about how to convince the British public of the need for the Government to talk to the kidnappers. Shaggy moustache and flamboyant bow-tie quivering in unison, he threw his hands in the air and cried, '*Il faut dire, "Honte au gouvernement Britannique! Honte au peuple Britannique! Honte à la Reine Britannique!"*' – 'You must say, "Shame on the British government! Shame on the British people! Shame on the British Queen!".' As Mary and I waved goodbye to him, I thought that I wouldn't put his advice into practice quite yet. We had a long way to go and to start by knocking the monarchy wouldn't go down too well at home.

In some parts of the media, though, one or two questions were being posed about the Government's approach. After the release of the two Frenchmen, Hugo Young had written an article in the *Guardian* that we seized on as if it were a lifeline. All he did was throw up a question mark – was Britain doing the right thing? – but to us it was the first sign that someone out there thought that government strategy might be wrong. His article sparked the interest of two *Newsnight* journalists, Gavin Esler and Martin Gregory, who asked the Foreign Office to give them a briefing. They had been shocked to hear that the policy was to do nothing, and I was astonished that the FO hadn't even bothered to disguise the fact. Esler and Gregory told us that they were planning a report on Terry Waite's anniversary in January and if we wanted publicity, they would interview us. I was relieved that they were prepared to question the policy and agreed.

Over New Year I had been able to escape a constant anxiety that time was running out. Knowing that John was alive, that fact was a spur to action of some kind. The idea that he was alive crystallized the need to let him know that we were trying to help him. Of John himself the picture was still vague.

I still had an enormous block when I tried to think of John as a hostage. It was hard enough to stare at his photograph and make it come to life, but it was impossible to imagine the figure in the picture living in the sort of conditions which Normandin and others had described. Even though I could now visualize a cell or a room, and a man chained to a wall, trying to occupy his mind and keep his fears at bay, when I thought of John it was like thinking of him lost in an abstract painting which I didn't understand. Before Auque's news, it was like looking at a huge, dark landscape whose features were indistinguishable from one another. Now it was as if my eyes had glimpsed the windows of a dimly lit house. The windows were obscured by curtains, but if I strained my eyes I thought I could make out the shadow of a figure standing behind them, never moving. As I watched the figure the lights in the windows would fade and the house would dissolve into darkness again, always out of reach; all that remained was a certainty that the figure was there, waiting.

The helplessness of that figure and the hopelessness it conveyed was always there. John's mother had been very ill over Christmas and over the New Year she had been admitted to hospital. Over the past year she had had various painful illnesses and eventually it had been diagnosed as a recurrence of cancer. It was unfair and wrong that life could be doing this to her; she needed her son and he needed to be here. Sheila was the kind of person who always gave so much to other people. Why was she denied this one thing now?

It was almost two years since John's abduction. So much had changed. I was upset about Sheila's illness, upset and angry. But I was also angry for myself, because I felt desperate about my own future. It had been my thirtieth birthday in November. It may only have been the milestone of hitting thirty, but I couldn't help feeling that it was proof that life was passing me by. I wanted to do the things John and I had looked forward to a year and a half ago, to travel as we had planned, to work abroad, have a family before too long. But life was still on hold. Outside events were in control.

I wanted John and I to have a chance together. Two French UNRWA workers were released from captivity in Beirut at the beginning of the year and I had watched their press conference imagining how I would feel if it were

John delivering the speech. I knew I would want him to be coming home to me. But the longer his captivity went on, the less likely that would be. I told myself that I had to face up to things; John might have forgotten me, he might have been changed beyond recognition by his experiences; he would not want me to mope. What I was holding out for hung on a pretty slender thread and I couldn't let my life be dominated by it. But it was one thing to tell myself that and another to act on it with any conviction.

Up until then most of John's friends and colleagues had heard any news in rather a fragmented way at parties or in the pub, which was frustrating for them and exhausting for me. I had discussed the possibility of a proper campaign with several friends over the past months and the idea had taken root in my mind. It now seemed to be the time to put the plan into action; the frustration and anger following Auque's and Normandin's release was the final shove I needed. I knew I could count on friends and colleagues to support a campaign. John's absence was still keenly felt. They were constantly asking me if there was any news of him and becoming increasingly anxious themselves about the lack of progress.

We wanted to change public opinion – we had the French campaign as an example – but other than that our aims were pretty vague. Somehow we had to convince politicians that they needed to do something, by proving it was in their interests to do so. The most obvious way to get through to them was via the media. I wanted to grab people by the throat and confront them with this terrible situation that was being allowed to continue. I saw a Greenpeace advert in the paper. It was extremely effective, didn't pull any punches, but had caught my eye and made me think. 'That's what we've got to do,' I thought, 'just make people think.'

Working in the WTN news room for the past four years had opened my eyes to how the media worked. Like news rooms everywhere, it was WTN's business to have the latest information and pictures on any given story. Even terrible disasters and news of death and destruction produced the automatic response, 'Have we got pictures?' before any compassionate noises. It was part of the job, part of the thrill of working in the immediacy of a news room. There were only a few occasions when I remembered the news room falling silent as news came in via satellite. The Sabra and Chatila massacres in Lebanon had been one; the scale of brutality was ungraspable. Even then, however, the pictures ran out, there was no new information and the rest of the world lost interest.

My own attitude to news changed with John's abduction. I could still do my job, but my heart wasn't in the day-to-day scramble for the latest pictures. I couldn't see the point of it any more. It was a relief when I was moved on to the Sports Desk; these were gains and losses of a different kind and they didn't involve people getting killed. I was still in the news room, though, and near enough to hear one of my own colleagues respond to a video of Terry Anderson in captivity with a dismissive, 'We're not running that; it's not newsworthy', as he tossed the cassette to one side. The tape showed Anderson sitting, struggling to keep himself alive and to communicate with the outside world, but the world wasn't going to see it. Anderson had done it before and so, according to my colleague it wasn't newsworthy.

When my colleague had said that, with me sitting right beside him, I felt like punching him in the face; it was that kind of attitude that any campaign would have to fight. I was appalled that we should find it in John's own news room. If that could happen at WTN, what hope was there that other news rooms around the country would publicize John's case out of sympathy with a fellow journalist, not to mention a fellow human being? Right from the beginning I assumed that we were going to have to work at interesting the press in the story. Just because John was a journalist we couldn't expect special treatment.

In early January 1988 about a dozen friends and colleagues, the same people who had been with me on the day John was kidnapped, met at my flat. We agreed that the lack of action was an outrage and that we had to draw people's attention to it. We decided to call ourselves the Friends of John McCarthy because that's what we were. We couldn't claim to be anything else; we couldn't speak for the families of Terry Waite or Brian Keenan. The umbrella group we'd formed in 1987 had fallen into abeyance, but the name still meant something. We decided to move up a gear. We didn't realize, as we sat around my flat being filmed by the *Newsnight* team, that it would consume so much of our time, and of our lives.

I went round all the departments at WTN, asking for support. I hated speaking to large groups of people and normally would have avoided it at all costs, but I found that I had thought so much about this that telling other people was a relief. Their reaction was so encouraging that it gave me the strength to carry on.

When we could find nowhere to meet at short notice, the WTN local, The Crown and Sceptre, said that we could use the kitchen upstairs. Our first official meeting was round a huge kitchen table surrounded by dirty dishes and grimy ovens. About fifty of us filed in, clutching our drinks. Chris took the chair and I went through the list of things that needed to be done to get us off the ground: a bank account, an address and telephone number somewhere, an eye-catching logo. At this stage, the urge to do something was unfocused, but it was extraordinary how people threw themselves into it. They were coming up with ideas for advertising on London Transport, in newspapers, contacting people they knew with professional PR experience, people in the media. We were virtually aiming for the impossible: to launch the revamped Friends of John McCarthy complete with campaign logo, notepaper and T-shirts, by our target date of 17 February, in four weeks' time.

Once the touchpapers had been lit, everyone showed the same commitment and enthusiasm as before, organizing posters, T-shirts, mugs, a regular meeting-place. In the past, I would have shared this kind of thing with Nick. But the shock of John's kidnap and the strain of the subsequent months had taken its toll on him. He really couldn't share the burden of campaigning any more and took a back seat.

I found myself snowed under from the start. I went to the NUJ to ask them to give us office space and the use of a phone. In the early days I had been a bit disappointed that the NUJ hadn't immediately leapt to John's defence, but ever since I had first been to see the General Secretary, Harry Conroy, and his assistant, Tom Nash, the union had done what it could to respond to what was asked of them. They had sent round a circular to all members asking them to mention John whenever possible in their reports on the Middle East; they had helped organize a petition among all members and accompanied Chris and me when we delivered it to the Iranian Embassy and Downing Street to mark John's six hundredth day in December. Now, they consulted their executive committee, and agreed to give us our most vital asset: the free use of an empty office.

Much of the initial cost of setting up the campaign was covered either by various committee members somehow doing things for free or came from the remainder of the money raised at the Comedy Store. The finances were in the hands of one of our most scrupulous colleagues, but not even her careful accounting could alter the fact that if we were to survive beyond the first month we would need to raise some money. In France Jean-Paul Kauffman's colleagues were paying a percentage of their salaries towards the campaign, and several colleagues at WTN had set up regular standing orders into our bank account. But if we were to pay phone bills, postage, future printing costs and fund a minimum wage for someone to run the NUJ office, we would need to hold some kind of fund-raising benefit.

Gina, Barbara, Ronnie and Chris Jury, a friend of theirs from Hull University Drama Department days, volunteered to arrange something for the second anniversary of John's kidnap on 17 April. From then on they met separately in wine bars, reporting back intermittently on the drunken evenings they had had. They guarded their independence fiercely and neither Chris nor I dared ask too often how much progress was being made.

I was busy doing interviews, as the media were beginning to pick up on the story. The interest of the BBC's *Heart of the Matter* was triggered by *Newsnight* and that, in turn, caught the attention of a researcher on *Wogan*, Mandy Nixon, who asked if I wanted to appear on the programme.

It was a huge breakthrough. Within weeks of forming the campaign we had a chance to advertise on a television show with a huge audience; Mandy even got Wogan to agree to display the campaign's recently acquired address and telephone number. There was no way I could have refused even if I had wanted to, so a few days later I found myself shaking in the BBC's hospitality suite, very glad to have Mary and Chris with me for moral support. I wore a suit that Mary had seen in a second-hand shop in Paris and insisted I bought so that at least I had one outfit I could put on for interviews without worrying whether it looked OK or not. She was right, it was perfect, but what I looked like was the least of my problems.

Although I had now done a few television interviews, I was still a relative novice and there was so much that I wanted to get across to all the people watching. I went through what I wanted to say over and over again, unable to respond to Mary's attempts to reassure me. The only thing I could do was discuss with her yet again the best way to express our case. Not for the first time, I was thankful that as a barrister she was an expert at this.

Wogan handled the interview very well, leading me gently through the facts of John's abduction and why we disagreed with the Government. Broadcasting regulations prevent anyone appealing for money on a programme like that, but he sidestepped the rules very smartly. 'You're not just asking for money, though, are you?' he said.

'It's people's support that you want, isn't it?' 'Oh yes,' I said gratefully, 'that's it exactly.'

Once the programme was broadcast, the BBC received forty telephone calls and hundreds of letters poured into our recently acquired PO Box, many containing donations. The letters were generous and heartwarming. One came from someone in prison who 'had nothing to give but enclosed stamp'; another from a pensioner who had sellotaped a pound coin to her letter and apologized for not sending more. One young man of John's age wrote to say that the pointlessness of his captivity had struck a chord with him. He said that John was the conscience of the nation and reassured me that John would not be forgotten by people in Britain. From another letter we discovered that a nun, Simone Donnelly, had already organized a mini-campaign by forming a prayer circle for John through the Catholic newspaper, *The Universe*. The letters gave me enormous encouragement. They were proof that the support we had been convinced was out there really did exist. I called Pat to tell him what sort of response we'd had and he was thrilled. Hearing him say, 'That's marvellous, Jill. I'll tell Sheila straightaway' made me feel that, at last, I'd been able to give them some good news. It gave us all the boost we needed to carry on to the launch and, after that, to the second anniversary of John's captivity.

On 17 February the campaign was launched with a press conference and a display of posters, T-shirts and other merchandise. Chris and I 'revealed' Roger Auque's news. We sold a few T-shirts, but otherwise barely caused a ripple. We also appealed to the Government to respond to an extraordinary press conference given by the Iranian chargé d'affaires in London on the anniversary of Terry Waite's imprisonment a few weeks ago, but no-one took much notice of that, either.

The chargé had said that if Britain wanted Iran to help in the case of its hostages in Lebanon, then Britain would have to help locate four Iranians who had gone missing in Beirut several years earlier. It was obviously a ploy on their part, because the Archbishop of Canterbury had investigated their disappearance and told the Iranians that these four men were dead. The main point, though, was that Iran was now offering to help with the British hostages and seemed to be acknowledging that they were alive. Roby was worried that through linking the four Iranians to the British hostages, the Iranian government was preparing the ground for announcing that the Britons, too, were dead. I worried about it too, but wasn't prepared to accept it. I didn't believe that John was dead.

The Iranians seemed to represent an increasingly important part of the equation. In the run-up to the launch Pat and I arranged a meeting with the chargé at the Iranian Embassy. We'd been trying to see someone there for months, but although I'd delivered petitions, I'd never managed to get through the front door.

Now, Pat and I found ourselves nervously waiting to be let in. When we were shown into the chargé's office, I studiously avoided shaking hands or having any eye contact, determined to alert him to the fact that I understood and respected their religious customs, in the hope that it might make a difference. He began to address us and I found the way he spoke mesmeric. He had a curious way of stressing words in the wrong place, sometimes swallowing them completely, but there was a hypnotic singsong quality to his voice which made it very hard to concentrate on what he was actually saying. Needless to say, he wasn't offering much comfort.

'Of course, the Islamic Republic of Iran condemns this practice of hostage-taking. It is against Islamic principles.'

'We do understand that,' Pat replied. 'We are simply appealing to you for help in the case of my son, John. If Iran could help us in this we would be very grateful.'

'Of course, it is not known who the kidnappers of Mr McCarthy are, so we are interested to know why you came to the Government of Iran for help.'

'We understand that Iran may be able to influence some

of the groups in Lebanon, some of the groups who follow Islam, and the teachings of Ayatollah Khomeini.'

I couldn't stand this ritual dance any longer and cautiously addressed the floor by the chargé's feet. 'We are very anxious to have news of John, to know if he is alive. We have had no news in almost two years now.'

He, in turn, addressed a spot two feet to the right of my head. 'Of course, you will know that we in Iran have hostages, too. Some of them are missing six years and their families do not know if they are alive.'

We went round in the same circles for half an hour and I left feeling a mind-numbing frustration, far worse than anything induced by meetings with the Foreign Office. However, glancing at Pat, it seemed to have gone pretty much as he had expected.

After that kind of stonewalling from officials, it was an enormous relief to be doing something positive to help John. The campaign was snowballing and life was getting increasingly hectic. There was so much to achieve and I fretted endlessly about the work that was needed to co-ordinate it all. After a month's frantic activity we now had an office, but we needed someone to run it. Everyone was working full time and doing campaign work on the side. It was obvious we couldn't cope, but who on earth could we rely on to sort us out?

Suddenly, at work one day, I thought of Cathy Comerford, an ex-WTN colleague who had left several years ago. She had been one of WTN's best newsdesk assistants, extremely well-liked, very bright and good at the job, one of the busiest in the news room. On impulse I picked up the phone and rang her, hoping I still had the right number. She answered, but was obviously in the middle of scolding several unruly children.

'Oh hi, Jill. What's up? Is there any news of John by the way? Roly, will you stop that AT ONCE! No, you cannot feed the cat again.' She broke off to berate her son for a few minutes. 'Now where was I? Oh yes, I was asking you about John.'

'There isn't any news,' I said, 'but that's what I was ringing about. We've decided to set up a campaign to put pressure on the Government and we need someone to run the office. I don't suppose there's any way you would be interested, is there?'

Cathy thought for about two seconds. 'I'd love to,' she said decisively. 'I can't think of anything else I would rather do. It's terrible what's happening to him, it really is, the Government ought to be ashamed of itself. I'll have to arrange babysitters, but it shouldn't be too much of a problem. To tell the truth I'll be glad to escape from the little horrors for a few hours! I'll give you a ring when I've sorted it out.'

With Cathy working two days a week the office started to take shape. I trusted Cathy, and Joan Willows, another ex-WTN colleague who offered to work back-to-back with her, as much as I was able to trust anyone. Intensely pig-headed about everything to do with the campaign, I was overwhelmingly protective of it. I had never been as stubborn or single-minded about anything else, or as insistent that things had to be a certain way. Now, because everything we did or said might have had some effect on John, I found it hard to relax about any aspect and always felt that we had to do more, be more efficient, keep up the pressure.

I tried to keep my feelings under control and remember that all these people were mostly helping us out of the goodness of their hearts, but sometimes it was difficult. I argued over the wording of the campaign slogan because I felt that 'Don't Forget the British Hostages in Beirut' was better than 'Free the Hostages' or 'Support the Hostages'. Afterwards I felt ashamed that I thought I knew better than they did, especially when they were doing everything for free. Every little detail seemed crucial and it was something I struggled with all the way through, but knowing that Cathy, Joan and I were all on the same wavelength and felt the same level of commitment was a great relief.

When it came to setting up the Friends, I found the

words 'realistic' or 'moderation' didn't have much meaning for me. I had a tendency to run around in circles getting more and more worked up. It was therefore essential to have a co-organizer, someone who would keep a cool head. I had asked Chris to be President of the Friends before the first meeting. He says now that if he'd known what it would involve he would have taken the first plane out of town, but thankfully he didn't. He was a good friend of John's, and I knew he would be totally committed. As he was a thoroughly professional journalist, he already knew the media inside out and I trusted his judgement.

Chris would talk things through with me, outlining all the possibilities and different lines of approach. He always stayed calm, but he had a knack of turning things around so that you thought you were getting your own way when in fact you'd just agreed with him. His other tactic was to agree with me and then stand well back from whatever foolish project I'd come up with. I realized he was probably right very early on, although I couldn't always restrain myself.

Chris's laidback manner was also perfect at meetings. After that first one in The Crown and Sceptre kitchen, Chris took the chair more or less every week for the next three years. I was so obsessive about most things that we'd quickly have got bogged down in details if I'd had my way. Chris avoided tedium very successfully; he resisted having an agenda for as long as possible and always refused point-blank to have a vote on anything, so meetings never got hung up on procedure, nor were they subjected to much prior lobbying. Everyone who wanted to speak did so and everything was agreed good-humouredly, without a show of hands and without causing lasting resentments. The pint glass of Tennants Extra that was always close at hand might empty rapidly, but it was the only outward sign that Chris was feeling the pressure.

The committee quickly provided everything that we needed. One person spent illicit hours at Saatchi's designing our logo; WTN allowed a lot of things to go through the system – printing, photocopying, artwork; Gina got the entire staff of her office converted to the cause within weeks and it seemed that everyone else had done the same: soon members' colleagues, friends and relatives were all helping out.

In March we marked John's seven hundredth day by erecting a cell-like cage in Covent Garden and persuading as many famous people as possible to come and stand in it for half an hour while the press filmed them. A friend of ours, Ed King, built the cage for £250 and Alastair Stewart from ITN, Jeremy Paxman, Pattie Coldwell and Simon Groome from the BBC agreed to stand in it. It was quite an act of faith; the Friends present were fired up with enthusiasm, but it was freezing cold, the media coverage was pretty disheartening and the public reaction was less than encouraging. Passers-by were clearly baffled by what they saw and it was only when curiosity proved too much that anyone came near enough to be buttonholed. Time and time again we would begin the long task of explaining who John was and what on earth we were doing.

Up in Doncaster my mum and dad had set up a stall in the car-park of the local Asda in an effort to raise signatures for a rolling petition. They'd been itching to do something to help for all this time, and as soon as the campaign started they rushed into action. They received much the same reaction as we did. 'Who?' 'Where?' The majority of people were sympathetic, but we had a long way to go before people would be shouting *'Honte à la reine Brittanique'* in the streets.

We knew, however, from the reaction to the *Wogan* show, that the support was there. As well as the letters that poured in, the other guests on the programme had all said privately that they would do what they could to help; Ian Hislop, the editor of *Private Eye*, had already printed a Friends of John McCarthy ad for free, and Gerald Scarfe had agreed to design a programme cover for the upcoming Benefit. I was doing interviews with any newspaper or magazine that approached me and some had printed contact numbers for the Friends. The interviews were mostly with women's magazines, and many of the letters we received were from women, who felt an instinctive sympathy for John and could easily put themselves either in my position or that of John's mother. The reality of what was happening to John either played on people's own experience of terrible loss and final separation, or the fear of it, which haunts us all. By the end of the campaign, when it seemed that the whole country was willing him on, it was as if he was everyone's brother, everyone's son, everyone's lover.

Reading the interviews was weird. I was getting used to the odd feeling of distance, which made it seem as if it was all about someone else, but it was alarming to see how most of the articles highlighted the love-story angle, rather than the conditions in which John was held or the reasons I'd given as to why the Government should be doing more. It was hardly surprising that this was the case, and it didn't stop me from giving interviews, but they seemed so far removed from what we were actually trying to do.

I sat in my flat and looked at the latest one. 'Come back, John, I still love you' alongside a huge photograph of me. Was this really the right thing to be doing? It was excruciatingly embarrassing to read the quotes and find myself coming over as a lonely, crusading 'woman who waits'. The interviewers always stressed the despair, that life was under a cloud, but the comradeship of the campaign and the fun we had along the way was just as real. It was odd coming over as a tragic heroine. I wasn't aware that I gave that impression. What was also disturbing was that I found being the centre of attention quite attractive. People listened to me, noticed me more, treated me differently. It made me uncomfortable, but I found that I grew more confident. I had the sense to realize that taking the publicity seriously would be dangerous, but nonetheless it was very seductive. As ever, Mary made sure I kept my feet on the ground.

Nothing that was happening seemed to have anything to do with real life. The most absorbing topic to me was what was going on in Lebanon and, increasingly, Iran. It was vital that we understood the political infighting between the 'moderates' and the 'radicals' there as it seemed more relevant to John and the other British hostages. Auque's news appeared to point to the fact that John was being held by an Iranian-backed group, and in March Hashemi Rafsanjani called a news conference in Tehran during which he repeated his request that Britain should help locate the missing Iranians in Beirut if it wanted Iran to help with the British hostages. Roby's fears of what that might mean weighed against the fact that John Simpson, the BBC's diplomatic correspondent, reported that he had spoken to senior Iranian politicians and was convinced that the British hostages were alive. There was no way of knowing if Simpson was right, but the report in itself was like an oasis in the desert. At last news of the hostages was being reported as a serious story on television. Simpson had broadcast a similar report nine months earlier, but the FO had dismissed it as media hype and not considered it interesting enough to follow up.

In April a Kuwaiti airliner was hijacked and flown to North East Iran. The hijackers were Islamic Jihad, and they threatened to kill members of the Kuwaiti Royal Family on board and all the Western hostages in Beirut if their comrades imprisoned in Kuwait were not released. I didn't think it likely that John would be killed – after all, he wasn't held by Islamic Jihad – but I felt the tension all the same. It was unavoidable; I saw the story unfolding minute by minute at work. Apart from anything else, we were terrified by what Mrs Thatcher would say; there were British people on board and her response might be crucial to their survival, as well as John's.

Chris rang me at work, sounding jubilant. 'Have you seen the wires? She's saying it's important to stand firm, not give in to terrorists, and the rest, but she's said, "That does not mean that you don't negotiate . . . people will be talking to the hijackers very carefully and very closely." Thank you Mrs T,' he added, 'you've admitted that you've got to talk.' We issued a statement pointing out that she wasn't talking to the kidnappers in Beirut, and sent a letter to that effect to every MP, but it was a busy time and no-one really noticed. We felt the same frustration when a British Oxfam worker, Peter Coleridge, was kidnapped in Beirut by Abu Nidal and then released within days, after pressure had been brought to bear by the aid agencies in Lebanon and Mustapha Saad. We tried to point out that the 'no deals' policy was obviously no deterrent to the kidnapping of Britons, but again, nobody really took much notice.

On the second anniversary of his kidnap, we made sure John was in the news. We handed out a video which WTN colleagues had culled together. It started with the terrible sound of a heavy door banging shut as a prison bar appeared over John's face, then Mrs Thatcher's voice could be heard saying, 'The role of Government is to create individual freedom, not deny it.' Another bar swung into place, another terrible clanging sound, and then Mrs Thatcher said, 'The Government is the servant of its people, not its master,' her voice echoing over and over again. This was followed by shots of John from some pop videos Barbara had made and then some footage that Nick and I had discovered in Damascus of John's farewell party in Beirut. I had seen these images of John before, but then came a video report from Danish TV back in 1981. Nick had unearthed it and passed it on. Claus Toksvig, then a Danish broadcaster based in London, had been reporting on unemployment in Britain. He decided to feature John, who was out of a job at the time.

This was the best; it was John exactly as I remembered him, walking down a road, waiting at a bus stop, hunched inside his big coat. Suddenly, as I watched the video in an editing suite at work, I heard his deep, warm voice filling the room and was transfixed. I realized that I had completely forgotten what he sounded like. It was so weird it made my hair stand on end; it was almost as if a ghost had walked into the room. He was talking about what it was like to be unemployed and, typical John, was making his depressing position sound not too bad. It was amazing to watch him walking and talking. For the thirty seconds or so that the video lasted, John was alive, but I couldn't hold on to it for any longer than that. The video ended and he was gone.

The anniversary publicity also involved a video of a young band called Sanctuary singing, 'John, we want you Home', which they had written for us, and a number of colleagues and others running in the London marathon wearing Friends of John McCarthy running vests, one bearing the number 17.4.86. The *pièce de résistance*, though, was to be the Benefit. It was held on the anniversary itself, and for me followed three days of interviews and other press events organized by Cathy and Chris. I was exhausted by the time that 'An Evening without John McCarthy' arrived, but the venue, the Camden Palace, wasn't far from my flat and, prompted by nerves, I turned up early, about an hour before things were due to begin. Arriving, I suddenly realized that I didn't have a job to do. I hadn't been involved in the organization and knew very little about what was going to happen. I felt rather at a loss.

Inside the ticket hall, a team of volunteers were putting up posters. Ed King was busily erecting the cage we'd had in Covent Garden; it was proving to be worth every penny of the £250 we'd paid for it. A friend of Gina's, Julie O'Dea, was in charge of the tickets; for the past few weeks, her flat had been a temporary box-office and she was running a tight ship; all committee members who took tickets were responsible for the money they owed. Chris had already been given a severe ticking-off when he'd admitted to the box-office that he'd lost count of the number of tickets and cheques he'd stuffed into all his suit pockets. I briefly saw Gina flit by talking into a short-wave radio and was momentarily stunned. Gina was completely preoccupied, in formidable, super-efficient mode; she waved hallo and then disappeared again, radio crackling.

I picked up a programme, which had been designed by one of the committee members, Sue Brown; it was a work of art. Gerald Scarfe's simple drawing of an empty chair was on the front and inside were pictures of John, information about the campaign, even a ready-to-send letter to MPs which you could tear out. Sue had designed it in the shape of a dove and the message read: 'How to give your MP the bird'. I looked at the line-up listed in the programme and at the stop-press late additions: Everything But The Girl, two of The Communards; Harry Enfield; The Oblivion Boys, the list went on. Barbara had pulled out all the stops. I walked inside the dance hall. Chris Jury, who had masterminded the whole thing and was entirely responsible for what was happening on stage, was taking some musicians through a soundcheck and, like Gina, was completely absorbed in what he was doing. At the back of the stage a huge banner made by the Hull University Drama Department read: 'Friends of John McCarthy'. It hit me for the first time that the bands and comedians were going to be performing here for free, for John, for us. It was terrifying.

I looked around at the place; I had been here before but it had never looked so huge. There was a big dance floor and several sprawling tiers of tables and bars. I knew that we all had sold a fair number of tickets to friends, relatives, colleagues, in fact, anyone who would buy them, but it wouldn't be enough to fill one tier. I walked up to the bar, passing several people I had never seen before who were obviously volunteers. Someone gave me a pass. Backstage passes! It was amazing.

Once there, I saw that Gina's sister Juliette had organized food and drink for the bands, all mostly donated for free. Drivers from the taxi firm WTN used were arriving all the time with equipment, food and people. I saw a couple of people with TV cameras; Tony had persuaded some cameramen to film the Benefit for free so he could make it into a video afterwards. Barbara and I were interviewed by one team upstairs in the top bar. I stood there clutching a drink, feeling completely lost. 'Would John enjoy tonight?' an interviewer asked. Barbara was confident that he would, it was just his sort of evening, but I wasn't sure if I knew what John would enjoy any more.

Chris arrived, notepad in hand, hair flying, and made sure I knew that we were both going out on stage at the end of the Benefit. It was the last thing in the world I wanted to do, but I couldn't refuse, not after the work that had gone into a production like this. I didn't know what I was going to say, but I would have to come up with something. The idea of standing out there was too awful to contemplate, and the knowledge that the hour would eventually arrive sent me into a state of high anxiety. Brian arrived, with his girlfriend and another friend, who seemed to realize that I needed to calm down and offered to walk around the building with me. I followed him, gratefully, and we wandered down some backstairs and out on to another floor just as Ray Gelato and his Giants of Jive were starting up.

I looked over the balcony, first at the stage and then back at the dance floor and beyond. There were people everywhere, rushing to the bars, crowding on to the dance floor, filling all the chairs and tables. The place was packed. A surge of adrenalin lifted me sky-high. All these people are here for John, I thought, and for us, as well as to hear the bands. It didn't seem possible. I put a lot of it down to Harry Enfield; just this week he'd really taken off. We'd booked him just as his catchphrases were being quoted by the entire nation, and all because Julie's mortgage broker knew someone who knew his phone number and he had agreed to appear.

We walked on, but now I had to stop every few yards because people were coming up to me; friends who wanted to introduce other friends, schoolfriends of John's, an ex-girlfriend, cousins. They all wanted to say hallo and shake my hand. I couldn't think of a single thing to say, but dimly realized that I now had my role for the evening; I had done nothing to bring this off, but I was to be the identifiable face of the campaign. It was nice, people were so kind, offering encouragement and congratulations for what had been achieved; I almost felt as if I had done it all. I felt quite heady; surely this overwhelming force of affection, compassion and concern must be able to produce something.

I couldn't really cope with meeting any more people and went to watch Everything But The Girl from nearer the stage. Shivers went down my spine when they sang, 'Come on Home' and again when Jimmy Somerville sang, 'For a Friend'. It was a moving song, and I could see people with tears in their eyes, but I kept wondering why I couldn't feel anything. The extraordinary atmosphere was keeping me so sky-high that my private feelings for John seemed to have detached themselves and slipped out of reach. It was such a collective experience that John wasn't mine any more, I had to share him with all these people, each with different motivations and reasons for being here. He was special to me but here was evidence that he was special to a lot of people. It was wonderful, but why did John not seem like an ordinary person any more, but a cause or a symbol to rally everyone around?

In my newspaper message to John I had said that hundreds of people would be attending a benefit for him tonight. I had wanted to give him hope and reassure him that he was loved, but the reality was quite overwhelming and a bit scary. The Benefit was an unqualified success, which was the main thing, but asking for the support of hundreds of strangers inevitably meant that the focus of their concern would be on John as well as on the terrible thing that was happening to him. I came down to earth a bit when Harry Enfield came on to thunderous applause. 'I don't know who this John McCartney is,' he said, 'and I don't care. You know why

I don't give a monkey's? 'Cos I got loadsamoney, that's why!' That would have made John laugh, I thought; I can imagine him here after all.

At the end of the evening Sanctuary went on stage and played their song for John. Terrified, I stood by the stage, knowing I had to go on after them. I clutched a drink and a grubby piece of paper. My 'speech' was written on it. Chris had insisted that if he was going to go out there, then so was I. I'd been searching for a way out all night, but nothing convincing came to mind.

All around me voices were saying, 'Good luck', as I walked on to the stage, but I was much too nervous to do anything but nod, grimly. Chris took the microphone and launched in. I can't remember what he said – I was too worried about what would happen when he stopped – but he looked supremely confident. The response from the crowd was fantastic, but when he introduced me I was hardly conscious of their cheers.

Once I'd started, I felt less hysterical. I went through a list of thanks and hoped I hadn't left anyone out. I was astonished by the number of people there and grateful for their warmth and support, but I felt I had to convince everybody to take the campaign home with them. I found it difficult to keep my voice steady.

'I've never really felt before tonight how much John is not alone. We've got 1,700 people here who have showed how much they feel about him. If everybody here just rang up the Foreign Office, rang up their MP, or wrote to the Prime Minister – it's everybody's right to do that – and said "What's happening to John McCarthy? We want him home." I didn't think we could possibly organize this evening, but we have. There's no stopping us now, so let's get John home.'

Chris was looking a bit alarmed. I was so high on adrenalin that for all I knew I was talking utter rubbish. Afterwards he told me that he'd thought I was going to start a revolution there and then. He took the microphone again and to renewed cheers raised his pint.

'Before we go there's one thing I would like to do. I want to propose a toast to an absent – and sorely missed – friend. Tonight I give you John McCarthy.'

7
Lebanon, May 1988–August 1990

The shooting started on 5 May. It sounded so close it
must have been in the street below us. At first there
were just a few 'pops', perhaps from pistols, then other
weapons joined in, from the familiar rattle of Kalashnikovs
to heavier machine-guns. By late afternoon, a full-scale
battle had broken out with rockets and grenades exploding
regularly and bullets thudding into the walls.

Mazzin came and told us to lie along the inside wall
together. We thought it would be more sensible to move
to the other side of the apartment; if a shell hit the wall to
which we were chained, we wouldn't stand a chance. I was
terribly conscious of just how vulnerable we were, in the
hands of our untrained guards, who were probably just as
frightened as we were. They couldn't be relied on to cope
with the situation and our safety at the same time.

'Who's fighting who?' I asked Mazzin.

'It's nothing,' he replied, 'just a family quarrel.'

Some family, some quarrel.

Overnight, the fighting calmed down a little but it
picked up again the next morning and raged on throughout
the day. We'd guessed that whatever local dispute had
provoked the initial spat it was now a battle between much
larger factions, probably Amal and Hezbollah. During the
day, there were visitors to the flat, one of whom came and
spoke to me. He spoke little English so I made 'bang-bang'
noises and said, *'Chou? Amal boom boom Hezbollah?'*

'Nam, yes.'

'Not family!'

'Non famille,' he laughed. At least twice a week we'd
heard the sermons broadcast from a nearby mosque and

were both sure that the preacher was Sheikh Fadlallah, one of the main spiritual leaders of Hezbollah. With the fighting so close, we had to be right on the border between Amal and Hezbollah territory.

Despite this, Mazzin maintained that it was still a local feud. His blind refusal to break the rules and give us any information was so bloody irritating. It couldn't have made any difference to them if we knew what was happening.

On the evening of 7 May we were moved. We weren't taped up this time, but we were blindfolded. Being hurried down stairs, trying to feel for the edge of the steps, unable to see, was very unnerving. I feared that at any moment I might fall and break my neck. The sounds of gunfire and shelling didn't do anything to calm my fears. We clambered into the back of a VW truck and drove for about five minutes, then waited outside an apartment block while the guards chatted with a woman. When she'd gone, we were bustled in and raced up the stairs. We must have climbed up eight flights. I collapsed in a heap as did George, one of the guards from the Pigsty, who was puffing as hard as me. That night we stayed in the guards' room with Mahmoud, but we had the feeling that other hostages were there, too.

The next day we were put in a different room and found brackets for the chains already attached to the wall. Others had indeed been here. We could still hear the fighting, but it was at a distance, while the sermons from the mosque were louder than ever. Another Friday 13th was approaching so I was certain we could expect another move, maybe the big one. We'd barely settled in when, sure enough, on 15 May, we were moved again.

Looking back I can see that some details of the various journeys have become confused in my memory. While preparing myself for what was coming I also had to keep track of what was actually happening, trying to picture the scenes I was living through, but couldn't see. Time was thrown completely out of joint by the instant transition from long periods of inactivity, when the most dramatic part of any day was a slow walk to the bathroom and back, to a chaos of orders, panic, delays and wild hurries, fear and physical discomfort. Within minutes one was torn from reading a book to being gagged and trussed up in a sack, carried down stairs by running men, waiting for the bag to slip or rip and one's head or neck to smash against the hard stone steps.

We were bundles, lifted up and put down wherever it suited our captors. We went in cardboard boxes, in fridges, in metal coffins fixed like mummies, in sacks like animals for market. We were turned, lifted, pushed, lowered, pressed and turned again in a direction that couldn't be guessed, only feared.

I know we were kept in thirteen main locations and I recall most of the dates we moved, but the minutiae have begun to merge. I don't remember how they got us out of the apartment, but I do remember that we stopped somewhere before leaving Beirut where we were taped up and transferred to a false-bottomed truck. For the first, and last time a guard travelled with us in the box. It was Mazzin. He had a pistol with a silencer on it. As usual we were advised that they were ready to do anything. Presumably he was there as a special precaution because of the Amal-Hezbollah fighting. Somehow I was relieved that a guard was with us because I thought that if there was an accident his friends might try to get him – and maybe us – out. It was one less thing to hyperventilate about. However, Mazzin was not the calmest of the guards and might easily panic and shoot us.

After an early start we were soon out of the city and climbing. It soon got hot. I tried to pass the time imagining the pleasant, and peaceful, countryside all around us as we drove through the mountains. Although the move was probably inspired by the fighting, it didn't mean that we wouldn't be going home soon. One of these months with a Friday 13th must come good eventually. There were lots of good omens and I was still inspired by the news of Jill and her campaign.

Every now and then Mazzin would run his hands over me, checking that I hadn't somehow ripped off the bindings and wasn't about to attack him. It took a great deal of effort not to wriggle about as much as I normally did, but I feared him panicking more than the physical discomfort.

The drive seemed interminable. I knew that I always overestimated the time these outings took, but I was certain that we'd been going for over two hours, and still we were crashing on. The heat was getting unbearable, our bodies soaked in sweat, aching, desperate for water and rest. Mazzin started feeling my stomach again. I could only imagine that Brian had managed to loosen his hands. In the event Mazzin was after the notebooks we'd stuffed down the front of our pyjamas. 'Why on earth should he want those now?' I wondered. Then he fumbled with the tape over my mouth. I'd worked it down by moving my jaw as much as possible. 'Don't cover my mouth, you bastard,' I thought, 'I'll lose control.' He didn't. In fact he pulled it further down making it easier for me to breathe.

On we went, it must have been three hours by now. We'd been turning on and off roads all along, dodging checkpoints I guessed. Then I realized that we kept returning to the same place and stopping for a few minutes, before moving off again around a similar route. 'We must be near,' I thought, 'they're waiting to get the all-clear to enter a certain area, where, please God, we'll stop.' I wanted to go to sleep, but was terrified of waking up in there, mummified, and going berserk. 'Don't sleep, don't sleep.' The heat, the fumes from the diesel engine, the physical and mental exhaustion were all dragging me down fast.

Suddenly Brian started shouting, 'How much fucking longer? Shoot me now and get it over with!'

'Hold on, Brian, for fuck's sake,' I thought. 'This guy's scared enough, don't push him now.'

But Mazzin seemed unconcerned. 'OK, OK, *seulement cinq minutes, cinq minutes*.'

He turned over to me and I felt the gun barrel at my head. 'Marvellous,' I thought. 'Brian goes bonkers and the little sod comforts him but sticks a gun in my ear.' I lapsed into a semi-coma, only vaguely conscious that we came round again to the familiar spot and waited, then headed off in a new direction.

We stopped. The end of the box was unbolted. Mazzin was out of there in a flash, laughing with his friends who seemed eager to know what it was like in the box. We were dragged out. I couldn't move. As they stripped off the tape I just lolled about, unable to get my brain to focus, let alone co-ordinate any muscles. After a few minutes I managed to get to my knees and use a pee-bottle, although after sweating so much, I can't imagine I needed to. Then we were lifted down through a trap door and laid on a mattress.

My mind refused to clear and I felt delirious, like in a dream where everything slows down and you can't reach your destination. Your legs are jelly, your mind sluggish, your will gone. 'Brian, are they going to shoot us?'

'Och no, John, we're going to a swimming-pool.'

'Really, did they tell you that? I'm not sure, doesn't sound right . . . Brian, are they going to shoot us?'

'No, we're going . . .'

I couldn't follow the words, couldn't appreciate the tone, light-hearted and reassuring. They gave us an apple each. The juice was marvellous, cutting through the taste of dust and diesel fumes. I felt a little better. I asked for a cigarette. Mahmoud gave me one. I could barely smoke it. Brian was lying down, dozing off. After a while I calmed down enough to rest myself.

Some hours later we were off again, in the truck, but untaped. A few minutes' drive and we were taken into a building. There were no sounds of traffic or neighbours. We must have been right out in the sticks. Inside I was guided down a weird stairway and told at one point to watch my step carefully. Below my blindfold I could see tiles and a toilet set in them. Down some more steps and into a room. We were underground. Brian was right behind me. Our mattresses were there. We sat down. Enormous chains were fastened to our ankles. Then a guard said, '*Kifak*, how are you, Andy?'

'OK thanks, Younis,' replied an American voice.

'*Kifak*, Abu Tariq?'

'I'm good, thanks,' replied another American voice. Who were these guys? There was another one with a name new to us. Were they *still* kidnapping people?

'Good night,' said the guards. 'Please, no noise.' A mixture of accents chorused 'Good night.' A metal door banged shut, then a piece of wood was tapped into place, then silence. I lifted my blindfold.

Brian was to my left. In front of us was a row of three men, sitting on mattresses, chained like us. They looked very familiar. The one to the right of my feet, nearest the door, bounced forward, hand out, 'Hi John, Terry Anderson.'

'Hallo Terry, fancy meeting you here.'

We all shook hands and grinned stupidly at one another. Terry, Tom and Frank all looked fine. It was so strange to meet and talk to them in the flesh. Hitherto we'd only seen their faces and spoken with our hands. Brian and I recounted the awful journey, but, of course, all the Yanks had been through the same ordeal. It turned out that Anderson had lived in the last apartment that we'd been in, moving out the day after we arrived. Like us, he reckoned that there'd been another man there. He said Fou-Fou agreed. 'Who's Fou-Fou?'

'Marcel Fontaine. The guards called him Fou-Fou and me Andy. He's gone home.'

'He's gone home?' There was a lot to take in here.

'All the French have. They went on 4 May,' said Tom. 'Are you sure?'

'I saw them arrive in Paris on the television,' Terry went on. This was terrific news. Before moving here, Terry had spoken to one of the big chiefs, whom he called the

Haj, and had been told that everything was now winding down, that we'd all be going soon. The fact that we'd all been put together was universally accepted as a sign that the end was so close that they didn't need to keep us apart any longer. *Allah Akbar!*

We'd been certain that Frank had been kept with a Frenchman in the apartment we'd been in from February to early May. He had – Jean-Paul Kauffman. Terry had been with Fontaine in Beirut. Tom had also been with Kauffman and the other long-term French hostage, Marcel Carton, in the place in the south, the one with the makeshift tent. Then Kauffman had been moved to join Frank and Carton came here with Tom. Tom confirmed our assumption that we were in the Beka'a Valley saying that Carton, an Arabic speaker, told him that some of the food wrappers had Baalbek addresses on them.

We talked for a while, catching up on our movements since we'd last been neighbours six months earlier, in November. Eventually we dropped off to sleep. For once we had definite news that things were looking up, and it was the perfect antidote to the gruelling journey.

The next day we started to get to know each other properly. Tom and Terry, but especially Terry, wanted to know everything about us immediately: where we'd been to school; what we'd studied; the history of the British constitution, or lack of it from an American point of view; what the real situation was in Ireland; why didn't Brian hit me when I responded to a proffered cigarette with, 'Fuck off out of my life, you wheedling Irish bastard'?

Brian and I noticed immediately that our three companions didn't have the same relaxed intimacy that we shared. They thought that we meant the insults and couldn't initially figure out why the injured party would fall about laughing instead of going into a sulk. Eventually they caught on and I think they enjoyed our banter. We certainly all seemed to laugh a lot.

Tom told us his life-story. He sat in the corner farthest from the door, a good-looking man in his fifties, with a twinkle in his eye despite three years' captivity, recalling incidents from his Scottish childhood in amazing detail. He would play all the characters like a one-man theatre. His memory was remarkable but it was often frustrating when an interesting story was interrupted while he talked about the family background of a man he'd met once in Iowa in the early 1960s.

Tom was a kind and gentle man, so his coolness towards Frank Reed was rather surprising. As far as I could tell Frank had recovered from the breakdown we witnessed in late 1986 and, despite the months alone and the awful beatings he'd received in the Pigsty, he still had a great sense of humour and told us hysterical episodes from his life, many of them against himself. He explained the theory of Mastery of Learning, about which he'd spoken before. It was an American teaching method that, Frank insisted, allowed students to progress through the stages of education confident that they had grasped all the basics of one stage before going on to the next. This sounded excellent to Brian and me. Repeatedly we had cursed ourselves and our schools for allowing us to think we'd grasped maths, physics and so on when now we couldn't remember any of the important or useful things. Frank was convinced of his arguments and fought bitterly with Tom, another academic, when he mocked the whole system.

Frank was withdrawn much of the time, often sitting for hours with his blindfold down. Bri and I assumed that he'd had enough of his countrymen and wanted to tune out. It was, however, obvious that there was some deep sadness within him. He spoke very warmly of his parents, but I felt that he'd been a lonely child. His career sounded very hit and miss; he'd switched from one subject to another at university, studying for a PhD but never completing it, and then shifted from job to job, looking for status rather than satisfaction. His first marriage had failed and, although his second, to a Syrian woman he'd met in Beirut, sounded disorganized, he talked fondly of his son Tariq.

Like Tom and myself, Frank was still proud of his appearance even in this hole in the ground. Terry, like Brian, didn't give a damn. Whenever we spoke about haircuts or what clothes they'd give us to go home in, Anderson would say, 'I don't care what I look like, I'll go out stark naked, I just want to leave.'

Going home really did seem a possibility. We had quite a few visitors over the next few days and Amin, particularly, was very encouraging. For once his 'soon and very soon' seemed more than empty optimism. Terry used his limited Arabic to have a long conversation with another visitor who suggested that an American would go home soon with the Irishman and then, after a little while, during which our governments were expected to 'make the next step', another American with a Briton and so on. This man also promised to see about getting us some magazines and a radio.

We talked endlessly about the possible timetable for release. My numbers game seemed to have been happily overshadowed by reality, although Franky clearly had his own mysterious method of divination, saying portentously, 'The number eleven, remember I told you that.' He would become even more mysterious when questioned. Tom believed that any day was the day. Brian and Terry remained slightly more cautious, Anderson saying, 'I'll give it a Ben,' a reference to Ben Weir who'd always said, 'I'll give it another month.'

And so we waited and continued to get to know one another. It took quite a while to put the Americans in proper perspective. They argued a lot, with Tom and Frank finally erecting an invisible wall between them. They hardly spoke more than a couple of words in six months. Terry was still talking to Frank, but Frank ridiculed everything he said to the point where they, too, hardly spoke. Terry and Tom argued as well, and there often seemed to be far more serious undercurrents than a simple difference of opinion. But maybe, having been on our own for so long, we were just oversensitive.

Both Tom and Terry had strong personalities, and Anderson, in particular, was very tough. A bright schoolboy, he'd joined the Marines at seventeen and gone to Vietnam. There, he'd worked for the Corps' news service, been wounded, gone home to study journalism at college and ended up with the Associated Press. He'd worked in Japan and married there, been bureau chief in South Africa and then taken over as the AP's chief Middle East correspondent in Beirut.

He was no taller than me, but was very heavily built. His physical presence was almost as much a part of his style of argument as his intelligence. Brian and I both found this wearing. We liked to talk about things, to search each other's memories for information and sometimes to have heated discussions. But the idea was never to defeat the other; we didn't want to score points. The Yanks appeared to need to do each other down, which, under the circumstances, was counter-productive.

One day when I couldn't answer a question about the workings of the British Parliament, Terry said, 'What's the matter, you dumb or what?' I was devastated. What could we possibly gain by undermining each other's self-confidence? Over the months it became clear that Tom's aggressive arguing with Terry was founded on a similar slight two and a half years previously.

Soon after his kidnap Tom had gone into a serious depression – he suffered from them periodically. He had been quite fazed by the guard-hostage situation and, feeling vulnerable, had decided that the other hostages, particularly Anderson and Jacobsen, thought him slow.

Terry had demonstrated his real worth by bringing Tom out of this decline. Tom freely acknowledged this just as Terry acknowledged his earlier insensitivity. Yet here they were needling one another as if the position of an aeroplane's wings on take-off, the true nature of Kennedy's presidency or the price of fish were matters that somehow impinged on their honour or real worth as human beings.

Having been deemed ignorant I dropped out of many of these discussions, finding them too oppressive. Brian then had to face the full force of the Sutherland-Anderson fact-finding machine on his own. They argued ferociously about Ireland, although neither of them knew too much about it. One of Bri's great loves, literature, became a nightmare for him as he had to defend even the most off-hand comment. He'd be stuck there with Terry and Tom sitting as close to him as their chains would allow, hardly letting him finish a thought before jumping in with an idea that took them miles away from Brian's original argument. I was very dismayed that I couldn't enjoy swapping ideas with Brian any more without things turning into a do-or-die debate. Late one night I whispered to him that I was worried that the Yanks were taxing him too hard, that his lucid arguments and eloquence were being weakened by constant niggling at everything he said. He, too, felt enough was enough.

The next day he started quizzing Tom on the possibility of setting up a pig-farm where the object was not to produce meat, but milk and cheese. I thought this was completely mad but became enthralled as Tom, Dean of Agriculture at AUB and an expert in animal science, outlined all the possibilities and problems – he even knew the average milk production of a sow. The problem seemed to have been solved. Talking over schemes like this was both entertaining and educative. Tom was a brilliant teacher. I found, through asking Anderson about his life, especially about his work as a journalist, that I liked the man much more when he wasn't trying to impose his intellectual will on the rest of us.

As I gained confidence in their genuine goodwill I found that my sense of humour returned and I enjoyed making them laugh. I felt useful when, during exercise periods, I could have Anderson choking with laughter, hanging on to Brian for support, as I imitated one of the guards and his absurdly curious use of English.

Here, in this dungeon we nicknamed the Pit, we were all free to make fun of the guards, in particular Abu Salim, he of clicking fingers fame. As a holy-roller he was something apart. He'd come down and try to get us to translate his prayers into English, or would turn up and recite Koranic verses he'd half translated with Mahmoud or one of the other English-speakers. He was such a two-faced little man that finding these hysterically funny didn't feel wrong. 'In my God, the rope red. Me in the ground, after, me in the rope, God.' We all used to bite our lips and nod wisely at these theological conundrums, holding our breath until he'd gone back upstairs before dissolving into laughter.

Abu Salim was a pain, which is why it was such a relief to take the mickey out of him. He got into the habit of coming down into our cell and asking an endless string of questions on vocabulary, which he normally directed at Terry. 'Tirry, what the meaning . . . ?' Terry would try and work out something to keep him happy and get rid of him.

One night when Terry, Frank, Brian and I were playing cards as Tom nodded off to sleep, Frank exclaimed, 'Incandescent, shit!'

'What's that, Franky?'

'When that boy was down here earlier he asked Tom what we call an ordinary light bulb if it isn't "flouress". Tom told him incandescent. Sure it's true,' Frank went on, 'but how the fuck's the guy gonna remember that?' We all fell about laughing at the idea of a man with virtually no English suddenly coming out with such a word.

'You're right, Franky,' I said, 'maybe we should just tell him "cup" every time he asks, "What's the meaning?" '

The next day Abu Salim was down again. He asked Terry to explain a word. Terry firmly said, 'Cup.' Abu Salim sounded perplexed. He knew cup was what we drank out of, but he accepted it. A few minutes later he asked another word. 'Cup,' said Anderson. 'Not cup!' barked Abu Salim. There was a long pause as we all tried to hold back the giggles. Terry gave him a different word and he went off content.

The Pit was about fifteen by twelve feet. The ceiling was so low that Frank could never stand up straight and even the shorties like Brian, Terry and I had to be careful not to bang our heads when we were exercising. Anderson, often eager to jump around and burn off some frustration, cut the little bald patch on the top of his head, and cursed himself. 'God, why must I be so clumsy?'

He wasn't clumsy at all, at least not physically. He made us some fine sets of playing cards and a neat Monopoly board. On a personal level, though, Terry's enthusiasm was sometimes gauche. He bombarded us in his zest for education, entertainment and, indeed, any intellectual exercise, but in the early days was oblivious to our hesitant reactions. Yet, when he did notice somebody was down, he was always very concerned and would try to cope with it, as with everything, head on. His strength of character was invaluable in dealing with the guards and his commitment to his fellow hostages was such that he would listen quietly and matter of factly on the occasions when we all had a heart-to-heart about the little ways in which we got on each others' nerves. As with Brian, and I hope myself, Terry worked on these areas to try and even off the rough edges.

Tom, on the other hand, didn't seem to have any rough edges. He was a gentle man by nature, but he would suddenly fall into a depression and lose all confidence in himself. This often happened when he thought that one or all of us were laughing at him, especially if he interpreted our teasing as mocking his intelligence. It was such a shame that he felt like that and couldn't recognize the true and deep affection that Terry, Brian and I had for him. Sadly, when he went into one of his depressions, he sometimes seemed to punish us by deciding that he wouldn't go on any more – he'd stop eating and that would be that. We all had the right to do this, but the rest of us would acknowledge the others' right to know what was going on and why.

On a couple of occasions, Brian had contemplated a hunger strike. But he'd known that while I might accept his desire to get out of the situation I could not accept his withdrawing support from me, just shutting me out, without letting me come to terms with his thinking. We had discussed the issue in great depth. Indeed by this time we were so in tune with one another that explanations were unnecessary. We were so confident of each other's love that should one of us make that final, selfish decision the other would feel his friend's sense of loss even more keenly than his own.

It did not feel the same with Tom. He had just turned away from us and read a book. He'd be jolly with the guards, telling them, 'It's OK thanks, I just want to lose a bit of weight,' and hold his belly, saying, 'Look at all this fat.' The guards knew full well what was happening and we knew that after a few days they were likely to get heavy about it. But we didn't have the energy to deal with them, given that Tom wasn't prepared to share his thinking with us. It eventually reached the point when one of us would simply talk to him about anything and everything until he'd break and say, 'OK, you want me to talk. Well, two weeks ago, John said something about AUB and Terry laughed. I couldn't hear exactly what he said, but I knew from Terry's tone that they were taking the piss out of me.' Then we'd try to remember the incident and painstakingly explain to Tom what had actually happened. It was an exhausting process and it was hurtful to think that Tom was so unsure of us.

He was terribly concerned about getting old. He was a good-looking man and was in good shape. His hearing was going a little which bothered him and he was worried that his memory was weak which was crazy, given his astonishing recall of detail. His stories were richly entertaining and his ability to remember whole courses that he taught became a very valuable source of information and entertainment.

Sometimes, if the lights had been left on, and I was unable to sleep, I'd look across to Tom and feel great sorrow to see that fine man lying on the floor in a bleak underground room, with a rough blanket over his legs and cockroaches crawling over him as he slept.

His curious insecurity would turn him permanently against some of his fellow hostages. When he'd started regaining his confidence he told us that he'd taken over from Terry in the endless arguments with David Jacobsen. Terry spoke evenly, if coolly, about Jacobsen, but Tom remembered him with something approaching venom. This streak was obvious in his relationships with Frank, who was certainly difficult to live with, and later with Terry Waite. One moment he loved them like a brother, then he'd turn away and never want to speak fondly to them again. Looking back, I'm sure that Frank's comment about the incandescent lights and another occasion when Tom was threatening to recite some Rabbie Burns and Franky had stated bluntly, 'We don't want to listen to that shit', were the real basis for Tom's antipathy. It hadn't helped that on both occasions the rest of us had laughed at Frank's remarks. We all lived on top of each other and at any time one of us was probably irritated in some way by one of the others, but Tom seemed to hold on to it for a long time, never expressing his resentment until he just flipped into despising somebody.

Brian and I weren't entirely sure how to deal with the Yanks' antagonisms. Sometimes it was like a sit-com, where two characters refuse to speak directly to each other, always using a third party to pass on comments. It was particularly odd as Frank was chained in the middle of the trio so when Terry and Tom were talking they would do so over Frank's head, almost as if he wasn't there.

In a sense this was true, although Brian and I didn't appreciate quite how detached Franky had become until we lived alone with him late the following year. He would sit for hours with his blindfold down, taking no part in the general conversations, or at best looking at Brian and me, shaking his head when his compatriots said something with which he disagreed. But occasionally he did speak to us, telling more funny stories, offering encouragement and giving me advice and demonstrations on how to improve my golf stroke.

Terry had played a fair bit of golf so would join in these chats, happy to acknowledge that Frank was the expert. I don't know what the guards thought when they looked through the closed-circuit television that was always trained on us here and saw three men, heads motionless, looking down fixedly at some spot on the ground, making curious, swinging arm movements.

Terry kept badgering the guards for magazines and a radio. He did it automatically whenever a guard was in the room. I often thought it was a pointless exercise, but, as he said, 'If you don't ask, you don't get', and he hoped that eventually they'd get so fed up with him that they'd deliver. He was right – they did, in early June.

When Mahmoud came in with a radio playing and said, 'Tirry, this is for you,' there was a moment's hush while we all thought, 'It must be a joke.' We were like nervous children, unsure that they'll be allowed to keep the lovely toy a relative stranger has just given them. We recovered our manners and began a series of, 'Thank yous', and, 'You are a good man, Mahmoud', and, within seconds, Terry had it tuned to the BBC World Service and its theme, 'Lili Bolero'.

When Mahmoud left we were like children again. 'Let me look, let me!' It was a very basic little radio but it worked fine. We could pick up the World Service, Voice of America (VOA) and a number of local stations which broadcast in English and French. The fact that our captors were confident and considerate enough to let us have the radio was almost as encouraging as the news we could at last listen to after two years of silence.

Britain was on the verge of restoring diplomatic relations, albeit only partially, with Iran. The minor disputes between the two countries, over reparations for damaged embassies in Tehran and London and some other outstanding debts, seemed all but settled and a group of

MPs were visiting the Iranian capital. The Iranians, too, were making very hopeful noises that improved relations, which must include British support for a UN resolution blaming Iraq for the Iran-Iraq War, would encourage them to help secure our release.

With Britain getting closer to Iran and with the US constantly improving its rapport with Syria, we felt that now we were all together, we could be released without having to wait for all the governments to restore relations. The only factor casting a shadow over all this was our concern, emphasized by Terry, that whatever governments might agree, Islamic Jihad would still insist on the release of the seventeen men held in Kuwait. Assuming this to be true, I thought that Brian and I might be in a better position. Our captivity had never been linked to theirs, as far as we knew. We also thought that if Iran, and its ally Syria, which controlled Lebanon, insisted on our release, there wasn't much chance of our captors refusing to co-operate.

At last, things seemed to be moving in a very positive direction. Listening to news from home on the BBC gave us a real sense of belonging again. Hearing British voices talking about anything from politics to music, even listening to old comedy shows, felt like the first step home.

Tom was chief radio monitor. From seven in the morning he'd sit there with the thing pressed to his ear; to preserve the batteries and to avoid alarming the guards, we always set it at the lowest volume. He'd often hear a mention of hostages on the early news he picked up from Radio Monte Carlo or VOA that might not be repeated later in the day. It was usually about Terry's sister, Peggy Say, and her efforts to get him home. Terry was very proud of Peggy's achievement. Terry's family, unlike he himself, hadn't had a great deal of experience of the world outside the States, so Peg had had an awful lot to learn.

From the letter Brian had received from the newspaper last November, we knew that his sisters and friends were working for him and we had also heard that Jill,

Nick Toksvig and other friends were active on my behalf. Nevertheless, it was amazing to hear John Bullock of the *Independent* say on the BBC's *Comment* programme that the Friends of John McCarthy had actually altered British government policy on the Iran–Iraq War.

I was immensely proud of this, having no idea that 'the Friends' was now a rapidly growing organization which had moved far beyond my immediate circle. In a strange way I felt almost embarrassed that such things were happening in my name. How could I live up to them when I got home?

Frank and Tom were never mentioned, even on the anniversary of their kidnaps, beyond being listed with all the hostages. I don't know what Frank thought, but Tom was clearly bothered, feeling forgotten and also angry that somehow he wasn't as important as the others. We tried to reassure him that this wasn't the case, that newspeople were merely going for the stories with the biggest hook. Doubtless his friends and family were working on his behalf and might well be involved with Peggy Say's campaign.

Frank had no real interest in the radio, beyond sometimes listening to the sports news. Terry, Brian and I also soon lost interest in monitoring it around the clock, although we'd listen to programmes that sounded interesting, together with a couple of news bulletins a day and then VOA at night as Tom went off to sleep and the rest of us played cards.

We even enjoyed one of the local stations. There was a woman newsreader, whose name sounded like Magda Tacker, and we soon called her Margaret Thatcher. Her sentences were amazingly convoluted, verbatim translations from interminable statements by Lebanese politicians. Nearly every broadcast would herald, 'The minister said, "We are on the threshold of the doorway to the window of opportunity . . ."' And then Magda would be off again explaining that, 'The road to Damascus was busy again today . . .'

It was from Magda that we heard early in September that a British Sunday newspaper had reported that an Iranian with close links to Hezbollah had said in Beirut that I was to be released immediately. For a couple of days I was extremely nervous. At one point there seemed to be a lot of people arriving upstairs and we wondered if they were there to take me out. Oddly I was uneasy about this, worrying over what I should do for my friends when I got home. I had no right to be released before Terry, Tom or Brian as they all had been kidnapped before me. Frank had suffered far more than me. What would my friends at home expect of me?

Brian and Tom asked me to get in touch with people for them; Tom even gave me long phone numbers for his wife in Beirut and daughters in the States. Terry wrote out messages for his girlfriend Madeleine and their daughter Sulome, his elder daughter Gabrielle and for his sister Peggy. These messages I memorized and was surprised to be able to recall and pass them on when I was released, two years later. This time, it was just another rumour.

Nonetheless, throughout the summer, the news continued to be very encouraging. Meetings had been held at increasingly high levels between Iran and Britain. Both sides were making hopeful noises about the hostages, although Britain's insistence that whatever improvements in relations there might be, the hostages were not to be seen as a direct part of that process, seemed rather contradictory. Despite obvious Iranian links with our captors, Britain appeared determined only to exploit the better relationship with Iran for British companies seeking contracts there, rather than using it to secure our release.

I couldn't see the logic of this except that it protected Thatcher from any hint of 'doing deals with terrorists'. No deals for hostages I could understand, yet the French had made future business and full diplomatic relations conditional on their hostages being freed and no more being taken. I got the distinct impression that 'no deals for hostages' was a hollow posture that sounded tough but which really served to free the Thatcher government from the bother of exerting the influence it could, through diplomacy and trade.

In early July an American warship in the Gulf shot down an Iranian airliner. Although our guards said it was irrelevant to our situation, we were worried that any hopes of freedom might just vanish. What bothered us was the initial reaction by Reagan and Thatcher, both of whom seemed to think that condemning the Iranians for the accident was perfectly reasonable. At a time when diplomatic relations between the West and Iran were looking so much better, how could they be so stupid?

Yet, despite Mrs Thatcher's resolutely 'gung-ho' attitude, it was increasingly clear that there had been a general shift in Britain's stance on Iran and the whole of the Middle East. To what extent this was the result of Jill's campaign will probably never be known, but it may be that it coincided with and reinforced a growing feeling in the Foreign Office and elsewhere that intransigence was no longer in Britain's interests. By extending ties the country stood to gain in political and economic terms, as well as improving the chances for the release of Nicholas Nichola and Roger Cooper, Britons held without trial in Tehran, and indeed for those of us held hostage in Lebanon.

Iran, too, was shifting politically. Power seemed to be moving towards Ali Akbar Hashemi Rafsanjani who was arguing that his country needed to mend bridges with the rest of the world in order to rebuild Iran, following the end of the long war with Iraq. There were also repeated statements from Iranian diplomats that they would help on the hostage issue as things improved.

On 13 September, Rudolf Cordes, a West German hostage, and then, on 4 October, Mithileshwar Singh were released. We were delighted for them and their families. Yet despite the general improvement in relations and these two releases, we weren't confident that we would soon follow. Singh, while holding a Green Card, was not a full US citizen and might simply have been released as a gesture. There were also hints that the West German government had paid some sort of ransom for Cordes.

Small things still gave us hope and the rare glimpses of colour we saw took on an almost spiritual quality. One day a guard came in with a bunch of roses. They were a subtle pink, their perfume was wonderful, and, kept in a cup until they fell apart, they lit up the bleak, dark cell. On another occasion they brought us a bowl of cherries. It seemed a shame to eat them. Their rich, warm colour was a powerful reminder of a world that was lost to us and I suddenly felt sure we would see it again.

Despite being held underground without daylight and with poor ventilation, we were able to relax a little in this place. The guards were above us and we always had good warning of their approach down the little staircase to the iron door. When the fans were going, we could talk in almost normal voices.

Our bathroom was inside the dungeon. It was about three feet square and maybe five feet high. There were taps for hot and cold water and a large plastic jug to flush the hole-in-the-floor toilet. We were allowed in there once a day, although the guards would normally let us go again if we were desperate. In the mornings we were let off the chains, four of us in pairs and then the fifth and last man on his own, to use the bathroom and to exercise for maybe half an hour. Normally we could have a rudimentary shower, using the plastic jug, whenever we liked, although hot water wasn't often available. Having experienced the agony of crotch rot the previous winter in the Pigsty, I felt better for taking a daily douche, even if in winter the freezing water left everything numb for an hour or so.

Inevitably, hygiene was not the guards' top priority and we all got a dose of diarrhoea. The guards' toilet was halfway up the stairs to their room. The stench from it filled our cell, making us feel nauseous and apprehensive that we, too, might catch whatever it was they were suffering from. Terry and I were worst hit and for a couple of days I was left off the chain so that I could use the toilet whenever I needed. Abu Salim decided that a third day wasn't necessary so I had to grin and bear it. In fact my chain was just long enough to let me get into the tiny bathroom, two feet from my mattress, to use the toilet.

When Terry succumbed Safi refused to leave him off the chain at night. It was the only time I saw Anderson close to tears. When the guard had gone he had to keep his blindfold on while he overcame his anger and humiliation. Fortunately, being so close to the bathroom, I was able to rinse out the plastic waste-basket he was forced to use whenever his cramps got too bad.

One afternoon in late October we heard on a local radio station that someone, claiming to speak for Islamic Jihad, had phoned to announce that two Americans would be executed. The caller had said the victims would be Anderson and Sutherland. A moment later Safi came down and Anderson simply said, '*Morituri te salutant*' – those who are about to die salute you – which under the circumstances struck me as being extraordinarily cool. Safi was obviously excited by something, but his usual *bonhomie* was so much in evidence that we couldn't imagine that he knew of anything ghastly in the offing.

Then they came and took Frank away. 'Fucking hell, surely they're not going to kill him.' Terry was confident that they wouldn't, but the rest of us couldn't rule it out. As far as we knew, Frank had never been claimed and, having been quite cut off in Lebanon for a number of years before his kidnap, had less 'publicity' value than the other Yanks. It was also possible that they saw his state of mind as a potential liability, particularly if he got desperate and tried to escape again. I was very apprehensive and the fact that they took away the radio at the same time made our suspicions worse.

A few days later, on 28 October, it was Terry's birthday. We asked to have the radio back in case there was any news from his family. We also said we were worried about Frank. The guard said, 'OK, for Terry and Abu Tariq,

322

but just for one day.' We listened, hearing a brief mention of Terry's birthday on VOA, but more importantly, heard nothing about Frank. They hadn't killed him, at least not yet.

The radio was reclaimed the next morning. We couldn't understand why and of course no reason was given by the guards. We tried to hope that they were going to release Franky and that they simply didn't want the rest of us to get angry and depressed. They could never understand that, whatever the news, it still helped us to feel less isolated.

Our depression over Frank's surprise departure and the loss of the radio deepened when 'Trust me' Ali turned up and wanted Terry to make a new video. He had never had anything to do with Bri and me, but the Yanks said he was very smarmy and had told them he was Iranian. He spoke fluent English and was always saying, 'If you do this for me, I can make things better for you. Trust me.' He was, by all accounts, a bit spooky and seemed a little distant from the other guards, perhaps because he was a representative from Tehran.

Now, he wanted Terry to tell the US government to start doing something for the hostages. Terry hated having to make these tapes and we knew how distressing it was for him. After the last time, he'd vowed not to do any more, but we all found our firm stances weakened as soon as the blindfold was pulled down and our well-rounded arguments got vaguer and vaguer as our minds raced with apprehension.

Terry was taken out of the basement and, when he returned, said that he couldn't tell us what he was doing. As he worked on his script he kept himself to himself. He had to – they were doubtless watching him on the closed-circuit television. He was clearly upset and simply said he was making a video. Tom told him he shouldn't do it, should tell them he wasn't going to co-operate any more. Tom's words struck me as unthinking and insensitive; Terry was so obviously unhappy about the whole thing.

The video passed. But the depression didn't lift. All the optimism of the summer had evaporated, and we now faced another winter and Christmas without our families in this cold hole in the ground. We filled the hours as best we could. Since Frank's departure, Tom had played cards with us more often and Terry and Bri started teaching me how to play poker. Brian and I lost fortunes back and forth between us, but Terry usually came out ahead – I still owe him two hundred dollars.

We still had lively discussions about the books we read, although even the supply of those seemed to be drying up, and Tom was teaching Brian French. Bri was eager to learn but frustrated by the idea of learning the verbs 'parrot fashion' and tried, unsuccessfully, to find a way round this.

Just before Frank disappeared, the guards had taken to making regular searches of our room, rifling through everything. We thought they must be making sure we had no hidden messages and Brian used to mock them, saying, 'The Kalashnikov is hidden in the bathroom.' After Frank had gone, they continued with the searches. It was an appalling invasion and drove us to fury. 'Why are you doing this? You know that everything in here has come from you. What are you looking for?'

'We are sorry, but this is orders.'

One day they got really excited. Terry had written out a very detailed plan for a farm-school project for juvenile offenders that he had been working on for almost two years. We had all enjoyed working through it with him. Tom had been a great help in advising him on the farming aspects and, of course, on the teaching. Frank had given more detailed advice on the educational side of things, as had Brian. I'd been of less practical help, but Terry had encouraged me to make general criticisms of the scheme.

Terry had invested so much in the project that he was damned sure he was going to try and get it home with him. So he kept the notes, in tiny handwriting, in a little plastic bag. When we were moving or when he thought a search was in the offing he'd hide it in his underpants.

They found it.

They searched us all, probing every inch of our bodies. It was horrible. They found the picture of Jill that Sayeed had given me more than eighteen months before. They took it. Then they took all the old magazines and Terry's home-made cards and games, even the dominoes. We were livid. They thought they'd got something really tasty from Anderson, maybe notes on the guards or the various locations. Terry was too angry to speak. I tried to tell Younis that they were all wrong and to explain what Terry's notes were really about. Needless to say, he didn't believe me. Younis told me that they'd taken my picture because I'd hidden it. I said it was mine to hide. They'd taken my girlfriend away from me in the real world, why must they take away her picture? No response.

This slide downhill continued for weeks. On my birthday in November we again lobbied the guards to have the radio for the day. They wouldn't help. What had gone so wrong that they wouldn't let us hear the news? Was the word from on high that all plans for release had been shelved? Had there been some awful dispute between London and Tehran or had the Americans done something unforgivable?

Shortly before Christmas I was taken upstairs. It was the first time I'd been out of the cell since 15 May. In the guards' room I was shown two videos. The first was of my parents appealing for news of me and – of course – for my release. I was really choked to see them. They looked so dignified in the sitting room at home. They even had their dog Emma with them. It was two and a half years since I had seen them and it gave me a lot of hope just to know that they were still in good shape, although they both looked much older. It reminded me yet again that our captivity was as much of a strain for them as it was for us, here in Lebanon.

Then there was a tape of Jill sending me a message. She looked quite different from the way I'd remembered her. Her hair was much longer and blonder, although I realized that the latter was probably due to the awful quality of the recording. I felt oddly disturbed by the new hair-do. Had she changed in other ways? With the work on the campaign and the success we'd heard she'd had with it, would she find me too limited when I got out? Would I be left way behind?

Here was the woman I wanted to marry, the woman I thought of every day as I looked beyond the cell to make plans for the future. Yet the glimpse of her on that brief video hadn't brought her back with the sharp focus that I craved. I wanted to see her smile, hear the little chuckle that so often bubbled from her as we spoke, and just watch her move about. Making the video had probably been a tense experience for her, the situation and subject preventing natural expressions, let alone laughter. Her message was one of love and support. It helped, but left me anxious as to whether we could still really know each other after so long apart. No matter how realistic and cautious I tried to be about changes at home, in my heart I only wanted reassurance that things would be as before.

When I got back to the cell the boys were keen to hear everything, but, tactfully, they left me alone to be with my thoughts. I felt shy of talking about my feelings with Terry and Tom and wished I could have half an hour alone with Brian. Once again the lack of privacy hit home hard. It wasn't that I disliked, distrusted or in any way doubted the sympathy of my friends. I just wanted to be private, to be able to choose whom I talked to, let alone where and when.

It was Christmas Eve – our third in captivity. Would there be cakes and 'Happy Birthday, Jesus' from the guards as there had been the previous two Christmases? This year there were to be no festivities, however meagre. It was to be one of the worst times in the whole five years. And of course it was all Brian's fault. At least that's the way Abu Salim and his cronies saw it.

That evening, Abu Salim came to chain Brian and me up after we'd been to the bathroom. He did me first and,

326

as usual, stepped over my mattress to Brian, who suddenly snarled, 'Don't you pull my leg, I'm not an animal.' The chain snapped on and there was a thump as Brian was hit, then some more noise and Abu Salim stormed out.

He returned a minute later breathing heavily. He went straight over to Brian, saying, 'So, you want escape?' and started raining blows down on him with a stick. Brian let out a hoarse screech at each cut.

I felt myself shrivelling up inside, knees drawn up under my chin, arms wrapped tight around them, my head buried in my arms. I prayed as I'd done a year before when Abed had attacked Bri. 'Please God, let it stop, stop it now!'

I could feel the same horror burning through Tom and Terry – the impotence, the rage, the fear and shame at doing nothing for our friend.

There was a vicious irony that it should be Brian, who always confronted the guards when they treated him subhumanly, who was now being abused like a dumb animal.

Bilal eventually called, '*Hallas.*' Abu Salim stopped and left. When the door clanged shut we all turned to tend to Brian. He lay there, trembling all over, panting hard. He said that he was all right. There wasn't much to say. We were all too shocked.

Both Tom and Terry decided to go on hunger strike. Tom said that Brian's beating was the end as far as he was concerned. He would rather die now than carry on under these circumstances. Terry agreed. I knew that Brian had already made the same decision, but, unlike the other two, he had no need to talk about it. He needed no justification, no support, no-one's approval. For the first time, I didn't feel I wanted to follow my friends.

Despite my anger and despair at what had happened to Brian, killing myself now wouldn't make amends for not helping him. The threat of violence was always there and there might well be more beatings. I knew that I wanted to survive, I wanted to go home. The short messages from

327

home, the frustrating glimpses of Jill and my parents on video still spurred me to hold on, for them as much as for me. Although 'real' life was now so often only fantasy and incomplete memories, there were moments when people, events, sights and sounds came back into sudden, sharp focus. These moments were so vivid, so powerful, that they overrode the endless tedium and the despair. I knew Brian understood my decision as I understood his.

I didn't have to explain.

We talked a little more, while Terry and Tom prepared themselves for the inevitable angry reaction from the guards and Brian lay down under an extra blanket as his body came to terms with the shock of the beating. It wasn't a good night for sleep.

The next morning, Christmas Day, Bilal and Abu Salim came down together. They dumped some bread and jam on the end of my bed and unchained me as usual. Terry and Tom said that they didn't want any food and when they asked Brian, he refused to answer. Then Abu Salim said, 'No eat, no *toilette*!' We argued, but they refused to let the others go to the toilet. This indignity, on top of the beating, was too much for me. I couldn't accept it; my resolve to carry on snapped and I said that if they were going to do this, then I, too, would not eat. The guards left. I was still off the chain so could at least go to the little bathroom and fill the others' water-bottles and empty their pee-bottles. Brian needed to shit so I gave him a plastic bag and then left it in the bathroom.

We sat and waited for the next move, which turned out to be a visit from Younis and Bilal, insisting that Brian was trying to escape.

In French and English we tried to explain. How could he be trying to escape when he was already chained? Why should he sit there when Abu Salim hit him for no reason? Why should any of us carry on playing their game when they treated a man like that? We tried to reason with them about the bathroom. They would only say that we must eat otherwise things would be 'very bad, not good for you'. They went away.

Later they returned, unchained Terry and took him upstairs. We heard him quietly talking to them, then a gun being cocked and a loud pop, followed by a moan. The moan, we all knew, came from Bilal. The pop was from an airgun, not a bullet, being fired. Bilal came down and said that Tom would be next, which was, of course, meaningless. I tried to make him understand that Brian hadn't done anything wrong. But he wasn't listening. Obviously, they had made up their minds that they would have to make us eat rather than tell their bosses what had happened.

Ten minutes later, Terry, in remarkably good shape for a dead man, was brought back down. Younis explained that whatever had happened we must eat. He left a plate of chocolate biscuits as a peace offering – at any other time it would have been a great treat – and went off with his friends. We talked about how ridiculous things had become. Eventually, Terry said, 'Well, I guess John's right, we may as well carry on,' and ate a biscuit. After a while, I took one. Later Tom did likewise. We had been defeated by the surreal, mock execution and chocky bickies. Under his blanket, Brian was silent.

I knew that this was probably the hardest moment of all for him. My decision not to eat had been made on the spur of the moment and was based not, as I well knew, on the terrible beating, but on the pointless cruelty of not allowing the others to go to the bathroom. I can't speak for Terry and Tom, but I imagine that as the night's anger and frustration ebbed away, their determination had been blunted by the morning's antics. Brian, alone of us all, knew how difficult it was to go through with a hunger strike. I was aware that he had been focusing all his will on this resolve and that to let go now would be an appalling submission. He would need time and peace to prepare himself for whatever he decided.

The next day he started eating again. Nothing was said, but we all knew he had gone against his own convictions to save us from the pain of losing his company and his vital support. It was a great statement of friendship and I wanted to thank him, but appreciated he would be offended.

On New Year's Eve Mahmoud showed up with Ali. They wanted to hear about the troubles. We told them the truth and as usual when a panic was over they apologized but warned that we must be patient. We kept our tempers, as if patience wasn't something we maintained at the expense of our fading energies.

By way of atonement they had brought us presents. There were playing cards, the New Year issues of *Time* and *Newsweek* and some videos. From the contents page of *Time* we saw that there was an article on heavy fighting between Lebanon's warring Shi'ite militias, Amal and Hezbollah, but the relevant pages had been cut out. We wondered if this had been going on since we were moved out of Beirut last May, but there was nothing else to indicate any serious set-back to our chances of release.

Even censored, the magazines were good to read. I particularly liked the arts sections and noted that a caption under a picture of Salman Rushdie said that his new book *The Satanic Verses* had been badly received in many Moslem communities. I thought he looked very smug.

January 1989 brought another Friday 13th so I was sure one of us would be on the move. My companions nodded patiently at yet another of my silly predictions. Yet on the 12th Anderson was moved. Amin was there muttering things about his shoe size, trying to give the impression that he was going home. After Terry had gone upstairs we heard the dreadful shriek of tape being torn and so, when Mahmoud came down and asked which was Terry's pee-bottle, we really couldn't believe that this was anything more than another move. As usual there was no chance to say a proper farewell, just hurried 'good lucks' and 'see you in New York'.

Nobody else was moved over the next couple of days so we talked endlessly about what it might mean. Had Terry been moved out before being released? Maybe they were holding him back in Beirut while the final details were worked out. Maybe he'd gone to join Frank. Speculating like this was always a pointless exercise but it occupied a portion of any day. We had to find a way of convincing ourselves that any move, no move, any news, no news, good treatment, bad treatment were all indicative of imminent release.

Terry's move at least meant there was now more space and I moved across to where Terry had been. Tom and Brian spent much of the time reading. When I tried I found I couldn't, but Bri took pity on me and we spent hours playing cards. I got very depressed – there was no particular reason, just a lowering of spirits as I realized again that, for the foreseeable future, we were going nowhere. There was also a new guard working with Abu Salim, from whom the man got the impression that we had to be treated heavily. The pair of them loved searches, making us face the wall and spread our arms and legs as they felt all over us for some exciting trophy. This really sapped my energies – it was so obviously just a sport for them – and I began to question whether I could go on.

Tom and Brian saw that I was down and worked very hard to bring me back up. They did it with such tenderness that I gained new strength from their friendship, suddenly seeing the value in continuing, if only to deepen that shared bond.

On 3 February Amin appeared again and took Tom off. There were more mutterings about shoe sizes as Tom anxiously asked where he was going. This time, we were allowed to say goodbye and Tom hugged us, saying, 'You're both towers of strength.' We returned the compliment with feeling. Then he was gone and it was just the Shilling-Taker and Bastardballs again.

Life took up its old monotonous routine. Because we were so comfortable together, in a way it was pleasant to be alone again. Tom's move reassured us that he, Frank and Terry were all right and were probably together. We wondered about Islamic Jihad's reasons for splitting us up again, keeping the Brits and the Yanks separate. It might suggest that all bets were off on the release stakes or, ever hopeful, it might be that they were planning on letting us go and didn't want us to be able to give any hint, however vague, as to the whereabouts of the Yanks. As time wore on that hope faded.

We amused ourselves playing ever more card games, later and later into the night, using up our sometimes meagre supply of candles. We carried on the French lessons and since I was really only one grade above Brian, we learnt together which was fun. Our only textbook was a French edition of *The Valley of the Dolls*. It was fairly easy to work out a translation. I would read through a passage and get it sorted out as best I could. Then Brian would sit by me and read it through. I was an utter martinet about his pronunciation (he didn't know when I didn't know) and would make him happily furious insisting that he repeat words over and over again until I was content.

We had fewer books and, although one unfortunate batch was dominated by Barbara Cartland's idiotic romances and an informative, though only distantly interesting, tome on breast feeding, there were still enough to keep us occupied. It was a pleasure to be able to talk about our reading without the combative air that our Yankee friends had always brought to such discussions. The best book of the lot was, to my surprise, *Jane Eyre*. I'd read it when I was doing my A levels at the crammer, but it was only now that I really appreciated it. I was amazed that someone brought up in nineteenth-century Yorkshire could understand so completely the deprivation and frustration of being a hostage.

Now that there were just two of us we were often left unchained for most of the day, certainly from breakfast to lunch-time. I enjoyed this comparative freedom and spent a lot of time pacing around the cell. Brian, also, went through frantic periods of exercising, often indulging in his favourite sport of shadow-boxing. I derived a great deal of amusement out of this because he got so carried away, huffing and puffing, and once he unleashed a mighty kick with 'Take that, you bastard', sadly forgetting that he was still chained at the time.

When the agony abated he was prepared to laugh with me. It wasn't just a joke, but a reflection of his need to fight back. Often, this attitude had left him physically the worse for wear, but not mentally, for he managed to give even the vicious beatings a meaning by analysing his reactions and those of the guards without pride, certainly with no feeling of humiliation, nor indeed with bitterness. He wanted to know what had happened, wanted to understand the dynamics of the situation and to store it away as part of his constantly changing, growing understanding of himself and of those around him.

But when he wasn't fighting shadows, he'd just spend the morning dozing on his mattress while I paced back and forth and sometimes did a few push-ups and other exercises.

The guards left us pretty much alone and, apart from the irritations of Abu Salim and his sidekick, there was no aggression. There was another new man who seemed to mean well. He'd first appeared a few months earlier for just a few minutes. He'd picked up some cream that they'd given me for a skin rash, stuck it under my blindfold and said, in a curious high-pitched waver, *'Champignons?'*

'Yes, *champignons*,' I replied, thinking that he sounded as old as Noah and immediately I'd named him Grandad. Now he was a regular. He was, I think, a bit simple, but quite harmless. He'd occasionally pop down to the dungeon just to say, *'Aujourd'hui, c'est Vendredi, Mars quatorze, mille neuf cent quatre vingt et neuf ans.'*

'Merci beaucoup, mon ami,' I'd reply and off he'd scoot, giggling merrily. His French aside, he was the first guy who understood immediately one of my pitiful Arabic sentences – so perhaps he wasn't that simple after all.

Late in March Mahmoud showed up for the first time since the Yanks had moved out. He was his usual self, cheerful, sympathetic but totally vague. 'What's happening with the negotiations, Mahmoud?'

'I don't know exactly, but I think they are good.'

'Mahmoud, are there really any negotiations? As far as we've ever heard your group has never told anyone you have us.'

'No, no, be sure they negotiate. But your British government want all things secret.'

Reasonable but as ever quite uninspiring.

He brought a two-week old copy of *Newsweek*. Like the last editions we'd had, it was censored, but enough remained to make it plain that all hell had been let loose over *The Satanic Verses*. The agitation mentioned just two months earlier now seemed to be consuming the whole Moslem world. There had been book burnings and riots from Bangladesh to Bradford. Leading Moslem clerics had condemned the book as a vicious, sacrilegious attack on their faith. Finally Ayatollah Khomeini had reclaimed his mantle as the most radical of the Imams by proclaiming a *fatwa* against Rushdie in February 1989, effectively condemning him to death.

Although most of the reports on the subject had been cut out, probably for the colour pictures of Imam Khomeini, we gathered that the EC countries had suspended relations with Iran and that the whole situation had grown completely out of hand. One chilling line read, 'The Rushdie affair cannot help but set back hopes for an early release for the western hostages in Lebanon.' Rushdie was apparently ready to apologize, but it didn't look as if that would convince the Ayatollah to withdraw the *fatwa* and Rushdie was in hiding somewhere in England.

Lucky sod, we thought. It was very hard not to compare his situation with ours. Our captors took political and spiritual guidance from Khomeini, who had condemned Rushdie to death. But we were in a dungeon in Lebanon and he was in a safe house in the Home Counties.

334

It was such a bizarre twist that we couldn't see how any-one would find a way around it. The British government had to protect and defend Rushdie's right to free speech. They had to condemn Khomeini's intrusion into the affairs of another state. There was no chance that Khomeini would withdraw the *fatwa*. The encouraging *rapprochement* between Tehran and London that we'd heard so much about the previous year was at an end.

The political shift between Iran and Britain seemed to have direct repercussions for us. From this point on, there were to be no more magazines, nor any news of any kind – even on our third anniversary in April, until after Brian's release more than a year later. We were once more cut off from reality in our underground prison.

But we were not completely isolated. From some time in high summer until we left the Pit the guards started bringing us a regular supply of videos. They'd bring down a little portable black-and-white television and wire it in to the video upstairs. There was an added pleasure to this as they used the cable that connected the spy camera on the wall, so, for a few hours at least, we had some privacy.

Initially we got the usual diet of karate and war films. Yet, surprisingly, when we asked for something else they obliged with a number of better films. Many were still about war, but they weren't quite as crass as before and were interspersed with some really enjoyable movies. We got them to show us *Moonstruck* three times, enjoying it more each time as we anticipated our favourite scenes. Even sad films took us back to a world that we under-stood, a world where people lived their lives, hoping for happiness and sometimes even finding it.

The one drawback to the Beka'a Video Club was that Abu Salim, who'd asked us to give him English lessons, would come down with a list of words and phrases he'd noted while watching the films and ask for an explanation, his main interest was obscene vocabulary.

Now that we were the only hostages there I had no reason to worry, or prevaricate, over the consequences of

335

an escape attempt. But even with the camera occasionally disconnected we realized that we would have to be incredibly lucky to overpower a guard in our room without alarming whoever was upstairs. Although we thought very seriously about escaping, it was more a mental exercise than anything else.

And so another seven months went by. We had been held for three and a half years and we still had no idea when we might be released. Ever since the journey to this place seventeen months ago I'd had occasional panic attacks at the thought of being 'mummified' and stuck in the base of a truck again. The attacks came without warning and didn't seem to be set off by any direct thought about being moved. The feeling of panic, the inability to move, the hyperventilation and the terrible fear would suddenly come over me. When I regained control, telling myself, 'It's OK, you're not taped, you're not in the truck,' I was always left with a residue of remembered fear, which built up in the back of my mind.

By this time I was so sure that any Friday 13th would mean a move that it came as no surprise when we left the Pit on Tuesday 10 October. The confidence with which I looked forward to that week and its promise of change, if not release, was undermined by nagging anxiety over the move itself.

I was taken upstairs first. Brian and I said farewell downstairs. Neither was sure if one of us would be going home or if we'd be split up and put with other hostages as had happened before with the Yanks and the Frenchmen. When I got upstairs I found Abu Salim, which did nothing for my confidence.

I was told to stand up straight and, as usual, one of the guards pushed my legs as close together as possible. Another set of hands was pulling my arms straight down by my sides. Other hands tightened my blindfold until it hurt and started fitting a cloth over my mouth.

I was breathing more and more heavily. I knew I couldn't face it again. I felt myself falling and begged

This photograph appeared with an article on the launching of the Friends of John McCarthy in *The Sunday Times*, 28 February 1988. *Anita Corbin/The Sunday Times.*

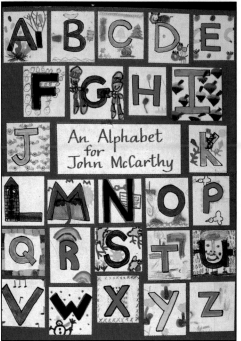

An Alphabet for John McCarthy, from the children of St John's C. of E. School, Heaton Mersey, Stockport. Their teacher, Ann Mettam, gave it to Jill at the fifth anniversary rally on 13 April 1991. In it are pictures, poems and letters from the children depicting all the things they thought John would be missing.

David Jacobsen, with his family, at Wiesbaden following his release, November 1986. *Piel/Frank Spooner.*

Frank Reed, with his wife and daughters, at Andrews Airforce Base following his release, May 1990. Robert Polhill, released only a few weeks before, is on the far right. Terry Anderson's sister, Peggy Say, is in the centre. *UPI/Bettmann.*

Brian Keenan with his sisters, Brenda and Elaine, on his return to Dublin, August 1990. *Syndication International.*

Jackie and Sunnie Mann with Group Captain Ian Corbett at RAF Lyneham, September 1991. *Syndication International.*

Tom Sutherland at Voice of America, shortly after his release, December 1991. *Reuters/Bettmann.*

Terry Waite with Lord Runcie at RAF Lyneham, November 1991. *Syndication International*.

Terry Anderson with his daughter Sulome arriving in New York following his release, December 1991. *Reuters/Bettmann*.

Arriving at RAF Lyneham, 8 August 1991. *Today/Rex Features.*

With Nick Toksvig and
Chris Pearson, the Russell
Hotel, 8 August 1991.
Sun/Rex Features.

With the Friends. (*L-r*) Mary Delaney with Anna, Lawrence Harrison,
Ronnie Wood, Sue Brown, Chris Pearson. © *Express Newspapers*.

At the Royal Scot Hotel,
9 August 1991. *Syndication
International.*

With Perez de Cuellar,
RAF Lyneham,
11 August 1991.
© *Express Newspapers.*

Leaving Lyneham for Merrow Farm, August 1991.
© *Press Association.*

New Year, 1993. © *David Secombe*.

them, 'Please, don't put me in the truck.' 'OK, John, no worry, just ten minutes.' It didn't help. I knew their ten minutes might last hours. I asked again about the truck. 'No truck, no problem.'

It wasn't until they made me squat down and then taped my wrists to my ankles and stuck me in a large sack that I accepted that it wasn't going to be a truck, but a car-boot move. I was so elated and relieved I could have kissed them, but immediately felt ashamed that I'd let them see my fear. I'd lost control. If they'd known it, if they'd wanted to, they could have got me to do anything in those minutes.

After the truck, the car boot even with Brian sharing it, was relatively comfortable. I managed to wriggle my hands out of the tape so I could pull down the gag, poke my head out of the sack and breathe more freely. With free arms we could move more and brace ourselves against the bumps on the road. Brian and I didn't talk, but occasionally gave one another a reassuring pat. Despite the fact that it was October and cool in the mountains, the heat in the small space was stifling.

We stopped briefly a couple of times, presumably for checkpoints and, as on other occasions, the driver would sometimes get out and speak to the people manning them. Looking back, it seems odd that, although this happened many times in the moves over the years, the cars and trucks were never searched.

When we came to a final stop we were carried up many flights of stairs, taken into an apartment and dumped on the floor. There were mattresses but no blankets, only thin sheets. Our pyjamas and underwear were soaking with sweat after the journey in the boot and now, in the night cold, I was freezing. But we were in an apartment, not a prison. The guards gave us a cigarette each and then left.

The door closed and a deep American voice came out of the darkness. 'Hi there, you guys, I thought you'd gone home ages ago.' It was Franky. He had been there since he left the Pit a year earlier and Tom had spent a week or so with him back in February. He sounded pretty good. I tried to imagine how I'd have coped with a year's solitary confinement. It was unimaginable – ten weeks had been hard enough.

At dawn the next day we were awoken by the call to prayer from a nearby mosque. I inspected the room in the faint light coming in around the shutters. I realized that this was the same place Brian and I had been held in for a week in May 1988 before going to the Pit. It was the first time we'd returned to any location and I thought it must be a good sign. The last stay here had been brief; perhaps it would be the same this time. As far as we knew, the only block to Britain's continued improvement in relations with Iran had been the Rushdie affair. Maybe that, and any other lesser problems had now been sorted out and we might be on the verge of going home. If we'd been put back with an American maybe it meant that at least one of us could expect to be released.

We asked the guards for news as soon as they appeared. Big Bilal from the Scullery was here with a new man and, according to Frank, they were generally reasonably behaved. Their opposite numbers were George, who treated Frank, or Abu Tariq as they still called him, well and Mazzin. Mazzin's presence filled us with foreboding. We knew him to be cowardly and because of that prone to bullying. However, we also knew that we'd got rid of Abed. We reckoned that we could probably deal with any nonsense from Mazzin, not that we wanted to waste our energies in a battle of nerves with him.

Nonetheless, both Brian and I found the change in conditions a tonic. Although we'd been left pretty much to our own devices in the last months in the Pit, the year and a half underground had become increasingly depressing. Living in an apartment again, with a proper bathroom, the sounds of street life, good food and a glimmer of daylight round the shutters, felt wonderful.

Our meals now regularly consisted of hummus, salad, chips and often meat, chicken or fried steak (which George called 'buffteak' which was closer to the mark – and particularly apt when we were trying to cut it with the inevitable plastic knife), and glasses of Pepsi. It was not *haute cuisine*, but it was both edible and nourishing. We were still hostages, but being better looked after took the edge off the horrors of captivity. Now that we were being treated as human beings, rather than sorry creatures penned up in a basement, we could relax a bit, which gave us a chance to replenish our flagging energies.

Each morning after the bathroom run, the three of us were let off the chains for an hour or so to exercise. Inspired by renewed hope, Brian and I pushed ourselves hard, doing umpteen push-ups and jogging round the cell. Franky contented himself with strolling around with his blindfold still over his face. Although in good spirits, Frank was even more withdrawn than he had been in the Pit. He would speak when spoken to and would answer any questions we had, but would then drift off into some sort of reverie, usually with his blindfold down, sometimes talking to himself. We knew that Frank got on better with us than he had with his fellow countrymen and hoped that being with us would help bring him back to himself.

After a few days he started telling us about the year spent in isolation. Although, like us, he'd had no news, either from the guards or television or magazines, he somehow felt he had a lot of information that came to him through the ether. He believed that he was the last hostage left. This belief was obviously challenged by our presence, but he insisted that Tom and Terry had gone home. Sometimes he would even say that Tom had not only gone home but had subsequently died of cancer. When asked how he knew this, he would become very vague, saying, 'There are things I can't tell you guys, you'll just have to take my word for it.' So desperate were we for hard news on our fellow hostages, and indeed for ourselves, that Brian and I found this very trying.

339

We appreciated that long months of solitary on top of the awful treatment he'd received before must have put incredible strains on him. Gently we tried to talk him round to looking at things in another way. We understood his need to feel that he was special, that someone was looking after him, and wished he could draw strength from us, rather than locking himself in his fantasies.

We encouraged him to read books and watch some television.

We felt it was our duty to try and bring Frank back to himself. This wasn't just altruism. It was dispiriting to live with such an example of what might conceivably happen to us.

Frank's inability to stand up for himself was brought home to us by Mazzin's relationship with him. It soon became clear that he had enjoyed having a free hand with Frank. He would badger him about anything, often hitting him on the least pretext.

Mazzin tried to impose the same treatment on us. He'd come and witter on about where, exactly, we should put this cup, that bag of tissues and just adored pulling down our blindfolds, even though they always covered our noses, let alone our eyes. We were always neat anyway. It was essential to be able to put a hand out for something in the dark without knocking over a jug of water, or sending a pee-bottle flying. I had long found that keeping my own little area and few belongings in order was a vital way of keeping ahold of myself, keeping my mind and spirits in order.

Being told by Mazzin to be tidy was infuriating, but our anger soon dissipated. However, his abuse of Frank was more serious and an increasing strain. We told Frank that we would support him if he stood up to the little tyrant, that he would feel better if he did, citing our own experiences, mine in particular. I now felt far more confident and comfortable knowing that I could refuse to go along with the guards' antics if they really upset me. I reminded him of how we'd got rid of Abed without any unpleasant repercussions, but he couldn't accept it.

Things came to a head a few weeks before Christmas, when Mazzin decided it would be fun to frogmarch us to and from the bathroom. Brian, furious, would huff and puff as Mazzin unceremoniously threw him back down on his bed. Like Abed before him, I reckoned Mazzin was hoping for a violent response in order to have an excuse to beat us up. So, when he treated me like this, I laughed aloud. It provoked him to impotent fury, but there was nothing he could do. I wasn't resisting, just showing a lack of respect for his 'hard man' image. Doubtless he was trying to convince himself as much as us.

Brian and I put all Mazzin's power games down to repressed homosexuality and his next trick seemed to confirm that. On shower day he made Frank strip off all his clothes before going to the bathroom. When he told me to strip I refused, saying that I would change my clothes only if he left the room. He wasn't happy, but could only agree when I said I was sure that he wouldn't want to look at a naked man.

We had no right to involve Frank in any battle of wills between Mazzin and his colleagues, so we had to avoid a confrontation. We simply had to tell Mazzin that his treatment of us and particularly of Frank was unacceptable to us and that we wanted to speak to his *chef*. As my French was better than Brian's, we agreed that I would do the talking and that I'd choose a moment when Mazzin was in one of his *camarade* moods so that neither of us would be starting from a point of anger.

I spent a couple of days rehearsing my speech in my head, and checking various ideas with Brian. This done there was no point in delaying the moment.

'*Mazzin, mon camarade, je veux parler avec vous.*'

'*Oui, monsieur John, qu'est ce que tu veux?*'

I told him that if he didn't cut out the vicious behaviour, Brian and I were going to cut out the co-operation, we'd stop eating. He would then have to tell his *chef* that two healthy, innocent and well-balanced hostages were killing themselves because of his idiocy. Did he think his *chef* was going to be pleased with his achievement?

I hope this came across in calm, polite and unthreatening language. Mazzin didn't lose his temper, although I could feel he was itching to have a go at me, but, as before, he knew he had no justification for doing so. He tried to argue that Abu Tariq had to be forced to wash and exercise. I said that wasn't the point, that Frank had lost his mind a little because Mazzin and the others in the past had treated him so badly. I pointed out that Abu Tariq was an older man who deserved respect and that his desire for a quiet life didn't give Mazzin the right to abuse him. Back and forth we went until Mazzin stormed out, clearly upset, but still under control.

We heard him talking, but heard no response, so we guessed that he was on the phone to one of the *chefs* rather than just moaning to George. After a while he returned, came over to me and, though I half expected a smack, said, '*Maintenant, il y a un nouvel relation entre nous. Maintenant nous serrons camarades.*'

We'd done it — but now we'd have to be friendly with the little swine!

A few days later Mahmoud showed up. We hadn't seen him since March, nine months previously. We asked him for news about our situation but as usual there was nothing he could, or would, tell us. We asked him for general news. He told us there had been a revolution in Eastern Europe and that the Soviet Union was finished, but he couldn't remember any more details. Then he changed tack and asked us if we had any problems with his friends. I told him that we had but that we'd talked about it with them and now things seemed all right. He wanted to make sure he knew who'd been the problem and wouldn't let me off the hook. Eventually I told him it had been Mazzin, who was duly summoned. After I'd explained the problems, Mazzin tried to wriggle out of it by going on about blindfolds. Patiently, I went through the same arguments that I'd used with Mazzin himself, emphasizing that we didn't want any trouble but wouldn't tolerate abuse, and that we felt Islamic Jihad didn't want to cause us unnecessary distress. 'Why you say Jihad Islami?'

'Well, Mahmoud, isn't that who you are?'

'No.'

'But we've been with Terry and Tom who are held by Jihad Islami, yes?'

'Yes.'

'So then we're held by Islami Jihad, yes?'

'No.'

'But you were there and your friends, you're the same people, so you must be the same group now.'

'No, why you think that?'

Baffling. There was no point in quibbling over semantics so we went back to Mazzin. Mahmoud assured us that there would be no more problems and said if we were upset we shouldn't get angry but must talk to a *chef*.

He went over to Frank who just said, 'I'm OK, Mahmoud, we all just want to go home.'

'But do you have problems with my friend?'

'Oh, it's not important, Mahmoud, we just want to go home.'

Frank's first words as the boys left were, 'There's no point in talking to these guys, they do what they like.' Brian and I swallowed our anger. 'Well, anyway, sounds pretty strange about Eastern Europe.'

'You can't always believe what they say,' said Frank, 'nothing's happened there, believe me.'

Mahmoud came in again later on and when we asked for books he said that we could have encyclopedias. He said there were about fifteen volumes. We guessed that this was the same set we'd seen long ago on the journey from the Scullery when Abed had wanted to stop us reading them. The Yanks had in fact had them for some months in the Scullery apartment.

At first the books came one at a time. They were very welcome but it was frustrating not being able to refer from one to another. Eventually we had the lot, half an edition of the *Encyclopedia Americana*. They were fascinating and it was wonderful to have them, even if most of the sections were forty or more years old. We spent hours mulling over maps and descriptions of countries.

Although Peru in 1990 probably bore little resemblance to the place described *circa* 1948 in our tomes, we were immediately obsessed with an area sloping down to the Amazon Basin to the east of the Andes. We decided we'd set up a farm there rearing llama and vicuna and corner the cloth market, assuming there was one. As we read more and more of the encyclopedias Brian became convinced that the best animal for the terrain would be the yak. He was confident that a letter to the government in Peking would secure us a gift from the People's Republic of a brace of breeding yaks. We fell out slightly when he decided that Patagonia, rather than the eastern slopes of the Andes, was better suited to his purposes.

Closer to home, Brian decided that he would refor-est Ireland. Here he found Frank a great help as he had a fair knowledge of native North American trees and shrubs which, when checked with the big books, sounded as though they'd do well in the peaty soil of Eire.

My main interest was in travel. At first, I wanted to take train journeys across the continents. Then I discovered a section on sailing vessels and decided that travelling the world by schooner was going to be my main occupation post-release. We learned that there were still, or had been in the late 1950s, a fair number of working schooners in Nova Scotia. Frank confirmed that as a boy visiting relatives in the region there had been many of the old ships still about, so Brian and I decided we'd go there, then sail down the US coast to the Caribbean, through the Panama Canal and head west to the Revillagigedo Islands which Brian had decided were his.

At the same time, we were lucky to get a couple of novels featuring sailing scenes. As neither of us knew anything about it we tried to glean as much information

344

on the technical side of sailing as possible and build it in to our globe-trotting plans.

Some time in the spring we watched the Oscars ceremony on the television. We were feeling rather disgruntled at how many good films we'd obviously missed when a man came on to the stage to read the nominations for one of the categories. His opening remark was, 'Who'd have thought six months ago that Nelson Mandela would now be free and that the Berlin Wall would have come down?' I swivelled round, eyes wide, to face Brian.

'Mandela's free! Fuck!'

'The Berlin Wall! Mahmoud was right! The world is going to be a different place when we get back to it, John.'

Without any more information to go on it was impossible to revise my image of the way the world worked or had done all my life. It was only months later when I could listen to the radio and talk over the events with Terry and Tom, that it began to sink in. Gradually, watching world powers responding differently as new crises emerged, it fell into place. But in our news void that spring these dramatic changes could only be interpreted as an almost mythical message of hope.

Early in March we saw the film *55 Days at Peking*. As soon as the title came up I thought, An omen! Fifty-five days to go! I decided there would be a release at the end of April, on the 29th or 30th. It was probably the idea of having to hang on for no more than two months that convinced me of the value of these silly prophesies, but I was a true believer.

The days went by, unchanging. Frank spent most of his time with his blindfold down or under his blanket, Brian and I read and exchanged ideas, plans and insults. The guards left us alone and we often watched television, although we were still denied the news.

At the end of April I had almost forgotten my prediction for a release when Bilal and his partner, for whom we had no other name than Frank's 'Jerk', excitedly started spring-cleaning both the apartment and us. We could hear them banging about, shifting things and wondered nervously if we were in for another move. But then they came in, rolled up the carpet, cleaned the floor, put plastic mats down, told us to have a shower and gave us clean clothes and clean sheets. Jerk gave Frank a dressing-down for not having a proper shower. Soon after they'd finished one of them returned, unchained Frank and took him out. We heard them settling down in the next room which until then had been empty. It was 29 April.

I reminded Brian that I'd predicted this and that Frank must be going home. He reminded me that I'd predicted many, many things over the years and that so far nothing had come to anything apart from purely coincidental moves. 'Unbelieving swine!' Still, he was right.

We listened hard every time the door to Frank's new room opened. We were almost sure that he'd gone. But where? That night we watched TV as usual, resisting the temptation to sneak a look at the news. In any case, the guards kept popping in around news time. We asked them, 'Has Abu Tariq gone home?' 'No,' came the only reply.

Later in the evening the film we were watching faded out and was replaced by scenes around a podium loaded with microphones. The CNN caption read, 'US Embassy, Damascus.' It could only mean one thing. Frank was out. The mad old bastard had done it. If only we could know for sure, but at that moment a guard came in and took away the television.

We were troubled at how Frank would cope back in the big world. He would have to break out of his semi-catatonic state to be able to deal properly with his family responsibilities, let alone all the media attention. We hoped that the US medical team whom we supposed would attend him at Wiesbaden, as we'd heard had happened with other American hostages, would recognize that he needed a long rest.

The year before in the Pit, we'd talked often about what would happen when we went home. We realized that each of us would be a big story for a few days, but that would pass and then we'd be able to get on with the real work of getting to know our families and friends again. Tom had been keen to take advantage of the medical facilities at Wiesbaden, if only to get his teeth sorted out. Terry didn't want any truck with service medicos, he just wanted to get back to the States and see Madeleine, Sulome and Gabrielle. Brian, although fascinated by psychology, always wanted to sort himself out, not put his mind into another's hands. I'd been thinking for a long time that I'd welcome the chance to talk with a psychiatrist, although not about captivity – I felt I'd worked my way through that enough – but about my past and how I came to be the person I was when I was taken hostage.

It was hard not to think of life as it had been back in 1986, or in Terry's and Tom's case, 1985. I still imagined returning to work at WTN in London, picking up with Jill as though all these years had not altered anything. Of course, we all realized that everything might have changed. Certainly Terry, Brian and I knew that close friends had been campaigning for us and that that experience could have changed them, just as we'd been changed by what we had gone through. But it was hard for us to see exactly how we had altered, beyond having some rough edges polished off and getting a better focus on some of our ideas and ambitions. So I tended to stick with how things had been; it was more comforting to think I'd be able to pick up where I'd left off.

Frank's departure was a relief in many ways: for the first time in two years someone from our group had gone home; Frank would now be free from fear while Brian and I could carry on together. His vulnerability had put a terrible strain on us, our determination to survive had been badly dented by the constant spectre of emotional collapse.

We carried on using the encyclopedia to make plans, taking ourselves out of that room to beautiful, exotic places, places of joyful freedom, sailing oceans, crossing mountain ranges and doing something worthwhile. All we had to do was get out of that place and our dreams would immediately be attainable.

A rather more down-to-earth plan was Brian's notion of rejuvenating Ireland (apart from reforesting it) by developing unorthodox uses for peat. Every day he'd come up with some new scheme. He started with making building bricks from it. Then it was furniture and so on. I'd listen, almost politely, to the latest idea, then do my best to knock it down. Brian's enthusiasm was such that I couldn't keep up my negative stance and was soon busy designing peat-moulding machinery, marketing plans and discussing the number of people who could be employed in such schemes. And, thus occupied, time passed.

Occasionally, we heard rocket fire and guessed, from the heavy propaganda on both the Christian television stations, that it was between Geagea's Lebanese Forces militia and the army of General Aoun, who was still apparently claiming to be the true President of Lebanon. As far as we could tell the Moslem factions were out of the fray for the time being. The Geagea-controlled television station, LBC, went so far as to show every film ever made about Hitler. Commercial breaks were replaced with old clips of Aoun ranting from a balcony to adoring crowds, just like a Nuremberg rally.

One of the films was a three-part drama about Hitler's last months in the Berlin bunker. Starring Anthony Hopkins, it was based on a book by an American journalist who'd been one of the first people into the bunker after the allied victory. The film started with this character telling the audience how long the Führer had spent in the bunker that last time, just over one hundred days. When the film was repeated a couple of weeks later I decided that this was another omen. After the bizarre accuracy of *55 Days at Peking* I was confident that I could predict when Brian and I would go home. It was by then mid-May, so I calculated that the great day would be 23 August. It seemed a shame that it couldn't be in time for my mother's birthday on the 8th but at least it was a good target for which to aim.

348

We'd both been inspired by Frank's release to step up our fitness campaign. Now I had an added impetus, although Brian's response to my prediction was, as always, 'McCarthy, will you stop putting my head away!'

While waiting for the great day we watched nearly every match of the 1990 World Cup, particularly the progress of England and Ireland in the early rounds. It was only now that I realized that Lineker wasn't Arabic for goal!

It was frustrating that any English commentary was usually blocked out by Arabic, although one of the commentator's forlorn attempts to pronounce Paul Gascoigne's name was a rich source of amusement. He started out doubtfully with Gass-coh-een, moved on to Gass-kern and after half-time, when he'd obviously consulted with his equally confused colleagues, went for Jax-oh-in. By the final whistle he'd done the sensible thing and switched to Gazza.

Whenever Italy played I couldn't help noticing that Brian looked remarkably like Salvatore Schilacci, but he didn't seem too pleased when I pointed this out. Salvatore may not be the world's most handsome man, but it was the glint of ferocious determination in his eyes and the sweet smile he reserved for his team-mates in quieter moments that reminded me of Bri.

Football fever got to us and Brian fashioned a small ball out of an old pair of underpants and a defunct blindfold. We tried football in the exercise periods, but soon developed a more entertaining and satisfying game, a variation on volleyball. We stood at opposite sides of the room and scored points when one of us failed to keep the ball moving after the permitted single bounce. The most heroic plays were made as we leapt to stop the ball hitting the wooden door to the hall or banging into the metal shutters over the window, which would have brought the guards running in.

Shortly after Frank's release our belief that there was another hostage in the apartment was borne out when he was moved into the room next door where Frank had spent his last day. We never heard a voice, but one evening there was a tapping on the wall. We tried to keep track of the number of taps and translate them into words. The tapping was repeated and we 'heard' the words clearly. 'My name is Terry Waite, I have been alone for over three years.' But we couldn't respond as our chains were too short to stretch across the room. The next day, while we were exercising, Brian kept watch under the door for the guards' feet as I tapped out, 'We are Brian Keenan and John McCarthy. A Yank went home in April.' Terry didn't respond, but we couldn't say any more. It wasn't a safe time to communicate as the guards often popped in to see that we were still exercising.

At last we knew what had happened to the Archbishop's special envoy. As we'd guessed the Jihad had nicked the negotiator.

As part of the improved conditions Bilal's partner started taking us to the kitchen once or twice a week to sit with them and get a bit of sun. Initially he would remove the blindfold and tape a little tissue over our eyes. There would be coffee and extra cigarettes. To start with these outings on the 'sun-deck' were a welcome change, but they became an increasing strain as we really had nothing to say to the guards. What we did say didn't encourage them to chat as we'd always turn the conversation round to why they were keeping us like this. They couldn't answer and became huffy that we weren't satisfied with the good treatment we were receiving. However, they didn't stop our excursions, they just got quieter. They both jumped one day when the phone rang and I leaned towards it, saying, 'That'll be for me.'

The feel of the sun on our skins again was wonderful and even with our eyes covered the brightness of the sunlight was dazzling after so long in the gloom. It was only natural that we should interpret all this as preparation for release, that we would go home looking fit and not too pale.

Our exercise periods were indeed much longer now and I padded around the room as much as I could, but Brian would often get bored and go back to a book. Once, as he sat cross-legged on his mattress reading, deep in thought, I grabbed both his ankles, and yanked his legs, saying, 'Excuse me, but I have to take this wheelbarrow out to the garden.' His eyes flashed Schilacci-like and he said crossly, 'You are one agitating bastard, McCarthy!' I backed off.

We lost our football when Bilal searched the room. We'd hoped that such irritations were behind us, but then they started taking toothpaste and soap away from us after we'd been to the bathroom. We guessed, wrongly, that Frank had been talking back home. Then Jerk came in one night and tightened our chains. Mine was so tight that it cut into the skin. I was furious, but he wouldn't loosen it. I fumed and later told Brian, 'That's it. If, after all this time, we're back to this sort of malarkey, they can fuck it, I'm going on hunger strike.' Brian urged me to calm down. 'Let's see what happens tomorrow, they're probably just in a fit about something, take it easy.'

I did and the next morning the chain was loosened again. We had changed a lot over the four years we'd been together. At the outset of our friendship it was always Brian who exploded and damn the consequences. Now I was ready to take on the guards and he was calming me, rather than me him. We'd found a balance. We had grown together not just in terms of affection but in our attitudes, in our views on personal dignity and in a mutual trust that helped us deal with the curious life we now shared.

In June or July we had a visit from 'Trust Me' Ali. Or at least I did. I was taken out to another room, sat down and then heard that thick voice, full of soft, sickly fruit. I was terrified. My mind raced, what does he want? A video? Let me be strong.

But I didn't feel strong, I was confused and he was being pleasant and solicitous. 'Would you like coffee? A cigarette? If you help me I can maybe help you. I want you to write a letter to your government.'

I tried to muster the arguments I'd arrived at with Brian nearly four years earlier, in the autumn of 1986, after having heard Jacobsen making a tape. Only if they told us why we were being held, would we co-operate.

'Here are pen and paper.' I took them. 'Write this.' I wrote:

> My name is John McCarthy. I am OK, but I am living in very difficult and bad conditions. You must understand the following. My release with the others is impossible if the prisoners in Kuwait and in some European countries are not released. You must keep this letter secret otherwise my life will be in danger.

So without any questions from me, we'd finally been told why we were there. We'd known more or less since I'd heard the words Jihad Islami in the Land of Grey and Pink, but they'd never actually said it. We'd always felt that the demands for the prisoners in Kuwait only affected the French and the Americans. The guards had always said that they weren't bothered about anyone in British gaols, so we'd hoped it would be easier for us to get out than for the others. But this didn't sound good. It looked as if we'd travelled a very long way to get nowhere. I faithfully promised not to breathe a word to 'my friend', went back to the room and sought Brian's opinion.

It was a nightmare, a warped nightmare. Were they really going to use us, and for this? After so long thinking that the reason for our kidnap had been bad feeling between Britain and Iran, and knowing that, before the Rushdie affair at least, fences had been mended, it was hard to believe now that it had all been a mirage. Our high hopes were shattered. It was a more fundamental problem after all.

I couldn't really assess how I'd handled Ali. Had I stuck to my principles or had I simply followed orders? I told myself that not only had I not had a choice, but that in fact I hadn't really needed to make one. The letter was so clear. Whether I'd stuck to my guns or not, it had been a harrowing experience and I felt abused.

As 23 August approached, I couldn't resist recalling my prediction for a release. Brian would have none of it. He didn't need me building up yet more false hopes which did nothing except try his patience. Yet I was positive. In the morning of the 23rd we went for our sessions on the 'sun-deck'. When we were both back I said, 'Today's the day, boy, believe me.'

'Roll it up and put it away, Snake,' came the response.

'Well, fuck you then. I'll go on my own.'

It was really no surprise that Brian was taken out of the room that afternoon. Usually I would have been very worried. 'Where's he gone? What's happening, are we moving again? Don't separate us.'

But this time I was calm. I knew what was going on. Then I thought, 'The scheming little Irish bastard, he's bloody gone and he didn't even believe me. There really is no justice!'

8

London, April 1988–August 1990

'An Evening without John McCarthy' was a great success. That night Gina had driven home with a binliner full of cheques and banknotes and reported back to the meeting that we had raised about £15,000. Everyone gave the Benefit committee a round of applause; it had been an enormous achievement. Other publicity and fund-raising events had also been successful and, although I didn't quite know where we should go from here, the atmosphere around the table every week took on a more confident, practised tone. We had now collected enough cash to finance the campaign for at least six months. It was as far ahead as any of us could bear to look.

Among other things, the money meant we could continue to buy half-page spaces in the Beirut newspapers for our messages to John. Ghassan Salem in the WTN office in Beirut sent us a copy of the newspaper containing our April missives, and seeing them in print made me believe that John might actually read them, that they didn't go into a vacuum after all.

The Benefit had given me some idea of the kind of responsibilities I now had as the public face of the campaign. Speech-making was an occasional nightmare, which I could just about get through if I rehearsed long enough, but there were other, unexpected tasks. During the evening at the Camden Palace I had gone backstage to thank those who had taken part and had felt at a loss to know how to express my gratitude, or how to cope with my new role. The campaign was for John, but I had to learn that people were also responding to my appeals for help and that I was the one they expected to acknowledge

354

their efforts. It was only natural; both friends and strangers needed to be thanked and I didn't want them to feel that they were being taken for granted. I was the one receiving the public acknowledgement, after all.

Over the anniversary I had been encouraged by the coverage John's situation had received; most newspapers and television bulletins had carried reports of our activities or interviews with me. When it was over, though, I wondered what difference our efforts had really made. The work we had put in had left us all drained, but like the press conference in February and the demonstration in the cage in March, it seemed to have changed nothing.

I spent several days in a black depression, uncertain that I could go through it all again. The let-down after each event seemed to be getting progressively worse; I'd played a role, but I'd used real feelings and, when it was over, all that was left was emptiness.

In interviews, I stuck to the same line I had adopted from the start. Whenever they asked me how I thought John was coping, I replied, 'He has an excellent memory for books, films, everything. He will have a lot to draw on. If anyone can get through to the guards, John can. If it's possible, he will establish a relationship with them. He has a great sense of humour, which will keep him going.' I still believed it, but my voice began to lack conviction. Two years had passed without any proof that John was alive, nor had there been any definite news. How on earth could I know how he was coping?

I tried to think of the immediate future, but a summer of silence from Lebanon stretched ahead, promising nothing. I could only hope that what I believed was true and try to convince others that it was time to take action on John's behalf. At least during the coming months we could remind people about John and attempt to persuade the Government that a more aggressive approach was needed. If John wasn't home by the end of the summer the Friends would attend the party conferences in October and would mark his birthday in November. If another Christmas came and still he wasn't home, then we would mark that, too.

It seemed that the only arrangements I made now revolved around the campaign. My personal plans were inevitably last-minute and I would rely on friends like Barbara to organize evenings out. Sometimes I would take a holiday and, rather than being miserable in London, Mary and I would end up being depressed in Menorca instead. After the break I would come back feeling more positive and determined to achieve a better balance in my life. This resolve would last until I walked into my flat and the phone began to ring.

Friends and colleagues would call just to show that they were interested in what was happening with the campaign, and sometimes I would find myself repeating the same news about fifty times. Mary would spend an evening at the flat with me and, when the telephone rang for the twelfth time, she would say, 'Jill, I can't bear to hear you say that one more time!' She would try to field the calls, but that hardly ever worked. People were offended and she'd be accused of being over-protective.

I had recently received a letter from a friend at WTN who had been posted abroad. My letter to him had been full of little else but campaign news and he'd expressed concern that I was pouring so much energy into that one area of my life. 'But what am I supposed to do about it?' I said to the blue sheets of his air-mail letter. Nothing else seemed important. Mike had also suggested that I was in danger of being irrevocably cast as John's girlfriend by the media and if I wasn't careful I would have no life of my own. I thought he was worrying unnecessarily; I might have done interview after interview, but, although the personal angle had sparked off media interest, I wasn't the focus of the story. Once the hostages were seen as a serious concern, my relationship with John wouldn't need to be mentioned. It was irrelevant to the main message of the campaign.

The media, at least, were beginning to consider the Friends' opinion when reporting any aspect of the hostage story. After each international development, we issued a statement and our constant appeals to the Government encouraging dialogue and more flexibility in dealing with the problem were, occasionally, also reported. We were making progress.

It soon became clear that if the campaign were to be a success, I would have to trust the Friends to do much of the work. It was obvious I couldn't do everything, which I found difficult to accept. I didn't feel that I could leave anything to chance, and I was very protective of the campaign, largely because John's life was at stake. For most of my life I had tended to fit in with people, and try not to upset anybody, but now I found that there was something I cared about more than being liked. If I thought something was right I had to fight my corner.

Cathy's understanding of my possessiveness over the campaign helped me relax a little; she would discuss everything with me, yet she and Joan took care of all the details themselves. Over the months I learned that if something were at all possible, it would be done and there was no need for me to fret about whether all the options had been tried. Cathy was like Superwoman, racing around at a hundred miles an hour, operating amid complete chaos and producing the reality out of the fanciful ideas dreamed up at meetings. Small wonder that I felt a fraud when described as the force behind the campaign.

As the media was only really interested in me, I did most of the interviews and was inevitably credited with the campaign's successes. In fact, a large part of the work was done without my being involved at all. Just as benefits were organized without my help, so were vigils, publicity stunts, our visits to the political party conferences and many other events. They all materialized without my having to do anything but turn up on the day, leaving me able to concentrate on interviews and meetings. It didn't matter to anyone else in the campaign who got the credit for their efforts, as long as we achieved what we set out to do, but without the Friends the campaign would not have lasted, let alone been such a success.

Everything we did took a long time to organize because everyone was working full-time. The meetings were like a long-running soap opera with familiar characters and a plot which developed little by little each week. Over the coming months I realized that it was mostly women sitting around the table every week. There were some men who were always there, too, but it was interesting to see that they were usually the minority. In the past I had always thought of men as the ones who got things done; now I was learning differently.

On the evening of 4 May, my telephone never stopped ringing. The last three French hostages in Lebanon had been released, and the media had gone mad. News programmes were desperate for interviews and I rushed off to do them, delighted at this apparent breakthrough. Whenever anyone was released, by whatever group, it seemed that John was nearer freedom too. I was happy for Joelle as well and called her as soon as I could. Judging by the noise in the background it seemed as if her house were full of people. Her voice sounded dazed, and for a moment I didn't know what to say. Then I burst out, 'Joelle, it's marvellous, you did it, you did it—' She laughed, saying she hadn't been able to believe the news; she'd torn a journalist to shreds for daring to suggest that Jean-Paul was free and then minutes later it had been confirmed.

'What's it like?' I asked her. 'How do you feel?' I had wondered so often how this moment would be. 'It's as if the last three years didn't happen,' she said. 'Really, Jill, it's just as if they didn't exist.' It was exactly what I wanted to hear.

'When are you coming to Paris to see Jean-Paul?' she asked.

I thought it unlikely that he would have news of John, but it would still be worth talking to him, to see how he was and to find out how his experiences compared to those of Normandin, Sontag and Jacobsen. 'I'll come as soon as I can,' I replied, hoping I could take a few days off work.

I watched in tears as the television news showed Jean-Paul Kauffman, Marcel Carton and Marcel Fontaine arriving home. The British press had taken the same line as they had when Normandin was released the previous November: disgust that the French government had cynically allowed itself to be manipulated by Iran for the release of its hostages; certainty that more Frenchmen would be taken now that their government had shown itself to be so weak; and the need for Britain to demonstrate that hostage-taking did not pay. The *Sun*'s editorial wondered what France would hand over next. 'The Eiffel Tower?' it asked. 'Thank God Britain has in Mrs Thatcher a leader who will never bow to terrorists.' Its final words on the matter were, 'Unlike the French, we do not crawl at the feet of scum.'

It was very disheartening. We'd tried so hard to put across the idea that talking to the Iranian and Syrian governments wasn't necessarily giving in. The Friends held a press conference to say how happy we were that the three Frenchmen had been released, but how dispiriting it was that, two years after John's kidnap, our own government still could not tell us whether he were dead or alive, let alone who was holding him and why.

I then plunged into the emotionally charged atmosphere in Paris, where the world's media were out in force to capture what shots they could of the freed men. I was nervous and glad that, once again, Mary had dropped everything to accompany me. In the mayhem I was worried that we wouldn't find Joelle, but she found us and, holding my hand very tightly, extracted us from the offices of the BBC. She explained that she and Jean-Paul were going away for a few days, but that I would have a chance to talk to him if I drove with them to the airport. Even at this time, regardless of all the pressure she was under, she remembered how important it was for me to know if there was any news.

359

We drove to the hospital to see Jean-Paul. It was like stepping into a film: a huge crowd of press and TV cameras were waiting at the gates and Mary and I looked at one another in amazement as Joelle ducked, hoping that she wouldn't be recognized. We saw the crowd surge forward as we disappeared through the gates. My heart was still pounding as we walked into Jean-Paul's hospital room. He was painfully thin, but it was the amusement in his eyes that I first saw. Despite all he had gone through, Kauffman began teasing us, saying he would welcome visitors like us any day. He seemed quite frail and moved with difficulty as we headed for the car, watching with a bemused expression as Joelle ripped campaign stickers off the rear window. As we roared out of the hospital's back entrance, a television cameraman pursued us on a motor bike, wobbling precariously alongside as he tried to jam his lens up against the car window. Jean-Paul stared at him through dark glasses, still wearing the same wry smile, looking for all the world like Jack Nicholson.

Amid the distractions of the paparazzi and the drama of the police escort, it didn't really seem appropriate to start questioning Jean-Paul about his captivity. Aware of my reticence, Joelle took charge and asked if he had any news of my boyfriend, a Briton called John McCarthy. Jean–Paul tipped his head back and thought for a second. '*Oui, oui, John Mac-arty oui, il est allé à un très bon école près de Londres, je pense, et il parle comme ça . . .*' Here he held his hand to his throat and made deep noises to indicate a posh English accent. Mary clutched my arm and I stared at Jean-Paul. '*Tu l'as vu?*' I said in a shocked voice. '*Non, je ne l'ai pas vu, mais j'étais avec Tom Sutherland et il le connaît.*'

I tried to take in what he was saying. Tom Sutherland, one of the American hostages, had spoken to John, or at least heard him speak, I wasn't sure which. Tom had also communicated with John via notes left in a prison toilet. The news was so unexpected and so sudden; I could hardly collect my thoughts enough to speak. '*Tom m'a dit que ce*

John Mac-arty, il était doux comme un agneau.' Jean-Paul
told me. Gentle as a lamb – that was the John I knew.
I was desperate for more, and as we neared the airport,
Jean-Paul tried to remember what else Tom had told him.
He recalled that Tom had said that John was with Brian
Keenan – further proof that he was alive! Keenan had
joked to Tom about how terrible it was not to be able to
escape from the Brits even as a hostage. I could imagine
John laughing and coming back at Keenan with an insult of
his own. It was reassuring to know that regardless of John's
conditions, there was still humour. I asked Jean-Paul when
Tom had seen them both, and he tried hard to remember.
'August 1986,' he said. The news was nearly two years old,
and my heart sank a little, but it didn't matter. If John
were alive then, he must be alive now.

Jean-Paul could remember nothing else, but said that
Tom was a kind, sensitive, educated man whom he had
greatly respected. It was comforting to think of a kindly,
paternal Tom sitting next to John, chatting to him, even if
the scene only existed in my imagination. I wanted to call
everyone in London straightaway, to tell them what I'd
heard, but as we reached the airport, Jean-Paul suddenly
became deadly serious. Nobody must know that Tom had
communicated with John, absolutely nobody. If anyone
found out that they had hidden notes for one another, it
could be bad for both of them. Jean-Paul's urgent tone
was enough to convince me of the gravity of the situation
and I promised that I would say nothing.

I felt reluctant to say goodbye to Jean-Paul; he was a link
to John and I didn't want to let go. He and Joelle allowed
me to get on to the plane with them and sit talking for a few
minutes more before it took off and then we said goodbye.
On the way back into Paris Mary and I celebrated the
exclusivity of a photograph she had taken of Jean-Paul and
Joelle embracing and I tried to absorb what I had learned.
Jean-Paul's news meant that John was with Islamic Jihad.
The name itself was terrifying to me, but all I could feel
was relief. At last we knew for sure who was holding him.

It was late by the time we got back to Paris. I did a television interview, during which I did nothing but smile and say that Jean-Paul had given me good news. I was bursting to say what that was, and to tell the world that John was alive, but knew I could not. Back in the hotel room, I went over the news again with Mary. Each fragment of information had produced faltering images of John in my mind. I tried to hold on to them and get a sense of John himself, but they were too brief. As we talked, though, I could almost feel his presence in the room. My image of him was still too vague to grasp properly, but he was no longer a shadow behind a curtain, more a recognizable figure walking purposefully about. His spirit was close, and I felt that suddenly I had been reconnected to the love I remembered and still felt.

I was sure that Kauffman's news would change everything. This was the first direct sighting of John and Brian in more than two years and as much proof as anyone could need that they were still alive. Sir Geoffrey Howe had said on the second anniversary of John's kidnap that the Government was hampered in its efforts to secure the release of the hostages because it didn't know who was holding them. We knew now that they were held by Islamic Jihad, who had long been linked with Iran. Iranian involvement had been suspected for some time, but now the Government finally had a concrete reason for insisting that Tehran use its influence with the kidnappers.

A few days later I returned to Paris to attend a news conference which Jean-Paul and Joelle gave on their return from holiday. The venue, which was a preview theatre, was heaving with press all jostling to get the best shots. While we were waiting, I saw Peggy Say, Terry Anderson's sister, and climbed over a couple of rows to speak to her. She seemed very tough and streetwise in relation to the media; I remembered that she had been publicizing Terry's captivity for three years now and had been through a hell of a time. I was envious of the fact that most

Americans were keenly aware of what their hostages were experiencing and felt very strongly that something should be done to get them home, but she explained that it wasn't like that any more. After Irangate it had been impossible to interest anybody in the hostage issue. 'Everyone's had it up to here with hostages in the States,' she said. 'They just don't want to know.'

My eyes were also opened to another of Peggy Say's problems. After the press conference we went off to have a quiet meeting with Jean-Paul Kauffman on our own; Peggy wanted to ask about her brother and I wanted to pick up as much general information as possible. As we posed briefly for the photographers outside before going into the meeting, I heard a voice behind me say, 'What a great day!' and turned to see David Jacobsen, the former American hostage. He positioned himself firmly in between Peggy and Jean-Paul and placed his arms around their shoulders.

Jacobsen joined our private meeting, and as Peggy tried to ascertain as much as she could about Terry, he wanted to talk about his experiences and to reminisce with Jean-Paul about the different guards. They mentioned Frank Reed; Jean-Paul admitted he was worried that Reed was coping very badly with captivity; he had been severely beaten for trying to escape and had spent most of his time huddled in a corner when they had been together. Peggy said she would try to contact his family and shortly after that we left; Jean-Paul was very tired by the end of the meeting.

Later, in my hotel room, I had a call from David Jacobsen who, I learned from Peggy, had been flown to Paris by CBS, one of the American networks. Jacobsen asked me if I remembered which parts of the meeting had been confidential.

'It was all confidential,' I said. 'It was a private meeting.'

'I don't think the bit about Frank Reed was confidential,' he replied. 'The American public have a right to know if one of their citizens is being ill-treated like that.'

'You can't say anything,' I said in alarm, 'that information was for his family. You have to clear it with them first before you do anything.'

'The American people have a right to know.'

Concerned at what Jacobsen might reveal, I phoned Jean-Paul and Peggy Say and somehow they stopped the news from being leaked. Months later, I met Jacobsen again during a discussion programme in France. He glowered at me, saying, 'If I ever find out who it was who said I would do such a thing, I will tear them limb from limb. I would never have betrayed that confidence.' I blushed, remembering what I had thought at the time, and hopped into a lift which arrived conveniently at that moment. Later I wished that I had been more sympathetic; Jacobsen must have found the pressure unbearable after his release. I'd heard he had received no psychiatric counselling, but had been left to adjust to the outside world as best he could. He must have been tormented by the knowledge that the price of his freedom had been arms sales to Iran, and that his fellow hostages remained in captivity.

Back at home the newspapers were still vehemently anti-French and David Mellor, the new Foreign Office Minister, had gone out of his way to repeat that there would be 'no deals' between Britain and the hostage-takers. But I took heart from the fact that several newspapers had recently printed articles questioning the Government's policy. An *Independent* editorial had said in January that 'calculated inaction cannot continue indefinitely' and over the past month several other articles had been blatantly critical.

It was encouraging to see that kind of debate at last, and to discover that we had been gathering support from other journalists over the past few months. Tim Marshall, an IRN reporter I had met in Paris, formed a French branch of the Friends; John Pilger had written a very good letter to the *Guardian* questioning government policy; and Martin Gregory had become a committee member after producing his *Newsnight* story in January. John Simpson, and his partner Tira Schubart, had gone out of their way to be as helpful as possible, telling Chris and me what they heard on their visits to Iran, suggesting the idea for the cage, and donating an answering machine to the campaign office. A colleague of theirs at the Foreign Affairs department of the BBC sent me photocopies of a magazine called *MidEast Mirror*, which reported what the Iranian newspapers were saying at any given time. I spoke regularly to Julie Flint, the *Guardian*'s Beirut correspondent, who was helping us and WTN from her end. Peter Bevington, a journalist in Doncaster, was helping my mum and dad to organize benefits and publicity stunts up there.

The few questioning articles that appeared, together with the growing support for the campaign, were very encouraging. At our most optimistic, we thought the Government might be a bit on the defensive. The Foreign Office had been criticized in the press for failing to send anyone to Paris to debrief Kauffman, and, after a few weeks, had relented and flown someone over to see him. In addition, Chris and I were invited to a meeting with David Mellor, the first Foreign Office Minister we had seen so far. We knew that Mellor wasn't averse to publicity – he had already caused a storm by criticizing the Israelis for their treatment of Palestinians in the Occupied Territories – and we decided it might be worth encouraging him at this point rather than criticizing him. If he wanted publicity, what could be better for him than getting the hostages freed?

During the meeting Mellor stressed that he felt strongly about the issue and promised that if any information came out of the French debriefings, the situation would be reassessed, and that if any new lines of enquiry seemed obvious, they would be followed up. A few weeks later, Mellor wrote to me saying how pleased he had been to meet us, but wondered if we could refrain from asking people to write to the Foreign Office expressing their concern about the hostages. He said that his colleagues were having to spend their time answering letters rather than working on the problem itself. It was a bit galling to hear a minister implying that the Friends and our supporters might be responsible for the Foreign Office's lack of action. Letter-writing was the acceptable face of the campaign, and yet even that was too much for them.

Incredibly, Kauffman's evidence about John didn't seem to cut much ice with the FO. In mid-June, when the officials returned from debriefing him, I asked them what they intended to do with his information.

'What do you mean?' said Ivor Roberts.

'Well, John must be with Islamic Jihad. That means it's definitely Iran. What are you going to do?'

'Kauffman's evidence isn't conclusive. It dates back to 1986, and his story has many inconsistencies. We have raised the matter with the Iranian Embassy here on several occasions. We may raise it again in the near future.'

I felt as if I'd run up against a brick wall yet again. Why were they always so quick to pour cold water on any evidence that John was alive? Why were they so reluctant to take an aggressive stance with the Iranians?

There had been another disquieting meeting a few days earlier. Pat, Chris and I had lunch at the Athenaeum Club with Sir John Gray, who had just finished his term as British Ambassador to Lebanon. Unlike the desk officials, he was easy to talk to and prepared to be quite open about what he had or had not been able to achieve. He told us he believed that clever diplomacy was the answer to the hostage problem; but policy didn't allow it. He had wanted to try all sorts of avenues in Beirut, but had been explicitly prevented from doing so by his superiors in London. It seemed to me to confirm that government policy was to do nothing.

Pat did not believe that this was the case, and was confident that the FO was still taking the correct line. He did not believe that criticizing the Government was helpful and the most outspoken that he had been was on *The Heart of the Matter* a few months before. He

had said that he was surprised that stronger representations had not been made to other governments. When
the interviewer, Joan Bakewell, had turned to Sheila, asking, 'We do rather feel a British passport means something
in the world, don't we?' Sheila's reply was not angry,
but she was a little more critical.

'It says "without let or hindrance", but that doesn't
mean anything, does it? The words in the passport now
might just as well not be there. We can't abandon him.
Our Government really must ask for help. We're not
getting anywhere which is why we are getting rather more
desperate now, the two of us. We can't get into three or
four years.'

These interviews were all the more powerful because of
Pat and Sheila's obvious reluctance to criticize or com-
plain. They supported our campaign in so far as it kept
John's name alive, but Pat was uncomfortable whenever
we attacked the Government.

Over the next few years I was occasionally exasperated
that he did not agree with some of the things the Friends
said or did, and wished he himself would be more critical
of the Government. After a while, though, I realized
his approach was one of encouragement and gentle per-
suasion rather than our more outspoken tactics. It was
only after John was released that I fully appreciated that
his approach had complemented that of the Friends. Pat
worked at communicating with Foreign Office officials on
a personal level, winning their respect and confidence,
which then rendered any criticism he did make of them
all the more powerful. I realized that in some way he
had acted as an intermediary between the Friends and
the Foreign Office, urging the officials there to be more
open with us and therefore save themselves more bad
publicity. If, at any point, the FO had decided not to
meet the Friends, I believe that Pat would have been in
a position to make sure that they had to. In 1990 William
Waldegrave, the Foreign Office Minister at the time, paid
tribute to Pat in the House of Commons.

'He is one of the most remarkable people I have met,' he said, causing speculation that Pat was about to be honoured with a knighthood!

By now I knew Pat and Sheila better. I spoke to Pat every few weeks. He passed on the latest word from Roby and the FO while I filled him in on campaign news. Sheila had suggested that we go shopping together one day, but the trip had had to be postponed for quite a time because she had been very ill, particularly over the New Year. Not long after Kauffman's release, I went out to Essex. As I stood waiting to be picked up from the railway station, I saw Pat's car approaching and heard Sheila cry, 'Oh, lovely, you're wearing your hair loose!' as she got out. She carried on talking as I walked over to the car.

'It's so nice to see your hair like that . . . I have such a problem with mine. Did John ever tell you I've got two crowns?'

Sheila sounded so bright and chatty, but I had not been prepared for the shock of seeing her looking so thin. I knew that she had lost weight, but had not realized how much. Later, the shopping trip was curtailed when Sheila felt unwell. Pat had not told me the nature of her illness, and I tried not to think of how ill she must be, concentrating on her high spirits instead. Despite that, I worried about how painful it would be for John to see her like this when he came home.

Terence took me back to the station. I didn't see him often because he was very busy looking after Sheila. He couldn't attend campaign functions because of his work at the College of Arms. As a Herald, Terence was a member of the Royal Household and we worried that if it became public, John's kidnappers might think they were holding a member of the Royal Family. Each time I did see him, however, I had to stop myself from staring at him. Terence looked so like John and they shared many of the same mannerisms, gestures and idioms of speech. It felt like a rare luxury to be able to see and hear them.

That summer the campaign was going full steam ahead. The Friends were co-operating with several television companies making documentaries about the hostage issue, lobbying the Government via our growing number of supporters and organizing more publicity stunts and fund-raising events. Around the country, several smaller groups were operating independently, but were co-ordinated by Cathy and Joan who kept them supplied with FOJM (the Friends of John McCarthy) merchandise and information packs. Hull University, the Doncaster Friends, the congregation of the church at Broxted next to John's former home and his old school Haileybury were all beavering away. One person who kept our campaign office busy was Pat's local butcher, who frequently asked us for regular supplies of FOJM carrier bags.

I was working on the documentaries and the interviews, and had noticed that I was beginning to be recognized in the supermarket or on the bus. It was odd, but everyone was sympathetic and it happened so rarely that it did not bother me. It was a sign that people were generally more aware of the hostage issue, and I was usually quite pleased when it happened. I wasn't quite so happy with the way I was being labelled as the 'waiting woman' in many of the interviews I gave, but again, it didn't really seem like a problem.

By now I had been given a six-month sabbatical from WTN to work full-time on the campaign. There was no further opposition to the idea of publicity, although I found the Friends' relationship with WTN a little awkward. The company felt it should not officially support us because it would have compromised Roby's relationship with the FO, but in practice WTN turned a blind eye to the use of its facilities and allowed some of our costs to go through their accounts. Many of the people who worked there helped us in whatever way they could, and we were allowed to consult the company's lawyers, Biddle & Co., to make sure that we were operating on a sound legal basis.

The mundane business of setting up a formal organization took up time, too. Chris, Cathy and I found ourselves discussing matters such as the refusal of the Charity Commission to grant us charitable status, and the subsequent necessity for a bank account to set aside money for tax, as well as other procedures involved in forming a limited company. It was all uncharted waters for us, and we groped our way through the various problems that came our way, hoping we were getting something right.

Now that I had been granted the sabbatical, I found the campaign increasingly taking over my life. When I woke in the mornings it was with the knowledge that John was still captive, but that I was doing something positive to help him. I filled my days with meetings, interviews, letter-writing and phone calls associated with campaign business. I was on the media treadmill, but the hectic days spent getting up at 5 a.m. for the first interview and carrying on from there were sufficiently far apart to allow me to recover from the exhaustion that inevitably followed each burst of activity and gear up for the next one.

We had been through more speculation that the hostages were about to be released in the early summer. The Syrian army was stationed on the edge of the southern suburbs of Beirut, the area dominated by Hezbollah, and press reports had said that when the Syrians went in, they would release the hostages. The media had placed its bets on the hostages coming home in a few weeks. Despite vowing not to listen to any of it, I did. It looked as if John might really be coming home, and it brought the worries that plagued me into focus. Here I was going on national television as John's girlfriend when I did not know whether he would remember me, whether he would want to see me, or whether he would think that campaigning had been the right thing to do. When the speculation died away, I pushed the worries away, too, and resumed the job of trying to keep John's name in everyone's mind.

Jean-Paul Kauffman's belief that the Friends were right to campaign was a great encouragement to me, as was

Joelle's continued support. They were to stay in contact with me for several years, through the occasional letter or postcard, and Jean-Paul supported many events held by journalists in Paris to draw attention to the plight of John and Terry Anderson. In June Jean-Paul and Joelle came to take part in several publicity events and attended one of our meetings. I think everyone felt that he had somehow brought John that bit nearer, just by being there in the room with us.

Kauffman was incredulous that the British would not confirm that he had given them evidence that John was alive, and furious at their attitude. He had publicized the conditions in which the hostages were being held and his views on why the British government's policy was wrong in several powerful and moving articles.

In one he wrote, 'They are in a cell without windows, without air, without daylight. They are fighting the atrocious heat of Lebanon in May. Like me, they have suffered cold and hunger. I sometimes asked to be delivered of my suffering when I was a captive – to be killed. But the captors do not kill – they make you suffer.' He argued that France had won a victory over terrorism through its negotiations with Iran, that the honour of a civilized society was to help its citizens who had been taken hostage, that the reality of terrorism should be stared in the face. If we were at war with the terrorists, the hostages were the wounded and should not be left to die in agony on the battlefield. To those who invoked grand principles, he said that he wished to quote a line from Shakespeare's *Much Ado About Nothing*. 'I pray thee, peace! I will be flesh and blood: For there was never yet philosopher, That could endure the toothache patiently.'

In London, Jean-Paul and Joelle attended our latest publicity event. We lobbied Parliament and hired a boat which sailed up and down the Thames past the Houses of Parliament for an afternoon, displaying a banner reading '789 Days: How Many More?' Only weeks after his release, Kauffman put himself through the strain of media interviews, press conferences and worse. For a *This Week* documentary he relived some of the more brutal aspects of his captivity, advising on the filming of a reconstruction of the way the hostages were moved around, in narrow containers strapped under lorries. It was the first time a current affairs programme had examined the issue and, for the Friends, it was a milestone. As I watched the documentary, which was often harrowing, I felt a curious sense of relief. At last, the plight of the hostages was being taken seriously in political terms. In Britain, journalists told us that Kauffman's passionate testimony made an enormous difference to them and their understanding of the hostages' suffering.

There was no indication from the Foreign Office or anyone else of what was about to happen next. It came as a complete surprise when, one Sunday in June, I read in the *Observer* that Britain was to pay Iran one million pounds to settle a dispute over repairs to our respective embassies that dated back to the Iranian revolution in 1979. It was obviously good news, but I wondered what had brought it about and why they hadn't told us it was on the cards. Diplomatic relations between Britain and Iran were still open, but they were at the lowest possible level.

Over the summer, relations with Iran steadily improved after a delegation of MPs visited Tehran, led by John Lyttle, the Archbishop of Canterbury's Secretary for Public Affairs. His involvement was, in itself, encouraging. Ever since Waite's abduction, he had been working to secure the hostages' release. Chris and I had been to see him several times at Lambeth Palace. On our first visit we had expected a strait-laced churchman but as soon as his office door closed behind us, he made for the drinks cabinet, saying, 'I think it's time, don't you?' Our talks with him were always positive and, although he never revealed any confidences, we trusted him because he was so straightforward. For a while, Lyttle seemed to be the only person who really was working behind the scenes; the only person looking for an opportunity to start a dialogue with the Iranians. I always left Lambeth Palace feeling cheered by our meetings and reassured to know that he was beavering away on behalf of John and the others.

The FO had never given us any assurance that the hostages were deemed to be an important factor in the renewed discussions with Iran. Officials would only say they had been 'mentioned' whenever possible. I feared that they would restore full diplomatic relations with Tehran without getting the hostages home. I'd learned more about the realities of Britain's position during the making of the *This Week* documentary, when Julian Manyon pointed out something that, perhaps naïvely, came as a shock.

'Iran and Britain are quite happy with the relationship the way it is because commercially it's very good. The British are supplying arms, but not the parts that actually kill people. Trade is very good. Nobody wants to rock the boat. What you've got is a stalemate.' I could not believe that the Government was prepared to allow British companies to trade with the country that controlled the hostage-takers while at the same time insisting it would never do a deal with them on the hostages' behalf.

Whatever was going on behind closed doors at the Foreign Office, from mid-June onwards the hostages and the thaw in relations between Britain and Iran were frequently in the news. Some newspapers even said that the release of the hostages should be a condition of the embassy agreement. Chris and I visited the editor of the *Independent* who was considering publishing the ever-increasing number of days of their captivity on the front page. Lyttle's delegation of MPs had returned from Iran, calling for improved relations between London and Tehran. Several of them came to address our committee meetings and told us to keep up the pressure on the Government.

In July the US shot down a civilian Iranian airliner in the Gulf, tragically killing all 286 people on board, and it seemed that everything might be lost. The US had been escorting vessels of friendly nations through the Gulf for months to protect them from attack by either protagonist in the Iran-Iraq War, and one of the warships mistook the airliner for an F-14 fighter plane.

Over the next few days television pictures showed bodies and debris being washed up on the shoreline and distraught relatives of the dead in Iran, but before any of the facts of the matter were known, Mrs Thatcher issued a statement supporting America's right to defend its forces in the Gulf: 'We fully accept the right of forces engaged in such hostilities to defend themselves.' We held our breath again, fearing that this could harm John and the others – or at the very least wreck the talks between Britain and Iran. Lambeth Palace attempted to repair the political damage and some politicians described the Prime Minister's comments as a knee-jerk reaction. My dad shared their views. 'She's done it again,' he said. 'She just can't keep her mouth shut. Why does she do it? Is she deliberately trying to provoke them?' But the Iranians turned to the UN to settle the dispute, the first time they had done so since the beginning of the war in 1980. We breathed a sigh of relief.

A few weeks later I was up in Glasgow, staying overnight in a hotel before an early morning interview on the BBC. I turned on the TV news and to my astonishment heard the newsreader say that Iran was to accept the UN conditions for an end to the eight-year war with Iraq. Ayatollah Khomeini had said that, for him, the decision was like drinking from a poisoned chalice, but he was going to do it. I phoned Chris straightaway, hardly daring to think what it could mean. If it were true, another huge stumbling block had been removed. Perhaps Iran's revolutionary fervour was at an end. When I next saw Roby he told me, 'It's all over now; we're in the end-game.' Articles in the newspapers said that British firms were poised to cash in on any commercial boom in Iran – and Iraq – after the end of the war. They left a bitter taste. 'They had better not let the hostages down now,' I thought.

I allowed myself to believe that John was coming home in August, because Iran had made its most formal offer so far to help Britain with its hostages and a British representative, David Reddaway, flew into Tehran. Everyone was optimistic and I bought a card with a picture of a bear carrying champagne on the front and wrote a message to John to be given to him on his release. I wouldn't be going to meet him. I was resigned to this. When, for a few days in 1986, we had thought John would be coming home Roby had informed me that he would be going to meet John with Terence while Pat stayed at home with Sheila, and it would be best if I didn't come. I had realized as I'd sat in Roby's office that it wasn't worth fighting. Roby had said that it would be better not to put John through any more emotional upheaval than necessary. He would have enough to cope with. Reluctantly, I took the point. I didn't want to put John under any more pressure; but it all came down to the same thing. I wasn't John's wife and it had been decided without me.

I wrote a message in the card. I would give it to Pat as soon as we had definite word that John was coming home. 'Darling John, It looks as if you might be finally on your way home, although as yet I don't know when. I've tried to imagine what it will feel like to know you've been released, but there have been so many false hopes and disappointments I've hardly dared think about it.' I finished off by saying, 'I'm dying to see you as soon as you can bear it. PS. You're late.' And put my new telephone number at the top.

The speculation that the hostages would be released within weeks faded, and it seemed that it had been yet another dead end. For the rest of the summer and throughout the autumn, however, relations with Iran steadily improved, and it was clear that something had changed dramatically. I could only speculate as to the reasons why. Had the FO been misleading us and the media about its policy hitherto? Had it become embarrassed at its lack of progress? Was there anything in the rumours that the FO had wanted to do more, but had been overruled by Mrs Thatcher in her obsession with vanquishing terrorists? Whatever the reason, my worry now was how long the hostages would stay on the agenda. There was enormous pressure on the Government from British businesses desperate for lucrative contracts with Iran now that the Iran-Iraq War was over. With money and jobs at stake, we were terrified that the Government would rush into an agreement with Tehran and that the hostage issue would simply be fudged.

In the meantime the campaign continued. For me our meetings were the focus of the week and I looked forward to them in a way, but it must have been hard for the others to work up much enthusiasm in advance. Chris was working four nights in a row at the BBC so the meetings ate into his spare time. Week after week he was there, summarizing the latest political developments and going through a rough agenda of what everyone was up to. We relied on the committee to come up with ideas for how on earth we were going to interest the media the next time around. For much of the time it was a tedious slog, but being with friends meant we had a lot of fun too.

Each item would often end with a general cry of, 'Let's ask Cathy when she gets here'. She was co-ordinating much of what was going on, whether it was interview requests for me, merchandise for someone else's fund-raising, posters for a prayer vigil, or tracking down doves for release on International Hostage Day. Cathy would always arrive at the meetings having driven all the way across London to see to the children and then back again. She would flip backwards and forwards through her note-books, filling us in on news from the office. She, Chris and I usually spoke on the telephone several times a day so the meetings were partly a report to the rest of the group on what was happening and partly a forum for ideas.

The political party conferences in the autumn were the biggest headache. The Labour Party said that we could have a stand for a reduced rate, a couple of hundred pounds, and so all the posters and merchandise were transported up to Blackpool, together with Ed's cage and a shop-window dummy that we had acquired to sit inside it. A rota of volunteers stayed throughout the week in a bed and breakfast which Ronnie had found fifteen minutes' walk from the conference centre. Mrs Duxbury was to put us up for the next three years.

Inside the Labour Conference Hall quite a few people were startled by the sight of our dummy in its cage. It wore a wig, which we found fashioned into a different style every morning when we arrived. Even after all the publicity about the hostages over the summer, many people still asked, 'Does he write home often?' and 'Have you been to visit him?' Whoever was on duty would go back to basics, beginning with a quick explanation of why that wasn't possible. Nearly everyone was sympathetic, however, and we could now say with conviction that we knew John was alive. The Labour Party bigwigs had their photographs taken with us, but were still steering clear of getting publicly involved in the campaign. They had firmly backed the Government's position, which, in a way, made things a little easier for us; the Friends couldn't be accused by the Government of being partisan.

John's nine hundredth day fell during the conference and Malcolm Handley, a local journalist, had organized a stunt for us; all I had to do was to launch some balloons off the top of Blackpool Tower. When the day came I took the lift up to the top of the tower with Chris, some council officials, George Robertson from the Labour Party, and my mum, who was helping us out for the week. We got out of the lift and I looked around for the balloons, but they weren't there; they were higher up. We traipsed up the stairs, emerging at a point where the tower is completely open to the elements, and a council official cheerily pointed out that we were right at the top. I could see a crowd of photographers focusing their lenses on the balloons, which were sheathed in netting on a platform near the handrail. I climbed across to the side nearest the rail, wondering if I was stark, staring mad. 'What on earth am I doing here?' I thought, looking up at a

TV cameraman who had climbed even further up one of the legs of the tower to get a better view. I didn't feel at all safe, but didn't have the nerve to say so, so just bared my teeth into a smile. All of a sudden I felt a hand grip each of my ankles. I looked down and there, in his suit, was Chris, sprawled face down across the rickety wooden platform, neatly keeping out of shot. He'd obviously had the same thought as me; this was potential suicide. I was only too glad that someone was holding me as I let go of the balloons, which were whipped away by the wind and streamed off down Blackpool's seafront.

Competing with conference news and the rest of the world wasn't easy and the balloons only made a few seconds' item on the news that day. The real media excitement came when an American hostage, Mithileshwar Singh, was suddenly released the next day. He had never been held with any British hostages, but I wondered if it were a sign that things were on the move.

We carried on to the Conservative Conference in Brighton, although we'd been refused permission to have a stand inside. Instead we'd hired a bright red double-decker bus, kitted out as a mobile exhibition centre. The Labour-controlled council had allowed us to park on a lower section of the promenade, but thanks to the massive security operation it was some way away from the conference centre. Our advance team of Cathy, Lawrence, John Curran and Chris Jury had done a terrific job. They had filled the bus with posters and merchandise and fastened a huge banner to the outside which read: '912 Days: How Many More?' It was almost out of sight, except at night; John had persuaded ITN to floodlight it. Even then, we wondered if passers-by might scratch their heads and wonder why we didn't just move the bus, if it had been there for 912 days.

The bus was a work of art, as the policeman who was sent to keep an eye on things told us constantly. He was a bus fanatic and pointed out its most fascinating features to anyone who would listen. We had a lot of time to do this as nobody was interested in us. We had a wonderful video about John's situation playing on a loop upstairs, petitions to sign and merchandise to buy, but nobody came.

Nevertheless, I thought we had a fair chance of rallying delegates to attend a fringe meeting we'd planned because we had flown over four former French hostages for the occasion: Jean-Paul Kauffman, Marcel Carton, Marcel Fontaine and Roger Auque, who, since their release, had never been seen together. Flying them over and putting them up was a very expensive operation, but I was convinced it would be worth it. The whole thing turned out to be a wash-out; the photographers and TV cameramen outnumbered the two Conservative delegates who turned up and frightened them off.

As we were rather morosely having something to eat, Lawrence called from the bus to say that they'd just had a visit from a team of sniffer dogs. The Foreign Secretary was going to visit us! We rushed over and gathered inside the bus, waiting for Sir Geoffrey Howe to arrive. We hadn't met him before, and had no idea why he was coming to see us, but it must mean something. Here we were, being ignored by most of the Conservative Party, but the second most senior member of the Cabinet was coming out of his way to see us. It was extraordinary. We couldn't believe he would actually turn up.

For over two years the Government had tried to avoid talking to anyone about the hostages. The FO had refused to discuss them, hiding behind 'security matters'. Ministers routinely refused interviews on the topic and, all in all, the Government did its best to discourage any mention of the issue. It was this brick wall against which we'd been banging our heads. Now, in front of TV crews and legions of photographers, in a sweep of aides and security men, the Foreign Secretary stepped into our clapped-out bus. Not only was Howe willing to be seen with us, he was also about to encounter four belligerent former French hostages, whose release a few months earlier his own Government had vilified

379

as a craven and gutless surrender to men of violence.

Standing on the lower deck of the bus I shook his hand, momentarily taken aback at the diffident man facing me. It was hard to reconcile Howe in the flesh with the man I'd criticized for so long and I was speechless. Fortunately the four Frenchmen weren't going to pass up this chance to tell a British politician exactly what they thought.

They surrounded the Foreign Secretary; Auque began jabbing his finger in Howe's chest and Kauffman was soon in full flow. Howe blinked, turning from one to the other, and tried to hold his own in ponderous French, *'Oui, je suis absolument d'accord mais—'* only to be drowned out by a fresh torrent of French. He got a second going over from Jackie How on the way out, and then he was off, in a blaze of lights from the TV crews filming his visit. When he had gone, we were utterly bewildered but jubilant that he'd come to see us. We crowded into a BBC hotel room, waiting for the news. We watched the bulletin for the full half-hour, sure that our bus would appear, but there was no mention of either hostages or the Foreign Secretary's visit. The four Frenchmen sat with us, incredulous that in Britain an issue as important as this could be overlooked. As we drove them to the airport our triumphant mood evaporated.

Afterwards I couldn't work out why Howe had visited the bus. Over the next few months, I wondered if it was because, during that autumn, he thought things were so optimistic for the hostages that it would be a good time to be seen with the pressure group campaigning for their release. Britain and Iran had finally agreed in principle to restore full diplomatic links and on 4 December, as a prelude to this, Gordon Pirie, the British representative in Tehran, raised the Union Jack at the British Embassy there. Even as I watched this happen, I wondered how much longer it would be before negotiations over the hostages began and how long we would have to wait until such negotiations bore fruit.

At Christmas time the Friends sang carols in Covent Garden and rattled tins. Everyone's thoughts had revolved round the hundreds of people killed in the Lockerbie plane crash. It was an appalling tragedy, seemingly unconnected to the hostage issue in any way. Iran wasn't blamed and the growing warmth between London and Tehran seemed unaffected. On Christmas Eve Nicholas Nichola was released.

In the New Year British and Iranian foreign ministers held their first meeting in ten years. Waldegrave and Velyati talked about improving ties and the hostages were said to have been top of the agenda. In his statement to the press following the meeting, Waldegrave stated publicly that relations with Iran could not be normalized until the hostages were released 'because public opinion wouldn't allow it'. Chris seized on his words. 'That's us,' he said, pointing at the quote in the paper, 'I think that's us he's talking about.' We didn't know if the Friends had had anything to do with making the release of the hostages a condition of upgraded relations with Iran, but Waldegrave's statement was the kind of public commitment for which we had been aiming. We were all heartened by an opinion poll carried out for us that month on the cheap. If we looked at the results optimistically, the poll showed that two-thirds of the British public did not think the Government was doing enough for the hostages. We took that as a sign of growing public concern, reflected in the Government's new attitude.

Even though things were going so well, we decided to keep up the pressure. On 10 January the Friends held a vigil outside the Iranian Embassy to mark John's thousandth day in captivity. Glenys Kinnock came along to give us her support, as did Anthony Grey, the journalist held hostage in Peking in the 1960s, who had recently joined our campaign. Our banner was hung on the railings, recycled from its last airing on the Brighton Bus and now reading: '1000 Days: How Many More?'; posters of John's photograph were tied to the railings.

My spirits were high as friends, colleagues and supporters gathered on the pavement opposite the embassy. There were about two hundred of us, clutching our candles and chatting away, taking discreet nips from Gina's hipflask to stave off the cold. Everyone was in a great mood. We even noticed that several strangers had turned up, after hearing about it on the news, some of whom became firm supporters of the campaign. Others, however, who'd heard about it on Capital Radio, must have been disappointed. A friend reported hearing one man say, 'What's going on here?' and another reply, 'I don't know. I just heard the Jill Morrell Roadshow was here today.'

For the first time in almost three years there was a real air of expectation that the situation was going to be resolved. The speculation in the media was difficult to bear. I'd had severe mood swings all over Christmas as the slightest thing made me upset or angry. My brother Brian took the brunt of it. He'd tried to keep some distance from the campaign so that I could escape from time to time, but these days as soon as I walked into the flat I dropped any pretence of being a nice person and didn't have a civil word to say for myself.

In February, Brenda and Elaine heard that Brian Keenan was on the point of being released and the tension was notched up as high as it could go. There were photographs of the new British Ambassador in Beirut, Alan Ramsay, leaving the embassy 'in pursuit of information about the hostages'. 'It's about time,' I thought. I just had to hang on a little longer and it would all be over.

The *fatwa* against Salman Rushdie on 14 February came out of nowhere, spinning the world back to the Middle Ages. Over the last few months, I had seen reports in the papers and on the television of bookburnings in Bradford and riots in Pakistan, but had paid little attention to this strange row over a novel, of all things. After the death-threat was issued, it seemed absurd. I thought it was just the religious radicals in Iran flexing their muscles and that more moderate elements would resolve the problems with the British officials who were trying to prevent the situation getting out of hand. 'This can't affect the hostages,' I thought, 'it's just barmy.' Rushdie issued a semi-apology, but said he wished he'd made the book more critical. The Ayatollah repeated the *fatwa*.

There were a few weeks of confusion during which the Iranian News Agency issued three conflicting reports in one day, rejecting, accepting and then rejecting again Salman Rushdie's statement of regret. Diplomats were withdrawn from Tehran and London. I went to hear Sir Geoffrey Howe speak in the House of Commons. Sitting in the public gallery listening to him talk of taking a determined stand against Iran, I wondered how this could be happening. We couldn't lose all that we'd worked towards now. I still thought everything would be all right, but when I walked into ITN one day to see bodyguards at the door because a death-threat had been issued on one of the newsreaders, I realized that this was not just another diplomatic tiff. In early March, the Iranian Parliament voted to break off diplomatic ties with London. Ayatollah Khomeini said he would never allow the liberals to gain power in Iran again. I couldn't believe it. The radicals had won, reason had lost and John slipped out of our hands completely.

It was spring again, a time I still associated with John's imminent return. Despite everything, I felt the usual irrational surge of hope. I had been so sure it was going to end. John would have been home by now. Instead he would be marking his third year as a hostage in a bleak cell in Lebanon. It took me a while to realize that we weren't just back to square one; it was worse than that, it was the end of everything.

I couldn't even summon up the energy to blame Rushdie. Even when I knew that his book had been a gift to the fundamentalists in Iran, the only concern I had was that this nightmare could go on for years. There seemed no point in marking the third anniversary of John's kidnapping in April. The situation was ~~literally~~ hopeless and I had no idea how we were going to lift the campaign. How could I expect people to put so much time and effort into organizing events when even I couldn't see the point in carrying on? Even so, a voice in my head was saying: 'What else is there to do? It's still better than doing nothing.'

The hostage issue had been doing so well at the end of 1988, not just on the international scene, but in campaign terms, too. Support had been hard won, but every television interview and every drop of publicity brought another batch of letters from people all over the country. Cathy and Joan made the most of each one, writing personal replies and sending information-packs which asked people to write to their MPs, buy our merchandise and sign our petitions. We'd delivered thousands more signatures to Downing Street and my mum and dad had organized a candle-lit procession through our village the previous November, on John's birthday. In London we'd held a second fund-raising concert to mark the event at the Hippodrome in Leicester Square. It had been another six months of hard work for the Benefit committee, but they had pulled it off. Tickets were harder to sell than for the Camden Palace Benefit, but it had raised a fair amount of money and attracted some publicity. There had been so many camera crews roving around the dance floor that night that it was difficult to move without being interviewed. This time everyone got a turn in the spotlight – Barbara was making a programme about the campaign for BBC2's *Open Space*.

With only four weeks until John's third anniversary we had to come up with a new plan. But what could we do or say? We could hardly ask the Government to talk to Iran now. We had no idea what to do, but in the end we decided on a theme: 'Three Minutes for Three Years'. Cathy was to ask radio stations, churches, our supporters, anyone we could think of, to devote three minutes of their time to John. It was a good idea, but we were all weary and it was hard for anyone to be particularly enthusiastic. I felt we were in danger of sinking into apathy and falling apart.

The advertising agency Bartle Bogle Hegarty was just another place to go in search of help and advice. I had had so many meetings over the years and was used to people saying that although they were sympathetic about John's situation, they didn't really see what they could do to help. I viewed our appointment to see John Hegarty at the agency in the same light; there was no harm in giving it a try. Johnny Haddock, a photographer who'd just joined the campaign, had worked with John in the past and modestly suggested he try to arrange a meeting with him. Seated in BBH's glossy reception area one evening in February, with Ronnie and Johnny, I looked around at the television screens which covered the whole of one wall and the glamorous young things whizzing in and out and wondered how a company geared to promoting consumer products was really going to help.

John Hegarty, though, was keen to offer advice. He told us that he had a 'professional fascination' with our ability to sustain the campaign, and after praising what we had done so far, he got straight to the point. He was conducting the meeting sitting astride a life-sized toy sheep, but I tried not to be distracted by that, and to concentrate on what he had to say.

'The main thing I always feel when I see anything about your campaign on television or in the papers is enormous sympathy for John's situation, but a kind of powerlessness about what I can do to help,' he said. 'Your main problem is that people feel they can't do anything about it. What would you like them to do?'

I felt myself blush. 'There isn't much people can do,' I replied, 'but we want them to tell their MPs that the Government's got to do more for the hostages. We just want people to be concerned, I suppose, we want them to care.' I tailed off, feeling a bit lame.

'But what do you do about all the other issues vying for people's attention? It helps to give people something practical to do, like with Band Aid or Red Nose Day. In this case you're asking people to do – what? – for which there are no tangible results.' We all nodded earnestly; we knew this was exactly our problem.

He promised to think about it and see if he could come up with any ideas. As we left, I felt positive and encouraged by his interest in the campaign. He had been honest with us about how we were perceived and exactly where we were going wrong. He hadn't tried to fob us off with platitudes, but he had given us something to think about. I wondered if he would remember his promise. He was such a busy man, it would hardly be top of his list of priorities.

A few weeks later BBH contacted us and Chris, Ronnie and I went to meet Steff Tiratelli and Paddy Byng, the creative team. They gave us the kind of respect and time I imagined they gave their clients, and in the same business-like way they presented us with a slogan: 'Out of Sight, Not Out of Mind'. The idea echoed our constant aim that the hostages should not be forgotten and formed part of a newspaper and cinema promotion they had drafted. The copy on the newspaper advert read: 'Close Your Eyes and Think of England. John McCarthy's been doing nothing else for the past three years.'

It dawned on me that they were offering this piece of advertising to us. 'Do you know we have very little money?' Chris asked, voicing my thoughts. 'The only thing we might ask you to pay for is whatever raw materials we can't get for free,' Steff replied, 'but with a bit of luck that shouldn't be much of a problem. The agency really wants to help, and we'll do the best we can.'

Although we didn't know it yet, BBH would lift our campaign on to another level altogether. Their poster and cinema advert formed the basis of our third anniversary publicity, and I found that meetings with Paddy and Steff were a perfect antidote to the bleakness of the time. The cinema advert was brilliant and when I saw it, shivers ran up and down my spine. The whole thing lasted only sixty seconds and was very simple. ITN and the BBC had supplied free footage of scenes of chaos and destruction in Beirut and into this the photographs of the British hostages were faded in and out. The hymn 'Jerusalem' played on a solo piano provided the soundtrack. The last image we saw was of a tiny child, sitting in rubble, crying. It was a powerful reminder that ordinary lives – those of the hostages and the Lebanese people – were being destroyed by civil war. If anything was going to move people, I thought this would.

Throughout the summer of 1989, following the third anniversary in April, BBH begged and called in favours, persuading cinemas around the country to run the advert. The IBA refused to allow it to be shown on television on the grounds that the Friends was a political organization, so consequently the campaign got even more free publicity. Several newspapers and television programmes questioned the IBA's decision, especially as, at the time, Britain's water companies were being allowed to advertise in the run-up to privatization. Over the years the argument continued to resurface, but we kept quiet about the fact that even if the IBA had approved the advert, we could never have afforded the air time.

BBH also persuaded the press to print the poster, all for free. They gave the artwork to newspapers, asking them to run it if they found themselves with an empty space. Every now and then I would open the *Observer* or *Spectator* and see our advert taking up a quarter- or half-page. It had a knock-on effect. The more space BBH acquired, the more they were offered. People clearly liked the advertising; Paddy and Steff told us that within the industry there was a tremendous desire to help.

The advertising prompted hundreds and thousands of people to contact our office for more information. Some of them were under the impression that we were a huge pressure group housed in luxurious offices. One group of supporters refused to believe otherwise, until Cathy sent them a photograph of our headquarters, a tiny, chaotic

387

office crammed with merchandise, files and posters and the campaign dummy, sitting quietly in a corner.

The people who contacted us cut across the political divide. After the advert appeared in the *Daily Telegraph*, a newspaper generally held to reflect the views of the establishment, we received a couple of thousand letters asking for more information. The number of supporters on our books began to grow, and we could direct some towards local FOJM groups around the country, formed by many of our early supporters. The groups took a mountain of work off our hands by organizing events of their own.

One person, Rosemarie Gabriel, set up an FOJM office in Beverley. She organized concerts, recitals, talks and a petition which finally totalled 31,000 signatures. Quite often, though, it was children who spurred their families and friends into action. Emma Murphy wrote to us from Lancaster. She came down to work in the office in her school holidays, organized endless meetings and gave talks all over her area. These Friends turned into experienced campaigners themselves, sharing our own ups and downs, and the difficulties of trying to think up new ways of drawing attention to John's plight.

Over the next two years, the letters and donations we received touched our hearts. People's compassion for a complete stranger and their remarkable loyalty to the campaign kept us going. Thanks to our supporters, and BBH, the campaign held its nerve. Attendance at meetings, which had dropped to around five or six good friends in the early summer, began to pick up.

Despite all these positive indications the situation on the international front was still dire. Frantically I tried to think where we could turn next now that Britain was no longer in contact with the Iranian government. The only way round the embargo as far as I was concerned was to seek help abroad. Terence had been at Oxford with Benazir Bhutto, then Prime Minister of Pakistan and he managed to get a letter through to her, asking for help. The result was that the Pakistani Foreign Minister had raised the subject of the hostages with the Syrians and the Iranians. We had no idea what effect it would have, but it had to be worth trying to encourage other countries to take up the hostage issue with the Iranians. I wondered if the European Parliament might take up John's case.

The MEP for Glasgow, Jayne Buchan, offered to help and Barbara and I made a trip to Strasburg. We spent an exhausting two days racing after her through the corridors of the Parliament, lobbying the vast number of people she insisted talk to us. Her energy put us to shame. The President of the Parliament, Lord Plumb, supported the idea of a working group which could make approaches to Iran, but the problem was time and resources. To work, the idea needed full-time lobbying and the support of the British government – that wasn't on offer.

Chris and I had met Sir Geoffrey Howe and William Waldegrave in April. I had been encouraged when we walked into the meeting to see an official switching off a video recorder – Howe had been watching Barbara's *Open Space* programme – but the rest had been extremely depressing. I asked him what ideas they had for making progress now that the Rushdie affair had ended in deadlock. I got the usual reply – the Government was doing all it could.

'So, you're going to carry on doing the same things that haven't worked for three years then? You're not going to change anything?' I asked.

'What exactly is it that you want us to do, Jill?' Waldegrave snapped.

'What about a European approach, an official European body, to act as an intermediary. Some of those countries have good relations with Iran; they may be able to make some progress where Britain can't at the moment.'

'We don't think that would work. In any case, it happens, already, on an informal basis. We're quite sure that a behind-the-scenes approach is the best way.'

We had come to a bit of an impasse and Howe peered at his watch, saying he had a funeral to attend. The meeting came to a close and he shuffled off. Chris and I crossed Whitehall for our usual, morose, post-Foreign Office drink at the pub opposite. I was exhausted. *The Satanic Verses* had put paid to the Government's only strategy for getting the hostages out and now it seemed as if we had to wait for religious fanaticism in Iran to wane before anything more could be done. No other ideas seemed to be on offer.

The hopes we'd had at the end of 1988 had gone. The darkness was denser and blacker than before. Sheila was very ill. In March 1989 I went down to see her and Pat again. The day before, I had spoken to her on the telephone for the first time in quite a while. 'I thought I was finally going to break down mentally after Rushdie,' she said. 'Before that I was out driving my car again, but afterwards I couldn't see how I could keep going.' I knew she had been very ill over the past few months and was relieved to hear her say that she felt better now. When I got to Cornish Hall End her appearance shocked me, as it had the year before.

'Jill, dear, how nice to see you. Was the train on time? I call it British Fail, you know, did Pat tell you? Come and sit down. I'm so annoyed with this wretched back of mine. It gives me so much pain. The doctor says it won't get better, but I'm going to do some stretching when the weather gets warmer, so then we'll see—'

She was chatting away, as she'd always done, her eyes dancing with fun whenever something amusing struck her. 'Have you met our new cat, Mortimer? We got him after Monty died. He's not at all like him, though, he's very shy.' Mortimer promptly shot away, careering out of the back door. 'Oh my hat! Pat, dear, I think he wants to go out! Poor old Monty,' she said, after the cat had disappeared. 'John did love him so. He'll be so sad he's not here when he gets back.' As she talked, I had a sudden memory of John imagining Monty's voice and what he might be saying as he haughtily picked his way along the back of the sofa, or disdainfully allowed himself to be stroked. Suddenly, the house seemed emptier.

In the drawing room, sitting in his armchair by the fireplace, Pat showed me copies of letters he had received from the Archbishop of Canterbury, the Queen, Mrs Thatcher and Glenys Kinnock about a service for the hostages at Broxted Church. There was pride in his voice as he pointed to one from the Queen. 'Look at this, Jilly. Not bad, eh?' I sat opposite him, as Emma, a lovely black labrador, raced round the room, showing off in front of the visitor. I petted her, and told the McCarthys my news.

I was there to supervise the recording of an appeal to the kidnappers which Sheila had learned by heart. It was a difficult speech and it was formidably long, but it had to be shot in one go. I didn't believe she'd get through it, but I had forgotten that her nickname was 'One take McCarthy'. Her main concern throughout had been that the camera crew were comfortable and had been given a cup of tea. After she'd finished, I gave her and Pat a copy of the cinema advert that BBH had just made. Pat put it on the video and we watched it in silence. As John's photograph came up on the screen, Sheila covered her face with her hands and rushed from the room. I'd hoped to cheer her up, and I felt utterly helpless. The photograph of John was used in many of our campaign posters and videos and I was accustomed to seeing it - so much so that it had lost any personal meaning for me. However, I should have foreseen Sheila's distress. I couldn't bear to look at other old videos and photographs of John; it was too painful and reminded me of how much had been lost.

In May Sheila was given only a few months to live. Pat and Terence decided that Pat should record an appeal. It was not in Pat's nature to dwell on his problems in private, let alone in public; but it was an ordeal he faced with immense dignity. His face was expressionless and his voice firm as he read a statement asking that Sheila be reunited with her son before she died. After it was broadcast, we heard that many people in Lebanon had been deeply moved by it. From the kidnappers there was only continued silence. I only wished I could find something that might help Sheila to hang on, to nudge the people holding John. They might not free him, but surely they would let him communicate with his mother.

In Lebanon, however, the kidnappers were still in operation, despite our Government's hard line. Jackie Mann, a retired airline pilot, living in Beirut with his wife Sunnie, was kidnapped on his usual Friday morning trip to the bank. ITN's correspondent, Brent Sadler, had filed a report on him and Sunnie only a few weeks before. It had seemed to me to be a dangerous temptation to the kidnappers. When Jackie was abducted, I didn't think that they could possibly hold on to someone of his age, but they were to keep him captive for two and a half years. To me, his kidnapping was also proof that the 'no deals' policy was not a sufficient deterrent.

The future looked bleak. I seized on the only hopeful development in the Middle East in months; the fact that Yasser Arafat, the PLO leader, had recently renounced terrorism and accepted Israel's right to exist. Arafat was taking a gamble, distancing himself from the more extreme elements in the PLO and trying to negotiate a settlement for his people instead of staging confrontations. World leaders had, cautiously, welcomed the move. I knew that, in the past, Roby had attempted to see Arafat, but there was no harm in our approaching him. He might just think it was in his interests to help us. 'No idea is a bad idea,' as Pat had said back in 1986.

I knew that Arafat was a difficult man to get to see, but one person who might be able to help us was a Palestinian journalist I'd met in rather unusual circumstances. In 1986 Nasri Hajjaj was being held in Pentonville Prison while the authorities decided whether to let him stay in England with his English wife. He had come to Britain from Beirut and I had gone to see him in the hope that he might know something about John.

It was the first time I'd been in a prison. In the waiting-room I watched as other visitors, mostly women and children, had their bags of food and other gifts sifted through by prison officers and then the door to the meeting area clanged open. It was a huge room; Nasri was sitting at one of the tables and there was a barrier between us. He had no news of John and was sad he couldn't help, although he was sure John was alive and would be OK. I heard later that, after months in Pentonville, Nasri had been deported to a succession of other countries before eventually ending up in Tunisia, where he now worked for the PLO's news department. He had been very kind to me in the prison and when I called him, he remembered me and immediately offered to help, hopeful that Arafat would see us. By the time Chris and I flew to Tunis in mid-June I had placed all my hopes on the meeting. We were racing against time.

The receptionist at our hotel didn't bat an eyelid when Nasri told him the PLO had reserved our rooms. As we got into the lift Chris wondered if there would be a rack for guests' AK47s, as well as the usual hairdryer and trouser press.

Later, Nasri collected us for a meeting with Arafat's second-in-command, Abu Iyad. We drove through Tunis to a road lined with substantial-looking villas. Outside one of the houses was a barrier with a sentry post. We were waved through and entered the garden. It was dark as we walked up the path. Waist-high lamps were strung along it, like lights on a Christmas tree. Every so often the glow caught the machine-guns dangling from the hands of the guards who flanked the path.

In the house we waited in a marble hallway until we were shown in to see Abu Iyad. We made polite, clumsy conversation, translated back and forth by one of the three other men in the room. Abu Iyad told us that Arafat was away at present, but might be back the following day. A boy brought in some coffee and as he bent down to serve it, he casually batted away the machine-gun slung across

393

his back which had nearly collided with one of the cups.

Abu Iyad told us that the PLO was against kidnapping, was working for peace in the Middle East and was doing all it could for the hostages. I told him about Sheila, and how her only wish was to see John again, or receive a message from him. I said to him that the silence of the kidnappers was playing into the British government's hands and allowing them to get away with doing nothing. Abu Iyad listened to us patiently and courteously and then we left, feeling a little encouraged. As we walked out into the darkness, past the machine-guns, I wondered what on earth I thought I was doing here. I was a tourist in a dangerous world, where the risk of sudden and violent death was high. The violence of the Middle East caught up with Abu Iyad a year later. He was assassinated, probably by one of his own guards, on the eve of the Gulf War.

We hung around for the next couple of days. The tedium was broken when Nasri appeared from time to time to tell us, 'The Chairman has gone to Lagos' or, 'The Chairman has had to fly to Egypt', but it was difficult to avoid the feeling that we were wasting time and we decided to leave. We wrote letters to Abu Iyad and Arafat, addressing him as Abu Ammar – Our Father – on Nasri's advice, in the hopes that it might somehow make a difference. We had already booked a cab to take us to the airport when Nasri came bursting into the hotel. 'The Chairman is here,' he said, smiling. 'You will see him this evening.' Chris's face was a picture of frustration and despair.

'Can you face going through all this again?' Wearily, I shrugged my shoulders. We had to stay. I couldn't bear to think that we might miss our one real chance.

Our luck was in. An hour later Nasri picked us up and we drove to the PLO Ambassador's residence. We passed more sentries with heavy-duty guns, then we were shown inside the villa and ushered through a series of large, connecting rooms. In the last one, which was divided into a large seating area and a raised dining area, a crowd of people, mostly men, were sitting, chatting. In an alcove was Arafat, talking animatedly to two men who, we gathered, were his biographers. He was tiny and, without his customary headdress, bald.

We sat down and waited for something to happen. Nobody took any notice of us. I was nervous, but fascinated, trying to absorb the scene, wondering what to do next. We didn't know if we had two minutes to state our case and leave, or whether we had all afternoon. It became apparent that lunch was due to be served when about twenty people moved to a big table in the dining area. Chris and I were shown to seats near Arafat, who sat at the head of the table. I had no idea if we were supposed to introduce ourselves, if that would be rude, or what the form was. I was completely taken aback when Arafat started to serve me and everyone around him. He had a huge, beaming smile and when he used it, as he did now, he lit up the room. He was enormously charismatic.

He still hadn't taken much notice of Chris and me, but when one of the biographers asked us who we were and we started to tell him about John, Arafat held forth, still smiling, about kidnapping.

'When the PLO were in Beirut there were no kidnappings. No journalist was hurt when the PLO were there. Why are they doing this? It is a very bad thing. Only since the PLO left did this happen.' Someone mentioned the Iranians and Islamic Jihad. 'Your Thatcher, she says she hates Iran and won't talk to them. But if you go to Iran you see a bridge on which is written the name of a British company.' Arafat's smile widened even further. 'The British are helping Iran, and they are also sending them arms.' I hoped he would carry on talking to us, but the conversation drifted away and after lunch was over everyone returned to the lounge area.

Arafat sat himself in a corner of the room, opposite us. There were still a lot of people around; I couldn't think of how to catch his attention again. Nasri came over and gave me a little nudge. 'Go and sit next to him, Jill,' he whispered. 'Go on.' I moved across and just plunged in. 'Chairman Arafat, my friend, John McCarthy, has been held hostage for three years . . . his mother is very ill . . . we are desperate for news or a message from him—'

He made sympathetic noises and then suddenly looked away. He shouted in Arabic at a big general with a handsome moustache. The general nodded, and walked out of the room. Arafat turned back to me and addressed the room in general.

'You see,' he said, 'already we are working on this case. We are making contact with our people in Lebanon. I have told him to telephone to Fadlallah straightaway and ask for news of your friend.'

I was amazed. 'When will you hear?' I asked.

'One week, maybe two,' he said.

'Thank you, Chairman Arafat. John's family will be very grateful.' I wanted to believe that it could be as simple as that; orders barked down a telephone, followed by John being allowed to send a message home, or even being released. When my excitement had subsided, I agreed with Chris that it was probably just theatrics, staged for our benefit, almost as an act of courtesy. All the same, I hoped something would come of it.

'Do you know who you shook hands with back there?' asked Nasri, as we walked to the car waiting to take us back to the hotel. We looked blank; before we left, we had shaken hands with everyone in the room.

'The tall one with the beard, that was Abu Abbas,' he said.

'Wasn't he responsible for the Achille Lauro?' I asked.

Nasri nodded. His smile seemed to say, 'Do you get the picture? Do you see what all this is about?' Members of Abu Abbas's group had hijacked an Italian cruise liner and murdered a crippled Jewish passenger in 1985. I was horrified that I had shaken the man's hand.

As we drove back to the hotel in a PLO car, Nasri pointed out the spot where the Israelis had murdered Abu Jihad, Arafat's second-in-command, just over a year ago.

It made the problems of the Middle East seem that much more real, and emphasized that we were outsiders who couldn't hope to understand. Nasri then reached down to the armrest in the passenger door next to him. Smiling, he yanked it open and pulled out a huge gun, which he waved around playfully. I felt out of my depth; I was encouraged that we had managed to see Arafat, but any hope that he might be able to help John now seemed foolish and naïve.

Every so often I looked back over the previous few months and was amazed at how busy I had been and by how much had happened, yet there was still no news from Beirut. So much of the campaign's activities were far removed from what was happening in the Middle East, yet they had come to be part of our lives. Conversations at social occasions inevitably drifted to the campaign and I found it difficult to escape it. As time went on I wished that not all of my friends were involved. Yet we were still the same collection of people, still learning as we went along. Sometimes it seemed that we were selling a product, but no-one forgot the reason we were there. We had not been taken over by outside political groupings and were blessedly free from internal politics. The group never splintered into factions, nor were there many displays of ego. There were plenty of irritations, but few rows. Most of us had felt the rough edge of Cathy's tongue on the occasions when she felt that someone was severely out of line, but it generally cleared the air.

The friendships between us grew more intimate and deepened. We were all aware of the changes in everyone's lives: different jobs, greater responsibilities, bigger flats, first mortgages, first babies. I shared these with my friends, but was saddened by them, too. John was missing so much.

I couldn't really imagine what he would have thought if he'd known how we were spending so much of our time. I thought he would have been overwhelmed, uncomfortable that all this attention was focused on him, and incredulous at the experiences we'd had. I kept hoping he would think we were doing the right thing and wondered if he knew anything about it. Were any of the messages we put into Beirut newspapers twice a year getting to him? It was frustrating telling him so often how much we cared, yet not having any idea if he ever heard us. I was still desperately worried that what we were doing might endanger his life, or prolong his captivity. Sometimes I wondered if John was sitting there wishing that we would just keep quiet and realize that we were making things more difficult for him. It was all right for us, we could enjoy the camaraderie that came from sharing a purpose, the occasionally bizarre and often exciting things that happened to us and the slightly smug feeling that we were doing something worthwhile. But what about John? Was it doing him any good?

In the early evening of 8 July, John's mother Sheila died at Addenbrook's Hospital. It was the saddest moment of John's captivity. For years her will and determination to see her son again had been stronger than her illness, but she was finally defeated. Pat told me that she had seemed at peace, and that her final words had been, 'It's all right,' and he drew comfort from that. All I could think was that no matter what else happened, there was no hope of a happy ending now. I wanted somebody to pay for all that she'd been made to suffer and for letting her die with such sadness in her heart. I despaired that when John did come home he would not find his dear mother waiting.

Sheila's funeral took place at Broxted Church near the lovely house where the McCarthys used to live. John had loved the place and after the funeral I walked round the garden with John's cousin, Justin, who told me how it used to be when they were younger. Everything seemed so unbearably sad. Standing by Sheila's grave, the realization that this was finally the end hit me, but at that moment a complete stranger rushed over. 'I just wanted to say how much I admire your campaign.' She appeared quite oblivious of the fact that I was distraught. 'Not now,' I thought, 'not here.'

I had realized by now that I had become public property. At my grandmother's funeral the previous year exactly the same thing had happened as we were standing by her grave. My grandmother's death had also hit me hard and the idea that I should have to put on a public face at her funeral distressed me.

I'd been stopped in the street a few times but it had happened little by little and I had muddled along, treating each occasion as a bit of a rarity. Now I had an uncomfortable feeling that the focus was increasingly on me as well as my relationship with John. In the beginning I had accepted that but now decided not to talk about John and me or do any more women's magazine interviews. I simply wanted to talk about the issue in political, rather than personal, terms.

It was only when someone yelled, 'Don't worry, Jill, he'll be back soon!' out of a car window that I realized I wasn't invisible any more; it seemed to have happened overnight. It still pleased me that at least it meant they were aware of John's situation, and the comments most people made were kind and supportive, but it was strange to be an ordinary person one minute and a minor celebrity the next. It was a new role I was having to learn how to play. I was dumbstruck when a girl at a party said to me, as we were introduced, 'Gosh, I feel as if I'm in the presence of Mother Teresa or something.' It was a bit of a conversation-stopper.

It worried me that people might think I was putting myself forward as some kind of martyr. Every time I heard myself described as 'the woman who waits' I winced. I hadn't given up my life for anyone, nor was I expecting John and me to fall into each other's arms again on his return. I had no idea if John would feel anything for me, whether he would even have thought of me, let alone whether he would want a relationship when he got home. I had no idea what I would feel either, but the longer his captivity went on, the more I felt that a future together was unlikely. Everything was so distant. I couldn't trust anything any more. Always at the back of my mind was the worry that I was making an utter fool of myself. Marking John's third anniversary in captivity had been a turning-point for me. It seemed to cancel out our three years together. I knew I had to be realistic. I couldn't dismiss John as a future partner – nor did I want to, but I'd recognized a long time ago that the only way forward was to try other relationships. It was difficult – some people seemed attracted to the situation I was in, which was the last thing I needed. The uncertainty and tension I lived with put any relationship under great strain.

I muddled along, wrapped up in the campaign, but the public recognition didn't go away. The problem got worse and I found myself wondering what to do about it. It had felt natural to call myself John's girlfriend after his abduction and I hadn't thought twice about it. Now I didn't know if I was his girlfriend any more. Increasingly I found the label 'girlfriend' mawkish, even patronizing, and I certainly didn't want to give people the impression that I was the devoted little lady of popular myth. If I said nothing, they would continue to believe what they wanted, but if I spoke out, and John heard me denying that I was his girlfriend, I worried that he would think I'd given up on him.

I talked it through with Mary and other friends, all of whom knew how unhappy I was feeling. The campaign was overwhelming me, but I couldn't walk away from it, the objective was too important. But I did have the power to change some things, particularly how I presented myself in the press. Once again, I fell back on the support of friends within the campaign. I asked the people who formed its backbone to give up yet another evening to discuss the problems I was having. It was very hard to explain exactly why I couldn't cope with life as it was. I knew that part of me was reluctant to play down my public role; it made me feel useful and I liked to be in control of what was being said. Another problem was that the media still only wanted interviews with me; no-one else was considered sufficiently newsworthy. Eventually, we decided to spread the interviews among more people whether the media liked it or not, and when I was interviewed I would insist on being called a friend of John's rather than his girlfriend. I didn't want to make a big deal out of it, nor did I want to mislead anyone. However, when I tried to put the new system into operation a few weeks later, I found it wasn't going to be as straightforward as I'd imagined.

The Friends were launching a new BBH poster at a site on the Finchley Road, donated to us by John's godfather, Tony Jones, who ran a business there. The poster was a huge, hand-painted version of the 'Think of England' idea. It was very eye-catching, bound to come to the notice of drivers travelling through Mrs Thatcher's constituency. Pat came to the launch and was soon talking to a couple of journalists who had turned up. I spoke to a reporter from the *Evening Standard* and answered the usual questions. I mentioned that I was getting very tired and would be taking more of a back seat in the campaign in future and asked her to describe me as a 'friend'. Pat and I went off to pose for a photograph in front of the new poster, we had tea with John's godfather, and then I went back to the flat.

I knew there was something wrong when I saw the number of messages on my answering machine. Joan had rung to ask if I'd seen the *Evening Standard*; she sounded very harassed so I ran to the corner shop and bought a copy. The front-page headline read: 'Hostage girlfriend: I have to get on with my own life now.' Cathy and Joan were furious. 'What on earth possessed you to say all that?' asked Cathy. 'They've barely mentioned the poster except for a few lines at the end and the phone's ringing non-stop!'

'I didn't say all that!' I said, frantically re-reading the quotes, before adding, miserably, 'It's not fair! All I said was I was going to take a back seat.'

But whatever I'd said, it had been too much and for the next two days I had a very small taste of what it is like to be hounded by the press, reporters were pressing on the bell, the telephone was ringing non-stop, and I dared not go out. Cathy and Joan were annoyed and harassed and Chris was away on holiday, so I couldn't ask his advice. I didn't know what to do except to stay in and not answer the door or the phone. The next morning the *Daily Express* featured the decision on its front page, and inside they even devoted an editorial to the subject. Although it was kind – the leader writer understood perfectly that I wanted to get on with my own life and who could blame me – it was, and is, weird to find an opinion piece all about yourself in a major national newspaper. Several other papers took up the same theme. The attention and pressure was terrifying. I got through it, but knew that I had had the merest glimpse of what it could be like, and decided that it was an experience I would try to avoid in future if I could possibly help it.

Life now stretched into the future like a long tunnel, with no end in sight. The media treadmill was now more tiring; it seemed to take me longer and longer to recover from each bout of publicity. My life was built around John and yet I did not even know what he looked like, let alone what kind of person he was. Sometimes what I was doing appeared to make no sense whatsoever. I tried to be sensible about the public side of things, but I seemed to be trapped, seen as a crusading Joan of Arc type, not allowed to have any feelings and not able to go home and forget about it either. I had been misquoted in the media about my decision to step back and was now a target for feature writers. One said that I was one of a new breed of professional widows, who had 'the cash and the cachet' of being attached to a famous man, but none of the bother of having him around. Mary had been outraged.

'What's this about cash and cachet?' she had said. 'I feel like writing in and telling them a few home truths!'

The times when I could just be myself were now all the more precious. I looked back at photographs of John and me from 1986 and could hardly imagine us as twenty-eight-year-olds with no ties. I remembered the nights out, the parties and the dancing and wondered if life could be as irresponsible again. The world had changed so much since then. Mrs Thatcher had just marked ten years in power and it was every man for himself. The world was changing elsewhere, too. In 1989 it was difficult to keep track of what exactly was going on. Popular elections in the Soviet Union, pro-democracy demonstrations in Eastern Europe, the opening of borders between East and West; it was impossible to know how the world would look when the dust settled. What, if anything, would John know about it all? How was I going to remember and explain all the subtle changes so that we could share them?

During the summer, the hostage issue had again made the front pages. The Israelis swooped into South Lebanon and abducted a Shi'ite cleric, Sheikh Abdul Karim Obeid. They claimed that he had been involved in terrorist offences against Israel. The direct consequences of this were the death of an American hostage, Lt.-Col. William Higgins, and threats to the lives of other Americans, including Joseph Cicippio. Videos were released by the kidnappers showing Cicippio with a gun to his head and of Higgins's body. With Lebanon and the Middle East so unstable, it seemed that anything could happen.

The Friends put out a statement, expressing our regret at Higgins's death, urging restraint, and saying that we hoped there would be diplomatic moves to ensure there would be no more consequences for the Western hostages from the Israeli action. We also said that our thoughts were with the families of the other hostages, and urged the Israelis to reconsider their action in kidnapping Sheikh Obeid.

The FO's response to the news at our next meeting with them was to inform us that the British government wasn't currently engaged in negotiations, but that they had asked the US to represent the interests of the British hostages in any dealings they had with Iran. They didn't hold out much hope that any such dealings were taking place, despite Hashemi Rafsanjani's progress against the radicals and his election as President, following the death of Ayatollah Khomeini. Israel's abduction of Sheikh Obeid had so enflamed the situation in the Middle East that there would be no *rapprochement* for some time.

In the aftermath of Obeid's abduction and Higgins's murder there was a blizzard of speculation about the Archbishop's Envoy, with headlines in the *Express*, *Sun* and *Mirror* screaming: 'Waite Next'. I had learned to treat everything I read and heard nowadays with a certain amount of scepticism but nevertheless the swings between hope and despondency were wearing. More to the point, I hoped the press reports weren't provoking the kidnappers, or giving them ideas. Once again, the rumours died down.

I needed to take some control over my life. In the past I had sometimes had to be told hostages were not top of everyone's list all the time, and that the subject wasn't the most important thing in the world. Eventually, I had come to see this for myself, realizing that people lose family and loved ones every day and have to cope; not everyone could go on television to talk about their personal tragedy. This was brought sharply home to me when a member of the campaign, Deborah Korner, suddenly died two weeks after having a baby. I didn't know her well, but she was Gina's best friend. The finality of it and the tragedy for the baby, his father and for Gina forced me to take stock. At least with John there was the hope that he would come back.

I tried to put things into perspective and change my outlook. I resolved to be more of a support to other people and less obsessed with the campaign. I also decided to change jobs. At WTN my career was on hold. I had long since given up being a union official and I had to get away from the endless queries about John and the campaign. It was a wrench to leave a place I had loved. It was where John and I had met, a place about which he would be thinking, but I needed to make the break and so joined ITN as a producer on a six-month contract. Roby seemed genuinely pleased for me, advising me to use the opportunity well and learn as much as I could from ITN. In the past months he had talked to me in greater detail about the efforts he was making on John's behalf. He was still quite cryptic, but I was used to it now and realized it was just his way of operating. I also knew that his relationship with Pat had grown into one of genuine affection and respect and that, since Sheila's death, he had become even more of a support to him. That we had adopted a different approach didn't seem to matter so much now.

At WTN there had been a degree of responsibility towards me because of John. When I moved to ITN I wanted to be an ordinary employee. My immediate bosses there were sympathetic to the campaign, but I couldn't expect them to give me any more time off than anyone else. If I wanted my contract renewed I would have to work hard. It was quite odd, though, going to a new job where, apart from the usual insecurities, everyone knew who I was. I was an employee, but I was also newsworthy. It took me some time to learn to trust my new colleagues.

The campaign was still going strong. Gina had been trying to put together an information pack for schools in response to the many letters which we received from children, but it was taking a while to organize. We were all amazed by the amount of interest shown by children towards the hostages. They seemed to go straight to the heart of the issue. Pat's secretary's little boy, Matthew, who was only six, had even written a prayer for John:

I love you God
You are good
You could make everybody
stop fighting like Iran
so they could let Mr McCarthy's
son out of there
Thank you.
Amen.

BBC Schools Radio ran a poster competition for the
Friends. Some of the entries were stunning. One was
painted in stark grey and black and showed a man sitting
in a cell, head in hands, while a spider dangled above him.
The caption read: 'Where is the hope? Where is the light?
Where is the love?' The artist was just ten years old. If
children could understand what we were trying to do, it
made everything seem that much more worthwhile.

Nonetheless, at times, the Friends' tactics really did
seem futile. At the Conservative Party Conference in
Blackpool in October we tried to collect signatures for
our petition and sell our FOJM mugs, T-shirts, pens and
sweatshirts. The Conservatives once again had banned us
from the conference centre, so we set up in biting wind
on the forecourt of a church opposite. I enjoyed the
comradeship with other groups banned from the centre,
but amid the huge security operation, few delegates realized
we were there and hardly anyone came our way. But one
night, after a fringe meeting, Jackie managed to accost the
new Foreign Secretary, John Major. He told her that as
long as he was Foreign Secretary the hostages would be
top priority; it was the strongest commitment that we'd
had from a Foreign Secretary, but unfortunately he was
only in the job for another month, moving to the Treasury
when Nigel Lawson resigned as Chancellor.

Over the next few weeks there were reports in the
Tehran Times that negotiations between the US and Iran
were underway and that Iranian assets frozen in the US
were to be returned. Another report in the paper linked

the imprisonment of Roger Cooper with that of an Iranian, Kourosh Fouladi, imprisoned in the UK for a bungled bombing attempt. Fouladi was freed in September and I wondered if these few small signs would add up to something. It didn't seem likely, the rift between Britain and Iran seemed irreparable, but they were the only things to hold on to amid the continuing silence.

At our weekly meetings it went without saying that we would be marking another anniversary in April. A *World in Action* programme by Nick Davies had raised the hostage issue again, asking why every other government had succeeded in releasing some or all of its hostages except Britain and forcing William Waldegrave, still Foreign Office Minister, to defend accusations in several letters to the *Guardian* that the Government was leaving the hostages stranded by refusing to abandon the moral high ground. In his first statement on the situation since taking over at the FO, Douglas Hurd said that he had come to the conclusion that Iran was the key. Hurd had a high reputation as a diplomat and it was believed that the FO welcomed his appointment. However, I couldn't decide whether his statement was a good sign or just more hot air.

The Government still seemed reluctant to take any steps to improve our relationship with the Iranians or to send any helpful signals to Tehran. Although the Iran-Iraq War had ended the previous year, the two countries were still wrangling over border disputes. Back in the summer Britain, supposedly neutral, had considered allowing a British company to supply sixty Hawk jets to Iraq. The Government finally stopped the sale, but only after coming under pressure in the newspapers and a private appeal from Pat. For months Britain had refused to condemn the Iraqi government's murder of thousands of its own citizens with chemical weapons. Eventually the Government issued a mild reprimand, but I couldn't understand why Britain was bending so far backwards to be nice to Saddam Hussein. A few months later, Iraq executed Farzad Bazoft, an *Observer* journalist accused of spying and imprisoned the nurse, Daphne Parish, accused of helping him. Together with the Supergun affair, these incidents led to Iraq becoming Britain's Public Enemy Number One. The world seemed to have gone mad.

At the end of 1989 and beginning of 1990 it had seemed for a few brief months as if we were entering the dawn of a new age and that old wrongs were finally being righted. 'Good God, Jill, if you're like this now, what are you going to be like when the hostages come home?' a friend said in October, as I watched television pictures of the Guildford Four walk free with tears streaming down my face. I felt the same when thousands of people swept over the borders of Eastern Europe into the West and tore down the Berlin Wall. When Nelson Mandela was released in February it struck the same emotional chord and it seemed that only the hostages in Lebanon were untouched by the wave of freedom sweeping through the world. However, the impact of the changes in Eastern Europe was enormous, and it appeared there might be practical benefits for the hostages.

When communism crashed to the ground and left the West triumphant, Syria, which for decades had received arms and finance from the Soviets, found it necessary to make friendlier noises to Western governments. For years Iran had been able to proclaim its hatred for America and Britain because it had lucrative trade deals with the communist Eastern bloc, but that was no longer the case. The leaders of Eastern Europe no longer provided Iran with any protection; she would have to find a way of living with the West.

There had been no releases and no news of John since the freeing of Kauffman twenty months earlier. In January 1990 a Lebanese reporter working for the *Sunday Correspondent* rang me out of the blue to say that she had been at a Hezbollah funeral in Lebanon and overheard a man claiming to be John's guard. The reporter believed that she had really stumbled on some information that John was alive; she and her photographer also said that they were shown a building where the hostages had been held. I seized on it as another indication that John was alive and it revived interest in the hostages for a day or two. The Friends spent nearly an entire meeting poring over the newspapers, all of which had published the same photograph of the building in Beirut on their front pages.

'I can't see any hotel,' someone muttered, poring over a copy of *Today* with a puzzled expression on his face. Mary Lambe leaned over to enlighten him. 'I think Hostage Hilton is just a tabloid expression, actually,' she said, as the rest of us dissolved into laughter.

To coincide with the fourth anniversary of John's kidnapping we launched a book of short stories under the title *Friendship*. It was a wonderful volume, the brainchild of one of John's former flatmates, Pete Nunn, who'd spent more than a year trying to make it happen. Ralph Steadman designed the cover, provided a host of illustrations and even helped publicize it for us, while writers like Samuel Beckett, Edna O'Brien and Martin Amis gave us permission to use their short stories. We all attended an auction of Steadman's illustrations at which John Hurt read Beckett's story, 'Lessness'. Then the bidding got underway and it seemed to be going terribly well. It was only afterwards that we realized we'd been bidding against each other, but at least the campaign benefited by several hundred pounds.

On 17 April 1990, the fourth anniversary of John's kidnap, we held another candle-lit vigil opposite the Iranian Embassy and I did the usual round of interviews, as did Cathy and Chris. The Benefit committee had managed to organize another concert, this time at the Town and Country Club, but it was harder to persuade people to appear than it had been on earlier occasions. All the agents and promoters seemed caught up in Mandela fever but, despite that, there was a good line-up of bands and comedians. Even so, trying to sell tickets was a depressing experience. In the ITN news room I'd walked up to a crowd of journalists clustered around a TV monitor, taken a deep breath and asked: 'Does anyone want to buy tickets for a benefit for John McCarthy?'

'Who?' said one, with the tone of irritation that affects some people who think they're frightfully important because they work in television.

'John McCarthy,' I said, through gritted teeth.

'No, thanks,' he said, brusquely, turning back to the monitor. It felt like a personal insult and I rushed out of the news room, on the point of tears.

By the evening of the concert I was so tired and depressed I couldn't make myself attend. The same gloom seemed to have descended on everyone. Chris told me that the Benefit had been a disheartening affair; not many people came and we didn't make much money. A few television camera crews turned up, though, to record our reaction to the sudden release of an American hostage, Robert Polhill, from three years of captivity. He had been held by a group whose links with Islamic Jihad were unclear and had no news of any other hostages apart from two Americans, Jesse Turner and Alan Steen, with whom he'd been held. He said very little, flew back to the United States, was photographed with George Bush on the White House lawn, and that was that. Everything went quiet again.

In the weeks up to the anniversary I'd read so many different things in the newspapers that I was completely confused. Discussions between the US, Iran and Syria were said to be making progress, but the White House was denying it; Rafsanjani had said that progress was being made on the hostage issue but the groups in Lebanon were denying it; Robert Fisk, whose reports I paid attention to, said that the entire ruling council of Hezbollah had been meeting with Iranian diplomats to discuss the possible release of the Western hostages; and the *Tehran Times* issued its strongest call yet for their freedom. As was the norm, the Friends dutifully put out a statement asking the British government to respond positively to the news. In the week following Polhill's release, there was more confusion. British hostages were said to be in the worst position because of our lack of contact with Iran and Syria; the Irish Foreign Minister Gerry Collins met with his Iranian counterpart at the UN, who said he hoped Keenan would be released soon and Julie Flint wrote an article about the inexplicable silence surrounding the fate of the British hostages, hinting that they were probably dead.

I was shattered, spending days moping around in a black mood. Each year it seemed to take longer and longer to recover from the interviews and activity surrounding the anniversary. I took a week off work and planned a few days away on the coast somewhere. On the Monday, Frank Reed, another American hostage, was released. I thought it strange that two people had been released in just over a week but in my despair I couldn't get too excited. Reed was bound to have been kept with the other Americans; I was sure he wouldn't have any news of John.

On Wednesday morning I was getting ready for my trip when the phone rang. It was Joan from the campaign office.

'You'll never guess who I've just spoken to.'

'Who?' I asked.

'Someone rang here and said, "Can I speak to Jill Morrell, please? It's Frank Reed calling." So I said, "Oh sure, you are. Well, she's not here but I can give a message to her later if you like." Then I realized it was him. I couldn't believe it. I felt such a fool. Anyway, I'd better get off the line, he's given me a number for you to call him at the airbase in Wiesbaden.'

'What does he want?'

'I don't know, he didn't say.'

I looked at the number I'd written down and thought I'd better call Germany. I wouldn't hear anything about John but I imagined that I would be able to talk to Frank Reed about the conditions he'd been held in, so it was probably worth it. I picked up the phone and began to dial.

'Is that Jill?'

'Welcome home,' I said, puzzled by his familiar tone. 'How do you feel?'

'I'm fine, and I can tell you that John and Brian are fine, too. I left them just two days ago . . .'

'Two days ago?' John's alive, I was thinking. He's alive. This man had been sitting in the same room as John. He could touch him, he'd spoken to him; John's alive. It wasn't a case of a man who'd spoken to another man who'd seen John; this time there was no doubt. I knew for sure he'd survived. The four years of silence shrank to nothing at all. I couldn't think of anything to say, where to start. Two days ago, when Julie Flint's piece appeared, Frank Reed and John had been together. Two days ago, when the world had been ready to accept that the hostages were dead, John and Frank Reed had been in the same room. Frank, of course, couldn't understand the impact of what he'd said. He knew that John was alive and had no idea that, until a few seconds before, I hadn't known.

'Yep, we gotta get that goddamn Thatcher off her ass and get them out if I have to go to goddamn Syria myself—'

I had to bring him back to John. I still didn't know where to start. I interrupted him, babbling, 'How is he? Is he OK? Is he all right?'

'John's fine, he has biceps from doing press-ups every day.'

'John's got biceps?'

'Yeah, he's beautiful. His hair is shiny and gone a bit red from the tea . . . they give us this tea and we think it's coloured John's hair . . . he's got a small beard, makes him look older, he's a bit of a babyface . . . but he does his exercises, keeps himself fit.'

'What about his spirits? Is he OK?'

'He's fine. He and Brian, they jog each other along and keep each other up, you know, those buggers. John, he's the negotiator, the guards just love him, he can get anything he wants. We'd say to him, "John, we want some cigarettes" and John would get them for us . . .'

'Did he – did he mention me?'

'He talks about you all the time . . . he'll be so pissed that I got my hands on you first I can't tell you—'

'Does he know about the campaign?'

'Yeah, he knows about you and the committee and he's real proud. He got a few videos and those letters you put in the paper. He had a picture of you, hid it in his underpants, but those bastards took it away. The guards, those bastards, they beat me, I tried to escape twice, but they caught me and beat me—'

He spoke for fifteen minutes, telling me about John, Brian, his own captivity and his rage against the American and British governments. For four years I'd had no information about John and suddenly facts and anecdotes were pouring over me. I couldn't take them in, they were rushing around my head and then out again. The only fact that remained lodged in there was that John was OK; the rest of it was an oddly painted picture of a diplomatic Mr Universe.

Frank broke off and told me that Pat was on the other line waiting to talk to him. Before he hung up there was one more question I had to ask.

'Frank, we didn't have any proof that he was alive, nobody would believe us, and now you can tell them that it's true. Is it all right if I tell people, tell the press, I mean?'

'If you don't, I will, hon, I'm gonna tell the world, you can bet on that, I'm going to go on every talk show in the goddamn world . . . I thought I was the last one out but then I find when I get to Wiesbaden that that goddamn government of ours—'

I put the phone down and stared at the floor. My brother Brian was grinning at me from ear to ear. He'd heard my side of the whole conversation. 'That's brilliant, Jill, brilliant.' I nodded, grinning back, lost for words. Bits of what Frank had said kept coming back to me. John had kept a photograph of me. Which one? How had he got it? That meant he still thought of me. I still couldn't think coherently, but I'd been lifted sky high. He knew about the campaign, he'd got our messages, he was proud of what we were doing. I wanted to know more details, everything he was thinking, but I felt too dazed to think properly. My next thought was that I had to speak to Chris and tell him everything, then maybe it would make sense.

'I've just spoken to Frank Reed . . . they're alive. He says John's OK, he's doing press-ups and things . . . I can't take it all in—'

'I know, I've just had the Foreign Office on to me. They say Frank was with John and Brian until last Saturday . . . incredible. Apparently both Frank Reed and the State Department are insisting it's kept secret.'

'But I've just had Frank Reed on the phone saying he's going to tell the whole world. I asked him if it was OK to tell the press and he said if we don't he will. What shall we do?'

It was a terrible dilemma. We'd had the most exciting news about John in four years and we weren't sure if we could tell anyone. We spent an hour in this confusing limbo, with the Government saying everyone, including Frank Reed, wanted it kept quiet and Frank himself saying he wanted everyone to know John and Brian were alive.

During the afternoon, Frank Reed came out on to the hospital balcony at Wiesbaden to do a photocall in front of the world's TV cameras. The press had been told that he would just wave and then come back inside without saying anything, but one reporter decided to break the rules.

'How do you feel, Frank?' she yelled.

'I'm angry,' he shouted back. 'I'm angry that Johnny and Brian aren't home yet . . . I left them two days ago—' And that was that.

Ever since Jean-Paul Kauffman had told me that John had been seen alive in 1986 I'd always taken it for granted that he was and, perhaps naïvely, thought the media shared that assumption. In fact, most of the media entertained doubts that the hostages had survived and some were convinced they'd been killed. Frank's first-hand proof was to generate an overwhelming reaction. From one o'clock onwards the phone never stopped. I set off to do interview after interview. For years I'd been asked the question, 'But, Jill, how do you *know* John's alive?' and I would go through my feeble list of reasons. Now, after Frank Reed's revelations, I knew that I wouldn't have to answer that question ever again. The BBC and ITN devoted at least fifteen minutes of their bulletins to the news throughout the day, and we were stunned when Anna Ford ended a live interview with me by saying, 'Good luck with your campaign, Jill.'

Everyone seemed to go completely potty. Chris was holed up in an office at Sky, where he now worked, for the rest of the day doing interviews with radio stations around the country while I dashed around the major broadcasters, all thought about taking a 'back seat' pushed aside. Sitting in the Channel 4 News studio before the programme went on air, waiting to be interviewed by Jon Snow, he had turned to me, beaming from ear to ear, and said, 'I can't believe I'm reading this! It's fantastic!' Every newspaper in Britain had pages and pages devoted to the news about John and Brian. 'Alive and shackled' was the headline on *Today*'s front page alongside a drawing of how the artist imagined they now looked. John, he had decided, looked 'a decade older'. 'Alive, now let's get John McCarthy free!' said the *Star*. It was the kind of media interest that I had wanted for so long, but the scale of it left me breathless.

The media onslaught was great news for the campaign, but there was a part of me that wanted to run from it. Chris and I had decided to follow Brenda and Elaine, and their campaign organizer, Frank McCallan, to Washington. Frank Reed had flown there for his debriefing and medical check-up and we hoped to be able to talk to him again. But in the two days between his announcement to the world and the weekend trip to see him, I had felt that I'd had all the media pressure with which I could cope. So much of my life was ruled by forces beyond my control I resisted the idea of being taken over by the hostage-media merry-go-round as well. I told Chris I didn't want to go to Washington, that I couldn't face it. He said nothing while I prevaricated, trying to make up my mind, eventually deciding with only minutes to pack that I would go after all.

It was only during the flight to Washington, free from all pressure – ringing telephones, TV cameras, being on show and anything else – that I began to relax and look forward to what was ahead. It was important to me to hear more details about John from the person who knew him best. Others seemed to share that feeling; the US State Department was helpful to us and the Irish government was pulling out the stops for Brian Keenan's sisters, escorting them through a diplomatic immigration channel in Washington and into an embassy limousine that whisked them into the city. Yet when a reporter asked the British Foreign Office what they thought of our trip, the official replied rather snootily, 'We don't think it would serve any purpose at all.' 'Right,' I thought, 'if that's your attitude we'll do it without you.' On the plane I was too wrapped up in my own turbulent state of mind to notice that Chris was in tears in the seat behind me as the news sank in for the first time.

We caught up with Brian's sisters and Frank McCallan at a hotel in the city. To be with people who were in the same position as us, feeling the same excitement and anticipation at hearing the news, was wonderful. We sat in the hotel bar drinking vodka, not having the faintest clue what time of the day or night it was or what was going to happen next. The following day the roller-coaster set off again; with half an hour's notice we were taken to a different hotel to a welcoming brunch for Frank Reed. The event had been pulled together in twelve hours flat by No Greater Love, the umbrella group for all the hostage families in the US. Their organizational skills put the Friends to shame. On a quiet Sunday morning they'd managed to round up three senior senators, Daniel Moynihan, Robert Dole and Edward Kennedy, as well as Robert Polhill, who'd been released a fortnight earlier, and relatives of other hostages. They'd set up a press conference with something like thirty TV crews, which was going to go out live on CNN. It was hardly going to be a private occasion, and I was introduced to Frank Reed with a cameraman six inches away and an apologetic Alastair Stewart of ITN kneeling at our feet holding a microphone. It was wonderful to see Frank, though. I felt as warm towards him as if he had personally ensured John's survival. He looked fine, but it was only when I looked at a photograph of the plump-faced, sleek-haired, bright-eyed Frank Reed taken four years ago that I realized the image was barely recognizable as the man who had ruffled my hair a few minutes earlier.

After the press conference Frank went back to the hospital on an airbase just outside Washington. Chris and I were told we could have an hour alone with him later that afternoon. On the way to the hospital I felt jet-lagged and disorientated by the day's events, but when we walked into Frank Reed's room I was suddenly calm again. This was what we had come here for; finally we were going to be able to ask everything we could about John – and get the answers. Sitting in his pyjamas, smoking a cigarette, Frank Reed greeted each of us with a hug and then sat down to talk. He gave us impressions of how John was rather than precise details, but we made allowances for the fact that he'd just been catapulted back into the world from four years' captivity. Information about John was interspersed with ten-minute diversions about Frank's views on education, women, the Middle East and his own personal experience of captivity, and I felt guilty for trying to turn him back to John. At last, though, I was able to start filling in the four-year blank of what had happened to John and ideas and impressions swirled around in my head, refusing to be pinned down. Images that I had been blocking out for so long – John chained, transported around like a mummy underneath the bottom of a truck – were painful to visualize. He told me that once Brian had subjected a guard to a stream of

417

oaths and curses during a journey and when they arrived the guard vented his frustration by firing his gun wildly into the air. John's reaction was to laugh at this crazy sight. Black humour, but humour all the same, and it brought him into the room with us.

I had difficulty getting the measure of John as he was now from some of Frank's stories, and it confused me. Frank told us that his own ritual on waking each morning was to say, 'Fuck you, Thatcher, fuck you, Reagan' and because this had elicited no response at all from John, not even a smile, he'd wondered if it offended him. I imagined that it was the constant repetition that had got John down, but it was hard to tell. It sounded as if John was now very depressed. According to Frank he'd been lifted by daily reports on the radio that he, Brian and Terry Waite were going home at the end of 1988, so it must have been a terrible blow when it didn't happen. According to Frank, John thought England had given up on him and had said, 'Don't worry, I'm not English any more, I'm Irish.' It was awful to imagine the despondency which led to that remark but at the same time it seemed to reveal a defiance and rebelliousness. I felt angry that he'd been forced to conclude he'd been let down, and as guilty as if I'd let him down myself, but the fighting spirit behind it cheered me.

I rapidly revised my image of Brian Keenan. Frank told us how the Irishman had told endless shaggy-dog stories that went on for hours until John and he would be begging Brian to stop, and that Brian loved to 'rave on' about politics.

'Did John get into discussions like that?' I asked. 'He never used to enjoy that much.'

'It was almost as if they were setting one another up,' said Frank, 'like role-playing, almost to the point where John would sit back and then they'd start, and they'd always want me in, and I'd say, "No, go ahead" and they'd talk about whale-killing in Antarctica or something. The buggers would sit there and they'd have this rather esoteric philosophical discussion . . . the next thing you know, John would tackle Brian, jump on his back and horse around . . . it's a pity there wasn't a hidden camera that could have followed them because the whole thing was about two men living together, how they communicated with each other, how they supported each other . . . it's a beautiful story.'

Hearing about John goading Brian reminded me of his relationship with Nick; they had been very close and had almost had their own language and private means of communication. At times I had felt jealous; now I was thankful that John and Brian had developed a similar friendship; it must have given him great support and comfort. It was lucky that he and Brian had been able to strike up such a relationship, but then again, John was the kind of person who worked at making the most of friendships.

'The thing about John is he gets what he wants,' Frank said. 'He's a better spokesperson because Brian didn't want to talk to the guards. I didn't want to talk to them even though I could speak French but I didn't bother, I let John do it.'

I felt a bit irritated when Frank said that. 'Why leave it all to John?' I thought. 'Isn't that just an extra burden on him, to have to negotiate for you?' But at the same time there was pride that John was the one who'd found a way to reach the people who were holding him; I had hardly dared hope that he would.

It was clear that Frank was very fond of John and Brian. He kept saying that he 'missed those guys, or those chaps as you call them in jolly old England', but despite the English idioms, words and the anecdotes it was difficult to get a sense of what John was really thinking and feeling; I wondered if Frank really did know. When he told me that John talked about me often, I believed him, but when he said that John still loved me I doubted that he really knew, and guessed he was simply trying to make me feel better. Something wasn't quite right, but I couldn't put my finger on it. I was still taking in information about the world John inhabited and the John of whom Frank had allowed us a glimpse. Despite my reservations I felt warm towards Frank, who had just given us our best and most precious news in four years.

Later, on the way back to the hotel with Chris, one chilling image haunted me. Frank had told us how at night Brian would usually sleep and snore and John would be awake until early morning when he would doze from six until about ten. Frank described how he knew John was awake in the darkness: all he could see was the tiny red flame of John's cigarette moving to and fro. It frightened me to think about what was occupying his mind during those long hours.

Back at the hotel, we were waiting in the lobby when the BBC correspondent Keith Graves strolled in and promptly put his hands in the air as if in surrender.

'What can I say?' he said. 'I'm really glad that I was wrong, completely wrong.'

For years Graves had been the BBC's Middle East correspondent and he was now apologizing for having been convinced that the hostages were dead. I'd known that he'd been telling the BBC in London that all his contacts had assured him John and Brian had been killed. He'd never said anything like that on air, but had privately briefed the BBC that it was the case. Any journalist at the BBC who thought about covering the activities of the Friends or listening to what we were saying must always have had Graves's advice ringing in their ears; they must have thought we were well-meaning, but mis- guided. Graves told us that several days earlier he'd been advising a colleague yet again that the British hostages were dead when one of the TV monitors in front of him spluttered into life with pictures from Wiesbaden. Graves was interrupted by Frank Reed yelling from the balcony that he'd left John and Brian a few days be- fore. The fact that he told the story against himself so well made it impossible to bear him a grudge, and be- sides, he was only one of quite a few journalists who were now eating their own words.

Many Middle East experts and diplomatic correspondents had been convinced that the hostages were long since dead and they were encouraged in their thinking by the British government. Some of the hacks who'd admitted that they'd got it wrong told us disturbing stories of how the Government had been pushing the line that John, Brian and Terry Waite were all dead. I don't know whether the British government really believed it or whether it was a deliberate ploy to bury the story, but it made me angry and strengthened my belief that I had been right not to trust Foreign Office officials in the past.

Back in London, the news about John and Brian galvanized the campaign. Messages of congratulation came in from former colleagues and friends all over the world – New York, Malaysia, Australia – and, after a year in the doldrums thanks to *The Satanic Verses*, we felt purposeful again. We knew John had got our messages and had been cheered by the campaign's existence; after so long spent operating in a void we now had confirmation that what we were doing was worthwhile. The knowledge put me back in touch with my original motivation, which the details, responsibilities, routine and endless minutiae of campaign business had sometimes obscured.

Activity on the political front still seemed to be painfully slow. The Friends published the results of another opinion poll we'd commissioned prior to Reed's release. We were pleased by the results and especially when we saw them displayed in the *Daily Telegraph* eight days later: 75 per cent of the population were in favour of the Government negotiating the release of the British hostages. It seemed to indicate that the pro-Thatcher stance had softened enough to allow the FO room to manoeuvre. I read in the *Guardian* that Britain was now ready to open direct talks with Iran. A top Iranian official, Hussein Moussavian, Director-General of the Iranian Foreign Ministry, was reported as saying that the death-threat on Salman Rushdie might be lifted and a way might be found to 'facilitate' the release of the British hostages if Britain condemned the 'insults' in *The Satanic Verses*. Douglas Hurd had said he had 'high respect' for Islam, and Mrs Thatcher, who seemed to have been persuaded to adopt a more diplomatic approach by her advisers, announced during an interview on the World Service that she believed Iran had offered a significant olive branch which could lead to talks on diplomatic relations and the release of the hostages. She also said that Britain was as concerned about insults to the Muslim faith as it was about slurs on Christianity, but to me it seemed that *The Satanic Verses* remained an impossible stumbling-block as long as Iran still refused to lift the *fatwa* against Salman Rushdie. Once the excitement over Reed's release had faded, it seemed as if excitement was all it had been. Even his concrete evidence made no difference. John's release was no nearer and the reality was that nothing had really changed.

In July 1990, Chris and I were called in to see Andrew Green at the Foreign Office. He had taken over in 1989 as the senior official responsible for the hostages. Pat said at once that he was good news and was very encouraged by his commitment. I was still wary of trusting anyone at the FO, but found him very likeable. His manner couldn't have been more different from Ivor Roberts and he seemed genuinely concerned to solve the problem. He didn't tell us that much more than his predecessor, but we developed a very good relationship with him. Andrew and his colleague, Mark Canning, told us that they were prepared to be far more open and honest with Chris and me if we gave a solemn undertaking not to tell anyone else what we learned, not even the other members of the campaign. They still didn't tell us very much but there was a mood of greater frankness in the discussions and they revealed a little more about what they were thinking and what the Government was trying to do. Andrew told us that Britain had made it clear to the Iranians that it wanted diplomatic relations with Iran and all the benefits that would then accrue to both sides, but there were some problems still to be overcome: Roger Cooper, the *fatwa* on

Salman Rushdie and the hostages in Lebanon. Britain was doing its best to impress on Iran that these obstacles had to be overcome, they weren't just a wish-list. Ironically, our campaign, for so long loudly critical of the British government, was actually shoring up its negotiating stance. The British could say to the Iranians there was no way they would restore diplomatic relations and leave the hostages in captivity because British public opinion wouldn't stand for it. They could point to our loud and, until now, irritating campaign as evidence of this.

I'm not sure what had prompted the new openness, but Douglas Hurd's arrival as Foreign Secretary coincided with a new attitude towards the whole issue. Also, unknown to me, Pat had written a letter to the FO saying that, in his view, they were bungling the public relations side of things and that they really ought to be more open with us as we were, in his opinion, responsible people. We kept our promise, but nothing they had told us was that earth-shattering, until this hot afternoon in July.

We sat at our usual table in Andrew's office, politely sipping coffee, but there was an odd tension in the air. He looked at us intently.

'I'm going to show you something, but first I must ask you to understand that news of what I'm about to show you will not leave this room. Is that understood?'

Chris and I nodded; this had never happened before and was so unexpected I couldn't imagine what it was he was about to produce.

'We have received a letter from John.'

I stopped dead, the coffee cup halfway to my mouth.

'It has come through an intermediary we regard as reliable and Pat has confirmed it is John's handwriting.' He looked at us to see if we were concentrating. We were. 'I can't give it to you, but I can show it to you.'

He handed me a piece of paper and I stared at it. John's handwriting looked steady, albeit a bit rushed, and there was his signature, neat and rounded as ever. I read it quickly, then read it again and passed it to Chris. I didn't want to let go of it. Here was a tangible link with John, the first letter in more than four years, and I felt that if I held on to it it might reveal more than was apparent from the text. It had obviously been written under pressure and said that John's life would be in danger if word of it leaked out. We stared at Andrew.

'How did you get it?' I asked.

'Through a reliable intermediary,' he repeated.

'There's no date on it,' I said in a daze.

'No, that's right, so we can't be absolutely sure that it's as recent as we think, but we believe it is.'

I asked to see the letter again, and tried to memorize it. I think Andrew was worried that I would relay what was in it to someone else, but I just wanted to hang on to John for a few seconds longer. The letter was so precious. I didn't think much about what was in it. Through John, Islamic Jihad were demanding the release of their comrades imprisoned in Europe and they wanted more pressure on the Kuwaitis to release the convicted bombers there. Andrew said that he thought the kidnappers were worried that Britain and Iran were going to resolve the hostage issue and ignore the demands of the kidnap groups themselves. So, he felt, they were trying to start direct contact with the British government. The FO had decided that they would continue talking to Iran and would rebuff the kidnappers. Chris and I nodded our agreement, thanked Andrew for showing it to us and walked out in a daze.

I didn't know what to make of it. Was it a desperate message from the kidnappers? Was it that Britain had asked Iran for some kind of proof? Did it mean John was any nearer being released? I still wondered if the FO was telling us the whole truth. Getting proof that John was alive was the first, basic step that the Government had to take. We were so behind in beginning the process that other countries had started years ago; who knew how long the rest would take?

Chris and I went straight to the regular weekly meeting, keeping the secret to ourselves. We discussed the progress on an encouraging number of the campaign's activities; Flamenco evenings, sponsored swims, the upcoming party political conferences, John's thirty-fourth birthday and another wonderful BBH cinema advert. It showed newsreel footage of the release of Frank Reed, David Jacobsen and others to a backing track of Paul Simon's song, 'Homeward Bound', performed by Paul Young who had recorded it free especially for us. After months of work, Jackie had finally finished typing all our supporters' names and addresses into a computer we'd bought, which made the job of encouraging support around the country a little easier. There were signs that interest was growing from Gina's sighting of a FOJM T-shirt on a complete stranger in Greenwich market. Also, NUJ members were organizing events themselves – three of them were taking part in a sponsored cycle ride to the Berlin Wall and back, and, another, Mike Hill had walked from John O'Groats to Land's End to raise money.

On 2 August Iraq invaded Kuwait and threw everything into confusion again. With the West lining up against an Arab country, how could any progress be made on the hostage front with the groups on the ground in Lebanon? I assumed that as long as the crisis lasted, the hostages would remain in captivity. John's letter didn't look like a firm breakthrough any more, just the flimsy piece of paper it was. I rang up the Gulf Support Committee on behalf of the Friends when foreigners in Iraq and Kuwait were detained by Saddam Hussein, but their committee was doing a brilliant job and didn't need additional help or advice on how to help the detainees. The media were calling them 'hostages'. Of course, they were, but I couldn't help being irritated that some of these people, who were living in hotel rooms and phoning home every week, were called hostages as well as someone who spent his days chained to the wall of a basement.

Despite the invasion, rumours about Brian Keenan's imminent release resurfaced in mid-August. I thought, 'Here we go again, they'll fade and die like they have in the past,' but the tension and speculation were driving me mad. My heart went out to Brian's sisters as I watched them being mobbed by the Dublin media, with Irish government officials acting as their bodyguards. When a reporter shouted to them in a hotel lobby, 'Elaine, we've just heard that Brian is free; how do you feel?' I saw Elaine's stricken face. She looked startled, unable to answer; it hadn't yet been confirmed. But it was true, Brian had indeed been released. I was overjoyed for them and I knew that Brian, who'd spent most of his four and a quarter years with John, would be able to bring him that much closer to me. At the same time, the thought of being thrown into the media circus again filled me with dread.

'And now, we go back to our main story of the day, the release of the Belfast teacher, Brian Hostage,' said a newsreader on Sky TV, capturing the sense of chaos and confusion surrounding Brian's freedom. I took a deep breath and got back on the merry-go-round. This time, though, I was armed with a new political argument with which to hit the British government. It was one I'd seen Chris try out to great effect the night before on *Newsnight*. I was sitting in an edit suite at ITN with a camera pointing at me to record my first reactions to Brian's appearance in Damascus. I was a disappointment to the reporter, who asked me to do it five times. I think that she wanted me to gush and be emotional, but I was determined to say my piece. Now that an Irishman had been freed, Britain was the only government in the world that had failed to gain the release of any of its nationals that were being held in the Lebanon.

Afterwards, over a couple of glasses of wine at Mary's flat, we watched the news reports and cried at the sight of Keenan saying he wanted to eat all the food in the world, drink all the drink in the world and make love to all the women in the world, and at the way his voice broke when he talked briefly about John. Later there were more pictures of his return to Dublin. Stepping from the plane into bright lights and tumultuous applause from thousands of people, he looked touched and very bewildered.

The next day, Sunday, I got a message from the Mater Hospital asking me to call Brian Keenan. I hadn't expected him to get in contact so soon and I was very, very nervous when I was eventually put through.

'So, hie are you?' he said, as if he'd just been down the road to the shops rather than held hostage for four and a quarter years. I felt immediately as if he were one of us, in the land of the living, not halfway between the two.

'Welcome home,' I said, wishing I could think of something better to say. 'How are you? How do you feel?'

'I feel marvellous, I've got all these lovely nurses here, so I'm fine. You know that man of yours and I, we had a nickname for you; do you want to hear what it is?'

I was stunned. John had a nickname for me. He had thought about me. It was such a curious, strange idea I couldn't take it in.

'I don't know if I should tell you.'

'Tell me, for God's sake!' I laughed.

'We used to call you DD. Do you want to know what that stands for?'

'Just tell me!'

'Well, John and me thought that you would probably have spent all his money by now on a sports car and fancy jewellery and be driving around with a toy boy on each arm, so we called you Dripping Diamonds. How're you doing, Dripping?'

I was outraged. 'Dripping Diamonds! You cheeky swines!' I laughed. 'For your information I've got a Fiat 127!' I couldn't believe that talking to Brian was like talking to someone who was just calling up for a chat and a joke. He was so normal, sane and in control. He was teasing me! All my attempts to be realistic about the future went completely out of the window. I had to ask.

'Brian, what does John think about me?'

'From what I can make out he wants ten kids when he gets out. Don't worry. You're going to be fine.'

'Ten kids with me?'

'Well now, who else would he be talking about?'

I'd been light-headed ever since he talked about Dripping Diamonds. It was confusing, this sudden contact with John via a man I didn't know from Adam, and to think that Frank Reed might be right, John might still think of me in that way. It was impossible to tell how I felt.

'I thought you were coming over, anyway?' Brian said.

'You try and stop me. I'll be there like a shot.'

There was a crowd of journalists outside Dublin Airport when Brenda and Elaine came to meet Chris and me the following day. I spotted Brenda and started to run towards her, but stopped, suddenly self-conscious in front of all these people. 'Run!' she shouted, so I did, and we all hugged one another, laughing and crying at the same time. We learned later that this public reunion had been engineered for a purpose. While the press met us at the airport, Brian was able to slip out of the hospital for a few hours. He'd been taken for a drive in the country and finished up in a pub where he'd had a pint of Guinness and held a baby in his arms for the first time in four years. We joined Brenda and Elaine and their families for dinner at their hotel. The sisters were distracted; they'd had no sleep for three days, were trying to look after their families, satisfy the media and take in Brian's release all at the same time. It was mayhem.

Chris and I left for the Mater Hospital at about 9 p.m. to find the biggest media scrum we had ever encountered. The journalists and cameramen must have been on the steps of the hospital for hours, restless and impatient for something to report; people were pushing and shoving, hitting each other with cameras. Chris ran around the car to hold people back as they surged forward and he gripped my arm so as not to lose me. Somebody shouted: 'What are you going to tell Brian, Jill?'

'I'm just going to listen to him, I think.'

Brian was sitting cross-legged on his hospital bed in a nightshirt when we went in, talking in a very quiet voice on the telephone to Tom Sutherland's wife, Jean. It struck me again that this was not going to be like talking to any other hostage I'd met when we heard him say, 'We decided that we would talk to the families first and let them decide what we should tell our respective governments—' Brian seemed in complete control.

When he had put the phone down we went over to shake his hand, but Brian reached up and gave us each a huge hug. 'How do you want to do this?' he asked. I shrugged my shoulders and looked at Chris. 'From the beginning, I suppose,' we both said at once.

We sat down by Brian's bed, and Chris took out his notebook. 'What's that for?' said Brian, looking worried. 'It's just to take notes so that we can remember everything,' I said, but Chris was already putting the notepad away. It was perfectly understandable for Brian to react like that; I understood that he wouldn't know whom he could trust but I just wanted to have more than my memory to rely on when we left him. I feared that Brian would disappear once we walked out of the door; the possibility of him being on the end of a telephone didn't occur to me. I wanted to know everything all at once, and felt that when we left him in this room, that would be it.

We asked him again to start at the beginning, and we learned how he had first met John three months after his capture and heard how they talked together in whispers non-stop for hours and hours. I was constantly amazed at how composed Brian was; he wasn't so clear on dates or chronology, and he would often go off on a tangent for ten minutes or so as incidents or thoughts occurred to him, but he never failed to remember what he'd been talking about before the digression. It was a different level of mental discipline than that I'd encountered in Frank Reed. One minute he would be talking about how dirty the blankets were and how the mosquitoes had tormented him and the next he'd be remembering a film that he and John had seen together, telling us of the frustration of the power being cut ten minutes before the end. During one story he turned to Chris and said, 'What's your surname?'

'Er, Pearson,' said Chris, looking puzzled.

'Are you the one that used to work for Radio Foyle?'

Chris sat back and looked at Brian as if he were a mind-reader. He had indeed worked for the BBC in Londonderry some eight years before.

'Yeah . . . how did you know that?'

'John told me. We told one another everything, all about our friends . . . After a while we knew each other's friends so well John would say, "No, you're wrong, Brian, Joe or Frank or whoever, they wouldn't have done that, they'd have said such and such—" And what're you laughing at, miss?' He'd noticed I was laughing at Chris's confusion and his eyes turned on me. 'You've no cause to laugh . . . I know everything about you. I do. Everything. So watch yourself!'

Brian spoke of John with love and respect. I felt like an outsider as he described how well he knew him, how he'd shared things with him that no-one else could ever share, like a lover does. He told us about their confrontation with fear and despair and about the ill-treatment they'd endured. It wasn't deliberate torture, but brutality through ignorance, thoughtlessness and stupidity. The guards who chained them to the wall were mostly boys, who knew only war, Rambo movies and obedience to a higher cause which justified what they were doing. He told us they both had been beaten several times. Although these incidents were painful to hear, Brian made us laugh about them, so that we could understand something of the relationship he and John had established and how it had helped them both survive. Brian told us that after one beating, John had admitted that all the time the guard was hitting him he'd been thinking, 'All right, all right, now why don't you go and get Keenan and leave me alone!'

Brian gave us lots of information but we also saw evidence of his philosophical side, the part of his character to which Frank had alluded. He had intellectualized what had happened to him and it was sometimes difficult to follow his thoughts, thoughts that he must have honed over the years. The beatings were endurable, he said, they weren't the worst thing. When it was over, all the guard had done was beaten you; at the end your spirit was still there, so while the guard had demeaned himself you were in a much stronger position than before. I could just about rationalize that, but it was difficult. It was an effort to follow Brian's argument at times, especially given the softness of his voice; I had to strain forward and leap over philosophical fences to keep up and I wasn't sure if I altogether understood. John must have been able to hold his own; he had the mental agility to do so, but it was a side of him I didn't really know.

Two and a half hours went by; we had drunk several bottles of Guinness and then started on a bottle of champagne. Brian told us about his trip to the pub and how all the women had danced with him and then, casually, dropped a bombshell. 'Terry Waite is alive. He was in the next room to John and me.'

Chris and I were stunned. There had been so many rumours about Terry Waite over the last three and a half years, but no other hostages had had any firm news of him. Brian and John had tapped messages to him on the wall; they knew for sure it was him. Brian was concerned that Waite was ill and that his three and a half years of solitary captivity had left him in a bad way. Brian was going to tell Waite's family that Terry was alive but he couldn't announce it publicly. If the guards in Beirut got to hear that John and Terry were communicating with each other, it could have dire consequences for them. We asked Brian if he had any idea when John was coming home. We already knew from an outspoken doctor at the hospital that Brian had not wanted to leave John without saying goodbye. He had insisted on knowing when he would see him again, and finally the guards had said, 'Your friend, he go home two weeks'.

Brian had now been talking for five hours, it was three in the morning, and we'd heard a wealth of information about

John. I had thrown off all the roles I had had to play and asked normal questions, just as anyone's girlfriend would. A nurse came in and asked Brian if he was all right; there were empty beer and champagne bottles all over the room and Brian, Chris and Frank McCallan, who had been with us the whole time, were smoking like chimneys. 'Don't get too tired, Brian,' she said and walked out of the room again without a backward glance.

Chris and I took the interruption as a cue to say our goodbyes and told Brian we would leave and let him get some sleep.

'Go if you're tired,' he said, 'but don't worry about me, I'm fine.' He looked as fresh as when we'd walked in five hours before, but we decided to go anyway. I didn't really want to leave. The conversation with Brian had brought my feelings for John to the surface and I felt the spell would somehow break if I left the room. The warmth I felt was all directed towards Brian, towards this small figure sitting cross-legged on the bed, smiling at us. 'He seems so calm,' I thought, 'and strong. John's going to be OK.' I blew him a kiss from the door and we left the room, past the policeman posted outside, towards the lift. We stopped and wondered what to say to the crowds of journalists still camped outside on the doorstep. Brian had told us so much but we couldn't reveal any of it. It was his story, and up to him to tell it when he wanted to. We would have betrayed his confidence if we'd repeated anything of what he'd told us. I would just have to stall.

'OK?' said Chris, looking grim. 'Right, let's go.'

Sometimes when Chris was serious, usually for good reason, it had the perverse effect of making me smile, and it just about did the trick now. I took a deep breath and we went down to the lobby, where we could see the crowd through the glass of the hospital door; as we caught sight of them they saw us and shook themselves into life. For about half an hour I tried to duck their questions with inane and rather vague responses about what Brian had told us. Over and over again I repeated things like 'Well, that's a matter

Brian Keenan at the fifth anniversary rally, 13 April 1991.
Julius Domoney/Camera Press.

2 August 1991, and still counting. © *Times Newspapers*.

Cathy Comerford, Brian Keenan and Pat McCarthy, NUJ
Conference, April 1991. *Gladwin Photography*.

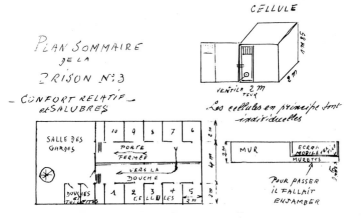

Camille Sontag's map of the Land of Grey and Pink.

FROM : JOHN McCARTHY
To : THE BRITISH GOVERNMENT.

My name is John McCarthy.
I am O.K. but I am living in
very difficult and bad
conditions. You must understand
the following.
My release with the others is
impossible if the prisoners in
Kuwait and in some European
countries are not released.
You must keep this letter secret
Otherwise my life will be in
danger.   John McCarthy.

JOHN McCARTHY.

Letter sent to the
Foreign Office,
received July 1990.

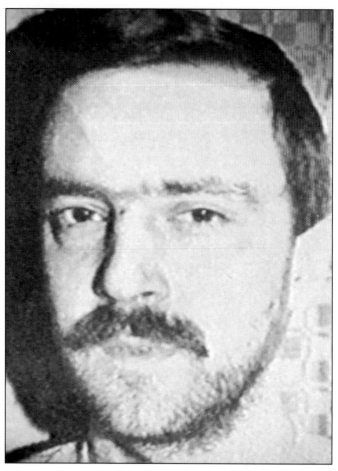
The only photograph of John in captivity, taken between February and May 1988, and issued by Islamic Jihad on his release. *Rex Features*

St Bride's, 8 August 1991.
© *Times Newspapers.*

Damascus, 8 August 1991.
Lionel Cironneau/Associated Press.

Damascus, 8 August 1991. *Lionel Cironneau/Associated Press.*

With Karen Talbot and Chris Pearson at the FOJM Press Conference, the Russell Hotel, 8 August 1991. © *Times Newspapers*.

Still working, FOJM office, 8 August 1991. © *Times Newspapers*.

Cartoon by Heath which appeared in the *Independent*, 9 August 1991. © *Heath/Independent*.

With Pat and Terence in Damascus, 8 August 1991. *Lionel Cironneau/Associated Press.*

Cartoon by Tom Johnston, which appeared in the *Sun*, 12 August 1991. *Tom Johnston/Sun.*

IF HE'S IN THERE ANY LONGER WE'LL HAVE TO START A CAMPAIGN TO GET HIM OUT!

With Terry Waite and Brian Keenan after receiving the CBE, 12 March 1992. *Rex Features.*

Wales, August 1991.

for Brian to talk about' and, 'I'm very happy to hear that John is OK and coping well—' I thought – any minute they're going to say, 'Stop talking such rubbish and tell us what really happened' but no-one did.

Back at the hotel, Chris and I sat in a quiet corner of the lobby and opened five mini-bottles of champagne that a BA stewardess had given us on the flight over. We talked for hours, our heads buzzing with information and images, too wound up to say good night.

9
Beirut, August 1990 – RAF Lyneham, August 1991

I sat alone, focusing on Brian's freedom, not on how life would be without him. After only a few moments I thought I heard the sound of a cry. Surely it couldn't be Brian? He was going home, yet suddenly I was full of doubt. Was he still a captive? Were they forcing him to make a statement? I sat there, expecting the door to be thrown open. But then, after some minutes of quiet, my confidence returned. I had just begun to consider the problems of coping alone when the guards did appear. Within seconds I realized that they had brought in Terry Anderson and Tom Sutherland.

As soon as the guards left we greeted each other warmly and I burst out with the great news.

'You just missed Brian, I'm sure he's gone home!'

'Oh yes, certainly, they've been talking about it for days on the radio,' said Tom.

'You've got a radio?'

'Sure we've had it for more than a year.'

'Typical Yanks,' I thought. 'Why had Brian and I been denied a radio?' But really I was too excited to care.

'What's going on out there then?'

Tom and Terry brought me up to date: the Berlin Wall had gone; Eastern Europe and the Soviet Union were stumbling towards democracy; Margaret Thatcher's popularity was waning; the 'poll tax' had provoked riots in central London; Ayatollah Khomeini was dead; and Iraq had invaded Kuwait and the United Nations were preparing to drive Saddam Hussein's forces out again. Amazingly the Iraqi army had released the seventeen men

434

held in Kuwait. This was a huge relief. The relationship between the US and Iran remained tense, but the release of those prisoners surely removed the major stumbling-block that lay between us and our own release. There had been new moves to get the *rapprochement* between Iran and Britain back on track after the break in communications following the Rushdie affair, more than a year before. There had also been calls for a restoration of diplomatic relations between Britain and Syria to help the hostages, who now included another Briton. Jackie Mann, a Battle of Britain veteran, now in his seventies, had been kidnapped in May 1989.

Tom then told me that he'd heard Jill speaking a number of times; once at length on a *Personal View* slot on the World Service, and that she had done very well. Over the year there'd been numerous mentions of the Friends of John McCarthy. The Americans were so incredibly well-informed. I teased them about the fact that Brian had always been convinced that they had received better treatment than us and wondered again why we had been refused a radio.

We'd been so carried away with all the news – and speculation about what might happen next – that the lights had gone out before I realized that they hadn't said a single thing about my family. I had always been worried that I'd never heard any news about Terence. Despite reassurances from Terry and Brian that he'd be keeping a low profile because he was a Herald at the College of Arms, I'd been unable to convince myself that he was really all right. When I asked Tom if he'd heard anything and he paused, opened his mouth to speak and then paused again, I thought the worst. Eventually he said, 'John, I don't know how to tell you.'

I sat there in the dark, waiting, trying to keep calm. He paused again. I thought, 'They must all be dead.' Terry suddenly stretched across the floor as far as his chain would allow, and said, 'Your mother died a year ago, John, after a long fight against cancer. I'm very sorry.'

Tom patted me on the shoulder. Gradually, they gave me what little more information they could remember. At first I could not take it in; I was so conscious of these two dear friends and their sorrow at having to break the news to me. I thanked them for their kindness. They settled back in their beds and left me quietly to myself.

I was shocked that I felt so numb. I didn't cry, but just kept telling myself, 'Mummy's dead. John, your mother is dead. Feel something, dammit, *feel something*!' For more than four years she had been living for me only in my fantasies. I had actually seen her only three times, heard her voice properly only once, in circumstances where, at best, I could only half-concentrate, ever aware of the gunmen at my back. They had known, but hadn't the nerve, nor the decency, to tell me. Now I knew that she was dead. But I also knew that despite her physical absence, her place in my fantasies was so vital that it would take a long time for my subconscious to accept that she had really gone.

Over the next few days I kept walking slap into the fact of her death. I played back scenes from the past a thousand times. I pictured myself with Jill at Cornish Hall End, sitting down for Sunday lunch and, then – there it was. No little figure at the end of the table chortling, telling some new story. No pretty woman leaping up in panic saying, 'Oh, my hat! The Yorkshire pudding!' I would never again hear her say, 'Felix, we should have called you Felix, it would have been so right for you; it means happy and you are happy.'

I had drawn strength and hope from those images. Now they lay shattered and I reeled away from them in horror. It made no difference that I had tried to prepare myself for the possibility that she might die. I'd known she had been ill before I was kidnapped, realized that the cancer might have returned, but optimism had been essential. Any dark thoughts had had to be banished – the story had to have a happy ending.

As I tried to focus on the fact of my mother's death, I would also try to imagine how my father and Terence would be coping. They would have been devastated, of course, and I wasn't at all certain that they would be able to carry on. I just could not visualize homelife without my mother. It wouldn't work. The Yanks said that it had been a long fight against the cancer. How much more she must have suffered because of my disappearance. I should have been there to look after her, offer her encouragement, been the attentive son I had vowed to be since the first days of my captivity.

For my father and brother the strain must have been appalling. At least now Brian was out and would be able to give them news of me. He'd be able to paint a far better picture of how I was than Frank could have done. The Yanks had not heard any bad news about either my father or Terence and I drew comfort from that. They must be all right. Perhaps they were already, after a year, coming to terms with my mother's loss. Home would be home still; just different, without her. But that was hard to imagine and I found it far easier to avoid such a painful idea. Then another picture of the past or vision of the future would cross my mind and I would crash into the same wall. My mother was dead.

As time went on I was able to adjust my images of freedom to exclude my mother's presence, although initially that meant banishing any thoughts of home. Remembered Sunday lunches at the Old Vicarage were no longer the joyful memories they had once been. But then I realized my mother hadn't really gone from me. Since my kidnap I had missed her physical presence but never her spirit. She'd been just as strong a support to me this past year, while I'd been unaware of her death, as she'd ever been. My sense of humour, which was based so much on her love of fun and her kindness, remained, as did the optimism it reflected and encouraged. I'd find myself chuckling at a memory before the wall hit me again and I'd feel guilty for laughing. But I couldn't deny her strong spirit. 'I'm a tough old soldier,' she'd said before going into hospital back in 1986, 'I'll be all right.' I had to let that spirit flow, let it take me onwards, not stifle it and lose direction now.

I remembered thinking about the 'afterlife' in my first months of solitary confinement. My lack of any firm religious belief had made it hard for me to accept any formal sense of continuing, but I could see that a person's spirit, their essential value, could carry on in others' minds and memories and influence them. My mother was still with me, would be when I went home and would be always.

Terry and Tom were great company for me in those first few days following Brian's release and after hearing the news about my mother. They were very supportive and gentle and I was able to retrieve my sense of humour and make them laugh. Tom told me that they hadn't had a really good laugh for ages. In their last place, just a few minutes away, they had spent most of their days quietly reading, or with Tom listening to the radio and Terry watching the television – colour, of course.

On the second morning Bilal came in and gave me a message. 'Before he leaves Brian said to say for you, "Up the Rebels".' I was sure Brian's message had really been 'Up the Republic' and loved him for it. Through those words I heard the echo of all the British-Irish insults we'd traded over the years and was able to laugh at them again. Bilal also handed over a radio, the same one we'd all shared in the Pit two years earlier. Before he left he added, casually, 'Tom, Terry, tomorrow I bring your bicycle.'

'*What* did he say?' I demanded after he'd gone.

'Oh, we had an exercycle at the other place,' came the reply.

I was amazed. Whenever the guards had asked us if we wanted anything, Brian had always joked with them, 'I'd like a bicycle and a grand piano, please.' He only asked for the piano in the really tiny cells. Now, after years of lobbying, he'd gone and the Americans had the bike. 'Yankee imperialist swine,' I told them. 'You always were so much better treated.' I wanted to share the joke with Brian and missed him dearly.

We now had permanent access to a television – another advantage of being with the Yanks. Together we watched Brian's arrival in Damascus, heard him speaking briefly about us, then saw his triumphant return home to Dublin. It felt very odd seeing him out there. I was nervous for him, the situation looked so strange. In the bright lights he appeared tense, not the laughing boy I liked to picture. I recalled my own apprehension in the summer of 1988, when there'd been rumours that I was to be released. I was sure that he must be going through agonies at leaving me behind – as he thought, alone – and at having to face the great world by himself. We'd often idled away time planning the show we'd mount to entertain the press corps had we been released together.

I heard him talk at his press conference a couple of days after his return and was extraordinarily moved. It was odd hearing his voice and knowing that he was so very far away. He seemed to speak in poetry and so touchingly of me. Gradually, I realized that he was not talking to me, but about me, and that the whole world was listening. The next day, exercising with Terry while Tom was in the bathroom, I said how weird I felt hearing Brian speak like that. Terry just said, 'He loves you, man.' I was still confused that Brian had focused on my sense of humour and mimicry and the thought that all I had done for him, and the others, was to crack jokes worried me. Terry looked at me curiously, and said, 'You making us laugh is probably the most important thing that any of us have done in here,' which encouraged me and stopped me fretting. Brian couldn't have expected me to hear his words, but even though he had gone home, he continued to help me as he always had.

Terry was still the same matter-of-fact, businesslike man I had first come across four years before and so I had no doubt that he'd meant what he said. He was also still discursive to the point of argument and I was wary of getting into the same kind of relentless discussions we'd had in the Pit. I realized, though, that unlike last time I couldn't just withdraw into myself and read, leaving Brian alone in the ring. I would have to deal with it myself now and was determined to find a comfortable way in which we could talk and debate ideas. I didn't want to be hounded for facts which I couldn't provide and end up feeling ignorant and useless.

I knew that I had to hold my own with Terry, more so than with Tom, who was gentler. Initially, the only way I could do this was to argue furiously over each little point, even arguing against what I really thought. I wasn't going to be used solely as a sounding-board. Looking back, I'm sure that on occasions I must have sounded ridiculous, but, soon enough, we found a more comfortable approach. The only thing that threatened our new-found equanimity was that Terry read so damned fast. It was impossible to keep up or to get him to slow down. He would be itching to get the books changed before Tom and I had read even half the current supply. Fortunately, another distraction was on hand.

Terry had often spoken of his love of chess. He now had a proper set, rather than one improvised from cheese wrappers, and asked if I'd like to learn. I did, but was worried that if I were inept, he would think less of me. After a couple of days, however, I'd stretch out to meet him at the board between us, in the middle of the floor, with a mixture of anticipation and apprehension. The mental exercise was refreshing, although the dramatically shifting consequences behind each slow move were mind-boggling. Terry was a brilliant teacher, gently explaining my mistakes and laying down memorable guidelines during each game which taught me the value of the various pieces. Chess became a fixation. I thought up moves all the time, eagerly looking forward to the next game. Once I'd grasped the rudiments Terry let me have a three-piece advantage. As I improved we cut it to two, then eventually we played evens. I was pleased that Terry didn't lose interest and was delighted when he started getting angry with himself as my playing began to make more demands on him. Better still were the times when I'd manage to fight off defeat for hours, while he happily chanted, 'Typical McCarthy. Always "wriggle and squirm, wriggle and squirm".'

The Yanks were amused to hear that Brian had called me 'one agitating bastard'. Terry corrupted it to 'Oab', which made an appropriate nickname. I felt him relax and show his sense of humour as I grew to know him better. His gentle side emerged ever-more naturally. One day, he remembered a phrase we'd heard on the radio when we were all together in the Pit. Some commentator had said that Americans meant well but would often blunder about in their enthusiasm and their checked jackets, being 'gauche and naïve'. With his new, relaxed self-awareness, Terry wouldn't hesitate to mock himself if he thought he'd been a little heavy handed in conversation. 'Oh dear, there I go again, being "gauche and naïve". That's me, G and N, always G and N!'

As soon as the Yanks moved in with me I had told them that Terry Waite was in the next room. Within a couple of days the two Terrys were tapping long messages to each other through the wall. It must have been very weird for Waite to hear of the amazing changes in the world through such a laborious method of communication. But just as our conditions had improved, so things were improving for our neighbour and, one day, he tapped triumphantly to Anderson, 'They have just given me a radio!'

After more than three years' solitary confinement the radio must have been an enormous encouragement for him, as, I hope, was the contact with us. However, any raising of Waite's spirits must have been desperately undermined when he became ill. We heard him coughing long into the night. He had developed a serious bronchial condition and it took a long time for the guards to get suitable medicine. Once again we felt the awful fear of illness. Our only hope, if we fell ill in this place, was to guess the right diagnosis and tell the guards what sort of medicine we needed.

We decided that we must try to get Waite moved in with us. The guards were much more open than they had been with Brian and me, perhaps because we now had access to the news. One morning, I asked Bilal to ask his *chef* if the man next door could join us. 'To be alone for a long time is very bad, the man must have company, friends, especially when he is so sick.' Bilal agreed to talk to his boss. Terry made the same request. We even nagged Mazzin who tried to maintain that the other prisoner was a mad and dangerous Arab. Our requests clearly fell on stony ground and, for the time being, Waite remained alone.

We'd been following the local news closely and watched as the various Lebanese factions, under Syrian leadership, united against the Christian General, Michel Aoun, who still maintained he was the rightful President. One morning in mid-October, I was woken by the sound of jet planes screaming low over the city, followed by two bombs shattering the morning quiet. Mazzin rushed into the room and for no apparent reason pulled my blankets off me, shouting, '*Tous les forces attaquent Aoun!*' I was terrified. The noise was so great that I could feel, let alone hear, the roar of hundreds of guns and cannons. It was impossible to think.

I asked Tom and Terry what the hell was going on. Tom had been listening to the radio since early morning, as usual, and reported any newsflashes to us. Terry calmed me down by trying to identify the sorts of weapons used, saying that it sounded as if all the fire was 'outgoing'. After a while I had almost got used to the bedlam, but I now understood why soldiers are trained to act unquestioningly to orders. Occasionally a blast would go off near us and it appeared that despite the onslaught Aoun's army was fighting back, which to me seemed incredible.

When more bombs fell near by, the guards came in and took us all into their living room on the other side

442

of the apartment and chained us together in a line – we later learned that Waite had been chained in the bath. It was a huge relief to have the radio; it was reassuring to know what was going on. When Tom announced that one of the local stations had just broadcast a newsflash in French saying that Aoun had surrendered, the battle was over, we all sighed in relief. Within seconds there was an almighty blast right next door, shaking the building and bringing down a cloud of dust. A few minutes later we went back to our room and began to clear up the mess.

The political situation in Lebanon may have improved, but there were no signs of change in Britain's relationship with Syria. At the end of October we heard the disappointing news that diplomatic relations were not to be restored and that Britain had also blocked moves to drop EC sanctions against Syria. British foreign policy now seemed to be running counter to everything else on the international scene. There was the promise of a new order, vividly evinced in the role played by the UN in co-ordinating a response to the Iraqi invasion of Kuwait. It seemed the perfect time to overcome old difficulties. Yet Britain – or at least Mrs Thatcher – seemed incapable of abandoning its tub-thumping approach to foreign policy.

On 3 November the apartment was suddenly full of guards, collecting up our belongings. We were moving. The tension was, as usual, immediate. My breathing quickened, I started coughing so hard I almost vomited, and I had an urgent – and constant – need to pee. I relaxed a little when they tied me up. My hands were taped to my ankles, which meant we weren't going in the truck bottom, or at least not straightaway. I heard Bilal saying, 'No talking in the car, John, I am with you, but please no talk', and then came the rush down stairs in the sack and the heave-ho into the boot. Someone else was in there, too. 'It must be a tiny car,' I thought. The boot seemed small and I could hardly move, unlike the days when Brian and I had enough space to wriggle about and get as comfortable as possible. We drove a little way then stopped, presumably waiting for the convoy to get clearance to head off. Then a deep voice with a clear English accent said, 'This is a very large boot.'

'No, it isn't.'

'Yes, it is.' There was a pause. 'Is that you, John?'

'Yes, Terry, how are you?'

'OK, thanks.'

After a few minutes wriggling we managed to free a hand each and to clasp them together. It was not the way I had expected to be introduced to the Archbishop of Canterbury's Secretary for Anglican Communion Affairs. Later I realized that it must have been a very large boot indeed to get both Terry and me inside it. Our exchange had been Terry's first direct contact with someone other than a guard in nearly four years.

Throughout the journey we tapped messages on one another's arms. This was awkward at the best of times, now made more so by the swinging of the car as we drove up into the mountains, but it helped clear my mind of images of slow death in the ravines. I told Terry that I'd ask the guards to move him in with us now that we'd actually travelled together. At one point, the car halted and a guard opened the boot and asked if we were all right. We both said, 'OK, OK', our English accents ringing out clearly.

Eventually we stopped altogether and I was carried into a room at ground level. Tom and Terry were there, and we guessed from the rattle of a chain that Waite was next door. In a hastily whispered conversation with Anderson, I let him know what had happened in the car and he agreed that I should speak to the Big M. When Mahmoud appeared, I told him that I knew that Waite had been with me in the car, as I had recognized his voice, and there now seemed no point in keeping him on his own. He said that he'd ask his boss. A few minutes later Terry spoke. 'That's the Haj's voice.' He called out the name and the man came over with Mahmoud. Terry made light of the situation. 'Translate exactly what I say, please,' he

444

told Mahmoud, before turning to the boss. 'OK, Haj, we know that you know that we know that Terry Waite knows that we know that you know that we know he's here. So we all know what we all know, so why not bring him in with us for some company?' The Big M laboriously went through all this and there was a murmur of laughter before the Haj said, 'OK, Tirry.'

A few minutes later Waite was brought in. It must have been extraordinary for him. He knelt beside us, blindfolded – as were we – and hugged us in turn. 'Tom, my dear fellow. Terry, good man. John, nice to meet you again!' His voice was choked with emotion, but he carried on, asking us about his family. Was there any news of them? We told him there was nothing new, but that Tom had heard his brother David and cousin John on the radio. Waite was worried about his mother. We'd heard nothing, but Anderson said that I'd lost my mother and he his father and a brother while we'd been away. Waite expressed his sorrow for us and soon the conversation turned to other things. Obviously, with the guards there, and our blindfolds on, talking was awkward. Besides, soon after, Waite was taken back to his room, but not before the guards told us that they would arrange for him to move in with us. We were all delighted. Not only would we have a new companion, but we'd also managed to crack the Jihad's lunatic barriers of secrecy. I was pleased that Terry and I had achieved this to-gether. It added to the growing bond between us and marked a further step forward in our relationship with the guards.

The following morning after we'd happily greeted Waite with, 'Good morning, Your Grace,' on his way through to the bathroom, the guards cleared off, leaving the door to our room open. I sneaked a look out and beyond through an open window. Although it was November the weather was fine and I saw a walled garden. Nothing was growing in it, but the yellow soil had been freshly tilled. The wall was too high to afford any view other than the blue sky, but that was enough. The move, coupled with the guards' change in attitude, promised a new beginning and perhaps might even herald the end of our captivity.

The guards spent much of the day away from our room, leaving the door connecting it with Waite's open, so we were able to talk. Tom was nearest to him, then Terry, while I was chained to the farthest wall next to the guards' room. We soon realized that two Terrys would cause confusion. As we had always called Anderson Terry, we decided it would be simplest to stick to that, addressing Waite as TW.

Tom and TW talked a lot, about their backgrounds, about the prospects of release and the inadequacies of our guards. Terry was, as ever, like a puppy with a new friend and bounced up all the time to join in the talk. TW and I spoke little beyond exchanging pleasantries. Both Tom and Terry apologized for hogging our new companion, feeling especially guilty that they were stopping the two Brits nattering together. I wasn't unduly bothered. Talking across a room in hushed tones, without the shorthand I'd had with Brian, wasn't the easiest way of communicating. In any case, I reckoned that we would have plenty of time to get to know one another when TW joined us. I had learned, too, over the years that it was better, in our circumstances, to develop new relationships little by little, rather than rush into a situation from which one might then have to retreat. Besides, my anecdotes seemed pretty parochial in comparison with the others' tales of world travel and encounters with VIPs.

I stuck to the couple of books and odd magazines which the guards had given us, though chess was still a major pastime. I could hold my own against Terry more often now and the great day came when I actually beat my teacher fair and square. I was delighted at my success, but more so at Terry's obvious pleasure. I valued his friendship increasingly as time passed.

446

As far as we could tell we were in some sort of farm outbuilding that had been done up for us. It was obvious that it was going to be freezing in the winter and although neither our room nor TW's looked big enough to accommodate us all, we kept badgering the guards to tell us when TW would join us. The answer was always, 'soon'. They let him come in a couple of times to see a video, but always insisted that we watched in complete silence, which rather destroyed the point of the exercise.

After a couple of weeks they came to move us. They chained us all together in TW's room and moved out our belongings. After dark they took us one by one. Still with the chain fixed to my ankle, I went out of the building, blindfolded of course, and was led up a steep, rocky path with a pistol sticking firmly in my back. It was only a short walk to the new building and soon the four of us were sitting together, chained to the walls of a perfectly normal room. They had promised, but it was still quite a surprise that they'd really done as we wanted.

I was on the inside wall, with the bathroom behind me. Terry was next to me, then Tom, and, on the far wall, TW. He was in such good form that the rest of us took it for granted that he was fine. I don't think that I fully appreciated what a great toll the long years alone had taken on him until I went home. Whatever he said about it and however he acted, he had had to use a huge amount of energy and determination to keep himself going. At the time we just assumed he was as well as he sounded and so expected him to fit in with the ways we'd evolved, over the years, as a group, to help us survive.

Tom started telling him his life story. From morning to night he would take TW from earliest childhood, through school, university, emigrating to the States, jobs, marriage and so on, all with the incredible detail that Terry and I had heard before. After a few days TW was clearly wearying of Tom's lengthy, sometimes rambling, anecdotes. TW, unused both to us and the delicacies of this bizarre and constricted communal living, tried to lighten his boredom with jokes at Tom's expense.

Anderson and I were still playing a lot of chess, listening to the radios or reading whatever we had with us. When Tom was in the bathroom we warned TW of Tom's great sensitivity to mockery, however gentle, and that even we could suddenly find that we were being given the cold shoulder unless we were careful. He could turn completely against people he didn't know so well, as he had done with Frank and with David Jacobsen. It was a particular concern now as Tom had clearly warmed to TW. They shared interests in music, travel and families. TW tried to accommodate Tom's need to talk, but I think it was already too late. Once Tom had lost his trust in TW the curtain came down.

Waite was a bluff companion, but moody and changeable after the long years alone. He would punctuate his conversation with anecdotes about his VIP status. I never knew how much irony there was in the pomposity with which he described his various comings and goings. He was great fun to be with when he was in good spirits, but he needed a lot of attention. He craved comfort as we all did, but those of us who had been confined with others knew it could only be given in small doses. He was desperately worried about what his actions had done to his family, but resorted to self-justification in order to overcome this, rather than a straightforward acceptance of his own fears and failings.

He must have found it strange that we, who had mostly had company over the years, often required solitude. There were times when we were all lying down, reading, when he would pipe up: 'John, did you hear that show on the radio this morning?'

'No, TW. I missed it.'

There would be a short pause. 'Tom, when do you think they'll bring us tea?'

'I don't know, TW. Soon, I expect.'

His words would fill the cell, allowing us no room to retreat from each other.

'Terry, do you think these people really are controlled directly by Iran?'

'I don't know, TW, and I've got to tell you I don't care.'

After a few weeks we explained that we had found the best way of surviving together was to give each other as much space as possible, mentally and emotionally. We didn't have physical space, so it was vital to allow each other private moments to read or think and find some sort of peace. TW said he understood and that he hoped we understood that he felt a bit of an outsider. He was sure we would all be able to work together.

Late in November I was delighted to hear the news of Thatcher's political demise. Although it probably meant little to the Yanks I felt sure that for the British hostages things must be looking up. Douglas Hurd's encouraging statements about the need to talk with all parties in the Middle East, coupled with various visits by MPs to Syria and their calls for renewed ties with Damascus, now seemed likely to bear fruit. Although I'd never heard of John Major, his quiet, thoughtful way of speaking suggested a more pragmatic approach than that of the Iron Lady.

Just before my birthday we heard that Jill and some other friends had staged an event to mark the occasion. They had mocked-up a cell, with someone chained inside, to remind people of the conditions in which we were held. A few days later I was given messages that they'd put in a Beirut newspaper. There were a number of short messages from friends, accompanied by the awful passport photograph of me. Jill sent all her love and hoped we'd be reunited soon. I especially liked a teasing note from Gina Filose and Barbara Mackie: 'We want to know when we are going to get that Italian meal you promised us!' I passed the clipping round and we all took heart that friends were still campaigning for us, that we had not been forgotten. The resumption of diplomatic ties with Syria on the next day, the 28th, was the icing on the cake.

The events in the Gulf still dominated the news and it seemed that the renewed ties with Syria must have been much influenced by them. We sympathized with the hostages held by Saddam Hussein, yet, to be honest, I did rather feel that, in comparison to us, some of them were going on a bit. They could spend their days by the pool, talking to news teams, even chatting with their folks back home on the phone, something of which I had often dreamed. I was still delighted though when they all went home some time before Christmas and we all hoped that the air of co-operation, or at least toleration, that now prevailed between the West and the Middle Eastern states over Iraq would speed up our release.

We had some unexpected local co-operation just before Christmas when the guards came in with a small pile of cards. They were sent from the congregations of two churches in Staffordshire. Some of them were addressed to the hostages in general, others to TW and some to me. They gave us a great lift, as did the fact the guards had given them to us. The messages from these strangers were very encouraging and we put the cards up around the shutters where they continued to give us heart until the New Year.

On Christmas Eve we heard Jill talking with Barbara Myers on *Outlook* on the World Service. The reception was abysmal so I couldn't hear it all, but I was alarmed to hear Jill describing herself as my 'former girlfriend'. Did that mean she had found someone else, or that her feelings for me had diminished over the years? She went on to say that she'd decided to make the change so that we would be free to see what happened when I came home. Until then it was impossible to assess what changes the years apart had made to us and the way we felt about each other. It seemed logical, but it still made me nervous.

I knew, of course, that she must need the comfort of other close relationships, but I'd always hoped it wouldn't happen. The extraordinary pressure that our relationship had imposed on her since she'd started the campaign had never occurred to me, nor could I have imagined how the media had zeroed in on our relationship as the 'peg line' for reporting any of her activities.

That night TW and I listened to a radio each to hear the repeat of *Outlook*. It was preceded by the Festival of Nine Lessons and Carols from King's College, Cambridge. It was the first time either of us had heard a carol service since being taken hostage, but this one seemed interminable. The anxiety of wanting to hear Jill again was such that even TW said, 'Why don't they get a move on?' Eventually the familiar, beautiful service ended and the next programme began. But it wasn't *Outlook*. I was furious. Being denied a second hearing and only half-understanding what I'd heard the first time made me worry more about what would happen between Jill and me when I went home.

I talked it over with my friends the next day and as usual Anderson managed to be direct, sensible and comforting. 'Look, John, none of us knows how our wives and girlfriends are going to be when we get out. We don't really even know how we're going to feel. But we're all intelligent human beings so we'll just have to work things out then, when we can talk about the past few years.' It was impossible to know what was happening back home. I found it easier to think that things would be all right, that whatever happened, we'd still be very close friends.

One morning, soon after Christmas, Hussein intercepted me on the way back from the bathroom. He held out a little pair of nail clippers that I'd managed to bring with me from the last place. 'Why you have these?'

Terry leant over, saying, 'Look this is very simple—'

'It's OK, Terry, I can handle this.' I didn't mean to sound dismissive, but I did want to show him that I could handle the guards for myself. Brian and I had done so for years and it wasn't necessary for Terry to jump in on my behalf. When I told Hussein that the clippers had come with our belongings, he just replied, 'No good'. Did they really think I could use this tiny, feeble device to attack them? I pointed out that they'd given them to me, so what was the problem? It didn't do any good.

Hussein and his friends, including Mazzin, had started a major search and our radios and magazines had already been removed. I was taken outside where I told them again that I couldn't see any problem and I suggested that if they were really so bothered, they should talk to their *chef* about it rather than letting things get out of hand. Having achieved nothing, I was taken back into the room. Tom and TW were furious at the loss of the radios and magazines and there had been talk of a hunger strike. Terry had said nothing since I'd cut in on him.

The most serious effect of this dispute was that TW had a new bout of asthma. It had come on almost as soon as I'd returned from being questioned in the guards' room. TW hadn't experienced one of these group problems before, although he had suffered beatings over the years. He was frightened for me and what may have started as a nervous reaction took serious hold. He had trouble breathing and began to hyperventilate. The guards, clearly guided by the malevolent Mazzin, dismissed TW's attack as a ploy to get his radio back. To us, it was obvious that he needed medicine.

The following evening our belongings were returned. Terry said that he thought we had all handled the problem abysmally, although I'm not sure what his plan would have been. It was no big deal, but we had really hoped that such incidents were a thing of the past. I was very distressed at having shut Terry out at a point of crisis, however minor, and apologized for the way I'd spoken to him. He accepted with good grace and after a quiet evening everything was back to normal.

After a couple of days, Mahmoud turned up with the relief shift. Ayeesa, who was now in charge of both shifts, was with them. They came in to talk to us and we discussed the potential threat the nail clippers had presented to the might of the Islamic Jihad. We explained that we carried enough responsibility for their security, with blindfolds, chains and whispers, without having to watch for them if they forgot to reclaim something as insignificant as a pair of nail clippers. It was only then that we were able to tackle the real problem. TW explained that if he did not have the right medicine, he might become very ill, as he had done before. They agreed to sort it out.

TW went rapidly downhill. The asthma attacks became more frequent, more vicious and lasted longer. He would be up much of the night, struggling to breathe. Terry worked very hard trying to get him to slow down his breathing, talking to him gently for hours, trying to show him that he must relax; that the more effort he made, the more adrenalin he pumped and the more tense he became, the more he would hyperventilate. On one occasion he passed out. After our conversation with Ayeesa and Mahmoud, the guards had fitted a buzzer so that we could call them if TW needed medicine. Most nights we'd have them in a few times. In a surprising display of humanity they installed an oil fire in the room. Sadly the chimney was so poorly positioned that we were often choked by the smoke. TW was sure that this was making him worse so the fire went off for good.

His hyperventilating frightened me. He would suck in air furiously and then blow it out like a demented horse; it made a tremendous noise. I recognized the symptoms only too well from the desperation of the gagged journeys, and knew that it just made the panic fiercer. I also knew that it was sometimes impossible to stop, and was ashamed when I heard, after my release, that asthmatics most often could not.

TW's illness put a great strain on us all. I found it hard to be sympathetic all the time, and harboured dark thoughts against him for being unable to rise above his condition and make light of it for a while. I wish I hadn't felt like that, but it seemed that every second of the day, and night, was focused on his asthma and I started to take his illness as some kind of personal slight. I simply did not have the energy for sustained support. Cursing the guards for the situation didn't relieve my frustration – I already spent a fair part of any day brooding on their inadequacies. Gradually, though, I realized that being angry with TW gave me something new to fight against, which rather perversely filled me with a new sense of purpose.

New distractions were always welcome and once Tom had taught us to play bridge we spent hours at it every day. As the bidding went round the four of us for the first time, I got the giggles. Tom and Terry looked at me askance. 'OK, Oab, what is it now?'

'I'm sorry, I don't know really. It's just that I've always wanted to do this. It always irritated me that I couldn't understand the game when it appeared in books and films, and now here I am, in a T-shirt and shorts, chained to the wall about to say, "Two clubs". It just tickled me.'

'Is that your bid then, weird person?'

'Yes, Terry, that's it. Two clubs.'

One afternoon as we were playing, a sonorous piece of cello music wafted through from the guards' radio. 'It's amazing what progress George has made with his playing,' I observed, in the manner of a proud papa. TW roared with laughter and spent the next few minutes doubled up. I was thrilled that I could make him laugh. The joke was rather lost on the Yanks and neither TW nor I could really say why we thought it was funny.

TW would reciprocate with many humorous stories about his travels around the world for the Church. At the time, his apparent inability to conceal his relish for VIP status made him hard to like. But since coming home I, too, have enjoyed meeting and talking to important and famous people, and am undeniably proud that they want to talk to me. Besides, looking back on his successes and acclaim must have been a vital way of bolstering his spirits in the long years of solitude, years when he was rarely treated better than an animal in a cage.

TW was at his best when he didn't feel that he was, or ought to be, the centre of attention. When he was able to see that others needed to hold the floor he would take a back seat and quietly offer advice and support. He helped ease the tension when Tom went on another hunger strike. Tom gave no reason for this apart from saying that he had simply decided to give up. It was terribly upsetting, particularly the way he seemed content to see Terry and me suffer great emotional distress at the thought of losing such a vital ally. By comparison, the anger of the guards would be of little consequence. We could not understand, nor accept, why he seemed to have turned against us.

I loved Tom and believed that he loved me. He was one of my few definite, positive points of reference and the fear that that would be taken from me as casually as an empty glass hurt. I tried to tell him but my voice, choked with barely restrained tears, failed me. All I could manage was a simple plea that he would change his mind and not give up on me. Terry, too, had to control his voice when he appealed to him.

'Tom, will you look at us, see what you are already doing to us? Doesn't that mean anything?' He went on, cajoling and even cursing him. TW remained quietly on the sidelines, until eventually he spoke. 'Tom, I know this doesn't have much to do with me; you are free to do as you like, but please listen to me when I say that I hear the real pain that your friends are going through. Please try and hear that, too.'

After an hour's awkward silence, Tom spoke.

'OK, I'll carry on.'

It was a great relief that he had been able to find the strength to keep going with us, and I was grateful to TW for his intervention.

455

It was so hard to keep up with each other all the time, to sense the ways in which we were getting on one another's nerves, or to catch the sadness and distraction in a man's eyes. Tom, Terry and I were already close. Generally we were able to watch and care for each other. This came less easily to TW who, I can see with hindsight, obviously had greater needs than ours. At times I would sit back exasperated and think, 'He's been here less time than any of us. What's his beef?' But he'd been alone for almost four years. Never any news; never a friendly word from another hostage, and only himself to fall back on. Doubtless he had put himself through the awful mill of self-analysis and consequent self-reproach that we had all experienced and I often felt that when he spoke of his commitment to the hostage issue he wasn't so much trying to convince us – after all, we had some idea of what he had suffered for it – as to reassure himself that it had been worthwhile. The tarnishing of his public reputation must also have hurt him deeply.

Since his release we have talked about this and I have seen a much more rounded man than I was able to perceive as a fellow hostage. Now he can reveal the enormous stress of the constant press probings, so often highly critical, and the uncalled-for attacks from Tom, who should have known better. To admit his fears then, in total and malign isolation, would have been too dangerous. It was perhaps safer to consign them to the back of his mind than to face a solitary breakdown.

We all shared the same concerns. We had all lived through the terrors of isolation, beatings, mummified journeys, illness, frustration, anger and fear. The others had yet another anxiety to cope with: they worried about what might be happening to their children. When another man was down, I always tried to find the energy to bring him round, with laughter, with the prospect of release, with the distractions of games or mad-cap projects. But sometimes their depression lingered and it was easy to become tired and forget the agonies they were experiencing. Their sorrow became another aspect of my own, another weight to bear. At such times I could only think: 'They must come out of it. They must. Otherwise we'll all go down.' It was only ever briefly that one of us would lose the will to survive. We had kept one another going for so long and in our heart of hearts knew we were lucky. The British teachers Padfield and Douglas had been killed in reprisal for the US raid on Libya in 1986. Another Briton, Alec Collett, probably died of natural causes, but in conditions of great discomfort and appalling stress. We were alive, we would go home; these three Britons, the Frenchman Seurat and the Americans Kilburn, Buckley and Higgins would not. However much we moaned, however long our families waited in anguish, we all had a chance that those men and the people who longed for them would never have. Ironically, we were the lucky ones, held for ransom not revenge, barter not blood.

We did not often speak of these men. Their fate was too close to our own, their end too imaginable and we preferred not to dwell on it.

By now I felt very close to Terry. The way our friendship had developed since our reunion last August meant that we could both sense each other's feelings and frustrations and feel confident that we could comfort one another. We had a shared sense of humour. As we lay in the dark one night Terry turned to me, and offered me the radio: 'Do you want to listen to *Questions of Faith*?'

'No, thanks, Terry,' I replied. 'I have only one question of faith.'

There was a pause before we spoke with one voice: 'Why me, God?'

Sometimes after a tense moment in the room or with the guards I might suddenly find his hands around my throat, his face close up to mine, saying: 'I'm sorry to have to do this, but I'm very frustrated. Someone has to die, and, as the others wouldn't understand, I've chosen you.'

457

The absurdity of such horseplay relieved many of our anxieties and reassured us that we really were in tune with one another. As with Brian I wished I could introduce Terry to my friends back home. I also looked forward to reintroducing the two of them, confident that any former coolness would disappear.

By the spring of 1991 the *rapprochement* between Iran and Britain was going ahead in fits and starts. Encouraging noises about talks on the hostage issue were often countered by statements from radicals in Tehran and Lebanon. The Rushdie affair remained an impasse. Whenever it seemed to have moved quietly to the sidelines, Rushdie would come out of hiding to denounce Ayatollah Khomeini's *fatwa* or make an appeal for it to be lifted. That was fair enough; his life was still on the line. I just wished he'd delay his appearances until we were out. But then, on 2 April, Roger Cooper was released. It was terrific news and we were all encouraged that he sounded remarkably well balanced, even cool, after his long, lonely ordeal. His freedom seemed to bring the chance of ours just a little closer.

I had been a hostage for five years now and on the fifth anniversary of my kidnap we listened to an *Outlook* report on the Friends of John McCarthy. It was strange to sit there listening to an interview with Chris Pearson, who was explaining the aims of the campaign. I was very impressed with his calm, balanced arguments, but I wasn't surprised. I'd seen him do professional news reports for BBC television long before I came to Lebanon. I just could not get used to the fact that now he was talking, not as a journalist, but as a leader of the campaign for my release. It was a bit of a shock to realize that that organization had now achieved national recognition. A man from an advertising agency explained how his company had played a part in this. Roger Cooper was also on the programme and we were touched that he should be involved in the campaign. It was from him that we learned that all those who supported the Friends had been asked to wear yellow ribbons.

We got a much clearer picture of the huge profile of the campaign when we heard the reports on the rally that Jill and the others had organized to mark the anniversary. Thousands of people had taken part in a march to Trafalgar Square. We heard some of them explaining why they'd gone along. I was amazed and delighted to hear complete strangers saying that they simply could not accept that I, and the other hostages, should have been left for so long in such terrible conditions. The rally was addressed by numerous famous people including Ted Heath. Brian was there, too, and spoke movingly, as ever: 'Five years, five words: bring these men home now!'

It was wonderful to hear him. By now he would know Jill, my family and friends and his involvement suggested that it was possible to make the leap from the cell to the wide world back home. I was in awe of what had been done for me. How would I live up to everybody's expectations? Little did I know that the rally was just the tip of the iceberg.

My spirits were soaring with optimism after the rally and were lifted still further by a news report from Iran. A senior Iranian politician linked the prospect of our release with that of Arab prisoners held in Israel. I was sure that the machinations behind the scenes would bear fruit; the governments concerned could take the credit for their humanitarianism, without getting their hands dirty.

A few weeks later, in early May, we were on the move again. After only a short trip in a car boot we found ourselves in a ground-floor room similar to the previous one. Once we were all there we heard chains being fixed in a nearby room. We wondered if these could be for Jackie Mann, the two Germans or some of the other Americans. Terry asked the guards to let us meet our fellow hostages. This time there was none of the 'OK, guys, so you know', as there had been with TW. Ayeesa abruptly told Terry that it was none of his business, and he wasn't to think about it any more. We never did discover who the other hostages were.

459

We soon settled into our normal routine. Terry and I would doze through the mornings while Tom and TW read, listened to the radios or did some exercises. The afternoons were spent in marathon bridge sessions. In the evenings Terry and I usually walked back and forth the two paces that our chains allowed until that became too boring, then watched television if the reception was any good. The frustration of missing the last half-hour of an engrossing film because of a power cut was terrible. It was even worse when the guards switched off the generator at the critical moment.

Despite such irritations, our conditions continued to improve. The food was much better and sometimes the guards would even nip out to the local shops to buy us ice-cream. We guessed that we were on the edge of a village or town, possibly Baalbek, as we could hear the call to prayer from at least one mosque, as well as the occasional air-raid siren. Mahmoud even said they would be bringing us air-conditioning. We assumed that he meant electric fans; we'd had them sometimes in previous years when the summer heat grew intense. But he actually meant what he said. After a ridiculous morning spent under our sheets – presumably to deny the engineer a look at us, although I can't imagine he had many doubts about who we were – there up on the wall was a brand-new air-conditioner. The difference it made was enormous. Within a few minutes of it coming on the room cooled down and the humidity evaporated. The afternoon bridge sessions were far more comfortable. Once we'd got used to having this luxury we became irritable whenever the power was off and we had to suffer a few hours in the hot damp air.

At night I found that the noise of the air-conditioner helped me relax. With the guards and my friends resting quietly, the machine's hum, coupled with the darkness, gave me a sense of privacy. I could almost pretend I was alone and let my mind wander away from the confines of the room. I still found it impossible to sleep until the early hours of the morning and could not break the habit of rehearsing past failures, too often countering them with wild fantasies of fulfilling even wilder ambitions.

A gap ran down the side of the shutter covering the window above my head. One night I noticed light coming through it. I put my eye up to the little crack; the light was very bright and I wondered if it were a security light that the guards had put up. Then I realized that it was, in fact, the full moon. As with my occasional glimpses of sunlight I was amazed at such natural brightness; it was so much stronger, so much more potent than any electrical illumination. It was comforting to think that that same moonlight would be shining down on England; perhaps Jill would look out of her window and share my thoughts for a moment.

When I did find peace of mind I would sleep well for a few hours, yet often wake confused. My dreams had become more violent over the recent months. I would wake up distressed at having witnessed myself beating a man, a guard, with all the callous, slow-motion bravado of a scene from a movie. Perhaps these dreams were a way of burning up some of my anger and frustration at the guards' treatment of us, which I always tried to contain when I was awake. Perhaps, too, they were a reflection of my growing confidence.

Even if I did manage to sleep well for a few hours I was always tired, no doubt the accumulation of years of disturbed nights. I tried to stay awake in the daytime, hoping to get just one good night's rest. There was also a serious drawback to sleeping in the day. After a nap I would wake up with an appalling sense of the loss, the void in my life, that the years of captivity represented. This had started early in my captivity and then my reaction had been, 'My God, three months gone!' Now I would wake in panic at the thought of over five wasted years.

Sometimes, though, my dreams brought happy escape. Dreams were the only place where people from better times came back to me in sharp focus. Often there would be someone I hadn't thought about for years, perhaps not since leaving school. Then there would be marvellous times with Jill. I would wake up feeling refreshed, my optimism restored. Often such dreams heralded uncanny coincidences. The following day I'd hear something about us or Jill's campaign on the radio and my feelings of hope would be endorsed.

The news continued to be promising. The idea of an exchange of prisoners held by Israel for Israeli soldiers held in Lebanon and ourselves gained acceptance from Israel, the leaders of Hezbollah and was acknowledged by John Major as offering a possible solution. In the last weeks of July we heard that the *Tehran Times* was predicting the imminent release of an American and a Briton. We felt certain that Jackie Mann would be the first to go as he was elderly and reputed to be in poor health.

In the early afternoon of 6 August we heard a report on Israeli radio that Islamic Jihad would be sending an envoy to the United Nations Secretary-General to seek his help in arranging the widescale exchange of prisoners. It never occurred to us that one of us would be involved. A few minutes later the guards came in and took the radios. We were all furious, but hoped it would be only a temporary set-back.

They returned almost immediately. They did not speak. They didn't have to. I just sensed what was happening. One knelt beside me and undid my chain. 'Come.'

I gave Terry a brief hug. 'Goodbye.'

'No speak,' ordered the guard as he pulled me to the door. They took me into their room and sat me on a bench. They taped my hands together behind my back and my feet together, but they said: 'No truck, no worry.'

Before they gagged me I told them that they should give the radios back. They were surprised that my friends would be happy that I was going. I said: 'They are very happy, *K'tir mazboot*, they do not mind that it is me. They hope they will follow me soon.' When they asked me not to think badly of them and wondered what I'd

462

say about them, I smiled. 'Well, I don't know,' I said. 'We'll just have to wait and see.'

For now, I was the one doing the waiting. I was nervous, but not frightened. Instead, I felt dazed. I kept saying to myself: 'I'm going home.' I was slowly beginning to realize that it was all coming to an end. I was now in a very different category from the three men in the room which I had just left. I was still bound, gagged and blindfolded, but now it was temporary, almost token, security.

They didn't bother with a sack when they put me in the boot. As we raced along I was conscious from time to time of a strange sound, like a muted alarm siren. I wondered if it came from a tail car. Perhaps this was some kind of marked convoy. I wriggled one hand out of the tape so they were both loose. I left my legs as they were, but I could stretch them out and with my hands free was able to ease the gag and blindfold and brace myself against the motion of the car. This was luxury.

I wondered if we were going back to Beirut or whether they'd drop me somewhere in the Beka'a Valley. When we started cruising downhill I realized that we must be going back to the capital. An inner voice cautioned me not to get too optimistic. 'It might just be another move. They might change their plans.' I thought about Brian. Had he felt like this on his last journey? He had not had the reassurance of hearing the radio news before he left.

When we reached Beirut, I was transferred to another car boot in a garage. After a while two men came and lifted me into a large, reinforced cardboard crate. We went upstairs and stopped in a room. They dumped some sheets on top of me. Everything went quiet. I moved a little to ease my aching arms. Someone rapped me on the head. Other men came in and carried me further upstairs. The sheets were lifted off me and my hands and feet were untaped and the gag removed. They left me sitting in the crate for a while before we moved into another room. As directed, I sat down on some folded blankets. They gave me some food and cigarettes. Ayeesa told me to sleep and that he would buy me some clothes the following day.

Sleep was the last thing I could do. My head was whirling with thoughts of what would happen tomorrow, how the hand-over would be arranged. I was in a normal apartment, in an area off the living room. There was no door so I had the blindfold on all the time, yet, by lying down with my head right back, I could see that the windows were not shuttered, and there was no chain. It was difficult to take in. There would be no more chains. I was so nervous that I couldn't let go completely. This might all go wrong, they might change their plan, the chains might be brought in or I might make the trip back to TW and the Yanks.

I had been chained for four and a half years. At some times I had been let off them for exercise, at others they would only come off when I went to the bathroom or was moved. Now I would be free of them. From now on if someone came into my room I wouldn't have to stop moving around, or be told 'Siddown' and be chained up for another twenty-four hours. Having this time to think about freedom was unnerving. While I was confident I hadn't become institutionalized in any way, I sensed that it was going to feel very odd making decisions again, finding the drive to get on with a normal daily routine rather than one dictated by my captors.

Most of all, though, I was thinking about what I could do for Terry, Tom, TW and the others. We knew from the radio that there were now very positive moves to wrap up the whole hostage issue. All I could do was to try to ensure that the situation was not left hanging. I didn't know exactly how, but at least I could appeal to everyone with the power to help not to delay things.

Eventually I dozed off. When I awoke it took me a few moments to realize how dramatically my situation had changed. The blindfold was still there but already my horizons were expanding. I felt a new, albeit undefined, sense of responsibility. At last I would be working for a future, not merely surviving the present.

Ayeesa brought me some food and said that he was going shopping. He measured me up for clothes and shoes. It was very exciting. I was suddenly and idiotically worried about whether they would fit or whether I'd like the style.

After he'd gone two other men remained. I had never come across them before and guessed they lived in the apartment. They took me to the bathroom, gave me shaving gear and told me to have a shower.

The hours dragged by. I wondered when on earth they were going to let me go. Ayeesa returned and I tried on all the gear: new underwear, a dark T-shirt, some lightweight slacks that fitted pretty well, socks and loafers. I was delighted. My first clothes in years; trousers and shoes that fitted. An hour or so later he returned and gave me a watch. 'This, eh, *cadeau* from me, John, good luck.' I thanked him. He could not have understood his present's significance for me. Since the day of my kidnap, I had been living in their time-scale. They had stolen my watch from me, and with it every other vestige of normal life. Even during the brief periods when we'd had a watch or a radio, time was only a meaningless progression of wasted hours. Now everything was going to be different.

Ayeesa told me that I would be free 'the night or *boukra*'. *Boukra* was a joke word for hostages. It did mean tomorrow, but in the sense of 'some time after today' rather than the very next day. When a guard said he'd bring us something *bad shwai* (after a little while) we knew he meant that he intended to bring it that day. *Boukra* suggested that he hoped to remember to think about it at some point in the future. Still, it was better than *bad ain*. To them, that meant 'after some more time', and to us, 'you'll be bloody lucky, chum'.

Now, finally, I was very close to being bloody lucky.

What I had not expected was a visit from one of Islamic Jihad's leaders and 'Trust me' Ali. I had my clothes and was all set to go. It was quite late at night so when I heard the new men arrive I assumed they were the 'honour guard' who would deliver me to freedom. When two men came in

465

and sat down and I heard Ali say: 'Hallo John', I became even more alert – and not a little alarmed. What did he want?

Ali said: 'This is my friend, he is the big chief.' Warily, I said: 'How do you do?' and we shook hands. Ali told me that they were all very sorry that I had been held for so long and that they hoped the improved conditions had made the last couple of years better. They hoped that I would now have a good life. He asked me if I had expected to be going home. I replied that we had heard on the radio that a Briton and an American were expected to be released. He agreed, and asked if I had heard that Islamic Jihad were sending an envoy to the UN. Yes, I'd heard that.

'My friends, the brothers, have been watching you and they tell me and the leaders that you have a good spirit. You work to be happy and be happy with your friends.'

'We all work together.'

'Yes, but my friends say your attitude to us is better, you are a gentleman.'

'Well, I hope so.'

'Good, so we have decided that you will be our envoy to Perez de Cuellar.'

'Fucking Ada,' I thought; I said: 'I see.'

'We want you to help us write a letter to him to get him to help us end the suffering of your friends and our friends. Then you will take it to him. What do you think we should say?'

I could not believe it. They had kept me locked up for more than five years and now they wanted my advice on ending the situation. In the space of one day I had transformed from pawn to plenipotentiary. I thought initially that they were just being formal, but in fact they did go through their letter with me and wanted my advice as to whether it was a good idea to include some particular ideas or if they should remain secret, to be communicated privately by me to Perez de Cuellar. This was beyond my experience, but I did tell them that to prove their good intentions the best thing would be to release pictures and messages from the hostages and the Israeli POWs. They assured me that all the hostages were alive and that they'd advise the 'brother groups' who held them to provide photographs. Where should they be sent?

I gave them WTN's London address and phone number, not knowing then that the company had moved. They repeated again and again that I must not let anyone but de Cuellar see the letter. I gave them my word. Ali said: 'You will be free at ten-thirty tomorrow morning. Good luck and goodbye.'

I spent another sleepless night, wondering how one demanded private meetings with the Secretary-General of the United Nations and how long it would take for me to get a passport so that I could go to see him in New York, and worrying that I had been too open with these men. They might decide that I was deceiving them in some way and have second thoughts about the whole plan.

My mission completely took my mind off happy thoughts about reunions with everyone back home. That would have to wait. This was terribly important. In my mind the fate of Terry, Tom, TW and the others I hadn't met depended on how well I carried out this task. Nothing else mattered. But my mind kept turning to more mundane concerns; I couldn't see the Secretary-General without a decent shirt, jacket and tie. I also knew I must get some rest otherwise I would collapse. I tried to sleep and managed to doze a little.

The next morning, having dressed at dawn, I was ready and trying to keep calm. I kept going over the conversation of the night before, remembering those aspects that might not be included in the letter and which I would have to talk about with de Cuellar. What was absolutely clear to me was that these people wanted this business concluded, and that they had a huge trust in Perez de Cuellar as a man of honour.

My new watch seemed to be running very slowly through those last hours. By ten o'clock I was just holding my breath, rocking backwards and forwards slightly as I sat cross-legged on the blankets. Occasionally my mind would slip into one of its familiar, long-held fantasies of freedom. I pictured myself going out with Jill; telephoning home; starting a shift in the news room. Then I would stop in shock as it struck me that within a few hours these day-dreams would be realizable; that in time such activities would be part of my normal routine again. The thought was so sweet, yet I hardly dared linger with it. At half-past ten no-one had arrived. Ayeesa was there with the two local men. Nothing happened. 'They've changed their minds. They'll come back and take away my clothes.'

At eleven o'clock there was a commotion. A new man came in to me. 'Come, Mister John. You are leaving.' He sounded older than the others.

'Am I going home?'

He laughed and squeezed my arm. 'Yes, of course, now you free!'

They asked me to climb into the cardboard crate.

'Wait!' exclaimed the new man. My heart stopped. 'I want photo,' he said.

I clambered out of the box and stood there. I waited for him to tell me to remove the blindfold for the camera. Nothing happened. Then he said: 'OK, we go.'

'No photo?' I asked.

'Yes, photo good, thank you.' It must look terrific in his album.

They carried me downstairs in the box and lifted me out and into the boot of a car. I was blindfolded, but this was the first time since the kidnap that I wasn't bound, gagged or in a sack. I waited anxiously. The minutes ticked by. There were footsteps, the boot opened. A large envelope was tossed in. 'For de Cuellar. Only him.' The boot slammed shut. We were off.

We drove for maybe ten minutes before the car stopped. The boot flew open. Two sets of arms grabbed me and pulled me out, a hand tore the blindfold off as I was bundled into another car. Someone pressed his hand over my eyes and said: 'OK?'

I replied, 'OK' and kept my eyes closed when he removed his hand. I sat in the back seat between two men. Two more were in front. A voice from the passenger seat said: 'You, de Cuellar, *haidarr*, this.' He shook the envelope.

'*Nam, uhnah* – de Cuellar *bas*, yes, just me and de Cuellar.'

'*Quiyees*, good.'

The car braked suddenly, the men on either side of me leapt out and we sped on.

We stopped again. 'OK, *ruh*, go.' I got out. There was an exchange in Arabic which I couldn't follow. A hand grasped my wrist, leading me away.

'OK, John,' a voice said. 'You can open your eyes, I am a Syrian officer.'

For five and a quarter years I had dreamed of meeting a Syrian officer. As far as we knew most of the released hostages had been handed over to the Syrians and gone home via Damascus. Now, at last, it was my turn. General Adnan Baloul was a relaxed, urbane man, smoking his pipe as we sped through Beirut in his elegant Mercedes coupé. When I asked for a cigarette he stopped in the middle of the traffic and waved his hand. The car behind, full of his bodyguards, drew up. '*Dachan*, smokes,' said the general. A packet of Marlboro was passed over. We were off again.

General Baloul pointed things out to me as we went along. 'Before we moved into the city, this was a no-go area, now it is open to everyone.' We went on, up into the hills above the city. 'I would like you to meet my boss, General Ghazi Kana'an at our headquarters.'

'Fine, but I'd like to get home as soon as possible.'

'Of course, John. You are envoy.'

'Well, yes I am, I have to see Perez de Cuellar.'

He waved a hand towards the buff envelope tucked down by my feet. 'That's the letter?'

'What? Oh yes, the letter.'

'What does it say?'

'Well, I'm not certain, exactly. I have to give it to de Cuellar personally, unopened.'

'Of course, of course,' he chuckled.

I settled back into the leather upholstery of the Mercedes, fascinated by the gadgets in the car. To be safely cocooned in the high-tech machine was a stark and brilliant contrast to the nightmare of being bound and gagged, blindfolded in the boot of a car. I was comfortable. I could sing and shout if I wanted and, above all, I knew where I was going and could watch our progress out of the city and into the hills.

It was an extraordinary sensation to be able to look about freely. I stared at the shell-damaged buildings and villagers in traditional costume at a crossroads. We crested a hill and there was the wide sweep of the Beka'a Valley. It was the first time I had seen it, although I was certain I had spent more than two years in, or under, the area. I kept having to pinch myself to remember that I really could gaze at the sights around me, that now my escort was looking after me for my own good, not his, or his group's.

We arrived at a small village where the Syrian Military Intelligence had its Lebanese headquarters. We went in and met General Kana'an. As he spoke little English Baloul translated for him. They asked a few questions to try and identify where I'd been held most recently with TW and the Yanks. Of course there wasn't much I could tell them. The two generals talked in Arabic for a few moments before Baloul said, 'The general wants to see the letter.'

'I am very sorry, I hope the general will understand, but I can only let the Secretary-General see this.'

'OK, no problem.' More chuckles and pleasantries and then we drove on.

I was looking everywhere, trying to get a sense of the size of the barren, rocky mountains through which we were driving. I marvelled at them, but could neither accept nor understand them. Until an hour ago my appreciation of scale had been limited to a room no more than twenty by fifteen feet and this dramatic scenery only made sense to me if I thought of it as two dimensional, as a gigantic painting.

I didn't start to feel truly safe until we had left Lebanon. Once we had crossed the Syrian border, there was no way that my kidnappers could recapture me. I could begin to look forward. I anticipated having to make a brief statement to the news teams and thought that then I would be handed over formally to the British Ambassador. After that, whether in Damascus or back in England I would start meeting the people whom I loved.

But first there was a detour to the Damascus headquarters of Military Intelligence where there was another, more senior, general who gave me tea and asked similar questions about our most recent location. Once more I had to refuse a general a peek at my letter. Then I was taken to the Syrian Foreign Ministry. I felt nervous, of course; the whole situation was so strange, but I think the main thing that bothered me was the persistent feeling that none of these people would want me to look at them. The hangover from the guards' paranoia was still very much with me and I automatically assumed that all Arabs were as nervous of being identified.

At the Foreign Ministry I was taken in through a side door and led up some stairs. Adnan Baloul handed me over to some ministry officials. I gave the general a fond farewell; I was sorry to lose this new friend so soon. It was to be the first of many such brief relationships over the next few weeks into which I poured a great deal of feeling.

I was ushered into a room.

'Mr McCarthy, welcome to Damascus, here is the British Ambassador, Mr Andrew Green.'

'Welcome home, John.'

I looked at the man in front of me – slim, nervous, with a sparkle in his bright blue eyes, as he stood there in his seersucker suit. I wanted to hug him, but felt

471

that might be bad form, so gripped his hand firmly and thanked him for his welcome.

We were led into another room where we were introduced to the acting Foreign Minister, Nasser Kaddour. We sat down for what seemed like an interminable exchange of diplomatic pleasantries. During the translation of some of these I turned to Andrew.

'I know my mother is dead, how is my brother?'

'He's fine, he is with your father on the plane coming here. Jill will see you at Lyneham.' He turned to one of his aides. 'Please radio this to Cyprus, "I have John, he is fine, he knows about his mother".'

During another pause for translation Andrew explained that there were a lot of journalists downstairs who would like to see me, but that I could do as I wanted. I said that I would prepare a brief statement.

A few minutes later, there was yet another lull and, feeling rather pompous, I explained my 'mission'. 'I'm Islamic Jihad's special envoy to the UN. Would it be possible for someone to get me a passport and arrange for me to go to New York?'

'Whatever you need will be arranged, John, don't worry.'

As Andrew continued his diplomatic chat with the acting Foreign Minister I scribbled some notes.

The room below was packed with film crews, photographers flashing lights and journalists with notebooks and microphones in hand. Mr Kaddour spoke first, followed by Andrew and then it was my turn. As I realized that my statement had no preface, all I could think to say was, 'Well, hallo.'

Looking back, having a role to play beyond that of 'released hostage' was a great advantage. It gave me a legitimate reason for delaying any response to questions from the press and also, by concentrating on my meeting with Perez de Cuellar, I was able to put a little distance between myself and the peculiar events through which I was living. There were too many weird new things to make sense of, let alone expect to speak coherently about the past five years. As I read my statement to the press I found myself stumbling and stalling when I spoke of my fellow hostages. If I had wandered from my script I would have broken down completely.

I was now in British hands. We drove to the ambassador's residence where another knot of journalists had gathered. We walked in past them. Andrew's wife, Jane, greeted me at the front door. She was charming; shy, yet quite relaxed – an ideal person to meet under the circumstances. She and Andrew took me inside and showed me around. On the stairs was a print of Haileybury and Jane explained that Andrew had also been there.

They had prepared a room for me with shaving things and some fresh clothes, donated by embassy staff in case I wanted a change. I shed Ayeesa's T-shirt in favour of something smarter and had a shave. I studied myself in the mirror. I looked OK, but found it hard to accept the remarkable difference in my surroundings. Everything seemed temporary, everything was moving, changing so rapidly. I felt that nothing would seem real until I had handed over that letter.

I went downstairs and out into the garden with Andrew and Jane. I talked about the recent months and about my concern to see through my duties as envoy to the UN as quickly and as effectively as possible. Andrew explained that he knew my father, Jill and Chris Pearson well as he had been running the 'hostage desk' at the Foreign Office prior to being posted to reopen the Damascus Embassy. I felt at ease with this couple; they were so English, restrained and humorous. When Andrew went inside to check some arrangements, Jane and I chatted about life in Damascus. Andrew returned to say that the plane from Cyprus had arrived and that my father and Terence would soon be here with Roby. I was surprised that Roby was coming too, having no idea what great friends he and my father had become over the years.

473

The Greens left me in the garden. I declined anything other than a soft drink, feeling wary of alcohol after such a long, dry spell.

Then they were there: Daddy and Terence came out on to the terrace and I bounded over to greet them. We stood in silence, arms wrapped around one another, weeping, swept away by complete relief. After a few moments we stepped back and congratulated one another on looking so well.

We sat and chatted for a little while, smiling at each other, perhaps a little vacantly, yet determined to carry on as if this sort of thing had been happening every day. I was greatly reassured to find them so unchanged and immediately felt that we would have the open, supportive relationships that I had longed for ever since being kidnapped. With Terence it was as though I had been reunited with a best friend who understood exactly how I was feeling. With my father the old, slightly formal, approach to one another was gone. I realized that I was even calling him Pat. They left me for a few minutes as Roby came out. I could think of nothing to say, so gave him a big, all-American hug. I would never have expected a man as self-possessed as Roby to be moved when he met me, but obviously he was.

Roby went back in so that the RAF medical team could come out to introduce themselves. Group Captain Fredoon Amroliwalla was in charge, assisted by Squadron Leader Elaine Proud. They asked if I was aware of any serious problems and reassured themselves that I was fit to travel. Wing Commander Gordon Turnbull then introduced himself.

'I'm a psychiatrist; I'll be there to talk things through, to debrief you, if you feel like it, though I get the impression you'll be counselling me before we get very far.'

What nice people. Everybody was so kind, and no-one seemed to be pressing me. Plans had been made for me, but everything was subject to my approval. Anything could be rearranged to suit me.

We had to leave almost immediately for the airport as the Syrians wanted the RAF plane out of the country before sundown. I said goodbye to Jane and the staff, was given a temporary passport and off we went: Pat, Terence, Roby and I in one car; Andrew and the others in another. On the way to the airport Roby explained the immediate plans: at RAF Lyneham there was a VIP suite which we could use as long as I wanted; the press would be there in force, but I had no obligation to speak to them; the Foreign Minister Douglas Hogg would be there to welcome me home officially, but privately.

'Isn't his wife, Sarah, head of the policy unit at Number Ten?' I asked.

Roby's flow of information stopped dead as he looked at me almost warily. 'Why, yes, I think she is.'

Having expected someone who was probably ignorant of the collapse of the Berlin Wall it must have been a bit of a shock to find me conversant with the intricacies of Downing Street staffing.

We exchanged farewells with Andrew and his staff beside the VC–10. I walked to the plane. At the foot of the steps stood two warrant-officers, their uniform shirts covered in emblems. They saluted as one, saying: 'Welcome home, sir.'

I stumbled up the steps, blinded by tears.

There was a cheer as I entered the plane. There seemed to be an awful lot of people on board: two full crews, more medical personnel, in case another hostage had been released with me, some Foreign Office staff and a man from Lambeth Palace called Francis Witts. He was a delightful fellow. I was relieved to find out that he'd only joined the Lambeth staff a few days earlier and was almost as baffled by the proceedings as me.

We talked about Waite. I had already gathered that most of the press were itching to ask TW about Irangate and many other things. I could not see the man I had got to know in the past few months waiting for matters to calm down; he would be on the first podium in sight, giving the press more to work with. I described the difficulties of living with Waite and explained my view that he would have to be convinced that keeping a low profile was the best policy until he'd readjusted to freedom.

I was invited up to the cockpit for take-off. I had never done that before and was thrilled. Looking back it seems odd that I should have felt so excited by this particular novelty on the day I had given my first news conference, to the world's excited press corps, in a foreign capital, about my role as the terrorists' envoy to the United Nations. But that had happened hours ago and was, in any case, just too bizarre to take in.

Having waved goodbye and blown a farewell kiss at Andrew, we took off for home. I went back to the party, sitting with Terence, my father and Roby. They started giving me news about some of my friends. Nick had lost his voice for some months immediately after my kidnap; recently he'd been working with some mutual friends in Switzerland. Pearson was now a senior producer with Sky television. Jill had left WTN and had been working for *Channel 4 Daily*; she had bought a flat of which I was a part owner. Other WTN colleagues had travelled the world, married and had children.

These things made me uneasy; everyone seemed to have left me behind. It would be quite a while before I realized, and could accept, that I had been living in a different time-scale. A month's activities for me barely equalled a quiet afternoon for most people. I became frightened and even jealous of others' news. I felt foolish talking about myself when I had done nothing for so many years.

My father told me that Brian had been very distressed by the press interest in him after his release. They felt that my best plan would be to take plenty of time to get my feet back on the ground. They said that after Lyneham they were looking for a quiet place in the country where we could have a week deciding what to do next. This all sounded fine to me. I was beginning to get a hint of the excitement waiting for me in England and, aside from wanting to keep my head clear for Perez de Cuellar, I was rapidly realizing that any sort of public performance would be very draining and would probably unleash the emotional floodgates. I was going to need time and space to put the hostage years in some sort of perspective and come to terms with this new sort of vulnerability.

Both my father and Roby spoke very fondly about Jill, but I was already aware that there had been differences over style, whether or not to campaign, high or low profile. I tried to absorb all these things, but, finding that much of it was too complicated, too confusing and strange, felt it better to let things drift for the moment. I wasn't responsible for the way anyone else had conducted themselves and couldn't imagine that any rifts that had formed were going to be relevant now. My captivity had ended and with it, for the most part, the stresses imposed on those close to me.

I was offered a drink. I thought for a moment then settled on a gin and tonic. One of the RAF psychiatrists took a photograph of me with my glass raised. Roby sidled up to him, saying, 'Let's make sure that photo doesn't appear in any of tomorrow's rags.'

'Of course not.'

The gin was marvellous. Drinking it with ice chinking in the glass, looking out over the great sweep of the arid Syrian landscape, I felt that I was washing away all the dust of the past five years, setting aside all the frustrated moments when such a simple pleasure would have meant so much. Yet Tom and the two Terrys would get nothing more that night than a cup of black tea. I felt foolish for relishing a luxury so much.

After half an hour or so food was announced. I was too nervous to eat, but thought a glass of red wine would be ideal. It tasted delicious but after two sips I felt so light-headed that I decided to go and lie down. Elaine Proud settled me into one of the beds. I couldn't sleep, my mind was spinning too much.

I would soon be seeing Jill and I was anxious that she should be happy with all the arrangements. Before that I had to face a big welcome as I got off the plane and meet various complete strangers. I had to protect the letter which Terence now clutched in his hands. I had to behave like an envoy, to show the Islamic Jihad that they were being taken seriously. How soon would my trip to New York be organized?

Elaine came up to me and I told her that I was too tense to sleep, yet felt so tired that if I didn't relax I was sure I would collapse down the plane steps. She checked with Fredoon who advised against a sleeping pill as it might send me out cold after two days with virtually no sleep. He prescribed a small whisky. I drank it down and felt better immediately.

As we flew over northern France, I was fascinated by the lights from the villages. They were so bright on that clear evening, it was as if it were all a wonderful show put on for my deprived eyes. Once over England the lights were even brighter. I was informed that ground control at Heathrow Airport had called through to say, 'Welcome home'. I was amazed. Then I was told that the blaze of lights ahead was RAF Lyneham, that every light at the base and in all the homes around had been switched on and curtains left open to be a beacon welcoming me home after my long absence.

Although I had been warned that a large reception awaited me at Lyneham I was quite unprepared for the mass of people and press that had assembled on the tarmac. I was stunned, aware initially only of a sea of lights and the roar of the cheering crowd; I felt both elated and embarrassed. Standing inside the plane I was anxious to acknowledge this great welcome, reminding myself that I must not raise clenched fists in triumph: I was not a hero. 'Who do they think I am?' I wondered, 'and what will they expect from me?' My fears vanished the moment I stepped out of the plane and into the warmth of their welcome. I was back in England; I was home. I waved towards the crowd, almost invisible behind the bright lights, then turned and beckoned to my father so that we could go down the steps together.

I had decided not to speak to the press yet and now felt certain it was the best move. I thought that I could cope with getting off the plane, meeting the station commander Group Captain Ian Corbett and then Douglas Hogg and his team. But beyond that all I wanted to do was see Jill and a few other close friends.

Ian Corbett took us round to the VIP suite where we were to stay. People were standing along the outside of the perimeter fence. They cheered as we walked in from the cars. It was at once uplifting and unnerving.

In the suite there was a sea of faces and an endless flow of champagne. I was introduced to Douglas Hogg. The small man stood close to me, formally welcoming me home on behalf of Her Majesty's Government. He asked me how I was and if I had everything I needed. Then he gestured diffidently to the letter in my hand.

'John, I wonder, wouldn't it be a help to you to know what it says, before you meet the Secretary-General?'

'No, thank you, Mr Hogg. I have a fair idea of what it says, and I'm honour bound to release it only to de Cuellar, personally.'

'Yes, of course, I understand, but as we have some Arabic experts just up the hall it seems a shame not to get a clearer picture of how things stand.'

'I'm very sorry, it may be unnecessary, but I will not let anyone but the Secretary-General see it.'

The various polite suggestions that I should hand the letter over, first from the Syrians and now from the British, amused me.

After a few drinks the party dispersed. As Duncan Slater, one of the FO team who had been on the plane, checked his bearings on the doorway, he said to Terence, 'Enjoyed talking, we must do this again sometime' and then was gone. Roby disappeared and returned with WTN's president Ken Coyte and Lorrie Grabham-Morgan, their marketing services manager. It felt better meeting familiar faces, it was more natural. We chatted for a few minutes and Lorrie explained that she was tracking down a safe house which we could use when we left Lyneham.

Then, at last, it was time for the big moment. Roby went off with Ken and Lorrie. He returned a few minutes later. I glimpsed Jill and Chris Pearson through the half-open door. Pearson seemed to push Jill into the room as he turned to hug both my father and Roby at once.

Jill and I looked at each other, smiling broadly, yet shyly.

'Hallo, how are you?'

'I'm fine and you?'

She looked so much as I had tried to picture her. She sounded just the same. I was so relieved. There before me was the woman I remembered, the one who had come back to me clearly only rarely, for the briefest moments, in dreams, remaining otherwise an elusive figure in memories and fantasies. Now I would be able to see this real Jill at any time and I felt certain that we stood a good chance of working our way back to the closeness we'd had five years before.

Pearson came in. 'My man,' he said as we hugged. We sat down and chatted, cracking a few jokes. I was burning to ask him so many things, but now, of all things, I simply had to know. 'Are Kylie and Dannii Minogue related?' He roared with laughter, the same deep rumble and shout I had sometimes heard echoing in my head.

'Yes. That's amazing, you've heard of them!'

'Yes, but I couldn't work out if there really was a connection.'

Chris was still laughing. 'At the press conference today someone asked what things I was expecting to have to tell you, and I joked, "I'll have to explain who Kylie Minogue is"!'

'You gave a press conference?'

'Oh yes. After we heard you were definitely coming home.'

'And you, too, Jill?'

480

'Yes,' she replied smiling.

Their news of the press conference added to the feeling of unreality; but I was reassured by the fact that they, too, found it all 'bloody odd' and seemed quite unchanged by the experience of campaigning for my release. For the first time since coming home I was confident that this new chapter in my life, however exhilarating or disturbing, would be manageable.

London, August 1990–August 1991

Brian's release changed everything. He was the first hostage whose return Britain and Ireland could celebrate as one of our own; the first hostage with British nationality to be freed by Islamic Jihad in four and a quarter years. Frank Reed's release a few months earlier had roused huge media interest, but, as usual, it had faded after a few weeks. When Brian returned home, a tidal wave of emotion and adulation rose up out of nowhere and never really went away. The campaign was swept along in its path. For years we had been trying to tell people what the hostages were going through, but it took Brian's eloquence and strength of spirit to convince them. The haunting images with which he described life as a hostage touched everyone and allowed them a glimpse of the half-world he had just left. No-one who heard him could be left in any doubt about the kind of despair John and the other hostages were still suffering, nor of the courage it took for them to cope with it day after day. He shone a light on his fellow hostages that allowed people to see them as individuals rather than pawns on a political chessboard and, at last, public concern was transformed from expressions of sympathy into calls for action. The number of people contacting our campaign office shot up.

Six days after his release, Brian faced rows and rows of TV cameras at a press conference in Dublin which Chris and I were invited to attend. Brian had kept away from the press until he'd had a chance to collect his thoughts. Now half the world's journalists had gathered to listen to what he wanted to say. I arrived to find that the whole of Ireland was still celebrating Brian's return and that once again we were caught up in non-stop madness. The atmosphere in Dublin was joyful, but it bordered on the surreal. We swept off to Brian's press conference in a four-car convoy with his family and friends. Police cars raced alongside us at high speed with sirens blaring, cutting a swathe through the city traffic as we swerved around corners, missing other drivers by inches, before finally screeching into the courtyard of Dublin Castle. Inside, Brian's immediate family were relaxing and horsing around; the media pressure was off them for a while, but, for Brian, it had just begun. This was his opportunity to make people understand, to make them care about the people he had left behind. I was worried that Brian might not be able to cope with insensitive or intrusive questions, and that the assembled journalists would neither understand, nor care, how vulnerable he was, but when Brian walked into the press conference the room erupted in applause. Everyone there was on his side. Their reaction took me aback; it was the first indication that something had really changed.

Around the country people were watching the press conference live. RTE, Ireland's national network, was transmitting the pictures into homes all over Ireland and into news rooms throughout Britain. Brian, dressed in a Friends of John McCarthy T-shirt, began to speak. In Dublin Castle, the room fell silent. All over Britain, journalists stopped what they were doing to listen. The press conference had been expected to last twenty minutes, but for the next hour and a half the force of Brian's words commanded complete attention. He spoke in no more than a painful whisper, but the journalists present had abandoned their cynicism; many of them were in tears.

Cameras were aimed in my direction whenever John's name was mentioned, and some newspapers carried a photograph of me apparently wiping away a tear. Unfortunately, though, I had hardly been able to hear anything Brian said; I was behind him and the sound was projected forward. It wasn't until I saw a video of the press conference back in London that I understood why everyone had been so mesmerized. Brian's love and regard for John came over so powerfully and eloquently, as did the extraordinary way they had helped each other survive. In every word Brian said I recognized the special person I knew and had loved, the person I had been unable to conjure up for so long for myself, let alone for strangers. It was the same John he had described to Chris and me from his hospital bed, but this time he spoke like a poet and was telling the whole world.

Those five hours we had spent with Brian had electrified me. At our next campaign meeting, just a few days later, I felt radiant and happy as we tried to share what we had heard; that John was planning a reforestation programme for Ireland; that his first words to Brian had been, 'Fuck me, it's Ben Gunn!' – it was a line that everyone could imagine John saying, and it meant that despite Islamic Jihad, despite everything he had gone through and was still going through, the John we all loved was still there. Brian's stories showed that John hadn't changed; he was coping well, and he was stronger than we had ever dared hope. I was very proud of him, particularly when Brian talked of John's sense of humour. For so long, I had said when interviewed that that quality would help him survive. But here was the evidence that I was right. I felt like saying, 'You see, that's what I meant.'

The lift it gave me lasted through a week of feverish activity; visits to Dublin, meetings and interviews, but by the time it was over I was exhausted and overwrought. My mind was drenched with impressions of John. Brian had brought him halfway home, almost close enough to touch; feelings that I had squeezed into a tiny part of myself, and kept in suspended animation for so long, had been revived by Brian's release. There was a possibility that John and I had a future. My thoughts were constantly split into two, between here and there, between now and then, as memories were revived and almost brought to life. I kept submitting to fantasies about the future, then squashing them down again, as the caution that had become second nature took over. I tried to be detached; I now knew that John still cared for me and I for him, but nothing could be resolved until he was home, and back in the real world.

So much of what Brian had told us confirmed that John was the same, and yet there was so much I still didn't know, which I couldn't fully understand about the ordeal, which had strengthened, deepened and changed him. I knew, too, that, for John, another overwhelming experience lay ahead; that of being freed from a world which offered no choices into one of infinite possibilities. Immediately after his release Brian had said that he wanted to drink all the drink in the world, eat all the food in the world, and make love to all the women in the world. Anyone could understand his desire to plunge headlong into life again, to make up for lost time and I thought it would be understandable if, once free, John also decided to take off in all directions at once. As for me, I had no idea if what I felt for John was real. The mental screen behind which my feelings had been hidden wouldn't stay in place any more and I felt more confused than I had been for years.

I may not have felt ready for John's release, but he was expected home within weeks. Brian's captors had promised it would be 'two weeks'. The FO were very upbeat and there were reports from Beirut saying that talks between Britain and Iran had reached their final stages; the three remaining British hostages would be released in September. The month passed, but the rumours persisted throughout October. Diplomatic relations between Britain and Iran were restored and there was speculation that links would also be renewed with Syria after a four-year break. I kept a lid on my expectations, but couldn't deny that things were going well. My daily campaign chats with Chris began to revolve around practical arrangements for John's release. Roby, Pat and the FO were handling it all and Pat was adamant that John would be better protected in every way than Brian had been. 'John's release will be very British,' he told me over the phone. 'There'll be none of that emotional stuff.' I agreed that there should be no public reunions and that Pat and Terence should fly out to meet him. We knew from Brian that John had no idea that his mother was dead; Pat and Terence would have the awful responsibility of breaking the news and no-one had any idea how John would react. As if that weren't enough, the pressure on him would be enormous, so it was best that our reunion should wait until later.

I worried, however, about how much later that would be, especially when I learned that John was going to be kept away from everyone on his return to England. To my relief, Roby, who would be accompanying Pat and Terence to meet John, told Chris and me that we would be allowed to see him; Roby said we 'had earned it'.

For a long time I had imagined watching John get off the plane following his release and then driving him off in a big fast car. Now I'd scaled the fantasy down. I just wanted to watch him get off the plane. I was determined to be there to see that, but I couldn't imagine anything beyond it. The uncertainty of what would follow was terrifying. I developed a desperate need to know what would happen on a practical level, making that the main focus of my fears. Nothing could be predicted, but I was still determined to reassure myself of everything. Where would John be taken on the day of his release? Would we be able to contact Pat to see how he was? When would he be back in England? At what time, when exactly, would we be allowed to see him? I worried that in the mayhem nobody would think to contact us and let us know.

The day of John's release was, in my imagination, taking on a nightmarish aspect; it was all beyond my control. Chris remained practical, accepting the FO's invitation to inspect the RAF base at Lyneham where John would land. When he reported back on the high-level security operation that would be in place, the armed guards and the layout of the VIP suite where John would be staying, I could see from his enthusiasm that he'd abandoned all caution; he'd let himself believe that John really would be home any day. It didn't help that the media was frantically trying to plan for John's release as well. We had been to several meetings with news organizations who wanted to discuss where we would be on the big day and to ask about their 'access to John'. We tried to explain: we weren't in any kind of position to grant 'access'; once John was free he would be able to make his own decisions about who he wanted to speak to and when. We politely refused offers of help and protection in the form of hideaways and transport; as attractive as those offers were, we knew that in practice it would mean that we'd been 'bought'. We wanted to be free to go wherever we liked and do whatever we wanted. On each occasion we left the news editor in question looking and feeling as worried as ever. It was a relief to be able to say: 'The person to talk to is Roby Burke at WTN; he's in charge of all the arrangements.'

We had all looked on Brian's release as a 'dry run' for when John came home and had learned from it, although just how little we had understood only became evident much later. Chris and I had been aware that the atmosphere in Dublin was highly charged and that there were tensions among Brian's family and friends; we weren't sure what the problems were exactly, but now some of those tensions surfaced in our own campaign group. A few weeks after Brian's release I'd learned that some of the friends on our committee had felt hurt and annoyed that they hadn't yet met him themselves.

Ruffled feathers were smoothed when Brian came over to London in October, and met friends like Barbara, Ronnie, Gina and Chris Martin, another old friend and John's former flatmate. He spent several hours chatting to them, and it boosted everyone when Brian said that John had talked about them over the years. It gave us all a thrill that Brian knew so much about us. He sat down between Gina and Barbara, saying, 'Now, who's the film producer?' and then, 'Which one's Ronnie? You can't swim, can you? John told me he nearly drowned you once.' Later, he and Nick, who was now working in Switzerland, met up in The Crown and Sceptre and hugged like old friends, almost as

487

if it were John who'd returned. Brian made him both laugh
and cry by insisting that he help him honour a promise
he'd made to John. 'When you get home make sure you
go and see Toksvig at The Crown and Sceptre, get him to
take you for a slap-up meal and get him to pay.' It was a
wonderful evening, but strange. We were like bees around
a honeypot, all eager to talk to Brian at once. We wanted
him to answer all the questions that presented themselves
and to listen to everything that we felt the urge to tell
him, on all kinds of subjects. When he spoke about his
captivity, we all fell silent, straining to hear every word,
as if he were a messiah. In a way he was – he had, in
effect, come back from the dead.

During the evening Frank McCallan, the organizer of
Brian's campaign group, beckoned Chris and me over
and spoke to us in an urgent whisper. 'You don't have
a clue. You just don't know what's going to hit you.'
He told us that we were all totally unprepared for what
was going to be thrown at us when John was released, by
which I thought he meant that our practical arrangements
needed tightening up. Chris and I had seen Brian's campaign committee in action after his release and had been
impressed by how brilliantly they seemed to be handling
everything. We'd realized that we had a lot to learn and I
said as much to Frank, but it dawned on me much later
that he'd been trying to tell us something else altogether.
He wasn't talking in practical terms, he was warning us
that John's release would have powerful and unimaginable
knock-on effects, emotionally.

I had no idea how hard it must have been for Brian in the
months following his release. Looking back I can see how
much he had to cope with. John's continued captivity must
have anchored him in an experience that he was trying to
leave behind. At the same time as trying to rebuild his life,
he had to help the other hostages; while he needed to flee
the spotlight he was compelled to remain in its glare. He
was famous, regarded by some as a kind of healer, and so
many people had expectations of him and were making

demands on him. Like everyone else, we imposed on him, too. Our need to talk to him that night in October was just one more responsibility he had to take on, and only a small example of the adulation he now faced wherever he went. I noticed when we went over to Ireland again in November that everyone seemed to want a part of him. After a while Brian appeared like a hunted animal, finding it difficult to reach any peace of mind or to trust anyone else, even Chris and me. Even the most innocent questions became intrusive and some distance entered our relationship. I was hurt, but I couldn't see it from Brian's point of view. Pat could and recognizing what was happening to Brian, he resolved that the same should not happen to John. Still, I wondered if John's home-coming would be as difficult and how I would cope if it was.

Gina had raised the awkward subject of 'feelings' in our meeting one night and suggested that we needed to talk through the emotions we might experience in the future, given the way some of us had felt after Brian's release. Some people were a bit uncomfortable with this idea, but others thought she was right and I was glad she'd brought it up. By then the rumours of John's imminent release had died down, taking with them some of my own anxieties, but I was still generally frightened of the whole prospect and witnessing Brian's difficulties made it worse. I wanted to know how to treat John and how I could best help him. I needed some guidance, a rule book that would tell me what to do. I still hadn't learned that there was no such thing.

There weren't many people around with knowledge of how to handle the release of a hostage, so we sought the advice of an expert in the psychological effects of indefinite political imprisonment. We talked to him about what John and we, his friends, might experience on his release. He told us that John would probably find it difficult to cope with all the information, facts and decisions of which he had been starved for so many years, that we would need to 'get into the cell with him' to talk on his wavelength. We shouldn't expect the John we had known to come back, but should try to imagine him as one of his distant relatives. I don't know if, afterwards, we were actually any more prepared for John's release than we had been; it was reassuring to think that we were and I worried less about what would happen and therefore felt less concerned about controlling it.

In November, for John's birthday, the Paris branch of the Friends held a party outside the British Embassy attended by Jean-Paul Kauffman. In London we staged a mock-up of John's conditions of captivity from detailed information supplied by Brian. The people who designed the 'cell' did a superb job, but we had resigned ourselves to not getting much media attention. For weeks the Conservative Party had been in turmoil; Mrs Thatcher had been forced out and the crucial second vote to decide her successor was on 27 November, John's birthday. Everyone was obsessed by that, not our photocall. I didn't know what effect her resignation would have on the hostages, but when she went, it felt, to me, as if someone had switched on the light after years in the dark. Although I knew nothing about the new Prime Minister, John Major, everyone expected a change of style. Two days after the resignation, Britain renewed ties with Syria. I thought it would be helpful, but with disarray at home and war looming in the Gulf, it was once again impossible to predict what would happen.

At Christmas we sent out special FOJM greeting cards designed by Sue Brown and John Hewitt to our supporters around the country. Thanks to Brian's release, the number of Friends on our files was now up to twelve thousand, and all had been painstakingly logged on to our computer. It had taken Jackie months to plough through the box files of letters piling up in our tiny office at the NUJ, but it was worth it when she finished; we were much more organized and could now mailshot all our supporters even if it did mean several sessions of stuffing thousands of wretched envelopes during meetings and at weekends.

The number of those supporters had grown steadily, increasing with each splash of publicity, but after Brian's release we became a cause that more people were prepared to rally round. Many got involved in the events organized by our major supporters across the country. Cathy and other campaign organizers co-ordinated them all, spending hours on the phone taking down orders for merchandise to be sold at various market stalls, exhibitions and concerts. They also advised them on how best to interest the local media, encouraging their attempts to make the Friends a nationwide campaign. I was touched to find that many of them were students; I'm sure I wouldn't have responded in such a generous way when I was at university and it gave me hope for the future that people so young could find room in their hearts to care about John.

A group of students at Hull had been supporting the campaign for some time, and recently they and other students around the country had really gone to town, running articles about John in university newspapers, holding parties to raise money, collecting signatures for our rolling petition. The Hull University Friends of John McCarthy were quite brilliant. They even got the Students' Union to rename their bar The John McCarthy Bar. Pat and Chris attended the grand opening, Chris telling the students that he and John had closed many a bar in their time but he had never opened one before.

Brian's release seemed to have lifted a barrier preventing us from developing into a mainstream campaign. As we became more acceptable, some companies and organizations felt able to support us. Camden Council had recently discovered that John lived within the borough and had given the go-ahead for a special neon display to be mounted on the council offices on Euston Road. It was Richard Steenhuis's idea, and it had taken a lot of pushing by him, but it was worth it. The number of days of John's captivity was now publicly marked on a huge building in a busy London road.

Even the BBC took up the cause; a month after Brian's release Simon Mayo lobbied his bosses at Radio One, convincing them that it would be a good idea to broadcast monthly updates about the hostage situation on his breakfast show. From September his lively producer, Rick, would telephone me on the first Monday of every month just before a quarter to nine. I would read out the number of days all the British hostages had been held and talk to Simon about the latest activities of the campaign, which again brought more letters into the FOJM office. Monday was my day off and one morning I overslept. I awoke to find three increasingly hysterical messages from Rick on my answering machine asking where I was. I could have died with embarrassment when my friend Jo told me she'd heard Simon Mayo on her car radio, saying: 'Jill, where are you? Get up and come to the phone, we can't talk to your answering machine, get up!' That kind of exposure was an enormous boost for the campaign and three months later, at the end of 1990, I came third in Radio One's Person of the Year poll. Fame at last! The Friends even seemed to be entering popular culture; a couple of bands recorded songs about the hostages, the Jonathan Ross Show invited me on to the programme and showed the BBH advert. One night, I was watching *Drop the Dead Donkey* and was amazed to see a Friends of John McCarthy poster on one of the walls of the news-room set.

Underpinning all this was the BBH advertising that we now took for granted. When I discovered that by the end of 1990 BBH's latest poster, WANTED, had received £70,000 worth of advertising space in the press, and £10,000 worth on poster sites around London I appreciated the scale of their support. The latest cinema advert, the one in which Paul Young sang 'Homeward Bound', had been shown on £600,000 worth of air time on cable and satellite television, and in cinemas around the country during May, June, September, October and November. Friends who had been in one of those cinemas, chattering through the usual sequence of adverts for Wrangler jeans, Pepsi and the local Indian restaurant, told me that when the BBH advert came on the entire cinema had fallen absolutely silent.

By the end of the year, despite the campaign's renewed lease of life, the prospects for John's release seemed, once again, to have faded away to nothing. War in the Gulf was looking increasingly likely. It was said that the number of casualties would be enormous; that there would be a bloodbath; that the repercussions in the Middle East were unimaginable. It seemed vital that we step up our political lobbying and we wrote to John Major, requesting a meeting. We didn't imagine he would see us, particularly given the impending conflict, but we thought that it was worth a try. It was impossible to know how much pressure the Government was under on the hostage issue or how many letters per day arrived on the desks of John Major, Douglas Hurd and Members of Parliament. We hoped that they were receiving thousands of letters and the FOJM postcards that for years we had shipped out to all our supporters. Our postcards were direct in their approach and read: 'John McCarthy is not forgotten. What are *you* doing to bring him home?'

We had become much more efficient in our lobbying of politicians; in the early days our political lobbying had taken the form of one-off meetings with sympathetic Labour politicians arranged by journalists like Phil Woolas, but for the past year our political activity had been in the hands of Leighton Andrews, the director of Salingbury Casey, a company of professional political lobbyists. Leighton had walked over to our stand at the Labour Party Conference in Brighton back in October 1989, when the campaign was still at a low ebb, and offered his expertise. Shortly after that we had met him at his offices in Victoria and I had left feeling relieved that, at last, we had someone who was willing to push our case inside Parliament. Our lack of organization on that front and our inability to get at the Government from inside the House had been bothering me for a long time. In the post-Rushdie depression of 1989 I had felt that our campaign was too superficial and lacked any real power to change things. 'What's the point of all those stunts if we're not getting at the MPs as well?' I'd moaned to Mary. She agreed that we had to be targeting all the MPs with marginal constituencies, together with the general public and the press, but I knew that the campaign office was already under too much pressure and could hardly be expected to take on that kind of work as well.

There was so much ground to make up; support for our campaign amongst MPs was virtually non-existent. I hadn't forgotten the reaction of John's own MP, Frank Dobson, who, back in 1986, had declined to get involved. The situation had hardly improved in 1989. We were able to count on one hand the number of MPs who had actively helped us: the Conservative Robert Hughes, an ex-BBC picture editor who had worked in Beirut; fellow Conservative Peter Temple-Morris, who had chaired one of our fringe meetings and was on the Parliamentary delegation to Iran; Charles Kennedy, the SDP Member who had been on *Wogan* at the same time as me in 1988 and offered his help, and Labour's George Foulkes and George Robertson, who were straightforwardly sympathetic. The issue had been raised occasionally in Parliament before Leighton's involvement, but once he brought his professional expertise to bear, lobbying for the Friends on an organized basis, things really took off.

At the end of 1989, with the help of George Foulkes, 150 signatures were gathered for an Early Day Motion (EDM) which ended '. . . those who enjoy freedom must use it to enable others to regain theirs'. By the end of 1990 Leighton had succeeded in getting twenty-nine questions raised in the House of Commons on the hostage issue and in persuading MPs to raise it in forthcoming debates and adjournments. The blandness of the EDMs frustrated me, but they had to be that way to ensure maximum support; at least the issue was being raised where it really mattered. Leighton and George Foulkes worked on an idea for forming a Parliamentary Friends of John McCarthy and eventually the small group of MPs who already supported us formed the cumbersome-sounding All-Party Parliamentary Group for the Release of Hostages, with the Archbishop of Canterbury as Patron, Temple-Morris, Foulkes and the Liberal Democrat Sir David Steel as the co-Chairs, and Hughes, Patrick Cormack, Tim Devlin and Sir Russell Johnston as Secretary, Vice-Chairs and Treasurer. The group's title was sufficiently general to allow it to encompass hostages of any kind, but our first meeting, in March 1990, had not been a resounding success. Only five MPs turned up and three of them were the chairmen. We soon learned that MPs became more enthusiastic when we asked all our supporters to lobby their members before the Parliamentary Group met, but the turning-point was Brian's release in August. He agreed to come over to address a meeting of the group shortly after his release prompting the biggest turn-out ever, about twenty MPs. Some of them were quite aggressive, but Brian, who was well-prepared, stayed calm.

From there, we went on to a disappointing meeting with Neil Kinnock. He hadn't been briefed properly and couldn't respond in any depth to Brian's argument that more effort should be made with the Syrians. I was upset and Brian, who'd met the Foreign Office Minister, William Waldegrave, earlier in the day, remarked on how depressing it was that the most encouraging meeting he'd had was with a representative of the Government who'd neglected the hostages for so long. 'Anyway,' he said, 'don't worry, it doesn't matter, none of them matter.'

Early in the New Year, 1991, the air war with Iraq began and I was convinced that while the fighting continued, the hostages would not be released. Ironically, the seventeen members of Islamic Jihad imprisoned in Kuwait had escaped within hours of the Iraqi invasion the previous August, so they were no longer a stumbling-block in any negotiations. However, no-one knew how long the war would last, what the outcome would be, how the Allies would behave after it was over, or whether Iran would remain neutral. I tried not to think of the last Gulf war, between Iran and Iraq, which had lasted eight years, cost millions of lives, and ended in stalemate. Regardless of all the talk of Allied military superiority and air supremacy, I thought it would be a long time before it was over.

Despite the war, or perhaps because of it, there had been progress on the diplomatic front. Relations had been restored with Syria immediately after Mrs Thatcher's resignation, which meant that we were soon able to write to the Syrian Ambassador, Mohammed al-Kouear, in London and request a meeting with him. For the first time in nearly two years we were able to do the same with the new Iranian representative, Sayed Shamseddin Khareghani. We had no idea how long it was going to take for negotiations with both countries to get underway, but at least Britain could not now maintain that talking to them was impossible. In early February the Iranian chargé granted Chris and me a meeting, but the gist of what he said didn't seem very different from his predecessor two years before. The two officials present told us that our Government had not made the right moves and my heart sank when they mentioned the case of the Iranian hostages in Lebanon. Long ago we had recognized this as a stalling tactic. 'If they're still trotting out this old line, what's changed?' I thought. Then one of the officials said: 'Of course, there is the question of the case of Kokabi, who is in prison here. He is like a hostage in Britain. His case is of great concern to the people of Iran.' This was the first time we had heard them mention Kokabi. He was an Iranian student who had been charged with a bungled bomb attempt on a bookshop during the row over *The Satanic Verses*, although the case had yet to come to trial. We went away fairly discouraged, wondering why Kokabi was so important to the Iranians. Was he going to represent yet another obstacle?

At the FO, Andrew Green confirmed that Kokabi was

just that. We gathered that he had been raised in a meeting between the new Foreign Office Minister, Douglas Hogg, and the Iranian chargé, Khareghani.

'Are you still saying that there'll be no exchange of ambassadors until the hostages are released?' asked Chris. We continued to worry that, given the pressures of the Gulf War, Britain would rush to upgrade diplomatic relations with Iran without ensuring the release of the hostages.

'Yes, absolutely,' said Andrew, with conviction. 'To do otherwise would, in my opinion, be immoral.'

Andrew seemed very cheerful. In fact, he and another official, Peter West, were all smiles. They introduced us to Hilary Synnott, who was to replace Andrew when he moved to his next job as Britain's new ambassador to Damascus in a few weeks' time. Hilary also seemed very affable, and we wondered what on earth had got into them. They said they thought that things might be going well, but that was all. There was nothing else to report, but the atmosphere in the room was so positive it was unnerving.

'That was almost . . . upbeat, wasn't it?' said Chris afterwards, as we headed for the pub. He looked puzzled. The FO, upbeat? It didn't make sense.

'What do you think that was all about, then?' I asked. 'Beats me.'

We shrugged our shoulders and stared doubtfully at our drinks. Where was the familiar, gloomy despondency that usually descended on us after meetings at the FO? The optimism, encouragement and cheerfulness we'd just encountered was infectious. I felt positive without really knowing why.

The Friends were now so busy that we needed to advertise for a full-time campaign organizer to run the office with Cathy. Over the past year and a half various members of the committee had done the job, along with a team of volunteers. But since 1989 I'd wanted someone full-time to develop the campaign and Cathy was far too busy keeping the office going and liaising with all our supporters. Recruiting the right person was very difficult. I needed someone whom I could trust and I was particularly wary following a disastrous but short-lived appointment the previous year. This time, as Chris, Cathy, Sharon Webber and I interviewed a succession of candidates in WTN's boardroom over several Saturdays in late January, we wanted to get it right. Sharon was the only one with any interviewing experience, so after a briefing from her we drafted a list of questions, but it still felt peculiar being a prospective employer rather than a nervous interviewee. One person impressed us all. Karen Talbot had been working for the Anti-Apartheid movement for several years and was looking for a change and a new challenge, especially now that Nelson Mandela had been freed. We asked her to take the job, and she agreed to start in late April, just after John began his sixth year in captivity.

Her appointment took a weight off my mind, as I had recently changed jobs. I was moved from a weekly programme I produced on my own to the news desk of *Channel 4 Daily*, the channel's breakfast programme. I wanted to do well. I was learning a lot and enjoyed being part of a team which was friendly and didn't take itself too seriously. The new job took up a lot of energy and concentration, taking my mind off the campaign.

Soon after Karen's appointment, our request for a meeting with John Major was finally, and surprisingly, granted. I went to my boss, Rachel Atwell, to ask for a few hours off.

'My, my, so he's agreed to see you, has he?' she said, looking surprised. 'Hmm. Good stuff. That's great news. Things must be moving.'

'Do you think so?' I said. 'It's probably just more PR.' I thought that he was probably agreeing to see us only so that he could appear more caring than Mrs Thatcher had been about the issue without actually having to do anything about it. Perhaps I was being too cynical. Rachel gladly gave me the time off and I talked to my colleagues about whether or not they would cover the meeting for *Channel 4*

Daily. We were short-staffed and there were the usual jokes about whether I would have to leap from one side of the camera to the other and interview myself.

On 27 February, Chris, Cathy and Jane Parritt, another member of the Friends and one of its temporary organizers, all gathered at the end of Downing Street and decided who should say what during the meeting with Major. As we stood on the doorstep of Number Ten, I felt nervous, but pleased that at last we were organized sufficiently to attempt a meeting like this. We'd delivered petitions to this door over the years, but it had always been closed too quickly to afford a glimpse inside. This time we were going in! Charles Powell, who'd advised Mrs Thatcher on foreign affairs, and was staying on for the new PM, met us just inside the door and showed us down a surprisingly long corridor to the back of the house, which was so much bigger than I expected. We had also assumed that we would be outnumbered by aides and press officers, as happened in meetings with Foreign Office Ministers, but when we were shown into Major's office, he was alone, sitting in a wing-backed chair. Charles Powell joined the meeting, but hardly spoke.

Mr Major was so nice it was disarming. He had a glass of milk while we all had coffee and told us how much he cared about the issue and how committed he was to resolving it. Chris asked if the Prime Minister would confirm that full diplomatic relations with Iran would not be resumed until the hostages were released.

'That is our position, yes, although we can't, of course, guarantee that it might not change should circumstances alter.'

It wasn't the kind of assurance we'd been hoping for and as we left I felt very tired. 'What was the point of that?' I wondered as I went back to work.

With the Gulf War still raging, I felt pessimistic about the chances of John's fifth anniversary in April receiving anything but a small amount of publicity. The prospect

499

of another anniversary was, as ever, both depressing and a target to work towards. This was the fourth time we'd tried to crank ourselves up to produce newsworthy events to mark the day. Each year it was more and more difficult to find the energy, and we were all similarly despondent. I looked pityingly on the strangers who had joined our meeting over the past months and who'd become regulars themselves. 'They don't know the half of it, that's why they're so enthusiastic,' I said to Chris gloomily after one meeting. However, I couldn't deny that it was encouraging to have new faces around the table and we all felt the benefit of a bit of 'new blood', as Barbara put it.

Week after week we faced the usual problem of how to mark the anniversary. This year BBH had used Brian's release to great effect. Their new cinema advert showed pictures of John, accompanied by Brian's voice, talking, at his press conference the previous August, about 'John-boy'. The same theme was behind the latest poster, which used more of Brian's words – 'John McCarthy's a great giver; it's about time others started giving to John McCarthy'. It was apparent how much Brian's love for John was still inspiring people; Paddy, Steff and the rest of their team at BBH had worked nights and weekends to pull it together. They were all good friends now, as well as a vital part of the campaign.

We were wondering what else we could do and I had my sights fixed on a rally, or a demonstration of some kind. I felt that we had to show the politicians how strong public opinion was, how everyone wanted the hostages home. Leighton Andrews and other campaign members were against the idea, saying a rally was old hat and didn't fit our image, which only made me even more determined. One of the committee teased me about it, but I could tell she was exasperated. 'The trouble with you, Jill, is that all you want to do is stand out in the street shouting, "Up the miners!" ' she said.

I had to admit there was an element of truth about her remark. I hated the idea that demonstrations were old-fashioned when they could be such a powerful way for ordinary people to make their voices heard. I knew we were living in a PR age and we had used that tactic time and time again, but it made me sad to think that marketing ploys were the only way of making a point. I also felt that however good our marketing, if that was all we had, then our campaign was superficial, lacking any real substance.

'If we can't show the Government that there's an awful lot of support for John on the anniversary of his fifth year in captivity, then we might as well pack up and go home.' Frustration was making me exaggerate, and I couldn't seem to find the words to explain my case. There were eleven of us at the meeting, and for the first time ever, Chris agreed that we should have a vote. The vote was 6–5.

An anti-rallier said: 'That's it, we've won!'

'No, hang on a minute, it's the other way round, isn't it?' said a pro-rallier. He turned out to be right, and on the basis of a narrow margin of one we decided to go ahead with a rally to mark the anniversary. Where, when, how and possibly why we were having it were decisions that we would leave for another, less fraught, occasion.

Cathy now had the nightmare task of pulling it together. We had never done anything like this before and weren't sure if anyone would even turn up. The thought that it might be a complete disaster made me go quite cold – it was firmly identified as my idea – but I felt quite do or die about it. We wrote to our supporters asking them to come to the rally but we couldn't afford to send out reminders. Our funds were running pretty low. The Inland Revenue hadn't yet decided whether we should pay tax. We were hoping that it would have mercy on us, but we daren't touch the money we'd put away to pay the bill should the worst come to the worst. We weren't in dire straits yet, but we'd had to make it clear to Karen Talbot that she would have to raise enough money to cover her own salary. Money was still arriving in the form of donations or merchandise sales, but we'd had no big fund-raising events for nearly a year, and the last hadn't been that successful.

We still had to think of other ways in which to mark John's fifth anniversary. It was such a huge landmark. How could we draw sufficient attention to the fact that he had now been held for half a decade? I wanted thousands of people to say to the Government, 'Enough is enough.' Someone had a vague idea about landing five hot-air balloons in Hyde Park, but we rejected that. Cathy and Jane wanted us to approach a PR company for help. Jane worked in PR and she'd really improved the presentation of the campaign, from the efficiently printed minutes she produced every week to coverage in various PR and trade magazines. She faced opposition from some people who didn't like the idea of giving up too much control to outsiders, and from me, currently on my high horse about the campaign using too many gimmicks.

I soon changed my mind when Cathy handed me a black folder from one company, Shillands, which had offered to organize the anniversary PR for us for free. Suddenly I forgot that I'd ever had any objections. Shillands had come up with several ideas but the one which really caught my imagination, as it had Cathy's, was called, 'Tie a Yellow Ribbon for John'. In the past we had steered away from the American-style Yellow Ribbon idea; it was too senti- mental. Not only that, I'd have been stuck firmly with the 'waiting woman' image if I'd gone around tying yellow rib- bons to trees every anniversary. Now that public concern for John was so widespread, however, it seemed like an idea that could involve everyone – if it worked. I liked it, but worried that it was too ambitious; Shillands proposed to put yellow ribbons everywhere and I doubted that they could do it. The idea of a major newspaper having a Yellow Ribbon Week for John was way out of our league.

As I leafed through the folder another idea caught my eye. If anything was going to bring home to people how long John had been held this was it – a radio or TV show depicting all the news events that he had missed since being kidnapped. Shillands had listed everything that had been such painful reminders over the years that the world was changing and that John wasn't here to share it. The wedding of the Duke and Duchess of York in July 1986; the sudden awareness in Britain of AIDS; the privatization of British Gas – 'If you see Sid, tell him'; the three big disasters of 1987 – Zeebrugge, Hungerford, King's Cross; the skier Eddie Edwards making the headlines with his failures in 1988; Paddy Ashdown taking over the SLD; Edwina Curry resigning over eggs; water privatization in 1989; the release of Nelson Mandela; the unification of Germany; the poll-tax demonstrations of 1990; Mad Cow Disease; Teenage Mutant Hero Turtles. The list seemed to represent a block of frozen time. I wished it would melt away so that John could come back to find everything just as it had been.

Plans for the rally and Yellow Ribbon Day were really taking shape. Cathy and Jane were working with Shillands and had news of developments to report every day. There was talk of London taxi-drivers wanting ten thousand yellow ribbons and major chains like Woolworth and The Body Shop agreeing to distribute them. I was going on *Wogan*; the *Late Show* wanted to feature the campaign; the *Sun* was interested in running Yellow Ribbon Week! The *Sun*! It was amazing.

The Gulf War had ended and I'd watched all the POWs coming home, wondering when it was ever going to be John's turn. There were rumours in the press from Beirut that some of the Western hostages were going to be released before Easter and that talks had resumed between Britain and other countries. The trial of the Iranian student Kokabi had been stopped on what seemed to be curious grounds. Defence witnesses were refused entry to the country and the judge ruled that the case should be discontinued and Kokabi deported. Even the Queen had been reported as expressing hope that the hostages would be released soon. I didn't know what was going on and sometimes I felt as if I never would. I couldn't stand the endless campaigning; occasionally I just wanted to go away, forget all about it and never come back.

Suddenly, just a few weeks before the anniversary, Roger Cooper was released from prison in Iran. I was back on the sofa at TV-AM, for what must have been the tenth or twelfth time in three years. There was a live link-up from Roger's home and on the screen he looked and sounded great, just as he had on his arrival back in London when he joked and chatted with the press as casually as if he'd just flown in from a long holiday. For five years the fate of Roger Cooper had been a barometer of the political climate in Iran. Initially, he'd simply been held without trial. Then, when the radicals got the upper hand, he'd been accused of spying and sentenced to 'death plus ten years'. It seemed that his release had been touch and go right up to the last minute. The obvious trigger had been the deportation of Kokabi back to a hero's welcome in Iran, but it must also have been the culmination of a series of smart moves by David Reddaway, the British chargé in Tehran.

I'd met Reddaway back in 1988 before he was sent out to Iran and had liked him a lot. He was like a breath of fresh air – he answered a straight question with a straight answer, which caused the other officials a bit of discomfiture – and there was no hint of the stuffed shirt about him. He was young, experienced and interested in the Iranians; I'd been encouraged by his willingness to look for communication and understanding with Tehran. I was glad that there would be somebody like him pushing John's case there and inside Whitehall, which sometimes seemed like it needed just as much of a shove in the right direction. When he arrived back from Iran the first time he dropped into a meeting to tell me how his trip had gone and then spent the rest of the evening with us in the pub. The Rushdie affair had put paid to what he had hoped to do, but I was glad when I heard that he was going back to Iran, and took it as a hopeful sign that we were getting somewhere. Roger Cooper's release confirmed that things were obviously going well. The question now was how far down the road were the British and the Iranians in their negotiations? Had they just started? How long would they take and what could go wrong?

Roger's return home had a similar effect to Brian's the year before. It brought the issue of the hostages to the fore again, throughout the country and in Parliament. A meeting of the All-Party Parliamentary Group a few days after his release was the best attended ever – thirty MPs showed up – and for once our campaign seemed to be a good thing to support. The All-Party Group had been to see Douglas Hurd and had plans to do so again. They were also considering seeing the Iranian chargé d'affaires, and wondering whether a Parliamentary delegation to Syria might not be a bad idea. The Shadow Foreign Secretary, Gerald Kaufman, talked about his visit to Syria the year before, just prior to Brian's release. He'd been astounded to discover that, for the past four years, the subject of the hostages had not been raised with the Syrians *at all*. 'Granted we didn't have diplomatic relations with the Syrians,' he told us, 'but in comparison with the British the Americans were constantly raising the issue with Damascus; there'd been a good deal of correspondence between President Bush, James Baker and President Assad that had, eventually, got through to the hostage-takers.'

Since Kaufman's visit to Damascus nine months ago so much had changed. Thatcher had gone, Britain had resumed diplomatic relations with Syria, and an opinion poll conducted in early April 1991 by BBH astounded us by showing that John's name was better known than those of the Chancellor of the Exchequer, Norman Lamont, the athlete, Linford Christie, or Chris Patten, the Conservative Party Chairman. When asked, 'Which of the following people have you heard of?' Some 91 per cent of people said that they had heard of John, with Lamont trailing behind at 82 per cent and Chris Patten at 79 per cent. The opinion poll also asked people to rank a list of issues in order of importance and the hostages came sixth, behind the Health Service, the Economy, Education and Unemployment, but ahead of Europe, Transport, Privatization and Sunday trading. John was a household name, the hostage issue was one of the most important things on people's minds, but was he any nearer freedom? We still had no idea.

The day after the poll results came in, branches of The Body Shop and Our Price began giving away yellow ribbons and the *Sun* claimed that 250,000 of its readers had received them. After all the long years trying to achieve this level of concern I was amazed at how quickly an idea could spread once the flame had been well and truly lit. The local organizer in Southampton, Belinda Cheeseman, distributed ribbons all round the area. When a local paper reported that she'd run out of funds, a man arrived on her doorstep, bearing a cheque for seventy-five pounds, and saying, 'This is for your campaign.' To see the *Sun* supporting the Friends as well was truly overwhelming and, for the time being, the campaign took on a life of its own.

While Shillands continued with their amazing job of promoting the anniversary, I went on *Wogan*, intending to advertise the rally. I wasn't as petrified as I had been two years earlier because I thought I knew what to expect, but it was still pretty nerve-racking. When Wogan asked me, 'How do you know John's still alive?' I was completely flummoxed. I'd never expected to have to answer that one again.

'Well, Brian Keenan was released last August and told us John was alive . . . there's not been any news since then, but—' I floundered.

The researcher had promised me there would be a question at the end about the anniversary so that I could talk about the rally, but before I knew where I was Wogan was saying, 'Thank you for coming on the show, and the best of luck with your campaign' and that was that. It was over and I hadn't mentioned the rally. I'd blown it. 'What a fool I am,' I thought, 'no-one's going to come, I'm going to look a right twit and Cathy and Jane will kill me.'

The rally took place on the afternoon of 13 April. My

mum and dad came down from Doncaster and Brian drove us down to Whitehall. We were late because I'd been nervously trying to finish my speech. On the way there, I felt grateful that it was such a lovely sunny day; at least the weather was on our side. We were due to march from the Foreign Office and then progress to Trafalgar Square. Brian dropped us off and we walked down King Charles Street to the steps at the other end where everyone was due to meet. It was difficult to see how many people were there, but when I got nearer I could see a medium-sized crowd. Not being very tall, it was hard for me to assess its size. I got swallowed up into it straightaway, turning every which way to have a quick chat to friends or say hallo to people I didn't know, who just came up and introduced themselves. There were yellow ribbons everywhere, fastened to lapels, tied up in hair, wound around necks and fluttering from babies' pushchairs.

For the millionth time in the three years since we had started the campaign I felt that I could relax in the knowledge that Cathy had organized everything, and that nothing had been overlooked. I felt as proud as if I'd arranged it myself and reassured by the fact that everywhere I looked I could see everyone I had ever met in the course of the campaign: Canon Oates, Paddy, Steff, John Hegarty, Jon Snow, Jean, a Frenchman who had never met John but had been involved right from the start, John's cousin Justin . . . There were also lots of people I didn't know, I realized, ordinary people whom Cathy was busily greeting as if they were old friends. 'Oh, hallo Emma, where's your mum?' 'Oh hi, Ann, did you get that letter I sent you?' She'd organized the police, the PA system, the speakers, the ribbons, the balloons, the marchers and the route, and she was still managing to do what she liked best, which was to talk to people.

As I looked around and saw that the crowd was, indeed, large enough to be noticed, I relaxed and my spirits lifted still further when I saw Roger Cooper, who had agreed to speak at the rally, and Brian Keenan's sisters, Brenda and

Elaine. It was like a huge reunion and seeing everyone, who had chosen to be there for John, really buoyed me up. More and more people arrived and I began almost to enjoy myself – or at least I would have done if I hadn't had to make another speech. Cathy came up and said that we were ready for off and I followed her to the other side of the crowd, towards the huge banner that read: 'Five long years: Why aren't they free?' I saw Brian Keenan walking along towards me with Terence and Pat; they'd stayed in the pub over the road until the last minute, which had sent us all frantic. Brian came over and gave me a hug, and then we set off, Brian, Roger and myself each carrying a box of petitions decked in yellow ribbons that we were to deliver to Downing Street along the route. After we'd been walking for a few minutes I risked a look behind me.

The crowd stretched down Whitehall, down King Charles Street and out of sight. I couldn't believe it. I couldn't believe that so many people were doing this, many who'd come from miles away, to show their support. It gave me the same huge lift as at the Camden Palace three years ago, but this time there was no Harry Enfield to attract the crowds, no evening's entertainment to pull them in, just a powerful, shared feeling that this was important. When we reached Trafalgar Square it seemed we almost filled it. Roger, Brian and I climbed up on to the raised concrete plinth around Nelson's Column from where the speeches were to be made, and milled around until the rest of the crowd had reached the square. Chris went over to the microphones to make the introductions and made a brilliant job of it. I got a huge round of applause, but I'd realized too late that I wasn't used to addressing a crowd of loyal supporters and my speech was all wrong. I was trying to convince them that the hostages mattered, but they already knew that. It was why they had come; they didn't need converting. The next speakers were better – ITN's Jon Snow and the BBC's Philip Hayton, then Anita Roddick, founder of The Body Shop, and then Sir Edward Heath, who had said at the last minute not only that he would come along, but that he would speak as well. Having a former prime minister there was a great *coup*, particularly since his visit to the Gulf to see Saddam Hussein and attempt to negotiate the release of the 'guestages'. It made me feel that if someone of his stature was prepared to support our campaign, then we really must be getting somewhere. The last speaker was Brian Keenan. As he strode to the microphone the crowd went wild. Here was John's biggest ally; his presence was worth more than anything. He ended his speech by holding up the fingers of his right hand one by one, saying: 'Five words for five years: bring these men home now.'

The rally ended with the release of hundreds of yellow balloons. Everyone poured out of the square, yelling and waving goodbye as if we'd all been to a great party. Lots of people headed straight for Brian and me. Inevitably, we got separated, and I began to feel a bit alarmed; people were pressing in, asking for autographs, handshakes and interviews or simply wanting to say hallo. Many of the supporters I had never met came over and one, Ann Mettam, thrust a huge yellow parcel in my hands.

'Jill, this is from the children at the school where I teach. I promised them I would give it to you today and they'd never forgive me if I didn't.'

I opened the parcel and there was a book of drawings and poems, *An Alphabet for John McCarthy*, depicting everything the children thought John was missing. On the first page was a message:

To John,
   We do not know how long it will be before you are able to read this.
   This book was made with our thoughts of some of the things you might have missed most, with our love, and most of all, hope.

I leafed through it, marvelling at the thought and imagination that had gone into it. I posed for a photograph with the book and Jon Snow came over to see what was going on. 'This is incredible,' he said, taking the book from me, 'look at it. We ought to do a story on this on *Channel 4 News* for the anniversary, don't you think?'

Ann was delighted and soon she and Jon were deep in arrangements. A few days later a five-minute item appeared about the children who had put the book together, featuring Camilla Cooper, the little girl who had insisted her class do something for John, and Timothy Archer, a five-year-old born on the day John was kidnapped. Timothy had a cheeky looking face and couldn't keep still.

'What did you do for this book?'

'Well . . . I helped.'

'What did you do?'

'I drew a picture.'

'What was your picture of?'

'A flower.'

'Do you know who John McCarthy is?'

A proud nod from Timothy, and a casual swing of the leg. 'Yeah. I was born on the day he was took,' adding as an afterthought, 'to prison.'

The day of the anniversary itself was just as successful as the rally, with taxi-drivers all over London sporting yellow ribbons from the roofs of their cabs and many other drivers throughout the country doing the same. BBH launched their new cinema advertisement, *Picture of John*, with Brian Keenan's moving words over still photographs of John. It ended with the caption, 'Brian Keenan's portrait of John McCarthy is the only picture of him in five years' and was duly banned by the IBA which then suffered a scalding reprimand in the *Sun*'s editorial. 'They don't need to wear yellow ribbons, they've already got yellow streaks down their backs.' Despite this astonishing vote of support, post-anniversary depression set in as usual. We hit a new low when John Lyttle died on 27 April. I hadn't realized that the man who'd done so much for the hostages from his small office at Lambeth Palace was so ill. Pat told me he'd been very weak for quite a while; he had liked Lyttle enormously and his death had left him very subdued. Even though I hadn't known him well, I, too, felt sad; he seemed to be firmly on the side of the good guys. I couldn't imagine another person taking his place.

At the end of the month, Karen Talbot took up her post of campaign organizer and it was a great relief to hand over some of the responsibility. It must have been a strange organization to step into. When Karen arrived she had no desk. The campaign office was still tiny, with just enough room for Cathy, boxes of merchandise, piles of files and a small army of volunteers. We had developed an eccentric way of working – no specifically defined areas of responsibility and precious little structure. Our finances were looked after by my friend Jo Sheehan and an accountant friend of hers who did all our books. We relied on mutual trust and personal motivation to keep us going, yet we were blessed with a top advertising agency, a political lobbyist and a PR company. It was a strange mixture, but Karen took everything on board very quickly and it didn't take me long to realize I could trust her. She was exactly what I felt we needed; experienced in campaigning, political lobbying, committed to the cause and the type of person who refused to let anything drop. She settled in very quickly and somehow we managed to look towards the summer. Someone had a good idea about planting a wood dedicated to John and the other hostages, and we thought that we might commission another opinion poll, then force ourselves to think about the party conferences in October once again.

In May there were several far-off rumblings about the release of Israeli soldiers in Lebanon in exchange for Shi'ite prisoners in Israeli-controlled gaols. The Israelis had said that they would be willing to trade their prisoners for the captured Israelis and Western hostages, but the idea of such a deal had cropped up regularly in the past and seemed too ambitious to have any hope of ever being concluded. Lynda Chalker, the Minister for Overseas

Development, went to Iran, the first minister to do so in thirteen years. Karen wrote to her on my behalf and she wrote back, saying that although her visit had been mainly concerned with the plight of Iraqi refugees, she had discussed the hostages. 'As Douglas Hogg made clear in the House of Commons on 24 April, there is no more important issue in our relations with Iran . . . We are determined to secure John's release, and that of Terry Waite and Jack Mann.' It sounded wonderful, but by then we were all very sceptical. Shortly afterwards, the new Foreign Office Minister, Douglas Hogg, announced he was to visit Lebanon to speed up the release of the British hostages. Cathy was quoted in the paper as saying his trip was a whitewash, which accurately reflected how most of us felt about its potential effectiveness.

One Sunday morning I went down to the flower market at Columbia Road looking for a plant for the flat. I spotted a huge parlour palm and asked the stall holder how much it cost.

'Twelve pounds,' he said.

I was writing out a cheque when he said: 'I know you, don't I? You're that John McCarthy's . . . aren't you?'

'That's right.'

'Have it for nothing and put the money towards the campaign.'

I was very touched and thanked him, assuring him that I would.

'You can give it to him when he gets back.'

There were more reports about prisoner swaps with the Israelis, but one morning I woke up to a series of messages on my answering machine. When I played them back I heard the sound of a baby crying; Mary had just given birth to her daughter, Anna. Mary was the first of my close friends to have a child. As I marvelled at Anna's perfect little fingers and bright eyes, I wondered when I was going to reach that stage in my life. It was yet another marker of how much time was passing. When John was kidnapped, Mary had just finished Bar School; now she'd been a practising barrister for five years, had settled down into a steady relationship and had just become a mother. The changes had been so subtle, I had hardly noticed them; but we had all grown up.

In May I met the Queen twice. Both meetings were engineered for me – the first by ITN when she visited our new headquarters and the second, by Doncaster Council, who included me in a civic reception at the Mansion House. Neither occasion was particularly noteworthy, but in Doncaster, the local paper had heralded the event on the front page: 'Campaigner to meet Queen'. After the reception I spent an uncomfortable fifteen minutes being grilled by the press about what had happened, but the Queen had said absolutely nothing when we were introduced.

'Did the Queen express any sympathy towards the hostages?' said one reporter.

'Oh, I'm sure she's sympathetic,' I replied. 'Who wouldn't be?'

By June, the post-anniversary blues were still affecting the Friends. It was hard to find the enthusiasm to attend yet another weekly meeting, but, ironically, help and support from outside seemed to be increasing. The *Daily Mirror* was planning to run a yellow-ribbon promotion; the producer of a West End show, *A Tribute to the Blues Brothers*, had offered us a Benefit gala night in August; and the Conservatives had finally granted us permission to attend their party conference in October. After years of being banned, they offered us a discount on our stand. This was all very encouraging, but the old, regular members of the committee were tired. Meetings seemed to be kept going by relatively new faces, people who didn't know John and had become involved in the campaign only fairly recently. One night I walked into a meeting and was momentarily disconcerted to see that there was no-one there I knew very well.

We were now working towards the next milestone,

John's two thousandth day, in October. Chris, Karen and I had several meetings about the possibility of organizing a trip to Iran and Lebanon. It was only an idea, but I felt that there seemed to be nothing else left to try. We were beginning to work out how much it would cost and wondered if we could get a newspaper or television station to fund part of it. I was reluctant to ask for more time off work; although my boss was sympathetic, I was worried about being made redundant. There were rumours that over a hundred jobs at ITN were to be lost and the future of *Channel 4 Daily* itself was looking uncertain. Like everyone else, I was preoccupied by the prospect of being jobless in a few months' time, and was scouring the newspapers for alternative employment.

Later that month, I was surprised to hear John Major make a statement in the House of Commons to the effect that the detention of the British hostages in Lebanon was linked to the release of Lebanese prisoners held in Israeli gaols. It gave credence to reports of a general prisoner exchange, but by now I had learned to wait and see what such statements actually produced; it still seemed too ambitious a project. Chris, Cathy, Jane Parritt and I had been to see Douglas Hogg on his return from Lebanon and he had given us the impression that something was going on involving an 'outside agency' which we took to mean the UN. He was quite cloak-and-dagger about it and we left feeling a little puzzled. We'd been told in the past that Britain had put resolutions before the UN on the hostage issue and they had produced nothing. This time, there seemed to be more to it than that, but we had no idea what; Hogg seemed to think that he'd said too much already. In early July, he announced to the EC that Britain was now in full support of lifting the arms embargo against Syria.

In late July the G7 summit meant that work became really hectic. I noted that the member countries had passed a worthy-sounding resolution on hostage-taking, but didn't think it would change anything. I'd got some holiday booked in early August and planned to get away. Before that, I wanted to go to the Benefit night of *A Tribute to the Blues Brothers* on 8 August. *The Blues Brothers* had been a favourite film of John's and mine; it had the makings of a good night.

On 5 August, I was sitting at my desk at work when Karen rang.

'Are you sitting down?' she said, quietly.

'What? Tell me,' I said, abruptly.

'Mark Canning's just rung from the Foreign Office. They're saying that there's a fifty-fifty chance that a British hostage is going to be freed in the next few days.'

My mind went blank.

'Are you all right?' she asked.

'I don't know.'

'Do you want to take that in and give me a call back?'

I put the phone down and asked my colleague, Mark, if he would cover me for a while. Then I went and sat in the smoking area. All I could hear was Karen's voice saying, 'There's a fifty-fifty chance that a British hostage is going to be freed.' I repeated the words to myself a few times, but it didn't help. They weren't making any sense. A colleague stopped as he walked by.

'Are you all right, Jill? Have you had some bad news?'

For the rest of the day I went through the motions at work. I couldn't risk telling any of my colleagues at ITN what had happened because any public speculation might have jeopardized whatever was going on in Beirut. The Foreign Office thought it was likely that Jackie Mann would be the Briton released because he was the oldest, and that seemed to make sense. By the time I met Chris and Karen after work to discuss what we were going to do I was convinced that nothing would happen.

'It'll probably turn out to be a hoax,' I said, 'there were months of rumours before Brian Keenan was actually released.'

Thinking like this helped me stay calm. I was of no use to Chris and Karen, who were making tentative plans involving mobile phones, press statements and other logistical details.

When I woke up the next morning I knew there was no way I could go into work and get through the day. I couldn't face the speculation, nor the usual round of interviews. Islamic Jihad issued a statement saying they were going to release a hostage who would be their envoy to the United Nations. With it, they released a new picture of the American, Terry Anderson, and the media assumed that he would be the one to go free. The phone rang; it was Chris.

'I've just spoken to Mark Canning; he says they're seventy per cent certain there's going to be a release, but now they think it's going to be John.'

I breathed in sharply.

'Are you OK?'

'Fine,' I said impatiently.

'The Iranian News Agency is saying that a Briton and an American are going to be released. Islamic Jihad have released another photo of Anderson; there are rumours that he's going to be the UN envoy the kidnappers have talked about.'

'What do you think?' My voice was tense and brisk.

'I dunno. It's weird—'

'What are we going to do? What about the buses to Lyneham, we've got to get the buses organized so everyone can go—' The buses were a detail that had been bothering me for months. We couldn't book them in advance because we had no idea how many we wanted, when we wanted them, where exactly they would be going, or for how long we would need them. But we had to make sure everyone could get to wherever John was going to be landing so that they could see him get off the plane.

'Don't worry. Don't worry about anything. Leave it to us.'

Normally when anyone said, 'Don't worry' to me I did exactly the opposite. Now I let go and gave up. I didn't have any choice. When I put the phone down I still refused to believe that John would be freed.

I told Brian, my brother, about the rumours. He stared at me. 'Really? I mean, how likely is it that, that—?'

'I don't know,' I said, bursting into tears.

I called in sick and spent the day convincing myself that the FO were wrong; Jackie Mann would be the one to be released. I was too tense to go to the Friends' meeting that night. If a release was in the offing the one thing that could scupper it was speculation in the media. We had to make sure the news wouldn't leak at all, and that meant I couldn't tell anyone about the staggering information I'd just heard. I couldn't face seeing anybody. Chris and Karen slipped away from the meeting and came around later that evening. We talked about what preparations we needed to make, but I was still convincing myself it was all a false alarm.

The next morning, I suddenly decided that the one thing I had to do before anything else happened was to get a saucepan stand. Brian, who by now was used to this kind of manic behaviour, saw the look on my face and said, as amiably as he always did, 'OK, Jill, just give me half an hour and I'll run you into town.' A few hours later, we were back at the flat, unpacking the purchases; shopping for kitchen equipment had calmed me down. The one thing I knew I had to do, though, was to get out of the flat. I couldn't cope with being under siege from the media, not now, not when I couldn't think straight. Geraldine and Mary had both said that I could stay with them if I needed to escape, but after seeing what had happened to Brian's family on his release I didn't think it was fair to cause them such disruption. I decided to camp at Tony's and Barbara's place just around the corner for a few days. They were on holiday in Turkey and I didn't think they'd mind me using their flat. I packed only a small bag; I'd probably be back home again as soon as we heard that it was Jackie Mann who'd been released or when the rumours died away. Once at Barbara's, I felt foolish; I'd over-reacted by coming here; nothing was going to happen. I called Mary.

'Do you want me to come over?' she asked. 'Rob and I can bring Anna over and stay the night with you if you want.'

'Mary, that would be fantastic. Are you sure?'

'It's no problem. Anna won't mind, she likes going places.'

For the rest of the day, there was a lot of speculation that Terry Anderson was going to be freed, but no-one in the media had yet considered that it might be John. I heard from Chris that Pat, Terence and Roby had managed to fly out of the country without being noticed and were on their way to Cyprus. They would fly on to Damascus if confirmation came through that John had been released. In the evening, Chris and Karen came over, armed with mobile telephones for each of us so that we could stay in contact all the time. We'd decided not to do any interviews with the press because it would add to the speculation, but the pressure suddenly became very intense. ITN had spoken to Sunnie Mann and she said that she'd been told by the British Embassy in Lebanon that Jackie wasn't coming out, it was going to be John. *News at Ten* began with the words: 'John McCarthy and Terry Anderson to be freed tomorrow'. We all put our heads in our hands and prayed that the speculation wouldn't destroy everything.

I didn't sleep much that night, and the following morning awoke feeling disoriented and nervous. I felt better after seeing Anna; it was soothing just holding her or watching her, and knowing that she, at least, had other priorities. Rob fetched some bacon sandwiches from a café and I made a cup of tea. It never occurred to me to switch on the television or radio to hear the news. For some reason, we were all convinced that nothing would happen until after midday. At ten o'clock, as we were tucking in, the telephone rang and I picked it up. It was Karen.

'Have you heard?' she said, triumphantly. 'He's out! He's on his way to Damascus now!'

I looked at Mary in amazement; a look of sheer delight shot across her face and she grabbed Rob's camera and began taking photographs of me holding the telephone. I started to laugh. It was only later that we discovered there was no film in the camera. Neither of us could speak coherently. 'Oh my God,' we kept saying. 'Oh my God.'

I wanted to speak to everyone all at once, to tell them the news. I put the phone down and dialled my mum and dad; Jean, my dad's cousin, answered the phone. I wondered vaguely what she was doing there and asked to speak to my mum.

'She's doing an interview right now, love,' she said. 'Brilliant news, isn't it? I'm so pleased for you, love. Shall you call back in a minute?'

'How did you know?' I asked, feeling slightly deflated.

'It was on the ten o'clock news. We had reporters here as soon as it was confirmed, they wanted your mum and dad to say a few words. It's like Piccadilly Circus here.'

I put the phone down and it rang immediately; it was Brian, back at my own flat. He'd woken to the sound of the telephone and doorbell ringing, windows being banged, and the letter-box being rattled – the press, in force.

'What's going on, Jill?' he asked.

'He's out, Bri, he's out!'

'What, really? Oh my God!'

I told Brian to come round as soon as he could but to make sure he wasn't being followed; I wanted to share the day with him, too.

Everything happened so fast. I was ecstatic. I felt as if I were floating miles up in the sky. In rapid succession came euphoria, then relief, then a blurry image of John sitting in a car somewhere between Beirut and Damascus; next anticipation and expectation; then nervousness and terror; and then back to pure bliss again. I phoned Chris at work, but he was under so much pressure that he hardly had time to speak; calls from the media were already flooding in. On top of that, he was worried that, although the kidnappers had put out a statement saying they had released John, the FO were saying they weren't sure. They'd had no confirmation from the Syrians that

John had been handed over. He was trying to damp down all the hysteria but, like King Canute before him, he didn't stand a chance. We agreed that we'd have to hold a press conference and arranged to meet there.

I washed my hair and Mary dried it, trying to get it in some sort of shape. 'Thank God I've just had it cut,' I said. Karen had organized a press conference in the space of an hour, and while we made our way there, with Mary, Brian, Rob and Anna following in a second taxi, she filled me in on what was happening. Pat and Terence were in Damascus; Cathy would hold the fort at the office, with Sue Barnard and another volunteer; Gina and Mary Lambe were arranging the buses to take everyone to Lyneham. Just down the road from the Russell Hotel we met up with Chris. I did a quick interview with ITN, and then the three of us walked, arm in arm, back to the hotel. I saw a crowd of photographers at the front entrance and just as a wave of panic hit me, a man stopped his car in the middle of the road, jumped out, ran across towards me, gave me a hug and ran off again. It happened so quickly I didn't have time to respond. His gesture was one of pure, spontaneous joy and it captured the moment perfectly. 'It's going to be all right,' I thought.

As we neared the hotel, the press scrum was enormous. Karen's grip on my arm tightened and Chris led the way through the chaos of cameras, microphones, lights and hundreds of people. Suddenly, Nick was coming towards me and we gave each other a hug. I hadn't seen him for ages and didn't know he would be there, but he was the perfect person to see. We bundled up to the room where the press conference was to be held, and all the Friends were somehow, miraculously, there. Everyone had heard the news, walked out of their jobs and headed for the Russell Hotel. We all gathered at the front of the ballroom, while a mass of snappers took photographs. I dimly noticed that the press were getting out of hand, that Chris was speaking, and that they were calming down. Later, when I watched a video of the whole day, I was astonished at Chris's composure.

'Look, some of you are probably going to speak to John McCarthy in the next few days and frankly it isn't going to happen if you don't behave yourselves.' He paused. 'Our joy is tempered by the knowledge that there are eleven other hostages and we feel for their family and friends as we know they are happy for us. Now I'll hand you over to Jill Morrell.' I heard people asking, 'How do you feel?' and, 'When are you going to see John?' and babbled some replies. I was on another plane altogether, trying to cope with the knowledge that, very soon, I was actually going to see John – see him, after five and a half years.

'Do you think you'll get back together?' said one reporter. His question was irrelevant.

'I don't know. It doesn't matter, it's not important—' was the only answer.

The rest of the day passed in a blur. I had no idea what the time was. I'd been holed up in a room at the Russell Hotel for about two hours, doing as many interviews as I could; I didn't feel, after all these years, that it was right to refuse anyone. Chris and I went round to ITN's headquarters, where, just before I was due to go on, we saw a photograph of John that the kidnappers had issued that day. It was the only picture of him they had ever released, and it was my first image of him in five years. It was chilling. John's eyes were lifeless and his face devoid of expression. It wasn't the John I knew, nor the John I'd been thinking about since Brian's release; it was a ghost. Instantly, the euphoria vanished. I carried on with the interviews, but the shock was lodged at the back of my mind; this wasn't a celebration any more. He looked so bad that I couldn't work it out. As far as we'd known, after Brian had been released John had spent the last year alone. Looking at the photograph, I feared he had lost his mind.

The euphoria returned when we all crowded into a tiny room at the Russell Hotel to watch the BBC news for the first television pictures of John; the presenter, Philip

Hayton, was grinning all over his face. I'd decided long before that this moment belonged to us; we wanted to share it among ourselves. No camera was going to film me watching John for the first time. John was making his statement to the press. 'Well, hallo,' he said, and those two words carried more of John than anything else he could have said. I couldn't believe how well he looked or how composed he seemed. He appeared exactly the same as when I last saw him. He was slightly tense, and looked nervous, but his statement was flawless. His voice sounded wonderful, slightly husky, but clear and strong, not the croaky whisper we'd heard from other hostages. He even seemed to have a tan. How on earth had he managed to turn up looking like that? It was absolutely, typically, unmistakably, John. Chris's voice was incredulous. 'For the last five years we've been trying to tell people he's been going through hell and he turns up looking like he's been on a health farm.' Someone else said, 'Frankly he looks a damn sight better than we do!' Everyone in the room cheered. We were all on the edge of hysteria, laughing, crying, hugging one another. It was wonderful, the only moment of the whole day that we had to ourselves. I glanced around at other people's faces to make sure that this was real, that it was John I was watching and that he was, finally, free.

John's release seemed to be one purely joyous moment that the whole country felt it could celebrate. Bells rang out in churches, announcements were made at the Oval cricket ground where everyone stood and cheered, and over the Tannoy at the London Underground. TV news bulletins were dominated by it, and extended their air time. Cars bearing yellow ribbons were tooting their horns at each other. The BBH building was wrapped in a huge yellow ribbon and the final poster, with the slogan: 'John McCarthy still counts', which had gone up only a few weeks before, was immediately amended. Now it read: 'John McCarthy is free. The other hostages still count.' At Broxted Church, the vicar, Jack Filby, served champagne at morning service. For months afterwards, people would tell me the story of where they were when they'd heard the news, as if it was a significant moment in their lives. After the last of the interviews was over, at about 7.30 p.m., Chris, Karen and I travelled down to RAF Lyneham in a chauffeur-driven hire car.

John was due to land tonight, at 9 p.m. I would be seeing him again in only a few hours; it was impossible to take in. Gifts of champagne and packs of Carlsberg lager (the brand John was holding in one of the campaign photographs of him) had been arriving at the office all day, and Karen had brought along a hamper of fruit and champagne sent to us by the *Wogan* programme. Chris opened the champagne; I'd had several glasses during the day, but the only thing intoxicating me was the adrenalin which was carrying me along. As we sped along the M4, I marvelled at what a perfect, perfect day it was. Everything had a clarity I hadn't seen for a long time. The trees, the sky, the sun; everything was bathed in a golden light. It looked beautiful.

My one regret was that I couldn't be everywhere, at once. In London, at the Whitehall Theatre, many of our friends were dancing in the aisles. *The Blues Brothers* Benefit suddenly became the event to be at that night. On the coaches down to Lyneham, other friends were drinking champagne, taking photographs and generally getting out of hand.

At Lyneham we made it through the gates of the base, suddenly overawed by the sight of men with guns and top-level security. There was no doubt that John would be safe here. We were shown into a large television lounge, somewhere on the base, and offered drinks. Ken Coyte, the WTN President was there, with Lorrie Grabham-Morgan, who'd helped enormously with the campaign. John's plane was due to land in about an hour. I drank a gin and tonic; then a half of lager; then a glass of wine; then someone brought in champagne. By this stage, I was having to visit the Ladies every fifteen minutes. I kept staring at myself in the mirror. How did I look compared to five and a half years ago? I had no idea. I knew I looked older, but how much, I wasn't sure. I kept thinking, 'What's it going to be like? What's going to happen?' The next couple of hours were agony.

An extended BBC *Nine o'Clock News* finished and Dave Mannion said, 'Right, now let's turn over to the real news,' and switched channels to ITV, where ITN's *News at Ten* was about to start. The screen was huge, filling one corner of the room. We watched Trevor MacDonald valiantly trying to fill time before John's plane landed. Someone said, 'The plane's landing now', and we all ran outside, across a stretch of grass, towards the tarmac. I wanted to see it happen with my own eyes, not through the lens of a television camera. But we couldn't see a thing. The plane was too far away. We all sprinted back towards the massive television screen, where all we could see was advertisements. Just ITN's luck. John's plane had landed during the commercial break.

We watched Trevor MacDonald try to do the impossible and keep talking as the plane, an 'RAC jet' circled the runway 'in a wide arc, more of a semi-circle, really' towards the building. Finally, with minute following excruciating minute, we saw Pat standing proudly at the door, and then John was coming down the steps. The moment was as magical as I had imagined it would be for all these years. He looked in control. Chris, Karen and I put our arms around each others' shoulders and watched as John stood for a couple of minutes at the bottom of the steps and then got into a car. I heard people screaming and realized that it was all our friends, yelling out their names. John seemed to hear, and wound down his window, but could evidently see very little. He smiled and waved, and then drove away.

There was more agony as we saw people being shown in to see him. Douglas Hogg went in to welcome him back, then Ken Coyte. We had no idea when our turn would come. I was getting more and more edgy, anxious that other people were trooping off to see John while we were kept in the waiting-room. After half an hour, Hogg popped up on the screen, giving a press conference about his meeting with John, telling the media how he was. Frustration was tempered only by my mounting nerves. More minutes ticked slowly by, and then an RAF officer came towards Chris and me and told us to follow him. I held Chris's hand tightly as we walked down the corridors for what seemed like miles. 'This is it, this is it,' I was thinking. Suddenly, we were at the entrance to the annexe containing John's suite. A group of men were standing outside and as we got nearer, I saw Pat, Roby and an RAF officer. They wanted Chris and I to go in together, but all at once I realized that Chris was deliberately blocking their way and at the same time shoving me through the door before they could stop him.

I was in the room. John was standing there, looking very small, but filling the whole room. He was smiling, shyly, and walking towards me. We hugged one another, and I was knocked sideways by the sensation of feeling him, of smelling his skin. I didn't know what year it was, where I was, or what I was supposed to say.

'You're back,' I said.

'Yes,' he said, 'I'm back.'

Minutes later, Chris came into the room, and he and John hugged. Chris was crying, saying something like, 'I missed you, it's good to see you', and then suddenly we were all sitting down, chatting, as normal as anything. I was aware that John was doing most of the talking and that his eyes looked dilated. I didn't say much; I felt no need to say anything at all. A wonderful peace had come over me. All tension was gone. Nothing mattered at all, only sitting here, listening to John talk, watching him move. It was like watching an old silent film and then seeing it come to life and fill the room. It was entrancing, magical, and, at the same time, it all felt very, very normal. At one point John reached over and took my hand, and the moment blotted out everything else. After fifteen minutes Roby, Pat and

Terence came in, and we spent another twenty minutes chatting, about what I don't remember. When it came to the time to leave, John pulled me into a separate room and we had another few minutes alone. All I remember is that John said, 'As far as I'm concerned, the plans we had still stand.' John wanted us to be together; finally I knew for sure. I was happier than I'd ever been. I didn't know what was going on around me, I didn't have a clue what the next few days or weeks were going to bring, but at that moment, I didn't care. All that mattered was that I still felt the same for John, John still felt the same for me; everything was all right. He was alive, he was safe and he was home.

Exile on Main Street

II
England, August 1991–August 1992

'What would you like for breakfast?' asked Ann, who looked after us during the day.

'Bacon and eggs please; I've dreamed about them for so long!'

But I was too nervous to eat and gave up after only a few mouthfuls and had a cigarette instead, probably the third that morning. Before being released I had cut down to two a day. Another week and I'd have been rid of the things. But no, the Jolly Jihadeers had, as ever, sent me in the least expected direction. And here I was, a day later, their envoy, free, but feeling sick through nerves and chronic nicotine poisoning.

I'd woken up late, opened the curtains and peeked out warily. There was no-one in sight, just some lawn and garages. I was safe, but I could barely take it in; my mind was too full, teeming with memories and my current responsibilities. It was impossible to assimilate all the information and emotions coming at me. I had to keep my head down, had to make 'total control' my motto, and, for the time being, let go of anything that seemed too confusing. Everyone I came across reassured me that there was all the time in the world to sort things out, but it was impossible not to be anxious.

I was given a note from Brian, in which he'd written, 'Be your own man, keep your counsel and do what you have to do. Choose your own course – Good luck!' Seeing his handwriting again was very comforting. I could feel his presence and welcomed the strength and advice the letter brought me, but didn't feel that I was quite ready to see him again. I didn't yet have the energy for what would undoubtedly be a very emotional reunion. Besides, advice was coming at me from all sides and I felt that any more, even from Brian – the only person who could really know what was happening to me – would make it impossible to judge if I was indeed being my own man. 'Total control, total control,' I kept telling myself. It seemed the only way to cope.

My life was going through complete upheaval and I was not at all sure how much control I had. In a sense I was a prisoner again, with RAF police following me at a tactful distance whenever I left the VIP suite and with the public and press waiting to see me. After Lyneham we'd be going on to a 'safe house'; we had already accepted that we would be on the run. It had never occurred to me that coming home would involve quite so much 'security'.

Perez de Cuellar had agreed to come to Lyneham, to save me flying to New York, which was a huge relief – although I was amazed that such an important man would rearrange his schedule to suit me. I was happy with the planned news coverage of our meeting and understood that I would have to say a few words myself. I was still enough of a journalist to appreciate how infuriating it must have been for the press not to have an opportunity to talk to me. A few questions after the meeting with de Cuellar would both fulfil my pledge to the Islamic Jihad to make the hand-over of the letter as public as possible and give the press something more than the limited briefings from the RAF and WTN.

I spent the rest of the day relaxing in the suite. It was still very strange to be 'free'. So many things were going through my mind, so many events and plans to try to put in place, that at times my brain just seized up and filled with a dense, grey cloud. I felt physically paralysed as well. At one point, I found myself stalled by the sitting-room window, staring out at some birds hopping around on the grass. After a few minutes I was aware of feeling calm and relaxed again and realized that it was because I had started concentrating on the birds, fascinated by the way they pecked at the ground for food. I made a mental note that whenever I blanked out all I had to do was observe the natural world around me, letting its mystery change my perspective.

As I pondered this, I heard my father talking to someone on the phone.

'Hallo, yes, this is Pat McCarthy. Oh, hallo there, John, how are you? Good, good, yes, we're fine, everyone is looking after us. Yes, he is, just a minute.'

'John, phone for you, it's the Prime Minister.'

I had a brief, pleasant chat with Mr Major who was calling from a holiday in Spain. When I put the phone down I looked at my father.

'You were calling him John. Do you know him then?'

'Oh yes, met him quite a few times, he was Foreign Secretary for a while, d'you see?'

I wasn't too sure that I did. It was difficult to take in the extraordinary *savoir-faire* with which my family and friends dealt with these amazing goings-on. Yesterday Jill and Chris had been talking about press conferences as if they were run of the mill. Now I discovered that my father was on first-name terms with the Prime Minister.

Later, when I spoke to Jill, she told me that she'd had another hectic day, giving yet another press conference. Her flat was besieged by reporters, so she was going into hiding.

Early in the evening Terence asked me what I would like for supper. My mind went blank at the prospect of choosing anything I wanted. I said that I couldn't think; why didn't he decide? No. He said that I had to get used to making decisions. I thought for a while and decided on lamb chops. The food was at once attractive and repulsive. It was good and there was plenty of it, yet it was far richer than the diet I was used to. I found I would sit down to eat and tuck in greedily, but if, after a few mouthfuls, I was distracted by something, almost anything, I would turn back to my plate and find my appetite quite gone, the food on my plate an offence.

Two days after arriving at Lyneham and my first meeting with Jill, she returned with Chris and Nick Toksvig. It had already been an exciting day – the Red Arrows had specially altered their course between shows for a fly-past in my honour, which was a great thrill and not how I'd ever expected to spend a Saturday morning. Now I was giving a dinner party. For five years I had had no say in what, where and with whom I did anything. Two days had altered life to such an extent that I could now not only choose what I ate, but with whom and what we would drink. I could even, in the highly unlikely event of anyone getting out of hand, ask my guests to leave. I cannot now remember what we ate or that we drank very much. I had to be alert for the meeting with Perez de Cuellar the following morning. We talked non-stop; Nick and I slipped easily into the past, retelling an endless stream of old jokes. When they'd arrived, by Cadillac of course, Jill and Chris had given Nick and me a few moments together. As with them on Thursday night the reunion was sweetly anti-climactic. We were laughing immediately, the bond of humour, a bond which had done so much to sustain me over the past few years, had not been broken. Despite the laughter, our evening was somehow restrained, although hilariously reassuring. I felt fine when talking about my experiences but found their stories left me feeling uneasy, something of an outsider.

Jill and I had talked on the phone about the years apart. She had been very open and that had given me some confidence, but I sensed I was really not going to be sure about her feelings for me until much later, probably not until I had a better hold on myself. Confidence in myself was the way towards confidence in relationships with others. As we sat at dinner I put my hand over Jill's, quietly asking her, 'Is that all right?'

'Yes,' she replied.

At about eleven o'clock my guests had to leave. I had a few minutes alone with Jill. There were no passionate hugs and kisses, it was far too soon for that, and neither of us wanted to rush things. We knew that we wanted to rebuild our relationship and take it slowly, 'one day at a time', as Jill had told the press. But for now, just to sit and look at one another, to be able to reach out and touch, knowing that the other was at last really there, was marvellous.

London, August 1991

The night after we went down to Lyneham, I could hardly eat or sleep; it was going to be the same for weeks. We had spent about twenty minutes with John and then met up with Karen for a drink in the Officers' Mess, where officials from the FO, Brian Keenan and others were all very merry. The two busloads of the Friends had already gone home, while we arrived back in London at about three in the morning after giving Brian a lift to his hotel in our hire car and getting lost in the wilds of Wiltshire. So many images and impressions flashed across my mind and then vanished. It had all happened so quickly and been over so fast, I could not relax. I woke early, and was immediately tense, as usual, before relief and joy washed over me. I lay there for about half an hour, trying to take in the idea that John was now on the end of a telephone. If I picked it up, I could talk to him. We could be connected. It seemed like a miracle.

It was another lovely day, but the media were bombarding the campaign office to find out when they were going to see John and what had happened the night before. We decided that we would have to hold another press conference. Mary came over with all the newspapers. I'd known John's release was going to be big news, but the scale of the coverage was phenomenal. It was an event of tremendous significance, in many different ways; John's mission, his courage and composure on release, the

533

groundswell of love and warmth it had caused, the interest in our relationship – the enormity of the event was just beginning to sink in. I had been trying to get the attention of the press for years, but now the roles were reversed; now it was they who wanted a story.

I hadn't really stopped to think why the media had besieged us the day before; it had seemed like another expression of joy at John's release. This time, I knew they wanted to know what it had been like when John and I saw one another and I felt very nervous as Mary, Anna and I made our way to the press conference in a taxi. When I saw the number of people and cameras waiting outside the hotel, I instinctively ducked down and asked the driver to carry on. I spotted Karen, got out, and we all walked towards the press together. The mayhem was the same as the day before, but this time I felt like the quarry whose scent has been picked up by the pack.

As we entered the scrum, I sensed that the atmosphere seemed different from that of the day before. It was oppressive and there was no warmth. The reporters were a different crowd from the one of the day before too; the usual faces were down at Lyneham, waiting for a glimpse of John. They started shouting questions, but it was impossible to stay outside on the pavement, the situation was too chaotic. Two passing policemen saw the crowds and came to see what was happening and they guided me into the hotel. The atmosphere became nasty – the reporters thought I wasn't going to answer questions and shouted, 'Is it true that you are pregnant and it's Chris Pearson's baby?'

I was in a state of shock as we got up to the conference room; we tried to work out how to cope. All the newspaper and television people were demanding individual interviews, but there was no way I could go all through that again. I was exhausted, and my mind was still circling somewhere about the clouds. Chris, Karen and I discussed what we should do, but as we talked, we were, of course, keeping the press waiting. Reported threats like, 'We made her and we can bring her down', drifted down the corridor and I burst into tears. We decided we would just have to get on with it. Everyone stayed in the room with me and their reassuring presence gave me the strength to get through the morning. We allowed five journalists in at a time and then the television companies, one by one. I fended off all questions about whether John and I had a future together in much the same way as I had the day before. It was too early to tell; everything was very confusing; John seemed fine, but would need space and time to relax; we were taking it one day at a time – as if any of it needed saying at all. Afterwards, on the way back to Barbara and Tony's flat, Chris and I ducked when we realized that we were being followed. The journalist pursuing us didn't spot which house we went into, but stationed himself at the end of the road for the rest of the day. I was trapped.

In the space of a few hours, the joy of John's release had been overtaken by fear and frustration. Friends were waiting at Barbara and Tony's to celebrate, but the atmosphere had gone flat. Someone had phoned to say that a reporter, who'd gone to interview John's former flatmate, Chris Martin, had snooped around and stolen a photograph of me in a towel. Suddenly everything was up for grabs, any kind of intimacy could be violated, as if it meant nothing. Personal feelings and emotions could be exploited and reduced to nothing more than a few lines of copy.

My nerves were on edge; I'd been wondering all day when I would get to see John again. Later, Chris managed to contact Roby and reported back that he had advised me to get away, out of the country; there weren't going to be any happy endings. Afterwards, I realized he had been trying to protect John, but at the time I felt that it was the final straw. The press and other people were in control. I began to get hysterical. It was the nightmare I'd imagined: under siege by the press, and unable to contact John. 'What's going on? How does Roby know what's going to happen between John and me?' It was difficult to keep a hold on myself and stay rational. I told myself that it didn't matter, that I would see John soon, that Brian Keenan's friend, Frank McCallan, had warned us a year ago that the emotional strains on John's release would be enormous, but I hadn't expected anything like this. I couldn't stay calm, especially knowing that the press would soon find out where I was. Later, when Geraldine suggested she and I went to stay at her parents' house in west London, it seemed like the perfect solution. The journalist positioned at the end of the road had disappeared by then, and Brian drove us over to the peace and quiet of the Chmerlings' house in Kew.

When we arrived I plucked up my courage and rang Lyneham, leaving a message for John with my new telephone number, but not knowing if it would get through. A few hours later, when I was lying awake in bed, he called. My despair vanished instantly. We spoke for about an hour, neither of us wanting to hang up. We understood later, after talking to the psychiatrists at Lyneham, that we were both aware that the last time we had said goodbye over the telephone it was another five and a half years before we spoke again.

I spent two weeks at Kew, talking to John every night on the telephone. Two days after his release, Chris, Nick and I joined John and Terence for dinner down at Lyneham. I could hardly wait for the hour to arrive, and spent ages deciding what to wear, as if it were my biggest date ever. We ate in style, the Lyneham staff serving us a huge meal in his VIP suite. As I sat there I felt the same overwhelming sense of relief and peace that I'd experienced on seeing him two days before. I hardly said a word, content to just sit and listen to John chatting to the others, and watch him talk and move about, seeing again all the gestures that were so familiar, like when he tipped his head back to light a cigarette and blow out the smoke. Nick and John were soon digging up all their old jokes and John spoke about his captivity, mainly light-heartedly, and making us laugh. He was anxious to play down his experiences. 'It was worse for you,' he said. 'I knew I was alive, but you didn't.' It was extraordinary that, despite all the pressures, John was looking at things from our point of view. But again, it was typically John.

I realized that he was working the hardest of any of us to keep the conversation going, and that he was incredibly alert. I knew the meeting with Perez de Cuellar the next day and doing something for his fellow hostages were the most important things on his mind, yet he was still obviously concerned for us, the other people whom he loved. I was astounded by how much he knew about the outside world, current affairs, new rock bands, the latest films; he seemed to know more than I did about any of them. At one point we talked about Tom Wolfe's *Bonfire of the Vanities* and John said, 'The film's not bad, have you seen it?'

Pat and Roby joined us and we spent a few minutes chatting to them. Pat looked like a man who had finally been able to let go for the first time in years and he was bursting with pride.

'I've realized that I'm quite vain about him really. I mean, to come out like that and then to say, "Well, hallo" – it said it all, didn't it, eh?'

We left reasonably early as John had a big day ahead of him; I understood now that he had more things to cope with following his release than I'd ever anticipated, and that, as eager as I was to spend more time with him, it was best that he stayed at Lyneham away from other pressures. Although he was handling everything brilliantly, he was also very vulnerable. The huge interest in his release and the reception he'd been given had overwhelmed him; he didn't understand it, and it was worrying away at the back of his mind. I appreciated how right Pat had been to insist that John's release be handled in this way; it was vital that he should have support and protection until he was ready to leave.

The weather was still gloriously hot and sunny, reflecting my mood and that of just about everyone I spoke to over the next few weeks. All anyone could talk about was the day of John's release, where they had been, how they had celebrated. I felt tremendously warm towards everyone, especially the friends who had worked for all those years towards John's release. It was a time for celebrating, for forgetting all the unhappiness of the years before, and I was still up in the clouds.

'Is it right to feel this happy?' I asked Mary.

All my anger had evaporated, all grudges were forgotten; I could have forgiven anyone anything. I began to see some of the FO officials we'd been dealing with over the past two years, like Andrew Green and Mark Canning, in a different light. Instead of eyeing them with suspicion I saw them as real people, whose delight at John's release was endearing and whose personal interest in bringing it about had been genuine. I could understand why Roby had been so single-minded about protecting John; John's interests had been paramount, and he had been ferocious in his defence of them, delighting in playing the bad guy and telling the media that John would not be available for interviews. Now that I could look back on John's captivity, I could see how much Roby had supported Pat throughout and how he had never stopped working towards John's release.

I stayed in hiding in Kew, relying on Karen, Chris and Cathy to take care of any practical arrangements and to deal with the media, who were still bombarding the Friends with calls. Close friends understood that it wasn't possible to see John just yet and were happy to wait, but others found that difficult to accept. I understood the intense desire to see him, having experienced it myself and I tried to explain why John needed the space.

My mum and dad came down to London and visited me every day. Brian arrived most afternoons with the day's newspapers, fresh clothes and mail, which mainly consisted of letters and messages of congratulations from friends, colleagues and well-wishers. Some had addressed their envelopes: 'John McCarthy, Freedom'.

Staying out of reach of the press was still the main priority. Brian had been caught by a crowd of journalists at

538

the flat in Camden one day and, although he had held firm under the pressure to tell them where I was, had been unable to avoid making some comments. He'd been asked to give the odds on the chances of John and me getting back together. He had no more of an idea than anyone else, but on being asked '100 per cent? 70-30? 50-50?', he plumped for the most non-committal. After his quotes appeared in the newspapers, expanded by the journalists' fevered imaginations, Brian was known by my friends as 50-50 for weeks, and the nickname is still coming back to haunt him. My mum and dad had been through a similar experience and they were all wary of being caught out again. They were staying, with Brian, in a hotel and had hired a car after Brian realized that he was being followed.

The coverage was warm and flattering, but overwhelming. Our photographs were everywhere and some papers quoted thoughts and feelings we had never had. Over the years, I had become accustomed to that, but it had never happened on this scale. For John, it was baffling; he had gone away as an ordinary, anonymous person, and had returned as a hero. He was disturbed when one paper wrote a profile of him that was as far away from the truth as could be imagined. I could easily understand why he didn't feel up to talking to the press quite yet. I had decided that I had no need to say anything further to them, although there was enormous pressure to do so. John's attitude put everything in perspective. He said, 'You don't have to do any of that any more; there's no need for it now, so only do it if you want to. We're not famous people; we don't do anything exciting – they can't report nothing.'

It took me a few minutes to register what he was saying, and then I understood that he was right and another weight lifted. I had given two press conferences and said everything I had to say; I didn't owe anybody anything more. I luxuriated in the feeling that those responsibilities were now gone. All I had to do was keep out of the way. I hardly dared venture out for fear of someone from the press finding me and forcing a move from the sanctuary of Kew. When I did go out, it was in Geraldine's baseball cap and dark glasses, and even then I was flabbergasted when a stranger spotted me at forty paces and came straight up to ask how John was.

RAF Lyneham, August 1991

The morning after my dinner party I woke with a start, anxious. I looked around and saw that Terence was still asleep in the bed next to mine. There were no metal shutters on the windows, only curtains. I began to breathe more easily – I was still free. But something was preying on my mind. Then I remembered. I was meeting the Secretary-General of the UN in a couple of hours. What jacket should I wear, what shirt and tie? Terence lent me everything and I soon looked presentable. He was now my constant source of reference. It was all something of a nightmare for the first few days. Pat and Roby sometimes seemed overprotective and I sensed that Chris and Jill resented this. When I spoke to Brian he seemed to trust no-one at all, not even Jill. I found myself trying to balance everyone, make them feel comfortable with each other. Terence was independent of all camps, had a fine mind and I was happy to talk everything through with him. I was also delighted that the strong bond we had formed in childhood had stood us in such good stead.

Finally, I was ready. We were driven over to the main reception area and walked across to where Perez de Cuellar stood with Douglas Hogg. I was less conscious of the mass of people watching us from behind the barricade than of the feeling that the man I was approaching would release me from my most pressing responsibilities. We posed for the cameras, holding the letter between us. The eyes of the world, and especially those of Mr Hogg, seemed to be focused on that buff envelope. I had kept a close hold of it ever since it had been thrown into the boot of the car with me.

After a few minutes, Perez de Cuellar and I left to talk in private and I told him the various details that the kidnappers might have omitted from their letter and he made notes on the envelope as we spoke. I felt a vast weight lifting from me. We sat in a huge reception room, yet the atmosphere was so intimate that the deep sense of calm and relief I was experiencing felt like an absolution.

When I started talking about Tom, Terry and TW, I was overcome with emotion. He simply said, 'Take your time, the world waits for us today, John.' When I tried to get myself back on track, he said, 'Take a little longer, there is no rush.' I was deeply impressed. This man had any number of incredibly difficult problems on his mind, yet here he was treating me as if I were the important person, as if there were no other issue in the world that mattered to him. I felt such sympathy from him; he was so kind, so natural.

After we'd spoken privately for a while we went back to speak to the press. Perez de Cuellar spoke first, then it was my turn. Unfortunately the radio microphone we were using had the effect of delaying my words over the loudspeaker system. This hadn't bothered de Cuellar, yet I found that I kept stopping to let my sentences catch up with me. The drawn-out delivery was attributed by most people to nerves and/or drugs. Luckily, someone switched off the microphone and during a brief question-and-answer session I was able to speak more fluently.

After the questions we headed off for lunch. It was fascinating watching these high-powered people going through their diplomatic paces. There were polite questions and cautious replies about when Her Majesty's Government would be ready to let the UN know their views on who should succeed Perez de Cuellar as Secretary-General. During the early part of the meal one of de Cuellar's aides took the letter and read it. She came back saying it was not dramatically different from what had been expected, and was virtually a general statement of policy. The FO types wondered, as it seemed so bland, if they could have a copy.

Now I realize that my envoy role was little more than a publicity stunt. I was vaguely aware of that at the time, but as I could not comprehend the extraordinary events going on literally around me, I could only base myself in the realities of which I was certain, my friends in chains and the intensity of their captors' last conversation with me. However much of a media circus it had been, this was no charade for Terry, Tom and TW. My feelings of responsibility for my friends, and the belief that I was helping them, distracted me from much of the madness that seemed to surround my return home. My public role over, I relaxed and felt free to look around, which meant I was vulnerable.

On returning to the VIP suite I looked at the Sunday papers. There was a lot about my home-coming and a headline in *The Sunday Times* caught my eye: 'A very British hero'. I felt very proud and read on. I realized that while the article had nothing but praise for John McCarthy, it didn't appear to be talking about me. I decided that it was too disturbing to continue and avoided reading about myself for a long time. It was seductive yet false. It left me feeling owned, recreated by someone else's imagination.

Over the weekend I spoke to the families of the fellows I had left behind. Before each call I would make notes to remind myself of stories that would encourage them, and reassure them that their men were coping well. With Tom's brother, Peter, speaking from his family home in Scotland, I think I may have gone too far. As I told him of our conditions, he kept replying, 'Aye well, that's nae so bad.' I was very surprised, but resisted the temptation to say, 'Actually, Peter, it's bloody awful.'

On Sunday evening I had a long talk with Brian on the telephone. We were both quite shy to start with. Gently he gave me advice on how to handle all the madness, explaining that through my release he was experiencing again some of the panic I was now feeling, which he knew all too well from his own home-coming. We were still being very quiet – and, for us, polite – when I said, 'Anderson calls me Oab.'

'Oab? What does that mean?'

'Oab stands for "one agitating bastard" if you remember.'

Brian burst out laughing at the idea of his own phrase still being in use. From that point on we relaxed and chatted away as of old. Here was someone who really knew what was going on. Yet he was as nervous as I, and at the back of my mind were the various rumours that Brian had become erratic and overly suspicious of everyone. I was as anxious for him as he clearly was for me.

The next morning Gordon Turnbull came into the suite holding triumphantly aloft a copy of the *Western Daily Press* with its headline: 'Mission accomplished'. He gave me a hug and said, 'That's behind you now, now you can think about yourself.' It was a huge relief and my talks with Gordon became more productive. I could now go over, in greater detail, the worries and fears of the last few years rather than concentrating on my 'mission'. I began to feel a little more confident that I would be able to apply whatever strengths I had developed as a hostage to normal life, especially if I were going to cope with the new reality of being famous.

I had taken to Gordon from the moment we met and found that I could talk to him comfortably about anything and everything. His pleasant nature and his method encouraged me a great deal and helped restore some of my self-confidence – I was getting things at least half-right. I trusted him – perhaps because I realized that he often felt self-conscious himself. He conducted our sessions as normal conversations, where advice was sought and given by both sides. After we'd admired the headlines, he told me that he had gone home the night before to find his wife, Alison, rather upset. She'd been 'doorstepped' by a journalist wanting 'background' on the man who was debriefing me. His knowledge of private details of the Turnbulls' lives, such as when and where they got married, had unnerved her. They had both felt very exposed, alarmed that their private life should have been thus hijacked. I could understand this and lost any restraint I still had at talking about myself.

I felt perfectly natural with Gordon and his team. They had worked with victims of the Hillsborough disaster, the Lockerbie rescue teams and the British POWs from the Gulf War. When they reassured me that my reactions were completely normal, it made my anxieties less daunting. Whereas as a hostage, I had been tense for twenty-four hours a day, now I was only tense for twenty-three. I found that for minutes at a time I would feel calm, relaxed and confident, then in a second it would all go; mostly for no apparent reason. Some passing thought would set off a whole stream of confused worries. What was the hullabaloo outside all about, when most of the people making it didn't really know me from Adam? Gordon went over this a number of times explaining that I was a symbol of how people hoped they would cope in similar circumstances. The fact that I'd walked out smiling after five years of captivity, when others had apparently found far shorter periods utterly traumatizing, and of course my being British, had given people a huge lift.

The question of Jill was always on my mind. It didn't help that half the media seemed interested only in whether we were getting back together again and how long it would be before we got married. It reinforced a decision I had already made, that I must take enough time to come to terms with things myself before doing anything publicly. The idea of going on to a safe house and then on to another hideaway with Jill seemed a sound idea to me. There really was no need for me to rush into words or print about my experiences or hopes. Indeed, it would only be counter-productive. Such ordeals would in no way help me clear my head; they would most likely do just the opposite.

For the time being, I could relax in the knowledge that Jill and I were getting to know each other again, mainly through telephone calls. We could chatter away without the added pressure of being together all the time and without feeling any need to make a decision about the extent of our relationship. A couple more weeks apart were nothing now that we could talk as much as we liked and arrange to meet with little fear that the press were going to track us down.

My first real outing, apart from the fly-past and the meeting with Perez de Cuellar, came when Gordon took me out for a drive in his car. We didn't leave the airbase but it is such a large and busy place that to me it was like being in the rush hour. I was amazed that I could remember how to drive, but it was a fabulous feeling, actually being in control of my own direction again, able to determine where I was going, by what route and how fast I'd get there. At one point we stopped as a large vehicle pulled off the road. A civilian stood on the huge truck and he looked over towards the car. He did a double-take, then pointed at me. We could see his mouth framing the words, 'Is that you John?' as he leapt to the ground and came trundling over. He was a great big man in blue overalls and, as he came up beside me, I saw his eyes were full of tears. We shook hands through the open window. 'Well done, John,' he said and let go of my hand while backing quietly away, as if to let me be myself, still gazing at me.

After he had gone, Gordon said, 'I think most people will be like that man. You noticed he just wanted to say, "Hallo", he didn't want to intrude. He even walked away behind us, not straight back to his lorry. Very nice, I thought.' It certainly was and, in a way, reassuring; the fellow hadn't tried to impose himself on me at all, he'd been discreet and polite. But this great burly stranger had wept because he had seen me. It was an odd thing to absorb.

Over the next few months, I found it very curious meeting people, strangers, who greeted me like an old friend. It was even odder when they spoke to me about Jill or my father and mother as if we had all known each other for years. Having been made public property to encourage increased efforts for our release, I had to face the fact that I was too familiar to many people for them to treat me in any other way.

Once you got to know someone things were much simpler; we were working, or playing together. It was that first moment, when they gasped, stammered and seemed to want to touch you, that was so disturbing. Being the focus of so much attention, no matter how warm and welcoming, is very, very frightening.

That evening I found I could hardly walk, my legs were aching so much. 'It must have been the driving, lad,' said my father. I must be in far worse condition than I'd imagined if twenty minutes in a car had had such an effect.

Late that night, Gordon and I were walking along a corridor in the mess. A large cardboard box had been left outside a door, probably by an officer who was moving. The hairs on the back of my neck stood up at the sight of it, my whole body tingled. As we neared the box, my breathing quickened. I imagined myself in the crate. I was moving, not my belongings though, I was the baggage. I was terrified, believing that if I ran the lid would open and I would see myself bound and gagged inside, see myself blindfolded and helpless. I forced myself to be calm and walked on steadily. Gordon asked me if I was all right. I said I was but that the box had unnerved me for a moment. He said no more then, but brought it up the next day, showing me that the important thing was that I had walked past the box, putting it behind me. My fear was now only remembered; I could move on.

Each day another sack of mail would arrive. I was told we were getting an average of three hundred notes from well-wishers each day. It was extraordinary that so many people wanted to tell me how happy they were for me. The great majority of the letters were from women and children and there were many lovely cards that children had drawn themselves. One girl sent me a piece of the Berlin Wall. There were books and tapes, many of them with songs which people had written for me and the other hostages, all of them inspired by Jill and the Friends' campaign. Many people opened their hearts to me, telling of the trials and sadness in their lives. Many said that I had helped them confront these difficulties. I felt so close to these strangers; by expressing their suffering they were helping me to explain my own experience and put it in perspective. I was privileged to be allowed such a look into their lives, but I could only read a few letters at a time. There was so much courage, so much feeling in them but my emotional balance was too unstable and I would put the pile away until there was enough time to appreciate them more calmly.

A week after our arrival the medical team departed and my father, Terence and I had a group session with them all before they left. We talked about problems that were likely to crop up and ways of dealing with the press, members of the public who might approach me in the street, others who might want to know everything. They asked me what my main concern was. There was only one answer.

'Jill,' I replied. 'I really want to get that straightened out, to see if it will work again.'

That was natural. The only advice, as much for Jill's benefit, I now realize, as for my own, was just to take plenty of time. We had that now, and the best decision was to decide not to make any long-term plans until we could feel more confident about our relationship and what else we might want to do.

I went with Terence and my father to see an old army friend of his, John Cowtan. We drove to his house in two cars with an RAF police escort. It was my first trip off the base since getting home. We drank buck's fizz on John's back lawn and it was a joy to be with someone who treated the whole thing as perfectly normal and even something of a joke. It made me feel much less self-conscious.

Two days later, after a brief statement to the press and a farewell bunch of flowers from a little girl called Natalie, we were flown in a helicopter to RAF Northolt where we met Roby and headed down to the safe house, near Guildford. Travelling in one car, rather than at least two, with only family and colleagues, we went deep into the countryside. I knew I was now going to have some time of my own; private space. As we left the village, following Lorrie's notes, I forgot for a moment that we were on the run, that at the back of all our minds was the fear that we'd wake up the following morning and find the drive filled with journalists and photographers. It is hard to tell how realistic that fear was, but I think it was true enough; certainly the requests for interviews were coming in thick and fast. Jill's flat was still a no-go area; her brother Brian and a friend of his had been followed all over London in the hope that they'd be going to see Jill. But that Saturday afternoon my mind was sensing release. The public role was over. Now there would be no strangers for whom to perform, even if those strangers had been nothing but kind and totally considerate. I was fascinated that the lane became so narrow, that the hedges and trees on either side met above our heads; it was as if we were travelling through some exotic and secret tunnel to a new and safer land.

Kew, August 1991

On Sunday, 11 August, I watched John on television as he handed over the letter to Perez de Cuellar. I knew how much of a relief it was for him to show the kidnappers and his fellow hostages that he had completed his 'mission' and could hand over the huge responsibility to the UN Secretary-General. When he spoke to the press afterwards his voice sounded blurred and, typical John, he joked,

'It's the drugs!' In fact it was the delayed sound relay that was making his speech sound peculiar, but I had several calls from people concerned that the FO and Lyneham were doping John up and even keeping him captive against his will. Friends came down to see me in Kew and we sat out in the garden talking about how John was, still marvelling at the week's events. One day I took my parents over to see Mary's baby, Anna. We were watching her play in the bath when the phone rang. It was John. Mary had answered the phone and stumbled for a few seconds, but recovered enough to say, 'It's great to hear your voice. I'll just get Jill.' It was such a normal thing for John to ring me at a friend's house, yet it was still extraordinary.

A few days after John's release, when he was still at Lyneham, I went to the Albany Empire in Deptford for what should have been a Benefit night to raise money for the campaign. Instead, I celebrated with my friends in a way that had not yet been possible. We let our hair down and danced until we dropped including Chris Pearson's father, Keith, who had to be cajoled off the dance floor by his wife, Frankie. The atmosphere was perfect. Glen Tilbrook was playing for us, as he had on several previous occasions; we were definitely among friends. At the end of the evening, Chris and I did our final speech-making 'double-act'. I thanked the friends who had turned up week after week at meetings when there was nothing going on at all and Chris raised his glass of beer to John publicly for the last time.

I'd never been in the position of making a speech where I didn't have to worry endlessly about what I said; this time, it didn't matter and I felt safe enough to hold out my shirt in front of me and joke, 'Oh, I just want everyone to know that I *am* pregnant, and Chris and I *are* having an affair, so there.' Everyone laughed and we left the stage only to discover that someone had phoned a newspaper and that a breathless reporter had just arrived. I ended the evening by sneaking out the back exit with Cathy, but was too happy to let the occasion be spoiled in any way.

When I got back I rang John and told him all about it. Our conversations were usually late at night and afterwards I found it hard to switch off. I had been to see one of the RAF psychiatrists and we had both recognized that their advice was sound. It was a good thing that we hadn't spent a lot of time together yet; the pressures of the situation were big enough without the extra strain of trying to work out our relationship. It was a relief to talk over what had happened during those five years. Even though it was a bit peculiar to be talking in such an intense way about some of the most painful aspects of that time over the phone, it was good to do it in such a controlled manner and have time to think about what the other had said before we talked again. Even after speaking to Frank Reed and Brian Keenan, I hadn't understood the extent of the tension of John's daily existence; for five and a half years he had lived in a state of controlled fear, and had never been able to escape the company of other people. He lived with the tremendous strain of trying to make his relationships with his fellow hostages – and his guards – work. I had told John about what Brian had said on his release about eating all the food in the world. 'Did you hear the end of the quote, though?' he asked, 'that was the joke: the last line was, "And maybe then I'll get a good night's sleep".'

A week after John came home, I watched on the television as he left Lyneham for his next, secret location, with Pat and Terence on either side waving proudly from the doors of the helicopter. Once there, he had a minder, Mike Pemberton, who would answer the phone. When I rang I had to use an alias they had chosen for John or would not be put through. It was all very weird. I was less wary about going out now, and went into Richmond to buy some clothes for John as he had little more than the ones given to him by Islamic Jihad and I wanted to get rid of them. I was so happy to be doing such a normal thing and as I sat on the bus a 1970s pop song kept playing in my mind – 'Bringing on Back the Good Times' by Love Affair. I went into a record shop to try to get hold of it, but the young chap behind the counter told me it had been discontinued. I suddenly realized how old I was, but I didn't care.

I bought several shirts, two pairs of jeans, a stylish jacket, some underwear, a pair of wellies and a waterproof jacket – the good weather might break at any time. Some of John's belongings were stored at my flat, and I asked Brian to retrieve them from the cupboard where they'd sat for four years and bring them over; there were a couple of shirts that had been John's favourites in the past and I knew he'd be pleased to see them. I looked through the rest of his things: a chequebook for an account the bank had discontinued and replaced three years ago; a cashcard that John had asked me to take care of while he was in Beirut; a pair of nail clippers, and a tiny silver snuff box. The rest of his things were stored either at his old flat in King's Cross or at Cornish Hall End. When I looked at the little I had to take him of what was left from his old life, I touched earth again for a while. Here was the material evidence of his former life stored in plastic bags and only now seeing the light of day. I wished that I could compensate somehow for all those years, all that lost time.

The day I spent down at the safe house was leisurely and normal. Getting down there had involved enormous secrecy, and I was very nervous about seeing John, but once there I felt very relaxed and happy. The house was a lovely family home and the McCarthys were obviously comfortable there. Terence shot some home videos and then we strolled around the gardens, stopping to watch two hot-air balloons suspended silently against the clear blue sky. John gazed at them in wonder.

'Look at that,' he said, 'what a perfect symbol of freedom.'

Every now and again, his senses seemed overloaded and he appeared to switch off. It was all so new to him. I found that I, too, was looking at everything with new eyes. As we walked across the lawn, I understood, with a shock, how hard he was having to concentrate just to keep his balance. I also noticed that the tips of John's ears were burning. His skin was vulnerable, like that of a baby. Later, when he tried on the clothes I'd bought, I beamed as he got rid of the Islamic Jihad trousers and paraded in his new jeans in front of the mirror; he was in ordinary clothes again, and it seemed to emphasize that he was really home. He was slightly thinner, but not much. Everything suited him; everything was a perfect fit. I stayed for dinner, leaving for London at about midnight.

Merrow Farm, August 1991

Merrow Farm was a lovely secluded place. Lorrie was there with Roby's wife Cathy and Mike Pemberton, who was going to act as 'minder' for us in the week we were to be there. It was a great old house, elegant yet so much a family home that, although it was not our own, we immediately felt at ease there. It was also an ideal place to meet some of the families of my fellow hostages. Anderson's sister Peggy Say and her husband David came down, as did Terry's fiancée Madeleine and their daughter Sulome. It was marvellous talking to them about the man they loved but had not seen for so long, and especially to Sulome who had never spoken to her father, nor even seen him. It was a great privilege to be able to talk to them about the man I knew and loved so well and to be able to reassure them, as far as it was possible, that like them his most fervent wish was that they would be able to be a family once more.

After a long chat Peggy and David prepared to head back to London. I noticed that there were two photographs of Terry glued to Peggy's attaché case. In one he looked very gaunt. Pointing to it, I asked, 'When was that thing taken?'

Peggy said that it had recently been distributed by Islamic Jihad. In that case, I told her, it was an old picture. They hadn't taken any for ages. 'That's what he looks like now,' I added, pointing at the other photograph. 'When did they put that out?'

She hugged me, beaming. '*They* didn't! That was taken before *he* was!'

I felt guilty that I was acting as go-between for Terry and Maddy. Terry should have been here telling her his news, his feelings, not me. But I found much peace talking with her. She was part of the inner circle of hostages, former hostages and their families. They knew the strangeness and the fears, and it was the happiest of my minimal duties at this time to speak to my friends' families and reassure them, as I genuinely could, that their men were in good shape, really hadn't changed very much, and certainly as far as I could judge not for the worse. There was also a value in talking intimately to these people that I could not see in talking to the press or to strangers. For me it was cathartic; they were a safe audience who needed to know about the hostages, who needed to know what difficulties release would mean for them all. Here my experience had a value. Otherwise I felt I was the best-loved freak in the land.

I was still finding it hard to concentrate even for short periods. As I sat talking with Maddy I realized that a moment's glance through the window had turned into a long confused stare at the trees blowing in the wind, trying to understand this commonplace, natural movement. I looked back at Maddy, who was smiling at me with great warmth and tenderness.

'I'm sorry, I was suddenly fascinated by the trees.'

'Yes, love, I know.'

I also found peace talking with Sulome. She was a pretty little girl and reminded me very much of Terry, both in her features and her quick intelligence. When I had telephoned Maddy the first time from Lyneham she had asked me to say hallo to her daughter. For a moment I'd been struck dumb. I had prepared things to say to Maddy and other relatives, but I hadn't thought about what I might say to a child. Within moments she was chattering away about her pets and her school, and told me that she loved swimming. I thought of her father and realized that I could tell her how proud he would be; he, too, loved being in the water. My sense of responsibility for her, and her chatter then, as now, at Merrow Farm, took my mind off my anxieties.

While at Lyneham I had walked nearly exclusively on man-made paths and roads or, of course, indoors. Here, at Merrow Farm, I began to get used to walking on uneven surfaces. The lush lawn was pleasant to walk on, yet I seemed to have the gait of an old sea-dog, rolling slightly, unused to dry land. I took Sulome into the paddock to meet a horse. As I walked over the rougher ground I realized I was finding it hard to balance and it frightened me. I could see the ground, see the ruts and hummocks, but lacked the co-ordination to cope with them. I tried to move carefully and positively. I didn't want my little friend to be alarmed at my confusion or to worry that her daddy was going to be a funny old fellow who staggered about. I was also distressed that untying the rope on the paddock's rickety gate, opening and closing it behind us seemed such a complex operation. Knowing that such actions should be automatic, yet finding them so difficult was incredibly frustrating.

It was the same trying to operate ordinary household utensils. Can and bottle openers left me feeling completely cack-handed. Any sort of knife, even a potato-peeler, left my fingers cut and bleeding. A simple process like making a cup of coffee seemed to have limitless pitfalls. How did the new-fangled kettle work? Why was it so difficult to put a spoon into a jar of instant coffee and empty it into a cup without depositing half the granules on the table? Why would the milk splash everywhere? Getting ice cubes separated from their tray was impossible. Although I was infuriated by my clumsiness, when I succeeded in some mundane task without undue concentration or mishap, I felt an enormous sense of achievement. However, I was, as yet, unschooled in everyday courtesies. I couldn't talk to guests and prepare food, not even a cup of tea, at the same time. Terence and my father would occasionally appear, asking if Maddy and I would like a drink, and eventually to tell us that lunch was ready.

Maddy wanted to learn from my experience of coming home and was interested when I suggested that, however confident Terry might seem immediately he got out, he would need a period of quiet, with a chance to talk to the psychiatrists. I had become something of a zealot on the subject. I knew that this time had been so peculiar for me, and far worse for Brian and other released hostages, that the next guys really must be offered some sanctuary.

Months later Anderson was to tell me that when they heard me talking on the radio about the strains of fame and the need to hide, he, Tom and TW had thought I had gone a bit loco. But as soon as he got to Wiesbaden, caught his breath and realized that he was the biggest story in the world, he, too, knew that he had to run from it, to give himself and his family the best chance of a steady transition back to normal life. Terry, TW and Jackie Mann benefited from this system, whereas Tom trotted happily into the limelight and followed its lead.

Terry was going to be fine when he came home. Like me he had worked for a large company who were ready to arrange anything that he and his family wanted. Although both were news organizations with big stories falling into their laps, there was no pressure to speak to them in interviews. On the contrary there was pressure to avoid all that until it was comfortable and really necessary. The support was very personal, no strings, no restrictions. It looked as though TW would have the same sort of support from his family and Lambeth Palace. Throughout TW's captivity, Frances Waite had always avoided the glare of publicity, understanding how important it was to get on with life and allow her children the most ordinary family environment possible. She clearly intended to follow the same path when her husband came home.

After I had seen Terry's relations, TW's folks and spoken to Tom's wife and daughters by telephone I realized that for the moment there was nothing more I could do. Essentially, the UN was now in charge of the hostage issue and all reports pointed to their release within a couple of months. Chris Pearson, Karen and Cathy were working hard and in total secrecy to organize another safe house for Jill and me after we left Merrow Farm. We were scheduled to leave at the weekend, and, as at Lyneham, by Thursday I was champing at the bit to be off to pastures new. I wanted to be alone with Jill.

That day she came down to the house, laden with new clothes for me. I loved everything and it was great fun trying them all on. Turning this way and that in front of a long mirror, I tried various combinations of my new jacket, shirts and trousers. I knew I was being vain, but carried on, elated at the renewed sense of appearance and the growing sense of regained identity that it echoed. I felt incredibly shy with Jill, yet at the same time found it hard not to assume the old intimacy. It was undoubtedly there, but the fact of our five years apart made me cautious. Often, when she chatted about the campaign or mentioned whom she'd seen and what she had done, I felt a rising sense of panic – this had nothing to do with me. It did, of course. It had all been for me, but it had happened without me. She was as beautiful and as sweet-natured as ever, yet I couldn't help thinking, 'I don't know her, can't know her until I know what she's been through.' But I didn't want to know. Fearful of her independence, I couldn't take an interest in her past. I mistrusted her for knowing my friends, even my cousins, better than I did. I was jealous of her experience at work and confused at her making me so famous that I lived in terror of being mobbed, photographed and obliged to be what was now expected of me, whatever that was. I was still so uncertain about what I was doing, even about who I now was, that I wanted to be reassured that there was something that had not changed.

My anxieties over Jill would sometimes lead me into dark thoughts against my captors. I would rage against them for denying me the chance to understand and share the ways in which she had developed. Yet I think this was in large part an attempt to avoid my own responsibilities, to blame them rather than confront my feelings of insecurity and inadequacy.

Many people expressed surprise that I did not appear bitter following my captivity. In all honesty, I could say that I wasn't, yet there were moments when I would turn in that useless direction. When I heard of my mother's suffering and anguish, I would only feel hatred for those men, whose treatment of me I could forgive, but whose callous, pointless abuse of her I could not.

Once my new wardrobe had been suitably admired, Jill and I joined my father, Terence and Mike for a drink. As we sat out in the garden in the perfect summer's afternoon, Mike leapt up to point out some hot-air balloons floating across the horizon. They were a brilliant symbol of freedom, but as I watched them I was suddenly afraid they would have scores of paparazzi on board. It was such a strain to feel hounded. I wasn't fully myself yet, only a part of me was functioning normally, and I longed to be free of such unnecessary pressures.

Wales, August 1991

At the end of the week, it was decided that John, Chris and I should go to Wales, to a cottage belonging to old friends of the McCarthys. Terence and John came to Kew for the evening. I was very nervous and grateful to my brother for keeping the conversation going whenever it looked like foundering. The next day, we headed off in yet another hire car, organized by Karen and Chris. As we drove off, my spirits soared even higher. It was another glorious day. I was sitting quietly, feeling very peaceful. John was wearing his new jacket. The Rolling Stones were on the car stereo and he was singing along. Every now and again Chris would ask John about another aspect of his captivity and I would listen to his replies. I found that after our conversations on the telephone I didn't want to ask much. I think I felt that with John sitting there looking so well, I just wanted to forget the horrors of what had happened to him.

Wales was idyllic; the view from the cottage was fantastic, looking out over a valley and stretching away to the hills in the distance. The weather remained impossibly perfect. When I woke up it was like Christmas morning every day; I would remember that John was here and experience the elation, relief and peace all over again. Often, as the days were so hot and clear, John would be transfixed by the view; the sight of the valley and hills beyond was astonishing to him. It hadn't occurred to me that, for years, he had never looked further than ten feet in front of him and that perspective was now something to be rediscovered. Sometimes it seemed impossible that he had actually been through five years as a hostage.

Time seemed elastic; there was no structure to the day and we barely paid attention to normal eating or sleeping hours. John paid no attention to time, the idea of it never occurred to him; he was more interested in talking and hours went by each morning as the three of us sat out on the terrace drinking coffee and eating bacon sandwiches. We ventured out several times, but once out of the car we were constantly worried about being spotted. We joked about Chris adopting his 'bodyguard' mode; he would stride ahead, looking to the left and to the right, scanning the crowds to see if anyone had noticed us and was likely to accost John. Chris went down to the supermarket most days and I cooked, enjoying it as much as I had before John was kidnapped. We ate food that he hadn't eaten for years, roast dinners of pork and lamb, that, in the end, were too much for him.

In the evenings we sat around and listened to *Exile on Main Street*, an album that John loved and had remembered while he was away; on the first night we danced to it outside on the terrace, taking photographs and drinking until the early hours. Nobody dances like John, he has his own style entirely, and it was extraordinary to watch him again, to remember instantly how it used to be. I learned that he had attempted his Mick Jagger impersonation in his chains; it was only now that I could visualize such things and the images were painful, as were others which he only mentioned in passing: the tightness of the chains, the constriction of the blindfold, the extremes of temperature and the casual brutality.

I couldn't bear the reality of what he had gone through; being handled so carelessly as if he had no feelings, no dignity, no rights and no capacity to feel pain. He'd been bundled in sacks, bumped down stairs, nearly choked to death. His captors had been so nonchalantly cruel, denying him basic comforts through thoughtlessness and ignorance, as well as through deliberate malevolence. It was mostly Chris who asked John questions, while I fiddled with the food or the dishes. One night as he talked about an incident I realized that I literally couldn't bear to listen. My head was spinning and I felt as if I was swirling down a black hole. I got up to go out of the room and fainted. It was partly due to the wine, but, after that I wondered if I could cope; it was too painful, too difficult, too much to take in.

Chris listened, and would occasionally try to fill in John on what had been happening with the campaign or current affairs. John tried to show an interest and would ask questions, but I could see that he found it too strange and couldn't really absorb it. There was too much; too many things that had seemed bizarre to us while they had occurred and seemed even more so to John now. When it came to talking about changes in our personal lives, I wanted to show off to him that I'd passed my driving test, bought a flat for us and changed jobs. He was pleased for me, of course, but the effect of my news was only to underline how long he had been away. John's achievements had been of a different kind, but at times it seemed to him that for the past five years he had accomplished nothing.

One night we decided to watch the news on television and as we lounged around in the comfortable armchairs I thought how normal everything could seem, and actually was, at times. If I looked at John now I could believe nothing had ever happened to him. Suddenly, the television and lights went off and we were in total darkness – a power cut. It was pitch black; we were in the middle of nowhere and there was no other light by which to see. John groped for a candlestick and some stubby candles next door and Chris tried to light one. 'Here, let me do that, I'm the expert,' John said, laughing, as he demonstrated how to avoid wasting the wax. I could not relax. The power cut had unsettled me, but to John it was all very familiar. He wasn't at all perplexed by the darkness or the frustration; the endless patience and self-discipline he had had to learn and the fatalistic attitude he had had to adopt were immediately apparent. For a minute we could have been in his cell in Beirut and I could not imagine how he'd survived. It seemed to me that John had been forced to confront himself and others in a way I hadn't had to, to strip himself down and reflect on things we were able to avoid in everyday life, particularly being so busy. I had avoided reflection. I had paddled around in the emotional shallows rather than plumbing the same depths as John. The realization made my head spin. How had he found the strength to manage?

As we sat out on the terrace and talked, John returned again and again to his fellow hostages and how concerned he was for their well-being. It was clear that his relationships with the other men had, for him, been crucial to his survival. It had been vital that they worked together, as a group, and he talked about his love for Brian Keenan and for Terry Anderson, which had grown over the past year. At times, he was quite distraught, anxious that the delicate balance between the men would have been damaged by his release. It seemed to me that John had put an enormous effort into making that balance work. I didn't know how to comfort his distress, other than to sit and listen. It made me realize how much extra pressure Brian Keenan must have felt on his release and I was again grateful to him and to Jean-Paul Kauffman for spending so much time with me so soon after they came home.

They must not have been able to enjoy their release, but John could. We were reasonably confident that all the other hostages were coming home and could concentrate on John's recovery. It would have been a different story altogether if John had not felt sure that the kidnappers knew it was all over and were going to release the rest of the men. Privately, I worried that the UN deal would fail and that the others would remain captive; I couldn't understand why John was so absolutely sure they were going to be released. He knew it would take a while, but was confident that it would happen. I hoped that John was right. Over the next few months as the hostages came home, I discovered that he was, and that from his cell in Lebanon he had made far more sense of political developments than I had and viewed them with an understanding that I had not been able to achieve. My vision seemed to have been blurred by having too much to look at, whereas his had been sharpened by having so little.

Wales, August 1991

It was a great relief to move on again. Life was beginning to calm down and some of the everyday things we all take for granted – getting up in the morning, choosing what to eat, walking around – now seemed more natural. The clouds fogging my brain were lifting for longer periods. Besides, I was so excited about being away with Jill, with Pearson as our chaperone, that my anxieties became less and less pressing.

Yet nothing was quite that simple. I still felt occasional moments of unease at Jill's close friendship with Chris. It was ironic that they had done so much, shared so much, on my behalf – yet I hadn't been there; I felt

561

somehow excluded. I was concerned that they had moved on from me, that I wasn't really a part of their life. I was the freakish old friend who had reappeared causing huge problems, none of which he could cope with for himself. I sometimes felt that I was an outsider, very much part of their lives, but only as a responsibility, never in a position to give anything back.

After much discussion, we'd settled on Wales as the next destination. We were borrowing a house from friends, Bill and Enid Thomas, whose children, Hugo and Hilary, I'd been at school with. We set off mid-morning. I sat in the front with Pearson, who was driving. Jill was in the back wearing an enormous baseball hat she was using as a disguise.

'Well, say something then,' said Pearson.

I went blank. No inane question about pop and soap opera stars came to mind. I was too excited, but also tired and apprehensive. I had the nagging fear that we would be pursued, that our private time, which was so vital, would be destroyed by the sudden appearance of the press.

Chris and Jill evidently shared my anxieties, but eventually we relaxed and turned our minds to our next jaunt. From Wales we were going to France and we spent the rest of the journey talking about the arrangements that were being made. The plans were reassuring, exciting, yet were feeding my paranoia about the media which was to linger for a long time.

When we arrived at Bill and Enid's house, I immediately felt happier. Hilary and her husband Mark were there to greet us; we drank champagne and chatted as they showed us around. The place was splendid, delightful inside and outside there was a fantastic view over a wide, lush valley topped by hills.

The weather, too, was perfect. Each morning I would get up late and go and sit with Pearson on the terrace, sipping coffee, revelling in the warmth of the sun and marvelling at the view. The clouds of confusion still descended, but I found they quickly lifted as I began to understand, as if for the first time, the natural world around me and my place in it. One morning, as we sat there, I realized that the little brown things across the valley were cows. The white dots higher up were sheep. My sense of perspective was slowly coming back. The valley and the animals in it were not painted on a huge screen, they moved. Some things I saw were a few yards away, others were far off. The joy was in seeing how the mosaic was made up.

It wasn't just my ability to perceive depth and distance that had suffered. Learning to drive again was terribly tiring and particularly hard on my eyes; there were frightening moments when I felt I could no longer focus. It was hardly surprising. Having looked no further than twenty-odd feet for most of my captivity, and having nothing interesting to look at, my eyes had become terribly weak. Driving, with its constant changes of focus was an intensive ocular fitness programme.

The mood swings, so relentless in captivity, were less frequent now I was free. In freedom, time can heal; in captivity, it destroys. Although the switches in mood may have been less common, they were there nonetheless. In captivity, I had worked hard to counter them, to dampen the anger, frustration and fear. Now, to avoid bursting into tears of confusion, I had to do the same. I had to have total control over myself.

Fear and confusion both interrupt your natural thought processes. Your mind senses that you simply cannot take any more and orders up an escape. With fear this may be blinding panic and an urgent desire to run. As a hostage, that was physically impossible, so I would bolt mentally, filling my head with a stream of random thoughts that blotted out the reality of what was happening.

The confusions of freedom bring, not panic, but a rush of images that switch your mind into neutral. I became fixed, physically, as if in a dense fog with all sense of direction gone. There was nothing to run to, and nothing specific from which to run. As I became more acclimatized to freedom, such confusion engulfed me less often and dispersed more quickly; I began to realize that I did have places to run to, more and more of them, all of them happier, fulfilling areas of my life.

There were the distractions of sight and sound – the constant reassurance of sunlight and trees, of music, of birds singing and water in streams. There were books, newspapers and magazines, the prospect of building a home, buying a car. Now, I had the freedom to think and act as I chose.

There were my old friends, too, and while in Wales I was able to start putting out feelers to them and spent hours chatting on the telephone. It felt more comfortable that way, particularly now that the initial euphoria of coming home had gone and with it any desperate need to see everyone at once. It took me a long time, far too long, to appreciate that my friends had changed very little, if at all. As I got to know them again I relaxed, but it took months. I was nervous even of talking to them, partly because of my great fear of the press. I was terrified of private moments being rehashed for public consumption, which was crazy and unkind, but, at the time, very real. When I was actually with someone these fears evaporated, but for the first few months I tended to stay quietly at home rather than arranging to go out and meet people.

Slowly, the idea that my friends and I had been living in different time-scales gained ground. That I had, unavoidably, done so little in five years, while they had done so much, didn't necessarily make me a failure. I had been unable to make the moves they had made, but had had to deal with other problems, unique to my situation. As this sank in, I came to feel more confident.

But the feeling of not quite belonging, of having gone through something that was almost impossible to communicate stayed with me. I still oscillated wildly between gratitude for all that had been done for me and anger when a new pressure appeared. At such moments I felt that I'd been set up in some way, that I wasn't my own man –

as I thought I had eventually become in captivity – but
the creature of the press, of the Friends, of relations, of
anyone who felt they had a claim of some sort and so
could call in the debt and warm themselves in the limelight
that, for me, could turn so cold.

One day we took a drive up to the coast and walked
around a resort town. I wasn't too worried about being
spotted, we were a long way from our base and if anyone
told the press they wouldn't be much the wiser. It was
still a novel and curious experience to walk along streets
but I could not get used to the crowded pavements. I
had lost the knack of negotiating people and obstacles,
of crossing a road. When I found myself stuck against a
shop window with a stream of pedestrians passing me I
felt nervous and shut in, wanting to run but terrified of
drawing attention to myself. Suddenly there was a young
woman standing on the far side of the pavement looking
at me through the heads of the passers-by.

'John?' she said.

'Um, yes,' I replied, my anxiety increasing as the sense
of being trapped was compounded by not knowing what
to do or say. We shook hands over the heads of some
children. I nodded my thanks for her courtesy and moved
away, desperate to be private again and take stock of my
strange, new life.

Towards the end of our stay we went for a drink at a
local pub. We were recognized and the bar-lady kindly
brought us over a round of drinks on the house.

'We all noticed you, but won't bother you. It's nice to
see you together.'

She was very quiet and sweet; and it was a pleasant
feeling to realize that people had understood our wish
to be private and wouldn't intrude. It was curious sitting there looking across the narrow river aware that
everyone knew who we were.

A couple of days later we went back to the pub and
encountered a very different type of person. A woman
came up and said, 'Hallo, it's nice to see you.' I thought I

was getting the hang of this and simply said, 'Thank you.' Then she turned to Jill. 'You're much softer in real life than you look on the telly, aren't you?' Jill mumbled an embarrassed reply. I couldn't believe that anyone could be so familiar, so personal. But to her, I suppose, we were in the public eye, there for her entertainment and as unreal as characters in a soap opera.

Normandy, September 1991

The cottage in Wales was a temporary measure, and after a week there, we left for France. Geraldine's parents had come to the rescue again by offering us their house in Normandy for two weeks. Moving anywhere involved huge practical problems because of our names and faces being, at the time, so instantly recognizable and because of the need to avoid the press. We relied on Chris and Karen to arrange tickets and a car. Karen was astonishing, organizing everything in a way which prevented our names being used. I was glad when Chris agreed to come with us for a week to get us safely over the Channel and install us in France. My head was still in such a whirl that I didn't think I could cope with all the details and arrangements on my own. Besides, John needed to talk so much and it was sensible to have two people there to listen. We drove back to London, stayed at Chris's parents' place for the night, and set off the next morning for the ferry. The trip over to France was uneventful, but when we went on deck we were constantly aware of people staring and worried that someone might call the press. It was too nerve-racking to wander about the boat, so John and I sat in a tiny cabin for a couple of hours. I couldn't believe that only weeks after being released, I had confined him to a room smaller than many of the cells in which he'd been held.

Once in France, and in no danger of being recognized, we began to relax again. The views in all directions stretched for miles, and the villages we passed contained lovely, timbered houses and occasionally an impressive château or two. When we arrived at the Chmerlings' house, we couldn't believe how perfect it was. 'This just gets better and better,' said John, staring at the shuttered windows, the wooden floors and the ornate antique grandfather clock ticking away in a corner. The weather was still hot. The village had its own château and a wood which hid a motionless lake. We explored the wood on bikes the Chmerlings had left, and drove around the towns in the area, tensing at the occasional overheard English voice, but forgetting about the press altogether.

We were able to do the ordinary things that we had done together before; going to restaurants and bars, and visiting supermarkets. I really enjoyed this, and I think John did, too. I was happy to see him browsing the way he used to, looking at everything from socks to handy tools and cooking implements, and studying the wines. Everything was as it had been before he went away, although I couldn't show off my French as much as I had in the past. I was a bit put out when I realized that, thanks to Tom Sutherland's teaching, John's French had improved a lot over the years. He kept asking me questions about grammar to which I didn't know the answers.

We laughed a lot, as we had done. There had been laughter right from the moment I saw him again, I was sure of his love and I felt restored by it. He said that he thought the campaign had been an impressive, wonderful thing and that he understood my reasons for starting it, just as he understood Pat's more low-key approach. I sensed that he wanted to banish any lingering tensions; it wasn't a question of who had been right. There had been no right way. John appreciated what we had gone through and, now, all that mattered to him was that his close relationships were firmly re-established. What I had to get used to again was John's merciless teasing – but it was good for me. It eased me out of the tendency to dwell on the negative trains of thought that I'd succumbed to over the years, and out of taking everything too seriously. I felt more like the old me. There was, too, a new me that I wanted John to get to know, but I knew that that would take time.

While we were in Wales and in France, John was determined to contact the relatives of his fellow hostages whom he had not yet seen. I could see that this was of paramount importance to him; he was quite single-minded about it, it was another mission that he had to fulfil. I knew how wonderful it had been for me to talk to Brian Keenan. I'd felt a special kind of bond with Brian because I could share John with him even though he wasn't there, and I knew that it would be the same for the relatives of Tom Sutherland, Terry Anderson and Terry Waite. Nevertheless, I felt quite jealous of the time John spent talking to Tom's many relations; it was another reminder of how separate our experiences had been.

John spent hours on the telephone trying to track all the relatives down and reassuring them about their loved ones. He was concerned that his fellow hostages should all experience the same kind of support and protection he had been afforded at Lyneham. He knew that the men whom he had left behind were not prepared for what would hit them on returning home and he wanted to convince their families of that.

I had suggested that he call up some of his own friends, and it had been quite a nerve-racking experience for him. I had suspected it would be, but I now realized he was worried that after campaigning for him for years they would expect too much of him, that he would feel odd and that things wouldn't be the same. I was relieved when a couple of calls went well, but was not prepared to push him any more until he was ready. He had too much on his mind; I just hoped people would understand. I didn't call many friends either; I didn't have the necessary mental energy, and I feared that conversations in any case would revolve around John, which would make him feel even more like a freak.

Nick came down for a couple of days and we drove around the countryside playing the soundtrack from

The Big Easy and a Van Morrison tape he brought for John, and then he and Chris left. John and I went sight-seeing and shopping for clothes; John seemed to have developed a fetish for shoes.

One night we went to try a restaurant about fifteen miles away that we had seen the day before; it was a small place and after a while we were the only people there, enjoying the waitress's extraordinary local costume as well as the local dishes. We left, happy and contented, at about nine-thirty. We stepped out of the door and a flashbulb went off. We stopped in our tracks, stunned; a man saying he was from the *Sunday Mirror* asked John how he felt about the prospects for Jackie Mann's release and how the holiday was going. 'It was fine, until now,' John said, between clenched teeth. We walked on and the photographer snapped away.

My heart was pounding. The holiday was ruined. They knew where we were. How long had they known? Did they know where we were staying? How had they found us? As we drove back to the cottage I was shaking, wondering if they would be waiting for us back there, too. There was no-one, but the next morning we dared not go out. Strange voices outside the window terrified us. I phoned the next-door neighbour and asked her if any visitors had come to the house. Sure enough, some Englishmen had turned up and asked her what we did during the day; she hadn't told them much and they had gone away. We calmed down. We didn't think the *Sunday Mirror* would give anyone else the information about where we were; there were two days left before they went to press and they would want to protect their scoop. By now, though, Chris had phoned us to say that other journalists were also in France, trying to track us down. My mum and dad had received phone calls from people posing as employees of the passport office and a car hire company. We had been due to go home anyway; we decided to leave a day earlier than planned.

On the way to France Jill and I stayed overnight with Chris's parents. We had recovered from the encounter in the pub and had a great evening with Keith and Frankie Pearson. I'd known them and their home since Hull days and the familiarity of both company and place helped me feel more relaxed than at any time since my release. Here, I met Karen Talbot for the first time. She was a quiet, nervous woman whose shyness covered a quick mind and great organizing talent. At first, I was uncertain what to say to her. She was the first Friend I had met. I still found it difficult to accept that complete strangers had done so much for me, yet my simple 'thank yous' seemed pitifully inadequate. Not only that, Karen had put in a terrific amount of work to ensure that Jill and I could move around with little fear of being pursued. Any embarrassment swiftly vanished as we talked and I thought, 'Here is a good friend'. That she didn't expect anything of me in return for her efforts on my behalf, made me feel easier about the whole campaign.

The next morning before we set off Keith asked if he could take a photograph of Jill and me, swearing that he wouldn't get it developed until he got the all-clear. He was so sweet sidling about a few feet from us and then turning abruptly to snatch a natural shot. The first kiss on film!

We had taken a cabin on the ferry to Le Havre so that we wouldn't be spotted, but it was small and there was no porthole. After a while both Jill and I began to feel rather claustrophobic, so we took it in turns to go for a stroll with Pearson. He was brilliant and took his role as 'minder' very seriously, walking slightly in front of me with his jacket flaring out so that people would be less likely to notice me in his wake. At one point, he left me to get a couple of beers. I leaned against the guard-rail and gazed out across the Channel. England was still visible, but I didn't hanker for it. Safe in the knowledge that I could now return whenever I wanted to, I was happy to turn towards another horizon.

Chris returned with the beers and we chatted for a bit, before lapsing into a companionable silence. It felt very good; we were now relaxed enough together to be confident of our renewed friendship.

Once in France, we felt quite safe. We were staying in a cottage owned by Geraldine's parents. It was the perfect hideaway, pretty and welcoming on a quiet street in a sleepy little village. Nobody recognized us and apart from being wary of English tourists we were able to relax. Being with Chris and Jill felt far more comfortable now and I began to feel part of the team again, joining them on shopping expeditions, rather than waiting nervously in the car. It didn't stop me, however, from locking all the doors and shutters religiously before going to bed each night. I had been very reassured to see the locks when we'd arrived at the cottage. After five years of being locked in, controlling my own security was very attractive.

Having settled in, Nick joined us for a few days. Just as we had at dinner in Lyneham, we picked up all the old threads. He was as funny as ever, but it struck me that he had calmed down a lot while I had been away; a gentle maturing that I was to notice in many of my friends. He gave me a tape of Van Morrison's *Greatest Hits* and we drove around the beautiful Normandy countryside, listening to it on the car stereo. All the songs seemed to be relevant to our curious situation, but one in particular, 'Wonderful Remark', stuck in our minds. Months later, it would provide the title for this book.

On Nick's first evening alone with us after Chris's departure, we went to a restaurant in the nearest town. He was looking after us as Pearson had done and it was so endearing to see him upset, yet really more amused, when, after assuring us that a restaurant looked quiet and safe, we found that the table behind us was occupied by two English couples.

'Brilliant, my first shift as minder, and what do I do? Reassure you that we won't be spotted? No, I have to get us a table right next door to a party of Brits!'

While Nick was with us, we decided to try out the Chmerlings' bicycles. We took a tour around the lake. Even more than driving a car, I relished the sense of movement and balance, the flowing control of cycling. The same feeling came over me as Nick and I kicked a football around the garden. I was delighted that since stumbling around the paddock at Merrow Farm I had regained enough co-ordination to run over the grass as I watched the ball and trapped it before kicking it back to him. As we played, Jill ran up and down, trying to fly a kite. Such incredibly normal pastimes, yet the simple pleasure of physical movement in fresh air, the co-ordination of mind and body in response to the moves of a friend were an absolute delight.

Despite the serenity of my surroundings, I was still often confused. Looking at some peaceful countryside, I would often think of my friends still in that room in Lebanon. It seemed impossible to rationalize the two images; I had grown so accustomed to one, and the other was so new, so vibrant and exciting. I felt guilty that my friends were not yet free, that as I drove a car, had a meal in a restaurant, got up in the morning and opened the shutters and looked out on the sun-soaked countryside, they remained captive, exactly as I had left them: TW against one wall, then Tom, then Terry, chained in a row, anxious, bored and hungry.

Memories of those dark rooms frightened me. Sometimes at night I would be transported back, to the long hours praying for sleep as the dawn came up on another wasted day. As I looked again down that bleak avenue I felt guilty not only for my friends but for myself, for not having resisted more. I would suddenly relive an incident with Abed, Mazzin or Abu Salim and be angry again at their wickedness; experiencing the old, awful frustration of having to bear it, and shame that I had done so.

One night I dreamed that I was strolling down a damp, ill-lit street and a man I partly recognized approached. He walked along, raincoat flapping, head down, his eyes shifting warily from side to side. He saw me and stopped. His eyes filled with consciousness. He told me a funny tale I'd heard so many times before. He stopped, his eyes clouded. He was gone, but still beside me. My heart bled for him, my fellow, but I couldn't wait and share his loss with him. That road filled me with a greater dread; I dare not follow him. I woke covered in cold sweat. As I remembered where I was I relaxed, but remained shaken. Who was the man in the raincoat? Why had he come to me? Then I realized that it was me, could have been me, forever damaged by the years of fear. I would be able to hold on; I must be able to now if I had done so then.

I was still anxious to do everything I could for the families of my fellow hostages, but had yet to see Jackie Mann's wife, Sunnie. She was visiting England and I took the opportunity to fly back for a few hours to meet her at Heathrow. Mark Canning at the FO and Lorrie Morgan at WTN arranged everything. Jill came with me on the train into Paris and we then went to the British Embassy, to meet Nick Cannon, the Second Secretary, who accompanied me to the airport. It was my first solo trip, but Nick was a charming companion and I felt certain that he'd look after me.

When we got to the airport I was alarmed to see a number of photographers waiting. They snapped a few shots of me then followed us into the terminal where we were met by the airport police and a British Midland representative. As we went up the moving walkway, I risked a look around, fearful of the press pack on my heels. There, just behind me, were a couple of very elegant plain clothes policemen and beyond them a dozen gendarmes who appeared to be armed to the teeth. The embassy's request for protection had obviously been taken very seriously.

As I sat with Nick chatting about my trip and holiday with Jill we were approached by a couple of journalists from British newspapers. They were very polite, but I was terrified, unable to think clearly and desperate not to talk about how things were going with Jill. It turned out that they'd found out my flight details from someone at Heathrow and would even be on the plane with me. My heart sank. I was already anxious about the flight and meeting Sunnie, without having to watch everything I said as well.

Thankfully, the cabin crew were very protective. I agreed to let the photographers take a couple of shots of me and then they left me alone. At Heathrow I was whisked off the plane and was met by Mark Canning before being driven around to the VIP suite to meet Sunnie. We posed for some photographs, then we went and had a chat. She was a remarkable woman. I'd heard a lot about her from Jill and Chris who had met her with some of the Friends and everyone agreed that she was a tough lady. I was amazed that she was so calm, confident and alert. She was very funny and very sweet and we chatted about her plans for herself and Jackie when he came home. It was a sad and bitter irony that, after holding on alone for so long, she was to have less than two years to share with Jackie after his release and their triumphant return to Lyneham.

I popped into the Gents before my return flight and met a couple of men who welcomed me home. They were soon joined by a very familiar-looking third man, who shook my hand and added his welcome to theirs. I told Mark that I'd met this fellow and he said, smiling, 'Oh, that must have been Kenneth Baker, the Home Secretary.' It was really all very odd.

Back in Paris Nick and more plainclothes policemen met me off the plane and we walked through the shopping area undisturbed. No journalists seemed to have been on the plane and as we emerged at the service entrance all was clear. At the embassy we met up with Jill, who had spent the day window shopping, and had some champagne with the Head of Chancery, John MacGregor, and his wife before heading back to Normandy.

It was a relief to be back in our sanctuary again, but I felt the tension had been worth it. Being able to use my experiences to offer a little comfort to Sunnie had given me a sense of purpose; I wasn't just an object of curiosity. Nonetheless, I greatly enjoyed the VIP treatment. It was fun calling up the Foreign Office and asking for their assistance in my travel plans, fun to have people lay on transport and override normal difficulties like customs and passport control. It made me feel very special. I liked it and, at the time, I needed it. I could at last understand how easy it had been for TW, having lost all status as a hostage, to look back fondly on his time as a VIP.

Jill and I spent a couple of days driving around seeing the sights, enjoying the marvellous summer weather. After a particularly happy day in Chartres, we went to a restaurant quite near the cottage for dinner. During the meal we chatted as we had done years before, pointing out amusing details to one another and trying to imagine what the other customers were like and what they got up to. I was no longer worried that any break in the conversation meant that I'd done something wrong and was happy to let those moments pass reflecting on the events of the day. I was sure that we were very close to reclaiming our former intimacy.

As we emerged into the quiet street, we were blinded by a flash of light. We froze. Then, as a camera kept whirring and flashing, we realized that we'd been caught. We tried to get away but a reporter followed us. Jill sagged against me as he asked, in a voice full of apology, 'How are you enjoying your holiday?'

'It was going fine, thank you. I'm afraid you've spoiled it.'

'I'm sorry, but, you know, it's the human interest. It's our job.'

After a few more questions and a few more photographs, they let us walk on alone, still apologizing.

We were in total shock. Our worst fears had come true. We'd thought they would never find us. How could they have done? Would the rest of the pack be following after them? I drove like a maniac back to our village. We scuttled into the cottage and locked and bolted all the doors and shutters. I was frightened and furious. Jill was terribly upset. I wanted to protect her. I was sure that, if another journalist came near me, I'd go berserk, releasing all the pent-up anger of five years, anger that I never risked directing at the guards but which, now, might hurt someone. I needed total control, yet I failed miserably.

After two large gin and tonics, I called Terence and then Chris. They were both sympathetic and calming but I was getting very drunk. Not only was it a bad idea in case the press did turn up, but, far more importantly, it wasn't helping Jill. She had already had to look after me so much. Now, although I could see that she was even more distressed than me, I was the one who drank too much.

We never did find out how the journalists, from the *Sunday Mirror*, found us. Luckily they told no-one else where we were, but it cast a huge cloud over our last few days in France. We were forever worrying that we'd be jumped on again. In fact, we spent months 'on the run', ever anxious that the press, who relish a chase, would be just around the corner. We may have been taking things a little far, but our paranoia did ensure that we had the privacy which we needed. Now, we decided that we'd have to talk to the media when we returned to England in the hope that they'd then leave us alone. We feared that the *Sunday Mirror*'s exclusive would have the rest desperate to catch us, too.

Chelsea, September 1991

On the return journey, John stayed in the cabin; the fears about being recognized were back again. We couldn't risk moving into my flat, so stayed at a place in Chelsea belonging to the father of a friend. By now I'd run out of vacation time and was dependent on the goodwill of my boss, Rachel, but I couldn't see how I could go back to work. It was impossible given that we were on the run. I wanted us to be normal, to calm down enough to work out what we wanted to do next, but we were just lurching from one day to the next. We scoured the streets before we dared step outside and kept our telephone number secret from everyone, even our friends, except Chris and our families. I missed them, and relied heavily on Chris, Karen, and our agent Mark Lucas, who became a friend as well as a source of good advice.

John and I decided that we would have to give a press conference so that all the newspapers could have a photograph of us together and talk to John about his captivity; it didn't seem fair to do an exclusive deal and we thought it would ease the pressure if we talked to everyone. I knew the press conference would be an ordeal for John; all eyes would be on him and he wasn't ready for that, let alone talking to strangers about his captivity. We also had to brace ourselves for questions about our relationship, about which there was a nerve-racking amount of interest. Before the press conference began, John was sick with nerves. We posed for the photographers, who called out, 'Show us your engagement finger, Jill' and, 'Give her a kiss, John'. I had expected it, but I couldn't believe that newspapers wanted to relegate us to cardboard cut-outs. Their readers' interest in us was warm and affectionate, but as far as the papers were concerned, our lives were simply not our own. At one point, John made everyone present guffaw and injected a bit of realism at the same time. One feature writer coyly asked, 'John, did you have any imaginary conversations in your head while you were away?' 'Yes, and I still do,' said John, quick as a flash.

The pressure from the media began to ease when it became clear that we had signed no exclusive deals and were not going to do anything remotely interesting for anyone to photograph, but the pressure of being famous remained. We wanted to start leading an ordinary life, but wherever we went we found ourselves being treated like film stars. When we went out people would stare and someone might recognize us and come over to say hallo. Everyone was warm, pleasant and full of good wishes, and many were simply overwhelmed at meeting John, as if he weren't quite human. He coped very well; he was always charming and courteous, and accepted what people had to say with good grace, but I knew it made him feel very strange. I had been through something similar myself and found it unnerving and confusing. I imagined that people only wanted to share the happiness they felt and to wish us or him well, or to tell us how much they had supported the campaign, and it was terrible to feel that their kindness was an intrusion. We got used to dashing for taxis and walking quickly without looking around us, and in crowded places I went on alert, ready to move on if anyone spotted us.

One day we dashed out to the Foreign Office for a meeting with Douglas Hurd, stopping off at John Lewis on the way to kit John out from head to toe in smart clothes, from shoes and socks to tie and cuff-links. He had hardly anything to wear apart from the items I'd bought on his release and a few bits salvaged from the past. It was impossible to go shopping; crowds of people bothered John, I could see him freeze, and it was impossible to concentrate on the task at hand as someone would always recognize him.

It was strange going to the FO with John, instead of going there hoping to hear news of him. This was a new experience altogether; an invitation for drinks with the Foreign Secretary. Douglas Hurd was genuinely interested in talking to John and blushed when he countered his question, 'Are you going to write a book about your experiences?' with 'How's your own writing coming along? You write novels, don't you?' I was proud of John for having the presence of mind, even amid the whirlwind that we were both caught up in, to turn a formal exchange into a real conversation. I could tell Hurd was impressed. In fact, everyone thought John was wonderful because of the way he'd conducted himself since his release. Of course, he was. I wondered if they had ever asked themselves why we had campaigned for him for all those years.

A few days later, we moved to the Camden flat. I was eager to show John the home in which he had a part share, and when he saw it I was anxious for him to say that he liked it. He did; he said that I'd made a wonderful job of it, but when I looked at it anew, as if through his eyes, I became painfully aware of all its shortcomings. Not only that; the place was full of my furniture, my decorations, my four-year-old memories. John must have felt like a visitor. Looking back I can see that it was far too ambitious to think that we could settle there, or that we could hammer out some kind of ordinary existence amid all the pressures of London, but I was too impatient. I wanted John to fit in with my life, but I didn't appreciate that not only was there no going back, it was also much too soon to attempt normality. I hadn't appreciated how difficult it was going to be. I tried to deal with all the things that were piling up and needed attention – gas bills, bank accounts, insurance policies – in between shopping and cooking, but the life we were having to lead did not allow for any settling down.

Chelsea, September 1991

When we got back to London we didn't dare go back to Jill's flat. We were very lucky to have been allowed to use a friend's flat in Eaton Square. From here we planned a press conference, with Chris, Roby and Mark Lucas, who was acting as our agent. Jill and I didn't want too much of a circus and were keen to limit our dealings with the press as much as possible. After lengthy discussions we decided to give a press conference for all the papers, and an interview with the BBC, ITN and Sky Television. We would kick off the day with a brief session with photographers from all the papers. Roby set everything up at WTN's studio in Camden Town, so that we could be based on home ground.

The first bit of business, with the photographers, wasn't too bad, although it is odd when there is a battery of people pointing lenses at you, shouting,

'This way, John. Jill, over here, love.'

'To your left, please.'

'Down here at the front.'

'Give him a kiss, oh come on!'

'No, we are *not* going to do that.'

After ten minutes we'd had enough; it was impossible to keep smiling any longer. We were guided into a little room and the snappers, grumbling, went on their way. Then came the bit I was really dreading – all the journalists, especially those from the tabloids, with their inevitable questions about 'wedding bells'. Jill and I sat at a desk and I read a statement about how I felt in general and how odd this was in particular.

Preparing the statement had allowed me to focus my thoughts. Reading it now I can see that while these ideas were still very fractured, I had started putting the pieces together again. Although virtually any plans, even going for a walk, usually involved a discussion with Jill and anything more complex often found me seeking the advice of other friends, I realized that I had been able to make some important steps.

My relationships with my father and brother had become very close while they looked after me, but, now that I began to appreciate the terrible strain they had been under while I was away, they became more so. I was also beginning to understand how Jill's life had been thrown into complete chaos and that even now it was at least as confusing as my own. I could also see quite how much, in terms of time and energy, Chris and so many of my friends had given to the campaign, let alone the thousands of others who had supported the Friends of John McCarthy. The effect of the campaign, at least in so far as it had made me famous, still confused me, but I had begun to rebuild my friendships, albeit mainly by phone. My emotional bases were expanding. Not only were my old friends exactly that again, but now I had new friends, like Karen, Gordon Turnbull and Mark Lucas.

I found that I brought the same intensity that I had established with my fellow hostages to these new friendships. Now, as then, I felt an urgent need to understand people immediately and find a way of working with them. My new friendships developed as we made plans together. Happily many of these working relationships grew deeper, but I became aware, nudged by Jill, that it was impossible to give this degree of attention to everyone. As I became used to meeting more and more people I redeveloped that basic sifting mechanism by which I could judge who was likely to become a close friend. It was impossible to give every chance encounter too much emotional value. I would just burn out.

Having read my statement the questions began. There were one or two sensible ones, about the other hostages and the prospects for their release, and then the 'human interest' brigade took over. They were all very polite, but it was disappointing to find that their real interest in the hostage and the campaigner was a scarcely concealed desire to know whether or not we had been to bed together yet. We handled it all as best we could. My greatest concern was to get across that whatever 'human interest' there might be in our situation, going in fear of them and their colleagues didn't help us to rebuild our lives. I asked them to bear this in mind when the other hostages returned.

After the press had left we had a bit of lunch in Ken Coyte's office. Old friends kept popping in for a chat, mostly just wanting to say hallo and crack a joke. Inevitably, though, there were one or two who wanted to tell me exactly what they'd done for the campaign and what their friends had done and how I'd have to go and have tea with them some time soon. 'Why are you telling me all this?' I thought. 'Why can't it wait? There's too much else going on here. Can't you, a friend, appreciate that?'

The sessions with the photographers and journalists had gone surprisingly comfortably. Much of my nervousness had eased off; I thought that being interviewed by one journalist at a time would be far simpler. Michael Buerk interviewed us first, for the BBC. I found the two television cameras disconcerting and was more aware that everything I said was being recorded than I had been earlier, with the print journalists. But he was very good and I think he drew a lot more from me than I had anticipated. At the end I was completely drained and, pulling Jill with me, rushed into the green room, where I threw up repeatedly.

I didn't think I could face any more, but Jill calmed me down to a point where I managed to get back into the studio without retching. After Michael Buerk's very serious approach, the interviews with ITN and Sky were easy. Both stations chose to go for the 'human interest' angle rather than probing any deeper.

The next day we were both delighted to be relegated to second place in the headlines. Jackie Mann had been released and had flown into RAF Lyneham. He looked a little shaky, but sounded remarkably alert. I was happy to think of him and Sunnie enjoying the Lyneham treatment. A month later I went to see Jackie at an RAF hospital where he was undergoing physiotherapy. He had been held in solitary confinement for two years and had often been brutally beaten. I was amazed how well he had coped with his ordeal. He reminded me of Camille Sontag who had seemed quite unconcerned at the antics of the guards. Despite poor health these elderly men had coped far better than many of the younger hostages. Like Sunnie, Jackie seemed to be so relaxed about himself that outside influences, however foul, couldn't touch his inner serenity. He is a great example.

Three days after our press conference I was reunited with Brian. He had bought a cottage in the far west of Ireland and I flew to Galway to meet him. We drove through the rugged, beautiful countryside, up to Mayo.

On the way we stopped at Patrick Sweeney's pub for a drink. It was here that Brian had talked for hours with my father, telling him about our life together in captivity.

Brian and I found that we were both much better than either of us had expected. I was aware that he had had a very difficult time since his release. For the sake of the rest of us he had kept himself in the public eye, dreading the attention, uncertain how to deal with all the incredible warmth and desperate to find enough space to discover himself again. He'd gone through agonies of doubt about whom he could trust and what he should say. The press had pictured him as a moody, unreliable recluse. He admitted that, in part, that was true, but he was, in fact, only a recluse from the press, who wouldn't leave him alone. He shared my fear of them, but had had to submit to their intense scrutiny so that those he'd left behind should not be forgotten. Now, with my release and the news that the others' was imminent, he was beginning to relax.

We fell into our usual banter, cracking jokes and teasing one another. It was terrific to be racing around Mayo together, stopping here and there for a drink or admiring the countryside while Brian explained the area's history to me. He put on a tape and it immediately struck a chord. Van Morrison's *Greatest Hits* was definitely the theme music for my home-coming.

We had tapes playing all the time. Now we could turn the volume as high as we liked, could feel the sound rather than trying to bring it back with whispers and tapping fingers. We could hear all the words, not just murmur a few remembered phrases. There was so much more in the songs that we could now share. We could dance, letting our bodies flow as the music moved us, free of the constraint of enforced quiet and the constriction of our chains.

In Brian's adopted town, Westport, the people were all very kind and relaxed. The only people who bothered us at all were a bus load of English tourists who insisted on taking our photographs. Brian stayed with me at Ann Corcoran's hotel. Ann had been a good friend to

Brian when he first discovered Westport on his wanderings around Ireland during the first, difficult, few months after his release. She managed to convey complete sympathy and support without in any way imposing herself on us. She, with her family and friends at the hotel, made my trip a very happy one. They understood Brian, which meant they understood me, too.

Being with Brian was, as usual, a great relief and an education. We were able to talk through many of the weird and confusing things that had happened to us since our release, and, as in captivity, could immediately understand and empathize with each other's anxieties. I found the attention of people in the street very confusing.

'They come up to me and just stare, eyes filling with tears. Some of them just want to touch me, as if I'll heal them.'

'I know, John, I know. It terrified me to start with, I wanted to tell them to clear off and leave me alone, tell them I needed to be my own man, not theirs.'

'Exactly. I don't know what the hell I'm meant to do. I can't fathom why they see so much in me.'

'Well, after I'd been back a while, I started to accept that I couldn't stop people coming up to me. Then I began to see that what they felt was healthy. We survived a situation so alien, so unimaginable to your ordinary man in the street, that they feel we understand their problems, that we can help them.'

'But we can't, can we?'

'Of course not. But we're folk-heroes, symbols if you like, of how to keep going whatever fate throws at you. It's all right if they look at us – as long as we don't get carried away with all the attention.'

'But it brings me down. I thought I'd sorted myself out while we were away. Now it seems I've got to start all over again.'

'Aye, I know. D'you remember, on our holidays, when I got really down and you said, "Choose joy, Brian"?'

'I remember.'

'I've often thought of that since I've been back and when I'm calm, I can do it. You'll get calmer every day, I can tell you. Choose joy, John, choose joy.'

Brian was right, as he so often had been. It was, as Gordon Turnbull had pointed out to me at Lyneham, that the way we had survived had encouraged people to look differently at their own lives and helped them to come to terms with their own problems. All we had to do was say a few words and walk on. There was no obligation to do more and it was important to remember that.

Brian's advice was a great help and rekindled my responsibilities to him. He needed my support as much as I did his. I wasn't coping as well as he was yet, but the desire to do so was a great impetus. I also realized that I wasn't the only one with worries. I knew from Chris and Jill that he had taken very strongly against a film about the hostages that Granada Television had proposed to make and which the Friends had thought would help the campaign. Brian's opposition stemmed from a decision we had made while in captivity. We had all agreed that we would not get involved in any dramatic representations of our years as hostages until we were all free. Until my return, Chris and Jill hadn't really been able to understand Brian's objections and had decided to take part in the project. It was only now, when I explained how important that decision was to us both, that they could see his point and agreed to back out. Still, Brian remained distressed and distrustful of Jill and Chris, which I found very upsetting. I was trying desperately hard to reconcile the world I now lived in with the world I had lived in as a hostage, yet my greatest friends from those two worlds were divided by a misunderstanding.

On my return from Ireland I went straight to meet Tom Sutherland's wife, Jean and his brothers, Peter and Willy, at a hotel near Heathrow. It was great to meet them all face to face. They were just as Tom had described them and as with the other families I felt as if I'd known them all my life. My only concern was that they didn't seem to take in the urgency of my appeals for them to get Tom away somewhere quiet once he returned home. They were determined to let Tom do as he wished, which was fine, but I argued that he might not know, or be able to judge, what was really best for him and the family amid all the excitement of his return.

The whirlwind of activity Jill and I seemed to have been thrown into showed no sign of letting up. The day after I saw the Sutherlands we went with Terence for a drink at the Foreign Office, with Douglas Hurd and the day after that there was to be a service of thanksgiving at St Bride's. I'd heard of the vigils they had had there for the hostages while I was away, yet had not fully appreciated the efforts of Canon John Oates and his team, nor known that there had been a memorial service for my mother there.

The service itself was very moving, especially the solo piano arrangement of 'Jerusalem', which Jill told me had been featured in one of the campaign advertisements. After the service, we met the Prime Minister, John Major, and Neil and Glenys Kinnock. We posed with them for the press before going on to lunch in the Oates' house next to the church. It was here that I first met some of my old friends and it seemed right that it should happen that way. It was a celebration of my release and the formality of the service somehow added to the pleasure of meeting up with them again. Gina was her same old self and I felt our conspiratorial confidences would be as entertaining, and as supportive, as they had always been. It was she who pointed out that much of the campaign had been great fun, so I wasn't to worry about all the work they had put in.

I knew that the balance had, perhaps inevitably, shifted in all my friendships. That my friends were so unchanged was a great relief, but I was still uncertain that I could be as true a friend as I wanted to be. I didn't think I'd be able to take on their worries when I was still so unsure of myself and my situation. I was wrong. It took longer than I thought it would, but once I began to see friends more regularly and we had time to talk, I found I enjoyed discussing their hopes and fears with them, just as before.

After the service at St Bride's we decided to move back to Jill's flat. I felt strange there. I loved the place but it harboured many anxieties for me. Jill's life, so independent of mine, seemed to threaten me in every room. My friends knew her home better than I did, which was strange in itself. I was jealous of her experiences, of simply buying the place, decorating and furnishing it. She had her own car, something I'd never had. Indeed, when I went away, she still hadn't been able to drive. I could understand my fellow hostages' needs, and that Brian needed my support, but I was sadly unable to appreciate Jill's concerns. I continued to think, because she had handled so many public appearances and press conferences, that events that were a great strain for me were, for her, relatively easy. I couldn't see that my constant demand for reassurance, my thinly veiled criticisms or dislike of many things, must have been an appalling strain as she worked to come to terms with what I'd been through.

I didn't realize for a long time that she was just as exhausted, confused and uncertain of where her life would now lead as I was. Even when I began to understand how difficult things were for her, I still found it hard not to think that my concerns were more serious. I was happy to be free again, of course, but I was also happy to coast for a while. I was slowly getting used to ordinary domesticity – proud when I could prepare a meal where the meat wasn't burnt to a frazzle and the vegetables still rock hard. Such minor achievements were enough for the time being. I had all the time in the world now and, while I was certainly nervous of committing myself to a formal routine, it was more that I enjoyed being free of anyone else's timetable.

Jill had lost the impetus of the campaign which, while being a huge responsibility, had kept her in touch with all her friends and given her an insight into the world she would not otherwise have had. Looking after me meant she was seeing very little of her friends. Likewise she was, for the time being, on extended leave from Channel 4 and was anxious that her life had no direction. I didn't help with this. On the few occasions she did go out with friends, I got terribly jealous. I often felt frightened of going out, yet was miserable when I was left at home.

Camden, September 1991

Settling into a routine was difficult but now we were back at the flat we could meet close friends whom John hadn't yet seen. I knew that they were very nervous and that John was, too; I felt torn between pushing him into something he wasn't ready for, and knowing how eager his friends were to see him. Nobody wanted it to be a big deal, but it was, and on each occasion John experienced the same trepidation. The structure of our friendships had changed so much. It was easier, in a way, for John to relate to my friends because that relationship was unchanged; his friends were more difficult because now so many were my friends, too, and everyone knew each other so much better. Before John was released I had worried that it might be difficult for him to come to terms with the campaigning and the slightly bizarre element it had introduced to his friendships. He insisted it wasn't, that he was just a little overwhelmed, but I suspected he was trying to spare my feelings. I knew he found it odd to have been regarded as an object for so long. I didn't know what to do, or how to deal with it. It was yet another thing to sort out later, when there was time. Other people, less close, began to express hurt that they hadn't seen or spoken to John yet. I knew how they felt, but they would have to be patient.

The days were difficult to grasp and bend to any particular shape. I couldn't impose any structure on them, or on John, because there was none. It took a long time to gear up in the mornings, towards what seemed like function after function; some would have been enjoyable

588

had we relaxed and others would have been more so. There was a Service of Celebration at St Bride's where John had been asked to read Simonov's poem 'Wait for Me' and then afterwards there was a drinks party in the church attended by a few friends and family. I'd forgotten that for some of the people there it would be the first time they had seen John since his release and it was an emotional occasion, but relaxed, enjoyable and fun.

Next was a small party at the Café Delancey in Holborn organized by the Friends. The people who were going to be there were those who had become closely involved in the campaign over the years and they were all colleagues or friends. I knew, though, that this was an ordeal for John; to be in a situation where he was once again the centre of attention. I felt very protective, and nervous, on his behalf; walking into the room was ridiculously nerve-racking given that I knew everyone there. For most people there it was enough just to see John and as people came up to say hallo I felt enormously grateful to those who managed as normal a conversation as possible. At the same time, I could understand why people might blurt out, 'I did a bungee-jump for you', but I also understood John's confusion and embarrassment. What on earth was he supposed to say in reply?

Letters from well-wishers were arriving every day, waiting to be answered, as were invitations to visit all kinds of people and places and accept this or that award. We turned down just about everything, and attended only those which we felt we just could not refuse, but we seemed to be stepping into our public personae every few days. Ordinary life still hadn't arrived and I began to feel loaded with responsibilities again, at the same time as being aware that I wasn't giving John the support he needed. I felt resentful that I had to be so strong when I wanted to relax. I was like a corkscrew that couldn't straighten out. I had always thought that when he came home I would want to look after him, but I felt I was failing at the job. I saw him fumbling with tin openers and corkscrews and couldn't bear it. I realize now that John's release uprooted and disorientated me almost as much as his abduction had done five and a half years ago. It was terribly confusing and brought with it a host of demands and difficulties. I had been aiming for his release for so long, but when it happened it knocked me for six. I wanted to get to know him again and build on what I had felt while he was away and when he was released. We couldn't even visit his home at Cornish Hall End, or think about going to see his mother's grave, without working out how we would avoid any press who might be waiting at the church, or who might get wind that John was coming. I hadn't anticipated that it would be such a long time before we felt that outside influences had loosened their grip on our lives.

We had talked about writing a book together and it seemed very important. I saw it as a way through the confusion, a way of putting the past into perspective and then moving on, as well as a way of setting our story in reality rather than in some sort of fairy-tale land. Our heads still in a spin, we visited a series of publishers with Mark and then decided that we were exhausted, we really needed to get away. We wanted to go somewhere hot, where we wouldn't be on show but could just be ourselves, somewhere we could relax. I called Karen, who with Cathy was winding down the Friends, and once again she was brilliant, arranging us a holiday, under assumed names, in Bequia, in the Caribbean.

Camden, October 1991

In the middle of October, the Friends had a big party at the Café Delancey in Holborn. I was so nervous that I very nearly didn't go. When we arrived and walked in I couldn't see a face I recognized. It was only after half an hour and a few drinks that I began to see more and more familiar faces until it dawned on me that I knew nearly everyone there. It was a great party and although, in a way, I was the centre of attention, I felt neither conspicuous nor out of place. It was a terrific and very happy celebration of a job well done.

A few days after the party I went round to Chris Martin's flat, where I had been living when I went to Lebanon. I had felt nervous, making one of my first 'solo' outings, but as soon as I was in the familiar surroundings, with Chris pottering about from room to room as he always had, I began to calm down. It was a pleasure being with him, feeling his affection for me and sensing that his desire to talk was as strong as mine. Most of my belongings were still there. He had everything neatly piled in my old bedroom, bags filled with old clothes and we went through some of them. Memories of times long past flooded back, a forgotten and battered pair of gym shoes reminded me of a day six or seven years earlier when Jill and I had been out with Barbara, trying to kit ourselves out for a black-and-white party. When I found a letter from my mother, I realized that we had looked enough for one day and decided to pick the things up another time. There was no need to rush.

Life was much quieter now and I felt my confidence growing. Jill and I went to the Harvest Thanksgiving service at Broxted Church with my father. We'd lived in the house next to the church, which is now a hotel, for six years and my mother is buried in the churchyard. I didn't yet feel ready to visit her grave, fearful that the acceptance of her death that I'd reached in captivity would be shattered by such a physical reminder of her loss. But it was nice to be in the church, participating in an ordinary service. Afterwards we chatted to the vicar, Jack Filby, and members of his congregation, who told me about the events they had staged to raise funds for the Friends and the champagne service Jack had organized on the weekend after my release. It was pleasant meeting people whom I had known during my university years and who had been good friends of my parents. There was one odd moment, though, which rather upset me. An old friend of my father's suddenly seemed shy of me, treating me like a celebrity. I wanted to give him a gentle shake and say, 'I'm Pat's son, John, I used to come round sometimes for a drink with my parents. That's all I am, just an old neighbour, nothing more.'

After the service we went back home to Cornish Hall End. I had planned to go there after leaving Merrow Farm in August, but had decided against it because the media were permanently encamped outside. I was also apprehensive that returning home so soon, uncertain how I would feel without my mother there, would have been an awful emotional strain. I was so confident, though, of my renewed friendships with my father and Terence that I'd decided to wait, so that I could go back with a clear head and absorb the changes in my own time.

I went into the house with some trepidation, yet as soon as I started moving from room to room, seeing all familiar things in their familiar places, I felt a great sense of peace. My mother was still here, as I'd anticipated in that room in Beirut, she was still with us. Now we could talk about her, even laugh at our funny memories of her, without becoming too sad.

I was glad that I hadn't visited her grave that morning. It was far better to feel comfortable at home with the rest of my family before taking that step. When I did eventually go, with my father and Terence, two Christmases after my release, I felt a very happy bond between us all as we planted some flowers and gently mourned.

There were still times when I'd find myself standing somewhere in the flat, unable to remember what I was doing, where I'd been going, although the clouds of confusion dispersed for longer and longer periods. Some of these moods were doubtless brought on when a hostage was released or there were rumours that one was coming home. I would worry for them and my own memories of my return flooded back and I felt again the old doubts and guilt at leaving my friends behind. I never seemed able to convey these thoughts to Jill. How could I? Even I found them incoherent. Unfairly, I sought complete solace from her, demanding her attention and constant reassurance that she loved me as a way of blocking out any other anxieties. Not only was it unfair, it was counter-productive. We both realized that we needed to get away again and at the beginning of November we left for a three-week holiday on the Caribbean island of Bequia.

Just before we left, we went to Bush House so that I could be interviewed on *Outlook* and send a birthday message to Terry Anderson and greetings to Tom and TW. Brian joined us on the line from Dublin. It was a strange experience speaking to my friends through this medium. We all had enjoyed *Outlook* while in captivity and had been very impressed with one of the regular presenters Barbara Myers, so I was pleased that she was on duty that day. I wasn't to know that very soon I would be able to talk to my old friends face to face.

Bequia was a magical place for me. Karen had arranged everything with British Airways so that we travelled first-class, under assumed names, luxuriating in anonymity. I had always wanted to visit a tropical island and now here I was. One morning I went for an early swim and, turning back to look at the island, I marvelled at the lush vegetation climbing up the steep slopes from the shore. I was really there. It was not a fantasy to escape the tedium of a Lebanese cell. I was there. I could learn windsurfing, go diving, go sailing. Anything was possible.

Bequia, October 1991

When we arrived in Bequia, by speedboat late at night, I thought we had come as near to paradise as we could get. The rooms were cabins half-hidden by exotic plants and trees; there was a small, private beach, and the hotel itself was an old colonial-style plantation house. When we ventured out to explore the area the next morning

I was still fearful after the last few months in Britain, and felt quite wary as we stumbled around, attempting to cross a path which the sea had shattered during a recent storm. Crossing the path, John cut his foot on some barbed wire and as he hesitated over his next move, we heard someone call, 'You've been in worse scrapes than that!' An English couple!

We discovered that there were quite a few English people staying at the hotel. They left us alone but I still felt that we were on show, and John was often too nervous to eat the rather rich food we were served. I was so tired; we had needed total escape, but we hadn't got it. Before we left, the strain of being recognized had seemed worse than ever. It had been so strange to be standing waiting to pay for something in a shop, thinking about mundane, ordinary things like what's on television tonight, and suddenly being asked by a complete stranger, 'How's John doing? Are you two going to get married?'

It was almost as if we were back to the campaign days when people would ask, 'What do you think John's chances of release are at the moment?' And I would reply, 'Well, I am cautiously optimistic . . .'

Happily, the English couple who had first spotted us became friends and I realized that being able to talk to them in the setting of the hotel was doing a lot for John's self-confidence. The Pagett-Browns and two other English couples we liked made him feel that he could strike up ordinary friendships again with strangers. I began to realize that he approached such new relationships on a much deeper level than he had before. Perhaps it was a reflection of the intense importance of his friendships in captivity. Other people responded equally intensely, and it boosted his confidence. I hadn't realized that John's self-esteem had been at such a low ebb; he'd said that he thought people were only interested in him as a freak, but I hadn't taken his fears seriously enough nor reassured him that this wasn't the case. I'd thought that John would find that reassurance in his friends, but hadn't appreciated the extent of his nervousness about taking up with them again. It was the normality of meeting people again that mattered; John could feel ordinary and comfortable with them.

The confusion I felt was symptomatic of the time; every few weeks I would look back and think, 'God, why didn't I see that a couple of weeks ago?' and then feel guilty for being so muddle-headed. A few days after we arrived in Bequia, we celebrated my thirty-fourth birthday at the hotel bar. John and I had just heard from Mark that the book deal had gone through, giving us the next twelve months to tell our story properly. I had just sent a fax to my boss, Rachel, in London, handing in my notice.

I sat at the bar, marvelling at what I'd done, but feeling slightly uneasy. I couldn't have concentrated on my job. John and I had been together virtually every day since his release, and the idea of working five days a week was just not possible. Yet I felt that I had left my old life behind without yet knowing what lay ahead.

John and I had talked about how we had lived in different time-scales for all these years and now that we were trying to live in the same one, they didn't always harmonize. John still sometimes operated on his old time-system and had no concept of what could be done with the hours that were passing. For me a busy lifestyle had become the norm and I was locked into thinking that time had to be spent profitably. I had always felt guilty doing nothing and found it difficult to relax. I missed the contact with people at work and on the campaign, and having an overriding purpose every day. I loved being with John again, and yet sometimes was confused and frightened by his lack of direction, his moods and anxieties. I tried to deal with them as best I could, but often felt useless, and then guilty. Sometimes I felt as if I were in another kind of limbo; when I looked back the past five years didn't seem real, and neither did this.

I felt guilty that I had made John famous, that everywhere we went people recognized us and that John was unable to do the little things that he had thought of doing for so long. I had made them impossible. I realized that I felt ignored, too. I wasn't the centre of attention these days, and was surprised to find how much I had become accustomed to it; I thought I'd hated it. 'What about me?' was the thought that kept sneaking its way into my head. I had to tell John how I was feeling, but felt anxious that I was loading even more worry and confusion on to him. I thought, however, that what I was experiencing was natural; I was bound to feel high and dry when reality took over. Where did the past end and the future begin?

Despite his own fears, John listened to mine and tried to deal with them. Ever since his release I had been amazed by how well he handled every situation; his instincts were absolutely right as were his judgements about people. I found that I trusted his opinion and was continually impressed by how quickly he had adapted to the outside world. I saw that he'd developed a layer of steel in him now, a strength to face whatever was thrown at him and the knowledge that nothing could ever again be as bad as what he had already been through and survived. His natural optimism and resilience would bounce him back so that he could, mostly, look to the future with confidence and hope. I saw how much more determined he'd become, too. In Bequia we had the chance to learn to scuba-dive and we were both quaking with fear as the morning dawned.

'I don't think I'll go,' I said. 'I'll try it in the pool, but I'd rather do some painting after that.'

'I'm going to have a go,' said John. 'I was thinking this morning: "This is silly. OK, you're nervous, but you've dreamed of doing this for years and now you've got the chance you can't pass it up because of a few nerves." '

Later, the sea turned grey and choppy and a storm blew up, but John still went out on the boat to do his first-ever dive; he came back shaking with cold, but enthusiastic and eager for more.

Not long after we arrived on the island, we met an English couple, Sue and Jimmy Pagett-Brown. They recognized us straightaway, but were both kind and tactful, avoiding talk of hostages or the campaign unless we brought it up. Sue taught Jill to paint and I was very impressed with her first attempts. I was seeing a new, creative side to her that I hadn't come across before. I could also see that she found it very relaxing and tried my best not to distract her. I did go diving, although I nearly gave up in panic, and we went sailing, to Mustique with the Pagett-Browns. We also tried windsurfing: Jill was brilliant; I was an exhausted and bitter failure.

It was in Bequia that Jill told me at last that I must look after myself more and, at the same time, try and be aware of her needs, for support, space and time. In theory, I was now able to accept such responsibilities; in practice, I still found it very difficult to set aside my own need for reassurance.

One morning in our third week we were woken by a knock on the door. I went and answered it. The man said, 'Phone call for Mr Childs.'

I was about to tell him he'd got the wrong room when I remembered that Childs was my alias. I jumped into a pair of shorts and trotted behind him to reception. It was Pearson.

'Tom and Waite are out!'

'Brilliant, fucking brilliant. How are they?'

'They both looked fine in Damascus. They both chatted on and on, they were really on a roll.'

'Any word on Terry?'

'Yeah, Waite said that they'll be releasing him within a month and that they'll release a couple more Yanks soon.'

'So, it really is working out.'

'Looks like it. Do you want to give a statement?'

I always found it odd when Chris, Cathy or Karen asked that. They knew from long practice that it made their lives much easier if they could fire off a statement to the Press Association, rather than having a stream of papers calling them. But how could I express the joy I felt in a couple of lines? Tom and TW were out, Terry looked certain to follow soon; then, we would all be free of chains, and any guilt at leaving a friend behind. I gave a standard sentence or two on how happy we were and wished them peace and quiet in which to get back to normal. We chatted on a while, then I let Chris get back to work.

Back in our room, Jill and I managed to tune in to the World Service and, hugging each other, heard the good news repeated. We automatically wondered if anyone would try to find us, assuming that the Waites and Sutherlands would follow Jackie's and my experience and keep a low profile until things had calmed down, and there would be no-one for the press to quote. On the whole it seemed most unlikely that anyone would bother to come so far. But, at breakfast, the hotel manager came over to us and told us that a journalist had been on to him to see if we were still there. It turned out that a group of British travel writers had been at the hotel during our first week and had recognized us. The manager had explained that we were there to avoid the likes of them and asked them to keep the secret. They had all agreed. Of course, now one of them felt he had a legitimate reason for checking us out. The manager had assured him that we'd moved on to another island, and were maybe even on our way home, for which we were both very grateful.

Later that afternoon, as we sat surrounded by palm trees and tropical plants, I remembered Jill taking me to the flower market in London's Columbia Road, just before we left for Bequia. As we moved along the crowded street, looking at the various displays, Jill stopped to say hallo to one of the stall-holders. He smiled at her, then turned to me, saying, 'I gave your girl a plant a little while ago, and then you came home – I reckon if I give you one for Terry Waite he'll be out soon, too.' It was a lovely gesture.

Back at home, John and I plunged back into another whirlwind of events every few days which we geared up for and then recovered from before moving on to the next. We were both finding that our moods were going up and down all the time and, although to a lesser extent, I found I was experiencing the same 'brain-freezing' that struck John every now and again, leaving me at a loss to know what to do. Our lack of direction still bothered me as we went from an Amnesty International dinner, to lunch with the Lyneham Base Commander, Group Captain Corbett and his wife, to a service at Broxted Church where we felt a bit as if we were in a goldfish bowl. On John's birthday he went to Buckingham Palace for lunch and came back chuckling at the bizarre nature of his celebrity status and the glimpses it afforded him of fascinating lives. In the evening, his former flatmate Chris Martin had organized a small party in his old flat. I had been back only once since John was kidnapped and I experienced an attack of nerves as we got into the lift. It was like Dr Who's Tardis, transporting us back to 1986 when we were both young, naïve, had no responsibilities whatsoever and paid no attention to what the future might bring. I'd wondered what it was going to be like, but everyone was relaxed and it was a relief to see John chatting to his friends again as normal, without being hampered by the fears and worries he'd had over the past few months.

A few days later Terry Anderson was released; Tom Sutherland and Terry Waite had returned home a couple of weeks earlier. Chris sent us round a video of his press conference. For a few seconds, at the beginning, Anderson broke down but recovered his composure and proceeded to deal with the questions, some quite tricky, with great presence of mind. Someone from the British press asked him what he thought of John, and Anderson paused for a minute.

'John—' he said, taking a deep breath, 'I think John was the best of us.'

I turned to John, smiling, then saw he was in tears. I held him tightly, but I didn't understand, what was the matter?

'I just didn't know, I just didn't know if I'd done all right,' he said. 'Only he knows, you see, only he knows what it was like.'

It had been fairly clear to me that John had worked hard to keep his companions going, that his sense of humour would have lifted them time after time, and that they would have recognized, as I and his friends already knew, that John gives more than anyone else. He can never see that, though; his other great quality is modesty.

Anderson's release seemed to unsettle John for a while; he began to return to the interrupted sleeping patterns of captivity and the fogginess that had clouded his mind during the days immediately following his captivity. Keenan said, on John's release, that he'd returned to sleeping like a hostage; his words came back to me now.

I was hugely relieved that all the Western hostages, apart from the two West Germans who were to follow several months later, were now finally free. It closed a chapter in all our lives. We'd already decided that the campaign should probably end, but now we could all move on. People had said to us that we mustn't let the spirit of the campaign die, and that we must use it to further another cause, but I wondered how something as unique as that could continue. The captivity of the hostages seemed to have touched something deep inside the people who supported the campaign and those who wrote to John and me in their thousands after he came home. The letters were wonderful, full of warmth and love, for people the writers had never met. John and I wrote a letter to all the Friends around the country, hoping it would go some way towards thanking them for all they had done.

We set about answering all the letters which were piled up in the campaign office, at Pat's house, and at the flat, but it was impossible to read more than ten at a time; the emotions expressed were too powerful; it was too overwhelming.

Cathy and I began to clear out the Friends' office, peeling off the Sellotape from the childrens' posters, thumbing through the photographs of campaign events over the years. It was strange that it was all over. Many of the supporters had written to tell Cathy how they had celebrated John's release with street parties and church services. One woman, Clancy Firth, had made sure that no-one in her home town of Sutton-in-Ashfield forgot John and on 8 August her telephone never stopped ringing with messages of congratulation, one caller joking that she thought Clancy would surely be on the plane to Damascus. The Murphys in Lancaster had finally completed the Education Pack, which, despite Gina's determination, had never actually got off the ground. The final version, which they named the Freedom File, made me wonder if there was any point in writing a book, they'd already done such a good job. I didn't want to throw anything away, it all seemed too precious, but on the other hand, what was to be done with everything? I took all the files, some photographs, drawings and other mementoes and Cathy cleared out the rest, storing all the letters from our supporters over the years in a cupboard. We couldn't bear to throw them out, so there they stayed, a lasting testimony of the love, determination and commitment granted to us willingly over the years. Although the euphoria of John's release was over, I felt, looking at the office and at all the letters, that I would remember the groundswell of sheer joy on that day for ever.

Much of that joy had been shared by the students of Hull University, and it was expressed in its purest form when John and I went up to Hull in mid-December on the occasion of his receiving an Honorary Doctorate from the university. The day was wonderful from start to finish, from the Vice-Chancellor's kind and witty speech to the reception John got on entering The John

McCarthy Bar. There was a fair number of press and crowds of people everywhere we went, but because the atmosphere was so special it was uplifting rather than intimidating. When John toured the Students' Union, with me following behind, I saw two girls walking away from him almost swooning, as if he were a pop star, and as we passed the cheering students who lined the route to the bar, one girl broke ranks to give John a kiss. It was wonderful to be there, really it was the first time we'd done anything of that kind that we'd actually enjoyed.

Camden, November 1991

By the time we came back from Bequia, things had quietened down again after Tom and Terry Waite's release. We had heard from Mark Lucas that the book deal we'd been discussing had come through. It was important to us both to tell our story in our own way, without worrying that it was being filtered through other people's ideas of us, and we now knew what we'd be doing for the next year, although Jill still hankered after a regular job. We didn't expect to start work on it until the New Year so were free to do as we liked.

My first birthday since coming home was rather different from those I'd experienced in Lebanon. The strangeness of the party in the Land of Grey and Pink with Sayeed, his cronies and Brian singing 'Happy Birthday' came back to me as I struggled into a suit and tried to keep calm at the prospect of having lunch at Buckingham Palace.

As soon as I got there I started to relax. The lunch was, of course, nothing to do with my birthday, but Sir Paul Greening, Master of the Household, told me that Cameron Mackintosh was another guest, which was a happy coincidence. The Mackintoshes had been neighbours of ours at Wood End so, although I hadn't seen

Cameron for years, I was relieved that there was someone present whom I knew. I was introduced to the other guests, then Cameron and I probably broke all sorts of protocol by indulging in a bear hug.

The Queen and the Duke of Edinburgh were announced and we formed a line and were introduced to their Royal Highnesses. Their faces were so familiar that I didn't feel overwhelmed at meeting them. The party broke up into groups to chat as the aides guided guests to meet the royal couple and after some general conversation we went into lunch. I have never seen so many people serving one table. I found that I was, after all, still very nervous and found the food almost too much, delicious though it was.

I was taken aback when a young man bent right down to serve me the next course and turned his face close to mine and beamed a huge smile of welcome. This pleasant, but funny, feeling of being somehow special lingered and after we'd had coffee and said goodbye to their Royal Highnesses, Sir Paul came up to me, saying that they'd heard it was my birthday and that they had a present for me. It was a print of Buckingham Palace. I was very moved that they should bother, and further surprised when he asked if I'd mind waving to the first-floor window as I left; his staff were very keen to get a better look at me. I did and saw a windowful of smiling faces.

That night, Chris Martin had arranged a party at the flat I had shared with him and Pete Nunn before I left for Lebanon. Chris had invited only our closest friends and it was a really good party; I managed to have a long chat with everyone. Barbara Mackie later said, 'You really "worked" the room, John!' I suppose I did, but it was important to me to show them that they were all my friends and that, even though I hadn't felt up to seeing them much, if at all, it wasn't through any lack of fondness. Talking about things we'd always had in common narrowed the gap of my years away, without hiding the fact. So with Roger Everatt, my old college friend whom I'd not seen since coming home, I talked about Van Morrison. He'd spent years trying to get me to listen to his music, but it had taken the Jihad, Brian Keenan and Nick Toksvig to make it happen. I told him how Brian had whispered the man's songs to me in our cells and how Brian was sure that he remembered Roger, who had spent one term at Coleraine University where Brian had done his first degree. Roger, for his part, told me how odd he'd felt at seeing me, a close friend, coming off the plane at Lyneham. 'That's the most famous person in the world – and it's John!' Quite a birthday.

The following weekend I went down to Lyneham to see TW. I was surprised to see him looking so haunted. But then I remembered that I had been in a state of shock for weeks after coming home. More to the point, I hadn't had to worry about press criticism of my past. Terry and I had a chat in his room. I was puzzled and a little disappointed at first. He went on about all the presents he'd been sent, his speech on his arrival home and the radio message he'd recorded for Anderson. But I soon realized that this wasn't bragging, this wasn't the VIP showing that he'd returned to his rightful domain and acclaim. He was, in fact, very unsure of himself and was almost seeking my approval for what he was doing. He would ask me how things were going, but, as I began to reply, would cut in on me, his eyes darting anxiously around the room.

'Yes, yes, but don't you find it frightening? The things they say in the press are terribly hurtful. I don't know what to think, don't know what I should do.'

'I think you're doing the right thing, TW. You don't have to perform for anyone. There'll be plenty of time to answer all your critics. Now you can just relax and enjoy getting to know your family again. I did that and I know I'd have been a complete wreck if I'd responded to all the razzmatazz when I got home. Mind you, I still get nervous.'

He would listen and, for a moment, look calm. But then his face would tense again and his eyes flicker as he confided another worry.

I was touched by this and, over the following months, was pleased that he felt able to share his worries and concerns with me as he had been unable to do in captivity – a shy man, unused to expressing his private feelings.

The following Wednesday Jill and I enjoyed another VIP perk. We had a private shopping spree at Selfridges after the store had closed. I still found it uncomfortable when I sensed someone had spotted me and felt so self-conscious that the idea of buying anything was displaced by the immediate need to get away from the scene. Having acquired some new clothes, we went back to the flat to hear that Terry Anderson was now a free man, that the spate of reports about his release had at last come true. I was so relieved that my friend would soon be meeting up with Maddy and Sulome that my mind barely focused on the fact that two German hostages were still in captivity.

For me, it was at last over. My friend was free of the nightmare that he had suffered and had done so much to help me endure. Terry was free. I couldn't take it in. It had been so long coming, it had sometimes seemed that it would never happen. 'He's done it! He's done it!' I chanted as I danced around Jill. 'Now we can relax.' Yet, over the next few days, I was very tense and found it difficult to sleep, worrying about Terry.

The Sunday after his release, Jill and I went up to Broxted for a service to dedicate a memorial hatchment for my mother. My father, Jill and I sat together. Terence hadn't joined us, fearing that the day would be spoiled by too much press attention. He was right. None of us could concentrate either on the service or on thoughts of my mother, as there was a group of photographers ten feet in front of us constantly snapping away. My father read a lesson and I read Simonov's poem, 'Wait for Me', as I had done at St Bride's. We were bitterly disappointed that what should have been a private service for friends and family had been taken over by the press.

I realized that I was getting better and that there was less and less to fear about being in the public eye when we went up to Hull for me to be awarded an honorary Doctorate of Letters. Although I was intensely nervous, the ceremony with all its pomp, and even the fact that I was kitted out in robes and hat, took much of the pressure off. I enjoyed it very much. When I thought of my idle performance as an undergraduate, I had felt a little shy about receiving such an accolade, but the Vice-Chancellor, David Dilks, gave a kind, and very moving, address. I was relieved that he pointed out that I wasn't remembered as a dedicated student and that my busiest hours had been spent not in the library but in the Students' Union bar which was now named after me.

After lunch we went to see The John McCarthy Bar. There were hundreds of students waiting for us. I felt like a pop star as we walked single file down a narrow gap left between the crowds of people, but I didn't feel in the least bit anxious. No-one pressed in on me and the mood was relaxed and happy. Inside I took stock of 'my' bar. It had changed a good deal since my days, being now an elegant place with proper tables and even carpets. We met the Union officials. I was a bit surprised to see that many of them wore suits and talked earnestly about the successful business they were running.

The students were all incredibly sensitive to our nervousness and wouldn't let anyone in until we said that it was all right. Jill and I sat with Geraldine and had a drink with Phillippa Breeze and other members of the Hull Friends of John McCarthy, talking about their campaigning, their studies, and my memories of Hull, while they passed over bits of paper for Jill and me to autograph.

I couldn't get over the fact that I had enjoyed the day so much. A month before, I would have been a gibbering wreck, but the students and faculty had been so natural that I was refreshed and encouraged that I had spent the day with barely a hint of nerves. Looking back, I can see that the Hull Convocation took place on Friday the 13th. Perhaps my mad hostage numbers game was still trying to tell me something: that I had entered a new era in

my return to life, an era in which fears of my curious
fame should be played down.

Camden, December 1991

Back in London, John and I attended the last meeting of
the Friends, which was held in The Crown and Sceptre.
All our friends had now got used to John being around.
It wasn't a big deal. Not many people were at the 'meeting', but as John went to the bar he was surrounded by
people who'd recognized him and wanted him to sign
autographs or visit their restaurant on the spot for a
drink. I couldn't laugh about it; I knew how John would
be feeling and that it would be unlikely that he would
come here, his old local, again.

It was alarming how little remained of the old life now
John was back. I filled him in as much as I could on what
had happened, showing off how organized I'd become and
how I could handle all kinds of problems by myself. John
made a good job of appearing enthusiastic, but I realized,
too late, that I was undermining his confidence even
further and that it worried him that I was so independent.
I tried to put myself in his shoes and not talk about
things that might upset him, and then I got even more
confused. I wasn't sure if I was living in 1986 or 1991
and felt pulled between the two. John was taken aback
at the overtly sexual nature of TV advertising and the
way women had become more sexually independent and
confident in general and I couldn't work out if it was a
change in him or in the world; I certainly hadn't noticed it before. I sometimes felt as if I'd been away for
five years and I appreciated how little I'd noticed of the
world around me. I also realized that I and many of
our friends had become more politicized over the years,
but whether that came from coping with Thatcherism,
the campaign, or simply growing up, I couldn't tell.

I felt that all the pressures had mounted up again and

that we needed to get away. After Christmas we returned to the sanctuary of France, staying there for New Year. We spent the time making fires, cooking, and not worrying about being recognized, which was a huge relief as it made us both much calmer. Back in London, in mid-January we resumed a hectic pace of life. The first event, however, was a great party; another of Sue Brown's Flamenco Nights at the 100 Club, this time to celebrate the end of the campaign and formally thank many of those who had worked on it. We were both nervous, but John seemed more relaxed and enjoyed himself more, while I was able to thank Cathy, Joan and others for the fantastic job they had done. During John's speech he said that his love for me had sustained him over the years. It underlined how safe and comfortable it now felt to be talking in public about our feelings. During the campaign it had sometimes seemed as if we glibly bandied around John's name and those of the other hostages as if they were products rather than people; I remembered my panic at the prospect of John becoming less my boyfriend and more a symbol for others. However political and organized the campaign had become, though, I felt that it was now ending, as it had started, as an expression of love. Afterwards, it was wonderful to see John with his arms around Cathy, Karen, Anne Lohmeyer, Jane Parritt, Sue Barnard and Jackie How, the women who had run our campaign office over the years and know that for him it was now a genuine pleasure to thank people, and not an enormous strain.

Camden, December 1991

On 17 December Jill and I went to the carol service at the FO. I was very pleased to have a chance to talk to Douglas Hurd again and meet his family. After the celebration Jill and I went to The Crown and Sceptre for the last meeting of the Friends. I had spent so many hours in this bar and now I was here again with friends with a capital F.

I felt slightly uneasy when recounting the fact that we had just come from the FO. I was cautious that I was beginning to sound like the captive TW and getting too carried away with my new status, especially as the FO had been the target for most of the campaign's activity.

Christmas was quiet, but enjoyable, spent with my father and Terence at Cornish Hall End. Jill stayed for a couple of days, before going on to her parents in Doncaster. She came back down before the New Year, as we had decided to spend it in Brittany. It was a good holiday, and we seemed closer and more confident in each other than we had done for a while.

I still had mood swings, though, but they were less common or severe. Jill also was able to relax much more. I realized that I had put a terrible strain on her after my first month home by relying so much on her company and approval. In many ways, I was jealous of her, of her confidence, her experience and even her friends. I often feared that she despised me. I had found it so hard to cope since I got back, even with tiny things. I couldn't seem to do anything right. Perhaps, too, she was jealous of the fact that she thought people were no longer interested in her but only in me. Superficially, this was true. I was the one who had been just a photograph for years, now I was a real person. My experience had, on the surface at any rate, been more peculiar. Maybe people felt that they knew her and what she'd been doing, whereas life in a cell, despite the testimony of other former hostages, especially Brian, was still rather unfathomable.

I noticed that Jill began to stay in and leave me to go out on my own to friends' parties. I now appreciate that it was only then that she felt able to do so, finally feeling that she did not have to accompany me everywhere in case I got confused. The relief must have been enormous, but she needed much more support than I appreciated and I felt cheated that just as I began to feel so much more confident, she should allow herself moments of depression. When I, too often, took refuge in getting drunk, she must have been at her wits' end.

The 'hangover' from the previous five years made it impossible for either of us to take on fully the other's experience, yet at the same time each of us was with the person best placed to help. It wasn't until I was clear-headed enough to recognize that I did feel drained for a couple of days after any of our public appearances, and that this was because I felt I had somehow exposed myself too deeply, and was nervous of that, that I was able to understand what Jill had lived with for so long.

I had been amazed to hear of the number of events she had attended, the number of people she'd lobbied, the number of interviews, yet I hadn't realized that she felt then and still did feel that she'd given too much of herself. As I began to appreciate that each anniversary, each birthday, each Christmas she had had to find the energy for a round of interviews and events, I appreciated that her ordeal had been in many respects more difficult than mine. At last I understood that my current worries about being a celebrity were a mere fraction of the worries with which she'd lived for years. Now, we did not have to go anywhere or attend anything unless we wanted to, but before she'd had to, or felt she'd had to. She had cranked up the physical, mental and emotional strength to go out there and do it time and again, never knowing if there was any point, if it were good for me or if it would ever end. Now I was back and, as I became the focus of attention, she found that she had to dredge up yet more energy to look after me, when she should, at last, have been able to relax. She must have felt I had stolen everything from her: her independence, her career, her friends, her special role.

She'd made the brave decision to stop calling herself my girlfriend more than two years earlier; now I believe she felt that she had once again been relegated to that role and that as far as anyone else was concerned she held no other interest. What she did not perhaps appreciate, although I mentioned it often enough, was that many of the people who came up to me, did so to let me know what a 'one in a million that girl is'. I heartily agreed, but didn't necessarily need anyone else to nudge me into acknowledging all she had done for me.

I found that I spent much more time talking to my women friends than I had done in the past. I so wanted to understand Jill and respond to her needs and felt that I had to find out how women ticked. I hadn't seen or spoken to any for so long. It was easier to get to grips with the changes my male friends had undergone – after all, I, too, had changed and grown – but the ways in which the women I knew had developed were a mystery. As I began to build up a social life again, I opted to spend a lot of time in female company. I had always enjoyed the company of women but, more to the point, I was now very comfortable with the idea of expressing my feelings – as a hostage it had been essential and, with the help of Gordon Turnbull, it seemed natural to be as open as possible. Most men feel rather ill-at-ease with such frankness, so talking to old friends like Gina, Ronnie and Barbara, and new friends like Mary, Cathy and Karen, was both a delight and a considerable source of support and sound advice.

On our return from Brittany, Jill and I again seemed to be caught up in a hectic round of parties and official lunches. In mid-January the Friends had a final, thank you party. Sue Brown organized a Flamenco night at the 100 Club on Oxford Street. I was nervous about it, but only because I was going to make a speech. I'd thanked the Friends for their amazing efforts and the vital support they had given me and the other hostages in all my brief public appearances, and had written to them, through the campaign office. In fact, I was still working my way through replying to the great mound of well-wishers' letters, but being able to say a few words at the party was very important to me. I could stand in front of many of the central players and those people who had formed local groups around the country and thank them again, personally. In the private atmosphere of the party, it was also a pleasure to thank Chris, Cathy, Karen and

Jill for their particular support since my return.

The party was a great success, with a tremendously happy atmosphere. I was grateful that enough time had passed since my home-coming for me to enjoy the evening, without being overwhelmed by emotion. I was pleased that so many people were there, many old friends whom I hadn't yet seen, and many new friends about whom I had only heard. There were even members of the FO there; it seemed quite natural that, despite having once borne the brunt of the campaign's criticism, they should now be welcome to share the fun.

The following weekend Jill and I flew up to Scotland to attend Tom Sutherland's welcome home party. It was a pleasure to meet up with more of Tom's family and friends – I stopped one of Tom's English friends dead in his tracks by pausing for a moment after he had introduced himself, then saying, 'Do you still drive a Jaguar?' He looked flabbergasted. 'How do you know that?' I explained that I remembered Tom telling me that he'd enjoyed driving it once on holiday, but that he thought the petrol consumption outrageous. The man laughed. 'Always the mean Scot, even after years in the States. That's Tom all right!'

Jill and I were amazed and concerned at Tom and Jean's appetite for this type of celebration. Tom spoke happily of all the public events he'd been to as a celebrity. 'We're having a ball!' he would say when I suggested that he really should take it easy. I tried to get him to think about taking a quiet holiday away from all of the hullabaloo so that he could spend more time with his family. I also took the opportunity to bring up the problem of the Granada film. I knew that they had approached Tom and explained how Brian and I felt about the project. He took the point and agreed not to talk to them, but he really couldn't see the need for a holiday. He was enjoying his freedom too much.

The Granada film was a recurring irritation. While I appreciated that their original intention had been to make a campaigning film which would have brought our plight

612

to wider public notice, I couldn't understand their urgency now that we were free. None of us had yet fully come to terms with our experiences and, until we had done so, were not in a position to help anyone else make sense of what we had gone through. The fact that it went ahead was an unnecessary strain at an already difficult time.

I was, therefore, very disappointed when Tom, eager to accommodate all-comers, spoke to Granada, after all. I was deeply troubled that he was taking the attention and adulation too much to heart. I tried to explain that while all the warmth and affection was quite genuine, it wasn't based on who we really were, but on the symbolic value which we seemed to have acquired. People want to believe in heroes, but that didn't have anything to do with how we had actually survived our ordeal.

Our survival was, in fact, a case of necessity rather than old-fashioned heroism and it was Frances Waite who summed that up for me. Jill and I were invited to attend a luncheon at Lancaster House for Perez de Cuellar who had just received an honorary knighthood from the Queen. Terry and Frances were there, too. Despite the grandness of our surroundings, it was a very relaxed and pleasant affair. I was touched when, as we sat down to lunch Señora Perez de Cuellar called down the table, saying, 'My husband still has the envelope for your letter with the notes he made on it, he will keep it always.' I was moved that our meeting had indeed meant as much to him as I had felt at the time.

As we prepared to leave I was talking to Frances when someone came up to me saying he couldn't imagine how we'd survived. I was fumbling for an appropriate response when Frances observed bluntly: 'They had to.' She was, of course, absolutely right and I was impressed with her directness and good sense. Thereafter whenever I was asked that question I would simply say: 'We had to, we had no choice. It would be the same for anyone.'

A few days later, I was again reunited with Keenan. We were both in search of a lavatory. A tall, slim man in a morning suit came up to us to ask if he could help us. We explained our dilemma and he abruptly pushed at the wall next to him to reveal a hidden room. As we straightened our ties, Brian observed, 'Those Jihad boys could have learned a thing or two about secret bathrooms if they'd come here to Buck House.'

We'd met a few minutes earlier in a large reception hall where other recipients of the CBE were gathering.

'Where the fuck have you been, McCarthy?' he'd muttered. 'I've been here, alone, for ages!'

It was a very strange experience to be there with Brian. The interlude in the secret lavatory seemed to epitomize the extraordinary change in our lives. Just months before we had been nobodys, chained in a dungeon. Now we had become celebrities receiving high honours in a palace. It was also bizarre introducing TW and Brian under these circumstances. They'd lived a few feet apart for months, yet had always been separated by a concrete wall and the limitless void of our captors' obsession with secrecy. Now we were all signing programmes for our fellow CBEs, embarrassed that we should be the focus of attention when we had done nothing to warrant such an honour. All the other people there had worked for their award, for charity, in social services, in industry, to benefit society.

I looked over the heads of those gathered around us to see Gary Lineker similarly occupied. I wondered what he'd think of my crazy belief that Lineker was Arabic for goal. He looked up and smiled at me, suggesting that he might like to talk to me and also that he was resigned to the duty of being a national hero.

We moved downstairs to an enormous ballroom, where the investitures were to take place. A military band provided background music, as we queued in an orderly fashion in an ante-room. I watched Brian exchange a few words with Her Majesty and then it was my turn. Concentrating on the instructions I'd been given, I took the ritual two steps forward. As the Queen placed the medal around my neck, she said, 'I hope we're not making you too nervous.' Stammering a little, I managed a reply. She went on, 'Your pal just told me that this was more frightening than anything you met in Lebanon.'

Outside I met Brian's sisters, Brenda and Elaine. It was a real pleasure to see them face to face. I had only ever spoken to them briefly on the telephone. I felt I knew them, not only from Brian but also from Jill who met them many times when their campaigning paths crossed. Our meeting was sadly brief as Brian, TW and I had to go to pose for the photographers, but it was important that they, along with Jill, my father and Frances Waite, were there. I think all three former hostages felt better for being able to share our honours with those who had kept us going, made people aware of our plight. It also gave some recognition to all those who had supported them over the years.

Camden, January 1992

The day after the Friends' final Flamenco Night, we raced up to Scotland to see Tom and Jean Sutherland, who were over on a visit following his recent release. I was happy to meet him; he was just as I imagined, and I was amazed at his stamina. I couldn't take the pace after just one night's partying and a day in his company, but Tom's appetite for big occasions and press interviews seemed enormous and he paid no attention to John's advice that he should take it a bit easy. I know John was concerned that at some point Tom would hit a terrible low, as he had in captivity, and I tried to put in my two penn'orth as well, but Tom seemed to thrive on constant activity and hasn't seemed to suffer any side-effects as far as we know. Tom couldn't understand John's wariness of the press and had answered questions put to him about Terry Waite or whether the various campaigns had actually been of any benefit to the hostages.

Tom later co-operated with Granada Television over the drama-documentary, *Hostages*. John was appalled at the idea of his captivity being dramatized so soon, in front of millions of people; it distressed him to think that someone else would tell his story before he'd had a chance to come to terms with it himself, and I supported his stance. Before his release, I had agreed to help Granada; the friends had been persuaded that a dramatization of events would help him and the other hostages by making the issue more understandable and so putting more pressure on the Government. I saw it as a campaigning film and had not been able to understand why Brian Keenan was so vehemently against it; I had put it down to his general mistrust of the media.

When John was released a few months later, I believed that the situation had changed so dramatically that the film would be redundant. Chris told Granada that we would no longer be involved, and we believed that the film would not go ahead. When we realized that it was going to be made, and would be the story of the hostages in captivity, John wrote several letters to Granada, setting out his objections. He understood why I had co-operated in the first place, but I felt guilty that I had contributed to something that was putting him under such strain; our correspondence with Granada, the stories in the press and the prospect of the programme itself cast a shadow over us until the film was shown.

We had decided not to watch it, but on the night changed our minds and watched it with friends. It was weird seeing other people play us, but it all fell into perspective in the opening few minutes when John had been curiously transformed from producer to reporter. We all burst out laughing; it was simply incorrect. That set the tone for the evening and a sense of relief enveloped me when it was all over.

We had another brush with the press at the opening night of Sandi Toksvig's *A Midsummer Night's Dream*; the photographers were unpleasant and it spoiled the evening, reinforcing our view that we should avoid public events, unless absolutely necessary. When we went up to

Doncaster, a few days later, to see my mum and dad and thank Doncaster Council for all it had done, I was relieved that the Leader, Gordon Gallimore, understood that we wanted to keep the occasion private. We were given a tour of the Mansion House and wrote a letter to the people of Doncaster for the local paper thanking them for their staunch support of the campaign. Gallimore and my mum told us how, on the day of John's release, the entire town centre had been covered with yellow ribbons.

Much of it was down to my mum and dad, and now that my head was beginning to clear I realized the true extent of their loyalty and how much it had meant to them to be part of the campaign. My mum, like me, had, over the past five years, grown in confidence from being thrown in at the deep end. Both she and my dad had been thrust into the local limelight when the campaign in London started and had lived with its ambiguous effects as I had. For a long time I'd been too weighed down with my own responsibilities to appreciate their problems, and the pressures after John's release meant that I had not seen them enough. I know they longed for us all to be a normal family again and I had found it difficult to explain why, as yet, it couldn't be. I didn't really understand it myself. They were delighted to have John at home at last and I was proud of my dad for quelling his enormous desire to ask John millions of questions. He waited until the subject came up naturally and then the interrogation he gave John would have put Michael Buerk to shame!

Antigua, March 1992

Two days after receiving the CBE, Jill and I went to Antigua to spend ten days with Terry, Madeleine and Sulome. I was really happy for Jill to get to know them. They were good friends, normal people like us who were coping with difficulties almost identical to our own. Beyond that it was wonderful to be doing things with

Terry after years of talking about things and doing nothing. It was a relief, as it was with Brian, and increasingly with TW, to be able to speak about past and present experiences knowing that my references would be understood, that I didn't need to explain details. One afternoon Terry and I sat on the beach with a glass of wine. He suddenly stood up and asked if I could sail.

'No,' I replied, jumping up with him. 'But I'd love to learn.'

Within a few minutes we were underway in a tiny sailboat, Terry explaining what he was doing, then letting me try my hand, just as he had when he taught me chess. It was a glorious moment, moving freely with the wind over the turquoise water, looking at him so healthy, tanned and happy. We talked of many things, among them fame, fear and the pleasures and difficulties of renewing relationships.

Suddenly there was a crash. The boat slewed round, the sail flapping out of control. We had run on to a reef. Terry went over the side to ease us off.

'Goddammit, this coral's sharp! Bloody hell, McCarthy, you oab, I didn't survive six years in a cell to be flayed alive because you can't steer!'

Terry and Madeleine had been in Antigua for three months and Jill and I realized that because of that they had made a lot of progress together; we resolved to find ourselves somewhere quiet in the country when we got home. Terence again came up trumps and through a friend found us the perfect cottage. It was comfortable to live in, quaint to look at and, above all, in a very peaceful village within easy reach of London. As soon as we moved there I felt happier and more confident every day. I knew that I was safe there. When I got wound up I could go for a walk – something I rarely felt like doing in busy Camden. There, wary of being spotted, I found that I always walked quickly along the streets, head down, avoiding eye contact and often turning my face to reduce the risk of recognition. I was still too uncertain of myself to feel comfortable with the often emotional greetings from strangers. Now, after just a few minutes I would feel the tension draining from me as I watched the trees and saw birds and animals all around me.

Jill relaxed as well; our relationship, based on mutual security in our new cottage, grew far stronger. I was more comfortable than in the London flat as this was a home we had both chosen and, after a while, Jill realized I was able to look after myself and so could take herself off to London to see her friends or work on our book at the flat. I was so much stronger emotionally that I was little troubled by her absence and found that I now actually enjoyed my occasional visits to town and the dramatic change of pace they offered. I knew I could always return to the quiet of the cottage whenever I wanted. More importantly, I recognized that I had recovered; I was happy to spend an evening alone by the fire, quietly reading.

I even felt able to visit my old school with very little anxiety. Haileybury had changed so much; the attitude of the teaching staff and their relationship with their pupils seemed quite different from what I remembered. I enjoyed the service in the chapel and was perfectly happy answering questions from pupils and staff afterwards.

As with our visit to Hull, Jill and I both found that the day, busy though it was, left us with none of the 'hangover' feelings of doubt and confusion that we had so often felt in the past. Going back to school and sensing it was a good place seemed to indicate that I had finally come full circle. I was no longer the nervous youth I had been and could look at my life with the understanding and confidence that the past few years had brought me.

Camden, March 1992

Life slowly began to get back to some kind of normality. I started to find the time to see my friends again. I had a belated birthday night out with my girlfriends and met

619

up with them occasionally over the months, although not nearly as much as I had done before.

When we went to Antigua to see Terry Anderson, Madeleine and Sulome in March, I realized on the first day that I should have organized a similar retreat. As soon as Terry had given his first press conference, AP had hired two serviced apartments on the northern coast of the island. It was perfect: there was no-one else around, so they weren't recognized; the apartments were private and they could be a family at last; and they could bring friends over to stay in the extra apartment and get to know them again in a completely relaxed atmosphere. Terry had spent almost three months there by the time we saw him and he looked great, he hadn't been hounded, and he had not been available to attend any functions – they were waiting until he felt able to deal with them.

I liked Madeleine and Terry a great deal. Madeleine took me fishing and I relaxed in her company. She seemed to be coping with Terry's return very well and, looking at her, my doubts about whether campaigning had been right sometimes returned. Madeleine had kept a low profile, she had not had to worry about Terry being forgotten as his sister, Peggy, had campaigned for his release; she and Terry seemed to have none of the tensions that might have occurred had they *both* been well known. I enjoyed getting to know Terry as well. I'd been nervous of meeting him after hearing from John how intelligent he was, but he wasn't the combative person I'd expected; he was relaxed and easy-going. He hated to sit around, though. On our first day there he said, 'Anybody want to do some snorkelling?'

'I'll go in a little later, I think,' I said, turning back to my book.

He waited about sixty seconds and then jumped up, saying, 'Ready now?'

The combination of seeing Terry and Madeleine so relaxed in Antigua and the necessity to get on with writing the book prompted John and me to look for somewhere to stay in the countryside. It was a difficult job, but Terence came to our rescue through a friend of a friend and we had the perfect place – a quiet cottage in a pretty village, with easy access to London. I was very tired by now, and felt that I was limping from event to event, but being away from the busyness of Camden made all the difference.

John really began to relax here and I realized how much I had expected of him. A few minor operations were the only temporary setbacks and over the next few months he had the mental and physical space to recover. I continued to worry and feel responsible but realized that much of it was unnecessary. John supported me now, listening patiently to my concerns and talking them through. We had time to enjoy ourselves again.

I saw the book more and more as a way of coming to terms with what John had been through, of us catching up with one another and of escaping those five and a half years and the limbo of the time that followed. 'How am I going to write about all that?' I thought as we unloaded stacks of files and letters and newspaper clippings from the car. 'How am I going to pay tribute to everyone?' However, we hoped that by writing honestly about our experiences, we could put them into perspective and people might stop concentrating on our romance, or the possibility of whether we might or might not get married, and let us work it out for ourselves like anyone else. We started work – at a leisurely pace – had friends down to stay occasionally, and I went up to town more often to see them, realizing that it was up to me to make the effort, too. I still struggled to come to terms with my impatience for life to return to normal and the sudden gap, since John's release, in the support on which, I appreciated, I had come to depend. Neither could I shake off the feeling that everyone else was moving on; Barbara had moved to Birmingham to start a new job; Cathy had decided to take over the family business, publishing *Stage and Television Today*; Karen had begun working as press officer for one of the London boroughs; Chris and Vicky had announced their plans to marry in August and Ronnie and Lawrence, who had met through the campaign, were planning a wedding in September.

Chris, who had been a great support to John and myself in our attempts to deal with all the strangeness of the past months, organized a 'reunion' meeting of the Friends in The Crown and Sceptre. It was great to see everyone again, and the worries that we would find little to say to one another now that we were no longer working together, faded. Brian Keenan came to stay and I felt that any tensions that had existed between us in the past were resolved. He was relaxed, I was relaxed, the initial warmth that I felt towards him returned. It was fascinating to hear John and him talking about their time together and chat to him about the huge task of writing a book. He had finished his and it was encouraging to see that, since he had done so, he seemed so at ease with himself, it was like being with a different person. Terry Anderson came over to stay, too, for one night, and it was the same. As with Brian, it was interesting to share John's friendship with him and get to know someone whom I had heard so much about. Terry's stubbornness came in handy, too. That evening, we wanted to light a fire, but had no kindling, so Terry spent hours kneeling over the grate, blowing for all he was worth, on to a tiny flame. He simply refused to give up and, in the end, his determination won through. The fire flickered into life.

On 8 August, the anniversary of John's release, and also Sheila's birthday, we went to Cornish Hall End to see Pat and Terence. We had a quiet time at Cornish Hall End, and that evening went out for a meal. I missed Sheila's presence at the table. It was such a happy occasion, but at the same time very poignant. The anniversary of John's release can never be a completely happy day.

*   *   *

As spring turned to summer I felt ever stronger and happier and in mid-August Jill and I set off for Devon for my most important public duty to date. Chris Pearson and his girlfriend, Vicky Gillett, were getting married. I was to be best man. I was very honoured, but as the wedding day dawned I realized that I had not been so frightened since some of the darker days early in my captivity. My fears had nothing to do with my new status as a minor celebrity, or possible press attention; I was just terrified of making a speech that would please my friend and properly express my love for him.

Apart from almost forgetting the rings the day went perfectly. Vicky and Chris looked magnificent in church, and the Gilletts' home was the perfect setting for the reception. The whole weekend was a marvellous party. Vicky's parents had organized everything beautifully, and in such a relaxed manner that there was no formality or pomp in the proceedings. We were all friends, celebrating a very happy union. The only problem was that being so nervous about my speech I was unable to eat and could barely manage a glass of wine, convinced that I might collapse at any point. As the lunch went on I kept telling myself that I only had to hang on for an hour or so, read the speech and then would be able to stagger into the house and pass out on the first bed I could find.

Eventually we got to the speeches. Vicky's father, John, and then Chris, stood up and made funny and moving speeches off the top of their heads. I had to read mine. But once it was done, instead of falling over, I felt completely rejuvenated. I was alive and raring to go, so I changed out of my morning suit and took my part in the celebrations. My father was already right in the swing of things. It was marvellous to see him so relaxed, the awful tension of the last few years that had been so deeply etched into his face now quite gone, replaced with a boyish grin.

We stood together watching the antics on the dance floor. I said, 'You're looking extremely jolly!'

'Of course I am,' he replied, 'this is a terrific party; I'm enjoying it with you and tomorrow morning we can call Terence and tell him all about it. *Both* my boys are safe now – what more could I want?'

At some point in the evening Chris reminded me of the conversation we'd had with the taxi-driver on the way to church that morning. The driver had said: 'Is it right you've got Terry Waite coming today?'

'No,' replied Chris, 'we've got one of the other ones, John McCarthy.'

There was a pause before the driver said: 'How is John doing these days?'

'I'm fine, thank you,' said his other passenger. The car swerved slightly, as he scrutinized me in the rear-view mirror.

Devon, August 1992

The time for celebrating came a week after our trip to Cornish Hall End, down in Devon, when Chris married Vicky. The local motor lodge overlooking an estuary soon resembled a scene from *Eldorado* as everyone gathered there, leaning over their balconies to watch others arrive. We had a great time. Vicky's parents had organized an informal weekend around a lovely, traditional wedding. Vicky looked beautiful and Chris was obviously so happy, the strain that had been etched on his face for so long now gone. John was his best man, handsome in his morning suit but terribly nervous, probably more so than at any other time since his release. I realized, though, that his terror came from knowing he would have to make a speech later on and not from anything else.

I watched the three of them at the front of the church, their faces slightly tense with nerves. Chris had told me ages ago that he did not want to get married until John was home and it had made me realize how much his life, too, had been on hold. He had become a good friend and his wedding meant much more to me than it would have done several years before. I knew, too, how much it meant to him that John was his best man. 'Things have come full circle,' I thought, 'we're all here, happy for Chris and Vicky, and John is simply the best man for one of his dearest friends.'

Outside there was a danger of John being mobbed by the waiting cameramen. We had decided not to walk together, because of the press. I could see that John was getting bothered, but the only thing he was concerned about was not upstaging Chris and Vicky. Gina went over to make sure that he was OK. Luckily, the moment of tension passed without incident.

Later, back at the marquee in Vicky's parents' garden, John made his speech. He told the usual stories expected of a best man, but no-one could help but be moved when he said what a real friend Chris had been to him. With the speeches successfully completed, Chris and Vicky hit the dance floor, completely wrapped up in each other. Everyone danced for hours to just about every record the disc-jockey played. Pat took to the floor, too, and came into his own later when he entertained everyone who could match his stamina in a local bar until the early hours of the following morning and then was up like a lark not long after for a motor lodge breakfast, leaving the dying and wounded upstairs in their rooms.

We returned to writing the book and it acted as a therapy after such a confusing and strange time. As John began to write about his captivity, I experienced a sense of relief that I could now learn and try to understand everything that had happened to him. It was easier to take in this way, although I still mentally shied away from the worst of it. I tried to put the past into perspective, too. Our personal lives had been dominated by the experiences we were describing, but our stories represent only a strand of a tiny sub-plot of a convoluted chapter in the history of the Middle East.

During the first few years that John was held hostage, by a group loyal to Iran, that country was engaged in total war with Iraq, a Middle Eastern ally of the United States, Britain and France. Despite the brutality of Saddam Hussein's regime, Iraq provided a counter to the revolutionary government in Iran. It was in British and American interests for the war to continue, for Iran's fundamentalist fervour to be diverted into a fruitless confrontation.

Under UN guidelines preventing the sale of arms to either side, Britain was supposedly neutral in this war. But, as the Matrix-Churchill affair has shown, Britain did not really bother to support the arms ban. It turned a blind eye to British companies who were supplying equipment to Iraq; at the very least, the Government must have suspected the equipment was being used to make arms. Other Western countries were also supplying arms to Iraq and ostracizing Iran, and it was this state of affairs that Iran was trying to alter by taking Westerners hostage in Lebanon. With Britain the problems weren't too great, but the Iranians probably saw that it didn't do them any harm to have a couple of Britons 'on hold'. In the early years, when the lack of dialogue between Britain and Iran wasn't a concern for either country, the British hostages were the victims of a stalemate.

The Friends' campaign achieved its objective, to make the hostages an issue in Britain; a political problem that would have to be resolved before the resumption of any meaningful relationship with Iran. We were hindered in our efforts by Foreign Office briefings to journalists that the British hostages were very likely dead. Whether the FO believed this or not, the effect was to persuade journalists that the issue was not worth their interest. One reporter was told by embassy officials in Beirut that Terry Waite's grave could be found in a particular Hezbollah cemetery in Lebanon.

How much the campaign influenced events is impossible to know, just as it is impossible to know if we lengthened or shortened John's captivity. But the Friends eventually made the hostages important in Britain's dealings with Iran and thus a political problem for the Iranians, too. After the collapse of communism, when Iran turned to the West, it discovered that the hostages in Lebanon were not pawns, but obstacles to economic and political development. Eventually, in 1991, Great Britain, the United States and Iran all turned to the UN to allow them to solve their joint problem; it was a moment when all their interests happened to coincide.

When that happened, the kidnappers were the pawns left out in the cold and, ironically, they chose one of the captives they had held in chains for five years to be their envoy to the UN. It was a bizarre tribute to their respect for John that the kidnappers chose him. It must have been partly due to his constant and frequently successful attempts to communicate with them over the years, often through flashes of humour. Perhaps the 'Wonderful Remark' of the Van Morrison song which gave us the title of our book refers to the inspiration that people are able to give to one another.

Throughout the years John was away I felt as if life was out of control, and that whilst I could choose any number of diversions and turn to any number of sources of comfort and support, that feeling never went away. Each morning I had woken up knowing that it was still there, waiting to be dealt with and the longer it went on the harder it became. John's abduction left a hole that I filled with as much activity as possible, and that turned into a campaign on his behalf, a fight for what he calls remembered joy. That joy had been shared by all of John's friends too, and those friends grew in number as more people saw what we were trying to do and shared with us their own remembered joy. It was a campaign in defence of one individual but, in a sense, of us all; I will remember the shared spirit of it for ever. At one point I could not look to the future without fearing what would happen when I no longer had a task to fulfil. Now though, I can look ahead, knowing that all this is in the past and that whatever I want to do, I'm as free as anyone else to do it.

In September, John bought a big car, the first indulgence he'd afforded himself since coming home. I rang around the insurance companies trying to get a competitive quote; I hadn't realized how much of a problem it was going to be. Many companies were saying that they just couldn't insure the car, although it wasn't that flash. Eventually, I got through to one company who sounded quite promising.

'Can I have the name, please?'

'McCarthy, John.'

'Occupation?'

'Er . . . writer, I suppose.'

'Oh, what's he writing about then?'

'Just a real-life experience—'

'Does he hold a current driving licence?'

'Yes.'

'Has he been resident in this country for the past five years?'

'No.'

'He's been working abroad then, has he?'

'Not exactly, no . . . actually he was a hostage in Lebanon.'

Silence.

'How long for?'

'Five years.'

'I suppose that's what he's writing his book about then, is it?'

'That's right, yes.'

'Are you his wife?'

'No, I'm his girlfriend.'

'It can't have been very nice for you.'

'It wasn't very nice, no, not really.'

'Was there much publicity about that then?'

As I put down the telephone I started to laugh and went to tell John; he must be well and truly home.

Broxted, 30 January 1993

On the last Saturday of January 1993 Jill and I went to
Cornish Hall End, picking up Brian Keenan from Stansted
Airport on the way. The following day, we three, together
with my father and Terence, went over to Broxted Church
for a service to dedicate two new stained-glass windows.
Terry and Frances Waite were there, too, and Lord Runcie
had recorded an address. Sadly, he was unable to attend in
person.

The windows represented Captivity and Freedom and
had been designed by John Clark. Before starting work
on them, he had interviewed Jill and me as part of his
research for the project. Our two meetings with him had
been refreshing. He was never morbidly curious or intrusive, wanting only to understand our experiences and
use them to create arresting and powerful images,
images which would convey something of what had happened to us – and to others – to everyone who saw
them.

During the service I realized how far we had all come
in the year or so since our release. Brian and Terry had
lost the haunted look which I had known, and shared, in
captivity and immediately after coming home. They were
relaxed and happy to be there. Their obvious peace of
mind echoed mine and that which I saw in the faces of
family and friends around us.

The dedication of the windows, which had no names
or dates upon them, finally put the hostage years behind
us. The Window of Captivity, with its muted tones, was
appropriately set in a side wall of the church and was not
immediately obvious. In brilliant contrast, the Window of

Freedom was a blaze of colour shining down from the west wall.

The service coincided with the end of my own efforts to put my years of captivity in perspective. Since coming home I had learned many things; life as a hostage had been hard, but in retrospect I realized that it had also been very simple. Freedom was difficult, too, but extremely complex. In captivity I had thought that being allowed to make choices would be the ultimate expression of freedom and that my life would then automatically follow the paths of which I had always dreamed. Yet decisions, however mundane, and the unforeseen demands and expectations that came with freedom often seemed unmanageable. At first I had been in awe of the way my friends managed to organize their lives. Now, more than a year later, I realized that everyday life wasn't so baffling. I, too, could cope with doing the shopping, finding somewhere to live, or buying a car. I knew how the world worked again and I was confident I could take it on and move forward. Now, I rarely feel panic rising when an image from captivity flits through my mind. I can look at the more painful memories of the past six years with a calm and understanding that for so long seemed beyond my grasp. At last, I am getting close to where I should always have been.

Appendices

Chronology

LONDON		BEIRUT
1986	**1986**	**1986**
15 March John McCarthy leaves for Beirut		**15 March** Fly to Beirut
	28 March Leigh Douglas and Philip Padfield kidnapped	
	11 April Brian Keenan kidnapped	
	15 April US bombing of Libya	
17 April John McCarthy kidnapped	**17 April** Padfield and Douglas found dead John McCarthy kidnapped	**17 April** Kidnapped
	April Video allegedly of Alec Collett's body released	

633

28 May
Sheila's first appeal broadcast

25 June
Moved in with Brian Keenan

29 June
Philippe Rochot and Georges
Hansen released by
Revolutionary Justice
Organization

26 July
Fr Lawrence Jenco released by
Islamic Jihad

3 August
Moved

30 August
Camille Sontag kidnapped

9 September
Frank Reed kidnapped

12 September
Joseph Cicippio kidnapped

24 October
Nezar Hindawi sentenced to 45
years in prison for attempted
bombing of El Al jet at Heathrow
Britain cuts diplomatic
relations with Syria
Edward Tracey kidnapped

634

1 November
David Jacobsen released

2 November
David Jacobsen released

4 November
Irangate starts to break

11 November
Camille Sontag and Marcel Coudari released

24 November
'Party for John' at the Comedy Store

27 November
John's first birthday in captivity

27 November
First birthday in captivity Guards give a birthday party

14 December
Fly to Cyprus, then Damascus with Nick Toksvig

19 December
Heard about Jill's trip to Damascus

24 December
Auriel Cornea released by Revolutionary Justice Organization

25 December
John's first Christmas in captivity
Sheila broadcasts appeal

1987

1 January
Return to London

1987

13 January
Terry Waite returns to Lebanon
Roger Auque kidnapped

20 January
Terry Waite disappears

24 January
Four Americans
Mithileshwar Singh, Robert Polhill, Alan Steen and Jesse Turner kidnapped

26 January
Rumours reaching Lambeth Palace of Terry Waite's kidnap denied

25 December
First Christmas in captivity
Saw Sheila's appeal on Lebanese television

1987

28 January
Heard Terry Waite had disappeared

30 January
Terry Waite's kidnap confirmed

10 February
300 days
Press Conference

16 February
Moved
Photograph taken

5 March
Fly to Paris to see Joelle Kauffman

10 March
Moved

9 April
Interrogated

11 April
Moved

16 April
All-night vigil at St Bride's to mark first anniversary of John's kidnap
Messages to John in Beirut papers

17 April
First anniversary of John's kidnap

June
FOJM support group press conference

30 August
500 days in captivity marked by service at St Bride's

11 June
Mrs Thatcher elected for third term

17 June
Diplomatic sanctions against Iran

18 June
Charles Glass kidnapped

18 August
Charles Glass escapes

17 April
First anniversary
Told of vigil at St Bride's
Given photograph of Jill

29 April
Moved

20 November
Moved

24 November
Postcard from Tom Browne, nine months late

27 November
John's second birthday in captivity
Messages printed in Beirut papers
Jean-Louis Normandin and Roger Auque released

8 December
600 days
Petition handed in to Iranian Embassy and 10 Downing Street

25 December
John's second Christmas in captivity

31 December
All-night vigil at St Bride's

1988

13 January
First meeting of FOJM

11 February
First appearance on *Wogan*

27 November
Auque and Normandin released
Do Chae Sung, Korean hostage, released

27 November
Second birthday in captivity
Saw messages in Beirut papers

25 December
Second Christmas in captivity

1988

February
Moved
Conditions improve

1988

17 February
The Friends of John McCarthy campaign launched

17 February
Lt.-Col. William Higgins kidnapped

17 March
FOJM stage mock-up of John's cell in Covent Garden

6 April
Kuwaiti airliner hijacked by Islamic Jihad

17 April
Second anniversary of John's kidnap
'An Evening without John McCarthy', Camden Palace, raises £15,000
Messages printed in Beirut press

17 April
Second anniversary
Photograph taken
Messages received

4 May
Marcel Fontaine, Jean-Paul Kauffman and Marcel Carton released

4 May
Marcel Fontaine, Jean-Paul Kauffman and Marcel Carton released

5 May
Shooting starts

7 May
Fly to Paris to meet Jean-Paul
Kauffman

15 June
789 days
Boat Trip

7 June
Iranian delegation arrives in
UK to discuss reparations to
embassies

19 June
Delegation of MPs flies to Iran

3 July
USS *Vincennes* shoots down
Iranian airliner in Gulf, 286 killed

18 July
Iran accepts UN terms for
ending war with Iraq

30 September
Britain and Iran agree to
restore diplomatic relations

7 May
Moved

15 May
Moved
Share cell with Anderson,
Sutherland and Reed

June
Given radio

September
News of imminent release
broadcast on Lebanese radio

2 October
FOJM attend Labour Party Conference

3 October
900 days
FOJM balloons released from top of Blackpool Tower

11 October
FOJM attend Conservative Party Conference

12 October
Sir Geoffrey Howe, Foreign Secretary, visits campaign bus

4 October
Mithileshwar Singh released

7 November
George Bush becomes President of the United States of America

10 November
Britain and Iran sign agreement restoring diplomatic relations

Late October
Frank Reed moved
Radio taken

27 November
John's third birthday in
captivity
Messages in Beirut papers
FOJM benefit at the
Hippodrome

25 December
John's third Christmas in
captivity
Messages in Beirut papers

27 December
Nicholas Nichola released

1989

10 January
1000 days
Vigil outside Iranian Embassy

4 December
Britain formally opens
embassy in Tehran

21 December
Bombing of Pan Am, 103
over Lockerbie, 270 killed

27 December
Nicholas Nichola released

27 November
Third birthday in captivity
saw video of parents and Jill

25 December
Third Christmas in
captivity

1989

12 January
Terry Anderson moved

3 February
Tom Sutherland moved

March
Heard about *fatwa* against
Salman Rushdie

17 April
Third anniversary

1989

14 February
Ayatollah Khomeini issues
fatwa against Salman Rushdie

7 March
Diplomatic relations between
Britain and Iran severed

13 May
Jackie Mann kidnapped

3 June
Ayatollah Khomeini dies

17 April
Third anniversary of John's
kidnap
Concert at St Bride's
First BBH ad campaign
Sheila's last appeal

13 May
Jackie Mann kidnapped

13 June
Fly to Tunis to see Yasser Arafat

19 June
Pat McCarthy broadcasts
appeal

8 July
Death of Sheila McCarthy

28 July
Sheikh Obeid kidnapped by Israel
Hafshemi Rafsanjani elected
President of Iran

31 July
Lt.-Col. Higgins hanged

15 September
Iranian Kouroush Fouladi
released from prison in UK
after serving ten years on
terrorism charges

30 September
FOJM attend Labour Party
Conference

6 October
Memorial service for Sheila
McCarthy at St Bride's

9 October
FOJM attend Conservative
Party Conference

10 October
Moved in with Frank Reed

22 November
Berlin Wall comes down

27 November
John's fourth birthday in captivity
FOJM release doves outside FO
Messages in Beirut papers

25 December
John's fourth Christmas in captivity

1990

13 March
First meeting of All-Party Parliamentary Group for the Release of Hostages

17 April
Fourth anniversary of John's kidnap
Vigil at Iranian Embassy
New BBH advert
Launch of Friendship
Messages in Beirut press

1990

22 April
FOJM Benefit at the Town and Country Club
Robert Polhill released

---

27 November
Fourth birthday in captivity

25 December
Fourth Christmas in captivity

1990

17 April
Fourth anniversary

1990

22 April
Robert Polhill released

29 April
Frank Reed released

June/July
Made contact with Waite
Letter sent to British
government

23 August
Brian Keenan released
Americans and radio moved in
Heard about mother's death

30 April
Frank Reed released

2 August
Iraq invades Kuwait
Dawa prisoners escape from
Kuwait

24 August
Brian Keenan released

30 April
Frank Reed released

5 May
Fly to Washington to meet
Frank Reed,

2 July
John McCarthy Bar opens at
Hull University

7 July
John's letter arrives at FO

24 August
Brian Keenan released

27 August
Fly to Dublin to meet Brian Keenan

5 September
First regular update on Simon Mayo's *Radio One Breakfast Show* Monthly event from now on

27 November
John's fifth birthday in captivity
Messages
Petition to Downing Street and Iranian Embassy
Camden Council display mounted

25 December
John's fifth Christmas in captivity

September
Britain and Iran restore diplomatic relations

22 November
Mrs Thatcher resigns

27 November
John Major becomes Prime Minister

28 November
Britain restores diplomatic relations with Syria

3 November
Moved
Met Terry Waite

17 November
Terry Waite moved in

27 November
Fifth birthday in captivity
Heard about FOJM mock-up of cell
Saw messages in Beirut papers

25 December
Fifth Christmas in captivity
Christmas cards received

1991

2 April
Roger Cooper released

17 April
Fifth anniversary of John's kidnap
FOJM rally in Trafalgar Square
New BBH advert
Launch of Yellow Ribbon Campaign

1991

16 January
Outbreak of Gulf War

28 February
End of Gulf War

13 March
Deportation of Kokabi, Iranian student charged with terrorism

2 April
Roger Cooper released

June
Douglas Hogg visits Lebanon

1991

17 April
Fifth anniversary of kidnap
Heard about FOJM rally

May
Moved

6 August
Moved

8 August
John released

8 August
John McCarthy released

11 August
Edward Tracy released

24 September
Jackie Mann released

21 October
Jesse Turner released

18 November
Tom Sutherland and Terry Waite released

4 December
Joseph Cicippio, Alan Steen and Terry Anderson released

8 August
Released

650

Index

657

659

FOR SO MANY, THE TORTURE GOES ON...

WHY I SUPPORT THE MEDICAL FOUNDATION

BY JOHN MCCARTHY

When I came home after 5 years in captivity, I was fortunate to return to the security and support of my family and friends.

There are thousands of people who have survived not just captivity but brutal torture, who are not so fortunate. Not only do they have to cope with the physical and psychological effects of torture, they have to do so while in exile in a foreign and sometimes hostile country.

That is why the work of the Medical Foundation for the Care of Victims of Torture is so vital. It is a unique charity in the UK which offers a range of specialist help using a combination of medicine, social work and psychotherapy.

The staff have specialist skills and experience which means that the Medical Foundation is a place of security for people to begin to rebuild their lives after the most shattering and brutal experiences. For many clients it is, quite simply, a lifeline.

I am honoured to have recently become a patron of the Medical Foundation and hope that you will join with me in supporting its vital work with survivors of torture.

Thank you.

John McCarthy

PLEASE SEE OVER >

I would like to help the Medical Foundation's work with survivors of torture through a donation of:

£15   £25   £50   £100

£250   £other

(cheque or postal order)

Name . . . .

Address . . . .

. . . .

. . . .

. . . .

. . . .

Postcode . . . .

To make a credit card donation please call 0171 485 8587

Please send me further information ☐

THE MEDICAL FOUNDATION
FOR THE CARE OF VICTIMS OF TORTURE

96 - 98 GRAFTON ROAD • LONDON NW5 3EJ
TELEPHONE: 0171 284 4321

COMPANY LIMITED BY GUARANTEE
Registered in England (No. 2398586)   Charity Registration No. 1000340